READING THE
MIDDLE AGES

READING THE
MIDDLE AGES

SOURCES FROM
EUROPE, BYZANTIUM, AND
THE ISLAMIC WORLD

EDITED BY BARBARA H. ROSENWEIN · SECOND EDITION

VOLUME I: FROM *c*.300 TO *c*.1150

UNIVERSITY OF TORONTO PRESS

LIBRARY AND ARCHIVES CANADA CATALOGUING IN PUBLICATION

   Reading the Middle Ages : sources from Europe, Byzantium, and the Islamic world / edited by Barbara H. Rosenwein. — Second edition.

Also available in 1 volume.
Includes bibliographical references and indexes.
Contents: v. 1. From c.300 to c.1150 — v. 2. From c.900 to c.1500.
Issued in print and electronic formats.
ISBN 978-1-4426-0605-0 (v. 1 : pbk.).—ISBN 978-1-4426-0608-1 (v. 2 : pbk.).—
ISBN 978-1-4426-0606-7 (v. 1 : pdf).—ISBN 978-1-4426-0607-4 (v. 1 : html).—
ISBN 978-1-4426-0609-8 (v. 2 : pdf).—ISBN 978-1-4426-0610-4 (v. 2 : html)

   1. Middle Ages—Sources. I. Rosenwein, Barbara H., editor of compilation

D113.R38 2013   909.07   C2013-905938-5
                                                   C2013-905939-3

We welcome comments and suggestions regarding any aspect of our publications—please feel free to contact us at news@utphighereducation.com or visit our Internet site at www.utppublishing.com.

North America
5201 Dufferin Street
North York, Ontario, Canada, M3H 5T8

2250 Military Road
Tonawanda, New York, USA, 14150

UK, Ireland, and continental Europe
NBN International
Estover Road, Plymouth, PL6 7PY, UK
ORDERS PHONE: 44 (0) 1752 202301
ORDERS FAX: 44 (0) 1752 202333
ORDERS E-MAIL: enquiries@nbninternational.com

ORDERS PHONE: 1–800–565–9523
ORDERS FAX: 1–800–221–9985
ORDERS E-MAIL: utpbooks@utpress.utoronto.ca

Every effort has been made to contact copyright holders; in the event of an error or omission, please notify the publisher.

The University of Toronto Press acknowledges the financial support for its publishing activities of the Government of Canada through the Canada Book Fund.

For Amy

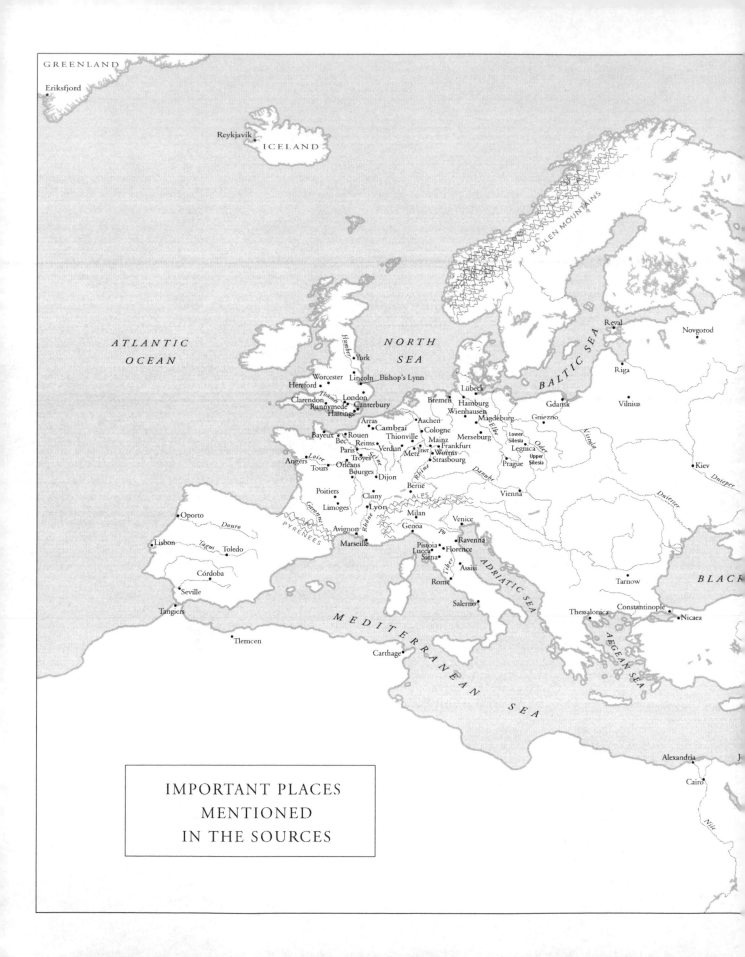

IMPORTANT PLACES
MENTIONED
IN THE SOURCES

Yet research continues, and it continues to be fruitful, because historians are not passive instruments, and because they read the same old documents with fresh eyes and with new questions in mind.

—Georges Duby, *History Continues*

Contents

The Western Church and Empire

Expanding Christianity

IV   POLITICAL COMMUNITIES REORDERED (*c*.900–*c*.1050)

Regionalism: Its Advantages and Its Discontents

Byzantine Expansion

Scholarship across the Islamic World

Kingdoms in East Central Europe

Preface

The major difference between *Reading the Middle Ages*, Vol. I, and other medieval history source books is its systematic incorporation of Islamic and Byzantine materials alongside Western readings. This second edition also includes new materials from East Central Europe. The idea is for students and teachers continually to make comparisons and contrasts within and across cultures. I have sometimes provided questions that I hope will aid this process, and Professor Bruce Venarde (University of Pittsburgh) has posed still other questions on the website for *Reading the Middle Ages* (www.utphistorymatters.com). Although this book may be used independently or alongside any textbook, it is particularly designed to complement the fourth edition of *A Short History of the Middle Ages*. The chapters have the same titles and chronological scope; the readings here should help expand, deepen, sharpen, and modify the knowledge gained there.

The sources in *Reading the Middle Ages* are varied; there are, for example, records of sales, biographies, hagiographies, poems, and histories.[1] There is also a new section on visual sources, "Containing the Holy." Some teachers may wish to assign all the readings in each chapter; others may wish to concentrate on only a few texts from each chapter. It is also easy to organize readings thematically by region: the index groups together all the sources pertaining to Italy, Spain, France, and so on.

The introduction to the first text in this book includes a discussion of how to read a primary source. The same project is repeated in chapter 4, this time with a very different sort of document. It should become clear to users of this book that the kinds of questions one brings to all documents are initially the same, but the answers lead down very different paths that suggest their own new questions and approaches. Each reader's curiosity, personality, and interests become part of the process; this, even more than the discovery of hitherto unknown sources, is the foundation of new historical thought.

This is the place for me to acknowledge—with pleasure and enormous gratitude—the many debts that I have incurred in the preparation of this book. All those who contributed

---

[1]   To make the texts translated from the Greek, Slavic languages, and Arabic more accessible, I have left out diacritical marks and non-Latin letters. Users of this book should, however, keep in mind that Arabic terms such as *sura* and names such as al-Bukhari should more properly be spelled *sūra* and al-Bukhārī, Slavic names such as Boleslaw are more correctly written Bolesław, and Greek terms such as *lorikion* and *komes* are more accurately *lōrikion* and *komēs*.

translations for this second edition deserve special thanks: Kristina Markman, Maureen Miller, Thomas F. X. Noble, William L. North, Frances Freeman Paden, William D. Paden, Carole Straw, and Bruce Venarde.

For advice, I thank Sheila S. Blair, Jonathan M. Bloom, Paul Cobb, Florin Curta, Zouhair Ghazzal, Monica Greene, Edin Hajdarpasic, Christine Meek, Maureen Miller, Faith Wallis, and Hiltrud Westermann-Angerhausen.

For special help, I thank The Emeryk Hutten-Czapski Museum, Jarosław Bodzek, Edyta Głogowska; Loyola's librarians Elizabeth Andrew, Jennifer Jacobs, and Linda Lotten; and the University of Toronto Press people with whom I worked: Martin Boyne, Judith Earnshaw, Natalie Fingerhut, Beate Schwirtlich, and Daiva Villa.

I offer special thanks to Riccardo Cristiani, whose thoughtful and careful reading of the entire manuscript led to numerous corrections and clarifications. His index for this book provides the user with numerous reference tools, such as dates for all persons and titles of all readings and their dates. He also helped coordinate all names, places, and facts in this book with those in *A Short History*. I thank Bruce Venarde for his creative questions, posted on the web site for this book. Elina Gertsman, Piotr Górecki, and Kiril Petkov provided indispensible counsel. Finally I thank my family, and with this book I thank in particular its newest and very dear member, Amy Rosenwein. May she enjoy reading medieval sources almost as much as she loves playing the violin!

Abbreviations and Symbols

AH Anno Hijra = year 1 of the Islamic calendar, equivalent to 622 CE
b. before a date = born
b. before a name = son of (*ibn, ben*)
BCE before common era. Interchangeable with BC. See CE below.
BEF. On timelines = before
beg. beginning
bt. daughter of (*bint*)
c. century (used after an ordinal number, e.g. 6th c. means "sixth century")
c. circa (used before a date to indicate that it is approximate)
CE common era. Interchangeable with AD. Both reflect Western dating practices, which begin "our" era with the birth of Christ. In *Reading the Middle Ages*, all dates are CE unless otherwise specified or some confusion might arise.
d. date of death
d. dinar = *denarius*, penny
Douay The standard English version of the Vulgate (Latin) version of the Bible. Ordinarily the books are the same as in the AV version (see above). The chief differences are that (1) the Douay version accepts some books considered apocryphal in the AV; and (2) the Psalm numbers sometimes differ. The Douay numbers follow the psalm numbering in the Greek Bible, whereas the AV and other Protestant Bibles follow the numbering of the Hebrew text.
e.g. *exempli gratia* = for example
ff. folios (or pages) following; this means that the reference is to a particular page and those that follow
fl. *floruit* (used—when birth and death dates are not known—to mean that a person "flourished" or was active at the time of the date)
ibid. in the same place, referring to the reference in the preceding note
i.e. that is (from the Latin *id est*)
£ pound (from the first letter of the Latin word *libra*)
MS manuscript
pl. plural

r.   ruled
s.   shilling = *solidus*, sous
sing.   singular
...   Ellipses, indicating that words or passages of the original have been left out.
[]   Brackets, indicating words or passages that are not in the original but have been
            added by the editor to aid in the understanding of a passage.

A date such as Boethius (d. 524/526) means that the exact date of his death is not known or disputed, but it is, at least, within the date range of 524 to 526.

Abbreviations for the Authorized Version of the Bible

In *Reading the Middle Ages*, references to the Bible are to the Authorized Version (AV). (Psalms are cited in both AV and Douay versions.) The standard abbreviations for the books of the AV are set out below. The Revised Standard Version of the Bible, which is perhaps the best translation in English, derives from the AV, which is based on the King James Version.

Old Testament

Genesis	Gen.
Exodus	Exod.
Leviticus	Lev.
Numbers	Num.
Deuteronomy	Deut.
Josue	Josue
Judges	Judges
Ruth	Ruth
1 Samuel	1 Sam.
2 Samuel	2 Sam.
1 Kings	1 Kings
2 Kings	2 Kings
1 Chronicles	1 Chron.
2 Chronicles	2 Chron.
Ezra	Ezra
Nehemiah	Neh.
Esther	Esther
Job	Job
Psalms	Ps.
Proverbs	Prov.
Ecclesiastes	Eccles.

Song of Solomon (This is also often called the Song of Songs)	Song of Sol.
Isaiah	Isa.
Jeremiah	Jer.
Lamentations	Lam.
Ezekiel	Ezek.
Daniel	Dan.
Hosea	Hos.
Joel	Joel
Amos	Amos
Obadiah	Obad.
Jonah	Jon.
Micah	Mic.
Nahum	Naḥ.
Habakkuk	Hab.
Zephaniah	Zeph.
Haggai	Hag.
Zechariah	Zech.
Malachi	Mal.

Apocrypha

1 Esdras	1 Esd.
2 Esdras	2 Esd.
Tobit	Tob.
Judith	Jth.
The Rest of Esther	Rest of Esther
The Wisdom of Solomon	Wisd. of Sol.
Ecclesiasticus	Ecclus.
Baruch	Bar.
The Song of the Three Holy Children	Song of Three Children
Susanna	Sus.
Bel and the Dragon	Bel and Dragon
Prayer of Manasses	Pr. of Man.
1 Maccabees	1 Macc.
2 Maccabees	2 Macc.

New Testament

Matthew	Matt.
Mark	Mark
Luke	Luke
John	John
Acts of the Apostles	Acts
Romans	Rom.
1 Corinthians	1 Cor.
2 Corinthians	2 Cor.
Galatians	Gal.
Ephesians	Eph.

Philippians	Phil.
Colossians	Col.
1 Thessalonians	1 Thess.
2 Thessalonians	2 Thess.
1 Timothy	1 Tim.
2 Timothy	2 Tim.
Titus	Titus
Philemon	Philem.
Hebrews	Heb.
James	James
1 Peter	1 Pet.
2 Peter	2 Pet.
1 John	1 John
2 John	2 John
3 John	3 John
Jude	Jude
Revelation	Rev.

Leaf from a Byzantine Psalter and New Testament (1084).

On this page of an eleventh-century Byzantine Psalter and New Testament, Saint Peter stands in front of the sort of theatrical background that had been used in earlier manuscripts to announce an important author. Peter holds a scroll, reminding viewers of the Old Testament prophets. The text beneath him, which is the First Epistle of Peter, begins with an initial of the capital Greek letter Π, or Pi, formed by the figures of Christ blessing and Saint Peter bowing his head in respect.

(Ink, tempera, and gold on vellum; 16.3 x 10.9 cm. The Cleveland Museum of Art, Purchase from the J.H. Wade Fund 1950.154. Photograph copyright © The Cleveland Museum of Art.)

To test your knowledge and gain deeper understanding of the chapters, please go to www.utphistorymatters.com for Questions for Reflection.

VOLUME I
FROM *c*.300 TO *c*.1150

I

Prelude: The Roman World Transformed (c.300–c.600)

A CHRISTIANIZED EMPIRE

1.1 Toleration or favoritism? *Edict of Milan* (313). Original in Latin.

No edict (an order issued to governors throughout the empire) was issued at Milan. But Emperors Constantine (r.306–337) and Licinius (r.308–324) met there in 313 and agreed to the provisions of what would be promulgated a few months later—the so-called *Edict of Milan*. It gave notice that Constantine and Licinius agreed to tolerate Christianity along with other religions and that they determined to restore the properties that the Church had lost under Emperor Diocletian (r.284–305). The current owners of the property might be compensated from the emperors' private funds if they applied to their "vicar," an imperial administrator with regional authority.

The *Edict of Milan* is the first source in this collection. Let us use it to begin a discussion of how to read primary sources. Each primary source calls for its own methodology and approach; there is no one way to handle all of them. Moreover, as the epigraph of this book points out, readers should bring their own special insights to old sources. Nevertheless, it is usually helpful to begin by asking a standard series of questions.

Who wrote it, and for what audience was it written? Normally this is fairly easy to answer, but often it is not. In this case, it seems that Emperors Constantine and Licinius conceived of the statement, though civil servants in an imperial writing office drafted and published it. The immediate recipients were provincial governors, each referred to as "your Excellency" in this document; they were expected to publish—that is, publicize—the contents to the public.

When was it written? Your editor has given the date 313, which is the year in which the document was issued. At this stage in your historical work, you need not worry about

1

how this date was arrived at. It is more important for you to consider the circumstances and historical events in the context of which this date takes on meaning. In this instance, you should be thinking that the date is pertinent to the history of the Roman Empire; that it comes directly after Constantine won a major battle at the Milvian Bridge in 312; that he attributed his victory to a sign from the Christian God; that immediately thereafter he took over administration of the western portion of the Roman Empire and soon (in 313) allied with Licinius; and that a few months later Licinius became ruler of the eastern half of the Empire. Therefore you should expect the document to have to do with both imperial authority and religion, which is precisely what you will discover when you read it.

Where was it written? In this case "Milan" is not the right answer. In fact the *Edict* was issued by Licinius at Nicomedia (today Izmit), in the eastern half of the Empire. But sometimes you will not know so specific an answer, and you must work with what information you have.

Why was it written? Often you will find a provisional answer to this question right in the text of the primary source. Ostensibly the *Edict* was written, as it says, "to give both to Christians and to all others free facility to follow the religion which each may desire." But you should go beyond this obvious answer to ask what other motives might have been at work, what sorts of negotiations may have been involved in its writing, and who benefited.

What is it? In this case, you know that it is *called* an *Edict* but is something a bit different. You might choose to call it an "imperial ordinance," an "official document," or even a "policy statement."

What does it say? This is the most important question of all. To answer it, you need to analyze the document for its various provisions, taking care to understand them fully and seeking further information (if necessary) about its vocabulary.

What are the implications of what it says? This requires you to ask many questions about matters that lie behind the text. Important questions to ask are: *What does the document reveal about such institutions as family, power, social classes and groups, religion, and education and literacy in the world that produced it? What are its underlying assumptions about gender; about human nature, agency, and goals; about the nature of the divine? Does the source apply to men and women in the same way?*

How reliable is it? If the document is authentic—if it really is what it purports to be—then at the very least you can know that it was issued by its writer(s). In this case, you can be sure that Constantine and Licinius did indeed want the *Edict of Milan* promulgated. You may wish to speculate about how much of it was Constantine's idea and how much Licinius's by considering what else you know about their religious convictions and political motives. The document certainly tells you about the ideals and intentions that they wanted the world to believe they had. But it alone cannot tell you whether the provisions were carried out. To know that, you need other documents and evidence about the nature of Roman imperial power at the time. One document that may help here is the *Creed* declared by the Council of Nicaea (p. 13 below), since Constantine presided over that council.

Are there complicating factors? Medieval texts were all handwritten, and they were "published"—in the sense of being made public and distributed—in relatively small numbers. In many cases we do not have them in their original state. The *Edict of Milan* was issued in multiple handwritten copies in Latin. However, none of these has survived. We know its contents because it was incorporated into the writings of two Christian apologists:[1] Lactantius's *On the Deaths of the Persecutors* (written perhaps in 318) and Eusebius's *History of the Church* (the first edition of which was published at some time between 303 and 312). Eusebius's text of the *Edict*, which he translated and presented in Greek, is not entirely the same as the one given by Lactantius. Scholars think that the one in Lactantius is the original, and that is the one printed here. But you should not be content with that. You should instead ask yourself at least two questions about these intermediary sources: *What motives might lead a later source to reproduce a text? What new meanings does the original source take on when it is embedded in a larger document with its own agenda?* You might also consider the fact that the *Edict* was not considered important enough to be drawn upon by the legal experts who compiled *The Theodosian Code* (438; see below, p. 4) or the later *Codex Justinianus* (529).

You should ask these questions of every source you read. Soon you will see how different the answers are for each document, for every one of them poses special challenges. If you like, look ahead to p. 167 to see this point clearly demonstrated in connection with a very different source, al-Tabari, *The Defeat of the Zanj Revolt*.

[Source: *Church and State Through the Centuries: A Collection of Historic Documents with Commentaries*, trans. and ed. Sidney Z. Ehler and John B. Morrall (Westminster, MD: Newman Press, 1954), pp. 5–6.]

We, Constantine and Licinius the Emperors, having met in concord at Milan and having set in order everything which pertains to the common good and public security, are of the opinion that among the various things which we perceived would profit men, or which should be set in order first, was to be found the cultivation of religion; we should therefore give both to Christians and to all others free facility to follow the religion which each may desire, so that by this means whatever divinity is enthroned in heaven may be gracious and favorable to us and to all who have been placed under our authority. Therefore we are of the opinion that the following decision is in accordance with sound and true reasoning: that no one who has given his mental assent to the Christian persuasion or to any other which he feels to be suitable to him should be compelled to deny his conviction, so that the Supreme Godhead ("Summa Divinitas"), whose worship we freely observe, can assist us in all things with his usual favor and benevolence. Wherefore it is necessary for your Excellency to know that it is our pleasure that all restrictions which were previously put forward in official pronouncements concerning the sect of the Christians should be removed, and that each one of them who freely and sincerely carries out the purpose of observing the Christian religion may endeavor to practice its precepts without any fear or danger. We believed that these points should be fully brought to your attention, so that you might know that we have given free and absolute permission to practice their religion to the Christians. Now that you perceive what we have granted to them,

---

[1] An "apologist" is someone who justifies or argues in favor of a doctrine or ideology.

your Excellency must also learn that for the sake of peace in our time a similar public and free right to practice their religion or cult is granted to others, so that every person may have free opportunity to worship according to his own wish. This has been done by us to avoid any appearance of disfavor to any one religion. We have decided furthermore to decree the following in respect of the Christians: if those places at which they were accustomed in former times to hold their meetings (concerning which a definite procedure was laid down for your guidance in previous communications) have been at any previous time acquired from our treasury or from any other person, let the persons concerned be willing and swift to restore them to the Christians without financial recompense and without trying to ask a price. Let those who have received such property as a gift restore whatever they have acquired to the Christians in similar manner; if those who have bought such property or received it as a gift seek some recompense from our benevolence, let them apply to the vicar, by whom their cases will be referred to our clemency. You are to consider it your duty that all these things shall be handed over to the Christian body immediately and without delay by your intervention. And since the aforesaid Christians are known to have possessed not only those places at which they are accustomed to assemble, but others also pertaining to the law of their body, that is of the churches, not of private individuals, you are to order in accordance with the law which we have described above the return of all those possessions to the aforesaid Christians, that is to their bodies and assemblies without any further hesitation or argument. Our previous statement is to be borne in mind that those who restore this property without price may, as we have said, expect some compensation from our benevolence.

You ought to bring into play your very effective intervention in all these matters concerning the aforesaid Christian body so that there may be a swift fulfillment of our Edict, in which the interests of public quiet have been consulted by our clemency. Let all this be done, so that as we stated above, the divine favor, of which we have experienced so many instances, may continue with us to bless our successors through all time with public wellbeing. In order that the character of this our perpetual benevolence can reach the knowledge of all, it will be well for you to circulate everywhere, and to bring to the awareness of all, these points which have been written to you as above, so that the enactment of this our benevolence may not be hidden.

1.2 Law: *The Theodosian Code* (438). Original in Latin.

The Theodosian Code, a massive compilation of imperial edicts and letters issued in 438 under Roman Emperor Theodosius II (r.408–450), was meant to serve as an authoritative standard for determining legal cases throughout the Empire. Covering topics as diverse as legal procedure, marriage, the army, and the Church, the *Code* was immediately adopted by Roman judicial authorities and was later influential on the laws drawn up in the barbarian successor states. The *Code* divided its topics into "Books," which were further subdivided into "Titles." Under each Title were arranged excerpts from pertinent imperial legislation. These were followed, when the compilers thought necessary, by legal interpretations. The passages below concern two issues: marriage (and divorce) and asylum. The first demonstrates the *Code*'s attempt to control social and moral behavior. The topic of asylum reveals that emperors not only came to recognize the holiness of the altar but also bowed to bishops' desire to allow even criminals the opportunity to do penance.

[Source: *The Theodosian Code and Novels and the Sirmondian Constitutions*, trans. Clyde Pharr (Princeton, NJ: Princeton University Press, 1952), pp. 76–77, 264–66 (slightly modified).]

Book 3, Title 14: *Marriages with Foreigners*

1. EMPERORS VALENTINIAN AND VALENS AUGUSTUSES TO THEODOSIUS, MASTER OF THE HORSE. [368–373]

No provincial, of whatever rank or class he may be, shall marry a barbarian wife, nor shall a provincial woman be united with any foreigner. But if there should be any alliances between provincials and foreigners through such marriages and if anything should be disclosed as suspect or criminal among them, it shall be expiated by capital punishment.

Interpretation: No Roman shall presume to have a barbarian wife of any nation whatever, nor shall any Roman woman be united in marriage with a barbarian. But if they should do this, they shall know that they are subject to capital punishment.

Title 16: *Notices of Divorce*

1. EMPEROR CONSTANTINE AUGUSTUS TO ABLAVIUS, PRAETORIAN PREFECT. [331]

It is Our[1] pleasure that no woman, on account of her own depraved desires, shall be permitted to send a notice of divorce to her husband on trumped up grounds, as, for instance, that he is a drunkard or a gambler or a philanderer, nor indeed shall a husband be permitted to divorce his wife on every sort of pretext. But when a woman sends a notice of divorce, the following criminal charges only shall be investigated, that is, if she should prove that her husband is a homicide, a sorcerer, or a destroyer of tombs, so that the wife may thus earn commendation and at length recover her entire dowry. For if she should send a notice of divorce to her husband on grounds other than these three criminal charges, she must leave everything, even to her last hairpin, in her husband's home, and as punishment for her supreme self confidence, she shall be deported to an island. In the case of a man also, if he should send a notice of divorce, inquiry shall be made as to the following three criminal charges, namely, if he wishes to divorce her as an adulteress, a sorceress, or a procuress.[2] For if he should cast off a wife who is inno-

cent of these crimes, he must restore her entire dowry, and he shall not marry another woman. But if he should do this, his former wife shall be given the right to enter and seize his home by force and to transfer to herself the entire dowry of his later wife in recompense for the outrage inflicted upon her.

Interpretation: The right to send notice of divorce is extended to a wife or husband for certain approved reasons and causes; for they are forbidden to dissolve a marriage for a trivial charge. If perchance a woman should say that her husband is either a drunkard or given to licentiousness, she shall not send him notice of divorce on that account. But if perchance she should prove that he is either a homicide, a sorcerer, or a violator of tombs, the husband who is convicted of these crimes appears to be justly divorced, without any fault of the woman; and she may recover her dowry and depart. If the woman should not be able to prove such crimes, she shall be subjected to the following punishment: namely, that she shall forfeit both the dowry which she had given or which had been given on her behalf and the gift[3] which she received, and she shall also be liable to exile by relegation.[4] But if a man should cast off his wife, he also is not permitted to divorce her for a trivial quarrel, as often happens, unless perhaps he should be able to prove that she is guilty of certain crimes, that is, if he is able to prove that she is an adulteress, a sorceress, or a procuress. But if he cannot prove this, he shall restore her dowry to the woman, and he shall not presume to take another wife. But if perchance he should attempt to do so, the woman who was cast off, though innocent, shall have the right to vindicate [claim] for herself her husband's home and all his substance. It is recognized that this is ordained in order that if a woman should be unjustly divorced, she is ordered to acquire the dowry of the second wife also.

2. EMPERORS HONORIUS, THEODOSIUS, AND CONSTANTIUS AUGUSTUSES TO PALLADIUS, PRAETORIAN PREFECT. [421]

If a woman should serve notice of divorce upon her husband and separate from him and if she should prove no grounds for divorce, the gifts shall be annulled which she had received when betrothed. She shall also be deprived

---

[1]   This is the "imperial 'we'"—the emperor refers to himself, as representative of the state, in the plural.

[2]   I.e., a madam or prostitute.

[3]   The betrothal and prenuptial gifts.

[4]   There were two forms of punishment by exile: in the harshest, the exile lost all civil rights. In exile by relegation, he or she retained these rights.

of her dowry, and she shall be sentenced to the punishment of deportation. We deny her not only the right to a union with a subsequent husband, but even the right of postliminium.[1] But if a woman who has revolted against her marriage should prove merely flaws of character and ordinary faults, she shall lose her dowry and restore to her husband all gifts, and never at all shall she be associated in marriage with any man. In order that she may not defile her unmarried state with wanton debauchery, We grant to the repudiated husband the right to bring an accusation.[2]

1. It remains to say that if a woman who withdraws[3] should prove serious grounds and a conscience involved in great crimes, she shall obtain possession of her dowry and shall also retain the betrothal bounty, and she shall regain the right to marry after a period of five years from the day of the divorce. For then it will appear that she has done this from loathing of her own husband rather than from a desire for another husband.[4]

2(1). Certainly if the husband should be the first to give notice of divorce and if he should charge his wife with a grave crime, he shall prosecute the accused woman in accordance with the law, and when he has obtained his revenge, he shall both get possession of her dowry and recover his bounty [gifts] to her, and he shall acquire the unrestricted right to marry another woman immediately. 3. If it is a fault of character and not of criminality, the husband shall recover his gifts but relinquish the dowry, and he shall have the right to marry another woman after a period of two years. 4. But if the husband should wish to dissolve the marriage because of a mere disagreement and should charge the repudiated woman with no vices or sins, he shall lose both his gifts and the dowry and be compelled to live in perpetual celibacy; he shall suffer punishment for his insolent divorce in the sadness of solitude; and the woman shall be granted the right to marry after the termination of a year. Moreover, We order to be preserved the guarantees of the ancient law in regard to the retentions from dowries, on account of children.

Interpretation: If a woman should be the first to serve a notice of divorce upon her husband and should not prove the statutory grounds for divorce, she shall forfeit the betrothal bounty, and she shall not recover that which she gave her husband as dowry. In addition, she shall also be sent into exile by relegation, and she shall not have the right to marry or to return to her own.[5] Indeed, if she should prove slight faults in her husband, for which she appears to seek a divorce, she shall forfeit her dowry and shall restore the betrothal gifts, and she shall not have the right to marry another man. If, however, after divorcing her husband, she should become involved in adultery, her husband shall have the right to prosecute her even after the divorce. But if a woman who has separated from her husband should prove that he is guilty of grave and definite crimes, she shall both recover her dowry and vindicate that which her husband bestowed upon her as a betrothal bounty, and she shall have the unrestricted right of marriage after five years.

Indeed, if the husband should be the first to serve notice of divorce, he shall secure his revenge on grounds approved by law, he shall vindicate the dowry of his repudiated wife, shall recover his betrothal gifts, and shall have the right to marry another woman immediately if he wishes. If indeed there were no definite crimes, but, as often happens, the husband is displeased with the frivolity of his wife's character, he shall recover his gifts and shall restore to her immediately anything which he has received from her, and after a period of two years he shall have the right to marry another wife. But if no defect of character should be proved but merely mental discord, the innocent woman who is rejected by her husband shall both vindicate the gifts made to her by the man and shall recover her dowry. But he shall remain alone forever and shall not presume to associate himself in marriage with another woman. The woman, however, is permitted to proceed to another marriage after a year if she should so wish. But for the sake of their common children, if there should be any, the Emperor orders those rules to be observed which have been established in the law concerning retentions according to the number of children, which law Paulus sets forth in his *Book of Responses* under the title, *A Wife's Property*.[6] …

---

[1]   The right to return home and resume her former life.

[2]   On grounds of immorality.

[3]   From her marriage.

[4]   The husband of another woman?

[5]   That is, she shall not have the right of postliminium—to return home and resume her normal life.

[6]   The juridical writings of Julius Paulus (*fl. c*.200) were considered authoritative.

Book 9, Title 44: Those Persons Who Flee for Sanctuary to the Statues of the Emperors

1. EMPERORS VALENTINIAN, THEODOSIUS, AND ARCADIUS AUGUSTUSES TO CYNEGIUS, PRAETORIAN PREFECT. [386]

We suffer those persons who have taken refuge at the statues of the Emperors, either for the purpose of avoiding danger or of creating ill will, neither to be taken away by anyone before the tenth day nor to go away of their own accord; provided that, if they had definite reasons for which they had to flee to the statues of the Emperors, they shall be protected by law and the statutes. But if they should be revealed to have wished to create ill will against their enemies by their own artifices, an avenging sentence shall be pronounced against them.

Title 45: Those Persons Who Flee for Sanctuary to the Churches

1. EMPERORS THEODOSIUS, ARCADIUS, AND HONORIUS AUGUSTUSES TO ROMULUS, COUNT OF THE SACRED IMPERIAL LARGESSES. [392]

If public debtors[1] should suppose that they may take refuge in the churches, they shall either be dragged out of their hiding places at once, or payment of their debts shall be exacted of the bishops who are proved to have harbored them. Your Eminent Authority shall know, therefore, that no debtor hereafter shall be defended by clerics, or else the debts shall be paid by the clerics for a debtor who they suppose ought to be defended.

2. EMPERORS ARCADIUS AND HONORIUS AUGUSTUSES TO ARCHELAUS, AUGUSTAL PREFECT. [397]

If Jews should be harassed by some criminal charge or by debts and should pretend that they wish to be joined to the Christian law,[2] in order that they may be able to avoid criminal charges or the burden of debts by taking refuge in the churches, they shall be driven away, and they shall not be received until they have paid all their debts or have been cleared of criminal charges by proof of their innocence.

3. THE SAME AUGUSTUSES TO EUTYCHIANUS, PRAETORIAN PREFECT. [398]

If, in the future, any slave, maidservant, decurion,[3] public debtor, procurator,[4] collector of purple dye fish, or anyone, finally, who is involved in public or private accounts should take refuge in a church, and if he should be either ordained a cleric or defended in any way by clerics and if he should not be returned to his former condition immediately by the issuance of a summons, decurions, indeed, and all others who are called by a customary function to the duty that they owe shall be recalled to their former lot by the energy and wisdom of the judges, as if by forcible seizure. We no longer permit such persons to have the benefit of the law which did not forbid decurions to be clerics after surrender of their patrimonies had ensued. But also those persons who are called stewards, that is, those who customarily manage ecclesiastical accounts shall be compelled without any delay to the repayment of a public or private debt to which it appears that those persons are obligated whom clerics received to be defended and did not suppose should be produced immediately.

4. EMPERORS THEODOSIUS AND VALENTINIAN AUGUSTUSES TO ANTIOCHUS, PRAETORIAN PREFECT. [431]

The temples of the Most High God shall be open to those persons who are afraid. Not only do We sanction that the altars and the surrounding oratory of the temple, which encloses the church with a barrier of four walls on the inside, shall be set aside for the protection of those persons who take refuge, but also the space up to the outside doors of the church, which people desiring to pray enter first, We order to be an altar of safety for those who seek Sanctuary. Thus if there should be any intervening space within the circumference of the walls of the temple which We have marked off[5] and within the outer doors of the church behind the public grounds, whether it be in the cells or in the houses, gardens, baths, courtyards, or colonnades, such space shall protect the fugitives just as the interior of the temple does. No one shall attempt to lay sacrilegious hands on them to drag them out, lest a person who dares to do this, when he sees his own peril, may himself also take refuge and seek aid. Moreover, We

---

1   Most of the public debtors were delinquent taxpayers.
2   I.e., become Christians.
3   A decurion was a member of a provincial city senate.
4   In this case, probably an imperial procurator—a fiscal agent or administrator—is meant.
5   By the boundary of walls mentioned above.

grant this extent of space for this purpose, namely, that it may not be permitted that any fugitive remain or eat or sleep or spend the night in the very temple of God or on the sacrosanct altars. The clerics themselves shall forbid this for the sake of reverence for religion, and those who seek sanctuary shall observe it for the sake of piety.

1. We also command that those persons who seek sanctuary shall not have within the churches any arms at all, in the form of any weapon, either of iron or of any other kind. For weapons are barred not only from the temples and divine altars of the Most High God, but also from the cells, houses, gardens, baths, courtyards, and colonnades.

2. Hereafter if any persons should flee without arms to the most holy temple of God or to its sacrosanct altar, either anywhere else in the world or in this fair City, they shall be prevented by the clerics themselves, without any injury to such persons, from sleeping or from taking any food at all within the temple or at the altar. The clerics shall designate spaces within the ecclesiastical enclosures which shall be sufficient for their protection and shall explain that capital punishment has been decreed if anyone should attempt to enter forcibly and seize them. If the fugitive should not agree to these restrictions and should not obey them, reverence for religion must be preferred to humanity, and reckless lawlessness must be driven from these holy places to those that We have mentioned.

3. We warn beforehand those persons who dare to enter the temples with arms that they shall not do this. Then if they should be equipped with weapons in any place in the church, either near the enclosure of the temple or around it or outside it, We command that they be notified immediately and very severely by the clerics alone, under the authority of the bishop, to lay aside their arms, and they shall be given the assurance that they are defended by the name of religion better than by the protection of arms. But if, warned by the voice of the Church and by the declarations of so many and so important persons, the refugees should be unwilling to relinquish their weapons, then the case of Our Clemency and of the bishops is cleared in the sight of God; armed men shall be sent in, if the case so demands, and the refugees shall know that they will be dragged forth, dragged away, and subjected to all kinds of misfortunes. But no armed persons shall be dragged out from the churches without consulting the bishop or without Our order or the order of the judges either in this fair City or anywhere else, lest, if many persons should be generally permitted to do this, confusion may arise.

Interpretation: Churches and places dedicated to God shall so protect accused persons who flee to them, driven by fear, that no one shall presume to bring force and violence to holy places in order to seize accused persons. But We command that whatever space belongs to the church, either in the colonnades, or in the halls, in the houses, or in the courtyards adjacent to the church shall be guarded just as the inner parts of the temple, so that the compulsion of fear may not constrain accused persons to remain around the altars or to defile places to which reverence is due. Certainly, if they should take refuge in holy places, they shall lay aside at once whatever arms they have brought with them, and they shall not suppose that they are defended by the protection of arms more than by reverence for holy places. But if they should be unwilling to lay aside their arms, and if they should not have confidence in the priest or the clerics, they shall know that they will be dragged out by the force of armed men. But if anyone should attempt for any reason to drag out from a holy place any accused person at all, the offender shall know that he will be condemned to capital punishment.

5. THE SAME AUGUSTUSES TO HIERIUS, PRAETORIAN PREFECT. [432]

We believe that a sanction should be promulgated, which shall be valid forever, concerning those persons who take refuge at the altars of holy religion, to the effect that if the slave of any person, relying only on reverence for the place, should seek refuge in the church or at the altars without any weapon, he shall be sent away after not more than one day in such place; furthermore, notice shall be given by the clerics whom it concerns to his master or to the person for fear of whom the slave appears to have avoided imminent punishment. The master shall grant pardon for his wrongs, and, with no remnants of anger remaining in his heart, in honor of the place and in respect for Him to whose aid the slave has fled, he shall take the slave away.

But if, armed and suspected of this by no one, the slave should rush in suddenly, then he shall be dragged out immediately, or at least notice shall be given at once to his master or to the person from whom such frantic fear has driven the slave, and the opportunity to drag him out at once shall not be denied. But if, relying upon arms and driven by madness, he should conceive the intention of resisting, his master shall be granted the right to drag him out and take him away by whatever means he can effect it. If it should happen that the slave should be killed in the struggle and battle, the master shall incur no blame, nor shall there be an occasion for anyone to originate a criminal action, if a person is killed who has changed from a servile status to the legal condition of a public enemy and a homicide.

If these regulations, so usefully constituted, should be perverted either by negligence or connivance, or in any other manner by those persons who are placed in charge of such matters in accordance with the duties of their office, just punishment will not be lacking, and, under the decision of an episcopal trial, they shall be removed from that place which they could not protect, they shall be cast back into the rank of plebeians,[1] and they shall receive the force of judicial severity.

1.3 Plague: Gregory the Great, *Letter to Bishop Dominic of Carthage* (600). Original in Latin.

The Plague of Justinian lasted from 541 to *c*.750. Named after the emperor under whom it first appeared, the plague spread across the Mediterranean and beyond, from the Middle East to Europe. Pope Gregory the Great (590–604) was well known for spearheading a drive to convert English to Christianity (see Bede, below, p. 94), for his commentaries on the Book of Job and other exegetical works, and for his "biography" (in fact the second book of his *Dialogues* on the holy men of Italy) of Saint Benedict of Nursia (for whose Rule see below, p. 17). He was also a devoted pastor who wrote a *Pastoral Rule* that served as a handbook for priests throughout the Middle Ages. In his letter to Dominic, who held the important position of bishop of Carthage, Gregory set forth in brief many of the ideas about the purposes of tribulation in this world that earlier had been elaborated in detail by Augustine (see the *City of God*, below p. 14). To counter the plague at Rome, Gregory organized penitential processions there at the beginning of his papacy and probably again *c*. 602; these fulfilled the "good deeds and tears of penitence" that he mentioned in his letter to Dominic. He also wanted bishops like himself and Dominic to restrain the members of their churches from "wicked deeds." Gregory did not concern himself with disposing of thousands of dead bodies, but at Constantinople Emperor Justinian ordered a court official to pay high wages to pit diggers and corpse bearers to handle the burials.

[Source: *Gregorii Magni Registrum epistularum libri VIII-XIV* 10.20, ed. Dag Norberg, Corpus Christianorum, Series Latina 140A (Turnhout: Brepols, 1982), pp. 850–51. Translated by Carole Straw.]

Gregory to Dominic, Bishop of Carthage

We already know how great a plague has invaded Africa;[2] and since neither is Italy free from the stroke of the sword, the groans of our grief are doubled. But amidst these evils and other innumerable calamities, dearest brother,[3] our heart would fail in tribulation without hope unless the Lord's voice had forearmed our frailty. For long ago, the trumpet of the gospel warned faithful listeners of the impending end of the world: pestilence, war and many other things would happen, which up to now, as you know, we only feared. But since we suffer these things that were foreknown, surely we ought not to be struck down by them as if they were from the unknown. For often even the

---

[1] This was the lowest class in Roman society. Plebeians had few rights and were subject to taxes and compulsory service.

[2] Gregory is using the "royal we" here; he means himself.

[3] Why would Gregory invoke the metaphor of brotherhood with Dominic even though they were not blood brothers?

kind of death is a consolation, considering other ways of dying. How many maimings and cruelties have we seen for which only death was the remedy, when life was torture? When the choice of a death was offered David, did he not decide that his people should die at the hand of God, rejecting famine and the sword?[1] Gather from this how much grace there is in those who die from a divine blow, when they die in the way that was offered as a gift to the holy prophet. And so let us give thanks in every adversity to our Creator and, trusting in his mercy, patiently endure everything since we suffer quite less than we deserve. Moreover, since we are scourged in earthly life that we may by no means be left without the consolation of eternal life, so the more we know the nearness of the judge to come announced in these signs, the more we should safeguard our accounts—which we must render to his examination—with the zeal of good deeds and tears of penitence, so that, through his benevolent grace, such great blows do not become the beginning of damnation, but the blessing of purification. But since the nature of our weakness is that we are unable not to grieve for those dying, let this teaching of your fraternity be a comfort to those in tribulation. Let it sink in that the goods promised them will endure, so that, strengthened by the most certain hope, they learn not to grieve for the loss of earthly things, in comparison to the gift awaiting them. Let your tongue (so we believe) compel them more and more away from the commission of wicked works, let it set forth in full the reward of the good and the punishment of evil so that those who love good the less should at least thoroughly fear wrong doing and restrain themselves from what must be punished. For those subjected to the scourge to commit crimes against the Punisher[2] worthy of the scourge is to be extremely proud, and it is to inflame his wrath to sharper fury; and it is the first order of madness not to want someone to cease justly his evil deeds, and to wish unjustly that God would check his vengeance. But since we need divine assistance in these things, let us, beloved brother, with joined prayers beseech the clemency of almighty God that he both may grant that we present these things worthily and also goad the hearts of the people mercifully to do these things, so that as we govern our actions wholesomely in fear of God, we may merit both to be rescued from the evils assailing us and also to come to heavenly joys, led by his grace, without which we can do nothing.

HERESY AND ORTHODOXY

1.4 Heretics: *A Donatist Sermon* (*c.*318). Original in Latin.

Emperor Constantine's (r.306–337) recognition and favoring of the Christian church ironically brought numerous tensions within Christianity to the fore. No longer united against a common foe, Christians formed splinter groups that maintained a particular interpretation of doctrine or demanded a certain standard of behavior. In North Africa, the key issue after Constantine's conversion was how to deal with those who had handed over their Bibles, church furnishings, and other emblems of their faith to escape persecution and death during Diocletian's persecutions. The Donatists scorned the *traditores* (from the Latin verb *tradere*: to hand over), and, when Constantine ended the persecutions, they refused to allow such people to pick up their Christian lives again as if nothing had happened. In particular, they denied the pastoral rights of priests and bishops who had been *traditores*, and they were equally wary of anyone even *ordained* by men so compromised. In 311, when Caecilian—whom the Donatists suspected of collaborating with the persecutors—was ordained bishop of Carthage, the Donatists insisted on

---

[1] In 2 Sam. 24, David orders a census to count the number of fighting men in Israel and Judah. Then he repents. God gives him three ways to die: seven years' famine, three months' flight from the enemy in hot pursuit, or three days of pestilence. Afraid of falling into human hands, David chooses death at God's hand, namely by pestilence. Many die, but he does not.

[2] I.e., God.

their own bishop, Majorinus. An appeal by the Catholics to resolve the crisis provoked Constantine to send troops. The Donatists interpreted the resulting bloodshed as a new persecution of Christians, strengthening their resolve. In this sermon, given a few years later to commemorate the event, the preacher hoped to fire his listeners to remain—or join—with the Donatists. He saw the "Catholics" and the emperor as inspired by the Devil, and he made fun of their epithet "heretic" for what he understood to be the true "Church of Christ."

[Source: *Donatist Martyr Stories: The Church in Conflict in Roman North Africa*, trans. Maureen A. Tilley, Translated Texts for Historians, 24 (Liverpool: Liverpool University Press, 1996), pp. 54–57 (notes modified).]

The Lord himself does not wish the death of the one who is perishing but rather that that person should return and live.[1] He was ready to receive the confession of those who were sorry. Knowing this, when the contriver [i.e., the Devil, working largely through his creature, Constantine] came face to face with times of peace, by worldly seduction, he revived those minds he had overcome in battle by fear of torture.[2] He took away their humility, the only way to tame the anger of an indignant God, and he substituted pride, which he knew for certain would gravely offend God. He promoted the idea that the lapsed, the deserters of heavenly sacraments, could illicitly hold ecclesiastical office again.[3]

As much as he recently took pleasure in their weakness of faith, so now he rejoices in this fraud. He is even more secure when they are called "bishops" or "Christians," than when they fell to ruin in their denial of the Christian name. He has these nominal enemies while he remains secure in deception. As we have already said, this is how he holds onto those he deceives by this false use of the Name. Not only does he delight these miserable men with vainglory but he also ensnares the greedy by royal friendship and earthly gifts.

Nevertheless, this rapacious robber was frustrated that he did not control everyone by this ruse. So the enemy of salvation concocted a more subtle conceit to violate the purity of faith. "Christ," he said, "is the lover of unity. Therefore, let there be unity." Those people who were already fawning on him and were deserted by God came to be called "Catholics." By prejudice in favor of the name, those who refused to communicate with them were called "heretics." He sent funds so that he might weaken their faith or provide an occasion for avarice through the publication of the law.[4] But when the course of justice holds firm and inflexible in the face of these seductive temptations, judges are ordered to intervene; the secular powers are forced to use coercion. Homes are encircled with battle standards; at the same time, threats of proscriptions[5] are launched against the rich. Sacraments are profaned; crowds are bedecked with idolatry; holy assemblies are transformed into splendid banquets.

O most faithful brothers and sisters, it is a crime even to publish what was said and done among the banquets of lascivious youths where despicable women were present.

How swiftly and completely did the situation change! The basilica, shameful to say, was turned into a fast-food restaurant. What grief to see such a crime in the house of the Lord, this place accustomed to pious prayers, now profaned by impure deeds and illegitimate incantations! Now I ask you, what person in whatever desperate condition would allow this to be done in their own home? No one would consent except the sort of person who

---

1   See Ezek. 33: 11.

2   Those who were wavering, about to abjure their alliance with the *traditores*, were deterred from repenting of their association with them by the prospect of being persecuted for being Donatists.

3   Donatists did not allow Catholic leaders who joined the Donatist fold to continue to preside over their congregations. They were admitted to the Donatist church as members of the laity. Catholics, on the other hand, recognized pastoral necessity and political prudence in cases where an entire Donatist congregation went over to the Catholic side under the leadership of its priest or bishop. Donatists treated schismatic Donatists returning to their church on a case by case basis.

4   The author is again referring to imperial gifts.

5   Confiscations of property.

would actually do it. Who denies that such deeds have the children of the Devil as their authors? Who calls the authors of the actions Christians, except the person who wishes to excuse the Devil himself or to disavow Christ the Lord? What diligence by the Serpent! So many evils let loose! How many hatched so that its family might assume the divine Name and hide itself from that Name, the Name it disgraces by its deeds! O the strength of the divine patience so worthy of praise, bearing up while the villainy of evil is spreading! Divine patience puts up with having the deeds of the crafty enemy imputed to itself or to its Name. Let no one think that something trivial happens when so many schisms and heresies arise. Satan's disguise surely dishonors God and Christ through his wicked ministry and adulterous work.

But lest we wander too far from the main point, let us omit their defilement of holy virgins. I repress any mention of their slaughter of the priests of God. I keep silent about their assaults, their pillaging, their booty. This way even they may know that we deliberately select few things from among many and we expose it quickly and modestly, seeing that we are eager not to exact vengeance on our enemies but to free the souls of these miserable people from the jaws of the ravenous wolf, indeed from the very mouth of the Dragon.[1]

Therefore, the one who corrupts holy discipline could violate the chastity of faith under the by-word of unity, i.e., by compelling unity with himself, not with God. Neither the rulers of this world nor those of darkness arrange things to happen in such a way that what is ordered might reveal the person giving the order. What glorious examples, how many glorious examples of "the Church of God" or "the Church of Christ" issue among them? What signs of Christian confession? What exiles, public tokens of true faith and perfect devotion, might there be? By these deeds truth obviously could not lie hidden unless someone in defiance of conscience determined to place their hope in deceit just as the prophet said.[2]

Let us proceed to the final events. They erupted in open threats and unmistakable fury once their subter-

fuges failed and their snares wore out. At that time you could have seen bands of soldiers serving the Furies of the traditors. They were brought together to perform a crime, but they were thinking only of pay. They stood around with most attentive curiosity lest mercenary cruelty be allowed to do something too gently. The cruel mercenaries asserted that attention to so improper a spectacle was not so much defense of a perverse claim, as the exaction of blood according to some contract.

Although the people of God might have anticipated the coming slaughter and known about it from the arrangements being made, they did not flee out of fear of an imminent death. On the contrary, they flew undaunted to the house of prayer with a desire to suffer. There faith grazed on the sacred readings, and prescribed fasts fed them with continual prayers. When these souls are delivered into the hands of the iniquitous, by their prayers they are actually commended into the hands of God.[3] Behold, in imitation of the Lord's passion, this cohort of soldiers marshaled by latter-day Pharisees sets forth from their camps to the death of Christians. Against innocent hands stretched out to the Lord, their right hands are armed with cudgels.[4] But it may be said that those who are not slaughtered by the sword are less martyrs for having been beaten to death in this impious massacre.[5]

The sword of the tribune had not yet pierced though the honored throat of the holy bishop of Siciliba, but it pricked him and the rage of the devil revealed who his agents were. In the same way the patience of the glorious bishop revealed the Church of Christ. No one else appears as servant of Christ the Lord as much as someone who suffered the same things as the Lord. It says: "No servant is greater than his master; if they persecute me, they will persecute you."[6] This is why these blind "servants of God" who are loved by the world show how the Lord himself was "loved" by the world. If the world does not love even those who are its own, it is necessary for it to hate those whom the Lord Jesus chose from out of the world. It says: "If you were from the world, the world would love what is its own; but because you are not from

---

[1] Matt. 7: 15; see Ezek. 22: 27.

[2] See Jer. 7: 4 and 13: 25.

[3] See Luke 23: 46.

[4] See Matt. 26: 47.

[5] This alludes to the belief that the only true martyrs were those who had actually shed blood. Thus a person beaten to death without the breaking of the skin would be considered less than a martyr. The author obviously repudiates this differentiation among those dying for their faith.

[6] John 15: 20.

the world, since I have chosen you from out of the world, for that reason does the world hate you."[1]

Finally, bloodshed marked the end of this hatred. Now the soldiers endorsed the contract and the covenant of crime in no other way than by the seal of blood. Everyone kept their eyes shut tight while each age group and sex was killed, cut down in the midst of the basilica. It is this very basilica, I say, between whose walls so many bodies were cut down and buried. Here, in the inscriptions, memory preserves the name of the persecution as Caecilianist[2] until the end of time, lest after his episcopate the parricide deceive others who were not privy to the things done in his name.

1.5 Orthodoxy's declaration: *The Nicene Creed* (325). Original in Greek.

A dispute between Bishop Alexander of Alexandria and Arius, an Alexandrian priest, concerning the relationship between the Father and the Son (Jesus Christ) within the Godhead had such far-flung repercussions that Emperor Constantine (r.306–337) called the Council of Nicaea (325), the first "ecumenical" (universal) council, to adjudicate the matter. We do not know precisely what Arius taught, but he clearly subordinated the Son to the Father. The Council declared that the Son was of the "same substance" (*homousios*) as the Father and thus not subordinate, a formulation that Arius could not accept. Although Arius was excommunicated, some of his supporters remained in high positions. When Constantius II (r.337–361) came to the imperial throne, he favored the position that the Orthodox called "Arian" and supported Ulfila, whose missionary work among the Goths led to their adoption of "Arianism." Although—or perhaps because—the Goths were allowed into the empire in 376, the Council of Constantinople, held in 381, affirmed the ban on Arianism, in effect branding as heretics the Goths and other barbarian tribes who adopted the Arian positions.

[Source: John N.D. Kelly, *Early Christian Doctrines,* 2nd ed. (New York: Harper and Row, 1958), p. 232.]

We believe in one God, the Father almighty, maker of all things, visible and invisible;

And in one Lord Jesus Christ, the Son of God, begotten from the Father, only-begotten, that is, from the substance of the Father, God from God, light from light, true God from true God, begotten not made, of one substance [*homousios*] with the Father, through Whom all things came into being, things in heaven and things on earth, Who because of us men and because of our salvation came down and became incarnate, becoming man, suffered and rose again on the third day, ascended to the heavens, and will come to judge the living and the dead;

And in the Holy Spirit. But as for those who say, There was when He was not, and, Before being born He was not, and that He came into existence out of nothing, or who assert that the Son of God is from a different hypostasis or substance, or is created, or is subject to alteration or change—these the Catholic Church anathematizes.[3]

---

[1] John 15. 19.

[2] A reference to Caecilian, appointed bishop of Carthage against Donatist wishes.

[3] I.e., excommunicates.

PATRISTIC THOUGHT

1.6 Relating this world to the next: Augustine, *The City of God* (413–426). Original in Latin.

As a young man, St. Augustine (354–430) wanted to be an orator and teacher—that is, a rhetorician—but his restless quest for life's meaning led him to make a dramatic conversion, chronicled in his *Confessions*. Later, as bishop of Hippo in North Africa (395–430), he became the most influential churchman of his day and for centuries to come. Counted among the Church Fathers, Augustine formulated many of the key themes of Western Christianity until at least the twelfth century. Perhaps the most enduring of his works was *The City of God*, which, by postulating two cities—the City of God and the City of Man—permitted Augustine to explore the mingling of the sacred with the secular realms, the uses of adversity in the world, the vision of Heaven as a place of total peace, and the idea that the life of man on earth is a pilgrimage—a holy trek—from home (the here-and-now) to a longed-for place of succor (the City of God). In spite of these universal and timeless themes, the book was written in response to a very specific historical event: the sack of Rome by the Visigoths under King Alaric in 410.

[Source: Augustine, *Concerning the City of God against the Pagans*, trans. Henry Bettenson (New York: Penguin, 1972), pp. 5–7, 13–17, 858–59, 881, 891–92.]

Book 1

PREFACE. THE PURPOSE AND ARGUMENT OF THIS WORK

Here, my dear Marcellinus,[1] is the fulfilment of my promise, a book in which I have taken upon myself the task of defending the glorious City of God against those who prefer their own gods to the Founder of that City. I treat of it both as it exists in this world of time, a stranger among the ungodly, living by faith,[2] and as it stands in the security of its everlasting seat. This security it now awaits in steadfast patience, until "justice returns to judgment,"[3]

but it is to attain it hereafter in virtue of its ascendancy over its enemies, when the final victory is won and peace established. The task is long and arduous; but God is our helper.[4]

I know how great is the effort needed to convince the proud of the power and excellence of humility, an excellence which makes it soar above all the summits of this world, which sway in their temporal instability, overtopping them all with an eminence not arrogated by human pride, but granted by divine grace. For the King and Founder of this City which is our subject has revealed in the Scripture of his people this statement of the divine

---

[1] Marcellinus (d.413) was an intimate disciple of St. Augustine sent by the Emperor Honorius to preside over the council summoned at Carthage to settle the dispute between Catholics and Donatists. Marcellinus was anxious to convert Volusianus (d.437), proconsul of Africa. Volusianus showed interest, but among his objections to Christianity was the charge that it had undermined the Roman Empire. Marcellinus wrote to ask for help from St. Augustine (who had already corresponded with Volusianus), and this led eventually to the writing of *The City of God*.

[2] See Hab. 2: 4; Rom. 1: 17; Gal. 3: 11; Hebr. 10: 38.

[3] Ps. 94: 15; Douay Ps. 93: 15.

[4] See Ps. 118: 7; Douay Ps. 117: 7.

Law, "God resists the proud, but he gives grace to the humble."[1] This is God's prerogative; but man's arrogant spirit in its swelling pride has claimed it as its own, and delights to hear this verse quoted in its own praise: "To spare the conquered, and beat down the proud."[2]

Therefore I cannot refrain from speaking about the city of this world, a city which aims at dominion, which holds nations in enslavement, but is itself dominated by that very lust of domination. I must consider this city as far as the scheme of this work demands and as occasion serves.

1. THE ENEMIES OF CHRISTIANITY WERE SPARED BY THE BARBARIANS AT THE SACK OF ROME, OUT OF RESPECT FOR CHRIST

From this world's city there arise enemies against whom the City of God has to be defended, though many of these correct their godless errors and become useful citizens of that City. But many are inflamed with hate against it and feel no gratitude for the benefits offered by its Redeemer. The benefits are unmistakable; those enemies would not today be able to utter a word against the City if, when fleeing from the sword of their enemy, they had not found, in the City's holy places, the safety on which they now congratulate themselves.[3] The barbarians spared them for Christ's sake; and now these Romans assail Christ's name. The sacred places of the martyrs and the basilicas of the apostles bear witness to this, for in the sack of Rome they afforded shelter to fugitives, both Christian and pagan. The bloodthirsty enemy raged thus far, but here the frenzy of butchery was checked; to these refuges the merciful among the enemy conveyed those whom they had spared outside, to save them from encountering foes who had no such pity. Even men who elsewhere raged with all the savagery an enemy can show, arrived at places where practices generally allowed by laws of war were forbidden and their monstrous passion for violence was brought to a sudden halt; their lust for taking captives was subdued.

In this way many escaped who now complain of this Christian era, and hold Christ responsible for the disasters which their city endured. But they do not make Christ responsible for the benefits they received out of respect for Christ, to which they owed their lives. They attribute their deliverance to their own destiny; whereas if they had any right judgment they ought rather to attribute the harsh cruelty they suffered at the hands of their enemies to the providence of God. For God's providence constantly uses war to correct and chasten the corrupt morals of mankind, as it also uses such afflictions to train men in a righteous and laudable way of life, removing to a better state those whose life is approved, or else keeping them in this world for further service.

Moreover, they should give credit to this Christian era for the fact that these savage barbarians showed mercy beyond the custom of war—whether they so acted in general in honor of the name of Christ, or in places specially dedicated to Christ's name, buildings of such size and capacity as to give mercy a wider range. For this clemency our detractors ought rather to give thanks to God; they should have recourse to his name in all sincerity so as to escape the penalty of everlasting fire, seeing that so many of them assumed his name dishonestly, to escape the penalty of immediate destruction. Among those whom you see insulting Christ's servants with such wanton insolence there are very many who came unscathed through that terrible time of massacre only by passing themselves off as Christ's servants. And now with ungrateful pride and impious madness they oppose his name in the perversity of their hearts, so that they may incur the punishment of eternal darkness; but then they took refuge in that name, though with deceitful lips, so that they might continue to enjoy this transitory light....

8. BLESSINGS AND DISASTERS OFTEN SHARED BY GOOD AND BAD

No doubt this question will be asked, "Why does the divine mercy extend even to the godless and ungrateful?" The only explanation is that it is the mercy of one "who makes his sun rise on the good and on the bad, and sends rain alike on the righteous and the unrighteous."[4] Some of the wicked are brought to penitence by considering these facts, and amend their impiety, while others, in the words of the Apostle, "despise the riches of God's goodness and forbearance, in the hardness and

---

[1]   1 Peter 5: 5.

[2]   Virgil, *Aeneid* 6. 853.

[3]   This refers to Alaric's clemency toward those who took sanctuary in Christian shrines, and especially in the basilicas of St. Peter and St. Paul.

[4]   Matt. 5: 45.

impenitence of their hearts, and lay up for themselves a store of wrath in the day of God's anger and of the revelation of the just judgment of God, who will repay every man according to his actions."[1] Yet the patience of God still invites the wicked to penitence, just as God's chastisement trains the good in patient endurance. God's mercy embraces the good for their cherishing, just as his severity chastens the wicked for their punishment. God, in his providence, decided to prepare future blessings for the righteous, which the unrighteous will not enjoy, and sorrows for the ungodly, with which the good will not be tormented. But he has willed that these temporal goods and temporal evils should befall good and bad alike, so that the good things should not be too eagerly coveted, when it is seen that the wicked also enjoy them, and that the evils should not be discreditably shunned, when it is apparent that the good are often afflicted with them.

The most important question is this: What use is made of the things thought to be blessings, and of the things reputed evil? The good man is not exalted by this world's goods; nor is he overwhelmed by this world's ills. The bad man is punished by misfortune of this kind just because he is corrupted by good fortune....

Book 19

5. SOCIAL LIFE; ITS VALUE AND ITS DANGERS

The philosophies hold the view that the life of the wise man should be social; and in this we support them much more heartily. For here we are, with the nineteenth book in hand on the subject of the City of God; and how could that City have made its first start, how could it have advanced along its course, how could it attain its appointed goal, if the life of the saints were not social? And yet, who would be capable of listing the number and the gravity of the ills which abound in human society amid the distresses of our mortal condition? Who would be competent to assess them? Our philosophers should listen to a character in one of their own comedies, voicing a sentiment with which all mankind agrees:

I married a wife; and misery I found!
Children were born; and they increased my cares.[2]

Again, think of the disorders of love, as listed in another quotation from Terence:

Wrongs and suspicions, enmities and war—
Then, peace again.[3]

Have they not everywhere filled up the story of human experience? Are they not of frequent occurrence, even in the honorable love of friends? The story of mankind is full of them at every point; for in that story we are aware of wrongs, suspicions, enmities and war—undoubted evils, these. And even peace is a doubtful good, since we do not know the hearts of those with whom we wish to maintain peace, and even if we could know them today, we should not know what they might be like tomorrow. In fact, who are, in general, more friendly, or at any rate ought to be, than those within the walls of the same home? And yet, is anyone perfectly serene in that situation, when such grievous ills have so often arisen from the secret treachery of people within those walls? And the bitterness of these ills matches the sweetness of the peace that was reckoned genuine, when it was in fact only a very clever pretense.

This explains why some words of Cicero come so close to our hearts that we cannot but sigh when we read:

No treachery is more insidious than that which
is hidden under a pretense of loyalty, or under
the name of kinship. For against an open adversary you could be on your guard and thus easily
avoid him; but this hidden evil, within the house
and family, not only arises before you are aware
but even overwhelms you before you can catch
sight of it and investigate it.[4]

Hence also that inspired utterance, "A man's enemies are those of his own household,"[5] is heard with deep sorrow of heart. For even if anyone is strong enough to bear these ills with equanimity, or watchful enough to guard with foresight and discretion against the contrivances

---

[1] Rom. 2: 4–6; "the Apostle" refers always to St. Paul in the works of the early Fathers of the Church.

[2] Terence, *Adelphi* 5.4.13–14.

[3] Terence, *Eunuchus* 1.1.14–15.

[4] Cicero, *Actio in Verrem* 2.1.13.

[5] Matt. 10: 36.

of pretended friendship, nevertheless he cannot but feel grievous anguish, if he himself is a good man, at the wickedness of the traitors, when by experience he knows their utter viciousness, whether they were always evil and their goodness was a sham, or whether they suffered a change from good-nature to the malice that they now display. If, then, safety is not to be found in the home, the common refuge from the evils that befall mankind, what shall we say of the city? The larger the city, the more is its forum filled with civil lawsuits and criminal trials, even if that city be at peace, free from the alarms or—what is more frequent—the bloodshed, of sedition and civil war. It is true that cities are at times exempt from those occurrences; they are never free from the danger of them....

20. THE FELLOW-CITIZENS OF THE SAINTS ARE IN THIS LIFE MADE HAPPY BY HOPE

We see, then, that the Supreme Good, of the City of God is everlasting and perfect peace, which is not the peace through which men pass in their mortality, in their journey from birth, to death, but that peace in which they remain in their immortal state, experiencing no adversity at all. In view of this, can anyone deny that this is the supremely blessed life, or that the present life on earth, however full it may be of the greatest possible blessings of soul and body and of external circumstances, is, in comparison, most miserable? For all that, if anyone accepts the present life in such a spirit that he uses it with the end in view of that other life on which he has set his heart with all his ardor and for which he hopes with all his confidence, such a man may without absurdity be called happy even now, though rather by future hope than in present reality. Present reality without that hope is, to be sure, a false happiness, in fact, an utter misery. For the present does not bring into play the true goods of the mind; since no wisdom is true wisdom if it does not direct its attention, in all its prudent decisions, its resolute actions, its self-control and its just dealings with others, towards that ultimate state in which God will be all in all,[1] in the assurance of eternity and the perfection of peace....

26. ..."Blessed is the people, whose God is the Lord."[2] It follows that a people alienated from that God must be wretched. Yet even such a people loves a peace of its own, which is not to be rejected; but it will not possess it in the end, because it does not make good use of it before the end. Meanwhile, however, it is important for us also that this people should possess this peace in this life, since so long as the two cities are intermingled we also make use of the peace of Babylon—although the People of God is by faith set free from Babylon, so that in the meantime they are only pilgrims in the midst of her. That is why the Apostle instructs the Church to pray for kings of that city and those in high positions, adding these words: "that we may lead a quiet and peaceful life with all devotion and love."[3] And when the prophet Jeremiah predicted to the ancient People of God the coming captivity, and bade them, by God's inspiration, to go obediently to Babylon, serving God even by their patient endurance, he added his own advice that prayers should be offered for Babylon, "because in her peace is your peace"[4]—meaning, of course, the temporal peace of the meantime, which is shared by good and bad alike.

1.7 Monasticism: *The Benedictine Rule* (*c.*530–*c.*560). Original in Latin.

St. Benedict (d.*c.*550–*c.*560), founder of several monasteries near Rome, wrote the most famous *Rule* for monks. In large measure it is an organized and institutionalized presentation of biblical directives, especially those inspired by the gospels. The key virtue of the monk in Benedict's *Rule* is obedience. The key duty is the Work of God, the hours of daily chant—known as the offices[5]—centered on the Psalter, all 150 psalms of which the monks

---

[1] 1 Cor. 15: 28.

[2] Ps. 144: 15; Douay Ps. 143: 15.

[3] 1 Tim. 2: 2.

[4] Jer. 29: 7.

[5] These are Vigils (the Night Office), Lauds, Prime, Terce, Sext, None, Vespers, and Compline.

were to complete each week. Within a half-century or so, Benedict's *Rule* had been incorporated alongside others in many Western monasteries. In the ninth century, it was adopted as the official norm for the monasteries of the Carolingian Empire. Compare its notions of human virtue and life on earth with those expressed in Augustine's *City of God*, p. 14 above.

[Source: *The Rule of St. Benedict*, ed. and trans. Bruce L. Venarde (Cambridge, MA: Harvard University Press, 2011), pp. 3, 7, 11, 13, 15, 17, 19, 21, 23, 29, 31, 33, 35, 37, 45, 47, 57, 59, 61, 79, 85, 87, 89, 97, 123, 125, 139, 141, 143, 161, 163, 177, 179, 187, 189, 191, 193, 229 (notes modified).]

In the name of our Lord Jesus Christ, here begins the prologue of the Rule by the great father Saint Benedict

Listen carefully, my son, to the teachings of a master and incline the ear of your heart. Gladly accept and effectively fulfill the admonition of a loving father so that through the work of obedience you may return to him from whom you had withdrawn through the sloth of disobedience. To you, therefore, my word is now directed—to whoever, renouncing his own will in order to fight for the Lord Christ, the true king, takes up the brilliant and mighty weapons of obedience....

Therefore our hearts and bodies must be prepared to fight for holy obedience to his instructions and what is not possible in us by nature let us ask God to order the aid of his grace to supply us. And if, fleeing the punishments of hell, we desire to attain eternal life, while there is still time and we are in this body and there is time to carry out all these things by the light of this life, we must hurry and do now what would profit us for eternity.

Thus we must found a school for the Lord's service.[1] In its design we hope we will establish nothing harsh, nothing oppressive. But if, according to the dictates of fairness, there emerges something a little severe in the interest of amending sins or preserving love, do not at once be frightened by fear and flee the path of salvation, which can only be narrow at the start. Instead, by progress in monastic life and faith, with hearts expanded in love's indescribable sweetness, we run along the path of God's commands so that, never turning away from his instruction and persevering in his doctrine in the mon-

astery until death, through patience we may share the sufferings of Christ and also deserve to be sharers in his kingdom. Amen.

Here begins the text of the Rule. It is called that because it rules the conduct of those who obey it.

Chapter 1
The Kinds of Monks

It is clear there are four kinds of monks. First are the cenobites, those in a monastery serving under a rule and an abbot. The second kind are anchorites, that is, hermits, those no longer fresh in the fervor of monastic life but long tested in a monastery, who have learned, by now schooled with the help of many, to fight against the Devil. Well trained among a band of brothers for single combat in the desert, by now confident even without another's encouragement, they are ready with God's help, to fight the vices of body and mind with hand and arm alone. The third, a very vile kind, are the sarabaites, tested by no rule nor instructed by experience, like gold in the furnace; but softened like lead, still keeping faith with worldly ways, they are known to lie to God by having tonsures.[2] They go around in pairs or threes or, of course, singly with no shepherd, shut in their own sheepfolds, not the Lord's, and the pleasure of their desires is their law, since they call holy whatever they have thought or chosen and they deem forbidden what they have not wished to do. The fourth kind of monks are those called gyrovagues,[3] who spend their whole lives lodging in different regions and

---

[1] In the Latin of this period, "school" could mean not only a place where instruction was received, but also the group receiving instruction, as well as, more generally, a vocational corporation (such as a guild) of people devoted to a common craft or service. A similar usage can be seen in the English "school of painters" or "school of porpoises."

[2] The tonsure is a haircut, reminiscent of male-pattern baldness, characteristic of monks. Interestingly, Benedict does not mention it elsewhere in the *Rule*.

[3] A combination word from the Greek for "circle" and the Latin for "to wander," reminiscent of the English idiom "to go around in circles."

different monasteries three or four days at a time, always wandering and never stable, serving their own wills and the lure of gluttony worse than sarabaites in every way. It is better to keep silent than to discuss the utterly wretched monastic ways of all these people. Therefore, leaving them aside, with God's help let us proceed to specifications for a very strong kind of monk, the cenobites.

Chapter 2
What Sort of Man the Abbot Should Be

An abbot who is worthy to lead a monastery should always remember what he is called and fulfill the name of "superior" in his deeds. For he is believed to act in the place of Christ in the monastery when he is called by Christ's title, as the apostle says: "You have received the spirit of the adoption of sons, in which we cry out 'Abba, Father.'"[1] Therefore, the abbot must not teach or establish or decree anything that is outside the Lord's commandments, but instead, his decrees and his teaching should sprinkle the yeast of divine justice in the minds of his disciples. The abbot must always be mindful that there will have to be a trial in God's fearsome court concerning two matters: his teaching and his disciples' obedience. And an abbot should know that whatever use the father of the household finds lacking in the sheep will be blamed on the shepherd. It will be equally the case that if all assiduous diligence is applied to a shepherd's unsettled and disobedient flock and every effort to cure its unhealthiness is applied, let their shepherd, acquitted in the Lord's judgment, say to the Lord, with the prophet, "I did not hide your justice in my heart and I spoke your truth and your salvation,[2] yet they scornfully rejected me."[3] And then in the end the punishment for disobedient sheep in his care will be death itself prevailing over them....

Chapter 3
Summoning the Brothers for Counsel

Whenever there is important business to do in the monastery, the abbot should call the whole community together and tell the brothers what it is about, After hearing the brothers' counsel, he should mull things over and do what he judges most beneficial. We said that all should be called to counsel because often the Lord reveals what is best to a junior brother.[4] Thus the brothers should give advice with all humble deference and not presume to defend their views too insistently, and instead let the decision depend on the abbot's judgment so that all may comply with what he has deemed most salutary. But just as it is fitting for disciples to obey their master, so too is it seemly for him to arrange everything justly and prudently.

Everybody therefore, should follow the Rule as a master in all things and nobody should rashly deviate from it. Nobody in the monastery should follow his own heart's will, nor presume to argue with the abbot insolently or outside the monastery.[5] Anyone who so presumes should be subject to the discipline of the Rule.[6] However, the abbot himself should do everything in fear of God and in observance of the Rule, knowing beyond all doubt that he will have to render an account concerning all his decisions to God, the most just judge.

If minor business concerning monastic interests is to be done, let the abbot take only the advice of the senior monks, as it is written: "Do everything with counsel and you will not regret it later."[7]

Chapter 4
The Tools of Good Works

First of all, "to love the Lord God with your whole heart, whole soul, and whole strength," then "your neighbor

---

[1] Rom. 8: 15.

[2] Ps. 40: 11; Douay Ps. 39: 11.

[3] Ezek. 20: 27.

[4] Junior could mean "younger" or "lesser in rank."

[5] The meaning here is obscure; as it stands, it means that respectful disagreement with the abbot is permitted only within the cloister but never outside. Some manuscripts read "inside or out," which would restrict much more severely the brothers' opportunities to question the abbot's decision.

[6] This discipline is described in chapters 23–30. It mainly involved "excommunication," that is, an internal shunning and restriction of privileges in the community.

[7] Ecclus. 32: 24.

as yourself."[1] Then "not to kill, commit adultery, steal, covet, or give false testimony; honor all men,"[2] and never do to another what you do not want done to yourself.[3] "Renounce yourself to follow Christ. Punish your body,"[4] do not embrace pleasure, love fasting. Give relief to the poor, clothe the naked, visit the sick, bury the dead. Help those in trouble, comfort those in mourning. Make yourself a stranger to the ways of the world, put nothing above the love of Christ.

Do not give in to anger, or waste time holding a grudge. Keep no deceit in your heart, nor give false peace, nor abandon charity. Do not swear oaths, lest by chance you perjure yourself, speak truth with heart and tongue. "Do not return evil for evil."[5] Do no injury, but even bear patiently those done to you. "Love your enemies."[6] Do not curse in return those who curse you, but bless them instead. "Endure persecution for the sake of justice. Do not be proud, nor overly fond of wine,"[7] nor a glutton, a sluggard, "slothful," a grumbler, or a detractor....

Look: these are the tools of the spiritual craft. When we have used them day and night without ceasing and given them back on the Day of Judgment, we will receive in return the reward God himself promised: "What the eye has not seen nor the ear heard, God has prepared for those who love him."[8] The workshops where we should industriously carry all this out are the cloisters of the monastery and stability in the community....

Chapter 7
Humility

Divine Scripture calls out to us, brothers, saying, "Everyone who exalts himself will be humbled, and he who humbles himself will be exalted."[9] When it says these words, it shows us that all exaltation is a kind of pride, which the prophet shows he guards against, saying, "Lord, my heart is not exalted, nor my eyes lifted up, nor did I move among great affairs or marvels that are beyond me." But what "if I did not understand humbly if I exalted my soul, would you refuse me in my soul like a weaned child on his mother's lap?"[10] So, brothers, if we want to reach the summit of the greatest humility and arrive quickly at that heavenly exaltation toward which we ascend through humility in this present life, as we ascend through our deeds we must raise the ladder that appeared to Jacob in his dream, on which ascending and descending angels were shown to him. We understand without a doubt that this descent and ascent can be nothing other than to descend by exaltation and ascend by humility. That raised ladder is our life in the world, which, in humble hearts, should be hoisted by the Lord to heaven. For we say that the sides of the ladder are our body and soul, in which our divine calling has placed the various rungs of humility and discipline we must climb.

The first step of humility, therefore, is that, placing the fear of God before his eyes at all times, one should altogether shun forgetfulness and always remember everything God commanded so that he always turns over in his mind both how hell burns those who scorn God for their sins and the eternal life prepared for those who fear God. Guarding himself at all times from sins and vices, those of thought, the tongue, the hands, the feet, and of his own will, but also the desires of the flesh, let him consider that he is always observed by God from heaven at all times and that his actions everywhere are seen by the divine gaze and reported by angels at all times....

Chapter 8
Divine Offices at Night

In wintertime, that is, from the first of November until Easter, reason dictates that monks should rise at the eighth hour of the night, so that after resting a little past

---

1 Matt. 22: 37, 39; Mark 12: 30–31; Luke 10: 27.

2 Rom. 13: 9; 1 Pet. 2: 17.

3 Tab. 4: 16.

4 Matt. 16: 24; Luke 9: 23; 1 Cor. 9: 27.

5 1 Thess. 5: 15.

6 Matt. 5: 44; Luke 6: 27.

7 Matt. 5: 10; Titus 1: 7.

8 1 Cor. 2: 9.

9 Luke 18: 14.

10 Ps. 131: 1–2, Douay Ps. 130: 1–2.

midnight, they should rise with digestion complete.[1] The time remaining after Vigils should be for study of the Psalter and readings by brothers who need it. From Easter to the abovementioned first of November, the schedule should be regulated so that, Vigils complete, there is a very brief break during which the brothers may go out for the necessities of nature, then Matins follows immediately, at first light.

Chapter 9
How Many Psalms Should Be Said[2] at the Night Offices

During wintertime as defined above, first this verse is to be said three times: "Lord, you will open my lips, and my mouth will proclaim your praise."[3] To that should be added Psalm 3 and the Gloria.[4] After that, Psalm 94 with an antiphon,[5] or at least chanted. Then an Ambrosian hymn[6] should follow, and then six psalms with antiphons. That done, after the verse is said, the abbot should give a blessing, and with everyone sitting down on benches, three readings should be recited in turn by brothers from the books on the lectern, and three responsories[7] should be chanted in between the readings. Two responsories should be said without the Gloria, but after the third reading, the chanter should say the Gloria. When the chanter begins it, all should rise from their seats at once out of honor and reverence for the Holy Trinity. Books of divine authority should be read at Vigils, from both the Old and New Testaments, and also commentaries on them written by well-known orthodox Catholic Fathers.

After these three readings with their responsories, there should follow the remaining six psalms, sung with an Alleluia. After those, there should follow a reading from the apostle, recited by heart, the verse, and the supplication of the litany that is, the Kyrie Eleison.[8] And Vigils should be concluded in this way....

Chapter 16
How Divine Works Should Be Done During the Day

As the prophet says, "I praised you seven times a day."[9] This sacred number seven will be completed by us if we fulfill the duties of our service at Matins, Prime, Terce, Sext, None, Vespers, and Compline, because he said concerning these daytime hours, "I praised you seven times a day."[10] Concerning nighttime Vigils, the same prophet says, "I rose in the middle of the night to confess your name."[11] Therefore at these times we should praise our creator "for the judgments of his justice,"[12] that is, at Matins, Prime, Terce, Sext, None, Vespers, Compline, and at night we should rise to profess his name....

Chapter 18
The Order in Which Psalms Should Be Said

... We urge this in particular: if this distribution of the psalms happens to displease someone, he should arrange it otherwise if he thinks it better, although in any case he must ensure that the entire Psalter is sung every week, the

---

[1] "Midnight" probably means "in the middle of the night," a time that varies according to the season.

[2] Benedict used verbs meaning "say," "sing," and "chant psalms" somewhat haphazardly, but it is likely that the psalms were sung rather than spoken. Certainly that was soon the case in most monasteries.

[3] Ps. 51: 17; Douay Ps. 50: 17. The "verses" that Benedict refers to are brief excerpts from scripture.

[4] That is, this short hymn of praise or doxology:

> Glory to the Father, the Son, and the Holy Spirit
> As it was in the beginning, is now, and will always be, forever. Amen.

[5] Here, "antiphon" probably means that Psalm 94 was to be sung interspersed with the repetition of a short phrase from scripture.

[6] I.e., a hymn by Saint Ambrose of Milan (d.397).

[7] Short, sung responses from scripture.

[8] Greek for "Lord, have mercy."

[9] Ps. 119: 164; Douay Ps. 118: 164.

[10] Ps. 119: 164; Douay Ps. 118: 164.

[11] Ps. 119: 62; Douay Ps. 118: 62.

[12] Ps. 119: 164; Douay Ps. 118: 164.

full complement of 150 psalms, and it is taken up again from the beginning, at Sunday Vigils. For those monks who sing less than the entire Psalter with the customary canticles in the course of a week show themselves lazy in the service of devotion, since what—as we read—our Holy Fathers energetically completed in a single day we, more lukewarm as we are, ought to manage in an entire week....

Chapter 22
How Monks Should Sleep

Each one should sleep in his own bed. They should get bedding suited to their monastic life according to their abbot's determination.[1] If possible, all monks should sleep in one place; if their number does not allow that, they should rest in tens or twenties with senior monks to take care of them. A candle should burn in that room continually until morning. They should sleep clothed, girded with belts or cords, so they do not have their knives at their sides when they sleep, lest by chance they wound another sleeper when dreaming and so that the monks are always ready and, arising immediately at the signal, may hasten to be the first to do the work of God, yet with all seriousness and modesty. Younger brothers should not have beds next to one another, but be interspersed among seniors. Rising for the work of God, they should gently encourage one another, to counter the excuses of the sleepy....

Chapter 33
Whether Monks Should Have Any Private Property

This vice in particular should be torn out at the roots in the monastery: no one should presume to give or receive anything without the abbot's permission, or have any private property, nothing at all, no book or tablets or stylus, but absolutely nothing, since the brothers my not have either their bodies or their wills under their own control. They should look to the father of the monastery for everything they need and not be allowed to have anything that the abbot has not given or permitted. "All things should be common to all," as it is written, "lest somebody say something is his,"[2] or presume it is. If anyone is caught indulging in this most wicked vice, let him be warned once, then a second time; if he does not amend, let him undergo correction.

Chapter 34
Whether Everyone Should Accept Necessities in Equal Measure

As it is written, "There was allotment to individuals according to their need."[3] By which I do not say that there should be favoritism,[4] God forbid, but consideration of weaknesses, so that he who needs less should thank God and not be upset, but he who needs more should be humbled by his weakness, not puffed up because of the mercy shown him, and in this way all members will be at peace. Most of all, the evil of grumbling should not show itself for any reason or in any word or sign whatsoever; anyone caught at it should be subjected to very severe discipline....

Chapter 39
The Measure of Food

For the daily meal, whether at the sixth or ninth hour, we believe that two cooked dishes for every table will suffice, taking into account individual weaknesses, so that he who cannot eat one may eat the other. Therefore, two cooked dishes should be enough for all the brothers, and if fruit or fresh vegetables are available, they may be added as a third course. A generous pound of bread should suffice for the day, whether there is one meal or both dinner[5] and supper.[6] If the brothers are to have supper, a third of the pound should be set aside by the cellarer for distribution at supper.

---

[1] The meaning here is uncertain: does the abbot hand out bedding appropriate to the level of communal asceticism, or does he treat each individual differently?

[2] Acts 4: 32.

[3] Acts 4: 35.

[4] See Rom. 2: 11.

[5] That is, the midday meal.

[6] The evening meal.

If the workload happens to be increased, the abbot will have the choice and the power to increase the portion somewhat, if it is expedient, but above all excess is to be avoided so that indigestion never steals up on a monk, because nothing is so inappropriate to every Christian as excess, our Lord says: "See to it that your hearts are not weighed down by overindulgence."[1] Younger boys should not be served the same amount, but less than their elders, frugality being maintained in all things. They should all abstain entirely from the consumption of the meat of quadrupeds, except the gravely ill.

Chapter 40
The Measure of Drink

"Everyone has his own gift from the Lord, one this, another that,"[2] and therefore it is with some uneasiness that we fix the portion of others' sustenance. Nevertheless, contemplating the frailty of the weak, we think that one *hemina*[3] of wine each per day is enough. Those to whom God gives the endurance to abstain should know that they will have their own reward. But if circumstances of the place or work or summer heat demand more, let it be up to the judgment of the superior, who must always take care lest excess or drunkenness creep in. Although we read that wine is not for monks at all, but since in our times monks cannot be persuaded of this, let us at least agree that we should not drink to excess but sparingly "because wine makes even the wise lose their way."[4] If the circumstances of the place are such that not even the aforementioned measure can be obtained, but much less or none at all, those who live there should bless God and not grumble. We caution this, above all: brothers should refrain from grumbling.

Chapter 41
At What Times the Brothers Should Eat

From holy Easter until Pentecost, the brothers should dine at the sixth hour and have supper in the evening.[5] From Pentecost through the summer, if the monks do not have work in the fields and excessive heat does not bother them, they should fast until the ninth hour on Wednesday and Friday. On other days they should dine at the sixth hour, and keep dinner at the sixth hour regularly if they have work in the fields or the summer heat is too great, according to the abbot's decision. The abbot must regulate and arrange everything so that souls are saved and what the brothers do they do without justifiable grumbling.

From the ides of September until the beginning of Lent, they should always eat at the ninth hour. But in Lent until Easter they should eat in the evening; Vespers should be done so that the monks do not need lamplight to eat, but everything should be finished in daylight. Both supper and dinner hours should always be adjusted so that everything may be done in daylight....

Chapter 48
Daily Manual Labor

Idleness is the enemy of the soul. Therefore, the brothers should be occupied at set times in manual labor, and again at other set times in divine reading. Therefore we think that the times for each should be established according to this arrangement, that is: from Easter until the [first] of October, brothers leaving Prime in the morning should work until almost the fourth hour at whatever is necessary; from the fourth hour until almost the sixth they should be free for reading. Rising from the table after Sext, they should rest in their beds in complete silence, and those who want to read to themselves should do so as not to disturb others; and None should be done a little early, at the middle of the eighth hour, and again they should work at whatever is needed until Vespers. They should not be upset if the circumstances of the place or poverty demand they do their own harvesting of produce, because then they are truly monks if they live by the work of their hands, like our Fathers and the apostles. Yet all tasks should be done in moderation out of consideration for the weak.

From the [first] of October until the beginning of Lent, they should be free for reading until the end of the

---

[1] Luke 21: 34.

[2] 1 Cor. 7: 7.

[3] The equivalent modern measure is unknown. Estimates generally range from a pint to a quart.

[4] Ecclus. 19: 2.

[5] That is, the traditional Mediterranean pattern in which the largest meal is in the middle of the day.

second hour; Terce should be done at the second hour, and then all should work at the tasks assigned to them until None. At the first signal for None, each should set aside his work and be ready when the second signal sounds. After the meal, they should be free for their reading or psalms....

Chapter 54
If a Monk Should Receive Letters or Anything Else

In no way should it be allowed for a monk to receive letters, gifts, or keepsakes, not from his relatives, any other person, or another monk, nor should he give them, without the abbot's permission. But if something has been sent to him by his relatives, he should not presume to receive it unless the abbot is informed beforehand. But if the abbot orders it to be received, it should be in his power to command to whom it should be given and the brother to whom it happened to have been sent should not be upset, lest "the Devil be given an opportunity."[1] Let anyone who presumes to do otherwise be subject to the discipline of the Rule.

Chapter 55
The Brothers' Clothing and Shoes

Clothing should be given to the brothers according to the nature and the climate of the place where they live, since more is required in colder regions, less in warmer ones. This consideration is the abbot's concern. However, we believe that in milder places, a cowl and a tunic for each monk will suffice—a woolen cowl in winter, a light or worn one in the summer—a scapular for work[2] and footwear: leggings and boots. Monks should not object to the color or coarseness of any of these items, but have what is available in the region where they live and can be purchased cheaply....

Chapter 58
The Discipline of Receiving Brothers

Easy entry to the religious life should not be granted to a newcomer, but as the apostle says, "Test the spirits to see if they are from God."[3] Therefore, if one comes knocking, perseveres, and, after four or five days, seems to suffer patiently ill-treatment directed at him and the difficulty of entry and persists in his request, let entry be granted him and let him stay in the guest quarters for a few days. After that, he should be in the novices' quarters, where they study, eat, and sleep. A senior monk should be assigned to them, someone suited to win souls, in order to watch over them very carefully.

The concern should be whether he truly seeks God, if he is attentive to the work of God, to obedience, and to reprimands. All the difficult and harsh things involved in the approach to God should be made clear to him. If he promises perseverance in his stability, after two months this Rule should be read to him straight through and let this be said to him: "This is the law under which you want to serve. If you can observe it, enter, but if you cannot, you are free to go." If he still stays, he should then be led into the abovementioned novices' quarters and have his patience thoroughly tested again. After six months, the Rule should be read to him so he knows what he is getting into. And if he still stays, after four months the same Rule should be read to him again. And if, after deliberating within himself, he promises to take care in all things and carry out every task given him, then let him be received into the community, knowing that it is stated in the law of the Rule that from that day forward it is not permitted to him to leave the monastery, nor shake his neck from the yoke of the Rule that he was free to reject or accept after such exacting deliberation.

Moreover, the one to be received should give assurances in the oratory, before everyone, concerning his stability, religious life and ways, and obedience. Before God and his saints, let him know that if ever he does otherwise, he will be damned by the one he mocks. He should make a petition concerning this promise of his in the name of the saints whose relics[4] are there and of the abbot who is present....

---

[1] 1 Tim. 5: 14.

[2] It is not clear exactly what this garment was. A plausible explanation is that it was an overshirt, smock, or apron-like garment meant to keep other clothes from getting dirty or torn during manual labor.

[3] 1 John 4: 1.

[4] Bones or other remnants of a saint.

If he has any property, he should either distribute it to the poor beforehand or, having made a solemn donation, give it to the monastery, keeping none of it whatsoever for himself, since indeed he knows that from that day forward, he will not even have control over his own body. Right there in the oratory, let him be stripped of the clothes in which he is dressed and put on the monastery's clothes. Let the clothing he removed be put in the wardrobe for safekeeping, so that if ever he gives in to the Devil's urging that he should leave the monastery, God forbid, then let him be thrown out, stripped of the monastery's clothes. However, he should not get back the petition that the abbot took from the altar, which should be kept in the monastery.

Chapter 59
Sons of Nobles and the Poor Who Are Offered

If it happens that a nobleman offers his son to the monastery, if the boy is young, his relatives should make the petition we discussed above, and they should tie together the petition and the boy's hand in an altar cloth, with the oblation,[1] and offer him that way. Concerning his property, they should either promise under oath in this same petition that they will never give him anything themselves, nor through a third party nor by any means, nor offer him the opportunity to own anything. Of course, if they do not want to do that and desire to offer something to the monastery for their own reward, let them make a donation to the monastery of the property they wish to give, keeping usufruct[2] themselves if they so desire. In this

way everything is closed off, so that the boy cannot harbor any hope by which, God forbid, he could be deceived and ruined, which we have learned through experience.

Let poorer people do likewise. Those who have no property at all should simply draw up the petition and offer their son before witnesses, with the oblation....

Chapter 73
Not Every Practice of Justice Is Set Out in This Rule

We have sketched this Rule so that those of us practicing it in monasteries may show that we have some honor in our ways and the rudiments of monastic life. But for one who hastens toward perfection in monastic life, there are the teachings of the Holy Fathers, observance of which should direct a man to the peak of perfection. For which page, which word of the divine authority of the Old and New Testament is not the most righteous guide for human life? And which book by the Holy Catholic Fathers does not resound with how we may arrive at our creator by a straight path? As for the *Conferences*, *Institutes*, and *Lives of the Fathers*, as well as the Rule of our holy father Basil,[3] what else are they but tools of virtue for good and obedient monks? For us, lazy, wicked, and neglectful, they cause a blush of shame.

Therefore, whoever you are, hastening toward your heavenly home, with Christ's help carry out this little Rule sketched as a beginning, and then at last you will reach those greater heights of learning and virtues we mentioned above, with God's protection. Amen.

---

[1] Apparently this means at the offering of the bread and wine during the Mass, an oblique indication of the circumstances of profession. Here as elsewhere, Benedict assumes his readers know a great deal already.

[2] Meaning that the gift is in trust; the donors receive any profit or return during their lifetimes, and then the property is transferred to the monastery.

[3] The *Conferences* and *Institutes* refer to the works of John Cassian (d.c.435), who spent the first part of his life as a monk in Bethlehem, Egypt, and Constantinople. Later he founded two monasteries, one for men and the other for women, at Marseille. The *Lives of the Fathers* is probably a reference to Athanasius, *Life of St. Antony* (see below, p. 27), along with other monastic biographies. The Rule of Basil was a collection of precepts written by Basil (d.379) in Greek for Byzantine monks, but it was available to Western monks through a Latin translation made by Rufinus of Aquileia in 397.

SAINTLY MODELS

1.8 The virginal life: Jerome, *Letter* 24 *(To Marcella)* (384). Original in Latin.

St. Jerome (*c*.347–419/420) was born in the Roman province of Dalmatia, near present-day Ljubljana. As a youth he went to Rome to study rhetoric and philosophy, and there, increasingly ashamed of his reckless student ways, he converted to Christianity. He subsequently lived in Trier, Aquileia, Antioch, and again in Rome; he spent the last decades of his life in a hermit's cell near Bethlehem. His most famous work is his translation of the entire Bible into Latin: the Old Testament from the original Hebrew and the New Testament from the original Greek. This so-called Vulgate Bible, completed around 405, was the standard in the Christian West for the next millennium. Jerome also wrote biblical commentaries, history, theological tracts, and more than a hundred letters. *Letter* 24 dates to his second period in Rome, during which time he was surrounded by a circle of elite women, including Marcella, a well-educated and wealthy widow who had already begun a life of Christian asceticism before Jerome arrived. The letter describes the way of life of the virgin Asella, Marcella's sister (although Jerome never says so explicitly). As a girl, Asella exchanged a gold necklace for a humble dark garment. She lived in a tiny cell and devoted herself to prayer and self-denial amidst the hustle and bustle of Rome, probably on a patch of family property. Jerome offers no specific rationale for why virginity is the ideal state for a Christian woman. What can you gather on this subject from the contents of the letter?

[Source: *Sancti Eusebii Hieronymi Epistulae pars 1: Epistulae I-LXX*, 2nd ed., ed. Isidorus Hilberg, Corpus Scriptorum Ecclesiasticorum Latinorum 54 (Vienna: Verlag der Österreichischen Akademie der Wissenschaften, 1996), pp. 214–17. Translated and introduced by Bruce L. Venarde.]

To Marcella, concerning the life of Asella.

1. Nobody should find fault that I praise or carp at certain people in my letters, since in exposing the wicked there is a reproach to others and zeal for virtue is spurred by preaching the best deeds of good people. The day before yesterday we had spoken concerning a certain Lea of blessed memory; immediately it pricked my conscience and came to mind that it is not fitting for me, having spoken of the second order of chastity,[1] to keep silent concerning a virgin. Therefore I must briefly sketch the life of our Asella, to whom I ask you not read this letter, since she finds praise of herself burdensome. I ask instead that you deem it worthy to read to young women who, instructing themselves by her example, may think that her way of life is the standard of perfection.

2. I pass over the fact that before she was born, she was blessed in her mother's womb. She was presented to her father, in his sleep, as a virgin in a bowl of gleaming glass more pure than any mirror; still wrapped in infants' clothing, scarcely ten years old, she was consecrated with the honor of future blessedness.[2] May everything that was before her work be attributed to grace,[3] although God, knowing the future in advance, blessed Jeremiah in the womb and made

---

[1] I.e., Lea, however holy, was a chaste widow, not a virgin, and thus she belonged to the "second order" of chastity. She was a wealthy Roman widow who gave up her privileges for a life of asceticism and prayer, directing a community of Christian virgins.

[2] This means that she vowed herself virginity at age ten. The reference to swaddling clothes, the material in which Mary wrapped the infant Jesus, is poetic license that stresses Asella's innocence.

[3] That is, before her "adult" work starting at age twelve, mentioned at the end of the paragraph.

John [the Baptist] leap in his mother's womb and before the creation of the world set [Saint] Paul apart to preach his son [Christ] [see Jer 1: 5, Luke 1: 41, and Eph 1: 5]. I now come to the things that she, by the sweat of her brow, chose, took up, held onto, began, and completed after her twelfth year.

3. Shut up in one narrow cell, she enjoyed the expanse of paradise. Likewise, the soil of the earth was her place of prayer and peace. Fasting was her pleasure and hunger her refreshment. When the human condition, rather than the desire to eat, drew her to food she stirred up hunger more than she suppressed it on a diet of bread, salt, and cold water. And since I nearly forgot what I should have said in the beginning, when she first took up her plan for living, she sold a gold necklace that is commonly called a *murenula* (because, the metal being made supple in little bars, a flexible sort of chain is woven together)[1] without her parents' knowledge. She put on a dark garment that she was unable to obtain from her mother; dressed in a pious portent of her undertaking, she quickly vowed herself to the Lord, so that all her kind would know that they would not be able to force anything out of one who had already condemned the world by means of her clothing.[2]

4. But, as I began to say, she always behaved with such restraint and guarded herself in the retreat of her room to the point that she never set foot in public, nor conversed with men. What is even more astonishing, she loved her virgin sister rather than seeing her.[3] She worked with her hands, knowing what is written: he who does not work does not eat [see 2 Thess. 3: 10]. In prayer and psalm-singing she spoke to her bridegroom. She hastened nearly

unseen to martyrs' shrines, and although she took joy in her plan, she was all the more greatly pleased that nobody recognized her. Not only fasting all year, eating every two or three days, in Lent she stretched out her sails to the fullest, nearly joining week to week in abstinence with a cheerful face. And because what is perhaps impossible for men to believe is possible with God's help, living this way she reached her fiftieth year, without stomach pain and free from bowel torments. The dry ground on which she lay did not harm her body, nor was her skin, roughened by sackcloth, subject to stench or abrasion. Sound in body and sounder still in mind, she thought her solitude a delight and found a monk's retreat in a busy city.

5. I have learned these few things from you, who know them better. Your eyes have also seen the hardness of camels' knees—the result of frequent prayer—on her holy little body. I offer what I can know. Nothing is more delightful than her seriousness or more serious than her delightfulness; nothing is sadder than her laugh or sweeter than her sadness. The paleness of her face, although it demonstrates continence, does not smack of ostentation. Her speech is silent and her silence speaks; her walk is neither fast nor slow; her bearing likewise. She gives no thought to neatness and her unstylish clothing is style without style. She has earned, by the quality of her life alone, that in a city of ostentation, lewdness, and pleasures, in which it is a misery to be humble, the good acclaim her and the wicked do not dare to disparage her. Let widows and virgins imitate her, married women cherish her, evil women fear her, and priests admire her.

1.9 The eremetical life: Athanasius, *Life of St. Antony of Egypt* (357). Original in Greek.

Athanasius, bishop of Alexandria (d.373), a ferocious upholder of the Nicene—and therefore anti-Arian—view of the Trinity, saw Saint Antony (or Anthony, d.*c*.356) as the living embodiment of his notion of salvation through Christ. His *Life of St. Antony*, which was translated into Latin in the later fourth century, was the first of what would become an enormously popular genre in the Middle Ages: the saint's biography, or hagiography. The

---

[1] *Murenula* is a diminutive for *murena*, the moray eel. The necklace, made of many tiny pieces of metal joined together, has the supple character of an eel in motion.

[2] It is a commonplace in writing about holy people that families resisted the desires of individuals to "leave the world." Asella's mother did not, it seems, want to offer her virgin daughter something that was, in the Roman world, a mourning costume.

[3] This is almost certainly a reference to Marcella, the addressee of this letter, who would have stayed in the family home before her marriage. Although Asella did sometimes leave her cell, as noted below, apparently her only destinations were Christian shrines.

virtues that Athanasius ascribed to Antony—seriousness of vocation even in childhood; resistance to all the temptations of the Devil; application to prayer, vigils, and fasts—were copied in nearly every subsequent saint's Life. This was not mechanical imitation, for Antony's Life was meant to be not just the story of one person but also the model for all Christians. At the same time, Antony's vocation as a solitary—a monk—became the ideal that even many Christians active in the hurly-burly of worldly life admired and strove to imitate. In what ways might the *Life of St. Antony* have influenced Augustine's ideas in the *City of God*, above, p. 14?

[Source: Athanasius of Alexandria, *Life of St. Antony of Egypt*, trans. David Brakke, in *Medieval Hagiography: An Anthology*, ed. Thomas Head (New York: Garland, 2000), pp. 7–14 (notes modified).]

LETTER OF ATHANASIUS, ARCHBISHOP OF ALEXANDRIA, TO THE MONKS IN FOREIGN PLACES CONCERNING THE LIFE OF THE BLESSED ANTONY THE GREAT

(Preface.) It is a good competition that you have begun with the monks in Egypt by seeking either to equal or surpass them in your discipline in virtue.[1] For at last there are monasteries among you as well, and the reputation of the [Egyptian] monks is the basis of their organization: therefore, this plan [of yours] deserves praise; may God bring it to completion through your prayers.

Inasmuch as you have asked me about the blessed Antony's way of life and want to learn about how he began the discipline, who he was before this, what the end of his life was like, and if the things that have been said about him are true, so that you might guide yourselves by imitation of him, I have received your charge with great enthusiasm. Indeed, for me as well it is of great profit just to remember Antony, and I know that once you have heard about him, in addition to admiring the man, you too will want to imitate his determination, since monks have in Antony's lifestyle a sufficient pattern for their discipline.

Therefore, do not disbelieve what you have heard from those who have brought reports of him; rather, think that you have heard only a little from them, for even they scarcely can have completely related such great matters. And since I too, urged by you, am telling you what I can by letter, I am sending only a few of the things that I have remembered about him. You for your part should not stop questioning those persons who sail from here, for it is likely that after each person tells what he knows, the account concerning him will still hardly do him justice. Therefore, when I received your letter, I decided to send for certain monks, particularly those who had spent the most time with him, in the hope that I could learn more and send you the fullest possible account. But since the sailing season was coming to an end and the letter carrier was ready to go, I hurried to write to your piety what I know—for I saw him often—and what I was able to learn from the man who followed Antony no short period of time and who poured water on his hand.[2] I have in every place kept my mind on the truth, so that no one, having heard too much, would disbelieve it, or, having learned less than necessary, would look down on the man.

(1.) Antony was an Egyptian by birth, and his parents were well-born and possessed considerable wealth. Since they were Christians, he was raised in a Christian manner. As a child, he lived with his parents and was familiar with nothing other than them and their house. When he grew to become a boy and became older, he did not put up with learning letters because he wanted to be removed even from the companionship of children. It was his complete desire, as it is written, to live in his house as an unformed person.[3] He would go to church with his parents. As a boy, he was not lazy, nor did he become rude as he got older. Rather, he was

---

[1] Athanasius presents his biography in the form of a letter to monks in places outside Egypt, most likely in areas of the western Mediterranean, such as North Africa and southern Europe. Many of the sentences in this opening section appear complicated and obscure to us because we do not know the exact situation in which Athanasius writes and because such a style is typical of prefaces to ancient works, in which the writer hopes to impress his readers with his rhetorical skill.

[2] See 2 Kings 3: 11.

[3] See Gen. 25: 27.

obedient to his parents, and by paying attention to the readings,[1] he preserved in himself what was beneficial in them. Although as a boy he lived in moderate wealth, he did not trouble his parents for diverse and expensive foods, nor did he seek such pleasures. He was happy merely with whatever he found and asked for nothing more.

(2.) After the death of his parents, he was left alone with one small sister; he was about eighteen or twenty, and it was his responsibility to care for the house and his sister. Not six months after his parents' death, he was going to church as usual, and he was thinking to himself and considering all this: how the apostles abandoned everything and followed the Savior;[2] how the people in Acts [of the Apostles] sold their possessions and brought the proceeds and laid them at the feet of the apostles for distribution to the needy;[3] and how such a great hope was stored up for these people in heaven.[4] Considering these things, he entered the church, and it happened that just then the Gospel was being read, and he heard the Lord saying to the rich man, "If you wish to be perfect, go, sell all your possessions, and give the proceeds to the poor, and come, follow me, and you will have treasure in heaven."[5] And Antony, as if the remembrance of the saints had been placed in him by God and as if the readings had been made on his account, left the church immediately and gave to the villagers the possessions he had received from his ancestors—three hundred *arourae* of fertile and very beautiful land—so that they would no longer trouble him and his sister.[6] He sold all their other movable possessions, collecting a sizable sum of money, and gave it to the poor, although he kept a little for his sister's sake.

(3.) But when he again entered the church and heard in the Gospel the Lord saying, "Do not worry about tomorrow,"[7] he could not stay: he went out and gave even that [little money remaining] to the common people. When he had delivered his sister to known and faithful virgins in order to be brought up for virginity, he at last devoted himself to the discipline outside the house, attending to himself and guiding himself with patience. For there were not yet so many monasteries in Egypt, and no monk knew the great desert; rather, each of those who wanted to attend to himself practiced the discipline alone, not far from his own village. Now, at this time there was an old man in the neighboring village who had practiced the solitary life from his youth: when Antony saw him, he imitated him in virtue.[8] At first he too began by remaining in the places around the village; then if he heard of some zealous one somewhere, like the wise bee, he went and sought that person, and he did not return to his own place until he had seen the man and had received from him, so to speak, travel supplies for the road to virtue.

And so, spending time there at first, he strengthened his intention never to return to the things of his parents nor to remember his relatives, but he directed all his desire and all his zeal toward the effort required by the discipline. Therefore, he worked with his hands, since he had heard, "Let not the idle one eat,"[9] and he spent some of the money on bread and some for the needy. He prayed continuously since he knew that it is necessary to pray in secret without ceasing.[10] For indeed he so devoted himself to the reading that nothing of what is written fell from him to the ground,[11] but he retained everything, so that his memory replaced books for him.

(4.) Conducting himself in this way, then, Antony was loved by everyone. He sincerely submitted to the zealous ones whom he visited, and he learned thoroughly the advantage in zeal and discipline that each one possessed in comparison to himself. He contemplated the graciousness of one and the devotion to prayers of another; he

---

[1] See 1 Tim. 4: 13.

[2] See Matt. 4: 20; 19: 27.

[3] See Acts 4: 35–37.

[4] See Col. 1: 5.

[5] Matt. 19: 21.

[6] Three hundred *arourae* may have been around two hundred acres; thus, Antony is portrayed as very wealthy by the standards of third-century Egypt.

[7] Matt. 6: 34.

[8] See Gal. 4: 18.

[9] See 2 Thess. 3: 10.

[10] See Matt. 6: 6; 1 Thess. 5: 17.

[11] See 1 Sam. 3: 19.

observed one's lack of anger and another's love of people; he attended to the one who kept vigils and the other who loved to study; he admired one for his perseverance and another for his fasting and sleeping on the ground; he watched closely the gentle nature of one and the patience of another; but in all he noticed piety toward Christ and love for one another. And when he had been filled in this way, he returned to his own place of discipline, and then he gathered into himself the virtues of each and strove to display them all in himself. Indeed, he was not contentious with those of his own age, except only that he should not appear to be second to them in the better things. And he did this in such a way that he did not hurt anyone's feelings; rather, they rejoiced in him. And so when the people of the village and the lovers of virtue with whom he associated saw that he was this kind of person, they all called him "Beloved of God"; some welcomed him as a son, others as a brother.

(5.) But the devil, who hates and envies the good, could not bear to see such resolution in a young man, but set out to do against Antony the kinds of things he usually does. First he tried to dissuade him from the discipline by suggesting the memory of possessions, the care of his sister, the intimacy of family, love of money, love of glory, the varied pleasure of food, and the other indulgences of life—and finally the difficulty of virtue and the great effort that it requires. He introduced the weakness of the body and the long duration of time. In short, he raised up a dust cloud of thoughts in Antony's mind, desiring thereby to separate him from his upright intention.

But the enemy saw that he himself was weak in the face of Antony's resolve and saw instead that he was defeated by the other's stubbornness, overthrown by his faith, and falling due to Antony's constant prayers. Then he took confidence in the weapons of the belly's navel[1] and, boasting in these—for they are his primary means of trapping the young—he advanced against the youth, troubling him at night and harassing him by day so that those who watched could sense the struggle that was going on between the two. The one would suggest dirty thoughts, and the other would turn them back with prayers; the one would titillate, and the other, as if seeming to blush, would fortify his body with faith and fasts.

And the miserable devil dared at night to dress up like a woman and imitate one in every way merely to deceive Antony. But Antony, by thinking about Christ and the excellence one ought to possess because of him, and by considering the soul's rational faculty, extinguished the ember of the other's deception.

Once again the enemy suggested the ease of pleasure. But Antony, like someone fittingly angry or grieved, thought about the threat of fire and the torment of the worm, and by setting these thoughts against [those of the enemy], he passed through these things unharmed. All this was a source of shame for the enemy, for he who had considered himself to be like God[2] was now being mocked by a youth, and he who boasted over flesh and blood was being overthrown by a human being who wore flesh. For working with Antony was the Lord, the one who for our sake took flesh and gave to the body the victory over the devil, so that each of those who truly struggle says, "Not I, but the grace of God that is with me."[3]

(6.) At last, when the dragon could not defeat Antony in this way but instead saw himself thrust out of his heart, he gnashed his teeth, as it is written.[4] As if he were beside himself, he finally appeared to Antony in his form just as he is in his mind, as a black boy. And as though he had fallen down, he no longer attacked Antony with thoughts—for the crafty one had been tossed down—but finally he used a human voice and said, "Many people I have deceived, and most I have defeated, but now coming against you and your efforts as I have against others, I have been weakened." Antony asked, "Who are you who say such things to me?" Immediately he answered with a pitiful voice, "It is I who am fornication's lover. It is I who have been entrusted with its ambushes and its titillations against the youth, and I am called the spirit of fornication. How many persons who desired to be prudent I have deceived! How many persons who professed to be so I have persuaded to change by titillating them! It is I on whose account even the prophet blames those who have fallen, saying, 'You have been deceived by the spirit of fornication.'[5] For it was through me that they were tripped up. It is I who so often troubled you and who as often was overthrown by you." But Antony gave thanks

---

[1] See Job 40: 16.

[2] See Isa. 14: 14; Ezek. 28: 2.

[3] 1 Cor. 15: 10.

[4] See Ps. 35: 16; 37: 12; 112: 10; Douay Ps. 34: 16; 36: 12; 111: 10.

[5] Hos. 4: 12.

to the Lord and took courage in him, and he said to him, "You are very despicable then, for you are black in your mind and as weak as a boy. From now on I will have no anxiety about you, 'for the Lord is my helper, and I will look down on my enemies.'"[1] When he heard this, the black one immediately fled, cowering before these words and afraid even to approach the man.[2]

(7.) This was Antony's first struggle against the devil, or rather this was the achievement in Antony of the Savior, "who condemned sin in the flesh so that the righteousness of the Law might be fulfilled in us, who walk not according to the flesh, but according to the spirit."[3] But Antony did not, because the demon had fallen, now become negligent and take no thought of himself, nor did the enemy, because he had been defeated, stop lying in ambush. For the enemy went around again like a lion, looking for some opportunity against him.[4] But Antony, since he had learned from the Scriptures that the wiles of the enemy are numerous,[5] practiced the discipline intensely, figuring that, even if the enemy had been unable to deceive his heart through bodily pleasure, he would attempt to trap him by another method. For the demon is a lover of sin.

Therefore, Antony more and more punished his body and enslaved it,[6] so that, even though he had triumphed in some ways, he would not be overcome in others; he resolved, then, to accustom himself to more severe training measures. Many people were amazed, but he himself endured the labor with ease, for his soul's intention, which had lasted for a long time, created in him a good habit so that, when he received even slight encouragement from others, he would show great enthusiasm for the task. He would keep vigil to such an extent that often he spent the entire night without sleep, and when he did this not once but many times, people were amazed. He

ate once a day after sunset, but there were times when he went two days and often four days without eating. His food was bread and salt; his drink, only water. Indeed, it is superfluous even to speak about meat and wine, for nothing of the sort was ever found among the other zealous ones. For sleeping he was content with a rush mat, but mostly he lay upon the bare ground. He would not anoint himself with oil, saying that young men ought to pursue the discipline with zeal and should not seek what would pamper the body, rather that they should accustom the body to labors and consider the Apostle's statement, "Whenever I am weak, then I am strong."[7] For at that time he used to say that the soul's intellect grows strong when the body's pleasures are made weak.

He had this truly wonderful thought: that one should not measure progress in virtue or withdrawal made for this purpose by the length of time, but by the desire and intention. Therefore, he himself did not keep track of the time that had gone by; rather, every day, as if he were just starting the discipline, he would make his effort toward advancement greater, constantly saying to himself Paul's statement, "forgetting what lies behind and straining forward to what lies ahead,"[8] and remembering also the voice of the prophet Elijah, saying, "The Lord lives, before whom I stand today."[9] He observed that in saying "today" he was not measuring the time that had gone by, but, as if he were always making a new start, he was zealous every day to show himself to God to be such that one should appear to God: pure in heart and ready to obey his will and nothing else. He would say to himself, "The ascetic ought always to observe his own life in the conduct of the great Elijah as if in a mirror."

(8.) Having constrained himself in this way, Antony departed to the tombs, which happened to lie far outside the village. He commanded one of his acquaintances

---

[1] Ps. 118: 7; Douay 117: 7.

[2] The symbolism of this scene is on two levels. First, the appearance of the devil as a boy reflects the homoerotic interest in male adolescents pervasive in the ancient world and condemned by Christian leaders such as Athanasius. Second, the devil's black skin illustrates the prejudice based on skin color present in late antique Egypt, which was a multiethnic society. Most Alexandrians such as Athanasius were descendants of the Greeks who founded the city in the fourth century BCE and so were of lighter skin color than those of more sub-Saharan African descent.

[3] Rom. 8: 3–4.

[4] See 1 Pet. 5: 8.

[5] See Eph. 6: 11.

[6] See 1 Cor. 9: 27.

[7] 2 Cor. 12: 10.

[8] Phil. 3: 13.

[9] See 1 Kings 17: 1; 18: 15.

to bring him bread every several days, and he himself entered one of the tombs; when the other had shut the door, he remained inside by himself. Then, when the enemy could not bear this but was afraid that in a short time Antony would fill the desert with the discipline, he came one night with a crowd of demons and so cut Antony with wounds that he lay on the ground speechless from the tortures. For he used to maintain that the pains were so severe that he would say that blows inflicted by human beings could not have inflicted such torture. But by God's Providence—for the Lord does not neglect those who hope in him—his acquaintance came the next day to bring him the bread. When he opened the door and saw Antony lying on the ground as if dead, he lifted him up, carried him to the village church, and laid him on the ground. Many of his relatives and the villagers sat around Antony as if beside a corpse. But around midnight Antony came to himself and got up; when he saw everyone asleep and only his acquaintance keeping watch, he motioned with his head for him to approach and then asked him to pick him up again and carry him to the tombs without waking anybody.

(9.) And so he was carried back by the man, and as usual, the door was shut, and he was once again inside by himself. He was unable to stand because of the blows from the demons, and so he prayed lying down.[1] After the prayer, he said with a loud voice, "Here I am: Antony! I do not flee from your blows. For even if you do more, nothing shall separate me from the love of Christ."[2] Then he sang, "Though an army encamp against me, my heart shall not fear."[3] This is what the ascetic thought and said.

But the enemy, who hates the good, was amazed that he dared to return after such blows. He called together his dogs and burst out, "See that we have not stopped this one with the spirit of fornication or with blows; rather, he bravely comes against us. Let us attack him in some other way." It is easy for the devil to change forms for his evil purposes, and so at night they raised such a tumult that it seemed as though that entire place was being shaken by an earthquake. The demons, as if they had shattered the four walls of the dwelling, seemed to enter through them, transformed into the appearance of beasts and serpents. And the place was immediately filled with the appearances of lions, bears, leopards, bulls, snakes, asps, scorpions, and wolves, and each of them was moving according to his own form. The lion was roaring, wishing to attack; the bull seemed to butt with his horns; the serpent writhed but did not approach; and the wolf rushed forward but was restrained. Altogether the ragings of their apparitions and the sounds of their voices were completely terrifying. Antony, whipped and tortured by them, felt even more severe bodily pain; but his soul was not trembling, and he remained vigilant. He groaned because of his body's pain, but he was sober in his thinking, and as if to mock them, he said, "If you had had the power, it would have been enough for one of you to come alone. But since the Lord has made you weak, you are trying to frighten me by your number. But it is a proof of your weakness that you imitate the shapes of irrational beings." And again he took courage and said, "If you are able and have received authority against me, don't delay, but attack! But if you cannot, why are you harassing me in vain? For faith in our Lord is our seal and wall for safety." And so after many attempts, they gnashed their teeth against him because they were making fools of themselves rather than of him.

(10.) Meanwhile the Lord had not forgotten Antony's struggle, but came to him in assistance. Thus, Antony looked up and saw the roof as if it were being opened[4] and a certain ray of light coming down to him. The demons suddenly vanished; his body's pain immediately stopped; and the building was once again intact. When Antony perceived the assistance, got his breath back, and was relieved of his pains, he asked the vision that appeared to him, "Where were you? Why didn't you appear at the beginning and make my pains stop?" And a voice came to him, "Antony, I was here, but I waited to see your struggle. Because you endured and were not beaten, I will always be your help, and I will make you famous everywhere." When he heard this, he got up and prayed, and he became so strong that he felt that he had more strength in his body than he had had before. At this time he was around thirty-five years old.

(11.) The next day Antony went out even more enthusiastic about the piety, and when he came to that old man [whom he had imitated earlier], he asked him to live with him in the desert. But when this man declined due to his

---

[1] It was contemporary custom to pray standing with one's arms extended.

[2] See Rom. 8: 35–39.

[3] Ps. 26: 3; Douay Ps. 25: 3.

[4] See Acts 7: 55–56.

age and because there was not yet such a custom, immediately he himself set out for the mountain. Yet again the enemy, when he saw his zeal and wanted to impede it, cast in his way an apparition of a large silver disk. But Antony recognized the trick performed by the hater of good; he stood and said to the disk, because he saw the devil in it: "How did a disk end up in the desert? This path is not well-trod, nor is there any trace of people having traveled through here. If it had fallen, it would have been missed thanks to its size; rather, the one who lost it would have turned back, searched, and found it since the place is a desert. This is the devil's work. You will not impede my intention in this way, devil! Indeed, let this go with you into destruction."[1] When Antony had said this, it vanished like smoke from before a fire.[2]

(12.) Next, as he went along, he again saw this time not an apparition, but real gold scattered in the path. He himself has not said nor do we know whether it was the enemy who showed this to him or whether it was some better power who was training the athlete and showing the devil that he truly did not care about money at all, but what appeared really was gold. Antony marveled at the amount, but as if stepping over fire, he passed by it so as not to turn back; rather, he ran so fast that the place became hidden and forgotten.

Having intensified his resolve more and more, he hurried to the mountain. On the other side of the river he found a deserted fort, abandoned for so long that it was full of serpents; he situated himself there and lived in it. The reptiles, as if someone were chasing them, immediately withdrew, but he barricaded the door, and since he had stored up enough bread for six months—the people of the Thebaid[3] do this, and their bread often stays fresh for a year—and since he had a water supply inside, he descended as if into a shrine, and he remained alone inside the monastic retreat, neither going out himself nor seeing anyone who came. And so in this way he devoted himself to the discipline for a long time, receiving only bread let down from above the house twice each year.

(13.) Those of his acquaintances who came, since he would not allow them to enter, often used to spend days and nights outside, and they would hear what sounded like crowds making a commotion, clamoring, raising up

pitiful voices and crying out, "Leave our places! What have you to do with the desert? You cannot endure our attack!" At first those outside thought that there were certain people fighting with him and that these people had gone in to him by ladders. But when they stooped and peeped through a hole and saw no one, then they reckoned that they were demons; they became frightened and called for Antony. He heard them, although he did not give a thought to the demons: coming near to the door, he exhorted the people to withdraw and not to be afraid, for he said, "In this way the demons create apparitions against the cowards. Therefore, seal yourselves [with the sign of the cross] and depart with courage, and let these [demons] make fools of themselves." And so they went away fortified with the sign of the cross, but he stayed behind and was in no way harmed by the demons, nor did he grow weary of fighting them. Indeed, the assistance of the visions that came to his intellect and the weakness of the enemies gave him much rest from his labors and made his intention even greater. For his acquaintances would always come, expecting to find him dead, but instead would hear him singing, "Let God rise up, and let his enemies be scattered; and let those who hate him flee before him. As smoke disappears, let them disappear; as wax melts before fire, let the wicked perish before God."[4] And again: "All nations surrounded me; in the name of the Lord I repelled them."[5]

(14.) For nearly twenty years he continued to discipline himself in this way, not going out himself and being seen by others only rarely. After this, when many eagerly desired to imitate his discipline, and others of his acquaintances came and were pulling down and wrenching out the door by force, Antony emerged, as if from some shrine, initiated into the mysteries and filled with God. Now for the first time he appeared outside the fort to those who had come to him. And they, when they saw him, were amazed to see that his body had its same condition: it was neither fat as if from lack of exercise nor withered as if from fasting and fighting demons, but it was such as they had known it before his withdrawal. The disposition of his soul was pure again, for it was neither contracted from distress, nor dissipated from pleasure, nor constrained by levity or dejection. Indeed, when he

---

[1]   See Acts 8: 20.

[2]   See Ps. 68: 2; Douay Ps. 67: 2.

[3]   The Egyptian province to which Antony had retreated.

[4]   Ps. 68: 1–2; Douay Ps. 67: 1–2.

[5]   Ps. 118: 10; Douay Ps. 117: 10.

saw the crowd, he was not disturbed, nor did he rejoice to be greeted by so many people. Rather, he was wholly balanced, as if he were being navigated by the Word and existing in his natural state.

Therefore, through Antony the Lord healed many of the suffering bodies of those present, and others he cleansed of demons. He gave Antony grace in speaking, and thus he comforted many who were grieved and reconciled into friendship others who were quarreling, exhorting everyone to prefer nothing in the world to the love for Christ. While he discussed and recalled the good things to come and the love for humanity that has come to us from God, "who did not withhold his own son, but gave him up for all of us."[1] he persuaded many to choose the solitary life. And so at last there came to be monasteries even in the mountains, and the desert was made a city of monks, who left their homes and enrolled in the heavenly commonwealth.[2]

1.10 The active life: Sulpicius Severus, *The Life of St. Martin of Tours* (397). Original in Latin.

Sulpicius Severus (*c.*360–*c.*420), a well-to-do and well-educated man of Aquitaine (southern Gaul), became a monk later in life. He met St. Martin (d.397) in 393 or 394 and, impressed by the holy man, wrote his *Life* shortly afterwards. It was a great success: St. Martin soon became the subject of a number of supplementary accounts—letters concerning his death; descriptions of his miracles—and was adopted as the patron saint of the Merovingian kings. Unlike St. Antony, Martin was a bishop, and thus Sulpicius needed to find a way to combine the model of the ascetic monk with that of the active life of a man in the world. Compare the virtues and lifestyles of Antony and Martin. What message did Martin's *Life* have for warriors? What ideals of behavior did it offer to bishops?

[Source: *Medieval Saints: A Reader*, ed. Mary-Ann Stouck (Toronto: University of Toronto Press, 1999), pp. 139–42, 144–49 (slightly modified).]

Martin, then, was born at Sabaria in Pannonia [modern Hungary], but was brought up at Ticinum [Pavia], which is situated in Italy. In terms of worldly dignity, his parents were not of the lowest rank, but they were pagans. His father was at first simply a soldier, but afterwards a military tribune. He himself took up a military career while a youth and was enrolled in the imperial guard, first under king Constantine,[3] and then under the Caesar Julian.[4] This, however, was not done of his own free will, for, almost from the earliest years of his holy childhood, this distinguished boy aspired rather to the service of God. For when he was ten years old, against the wish of his parents, he fled to a church and begged to become a catechumen [to begin instruction in Christianity]. Soon afterwards, in a wonderful manner he became completely devoted to the work of God, and when he was twelve years old, he longed for a life in the desert [to become a hermit]; and he would have made the necessary vows if his youthfulness had not been an obstacle. His mind, however, was always intent upon hermitages or the Church, and already meditated in his boyish years on what he later fulfilled as a religious. But since an edict was issued by the rulers of the state that the sons of veterans should be enrolled for military service, his father (who grudged his pious behavior) delivered him up when he was fifteen years old, and he was arrested and put

---

[1] Rom. 8: 32.

[2] See Phil. 3: 20; Heb. 12: 23. Compare with Augustine's idea of the City of God, above, p. 14.

[3] Constantine I (r.306–337).

[4] Julian was at this time Caesar in Gaul. Later, when emperor (r.361–363), he was known as "the Apostate."

in chains and was bound by the military oath. He was content with only one servant as his attendant, and then, reversing roles, the master waited on the servant to such a degree that, for the most part, it was he who pulled off his [servant's] boots and he who cleaned them with his own hand; and while they took their meals together, it was he who more often served them. For nearly three years before his baptism, he was a professional soldier, but he kept completely free from those vices in which that class of men become too frequently involved. He showed great kindness towards his fellow-soldiers, and wonderful affection, and his patience and humility surpassed what seemed possible to human nature. There is no need to praise the self-denial which he displayed: it was so great that, even at that date, he was regarded not so much as being a soldier as a monk. By all these qualities he had so endeared himself to the whole body of his comrades that they held him in extraordinary affection. Although not yet regenerated in Christ, by his good works he acted the part of a candidate for baptism.[1] This he did, for instance, by aiding those who were in trouble, by giving help to the wretched, by supporting the needy, by clothing the naked, while he reserved nothing for himself from his military pay except what was necessary for his daily sustenance. Even then, far from being a senseless hearer of the Gospel, he took no thought for the morrow.[2]

So it happened one day when he had nothing except his weapons and his simple military dress, in the middle of a winter which had been very bitter and more severe than usual, so that the extreme cold had caused the death of many, he chanced to meet at the gate of the city of Amiens a poor naked man. He [the beggar] was entreating the passers-by to have pity on him, but all passed the wretched man without notice, when Martin, that man full of God, recognized that the beggar to whom others showed no pity was reserved for him. But what should he do? He had nothing except the cloak in which he was dressed, for he had already parted with the rest of his garments for similar purposes. Taking, therefore, his sword, which he was wearing, he divided his cloak in half, and gave one part to the beggar, and clothed himself again with what was left. At this, some of the bystanders laughed, because he was now an unsightly object in his mutilated clothing. Many, however, who were of sounder understanding, regretted deeply that they themselves had done nothing similar. They especially felt this because, possessing more than Martin, they could have clothed the poor man without reducing themselves to nakedness.

The following night while he slept Martin had a vision of Christ wearing the part of his cloak with which he had clothed the beggar. He was told to regard the Lord with the greatest care, and to recognize [the Lord's] robe as his own. Before long, he heard Jesus saying in a clear voice to the multitude of angels standing round, "Martin, who is still only a catechumen, clothed me with this robe." Truly the Lord remembered his own words, which he had spoken [while on earth]: "Inasmuch as ye have done these things to one of the least of these, ye have done them unto me,"[3] when he declared that he himself had been clothed in that beggar; and he confirmed the testimony he bore to such a good deed by condescending to show himself in that very garment which the beggar had received.

After this vision the sainted man was not puffed up with vainglory, but he acknowledged the goodness of God in his own action, and as he was now twenty years old he rushed off to receive baptism. However, he did not immediately retire from military service, but gave into the entreaties of his tribune, whom he served as one of his private staff. For the tribune promised that, after his term of office had expired, he too would retire from the world. Martin was held back by this expectation, and continued to act the part of a soldier (although only in name) for nearly two years after he had received baptism.

In the meantime, the barbarians were invading the two divisions of Gaul, and the Caesar [Julian] brought an army together at the city of Worms, and began to distribute a donative [bonus] to the soldiers. As the custom was, they were called forward, one by one, until it came to Martin's turn. Then, indeed, thinking it a good time to ask for his discharge—for he did not think it would be proper for him to receive a donative if he did not intend to continue as a soldier—he said to Caesar, "Until now I have served you as a soldier: permit me now to be a soldier for God. Let the man who is to fight for you receive your donative; I am a soldier of Christ: it is not lawful for me to fight." Then the tyrant began to rage at what he said, declaring that [Martin] was withdrawing from military service from fear of the battle which was to take place the next day, and not from any religious motive. But Martin, full of courage, and all the more

---

[1]   In this era, infant baptism was unusual, most Christians were baptized in adulthood.

[2]   Matt. 6: 34.

[3]   Matt. 25: 40.

resolute in the face of this attempt at intimidation, said, "If this is attributed to cowardice and not to faith, tomorrow I will confront the battle-line unarmed, and in the name of the Lord Jesus, protected by the sign of the cross and not by shield or helmet, I will advance unharmed into the ranks of the enemy." Then he was ordered to be thrown back into prison, so that he might keep his promise by exposing himself unarmed to the barbarians. But the next day, the enemy sent ambassadors to negotiate peace, surrendering themselves and everything they possessed. From these circumstances, who can doubt that this victory was indeed due to the saintly man? For it was granted him that he should not be sent unarmed into battle. And although the good Lord could have preserved his own soldier even from the swords and spears of the enemy, yet he removed all necessity for fighting so that [Martin's] blessed eyes might not have to witness the death of others. For Christ could not have granted any victory on behalf of his own soldier other than subduing the enemy without bloodshed or the death of anyone.

After leaving military service, [Martin] sought out blessed Hilary [d.c.367], bishop of the city of Poitiers whose proven faith in the things of God was highly regarded, and he stayed with him for some time.... [Later, Martin left Hilary in order to return home to convert his parents. Hilary, meanwhile, was exiled and lived for a time in Italy. When he was allowed to return to Poitiers, Martin joined him there.]

After he [Martin] had been most joyfully welcomed by him [Hilary], he established for himself a monastery not far from the town [at Ligugé]. At this time he was joined by a certain catechumen who wished to have instruction in the teachings of the most holy man. Only a few days later, however, the catechumen fell suddenly ill, suffering from a high fever. It so happened that Martin was then away from home. He was absent for three days, and on his return he found the lifeless body; and death had been so sudden, that he had left this world without receiving baptism. The body had been laid out in public, and the grieving brethren were visiting it as their sad duty required, when Martin hurried up, weeping and lamenting. But with his soul completely filled with the Holy Spirit, he ordered the others to leave the cell in which the body was lying; and bolting the door, he stretched himself at full length on the dead limbs of the departed brother. After he had stayed lying there for some time in prayer, and had

become aware through the Spirit that the power of God was present, he rose up for a short time, and fixing his gaze on the dead man's face he waited with confidence for the result of his prayer and the mercy of the Lord. And after scarcely two hours had passed he saw the dead man begin to move all his limbs little by little, and his eyes trembling and blinking as he recovered his sight. Then indeed he raised a loud voice to the Lord and gave thanks, filling the cell with cries. Hearing the noise, those who had been standing at the door immediately rushed inside. And truly a marvelous spectacle met them, for they beheld the man alive whom they had left for dead.

Thus restored to life, he immediately received baptism and lived for many years afterwards; and he was the first one among us to give both substantial proof of Martin's virtues and to testify to them. He often related that, when he left the body, he was brought before the tribunal of the Judge [God], and had a dismal sentence pronounced on him which relegated him to the dark places among the crowd of common men.[1] Then, however, he added, it was suggested by two angels of the Judge that he was the man for whom Martin was praying; and so the same angels were ordered to lead him back and to give him to Martin, and restore him to his former life. From this time forward, the name of the blessed man became famous, so that he was treated as if he were already a saint by everyone, and was also held to be powerful and a true apostle....

At about the same time, Martin was sought after to be bishop of the church at Tours,[2] but when he could not easily be persuaded to leave his monastery, a certain Rusticius, one of the citizens, pretended that his wife was ill, and by throwing himself down at [Martin's] knees, prevailed on him to leave. A crowd of citizens had previously been posted along the road on which he traveled, and in this way he was escorted to the city as if under guard. In an amazing manner, an incredible number of people not only from that town but also from the neighboring cities had assembled to give their votes. They all had only the same wish, the same desire, the same opinion: that Martin was most worthy of being bishop, and that the Church would be happy with such a priest.

A few impious persons, however, including some of the bishops who had been summoned to appoint the prelate, resisted, asserting strongly that Martin's person was contemptible, that he was unworthy of being a bishop, that he was despicable in appearance, his cloth-

---

[1]   This is a very early reference to Limbo, the eternal home of the souls of the unbaptized.

[2]   In 371.

ing was shabby and his hair disgusting. This madness of theirs was ridiculed by people of sounder judgment, since even while they attempted to slander him they were proclaiming his extraordinary merits. And in truth, they were not allowed to do anything other than what the people wished for, in accordance with Divine will....

And now it is beyond my power to describe completely what Martin was like after he became bishop, and how he distinguished himself. For with the utmost constancy he remained the same as he had been before. There was the same humility in his heart and the same simplicity of clothing. Filled with both authority and courtesy, he kept up the position of a bishop properly, yet in such a way as not to abandon the life and virtues of a monk. For some time he lived in a cell adjacent to the church; but afterwards, when he could not tolerate the disturbance caused by the numbers of visitors, he established a monastery for himself about two miles outside the city.

This spot [Marmoutier] was so hidden and remote that he no longer had to wish for the solitude of a hermit. For on one side it was surrounded by the steep rock of a high mountain, while the rest of the land had been enclosed in a gentle curve of the Loire river; there was only one means of access, and that was very narrow. Here, then, he inhabited a cell built of wood, and a great number of the brothers were housed in the same fashion, but most of them had made themselves shelters by hollowing caves out of the overhanging rock. There were about eighty disciples who were instructed by the example of their holy master. There, no one possessed anything of his own; everything was held in common. No one was allowed either to buy or to sell anything, as is the custom among many monks. No art was practiced there, except that of the scribes, and even this was assigned to the younger brothers while the elder spent their time in prayer. It was rare for any of them to leave his cell, except to gather at the place of prayer. After a period of fasting was over, they all ate their meals together. No one used wine, except when illness compelled them to do so. Most of them wore garments of camel's hair; softer clothing was considered a serious fault there. This must be considered all the more remarkable, because many of them were considered to be of high rank, brought up in a very different fashion, and yet they had forced themselves to accept humility and patience; and we have seen many of these afterwards made bishops. For what city or church would not want a priest from the monastery of Martin?[1]

But let me go on to describe the other virtues that Martin displayed as a bishop....

While Martin was going on a journey he met the body of a pagan that was being carried to the tomb with superstitious funeral rites. Seeing from a distance a crowd approaching, and not knowing what it was about, he stood still for a little while. For there was nearly half a mile between him and the crowd, so that it was difficult to make out what he was seeing. Nevertheless, because he saw it was a group of peasants, when the linen cloths covering the body were blown about by the wind, he believed that some profane sacrificial rites were being performed. For it was the custom among the peasants of Gaul in their wretched madness to carry about through the fields the images of demons covered with a white veil.

Therefore he raised the sign of the cross against them and commanded the crowd not to move from the place where they were and to put down what they were carrying. At this, wonderful to relate, you might have seen the wretched creatures first become as rigid as rocks. Next, when they tried with a great effort to move forward, but were not able to take a step farther, they began to whirl themselves about in the most ridiculous fashion until they were defeated and had to put down the dead body. They were thunderstruck and looked at each other, silently wondering what had happened to them. But when the saintly man discovered that the peasants were simply performing funeral rites, and not sacrifices, with raised hand he gave them back the power of leaving and of lifting up the body. Thus when he wished, he made them stand still, and when he pleased, he let them go.

On another occasion, in a certain village he demolished a very ancient temple, and set about cutting down a pine-tree that stood close to the temple. The chief priest of that place and a crowd of other pagans began to oppose him. And although these people had, at the Lord's command, been quiet while the temple was being destroyed, they could not endure the cutting-down of the tree. Martin carefully impressed upon them that there was nothing sacred in the trunk of a tree, and urged them instead to honor God whom he himself served; the tree had to be cut down because it was dedicated to a demon.

Then one of them who was bolder than the others said, "If you have any trust in your God, whom you say you worship, we ourselves will cut down this tree, and you stand in its path; for if, as you say, your Lord is with you, you will not be hurt." Then Martin, courageously

---

[1] Compare the standards at Marmoutier with those described in *The Benedictine Rule* (above, p. 17).

trusting in the Lord, promised to do so. Upon this, all that crowd of pagans agreed to the condition; for they held the loss of their tree a small matter, so long as they got the enemy of their religion buried under its fall. Since that pine-tree was leaning to one side, so that there could be no question as to which way it would fall when it was cut, Martin was bound to the spot where the tree would certainly fall, as the pagans had stipulated.

Then they began to cut down their own tree, with great delight and rejoicing. A wondering crowd stood some distance away. Little by little the pine-tree began to shake, and, on the point of falling, threatened its own ruin. The monks at a distance grew pale and, terrified by the approaching danger, they lost all hope and faith, expecting only Martin's death. But he, trusting in the Lord, waited courageously, even as the falling pine made a cracking noise, even as it was falling and as it rushed down upon him: simply lifting his hand against it, he held up the sign of salvation. Then, indeed—you would

have thought it driven back like a spinning top—it swept round to the opposite side, so that it almost crushed the peasants, who had stood in what seemed to be a safe spot.

Then a shout went up to heaven: the pagans were amazed by the miracle while the monks wept for joy, and the name of Christ was proclaimed by them all together. And as it is well known, on that day salvation came to that region. For there was hardly one of that huge crowd of pagans who did not long for the laying-on of hands [to become a catechumen] and, abandoning their impious errors, they believed in the Lord Jesus. Certainly, before Martin's time, very few, indeed hardly any in those regions had received the name of Christ. Through his virtues and example that name has prevailed to such an extent that now there is no region that is not filled either with crowded churches or monasteries. For wherever he destroyed pagan temples, there immediately he used to build either churches or monasteries.

1.11 St. Radegund as ascetic: Venantius Fortunatus, *The Life of St. Radegund* (before *c.*600). Original in Latin.

Venantius Fortunatus (*c.*535–*c.*605?) was born and educated in Italy, where he trained in the late classical rhetorical tradition. He came to Gaul when he was about thirty years old to earn his living by writing poetry for wealthy Merovingian aristocrats, both lay and clerical. A few years later he settled at Poitiers, where he became a priest and a close associate of Queen Radegund (d.587). She had originally been a member of the royal house of Thuringia, a kingdom bordering on Frankish territory. When King Clothar I (r.511–561) invaded Thuringia, Radegund became one of his prizes of war and, eventually, his wife. But following the execution of her brother, probably with Clothar's connivance, Radegund founded—and retired to—a monastery (as medieval nunneries are often called, just like their male counterparts) at Poitiers, known as Holy Cross. Toward the end of his life, around 600, Fortunatus became the bishop of Poitiers. In his *Life* of Radegund, Fortunatus was concerned above all to praise her piety, charity, and asceticism. As we shall see, her community wanted other aspects of her work recognized, and so shortly after Fortunatus wrote his hagiography, another was written by a nun at Holy Cross. How might you compare the virtues of Fortunatus's St. Radegund with those of Athanasius's St. Antony (p. 27 above)? What ideals of queenship does Fortunatus's portrait suggest?

[Source: *Sainted Women of the Dark Ages*, ed. and trans. Jo Ann McNamara and John E. Halborg, with E. Gordon Whatley (Durham, NC: Duke University Press, 1992), pp. 70–81 (slightly modified).]

1. Our Redeemer is so richly and abundantly generous that He wins mighty victories through the female sex and, despite their frail physique, He confers glory and greatness on women through strength of mind. By faith, Christ makes them strong who were born weak so that, when those who appeared to be imbeciles are crowned with their merits by Him who made them, they garner praise for their Creator who hid heavenly treasure in earthen vessels. For Christ the king dwells with his riches in their bowels. Mortifying themselves in the world, despising earthly consort, purified of worldly contamination, trusting not in the transitory, dwelling not in error but seeking to live with God, they are united with the Redeemer's glory in Paradise. One of that company is she whose earthly life we are attempting to present to the public, though in homely style, so that the glorious memory that she, who lives with Christ, has left us will be celebrated in this world. So ends the Prologue.

Here begins the Life.

2. The most blessed Radegund was of the highest earthly rank, born from the seed of the kings of the barbarian nation of Thuringia. Her grandfather was King Bassin, her paternal uncle, Hermanfred and her father, King Bertechar. But she surpassed her lofty origin by even loftier deeds. She had lived with her noble family only a little while when the victorious Franks devastated the region with barbaric turmoil and, like the Israelites, she departed and migrated from her homeland. The royal girl became part of the plunder of these conquerors and they began to quarrel over their captive. If the contest had not ended with an agreement for her disposition, the kings would have taken up arms against one another. Falling to the lot of the illustrious King Clothar,[1] she was taken to Athies in Vermandois, a royal villa, and her upbringing was entrusted to guardians. The maiden was taught letters and other things suitable to her sex, and she would often converse with other children there about her desire to be a martyr if the chance came in her time. Thus, even as an adolescent, she displayed the merits of a mature person. She obtained part of what she sought, for, though the church was flourishing in peace, she endured persecution from her own household. While but a small child, she herself brought the scraps left at table to the gathered children, washing the head of each one, seating them on little chairs and offering water for their hands, and she mingled with the infants herself. She would also carry out what she had planned beforehand with Samuel, a little cleric. Following his lead, carrying a wooden cross they had made, singing psalms, the children would troop into the oratory as somber as adults. Radegund herself would polish the pavement with her dress and, collecting the drifting dust around the altar in a napkin, reverently placed it outside the door rather than sweep it away. When the aforementioned king, having provided the expenses, wished to bring her to Vitry, she escaped by night from Athies through Beralcha[2] with a few companions. When he settled with her that she should be made his queen at Soissons,[3] she avoided the trappings of royalty, so she would not grow great in the world but in Him to Whom she was devoted and she remained unchanged by earthly glory.

3. Therefore, though married to a terrestrial prince, she was not separated from the celestial one and, the more secular power was bestowed upon her, the more humbly she bent her will—more than befitted her royal status. Always subject to God following priestly admonitions, she was more Christ's partner than her husband's companion. We will only attempt to publicize a few of the many things she did during this period of her life. Fearing she would lose status with God as she advanced in worldly rank at the side of a prince, she gave herself energetically to almsgiving. Whenever she received part of the tribute, she gave away a tithe[4] of all that came to her before accepting any for herself. She dispensed what was left to monasteries, sending the gifts to those she could not reach on foot. There was no hermit who could hide from her munificence. So she paid out what she received lest the burden weigh her down. The voice of the needy was not raised in vain for she never turned a deaf ear. Often she gave clothes, believing that the limbs of Christ concealed themselves under the garments of the poor and that whatever she did not give to paupers was truly lost.

4. Turning her mind to further works of mercy, she built a house at Athies where beds were elegantly made up for needy women gathered there. She would wash them herself in warm baths, tending to the putrescence

---

[1] Clothar I (r.511–561) was the third son of Clovis and shared his kingdom with Childebert until the latter's death in 558.

[2] Not identified.

[3] Soissons was the capital of Clothar's kingdom.

[4] I.e., ten per cent.

of their diseases. She washed the heads of men, acting like a servant. And before she washed them, she would mix a potion with her own hands to revive those who were weak from sweating. Thus the devout lady, queen by birth and marriage, mistress of the palace, served the poor as a handmaid. Secretly, lest anyone notice, at royal banquets, she fed most deliciously on beans or lentils from the dish of legumes placed before her, in the manner of the three boys.[1] And if the singing of the hours started while she was still eating, she would make her excuses to the king and withdraw from the company to do her duty to God. As she went out, she sang psalms to the Lord and carefully checked what food had been provided to refresh the paupers at the door.

5. At night, when she lay with her prince, she would ask leave to rise and leave the chamber to relieve nature. Then she would prostrate herself in prayer under a hair shirt[2] by the privy so long that the cold pierced her through and through and only her spirit was warm. Her whole flesh prematurely dead, indifferent to her body's torment, she kept her mind intent on Paradise and counted her suffering trivial, if only she might avoid becoming cheap in Christ's eyes. Re-entering the chamber thereafter, she could scarcely get warm either by the hearth or in her bed. Because of this, people said that the King had yoked himself to a *monacha* rather than a queen.[3] Her goodness provoked him to harsher irritation but she either soothed him to the best of her ability or bore her husband's outbursts modestly.

6. Indeed, it will suffice to know how she bore herself during the days of Quadragesima [Lent], a singular penitent in her royal robes. When the time for fasting drew near, she would notify a *monacha* named Pia, who, according to their holy arrangement, would send a haircloth sealed carefully in linen to Radegund. Draping it over her body through the whole of Quadragesima,[4] the holy woman wore that sweet burden under her royal garment. When the season was over, she returned the haircloth similarly sealed. Who could believe how she would pour out her heart in prayers when the king was away? How she would cling to the feet of Christ as though He were present with her and satiate her long hunger with tears as though she was gorging on delicacies! She had contempt for the food of the belly, for Christ was her only nourishment and all her hunger was for Christ.

7. With what piety did she care solicitously for the candles made with her own hands that burned all night long in oratories and holy places? When the king asked after her at table during the late hours, he was told that she was delayed, busy about God's affairs. This caused strife with her husband and later on the prince compensated her with gifts for the wrong he did her with his tongue.

8. If she received a report that any of God's servants was on his way to see her, either of his own accord or by invitation, she felt full of celestial joy. Hastening out in the night time with a few intimates, through snow, mud or dust, she herself would wash the feet of the venerable man with water she had heated beforehand and offer the servant of God something to drink in a bowl. There was no resisting her. On the following day, committing the care of the household to her trusted servants, she would occupy herself wholly with the just man's words and his teachings concerning salvation. The business of achieving celestial life fixed her attention throughout the day. And if a bishop should come, she rejoiced to see him, gave him gifts, and was sad to have to let him go home.

9. And how prudently she sought to devote everything possible to her salvation. If the girls attending her when she dressed praised a new veil of coarse linen ornamented with gold and gems in the barbarian fashion as particularly beautiful, she would judge herself unworthy to be draped in such fabric. Divesting herself of the dress immediately, she would send it to some holy place in the neighborhood where it could be laid as a cloth on the Lord's altar.

10. And if the king, according to custom, condemned a guilty criminal to death, wasn't the most holy queen near dead with torment lest the culprit perish by the sword? How she would rush about among his trusty men, ministers, and nobles, whose blandishments might soothe the prince's temper until the king's anger ceased and the voice of salvation flowed where the sentence of death had issued before!

11. Even while she remained in her worldly palace, the blessed acts which busied her so pleased Divine Clemency that the Lord's generosity worked miracles through her. Once at her villa in Péronne, while that holiest of women was strolling in the garden after her meal, some sequestered criminals loudly cried to her from the prison for help. She asked who it might be. The servants lied that

---

[1]   See Dan. 1: 12, where Daniel and three other boys at court eat plain food, yet thrive.

[2]   A hair shirt was a coarse and rough garment, worn by ascetics next to their skin as part of their penitential practices.

[3]   *Monacha* (pl. *monachae*): female monk.

[4]   Lent.

a crowd of beggars was seeking alms. Believing that, she sent to relieve their needs. Meanwhile the fettered prisoners were silenced by a judge. But as night was falling and she was saying her prayers, the chains broke and the freed prisoners ran from the prison to the holy woman. When they witnessed this, those who had lied to the holy one realized that they were the real culprits, while the erstwhile convicts were freed from their bonds.

12. If Divinity fosters it, misfortune often leads to salvation. Thus her innocent brother was killed so that she might come to live in religion. She left the king and went straight to holy [Bishop] Médard at Noyon. She earnestly begged that she might change her garments and be consecrated to God. But mindful of the words of the Apostle: "Art thou bound unto a wife? Seek not to be loosed,"[1] he hesitated to garb the Queen in the robe of a *monacha*. For even then, nobles were harassing the holy man and attempting to drag him brutally through the basilica from the altar to keep him from veiling the king's spouse lest the priest imagine he could take away the king's official queen as though she were only a prostitute. That holiest of women knew this and, sizing up the situation, entered the sacristy, put on a monastic garb and proceeded straight to the altar, saying to the blessed Médard: "If you shrink from consecrating me, and fear man more than God, Pastor, He will require His sheep's soul from your hand." He was thunderstruck by that argument and, laying his hand on her, he consecrated her as a deaconess.[2]

13. Soon she divested herself of the noble costume that she was wont to wear as queen when she walked in procession on the day of a festival with her train of attendants. She laid it on the altar and piled the table of Divine Glory with purple, gems, ornaments and like gifts to honor Him. She gave a heavy girdle of costly gold for the relief of the poor. Similarly, arriving at the cell of St. Jumer one day on which the happy queen decorated herself [with finery] composed of what I would call by the barbarian term "stapio"—blouses, tunics, hair coverings, buckles, all made of gold and some with circlets of gems—she put them on the holy altar for future benefits. Again, proceeding to the venerable Dato's cell one day, spectacularly adorned, as she should have been in the

world with whatever she could put on, having rewarded the abbot, she gave the whole from her woman's wealth to the community. Likewise going on to the retreat of holy Gundulf, later Bishop of Metz, she exerted herself just as energetically to enrich his monastery.

14. From there her fortunate sails approached Tours. Can any eloquence express how zealous and munificent she showed herself there? How she conducted herself around the courts, shrines, and basilica of Saint Martin, weeping unchecked tears, prostrating herself at each threshold! After mass was said, she heaped the holy altar with the clothing and bright ornaments with which she used to adorn herself in the palace. And when the handmaid of the Lord went from there to the neighborhood of Candes whence the glorious Martin, Christ's senator and confidant, migrated from this world, she gave him no less again, ever profiting in the Lord's grace.

15. From there, in decorous manner, she approached the villa of Saix near the aforesaid town in the territory of Poitiers, her journey ever prospering. Who could recount the countless remarkable things she did there or grasp the special quality of each one? At table she secretly chewed rye or barley bread, which she had hidden under a cake to escape notice. For from the time she was veiled, consecrated by Saint Médard, even in illness, she ate nothing but legumes and green vegetables: not fruit nor fish nor eggs. And she drank no drink but honeyed water or perry[3] and would touch no undiluted wine nor any decoction of mead[4] or fermented beer.

16. Then, emulating Saint Germanus' custom, she secretly had a millstone brought to her. Throughout the whole of Quadragesima, she ground fresh flour with her own hands. She continuously distributed each offering to local religious communities, in the amount needed for the meal taken every four days. With that holy woman, acts of mercy were no fewer than the crowds who pressed her; as there was no shortage of those who asked, so was there no shortage in what she gave so that, wonderfully, they could all be satisfied. Where did the exile get such wealth? Whence came the pilgrim's riches?

17. How much did she spend daily on relief? Only she who bore it to the beggars ever knew. For beyond the daily meal, which she fed to her enrolled paupers twice

---

[1] 1 Cor. 7: 27.

[2] There is no reason to suppose that a deaconess was bound to celibacy; conceivably, Médard had found an ingenious solution to his particular dilemma in consecrating a woman who was still married to the king.

[3] Fermented pear juice.

[4] A drink made from fermented honey and water.

a week, on Thursday and Saturday, she prepared a bath. Girding herself with a cloth, she washed the heads of the needy, scrubbing away whatever she found there. Not shrinking from scuff, scabs, lice or pus, she plucked off the worms and scrubbed away the putrid flesh. Then she herself combed the hair on every head she had washed. As in the gospel, she applied oil to their ulcerous sores that had opened when the skin softened or that scratching had irritated, reducing the spread of infection. When women descended into the tub, she washed their limbs with soap from head to foot. When they came out, if she noticed that anyone's clothes were shoddy with age, she would take them away and give them new ones. Thus she spruced up all who came to the feast in rags. When they were gathered around the table and the dinner service laid out, she brought water and napkins for each of them and cleaned the mouth and hands of the invalids herself. Then three trays laden with delicacies would be carried in. Standing like a good hostess before the diners, she cut up the bread and meat and served everyone while fasting herself. Moreover, she never ceased to offer food to the blind and weak with a spoon. In this, two women aided her but she alone served them, busy as a new Martha until the "brothers" were drunk and happily satisfied with their meal.[1] Then, leaving the place to wash her hands, she was completely gratified with her well-served feast. And if anyone protested, she ordered that they sit still until they wished to get up.

18. Summer and winter, on Sundays, she followed a praiseworthy rule. She would provide an undiluted drink of sweet wine to the assembled paupers. First she doled it out herself and then, while she hurried off to Mass, she assigned a maid to serve everyone who remained. Her devotions completed, she would meet the priests invited to her table, for it was her royal custom not to let them return home without a gift.

19. Doesn't this make one shudder, this thing she did so sweetly? When lepers arrived and, sounding a warning,[2] came forward, she directed her assistant to inquire with pious concern whence they came or how many there were. Having learned that, she had a table laid with dishes, spoons, little knives, cups and goblets, and wine and she went in herself secretly that none might see her. Seizing some of the leprous women in her embrace, her heart full of love, she kissed their faces. Then, while they were

seated at table, she washed their faces and hands with warm water and treated their sores with fresh ointments and fed each one. When they were leaving, she offered small gifts of gold and clothing. To this there was scarcely a single witness, but the attendant presumed to chide her softly: "Most holy lady, when you have embraced lepers, who will kiss you?" Pleasantly, she answered: "Really, if you won't kiss me, it's no concern of mine."

20. With God's help, she shone forth in diverse miracles. For example, if anyone was in desperate straits because of pus from a wound, an attendant would bring a vine leaf to the saint speaking with her about what was to be done with it. As soon as the saint made the sign of the cross over it, the attendant would take it to the desperate one, placing it on the wound which would soon be healed. Similarly an invalid or someone with a fever might come and say that he had learned in a dream that to be healed he should hasten to the holy woman and present one of her attendants with a candle. After it had burned through the night his disease would be killed while the invalid was healed. How often when she heard of someone lying bedridden would she sally forth like a pilgrim bearing fruit or something sweet and warm to restore their strength? How quickly would an invalid who had eaten nothing for ten days take food when she served it herself and thus receive both food and health together? And she ordered these things herself lest anyone tell tales.

21. Weren't there such great gatherings of people on the day that the saint determined to seclude herself that those who could not be contained in the streets climbed up to fill the roofs? Anyone who spoke of all the most holy woman had fervently accomplished in fasting, services, humility, charity, suffering and torment, proclaimed her both confessor and martyr. Truly every day except for the most venerable day of the Lord, was a fast day for that most holy woman. Her meal of lentils or green vegetables was virtually a fast in itself for she took no fowl or fish or fruit or eggs to eat. Her bread was made from rye or barley, which she concealed under the pudding lest anyone notice what she ate. And to drink she had water and honey or perry and only a little of that was poured out for her, however thirsty she was.

22. The first time she enclosed herself in her cell throughout Quadragesima, she ate no bread, except on Sundays, but only roots of herbs or mallow greens

---

[1] See Luke 10: 40. Martha is customarily presented as the model of the active religious life for women, whereas her sister Mary symbolizes the contemplative life.

[2] Lepers wore bells to signal their approach.

without a drop of oil or salt for dressing. In fact, during the entire fast, she consumed only two *sestaria* [pints] of water. Consequently, she suffered so much from thirst that she could barely chant the psalms through her desiccated throat. She kept her vigils in a shift of haircloth instead of linen, incessantly chanting the offices. A bed of ashes served her for a couch, which she covered with a haircloth. In this manner, rest itself wearied her but even this was not enough to endure.

23. While all the *monachae* were deep in sleep, she would collect their shoes, restoring them cleaned and oiled to each. On other Quadragesimas, she was more relaxed, eating on Thursday and again on Sundays. The rest of the time when health permitted, except for Easter and other high holy days, she led an austere life in sackcloth and ashes, rising early to be singing psalms when the others awoke. For no monasterial offices pleased her unless she observed them first. She punished herself if anyone else did a good deed before she did. When it was her turn to sweep the pavements around the monastery, she even scoured the nooks and crannies, bundling away whatever nasty things were there, never too disgusted to carry off what others shuddered to look upon. She did not shrink from cleaning the privies but cleaned and carried off the stinking dung. For she believed that she would be diminished if these vile services did not ennoble her. She carried firewood in her arms. She blew on the hearth and stirred the fire with tongs and did not flinch if she hurt herself. She would care for the infirm beyond her assigned week, cooking their food, washing their faces, and bringing them warm water, going the rounds of those she was caring for and returning fasting to her cell.

24. How can anyone describe her excited fervor as she ran into the kitchen, doing her week of chores? None of the *monachae* but she would carry as much wood as was needed in a bundle from the back gate.[1] She drew water from the well and poured it into basins. She scrubbed vegetables and legumes and revived the hearth by blowing so that she might cook the food. While it was busy boiling, she took the vessels from the hearth, washing and laying out the dishes. When the meal was finished, she rinsed the small vessels and scrubbed the kitchen till it shone, free of every speck of dirt. Then she carried out all the sweepings and the nastiest rubbish. Further, she never flagged in supporting the sick and even before she took up the Rule of Arles[2] did her weekly tour of service preparing plenty of warm water for them all. Humbly washing and kissing their feet, the holy one prostrated herself and begged them all to forgive her for any negligence she might have committed.

25. But I shudder to speak of the pain she inflicted on herself over and above all these labors. Once, throughout Quadragesima, she bound her neck and arms with three broad iron circlets. Inserting three chains in them, she fettered her whole body so tightly that her delicate flesh, swelling up, enclosed the hard iron. After the fast was ended, when she wished to remove the chains locked under her skin, she could not—for the flesh was cut by the circlet through her back and breast over the iron of the chains, so that the flow of blood nearly drained her little body to the last drop.

26. On another occasion, she ordered a brass plate made, shaped in the sign of Christ. She heated it up in her cell and pressed it upon her body most deeply in two spots so that her flesh was roasted through. Thus, with her spirit flaming, she caused her very limbs to burn. One Quadragesima, she devised a still more terrible agony to torture herself in addition to the severe hunger and burning thirst of her fast. She forced her tender limbs, already suppurating and scraped raw by the hard bristles of a haircloth, to carry a water basin full of burning coals. Then, isolated from the rest, though her limbs were quivering, her soul was steeled for the pain. She drew it to herself, so that she might be a martyr though it was not an age of persecution. To cool her fervent soul, she thought to burn her body. She imposed the glowing brass and her burning limbs hissed. Her skin was consumed and a deep furrow remained where the brand had touched her. Silently, she concealed the holes, but the putrefying blood betrayed the pain that her voice did not reveal. Thus did a woman willingly suffer such bitterness for the sweetness of Christ! And in time, miracles told the story that she herself would have kept hidden.

[Fortunatus continues with accounts of Radegund's miracles.]

---

1   Presumably left there by the monks attached to a small service community nearby.

2   This was the strict Rule for nuns written by Caesarius of Arles (d.542).

1.12 St. Radegund as relic collector: Baudonivia, *The Life of St. Radegund* (c.600). Original in Latin.

We know nothing about Baudonivia beyond what she tells us in the preface to her *Life* of Radegund. She was a nun at Holy Cross who, around 600, was asked by her abbess and other members of her community to supplement the *Life* written by Fortunatus. As she says, they thought that Fortunatus had not recounted enough of Radegund's miracles. They also must have wanted more discussion of Radegund's interest in relics, since Baudonivia spends much time on this topic. We should not take literally her profession of intellectual inadequacy; this was a *topos*—a commonplace, or customary practice—of ancient and medieval writings, meant to make the reader sympathetic to the author. How would you characterize the different ideals of sainthood presented in Baudonivia's and Fortunatus's two *Lives*, and how might you account for those differences?

[Source: *Sainted Women of the Dark Ages,* ed. and trans. Jo Ann McNamara and John E. Halborg, with E. Gordon Whatley (Durham, NC: Duke University Press, 1992), pp. 86–87, 94–99 (slightly modified).]

To the holy ladies adorned with the grace of virtuous living, Abbess Dedimia[1] and all Holy Radegund's congregation, from Baudonivia, humblest of all.

I can as easily touch heaven with my fingers as perform the task you have imposed upon me—namely to write something about the life of the holy Lady Radegund, whom you knew best. This task should be assigned to those who have fountains of eloquence within them. For whatever such people are commissioned to write is laid out generously in flowing song. On the contrary, people who are narrow of understanding and lack the full fluency of eloquence to relieve their own sterility and aridity—let alone refresh others—not only have no wish to speak out on their own but become terrified when they are commanded to do so. For in myself, I know that I am weak-minded and have but few intelligent things to say. For good as it is for the learned to speak, it is best for the unlearned to keep silence. For the former know how to produce something great from very little while the latter cannot even make a little from a great deal. Therefore what the learned seek eagerly terrifies the unlearned. I am the smallest of the small ones she nourished familiarly from the cradle as her own child at her feet! So that I may, in obedience to your most gracious wishes, compose, not the full story but a partial account in writing of her famous works, and so that I may offer a public

celebration of her glorious life to the ears of her flock, in devout though unworthy language, I pray that you will aid me with your prayers, for I am more devoted than learned. In this book, we will not repeat what the apostolic Bishop Fortunatus[2] recorded of her blessed life but speak of what he omitted in his fear of prolixity, as he explained in his book when he said: "But let this small sample of the blessed one's miracles suffice, lest their very abundance arouse contempt. And even this should in no way be reckoned a small amount, since from these few tales we may recognize in the miracles the greatness with which she lived." Therefore, inspired by the Divine Power whom Radegund strove to please in this world and with Whom she reigns in the next, we will attempt to relate, in rustic rather than refined language, what she did here and to publish a few of her many miracles....

13. While Radegund was still at the villa of Saix, her faithful and devoted mind intent on Christ, she determined, with great devotion, to collect relics of all the saints. At her request, a venerable priest named Magnus brought her relics of Lord Andrew and many others which she placed above the altar. When, at night, she lay prostrate in prayer keeping vigil on her couch, a little sleep came over her while the Lord declared her wish granted, saying: "Know thou, blessed woman, that not only the relics brought by Magnus the priest are here,

---

1   The abbess was the female counterpart of the abbot in a women's monastery.

2   See above, p. 38.

but all those you gathered together in the villa of Athies are assembled here." When she opened her eyes she saw that a most resplendent man had told her these things and she rejoiced and blessed the Lord.

14. After she had entered into the monastery, she assembled a great multitude of the saints through her most faithful prayers, as the East bears witness and North, South and West acknowledge. For from all sides, she managed to obtain those precious gems which Paradise has and Heaven hoards and as many came freely to her as gifts as came in response to her pleas. In their company, she gave herself up to chanting hymns and psalms continuously in ceaseless meditation. At last, news came to her that the holy limbs of Lord Mammas the Martyr[1] rested at Jerusalem. She drank the information in greedily and thirstily; as the dropsical[2] only increase their thirst by drawing more water, so she, though refreshed by God's dew, was burning up.[3] She sent the venerable priest, Reoval, who was then a secular[4] and still abides in the flesh with us, to the patriarch of Jerusalem to ask Blessed Mammas for a token. The man of God received him benignly and, seeking the will of God, announced his request to the people. Three days later, after celebrating Mass, he approached the blessed martyr's sepulchre with all his people and, full of faith, proclaimed in a loud voice: "I ask you, Confessor and Martyr of Christ, that if the blessed Radegund is truly a handmaid of the Lord, you will make it known to all the nations by your power; permit that faithful soul to receive the relic she asks from you." At the end of the prayer, everyone responded, "Amen." Continually declaring his faith in the Blessed One, he went to the holy sepulchre and touched the limbs in such a way that the most blessed saint might indicate what he would give in response to the Lady Radegund's request. He touched each finger of the right hand and, when he came to the little finger, it came away from the hand it belonged to with a gentle pull. Thus the blessed queen's desire was satisfied and her wish granted. With

fitting honors, the apostolic man sent the finger to the blessed Radegund and from Jerusalem even to Poitiers God's praises resounded in her honor. Can you imagine the ardent spirit, the faithful devotion with which she threw herself into abstinence while awaiting the prize, the mighty relic? And then on receiving the heavenly gift, her joy was ecstatic. She devoted herself and all her flock to psalmody, with vigils and fasts for an entire week, blessing the Lord that she had deserved to receive such a reward. For God does not deny the faithful what they ask of Him. Frequently she would say sweetly, in a sort of veiled figure of speech that none could understand: "Anyone who has the care of souls must be sore afraid of universal praise."[5] But no matter how much she wanted to avoid it, the Giver of Virtue labored more and more to display her faith to everyone. Thus, whenever the infirm invoked her, they would be healed of whatever illnesses imprisoned them....

16... What Helena did in oriental lands, Radegund the blessed did in Gaul![6] Since she wished to do nothing without counsel while she lived in the world, she sent letters to the most excellent King Sigibert who held this land in his power asking that, for the welfare of the whole fatherland and the stability of his kingdom, he would permit her to ask the emperor for wood from the Lord's cross.[7] Most graciously, he consented to the blessed queen's petition. She who had made herself a pauper for God, full of devotion and inflamed with desire, sent no gifts to the emperor. Instead she sent her messengers bearing nothing but prayers and the support of the saints whom she invoked incessantly. She got what she had prayed for: that she might glory in having the blessed wood of the Lord's cross enshrined in gold and gems and many of the relics of the saints that had been kept in the east living in that one place. At the saint's petition, the emperor sent legates with gospels ornamented in gold and gems. And the wood where once hung the salvation of the world came with a congregation of saints to the city

---

1 A fourth-century martyr particularly venerated in the Eastern Church.

2 I.e., those affected by dropsy, or edema, in which fluids accumulate in the tissues.

3 See Horace, *Carmina* 2.2.13.

4 The "secular" clergy—priests and bishops—were "in the world," as opposed to the "religious"—the monks.

5 Baudonivia takes every opportunity to emphasize Radegund's pastoral and quasi-priestly activities. Priests were responsible for the "care of souls."

6 Saint Helena, the mother of Constantine, to whom the discovery of the True Cross was attributed, was much admired as a model of medieval queenship.

7 In the partition of Clothar I's lands among his sons, Tours and Poitiers had come to Sigibert (r.561–575). The Byzantine emperor was Justin II, and the date of the mission was 568–569.

of Poitiers. The bishop of that place should have wished to welcome it devoutly with all the people but the Enemy of humankind, to subject the blessed Radegund to trials and tribulations, worked through his satellites to make the people reject the world's ransom and refuse to receive it in the city. So one and another played the role of the Jews, which is not part of our story.[1] But they would see; the Lord knows His own. Her spirit blazing in a fighting mood, she sent again to the benevolent king to say that they did not wish to receive Salvation itself into the city. Until her messengers could return from the lord king, she entrusted the Lord's cross and the tokens of the saints for shelter in a male monastery that the king had founded at Tours for his own salvation, amidst the chanting of priests.

Thus envy inflicted no less injury on the holy cross than on the Lord Himself, who endured every malicious act patiently when He was summoned time and again by the minions of judges and governors so that the people He created might not perish. She cast herself into agonies of fasts and vigils, lamenting and wailing with her whole flock every day until at last the Lord respected his handmaid's humility and moved the heart of the king to do judgment and justice in the midst of the people. Thus the devout king sent word by his trusted man, the famous Count Justin, to the apostolic Bishop, Lord Eufronius of the city of Tours, to deposit the Lord's most glorious cross and the relics of the saints with due honors in the Lady Radegund's monastery. So it was done. The blessed woman exulted in joy with all her cell when Heaven conferred this gift and perfect present on the congregation which she had gathered for God's service, for she had felt in her soul that they might have all too little after her passing. Thus, though she would always be able to help them when she was in glory with the King of Heaven, this best provider, this good shepherdess, would not leave her sheep in disarray. She bequeathed a heavenly gift, the ransom of the world from Christ's relics, which she had searched out from faraway places for the honor of the place and the salvation of the people in her monastery.[2] Thus, with the aid of God's might and heaven's power, the blind receive light for their eyes, the ears of the deaf open, the tongues of the mute resume their office, the lame walk, and demons are put to flight in that place. What more? Anyone who comes in faith, whatever the infirmity that binds them, goes away healed by the virtue of the Holy Cross. Who could attempt to tell the greatness and richness of the gift the blessed woman conferred on this city? For this, all who live by faith do bless her name. And she solemnly called God to witness when she commended her monastery to the most excellent lord king and his most serene lady Queen Brunhild, all of whom she loved with dear affection, and to the sacrosanct churches and their bishops.

....

BARBARIAN KINGDOMS

1.13 Gothic Italy as Rome's heir: Cassiodorus, *Variae (State Papers)* (*c*.507–536). Original in Latin.

Theodoric and his successor kings of the Ostrogoths saw themselves as continuators of Roman traditions. Depending on classically educated men such as Cassiodorus (d.583) to work for them as writers and publicists, they issued edicts, gave orders, and negotiated with other rulers. The documents here were among the papers that Cassiodorus compiled into his twelve-book *Variae* (or *State Papers*) *c*.537, when the Ostrogothic king Witigis was at war with Emperor Justinian (r.527–565). In 2.27 (i.e., *Variae* book 2, document no. 27), Theodoric demonstrates his adherence to Roman law: even though he considers Jews "destitute of God's grace," he grants them the right, as enshrined in the laws of Theodosius (see above, p. 4), to maintain their synagogues. In 2.40 he responds to the request of Frankish King Clovis (r.481/482–511) to send a lyre-player, a symbol

---

[1]   This is most likely another attempt to parallel Radegund with Helena, whose efforts to find and glorify the True Cross were said to have been resisted by the Jews of Jerusalem.

[2]   Thereafter the monastery was named Holy Cross.

of classical refinement and rulership, by writing to Boethius (d.524/526). Trained in the classics like Cassiodorus, Boethius had just written a book on music theory. Writing in Theodoric's name, Cassiodorus borrows some of Boethius's ideas, thereby both flattering Boethius and burnishing the king's reputation for learning. In 3.1, Theodoric presents himself as a peaceful elder statesman mediating between the Visigothic King Alaric and the Frankish King Clovis. His aims were frustrated, however, as Clovis soon attacked the Visigoths and defeated them at the Battle of Vouillé (507). In 10.31, a much later text, Cassiodorus writes in the name of King Witigis, who overthrew Theodahad, the last king of Theodoric's line, and tried unsuccessfully to counter Justinian's conquest of Italy. Note how Witigis claimed the mantle of Theodoric.

[Source: *The* Variae *of Magnus Aurelius Cassiodorus Senator*, trans. S.J.B. Barnish (Liverpool: Liverpool University Press, 1992), pp. 34–35, 38–39, 45–46, 142–43 (notes modified).]

2.27 *King Theodoric to All Jews Living at Genoa (507–12)*

As it is my desire, when petitioned, to give a lawful consent, so I do not like the laws to be cheated through my favors, especially in that area where I believe reverence for God to be concerned. You, then, who are destitute of His grace, should not seem insolent in your pride.

Therefore, by this authority, I decree that you add only a roof to the ancient walls of your synagogue, granting permission to your requests just so far as the imperial decrees allow.[1] It is unlawful for you to add any ornament, or to stray into an enlargement of the building. And you must realize that you will in no way escape the penalty of the ancient ordinance if you do not refrain from illegalities. Indeed, I give you permission to roof or strengthen the walls themselves only if you are not affected by the thirty year limitation.[2] Why do you wish for what you ought to shun? I grant leave, indeed; but, to my praise, I condemn the prayers of erring men. I cannot command your faith, for no one is forced to believe against his will....

2.40 *King Theodoric to the Patrician Boethius (506)*

Although the king of the Franks, tempted by the fame of my banquets, has earnestly requested a lyre-player from

me, I have promised to fulfill his wishes for this reason only, that I know you to be skilled in musical knowledge. To choose a trained man is a task for you, who have succeeded in attaining the heights of that same discipline.

For what is more glorious than music, which modulates the heavenly system with its sonorous sweetness, and binds together with its virtue the concord of nature which is scattered everywhere? For any variation there may be in the whole does not depart from the pattern of harmony. Through [music] we think with efficiency, we speak with elegance, we move with grace. Whenever, by the natural law of its discipline, it reaches our ears, it commands song. The artist changes men's hearts as they listen; and, when this artful pleasure issues from the secret place of nature as the queen of the senses, in all the glory of its tones, our remaining thoughts take to flight, and it expels all else, that it may delight itself simply in being heard. Harmful melancholy he turns to pleasure; he weakens swelling rage; he makes bloodthirsty cruelty kindly, arouses sleepy sloth from its torpor, restores to the sleepless their wholesome rest, recalls lust-corrupted chastity to its moral resolve, and heals boredom of spirit which is always the enemy of good thoughts. Dangerous hatreds he turns to helpful goodwill, and, in a blessed kind of healing, drives out the passions of the heart by means of sweetest pleasures....

Among men all this is achieved by means of five *toni* [scales or modes], each of which is called by the name of

---

[1] This refers to a new law (a "Novel") by Emperor Theodosius II that prohibited Jews from building new synagogues but granted them the right to strengthen those already standing if they threatened to collapse.

[2] This probably means "if no one, for thirty years, has legally challenged the right of your synagogue to exist on that site, and in that form." Theodoric considered property arrangements in place before his conquest of Italy (489–493) to be valid.

the region where it was discovered.[1] Indeed, the divine compassion distributed this favor locally, even while it assuredly made its whole creation something to be praised. The Dorian *tonus* bestows wise self-restraint and establishes chastity; the Phrygian arouses strife, and inflames the will to anger; the Aeolian calms the storms of the soul, and gives sleep to those who are already at peace; the Iastian [Ionian] sharpens the wits of the dull, and, as a worker of good, gratifies the longing for heavenly things among those who are burdened by earthly desire. The Lydian was discovered as a remedy for excessive cares and weariness of the spirit: it restores it by relaxation, and refreshes it by pleasure....

3.1 *King Theodoric to Alaric, King of the Visigoths (507)*

Although the countless numbers of your clan gives you confidence in your strength, although you recall that the power of Attila yielded to Visigothic might,[2] nevertheless, the hearts of a warlike people grow soft during a long peace. Therefore, beware of suddenly putting on the hazard men who have assuredly had no experience in war for many years. Battle terrifies those who are unused to it, and they will have no confidence in a sudden clash, unless experience gives it in advance. Do not let some blind resentment carry you away. Self-restraint is fore-sighted, and a preserver of tribes; rage, though, often precipitates a crisis; and only when justice can no longer find a place with one's opponent, is it then useful to appeal to arms.

Wait, therefore, until I send my envoys to the Frankish king [Clovis], so that the judgment of friends may terminate your dispute. For I wish nothing to arise between two of my marriage kinsmen that may, perhaps, cause one of them to be the loser.[3] There has been no slaughter of your clansmen to inflame you; no occupied province is deeply incensing you; the quarrel is still trivial, a matter of words. You will very easily settle it if you do not enrage yourself by war. Though you are my relative, let me set against you the notable tribes allied to me, and justice

too, which strengthens kings and quickly puts to flight those minds which it finds are so armed against it. And so, giving first the honor of my greeting, I have seen fit to send you X and Y[4] as my envoys. They will convey my instructions, as requisite, and, with your approval, will hasten on to my brother Gundobad and the other kings, lest you should be harassed by the incitements of those who maliciously rejoice in another's war. May Providence prevent that wickedness from overcoming you. I judge your enemy to be our common trouble. For he who strives against you will find in me his due opponent....

10.31 *King Witigis to All the Goths (536)*

Although every promotion must be ascribed to the gift of God, nor is anything a blessing unless we know that He bestowed it, nonetheless, the case of royal office must be especially ascribed to the judgment of Heaven. For God Himself has certainly ordained the man to whom He assigns the obedience of His people.

Hence I thank my originator most humbly, and announce that my kinsmen the Goths, placing me on a shield among the swords of battle, in the ancestral way, have conferred on me the kingly office by God's gift. Thus arms bestow an honor based on a reputation won in war. For you must know that I was chosen not in privy chambers, but in the wide and open fields; I was not sought among the subtle debates of sycophants, but as the trumpets blared, so that the Gothic race of Mars, roused by such a din, and longing for their native courage, might find themselves a martial king.[5] For could brave men, nourished among the turmoil of war, long endure a prince so untried that they were anxious for his fame, although they trusted in their own courage?[6] For inevitably, the reputation of a whole people corresponds to the ruler which that race has earned. Now as you may have heard, I was summoned by the perils of my kindred, and came prepared to endure the common fortune with you all; but who were looking for an experienced king did not suffer me to be [only] their general. Therefore,

---

1   Tones were a way to categorize melodic practices, and theorists differed on their number.
2   The Visigoths, fighting as part of the Roman army, won a battle over Attila's Huns in 451.
3   Theodoric's wife was the sister of Clovis, while Alaric's wife was Theodoric's daughter.
4   The letters were drafted for specific situations but also for use as models for future correspondence. Here we have the form of the model.
5   Mars was the war god of the pre-Christian Romans.
6   The prince referred to here was Theodahad.

give your assent first to the judgment of divine favor, then to the judgment of the Goths, since, by voting for me unanimously, all of you make me king.

Put aside now your fear of punishment, discard suspicions that you will suffer loss: you need fear no harsh treatment under my rule. I who have waged war many times know how to love the brave. Moreover, I am the witness to each of your warriors. There is no need for another to recount your deeds to me: I am a partner in your toils, and know them all. Gothic arms will never be broken by any change in my promises to you: all that

I do will look to the benefit of our race; I will not have private attachments; I promise to pursue what will honor the royal name. Finally, I promise that my rule will, in all things, be such as the Goths should possess following the glorious Theodoric. He was a man peculiarly and nobly formed for the cares of kingship, so that every prince is rightly considered excellent only in so far as he is known to love his policies. Hence, he who can imitate his deeds should be thought of as his kinsman. And therefore you should take thought for the general good of our realm, with, by God's help, an easy mind as to its internal affairs.

1.14 Gothic Spain converts: *The Third Council of Toledo* (589). Original in Latin.

In 589, 63 bishops and other clerics, abbots, and nobles met at Toledo in Spain at the request of King Reccared (r.586–601). They were there to "restore ecclesiastical discipline" by converting the kingdom from the Arian form of Christianity to the Catholic. In 587, Reccared had announced his own conversion, and even before that, in 580, an Arian council at Toledo had accepted part (though not all) of the Catholic Creed on the Trinity, agreeing that the Father and Son were equal and co-eternal, but not the Holy Spirit. The Third Council of Toledo added Catholic teaching on the Holy Spirit and instituted all the canons (laws) of the Catholic Church. Since opposition to the conversion of 589 seems to have been very weak, it is likely that most Visigoths were happy to accept Catholicism, which brought them into agreement with the large Hispano-Roman population in Spain.

[Source: *Medieval Iberia: Readings from Christian, Muslim, and Jewish Sources*, ed. Olivia Remie Constable with the assistance of Damian Zurro, 2nd ed. (Philadelphia: University of Pennsylvania Press, 2012), pp. 12–20. Translated by David Nirenberg.]

In the name of our Lord Jesus Christ, in the fourth year of the reign of the most glorious, most pious and most faithful to God Lord Reccared, king, on the eighth day of the Ides of May, era 627 [589],[1] this sacred council was celebrated in the royal city of Toledo, by the bishops of all Spain and of the Gauls who are inscribed below.

This most glorious prince having commanded, because of the sincerity of his faith, that all the prelates of his kingdom should convene in one [council] in order that they might exult in the Lord, both for his conversion

and for the renewal of the Gothic people, and that they should at the same time give thanks to the divine dignity for such an extraordinary gift, this same most blessed prince addressed the venerable council saying: "I do not believe that you are unaware of the fact, most reverend bishops, that I have summoned you into our serene presence for the restoration of ecclesiastical discipline. And because throughout past times the threatening heresy [of Arianism] did not allow a synod [council] of all the Catholic Church to be convened, God, whom it pleased

---

[1] In the Spanish system of dating, used until the fourteenth century, the year 1 began in what is today 38 BCE. The calculation of the day of the month, however, followed the ancient Roman dating system: the eighth day of the Ides of May was the seventh day counting backwards from May 15, so May 8.

to eliminate the said heresy through us, admonished us to repair the institutions of the customs of the church.…"

Upon [hearing] this, the entire council, giving thanks to God and acclaiming the most religious prince, decreed in that instant a fast of three days. And all the bishops of God having come together again on the eighth day of the Ides of May, after the preliminary oration [prayer], each of the bishops was again seated in his proper place, when behold, among them appeared the most serene prince, having joined himself to the oration of the bishops of God, and filled thereafter with divine inspiration, he began to address [the bishops] saying: "We do not believe that your holinesses are unaware of how long a time Spain labored under the error of the Arians, and how, not long after our father's death, when it was known that we had associated ourselves with your holy Catholic faith, there [arose] everywhere a great and eternal rejoicing. And therefore, venerable fathers, we decided to unite you [in order] to celebrate this council, so that you yourselves may give eternal thanks to the Lord for the peoples newly come to Christ. The rest of the agenda that we present before your priestliness concerning our faith and hope which we profess, we have written down in this book. Read it, therefore, among yourselves. And [then] approved by the judgment of council and decorated with this testimony of faith, our glory shall shine throughout all times to come."

The … book the king offered was received, therefore, by all the bishops of God, and [it] being read in a clear voice by the clerk, the following was heard: Although the omnipotent God has, for the benefit of the populace, given us charge of the kingdom, and has delivered the governance of not a few peoples into our royal steward-ship, nevertheless we remember that we too are of mortal condition, and that we cannot merit the happiness of future blessedness unless we esteem the cult of the true faith, and, at least, please our creator with the creed of which he is worthy. For which reason, the higher we are extolled above our subjects by royal dignity, the more we should provide for those things that pertain to God, both to increase our faith, and to take thought for the people God has entrusted to us.…

Therefore, most holy fathers, these most noble peoples, who have been brought near to the Lord by our diligence, I offer to the eternal God through your hands, as a holy and propitiating sacrifice. Truly it shall be for me an unfad-

ing crown and a delight in the reward of the just if these peoples, who because of our dexterity have rushed to the unity of the church, remain rooted and firm within it. And truly, just as it was [entrusted] to our care by the divine will to bring these peoples to the unity of the Church of Christ, it is your duty to instruct them in the dogmas of the Catho-lics so that, instructed in the full knowledge of the truth, they [shall] know [how] stolidly to reject the errors of the pernicious heresy, and to keep to the path of the true faith through love, embracing the communion of the Catholic Church with an ever more ardent desire.…

To these my true confessions I added the sacred decrees of the abovementioned councils, and I signed them, with God [as my] witness, in all innocence of heart.…

I, Reccared, king, faithful to this holy and true creed, which is believed by the Catholic Church throughout the world, holding it in my heart, affirming it with my mouth, signed it with my right hand, [under] God's protection.

I, Bado, glorious queen, signed with my hand and with all my heart this creed, which I believed and professed.

Then the entire council broke into acclamations, praising God and applauding the prince.…

Here begin the decrees that, in the name of God, were established by the third holy synod in the city of Toledo.

1. THAT THE STATUTES OF THE COUNCILS AND THE DECREES OF THE ROMAN PONTIFFS BE MAINTAINED

After the condemnation of the Arian heresy and the exposition of the holy Catholic faith, the holy coun-cil decreed the following: that since in some Spanish churches, whether because of heresy or paganism, canon-ical discipline was passed over, license for transgression abounded, and the option of discipline was denied, so that any excess of heresy found favor and an abundance of evil made lukewarm the strictness of discipline, [because of these things,] the mercy of Christ having restored peace to the church, [we order that] all that which the authority of the ancient canons[1] prohibited, let it also be restricted by the revived discipline, and let that be performed which [the canons said] ought to be performed.…

2. THAT IN ALL THE CHURCHES THE CREED[2] SHOULD BE RECITED ON SUNDAY …

---

[1] Canons were the laws determined by Church councils.

[2] See the *Nicene Creed* (above, p. 13), to which was added the "filioque," which said that Holy Spirit proceeded from the Father and the Son.

4. THAT IT IS PERMITTED THE BISHOP TO CONVERT A CHURCH IN HIS PARISH INTO A MONASTERY . . .

5. THAT BISHOPS AND DEACONS SHOULD LIVE CHASTELY WITH THEIR WIVES

It has come to the attention of the holy council that the bishops, presbyters, and deacons who are coming out of heresy [i.e., Arians] copulate with their wives out of carnal desire. So that this shall not be done in the future, we decree what prior canons had already determined: that they are not allowed to live in libidinous union, but rather with the conjugal bond remaining between them they should mutually help each other, without living in the same room. Or if [his] virtue is strong enough, let him make his wife live in some other house, as good witness to [his] chastity, not only before God, but also before men. But if any should choose to live obscenely with his wife after this accord, let him be a lector.[1] [And concerning any of] those who have always been subjected to ecclesiastical canons [i.e., Catholics], if against ancient command they have had consort in their cells with women who could provoke a suspicion of infamy, let them be punished canonically, the women being sold [into slavery] by the bishop, their price being distributed to the poor. . . .

9. THAT THE CHURCHES OF THE ARIANS SHALL BELONG TO THE CATHOLIC BISHOPS IN WHOSE DIOCESES THEY ARE LOCATED . . .

10. THAT NO ONE COMMIT VIOLENCE AGAINST THE CHASTITY OF A WIDOW, AND THAT NO ONE MARRY A WOMAN AGAINST HER WILL

In the interests of chastity (the increase of which the council should most avidly incite) and with the agreement of our most glorious lord king Reccared, this holy council affirms that widows who wish to maintain their chastity may not be forced with any violence into a second marriage. And if before taking a vow of chastity they wish to be married, let them marry him who of their own free will they wish to have as husband. The same should be maintained concerning virgins, [for] they should not be forced to take a husband against their parents' will or their own. If anyone impedes the desire of a widow or virgin to remain chaste, let him be held a stranger from holy communion and the thresholds of the church.

11. THAT PENITENTS DO PENANCE

[We are] aware of the fact that in some churches of Spain men do penitence for their sins, not in accordance with the canons, but in a disgusting way: as often as they wish to sin, they ask the presbyter to be reconciled. Therefore, in order to eliminate such an execrable presumption, the council decrees that penitence be given in accordance with the form of the ancient canons, that is: that he who repents should first be separated from communion, and he should avail himself often of the laying on of hands, along with the other penitents. Once his time of satisfaction is finished, he should be restored to communion as the bishop sees fit. But those who return to their old vice, whether during the time of penitence or afterwards, shall be condemned in accordance with the severity of the ancient canons. . . .

14. CONCERNING THE JEWS

At the suggestion of the council, our most glorious lord has commanded [that the following] be inserted in the canons: It is not permitted for Jews to have Christian women as wives or concubines, nor to purchase slaves for their personal use. And if children are born of such a union, they should be taken to the baptismal font. They may not be assigned any public business by virtue of which they [might] have power to punish Christians. And if any Christians have been stained by them, [or] by Jewish ritual, or been circumcised, let them return to liberty and the Christian religion without paying the price [of their freedom]. . . .

16. THAT BISHOPS ALONG WITH JUDGES DESTROY THE IDOLS, AND THAT LORDS FORBID THEIR SERVANTS IDOLATRY

Because the sacrilege of idolatry is taking root in nearly all of Spain and Gaul, the holy synod, with the consent of the glorious prince, commands the following: that each bishop in his respective area, along with the judge of that region, should diligently search out the aforesaid sacrilege, and should not refrain from exterminating that which they find, and should correct those who participate in such error with any punishment available, save that which endangers life. . . .

17. THAT THE BISHOPS AND THE JUDGES CORRECT WITH BITTER DISCIPLINE THOSE WHO MURDER THEIR OWN CHILDREN

Among the many complaints which have come to the ears of the holy council, there has been denounced to it a

---

[1] A demotion to minor orders.

crime so great, that the ears of the present bishops cannot bear it, and this is that in some parts of Spain, parents kill their own children, [because they are] eager to fornicate, and know nothing of piety. Those to whom it is troublesome to have many children should first refrain from fornication. [For once] they have contracted marriage under the pretext of procreation, they make themselves guilty of parricide and fornication, who, by murdering their own children, reveal that they were married not for procreation but for libidinous union. Our most glorious lord king Reccared, having taken account of such evil, his glory has deigned to instruct the judges of those regions to inquire diligently concerning such a horrible crime, in conjunction with the bishops, and to forbid it with all severity. Therefore this sacred council sorrowfully urges the bishops of [those] regions that together with the judges they diligently inquire [about this crime], and forbid it with the most severe penalties, excepting death....

19. THAT THE CHURCH AND ALL ITS GOODS ARE UNDER THE ADMINISTRATION OF THE BISHOP

Many people, against that which is established in the canons, request the consecration of churches which have been built [by them] in such a way that the endowment they gave it not fall under the administration of the bishop, which thing was displeasing in the past and is forbidden in the future. Rather everything is [now] under the administration and power of the bishop, in accordance with the ancient edicts....

22. THAT THE BODIES OF [DECEASED] RELIGIOUS BE PROCESSED [TO BURIAL] AMID THE CHANTING OF PSALMS

The bodies of all religious who, called by God, depart from this life, should be carried to the grave amid psalms and the voices of the chanters only, but we absolutely forbid burial songs, which are commonly sung for the dead, and the accompaniment [of the corpse] by the family and dependents of the deceased beating their breast. It suffices that, in the hope of the resurrection

of the Christians, there be accorded to bodily remains the tribute of divine canticles.[1] For the Apostle forbids us to mourn the dead, saying: "I do not wish you to sadden yourselves about those who are asleep, as do those who have no hope."[2] And the Lord did not mourn the dead Lazarus, but rather shed tears for his resurrection to the hardships of this world. Therefore if the bishop is able, he should not hesitate to forbid all Christians to do this. Clerics, too, should not act in any other way, for it is fitting that throughout the world deceased Christians should be buried thus.

23. THAT DANCES BE PROHIBITED ON THE BIRTHDAYS OF THE SAINTS

That unreligious custom which the vulgar people practice on the feast days of the saints must be completely destroyed. That is, that the people who ought to attend to the divine offices instead dedicate themselves to unseemly songs and dances, injuring not only themselves, but also interfering with the offices of the religious. The holy council commends [this] to the care of the bishops and judges: that this custom may be banished from all of Spain.

HERE BEGINS THE EDICT OF THE KING IN CONFIRMATION OF THE COUNCIL

... We decree that all these ecclesiastical rules which we have summarized briefly above [should be] maintained with eternal stability as is amply explained in the canons. If any cleric or layperson does not wish to obey these decrees, [let them be punished as follows]: If they are a bishop, presbyter, deacon, or cleric, let them be subject to excommunication by the entire council. If they are laypeople of substance in their region, let them give [as a fine] half of their possessions to the fisc,[3] and if they are people of inferior status in their region, let them lose [all] their possessions and be sent into exile.

I, Flavius Reccared, have signed as confirmation these decrees that we established with the holy synod.

[There follow the signatures of the bishops, etc.]

---

[1] This probably refers to any of the poetry of the Old Testament, including the psalms.

[2] 1 Thess. 4: 12.

[3] The fisc was the property or treasury of the state, in this case the king.

1.15 Merovingian Gaul's bishop-historian: Gregory of Tours, *History* (576–594). Original in Latin.

Bishop of Tours from 573 until his death *c.*594, Gregory began his *History* with the Creation itself but soon turned to Gaul and to his own day, which he chronicled in the Augustinian spirit (see *The City of God*, p. 14 above), with both good and bad people and events intermingled. As the successor of St. Martin as bishop of Tours (see *The Life of St. Martin*, above p. 34), Gregory was responsible for the well-being of his flock. But his authority was checked and balanced by that of dukes, counts, and kings. In the excerpt below, in which the former count of Tours, Leudast (d.582), accuses Gregory of slandering Chilperic's Queen Fredegund (d.597), the role of Merovingian kings in Church affairs and the importance of bishops in royal policy are illuminated. Gregory's trial before King Chilperic at Berny-Rivière was a very dangerous moment for the bishop, who might well have been exiled or even executed for treason. Why, then, was he let off with a token sentence?

[Source: *Gregory of Tours: The Merovingians*, trans. and ed. Alexander Callander Murray (Toronto: University of Toronto Press, 2005), pp. 112–20 (slightly modified).]

Book 5

47. [King] Chilperic [r.561–584] heard all about the harm that Leudast [count of Tours] was doing to the churches of Tours and the entire population, and so the king sent Ansovald there. He came on the festival of Saint Martin, and as the choice of count was granted to me on behalf of the people, Eunomius was raised to the comital office.

Leudast, seeing himself set aside, went to Chilperic.

"Most dutiful king," he said, "up to now I have guarded the city of Tours. But now that I have been removed from office, look how it will be guarded. You should know that Bishop Gregory is preparing to surrender it to the son of Sigibert."

"Not at all," said the king on hearing this, "you bring this up only because you have been removed."

"The bishop speaks of even greater matters that concern you," said Leudast; "for he says that your queen [Fredegund] is committing adultery with Bishop Bertram."

At that point the king became angry. He punched and kicked Leudast, ordering him thrown into prison, loaded with chains.

48. Although this book should come to an end, I would like to tell something of Leudast's career. It seems best to begin with his birth, his homeland, and his character.

Gracina is the name of an island off Poitou, where Leudast was born to Leuchadius, a slave of a vinedresser

of the fisc [i.e., royal estates]. From there Leudast was summoned to service and assigned to the royal kitchen. But as his eyes were poor when he was young, and the bitter smoke did not agree with them, he was removed from the pestle and promoted to the baker's basket. Although he pretended to be happy among the fermented dough, he soon ran away and abandoned his service. And when he had been brought back two or three times and could not be prevented from attempting to escape, he was punished by having one of his ears clipped. Then since there was no way for him to conceal the mark imprinted on his body, he fled to Queen Marcovefa, whom King Charibert [r.561–567] loved very much and had admitted to his bed in the place of her sister. She received him willingly, promoted him, and appointed him keeper of her best horses. On this account, now overcome with self-importance and full of arrogance, he canvassed for the office of count of the stables. When he got it, he looked down his nose at everyone, holding them of no account. He was swollen with conceit and undone by the pleasures of the senses; he burned with greed and, as a favorite of his patroness, went here and there on her affairs. After her death, being well-provided with plunder, he tried to maintain with King Charibert his former position by giving gifts.

After this, due to the sinfulness of the people, he was sent as count to Tours, and there the prestige of the high office allowed him to be even more arrogant. He showed himself to be a greedy plunderer, a loud-mouthed

53

brawler, and a filthy adulterer. By sowing dissension and bringing false charges, he there amassed no small fortune.

After Charibert's death, when the city became part of Sigibert's share,[1] he went over to Chilperic, and everything that he had unjustly amassed was seized by the adherents of Sigibert. Then king Chilperic, through his son Theudebert, overran Tours. Since by this time I had arrived in Tours, Theudebert strongly recommended to me that Leudast should hold the office of count, which he had held before. Leudast acted very humbly toward me and was subservient, repeatedly swearing on the tomb of the holy bishop Martin that he would never act unreasonably and that he would be loyal to me in matters affecting my own person as well as in all the needs of the church. For he was afraid that King Sigibert would bring the city back under his authority, as later happened. On Sigibert's death, Chilperic succeeded to his rule and Leudast again became count. When Merovech came to Tours,[2] he plundered all Leudast's property. During the two years that Sigibert held Tours, Leudast took refuge among the Bretons.

When he assumed the office of count, as we have said, his capriciousness reached the point of his entering the bishop's house wearing body armor and mail, with a bow case slung from a belt, a lance in his hand and a helmet on his head, a man safe from no one because he was the enemy of everyone. If he presided over a trial along with leading members of the clergy and laity and saw someone pursuing justice, he would now immediately go into a rage and belch forth abuse on the citizens; he used to order priests dragged away in fetters and soldiers beaten with staves, and he showed such cruelty as to beggar description.

When Merovech, who had plundered his property, went away, Leudast came forward with false charges against me, claiming that Merovech had followed my advice in taking away his property. But after the injury had been done, he again repeated his oath and offered a covering from the tomb of the blessed Martin as a pledge that he would never be my enemy.

49. But as it is a long story to follow step by step Leudast's perjuries and other crimes, let me come to his attempt to overthrow me by unjust and execrable cal-

umnies and the divine vengeance wreaked upon him, fulfilling the saying, "Everyone who overthrows shall be overthrown,"[3] and again, "Whoever digs a pit shall fall therein."[4]

After the many wrongs Leudast inflicted on me and mine, and after the many seizures of ecclesiastical property, he joined forces with the priest Riculf, a man as twisted as himself, and blurted out the charge that I had accused Queen Fredegund of a criminal act;[5] he claimed that, should my archdeacon Plato or my friend Galien be put to torture, they would certainly convict me of having spoken in this way. It was then, as I have said above, that the king had become angry and, after punching and kicking him and loading him with chains, had him thrown into prison.

Now Leudast said that he had the support of the cleric Riculf, on whose testimony he made these charges. This Riculf was a subdeacon, just as unstable as Leudast. The year before, he had plotted with Leudast on this matter and looked for grounds for going over to him due to my anger. At last he found them and went to him. After preparing all their tricks for four months and having laid their traps, Riculf then came back to me with Leudast and begged me to take him back without penalty. I did it, I confess, and publicly received a secret enemy into my household.

On Leudast's departure, Riculf threw himself at my feet.

"Unless you help me quickly, I am lost," he said. "At the instigation of Leudast, I have said what I should not have said. Send me now to another kingdom; if you do not, I shall be arrested by the king's men and suffer tortures that will kill me."

"If you have said anything that does not correspond to the truth, your words shall be on your own head," I said. "I will not send you to another kingdom in case I fall under suspicion of the king."

After this Leudast came forward as Riculf's accuser, claiming that he had heard the previously mentioned testimony from Riculf the subdeacon. Riculf was bound and put under guard, while Leudast in turn was released. Riculf claimed that Galien and the archdeacon Plato were present on the very day the bishop had uttered his charge.

---

[1] King Sigibert I (r.561–575).

[2] Merovech (d.578) was a rebellious son of King Chilperic.

[3] See Jer. 9: 14.

[4] See Prov. 26: 27.

[5] Note there are two clerics called Riculf to be distinguished in the narrative that follows: the priest Riculf, and the subdeacon Riculf.

The priest Riculf, who by this time had been promised the episcopal office by Leudast, was so carried away with himself that his pride was the equal to that of Simon Magus.[1] On the sixth day after Easter [April 26], he who had taken an oath to me three or more times on the tomb of Saint Martin spewed out such abuse that he could scarcely keep his hands off me, confident, of course, in the trap that he had laid.

On the next day, that is, the Sabbath after Easter, Leudast came to the city of Tours pretending to have some business to attend to. He arrested Plato the archdeacon and Galien, tied them up, and ordered them taken to the queen, loaded with chains and stripped of their robes. I heard of this while in my quarters in the bishop's house and, saddened and disturbed, I entered the oratory and took up the Psalms of David so that some consoling verse might be revealed when I opened them. This is what was found: "He led them away in hope and they were not afraid, and the sea covered their enemies."[2]

Meanwhile, as they began crossing the river on a ferry whose deck rested on two skiffs, the boat that was supporting Leudast sank, and if he had not escaped by swimming, he might have perished with his comrades. As for the other boat, which was connected to the first and carried the bound prisoners, it was kept above water by God's help.

Then the prisoners were taken to the king and charges that carried a death sentence were immediately laid against them. But the king, on reflection, freed them from their bonds and kept them under guard, unharmed and unshackled.

At Tours, in the meantime, Duke Berulf and Count Eunomius concocted a tale that King Guntram [r.561–592] wanted to take the city, and for that reason, to prevent anything going wrong, they said, the city must be provided with a guard. They pretended to set watches at the gates to protect the city, but they were really guarding me. They also sent people to advise me to take valuables from the church and make off secretly to Clermont. But I would not take their advice.

Next the king summoned the bishops of his kingdom and ordered the case carefully investigated.

When the cleric Riculf was repeatedly being examined in secret and, as he often did, was uttering many lies against me and my associates, Modestus, a certain carpenter, said to him, "Unlucky man, who so stubbornly has these designs against his bishop, it would be better for you to be quiet, beg pardon from the bishop, and procure his favor."

At this Riculf began to shout out in a loud voice, "Look at this man who bids me be silent and not pursue the truth. He is an enemy of the queen and will not allow the reasons for the charge against her to be investigated."

These words were immediately reported to the queen. Modestus was arrested, tortured, whipped, put in chains, and kept under guard. He was bound to a post by chains between two guards, but in the middle of the night, when the guards fell asleep, he prayed for the Lord to be so kind as to exert his power on behalf of a wretched man and to let an innocent prisoner in bonds be freed by the visitation of the bishops Martin and Médard.[3] The bonds were broken, the post shattered, the door opened, and soon he entered the basilica of Saint Médard [in Soissons], where I was keeping vigils.

The bishops then assembled at the villa of Berny and were ordered to meet in one building. Next the king arrived and took his seat, after greeting everyone and receiving their blessing. At that point Bertram, bishop of Bordeaux, against whom, along with the queen, this charge had been brought, explained the case and addressed me, saying that the charge [of adultery] had been brought against him and the queen by me. I denied in truth having uttered these things, saying, I heard others say them, but I had not devised them.

Outside the building there was a lot of talk among people, who said, "Why are these charges made against a bishop of God? Why does the king prosecute such charges? How could a bishop have said such things, even about a slave. Lord God, help your servant."

The king said, "The charge against my wife dishonors me. If therefore it is your judgment that witnesses should be presented against the bishop, here they are. But if it seems that this should not be done, and that the matter should be left to the honor of the bishop, speak up. I will gladly pay heed to your command."

All were amazed at the king's wisdom and forbearance.

At that point, when all the bishops said, "The testimony of an inferior cannot be admitted against a bishop," the case came down to this, that I should say three masses

---

[1] Simon Magus figures in Acts 8: 9–24, where he is a magician who thinks that the power of the Holy Spirit exercised by the apostles is a type of magic that he can buy.

[2] See Ps. 78: 53; Douay Ps. 77: 53.

[3] Bishop Martin was St. Martin (see above, p. 34); Médard (d.c.545) was bishop of Vermandois; his body lay at the church at Soissons.

at three altars and clear myself of the alleged charges by taking an oath. And though these conditions were contrary to the canons, still they were fulfilled for the sake of the king. Also I cannot be silent about the fact that Queen Rigunth,[1] out of sympathy for my suffering, fasted with all her household until a slave reported that I had fulfilled all that had been required of me.

Then the bishops returned to the king.

"All that was imposed upon the bishop has been carried out," they said. "What remains to be done now, king, if not the excommunication of you and Bertram, the accuser of a brother?"

"Oh no," said the king, "I only reported what I had heard."

They asked who had said this, and he answered that he had heard these things from Leudast. He had already fled owing to the weakness of his plan or his resolution. All the bishops then decided that this sower of discord, traducer of the queen, and accuser of a bishop, should be shut out of all churches, because he had withdrawn from the hearing. To the bishops who were not present, they sent a letter to this effect, bearing their signatures. After this, each of them returned to his own see.

When Leudast heard, he took refuge in the church of Saint Peter in Paris. But on hearing the royal edict prohibiting anyone in Chilperic's kingdom from receiving him, and especially since the son whom he had left at home had died, he came to Tours in secret and carried away his more valuable possessions to Bourges. The king's retainers pursued him, but he escaped by flight. They captured his wife, and she was sent into exile in the district of Tournai.

The subdeacon Riculf was sentenced to death. I managed to obtain his life but I could not free him from torture. Nothing, not even metal, could have endured such beating as was given this wretch. With his hands tied behind his back, he was suspended from a tree from the third hour of the day; at the ninth hour, he was taken down, wracked on pulleys, beaten with staves, rods, and doubled thongs, and not by one or two assailants, but by as many as could reach his wretched limbs. Only at the critical point in the torture did he then reveal the truth and make known the secrets of the plot. This was the explanation he gave for the charge being made against the queen: when she was driven from power, Clovis would

obtain the kingdom, once his brothers and father had been killed;[2] Leudast would get a ducal office. As for the priest Riculf, who had been a friend of Clovis from the times of the blessed Bishop Eufronius, he would win appointment to the bishopric of Tours. The subdeacon Riculf was promised the archdiaconate.

I returned to Tours by God's grace and found the church thrown into turmoil by the priest Riculf. Now this man had been picked out from among the poor under bishop Eufronius and appointed archdeacon. Later he was raised to the priesthood and withdrew to his own property. He was always self-important, arrogant, and impudent. For example, while I was still with the king, he brazenly entered the bishop's house as if he were already bishop, inventoried the church silver, and brought the rest of the property under his control. He enriched the more important clergy with gifts, granted vineyards, and parceled out meadows; to the lesser clergy, he administered beatings and many blows, even raising his own hand against them.

"Acknowledge your master," he said. "He has gained victory over his enemies, and it is by his devices that Tours has been purged of that crew from Clermont."[3]

The wretched man did not know that, with the exception of five bishops, all the others who have held the bishopric of Tours were descendants of my ancestors. He was accustomed to repeating to his intimates the proverb that no one can expect to trick a wise man without using perjury.

Upon my return, when he continued to hold me in disdain and did not come to greet me as did the other citizens, but rather threatened to kill me, I ordered him taken away to a monastery on the advice of the bishops of my province. While he was closely confined, representatives of bishop Felix [of Nantes], who had supported the charge against me, intervened. The abbot was taken in by their perjuries; Riculf slipped away and went to Bishop Felix, who received him warmly, though he should have cursed him.

Leudast meanwhile went to Bourges, taking with him all the treasure that he had plundered from the poor. Not long after, forces from Bourges under their count attacked him and carried off all his gold and silver and whatever else he had brought with him, leaving him nothing but what he had on his person; and they would have taken

---

1   Rigunth (d.585) was the daughter of King Chilperic and Queen Fredegund.

2   This Clovis (d.580) was the son of King Chilperic and his first wife, Audovera.

3   Gregory of Tours's father's family was closely associated with Clermont, and Gregory spent much of his childhood there.

his very life if he had not fled. He regained his strength and in turn led some men from Tours in an attack against his plunderers; killing one of them, he recovered some of his property and returned to the territory of Tours. Duke Berulf heard about this and sent his own retainers outfitted for war to seize him. Leudast realized that he would now be captured, and so he abandoned his property and fled to the church of Saint Hilary in Poitiers.[1] Duke Berulf meanwhile sent the property that he seized to the king.

Leudast would leave the basilica and attack the houses of various people, taking plunder without trying to disguise the fact. He was also repeatedly caught in adultery in the holy confines of the very porch of the basilica. For these reasons, the queen, disturbed that a place consecrated to God was being defiled in such a fashion, ordered him to be expelled from the holy basilica. On being expelled, he went again to his supporters in Bourges, begging them to hide him.

50. I should have mentioned my conversation with the blessed Bishop Salvius earlier, but, as it slipped my mind, I do not consider it unwarranted if it is written later.[2]

When I had said farewell to the king after the council that I mentioned [at Berny], and was anxious to return home, I did not want to go without taking leave of Salvius with a kiss. I looked for him and found him in the courtyard of the domain of Berny. I told him that I was about to return home.

We had moved off a little and were speaking of one thing and another when he said to me, "Do you see what I see upon this roof?"

"Why, I see the roof-covering that the king lately had installed," said I.

"Don't you see anything else?"

"I see nothing else." I suspected that he was making some kind of a joke.

"Tell me what more do you see?" I added.

Drawing a deep breath, he said, "I see the sword of divine wrath unsheathed and hanging over this house."

Indeed, the bishop's words were not wrong; for twenty days later died the two sons of the king, whose deaths I have already described.[3]

---

[1] How does the description of this particular case of asylum in the Merovingian Kingdom fit with the provisions in *The Theodosian Code*, above, p. 4!

[2] Salvius was bishop of Albi 571–584.

[3] In an earlier chapter, Gregory had described the deaths of the two sons of King Chilperic.

TIMELINE FOR CHAPTER ONE

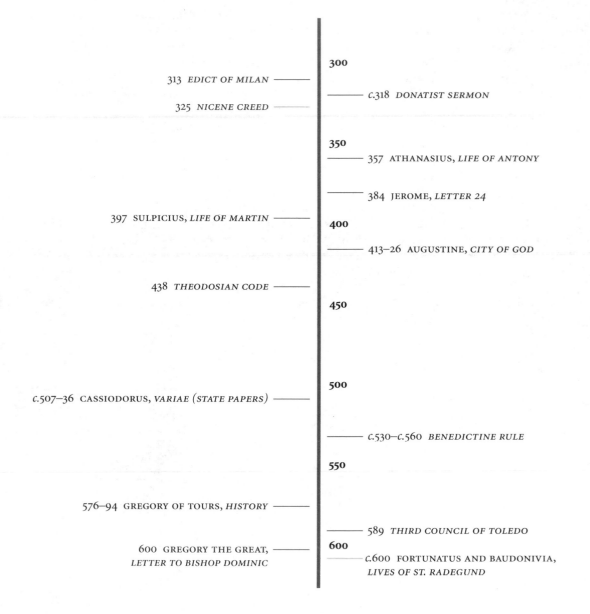

300

313 *EDICT OF MILAN* ——————

—————— *c.*318 DONATIST SERMON

325 *NICENE CREED* ——————

350

—————— 357 ATHANASIUS, *LIFE OF ANTONY*

—————— 384 JEROME, *LETTER 24*

397 SULPICIUS, *LIFE OF MARTIN* ——————
400

—————— 413–26 AUGUSTINE, *CITY OF GOD*

438 *THEODOSIAN CODE* ——————

450

500

*c.*507–36 CASSIODORUS, *VARIAE (STATE PAPERS)* ——————

—————— *c.*530–*c.*560 *BENEDICTINE RULE*

550

576–94 GREGORY OF TOURS, *HISTORY* ——————

—————— 589 *THIRD COUNCIL OF TOLEDO*

600 GREGORY THE GREAT, ——————
600

LETTER TO BISHOP DOMINIC

*c.*600 FORTUNATUS AND BAUDONIVIA,
LIVES OF ST. RADEGUND

*To test your knowledge and gain deeper understanding of this chapter,
please go to www.utphistorymatters.com for Questions for Reflection.*

II

The Emergence of Sibling Cultures (c.600–c.750)

THE RESILIENCE OF BYZANTIUM

2.1 Byzantine village life and the education of a saint: *The Life of St. Theodore of Sykeon* (7th c.). Original in Greek.

One of St. Paul's letters was written to the Galatians, a Celtic people that settled in north-central Anatolia. By the seventh century, they were thoroughly Christianized, as the anonymous *Life of St. Theodore* makes clear. Although the story is set in the time of Justinian, it probably best reflects the period of its writing, just before the Arab invasions of Anatolia. What evidence do you find that villagers were aware of the imperial court? How many local churches can you count? What sort of schooling was normal in a village?

[Source: *Three Byzantine Saints: Contemporary Biographies translated from the Greek*, trans. Elizabeth Dawes and Norman H. Baynes (Crestwood, NY: St. Vladimir's Seminary Press, 1977), pp. 88–96 (notes modified).]

(3) In the country of Galatia[1] there is a village called Sykeon under the jurisdiction of the town of Anastasioupolis which belongs to the province of Galatia Prima, namely that of Ancyra. Sykeon lies twelve miles distant from Anastasioupolis.

The public highway of the imperial post ran through this village, and on the road stood an inn kept by a very beautiful girl, Mary, and her mother, Elpidia, and a sister Despoina. And these women lived in the inn and followed the profession of courtesans.

At that time when Justinian of pious memory was Emperor [r.527–565] certain imperial decrees were being dispatched from the capital, and thus it chanced that a certain well-known man, Cosmas by name, who had become popular in the Hippodrome in the corps of those who performed acrobatic feats on camels, was appointed to carry out the Emperor's orders.

On this man's journey to the East he stayed for some time in the inn, and seeing Mary and how fair she was, he desired her and took her to his bed. From this union

---

[1] Galatia was an Anatolian province of Byzantium.

she conceived and saw in a dream a very large and brilliant star descending from heaven into her womb. She awoke all trembling with fear and related the vision she had seen in the night to Cosmas, the imperial messenger, and he said to her, "Take good care of yourself, dear, for perchance God will watch over you and give you a son who will be deemed worthy to become a bishop." With these words he left her in the morning and went on his way rejoicing.

(4) Next the woman visited a holy father who could foresee the future who lived six miles off near the village of Balgatia, and related to him what she had seen in her dream. The old man said to her, "I tell you of a truth that the son who shall be born of you will become a great man, not as men hold greatness, but he will be well-pleasing to God. For a brilliant star is held to signify the glory of a king by those who are expert in interpreting visions; but with you it must not be read thus. For it is the brilliant adornment of virtues and graces which God has sent down upon the babe in your womb that you saw in the likeness of a brilliant star; for thus He is wont to consecrate His worthy servants in the womb before they are born." When Theodosius, who had been appointed bishop of the town of Anastasioupolis, heard of her vision, he, too, by God's inspiration gave to her the same interpretation.

(5) When her full time was accomplished, Mary bore the servant of God; and after some days had passed, she carried him, as is the custom among Christians, to the Holy Church of the Orthodox and showed him to the priests who baptized him in the name of the Holy Trinity and named him "Theodore," thus showing by this name that he would be the "gift of God." When the child was about six years old, his mother wanted him to enter the Emperor's service in the capital, so she made ready for him a gold belt and expensive clothes and everything else necessary, and then she prepared herself for the journey. On the night when she intended to start, God's holy martyr, St. George, appeared to her and said, "What is this plan, lady, which you have made for the boy? Do not labor in vain, for the King in heaven has need of him."[1] And in the morning she arose and related her vision and wept saying, "Assuredly death has drawn near to my boy." After this she abandoned her journey. She wore herself away with increasing care of her son, and when he was eight years old she gave him to a teacher to be taught his letters. By the grace of God he was quicker at learning than all the other boys and made great progress.

He was beloved by all and in his daily life became known to all for his virtues; for when he played with the others he always beat them, but no oath or blasphemy nor any unfitting word ever escaped his lips, nor did he allow the others to use one. And whenever any dispute arose in their games, he at once withdrew and through his actions put an end to it.

(6) Now there lived in the house a God-fearing man called Stephen who used to make skillfully prepared dishes. The women by this time had become quite respectable, for they had abandoned their profession as prostitutes and followed the path of sobriety and godliness. They now relied upon the goodness of the fare when they entertained the many governors and officers who came to the inn, and they congratulated Stephen who had made the food so tasty. Whenever he received any money, either from the women or their guests, he spent it on the churches where he prayed regularly morning and evening. During Lent, although he prepared all the food for the women, he fasted till the evening partaking of nothing except perhaps a little boiled wheat and water.

The women loved him and looked upon him as a father because he was such a true lover of Christ. The boy noticing this abstinence was moved by divine love and desired to copy Stephen's mode of life, according to the words of the apostle who said, "Remember them that have the rule over you who spake unto you the word of God; and consider the issue of their life and imitate their faith… For it is good that the heart be established by grace; not by meats wherein they that occupied themselves were not profited."[2] "For meat commends us not to God."[3]

His mother and the other women, unconscious of his heart's desire, compelled him to eat with them when he returned home from school at the dinner hour; so when school was over he no longer came home for dinner but spent the whole day in the school fasting and in the evening he would come back and go off with the pious man, Stephen, to the holy churches and there pray and partake of the body and blood of Christ. Returning home he would share with Stephen his boiled wheat

---

[1] St. George (d.303) was martyred in Palestine. He had possibly been a soldier. In any event, he soon became a patron saint of the Byzantine army.

[2] Heb. 13: 7, 9.

[3] 1 Cor. 8: 8.

and water. However much the women and even Stephen himself urged him, he could not be persuaded to do as they wished. Then his mother asked the schoolmaster to send him home at the dinner-hour as she wished to persuade him to eat at least a little vegetable food, because he was getting run down from want of food and from eating only so late in the day. The schoolmaster accordingly sent him away with the other boys, but Theodore did according to the song of David which says: "In the Lord I have trusted; how shall ye say to my soul, Flee as a bird to your mountain?"[1]

(7) When he came out of school he went up the rocky hill which lay near the village. Here there was a shrine dedicated to the martyr St. George. The Saint would guide him to the spot appearing visibly before his eyes in the form of a young man. Entering the shrine, Theodore would sit down and busy himself with the study of the Holy Scriptures, and after midday he went back to the school and returned home in the evening. When his mother inquired why he had not appeared at dinner time, he tricked her saying either that he had not been able to say his lesson and was therefore kept in, or that he had a pain in his stomach and therefore had no appetite. So she again sent word to the master to send him home with the others, and he replied that since he had received her message he always did send him away with the others. Then she found out that he went up to the shrine and so she sent some of her servants to fetch him, and they brought him down to her. She threatened him and told him to come straight home from school to her, but he continued to act as he had been accustomed to do. His mother was very troubled about him, but in spite of all her threats and advice she was quite unable to make him change his fixed purpose, or to break the rules of abstinence which he had prescribed for himself.

(8) When he was about twelve years old an epidemic of bubonic plague fell upon the village and it attacked him along with the others so that he came near to dying. They took him to the shrine of St. John the Baptist near the village and laid him at the entrance to the sanctuary, and above him where the cross was set there hung an icon of our Savior Jesus Christ. As he was suffering great pain from the plague suddenly drops of dew fell upon him from the icon and immediately by the grace of God, freed from his suffering, he recovered and returned to his home....

(10) The boy had made very good progress in learning to read when one day he went into the church of the holy martyr Gemellus,[2] which was near his home, and spent the night there. And he saw himself as though he were in the presence of a king surrounded by a strong bodyguard and a woman clad in purple at his side, and he heard the king say, "Fight the good fight, Theodore, that you may receive full pay in the heavenly army, and on earth I will give you glory and honor in the sight of men." When he had heard this voice, he awoke.

He was twelve years old when his heart was stirred by the message given to him by the King, Christ, in this vision, and in his zeal to follow the path leading to those better things which pertain to salvation he began to shut himself up in one of the cellars of his home from Epiphany to Palm Sunday, and during two weeks in Lent, the first and the middle one, he spoke to no one at all but offered prayers to God alone, and practiced abstinence as he had done before.

(11) Now when the devil, the enemy of truth, saw that Theodore was industriously acquiring the spiritual weapons of virtue against him, he determined to destroy him. Accordingly one day he assumed the appearance of one of Theodore's schoolfellows, Gerontius by name, and took him and led him up to the cliffs of a place called Tzidrama, and, setting him on a lofty crag of the cliffs there, put the temptation to him which was put to our Savior, and said, "If you are willing, master Theodore, to display your powers of conquest, display them here and jump down from this cliff." But Theodore looked at the height which was really great and said to Gerontius, "It is high and I am afraid." The devil said to him, "In the eyes of all the boys you are considered braver than I, and you outshine me, but in this matter I am no coward and will throw myself down." The boy answered him, "Don't do it! You may lame yourself, or even be killed." As the other asserted he could do the feat without any danger, Theodore finally said to him, "If you will, then I will too." So the devil standing with him on the rock jumped down, and alighting on his feet shouted up to the boy Theodore, saying, "See, I have done it! If you dare, come down too, that I may see your bravery: if you can, as in all else, distinguish yourself in this test too." While the boy stood debating within himself full of fear at this utterly useless ordeal, and staggered at the boldness of the supposed Gerontius, who had never previously been

---

[1] Ps. 11: 1; Douay Ps. 10: 1.

[2] St. Gemellus (d.362) was martyred under Emperor Julian (r.361–363) in Galatia.

so bold, George, the martyr of Christ, suddenly appeared and taking Theodore by the hand, led him away from the place, saying, "Come, follow me, and do not listen to the tempting of him who is seeking your soul; for he is not Gerontius but the enemy of our race." And so saying the holy martyr brought him to his oratory.

(12) One day when Theodore was staying in the chapel of St. George his mother and his mother's mother came up to him and with much coaxing tried to force him to come down home saying that they expected the visit of some important friends. But the boy could not be persuaded by them to go down, for he fulfilled literally the words of holy scripture which says, "The friendship of this world is enmity with God, and whoever would be a friend of the world makes himself an enemy of God,"[1] and "No one can serve God and Mammon."[2] He also regarded the wealth of the world as nought, and wishing to get rid of it, he unbuckled his gold belt, took off his necklace and the bracelet from his wrist and threw them down in front of the women saying, "You suspect that these things may get lost and it is because of them you trouble me. Take them then and begone! for I will not leave this place." And the women took them and went, as they could not persuade him. For all his thoughts were towards the Lord Whom he imitated and in Whose footsteps he followed; he fled from his parents and ran to God; he gave up wealth and houses in order to be rewarded a hundredfold and inherit eternal life,[3] as the Lord who has promised this says: "He that wishes to come after me, let him deny himself and take up his cross and follow me!"[4]

For the boy nobly mortified his body, keeping it under and wearing it down, as though it were some alien thing which warred against his soul; and on his forehead he bore the Cross; and just as Peter and James and John and the rest of the apostles "left all and followed Jesus"[5] so this boy likewise believed in the witness of the Scriptures and sought earnestly to mold his life thereon.

(13) Further, he wanted to imitate David in his holy hymn-writing and accordingly began to learn the Psalter.[6] With difficulty and much labor he learnt as far as the sixteenth psalm, but he could not manage to get the seventeenth psalm by heart. He was studying it in the chapel of the holy martyr Christopher[7] (which was near the village) and as he could not learn it, he threw himself on his face and besought God to make him quick of learning in his study of the psalms. And the merciful God, Who said, "Ask and it shall be given you,"[8] granted him his request. For as the boy got up from the ground and turned to the icon of our Savior in prayer, he felt a sweetness more pleasant than honey poured into his mouth. He recognized the grace of God, partook of the sweetness and gave thanks to Christ, and from that hour on he memorized the Psalter easily and quickly, and had learnt the whole of it by heart in a few days.

And he would wander about to all the churches, "with psalms and hymns and spiritual songs singing and praising the Lord," and wherever a commemorative service in honor of a saint was being held, he attended it with joy. Similarly, on the occasion of the all-night service for the holy martyr Heuretus[9] held in the town of Iopolis, fifteen miles away, he left at the hour of supper and ran fasting to this service and after praying and partaking of the divine mysteries of Christ, he returned and reached his home at midnight. For he was an exceedingly swift runner, so much so that several times for a wager he ran a race of three miles with horses and outstripped them.

---

[1] James 4: 4.

[2] Luke 16: 13.

[3] Luke 18: 29.

[4] Matt. 16: 24.

[5] Luke 5: 11.

[6] The book of the 150 psalms.

[7] Nothing is known about St. Christopher, possibly a third-century martyr, except that he died in Anatolia and that a cult grew up around him from a very early period.

[8] Matt. 7: 7.

[9] St. Heuretus cannot be identified.

2.2 The argument for icons: John of Damascus, *On Holy Images* (730s or early 750s). Original in Greek.

Once Emperor Leo III adopted a policy against icons, later dubbed "iconoclasm," a spirited debate about holy images began. An early defender was John of Damascus (*c.*675–749), who became a major spokesman for the iconophile (icon-loving) or iconodule (icon-serving) position. John was born at Damascus when it was under Umayyad rule; his father, although Christian, was employed by the caliph, and John succeeded him in the same position. Eventually he became a monk at Mar Saba, near Jerusalem, where he spent the rest of his life practicing the ascetic life while studying, writing, and preaching. His book *The Fount of Knowledge* was a foundational text for Greek Orthodox theology.

[Source: *St. John Damascene on Holy Images*, trans. Mary H. Allies (London: Thomas Baker, 1898), pp. 1, 4–6, 8–17 (slightly modified).]

With the ever-present conviction of my own unworthiness, I ought to have kept silent and confessed my shortcomings before God, but all things are good at the right time. I see the Church which God founded on the Apostles and Prophets, its corner-stone being Christ His Son, tossed on an angry sea, beaten by rushing waves, shaken and troubled by the assaults of evil spirits. I see rents in the seamless robe of Christ, which impious men have sought to part asunder, and His body cut into pieces, that is, the word of God and the ancient tradition of the Church. Therefore I have judged it unreasonable to keep silent and to hold my tongue....

I believe in one God, the source of all things, without beginning, uncreated, immortal, everlasting, incomprehensible, bodiless, invisible, uncircumscribed [i.e., in no one place], without form. I believe in one supersubstantial being, one divine Godhead in three entities, the Father, the Son, and the Holy Ghost, and I adore Him alone with the worship of latreia.[1] I adore one God, one Godhead but three Persons, God the Father, God the Son made flesh, and God the Holy Ghost, one God. I do not adore creation more than the Creator, but I adore the creature created as I am, adopting creation freely and spontaneously that He might elevate our nature and make us partakers of His divine nature. Together with my Lord and King I worship Him clothed in the flesh, not as if it were a garment or He constituted a fourth person of the Trinity—God for-

bid. That flesh is divine, and endures after its assumption. Human nature was not lost in the Godhead, but just as the Word made flesh remained the Word, so flesh became the Word remaining flesh, becoming, rather, one with the Word through union. Therefore I venture to draw an image of the invisible God, not as invisible, but as having become visible for our sakes through flesh and blood. I do not draw an image of the immortal Godhead. I paint the visible flesh of God, for if it is impossible to represent a spirit, how much more God who gives breath to the spirit.

Now adversaries say: God's commands to Moses the law-giver were, "Thou shalt adore the Lord thy God, and thou shalt worship him alone, and thou shalt not make to thyself a graven thing that is in heaven above, or in the earth beneath."[2] They err truly, not knowing the Scriptures, for the letter kills whilst the spirit quickens—not finding in the letter the hidden meaning....

These injunctions were given to the Jews on account of their proneness to idolatry. Now we, on the contrary, are no longer in toddler harnesses. Speaking theologically, it is given to us to avoid superstitious error, to be with God in the knowledge of the truth, to worship God alone, to enjoy the fullness of His knowledge. We have passed the stage of infancy and reached the perfection of manhood. We receive our habit of mind from God and know what may be imaged and what may not. The Scripture says, "You have not seen the likeness of Him."[3]

---

[1] Latreia is the worship due to God alone.

[2] See Exod. 20: 4–5.

[3] Exod. 33: 20.

What wisdom in the lawgiver! How depict the invisible? How picture the inconceivable? How give expression to the limitless, the immeasurable, the invisible? How give a form to immensity? How paint immortality? How localize mystery? It is clear that when you contemplate God, who is a pure spirit, becoming man for your sake, you will be able to clothe Him with the human form. When the Invisible One becomes visible to flesh, you may then draw a likeness of His form. When He who is a pure spirit, without form or limit, immeasurable in the boundlessness of His own nature, existing as God, takes upon Himself the form of a servant in substance and in stature, and a body of flesh, then you may draw His likeness, and show it to anyone willing to contemplate it. Depict His ineffable condescension, His virginal birth, His baptism in the Jordan, His transfiguration on Tabor, His all-powerful sufferings, His death and miracles, the proofs of His Godhead, the deeds which He worked in the flesh through divine power, His saving Cross, His Sepulcher, and resurrection, and ascent into heaven. Give to it all the endurance of engraving and color. Have no fear or anxiety; worship is not all of the same kind. Abraham worshiped the sons of Hamor, impious men in ignorance of God, when he bought the double cave for a tomb.[1] Jacob worshiped his brother Esau and the Pharaoh, the Egyptian, but on the point of his staff.[2] He worshiped, he did not adore. Joshua and Daniel worshiped an angel of God; they did not adore him.[3] The worship of latreia is one thing, and the worship that is given to merit another. Now, as we are talking of images and worship, let us analyze the exact meaning of each. An image is a likeness of the original with a certain difference, for it is not an exact reproduction of the original. Thus, the Son is the living, substantial, unchangeable Image of the invisible God, bearing in Himself the whole Father, being in all things equal to Him, differing only in being begotten by the Father, who is the Begetter; the Son is begotten. The Father does not proceed from the Son, but the Son from the Father. It is through the Son, though not after Him, that He is what He is, the Father who generates. In God, too, there are representations and images of His future acts—that is to say, His counsel from all eternity, which is ever unchangeable. That which is divine is immutable; there is no change in Him, nor shadow of change.[4] Blessed Denis [i.e., Pseudo-Dionysius][5] who has made divine things in God's presence his study, says that these representations and images are marked out beforehand. In His counsels, God has noted and settled all that He would do, the unchanging future events before they came to pass. In the same way, a man who wished to build a house, would first make and think out a plan. Again, visible things are images of invisible and intangible things, on which they throw a faint light. Holy Scripture clothes in figure God and the angels, and the same holy man [Blessed Denis] explains why. When sensible things sufficiently render what is beyond sense, and give a form to what is intangible, a medium would be reckoned imperfect according to our standard, if it did not fully represent material vision, or if it required effort of mind. If, therefore, Holy Scripture, providing for our need, ever putting before us what is intangible, clothes it in flesh, does it not make an image of what is thus invested with our nature, and brought to the level of our desires, yet invisible? A certain conception through the senses thus takes place in the brain, which was not there before, and is transmitted to the judicial faculty, and added to the mental store. Gregory, who is so eloquent about God, says that the mind that is set upon getting beyond corporeal things is incapable of doing it.[6] For the invisible things of God since the creation of the world are made visible through images.[7] We see images in creation which remind us faintly of God, as when, for instance, we speak of the holy and adorable Trinity, imaged by the sun, or light, or burning rays, or by a running fountain, or a full river, or by the mind, speech, or the spirit within us, or by a rose tree, or a sprouting flower, or a sweet fragrance.

Again, an image is expressive of something in the future, mystically shadowing forth what is to happen. For instance, the ark represents the image of Our Lady,

---

[1] See Gen. 23: 7; Acts 7: 16.

[2] See Gen. 33: 3, and 47: 7, 10.

[3] See Jos. 5: 14–15.

[4] See James 1: 17.

[5] Today scholars call the man whom John referred to as Denis "Pseudo-Dionysius." He was a mystical theologian of the late fifth or early sixth century.

[6] This may be a reference to Gregory of Nyssa (d.c.394).

[7] See Rom. 1: 20.

Mother of God, as does the staff and the earthen jar. The serpent brings before us Him who vanquished on the Cross the bite of the original serpent; the sea, water, and the cloud [signify] the grace of baptism.[1]

Again, things which have taken place are expressed by images for the remembrance either of a wonder, or an honor, or dishonor, or good or evil, to help those who look upon it later on, so that we may avoid evils and imitate goodness. It is of two kinds, the written image in books, as when God had the law inscribed on tablets, and when He enjoined that the lives of holy men should be recorded and sensible memorials be preserved in remembrance; as, for instance, the earthen jar and the staff in the ark.[2] So now we preserve in writing the images and the good deeds of the past. Either, therefore, take away images altogether and be out of harmony with God who made these regulations, or receive them with the language and in the manner that befits them. In speaking of the manner let us go into the question of worship.

Worship is the symbol of veneration and of honor. Let us understand that there are different degrees of worship. First of all the worship of latreia, which we show to God, who alone by nature is worthy of worship. Then, for the sake of God who is worshipful by nature, we honor His saints and servants, as Josue and Daniel worshiped an angel, and David His holy places, when he says, "Let us go to the place where His feet have stood."[3] Again, in His tabernacles, as when all the people of Israel adored in the tent, and standing round the temple in Jerusalem, fixing their gaze upon it from all sides, and worshiping from that day to this; or in the rulers established by Him, as Jacob rendered homage to Esau, his elder brother, and to Pharaoh, the divinely established ruler....

Of old, God the incorporeal and uncircumscribed was never depicted. Now, however, when God is seen clothed in flesh and conversing with men, I make an image of the God whom I see. I do not worship matter, I worship the God of matter, who became matter for my sake, and deigned to inhabit matter, who worked out my salvation through matter. I will not cease from honoring that matter which works my salvation. I venerate it, though not as God. How could God be born out of lifeless things? And if God's body is God by union, it is immutable. The nature of God remains the same as before, the flesh created in time is quickened by a logical and reasoning soul. I honor all matter besides and venerate it. Through it, filled, as it were, with a divine power and grace, my salvation has come to me. Was not the thrice happy and thrice blessed wood of the Cross matter? Was not the sacred and holy mountain of Calvary matter? What of the life-giving rock, the Holy Sepulcher, the source of our resurrection: was it not matter? Is not the most holy book of the Gospels matter? Is not the blessed table matter that gives us the Bread of Life? Are not gold and silver matter out of which crosses and altar-plate and chalices are made? And before all these things, is not the body and blood of our Lord matter? Either do away with the veneration and worship due to all these things, or submit to the tradition of the Church in the worship of images, honoring God and His friends, and following in this the grace of the Holy Spirit. Do not despise matter, for it is not despicable. Nothing is that which God has made. This is the Manichean heresy.[4] That alone is despicable which does not come from God but is our own invention, the spontaneous choice of will to disregard the natural law—that is to say, sin.

2.3 The iconoclastic argument: *The Synod of 754.* Original in Greek.

The Byzantine Emperor Leo III (r.717–741) may have launched the period of iconoclasm, but he treated icons as an abuse, not a heresy. His son, Constantine V (r.741–775), took the next step, calling a church council in 754 to declare the veneration of icons a violation of "the fundamental doctrine of our salvation." The synod, whose proceedings survive

---

[1] See 1 Cor. 10: 1.

[2] See Exod. 34. 28 and Heb. 9. 4.

[3] Ps. 132: 7; Douay Ps. 131: 7.

[4] The Manicheans thought that the world consisted of two entities: evil (matter) and good (spirit).

only because they were included in the account of the later iconodule (pro-icon) synod of 787, compared "unlawful art" to the great heresies of Nestorius and Arius, who challenged the orthodox view concerning the nature of the persons of the Trinity. No representation of Christ, the bishops argued, could accurately portray the correct union of His two natures, man and God. The synod included no patriarch or papal representative, but it did involve over 300 bishops—a very large number. What evidence in this document shows that the synod constituted a major triumph for the emperor? How might you argue that iconoclasm was more popular in its day than later iconodule propaganda might suggest?

[Source: *A Select Library of Nicene and Post-Nicene Fathers of the Christian Church*, 2nd ser., ed. Philip Schaff and Henry Wace, vol. 14: *The Seven Ecumenical Councils* (Grand Rapids, MI: Wm. B. Eerdmans, 1971), pp. 543–45 (slightly modified).]

The holy and Ecumenical synod, which by the grace of God and most pious command of the God-beloved and orthodox Emperors, Constantine and Leo[1] now assembled in the imperial residence city, in the temple of the holy and inviolate Mother of God and Virgin Mary, surnamed in Blachernai[2] have decreed as follows.

Satan misguided men, so that they worshiped the creature instead of the Creator. The Mosaic law and the prophets co-operated to undo this ruin; but in order to save mankind thoroughly, God sent his own Son, who turned us away from error and the worshiping of idols and taught us the worshiping of God in spirit and in truth. As messengers of his saving doctrine, he left us his Apostles and disciples, and these adorned the Church, his Bride, with his glorious doctrines. This ornament of the Church the holy Fathers and the six Ecumenical Councils have preserved inviolate. But the before-mentioned demiurgos of wickedness [i.e., Satan] could not endure the sight of this adornment and gradually brought back idolatry under the appearance of Christianity. As then Christ armed his Apostles against the ancient idolatry with the power of the Holy Spirit and sent them out into all the world, so has he awakened against the new idolatry his servants our faithful Emperors and endowed them with the same wisdom of the Holy Spirit. Impelled by the Holy Spirit they could no longer be witnesses of the Church being laid waste by the deception of demons and summoned the sanctified assembly of the God-beloved

bishops, that they might institute at a synod a scriptural examination into the deceitful coloring of the pictures which draws down the spirit of man from the lofty adoration of God to the low and material adoration of the creature, and that they, under divine guidance, might express their view on the subject.

Our holy synod therefore assembled, and we, its 338 members, follow the older synodal decrees and accept and proclaim joyfully the dogmas handed down, principally those of the six holy Ecumenical Synods. In the first place the holy and ecumenical great synod assembled at Nicaea, etc.[3]

After we had carefully examined their decrees under the guidance of the Holy Spirit, we found that the unlawful art of painting living creatures blasphemed the fundamental doctrine of our salvation—namely, the Incarnation of Christ—and contradicted the six holy synods. These condemned Nestorius because he divided the one Son and Word of God into two sons, and on the other side, Arius, Dioscorus, Eutyches, and Severus, because they maintained a mingling of the two natures of the one Christ.[4]

Wherefore we thought it right to make clear with all accuracy in our present definition the error of such as make and venerate these, for it is the unanimous doctrine of all the holy Fathers and of the six Ecumenical Synods that no one may imagine any kind of separation or mingling in opposition to the unsearchable, unspeakable, and

---

[1]   Constantine V (r.741–775); his son Leo was only four years old at the time; he eventually ruled as Leo IV (r.775–780).

[2]   A church at Constantinople, the shrine of the Virgin at the west end of the Theodosian walls.

[3]   A shorthand way to refer to the other synods.

[4]   Nestorius, Arius, Dioscorus, Eutyches, and Severus represent the heresiarchs (the originators of the heresies) of early Christianity. Each had a different view of the nature of the persons of the Trinity.

incomprehensible union of the two natures in the one hypostasis or person. What avails, then, the folly of the painter, who from sinful love of gain depicts that which should not be depicted—that is, with his polluted hands he tries to fashion that which should only be believed in the heart and confessed with the mouth? He makes an image and calls it Christ. The name *Christ* signifies *God and man.* Consequently it is an image of God and man, and consequently he has in his foolish mind, in his representation of the created flesh, depicted the Godhead which cannot be represented and thus mingled what should not be mingled. Thus he is guilty of a double blasphemy—the one in making an image of the Godhead and the other in mingling the Godhead and manhood. Those fall into the same blasphemy who venerate the image, and the same woe rests upon both, because they err with Arius, Dioscorus, and Eutyches, and with the heresy of the Acephali.[1] When, however, they are blamed for undertaking to depict the divine nature of Christ, which should not be depicted, they take refuge in the excuse: We represent only the flesh of Christ which we have seen and handled. But that is a Nestorian error.[2] For it should be considered that that flesh was also the flesh of God the Word, without any separation, perfectly assumed by the divine nature and made wholly divine. How could it now be separated and represented apart? So is it with the human soul of Christ which mediates between the Godhead of the Son and the dullness of the flesh. As the human flesh is at the same time flesh of God the Word, so is the human soul also soul of God the Word, and both at the same time, the soul being deified as well as the body, and the Godhead remained undivided even in the separation of the soul from the body in his voluntary passion. For where the soul of Christ is, there is also his Godhead; and where the body of Christ is, there too is his Godhead. If then in his passion the divinity remained inseparable from these, how do the fools venture to separate the flesh from the Godhead and represent it by itself as the image of a mere man? They fall into the abyss of impiety since they separate the flesh from the Godhead, ascribe to it a subsistence of its own, a personality of its own, which they depict, and thus introduce a fourth person into the Trinity. Moreover, they represent as not being made divine that which has been made divine by

being assumed by the Godhead. Whoever, then, makes an image of Christ either depicts the Godhead which cannot be depicted and mingles it with the manhood (like the Monophysites),[3] or he represents the body of Christ as not made divine and separate and as a person apart, like the Nestorians.

The only admissible figure of the humanity of Christ, however, is bread and wine in the holy Supper. This and no other form, this and no other type, has he chosen to represent his incarnation. Bread he ordered to be brought, but not a representation of the human form, so that idolatry might not arise. And as the body of Christ is made divine, so also this figure of the body of Christ, the bread, is made divine by the descent of the Holy Spirit; it becomes the divine body of Christ by the mediation of the priest who, separating the oblation [offering] from that which is common, sanctifies it.

The evil custom of assigning names to the images does not come down from Christ and the Apostles and the holy Fathers; nor have these left behind them any prayer by which an image should be hallowed or made anything else than ordinary matter.

If, however, some say we might be right in regard to the images of Christ on account of the mysterious union of the two natures, but it is not right for us to forbid also the images of the altogether spotless and ever-glorious Mother of God, or of the prophets, apostles, and martyrs, who were mere men and did not consist of two natures; we may reply, first of all: If those fall away, there is no longer need of these. But we will also consider what may be said against these in particular. Christianity has rejected the *whole* of heathenism, and so not merely heathen sacrifices, but also the heathen worship of images. The Saints live on eternally with God, although they have died. If anyone thinks to call them back again to life by a dead art, discovered by the heathen, he makes himself guilty of blasphemy. Who dares attempt with heathenish art to paint the Mother of God, who is exalted above all heavens and the Saints? It is not permitted to Christians, who have the hope of the resurrection, to imitate the customs of demon-worshipers and to insult the Saints, who shine in so great glory, by common dead matter.…

Supported by the Holy Scriptures and the Fathers, we declare unanimously, in the name of the Holy Trinity, that

---

[1] The Acephali was another name for the followers of Eutyches.

[2] The "error of Nestorius" was to stress the independence of the two natures—divine and human—of Christ.

[3] The Monophysites, like the followers of Eutyches, rejected both the Orthodox assertion of the hypostatic (or "underlying") union of the "two natures" of Christ and the Nestorian assertion of a union that was not hypostatic but rather accidental.

there shall be rejected and removed and cursed out of the Christian Church every likeness which is made out of any material and color whatever by the evil art of painters.

Whoever in future dares to make such a thing, or to venerate it, or set it up in a church, or in a private house, or possesses it in secret, shall, if bishop, presbyter, or deacon, be deposed; if monk or layman, be anathematized[1] and become liable to be tried by the secular laws as an adversary of God and an enemy of the doctrines handed down by the Fathers. At the same time we ordain that no incumbent of a church shall venture, under pretext of destroying the error in regard to images, to lay his hands on the holy vessels in order to have them altered because they are adorned with figures. The same is provided in regard to the vestments of churches, cloths, and all that is dedicated to divine service. If, however, the incumbent of a church wishes to have such church vessels and vestments altered, he must do this only with the assent of the holy Ecumenical patriarch and at the bidding of our pious Emperors. So also no prince or secular official shall rob the churches, as some have done in former times, under the pretext of destroying images. All this we ordain, believing that we speak as does the Apostle, for we also believe that we have the spirit of Christ; and as our predecessors who believed the same thing spoke what they had synodically defined, so we believe and therefore do we speak and set forth a definition of what has seemed good to us following and in accordance with the definitions of our Fathers.

(1) If anyone shall not confess, according to the tradition of the Apostles and Fathers, in the Father, the Son and the Holy Ghost one godhead, nature and substance, will and operation, virtue and dominion, kingdom and power in three subsistences, that is in their most glorious Persons, let him be anathema.[2]

(2) If anyone does not confess that one of the Trinity was made flesh, let him be anathema.

(3) If anyone does not confess that the holy Virgin is truly the Mother of God, etc.

(4) If anyone does not confess one Christ both God and man, etc.

(5) If anyone does not confess that the flesh of the Lord is life-giving because it is the flesh of the Word of God, etc.

(6) If anyone does not confess two natures in Christ, etc.

(7) If anyone does not confess that Christ is seated with God the Father in body and soul, and so will come to judge, and that he will remain God forever without any grossness, etc.

(8) If anyone ventures to represent the divine image of the Word after the Incarnation with material colors, let him be anathema!

(9) If anyone ventures to represent in human figures by means of material colors by reason of the incarnation, the substance or person of the Word, which cannot be depicted, and does not rather confess that even after the Incarnation he [i.e., the Word] cannot be depicted, let him be anathema!

(10) If anyone ventures to represent the hypostatic union of the two natures in a picture and calls it Christ and thus falsely represents a union of the two natures, etc.

(11) If anyone separates the flesh united with the person of the Word from it and endeavors to represent it separately in a picture, etc.

(12) If anyone separates the one Christ into two persons and endeavors to represent Him who was born of the Virgin separately and thus accepts only a relative union of the natures, etc.

(13) If anyone represents in a picture the flesh deified by its union with the Word, and thus separates it from the Godhead, etc.

(14) If anyone endeavors to represent by material colors God the Word as a mere man, who, although bearing the form of God, yet has assumed the form of a servant in his own person, and thus endeavors to separate him from his inseparable Godhead so that he thereby introduces a quaternity into the Holy Trinity, etc.

(15) If anyone shall not confess the holy ever-virgin Mary, truly and properly the Mother of God, to be higher than every creature whether visible or invisible and does not with sincere faith seek her intercessions as of one having confidence in her access to our God, since she bore him, etc.

(16) If anyone shall endeavor to represent the forms of the Saints in lifeless pictures with material colors which are of no value (for this notion is vain and introduced by the devil) and does not rather represent their virtues as living images in himself, etc.

(17) If anyone denies the profit of the invocation of Saints, etc.

(18) If anyone denies the resurrection of the dead and the judgment and the condign [appropriate] retribution to everyone, endless torment and endless bliss, etc.

---

1 I.e., excommunicated from the Church.

2 I.e., excommunicated from the Church.

(19) If anyone does not accept this our Holy and Ecumenical Seventh Synod, let him be anathema from the Father and the Son and the Holy Ghost and from the seven holy Ecumenical Synods!

[At this point the making or teaching of any other faith is prohibited, and the penalties for disobedience are enumerated.]

The divine Kings Constantine and Leo said: Let the holy and ecumenical synod say, if with the consent of all the most holy bishops the definition just read has been set forth.

The holy synod cried out: Thus we all believe, we all are of the same mind. We have all with one voice and voluntarily subscribed. This is the faith of the Apostles. Many years to the Emperors! They are the light of orthodoxy! Many years to the orthodox Emperors! God preserve your Empire! You have now more firmly proclaimed the inseparability of the two natures of Christ! You have banished all idolatry! You have destroyed the heresies of Germanus [of Constantinople], George and Mansur.[1] Anathema to Germanus, the double-minded, and worshiper of wood! Anathema to George, his associate, to the falsifier of the doctrine of the Fathers! Anathema to Mansur, who has an evil name and Saracen[2] opinions! To the betrayer of Christ and the enemy of the Empire, to the teacher of impiety, the perverter of Scripture, Mansur, anathema! The Trinity has deposed these three!

....

2.4 Vilifying the iconoclasts: *The Chronicle of Theophanes Confessor* (before 818). Original in Greek.

The bitter feelings of the iconodules were given free expression in the *Chronicle* of Theophanes Confessor (*c*.760–817/818), which was in fact written by two men, Theophanes and a high church official named George Syncellus (d. after 810). Both lived during the turbulent period in which iconoclasm was first the norm, then condemned (in 787), and later revived (815–843). It is very likely that the *Chronicle* was written in secret, finished before Theophanes' death, and "published" only after 843. The passage here represents the iconodule take on the Synod of 754.

[Source: *The Chronicle of Theophanes Confessor: Byzantine and Near Eastern History, AD 284–813*, trans. Cyril Mango and Roger Scott (Oxford: Clarendon Press, 1997), pp. 591–92.]

In this year [754] Anastasius, who had held in unholy fashion the episcopal throne of Constantinople, died a spiritual as well as a bodily death of a dreadful disease of the guts after vomiting dung through his mouth, a just punishment for his daring deeds against God and his teacher. In the same year the impious Constantine [V (r.741–775)] convened in the palace of Hiereia an illegal assembly of 338 bishops against the holy and venerable icons under the leadership of Theodosius of Ephesus, son of Apsimarus, and of Pastillas of Perge. These men by themselves decreed whatever came into their heads, though none of the universal sees was represented, namely those of Rome, Alexandria, Antioch, and Jerusalem. Starting on February 10th, they went on until August 8th of the same 7th indiction.[3] On the latter day the enemies of the Theotokos[4] having come to Blachernai [Palace], Constantine ascended the ambo [pulpit] holding the monk Constantine, former bishop of

---

[1] Germanus I (r.715-730) was the Patriarch of Constantinople. He opposed iconoclasm and was sent into exile. Mansur ("Victorious") was the Arabic surname of John of Damascus, whose iconodule arguments may be read above on p. 63.

[2] I.e., Arab.

[3] I.e., 754.

[4] Theotokos means Mother of God in Greek.

Syllaion, and, after reciting a prayer, said in a loud voice, "Long live Constantine, the ecumenical patriarch!" On the 27th of the same month the emperor went up to the Forum together with the unholy bishop Constantine and the other bishops and they proclaimed their misguided heresy in front of all the people after anathematizing the most holy Germanus, George of Cyprus, and John Damascene [i.e., John of Damascus] of the Golden Stream, son of Mansur, holy men and venerable teachers.

THE FORMATION OF THE ISLAMIC WORLD

2.5 Pre-Islamic Arabic poetry: Al-A'sha, *Bid Hurayra Farewell* (before 625). Original in Arabic.

Al-A'sha (which means the "Near-Blind") was a member of the Bakr tribe—thus related to the caliph Abu-Bakr (r.632–634)—and well known for his satires and songs of wine and women. Like other pre-Islamic poetry, his was written down between the 7th and 11th centuries, and the written version probably, like a piece of jazz, reflects both the original idea and the riffs of subsequent poetry reciters. *Bid Hurayra Farewell* is a parody of a traditional Arabic ode. Like the others, it may be divided into three parts: a departure, a journey, and the poet's boast. (In the translation below these parts are labeled by your editor.) But here the departed beloved is overdrawn—"full at the bodice, at the waist sash nil"—and her delicacy over-emphasized—"she braces herself or she'd be thrown back flat." In place of the "journey" is a lover's lament that borders on the ridiculous—"I fell for her by chance. She fell for another who fell for another…"—and then a depiction of a storm mingled with thoughts about inebriation. "Foretell!" the poet says, and instead of recounting the places that he visits in his "journey," he prophesies where the rain will fall. Then the poet begins the journey, sometimes "barefoot," at other times "wearing boots," combining the normally separate adventures of the shoeless brigand and the well-shod warrior, the accounts of both veiled in a drunken stupor. Then suddenly the poet is serious: "How many a land, like the flat back of a shield…/Have I cut through." Finally comes the boast "To Yazid of the Bani Shayban," and the poet recalls battles and challenges his enemies to new ones.

[Source: *Desert Tracings: Six Classic Arabian Odes by 'Alquama, Shanfara, Labid, 'Antara, Al-A'sha, and Dhu al-Rumma*, trans. Michael A. Sells (Middletown, CT: Wesleyan University Press, 1989), pp. 60–66.]

[The Departure]

Bid Hurayra farewell.
The riders are departing.
Can you, man that you are,
bear bidding farewell?
    Brow aglow, hair flowing,   5

a gleam from the side teeth as she smiles,
    she walks gently as a gazelle,
    tender-hoofed in wet soil,
As if her walk
from the tent of a neighbor   10
were the gliding of a cloud
neither slow nor hurried.

You hear her anklets whisper
as she turns away
    like cassia[1] rustling   15
supplicant in the breeze.
She's not one of those
whose neighbors hate to see her face.
You won't find her,
ear to their secrets, listening.   20
    She braces herself
or she'd be thrown back flat,
    when rising to visit a neighbor,
by languor.
She entertains her companion awhile,   25
then slackens,
lower back and buttocks
quivering,
    Full at the bodice,
at the waist sash nil,   30
    a belle, seeming as she comes near
to divide in two.
How sweet a bedmate
on a cloudy afternoon,
not for some unbathed rude   35
to lay and take some pleasure,
    Wide-hipped, delicate,
elbows soft, walk tender,
    as if a thorn were caught
in the arch of her sandal.   40
As she rises
a fragrance of musk trails,
her sleeve-cuffs with the scent
of rose jasmine brimming over.
    No meadow of the meadows   45
of the roughland plateau,
    luxuriant and green, blessed
by dark-trailing big-dropped clouds,
Where the sun is teased
by a blossom in full flower,   50
drenched in color,
mantled deep in rushes and greens,
    Is ever more fragrant,
more redolent
    than she, or more beautiful   55
when evening shadows fall.

————————

[The Journey]

Hurayra said
when I came to pay her call
woe to you, woe,
you woesome male!   60
    I fell for her by chance.
    She fell for another
        who fell for another
    other than her,
For him a girl was falling   65
he didn't desire,
while a cousin on her father's side
was weakening for her, and dying.
    Then for me there fell another,
not to my liking,   70
    love in love on love,
beside itself, entangled, mad,
Each of us afflicted,
raving to this friend or that,
approaching, backing off,   75
ensnared, ensnaring.
    Hurayra shut us off,
not speaking,
    ignorance on the part of Umm Khulayd
of the bond she tied.   80
Didn't she see a man,
night-blind, wounded
by intimations of death shades
and by time, the demented, the undoing?

————————

    Have you seen it blocking the horizon?   85
I passed the night in watch,
    lightning kindled along its edges,
flickering,
With a dark trail behind it,
its middle full and moving,   90
girded and held together
by buckets of rain.
    No play diverts me
from foretelling the rain's direction,
    no pleasure from a cup of wine,   95
no languor.
I told them at Durna,
the drinkers, already sodden:

————————

[1] A cinnamon tree.

Foretell! But how
can a wine-faced drinker heed?   100
        Lightning lit up the slopes
    where the rain would fall,
        in Khabiyya, a blackening cloud
    against the horizon.
They said let it pour   105
on Leopard Streak and Camel Belly,
on Horse Trappings, Tired Man,
and Legland,
        Flowing over the Edgelands,
    then Boar with its tracts   110
        of rock and sand,
    until the hills and mountains burst,
Until the grouse meadows
and the tree-hedged
soft-curved dunes   115
take all they can bear,
        A gushing, quenching draught
    for abodes long since desolate,
        off the track
    shunned by horse and camel mare.   120

_____

You may well find me barefoot,
not a scrap of shoe leather to my name.
Wearing boots or shoeless,
that's the way I am.
        I might well steal upon   125
    some master of his house
        and catch him unawares. Wary once,
    now he finds no haven.
I might one day lead the reins
of youthful passion,   130
and it might follow,
a hot-blooded love-talker at my side.
        Many's the time I have set out at dawn
    to the wine shop,
        followed by a bob-skewing, quick-witted,   135
    path-wise fast-hander,
In a crowd of men like Indian swords
who know that everyone,
barefoot or bootshod,
will perish.   140
        I rivaled them down for the snip of basil,
    head on elbow, reclining,

and for a tangy wine
    from a porous, moistened jug of clay.
They don't come to   145
while there is any of it left,
except to call for more
after a third round or after a second,
        The glass-bearer
    busying here and there,   150
        shirt bottom tucked up,
    alert, agile.
How many a song—you'd think it sung
to a Persian harp—
when a singing girl in a nightslip   155
sings it,
        How many a gowned lady,
    trailing silk,
        how many a girl
    with a leather wine flask at her side,   160
Have I spent my time enjoying,
enduring trial
by amorous talk
and length of pleasure.
        How many a land   165
    like the flat back of a shield,
        wild, where jinn[1] are overheard
    in the corners, rustling,
That no one dares enter,
riding upon the burning heat,   170
except one who, in what he undertakes,
is unhurried,
        Have I cut through
    on a well-worn, rock-ribbed,
        easy-gaited mare, elbows well apart   175
    when you show her.

_____

[The Boast]

To Yazid of the Bani Shayban
bear this word:
Abu Thubayt,
stop gnawing at your heart!   180
        Stop carving at the grain
    of our ancient name
        that nothing can harm

---

[1] Jinn are half-spirit creatures.

as long as burdened camels groan,
Like a mountain goat   185
butting against a rock
to split it, the rock unharmed,
the horns weakening.
     I know you well
     when the battle signal calls us,   190
       when war blazes
     with arms, night raids, and plunder.
You inflame Mas'ud's kin
and his brothers against us,
sowing destruction when we meet,   195
then drawing away.
     Don't sit alone
     when you've stoked the fire!
       You'll implore refuge one day
     from its burning, praying.   200
There were among the people of Kahf,
when they fought, and the Jashiriyya,
those who were quick,
those who would take their time.
     You claimed we wouldn't fight you.   205
We are—tribe of ours!—
     for the likes of you,
     the killers,
Until the chief of the tribe
lies fallen, head on arm,   210
protected by child-bereft women's
flailing hands,
     Struck down by an Indian sword
     well aimed toward its target,

or a supple, well-tempered spear   215
     from Khatt.
We might well spear the chieftain
in the hollow of his thigh,
and a champion might perish
on our spear tips, unavenged.   220
     End it!
     Nothing curbs the overbearing
       like a gaping wound
     unstaunched by oil and gauze.
By the life of the one   225
to whom stamping camels
and long-horned cattle of every kind
are led in offering,
     Kill a chief
     who never stood in your way   230
       and we'll kill one of yours
     like him, one to our choosing.
Try us. You won't find us
after the battle
from the tribe's blood-right   235
turning away.
     Under the noon sun,
     the day of the Bowbend,
       around Futayma, we were the riders,
     not shirking, not giving way.   240
They called for a mounted attack.
We said we can do that.
They prepared to fight on foot.
We're a tribe that fights unmounted.

2.6 The sacred text: *Qur'an Suras* 1, 53:1–18, 81, 87, 96, 98 (*c*.610–622). Original in Arabic.

Muhammad (*c*.570–632), born in Mecca, orphaned, raised by an uncle, married to Khadija, heard (*c*.610) what he understood to be revelations from God. He recited them (Qur'an means "recitation"), scribes wrote them down, and they became the foundation of a new religion, Islam. The whole process of recording and arranging the Qur'an did not end until after Muhammad's death. The resulting book begins with a prayer (the *fatihah*, or "Opening"), followed by chapters (suras) that gradually diminish in length. While different from the odes of the pre-Islamic period (see *Bid Hurayra Farewell*, above, p. 70), the verses of the Qur'an are poetry, and they often take up the traditional themes: remembrance of the beloved (who is now God), the journey (turned into a spiritual quest), and the boast (a celebration of God's generosity and justice). The earliest suras generally are found toward the end of the book. Muhammad's first vision is described in Sura 53, "The Star"; his first auditory revelation was probably "Recite in the name of your lord who created…," which is found in Sura 96. Other suras come from the period after Muhammad made the *hijra*, or emigration, to Medina (622; the year 1 in the Islamic calendar). Most of those presented here are from Muhammad's earliest Meccan period. Note that there is relatively little punctuation (mirroring the Arabic); this is the translator's way of suggesting the open and multiple meanings of the verses.

[Source: *Approaching the Qur'an: The Early Revelations*, trans. Michael Sells (Ashland, OR: White Cloud Press, 1999), pp. 42, 44, 48, 50, 72, 96, 104, 106.]

1: *The Opening*

In the name of God
  the Compassionate the Caring
Praise be to God
  lord sustainer of the worlds
the Compassionate the Caring
master of the day of reckoning
To you we turn to worship   5
  and to you we turn in time of need
Guide us along the road straight
the road of those to whom you are giving
  not those with anger upon them
  not those who have lost the way

53: 1–18 *The Star*

In the Name of God the Compassionate the Caring
  By the star as it falls
  Your companion[1] has not lost his way nor is he
    deluded
  He does not speak out of desire
  This is a revelation
  taught him by one of great power   5
  and strength that stretched out over
  while on the highest horizon—
  then drew near and came down
  two bows' lengths or nearer
  He revealed to his servant what he revealed   10
  The heart did not lie in what it saw
  Will you then dispute with him his vision?

He saw it descending another time
at the lote tree of the furthest limit
There was the garden of sanctuary   15
when something came down over the
    lote tree, enfolding
His gaze did not turn aside nor go too far
He had seen the signs of his lord, great signs

81: *The Overturning*

In the Name of God the Compassionate the Caring
  When the sun is overturned
  When the stars fall away
  When the mountains are moved
  When the ten-month pregnant camels
    are abandoned
  When the beasts of the wild are herded together   5
  When the seas are boiled over
  When the souls are coupled
  When the girl-child buried alive
  is asked what she did to deserve murder
  When the pages are folded out   10
  When the sky is flayed open
  When Jahim[2] is set ablaze
  When the garden is brought near
  Then a soul will know what it has prepared
  I swear by the stars that slide,   15
  stars streaming, stars that sweep along the sky
  By the night as it slips away
  By the morning when the fragrant air breathes
  This is the word of a messenger ennobled,
  empowered, ordained before the lord of the throne,   20

---

[1] "Your companion" is ordinarily interpreted as referring to Muhammad.

[2] A term for the Day of Reckoning.

holding sway there, keeping trust
Your friend[1] has not gone mad
He saw him on the horizon clear
He does not hoard for himself the unseen
This is not the word of a satan   25
    struck with stones

Where are you going?
This is a reminder to all beings
For those who wish to walk straight
Your only will is the will of God   30
    lord of all beings

87: *The Most High*

In the Name of God the Compassionate the Caring
    Holy be the name of your lord most high
    Who created then gave form
    Who determined then gave guidance
    Who made the meadow pasture grow
    then turned it to a darkened flood-swept remnant 5

    We will make you recite. You will not forget
        except what the will of God allows
    He knows what is declared
        and what lies hidden
    He will ease you to the life of ease
    So remind them if reminder will succeed[2]
    Those who know awe will be brought to remember 10
    He who is hard in wrong will turn away
    He will be put to the fire
    neither dying in it nor living
    He who makes himself pure will flourish
    who remembers the name of his lord and   15
        performs the prayer

    But no. They prefer the lower life
    Better is the life ultimate, the life that endures
    As is set down in the scrolls of the ancients
    the scrolls of Ibrahim and Musa[3]

96: *The Embryo*

In the Name of God the Compassionate the Caring
    Recite in the name of your lord who created—
    From an embryo created the human
    Recite your lord is all-giving
    who taught by the pen
    Taught the human what he did not know before   5

    The human being is a tyrant
    He thinks his possessions make him secure
    To your lord is the return of every thing

    Did you see the one who stopped a servant
    from performing his prayer?   10
    Did you see if he was rightly guided
    or commanded mindfulness?
    Did you see him call lie and turn away?
    Did he not know God could see?

    But no. If he does not change   15
        we will seize him by the forelock
    the lying, wrongful forelock
    Let him call out his gang
    We will call out the Zabaniya[4]
    Do not follow him
        Touch your head to the earth in prayer
        Come near

98: *The Testament*[5]

In the Name of God the Compassionate the Caring
    Those who denied the faith—
        from the peoples of the book
        or the idolators—
        could not stop calling it a lie   5
        until they received the testament

    A messenger of God
        reciting pages that are pure

---

[1] "Your friend" refers to Muhammad.

[2] Muhammad is to "remind" people about God and justice. There is no notion of "original sin" in Islam, but people "forget" the purpose of human life and the Day of Reckoning.

[3] Ibrahim is Abraham in the Bible; Musa is Moses.

[4] The Zabaniya are probably a species of *jinn*, half-spirit creatures.

[5] This sura is from a later period in Muhammad's career, after he experienced the rejection of not only polytheists but also the "peoples of the book"—Christians and Jews—he had expected to join him.

Of scriptures that are sure

Those who were given the book   10
    were not divided one against the other
    until they received the testament

And all they were commanded
    was to worship God sincerely
    affirm oneness, perform the prayer   15
    and give a share of what they have
    That is the religion of the sure

Those who deny the faith—
    from the peoples of the book
    or the idolators—   20
    are in Jahannam's fire,[1]

eternal there
    They are the worst of creation

Those who keep the faith
    and perform the prayer   25
    they are the best of creation

As recompense for them with their lord—
    gardens of Eden
    waters flowing underground
    eternal there forever   30
    God be pleased in them
    and they in God

That is for those who hold their lord in awe

2.7 Umayyad diplomacy: *The Treaty of Tudmir* (713). Original in Arabic.

Although the Islamic conquests seemed to take place with lightning speed, they were at times piecemeal and even non-violent. Five years after Islamic forces entered Spain in 711, almost the entire peninsula was under the rule of the caliph. Yet documents such as the *Treaty of Tudmir* (713) suggest that in some cases the take-over was peaceful, accomplished via agreements with local rulers. In this case 'Abd al-'Aziz (d.716), son of Musa (the governor of much of North Africa and a leader in the conquest of Spain), came to an agreement with Theodemir, the local Visigothic commander of the region of Murcia (in the southeast corner of Spain). The Murcians were not to aid any enemies of the Muslims, and they had to pay a modest tax in money and kind. In return, they were offered local autonomy and permission to practice their Christian religion. The Arabic for Theodemir was Tudmir, which for years afterwards was the Arabic name for the region of Murcia.

[Source: *Medieval Iberia: Readings from Christian, Muslim, and Jewish Sources*, ed. Olivia Remie Constable (Philadelphia: University of Pennsylvania Press, 1997), pp. 37–38. Translated by Olivia Remie Constable.]

In the name of God, the merciful and the compassionate.

This is a document [granted] by 'Abd al-'Aziz ibn Musa ibn Nusair to Tudmir, son of Ghabdush, establishing a treaty of peace and the promise and protection of God and his Prophet (may God bless him and grant him peace). We ['Abd al-'Aziz] will not set special conditions for him or for any among his men, nor harass him, nor remove him from power. His followers will not be killed or taken prisoner, nor will they be separated from their women and children. They will not be coerced in matters of religion, their churches will not be burned, nor will sacred objects be taken from the realm, [so long as] he [Tudmir] remains sincere and fulfills the [following]

---

[1] The fire of eternal punishment.

conditions that we have set for him. He has reached a settlement concerning seven towns: Orihuela, Valentilla, Alicante, Mula, Bigastro, Ello, and Lorca. He will not give shelter to fugitives, nor to our enemies, nor encourage any protected person to fear us, nor conceal news of our enemies. He and [each of] his men shall [also] pay one dinar every year, together with four measures of wheat, four measures of barley, four liquid measures of concentrated fruit juice, four liquid measures of vinegar, four of honey, and four of olive oil. Slaves must each pay half of this amount.

[Names of four witnesses follow, and the document is dated from the Muslim month of Rajab, in the year 94 of the *hijra* (April 713).]

2.8 Taxation: *A Tax Demand in Egypt* (710). Original in Arabic and Greek.

The Umayyads generally adopted the administrative apparatus and offices of the regions that they conquered, and often they used the indigenous elite to carry out administrative duties. In Egypt, from which we have many papyri attesting to the fiscal system, the Arab governor of Egypt in the early eighth century was Qurra ibn Sharik (r.709–715). In the letter below, he is writing to Basil, *pagarch*—or provincial governor—of Aphrodite, located in the Thebaid just south of Asyut in Upper (i.e., southern) Egypt. Basil was neither Arab nor Muslim but rather a Christian local magnate who cooperated with his Islamic overlords. Qurra's letter shows that Basil was in charge of collecting the *jizya*, a poll tax imposed on non-Muslims. Qurra intended to use the revenue to pay his army.

[Source: *Islam from the Prophet Muhammad to the Capture of Constantinople*, ed. and trans. Bernard Lewis, vol. 2: *Religion and Society* (New York: Oxford University Press, 1987), p. 130 (slightly modified).]

In the name of God, the Merciful and the Compassionate.

From Qurra ibn Sharik to Basil, *pagarch* of Aphrodite. I praise God, other than Whom there is no God.

As follows: You know how much time has passed, and you still delay the *jizya*, and now the time has come for the pay of the troops and the families and for the departure of the armies on campaign, please God. When this my letter reaches you, take whatever *jizya* is due from your lands, and send whatever you collect, batch by batch. Let me not learn that you have delayed what you have gathered, and let it not be held back, for the people of your land have already completed their sowing. God is their helper in what is due from them to the Commander of the Faithful. Therefore, let there be no deficiency in your affair and no delay or holding back of what you have. Had the money been in my possession, I would have given the troops their pay, please God. Write and inform me what has accumulated with you, of what you have collected of the *jizya*, and how you have done this. Peace be upon those who follow the right guidance.[1]

Written by Jarir in the month of Rabi' I of the year 91 [January–February 710].

---

[1] A form of greeting used when addressing non-Muslims.

2.9 Praising the Caliph: Al-Akhtal, *The Tribe Has Departed* (*c.*692). Original in Arabic.

When Caliph 'Abd al-Malik (r.685–705) suppressed a major rebellion and established his rule, he needed a way to legitimize his authority and assert its roots in Arabic tradition. This he did largely by patronizing poets, for poetry was both highly valued and adaptive to a variety of purposes. In Syria, where the Umayyads established their capital, most of the population was Christian, but that did not prevent the Christian al-Akhtal (*c.*640-*c.*710) from becoming one of the caliph's most important poetic eulogists. In *The Tribe Has Departed*, al-Akhtal drew on traditional forms. The poem begins, as had many pre-Islamic poems (see al-A'sha, above p. 70), with the departure of women. The usual "journey" section (the parts are labeled here by your editor) takes up only one line. The "boast" section includes a declaration of victory; words of praise for the caliph and the Banu Umayyah, the caliph's clan; the poet's boast proper; and denigration of opposing clans.

[Source: Suzanne Pinckney Stetkevych, *The Poetics of Islamic Legitimacy: Myth, Gender, and Ceremony in the Classical Arabic Ode* (Bloomington: Indiana University Press, 2002), pp. 89–94, 96–97 (notes added).]

[The Departure]

1. Those that dwelt with you have left in haste,
     departing at evening or at dawn,
   Alarmed and driven out by fate's caprice,
     they head for distant lands.

2. And I, on the day fate took them off,
     was like one drunk
   On wine from Hims or Gadara
     that sends shivers down the spine,

3. Poured generously from a brimming wine-jar
     lined with pitch and dark with age,
   Its clay seal broken
     off its mouth,

4. A wine so strong it strikes
     the vital organs of the reveler,
   His heart, hungover, can barely
     sober up[1]

5. I was like that, or like a man
     whose limbs are racked with pain,
   Or like a man whose heart is struck
     by charms and amulets,

6. Out of longing for them and yearning
     on the day I sent my glance after them
   As they journeyed in small bands
     on Kawkab Hill's two slopes.[2] …

[The Journey]

17. They alighted in the evening,
      and we turned aside our noble-bred camels:
    For the man in need, the time had come
      to journey

[The Boast]

18. To a man whose gifts do not elude us,
      whom God has made victorious,
    So let him in his victory
      long delight!

19. He who wades into the deep of battle,
      auspicious his augury,
    The Caliph of God
      through whom men pray for rain

---

1 By invoking the inebriating power of wine, al-Akhtal here pays tribute to al-A'sha (above, p. 70), who was known for celebrating wine's heady effects.

2 Kawkab Hill is southwest of Damascus.

20. When his soul whispers its intention to him
      he resolutely sends it forth,
    His courage and his caution
      like two keen blades.

21. In him the common weal resides,
      and after his assurance
    No peril can seduce him
      from his pledge.

22. Not even the Euphrates when its tributaries
      pour seething into it
    And sweep the giant swallow-wort from its two banks
      into the middle of its rushing stream,

23. And the summer winds churn it
      until its waves
    Form agitated puddles
      on the prows of ships,

24. Racing in a vast and mighty torrent
      from the mountains of Byzance[1]
    Whose foothills shield them from it
      and divert its course,

25. Is ever more generous than he is
      to the supplicant
    Or more dazzling
      to the beholder's eye.

26. They did not desist from their treachery and cunning
      against you
    Until, unknowingly, they portioned out
      the maysir players' flesh.[2]...

29. Like a crouching lion, poised to pounce,
      his chest low to the ground,
    For a battle in which there is
      prey for him,

30. [The caliph] advances with an army
      two hundred thousand strong,

The likes of which no man or jinn[3]
      has ever seen.

31. He comes to bridges which he builds
      and then destroys,
    He brands his steeds with battle scars,
      above him fly banners and battle dust,

32. Until at al-Taff
      they wreaked carnage,
    And at al-Thawiyyah
      where no bowstring twanged.[4]

33. The tribesmen saw clearly
      the error of their ways,
    And he straightened out the smirk
      upon their faces....

44. O Banu Umayyah, your munificence
      is like a widespread rain;
    It is perfect,
      unsullied by reproach.

45. O Banu Umayyah, it was I
      who defended you
    From the men of a tribe
      that sheltered and aided [the Prophet].

46. I silenced the Banu Najjar's endless braying
      against you
    With poems that reached the ears
      of every chieftain of Ma'add,

47. Until they submitted,
      smarting from my words—
    For words can often pierce
      where sword points fail.

48. O Banu Umayyah, I offer you
      sound counsel:
    Don't let Zufar dwell secure
      among you,[5]

---

[1] Byzantium.

[2] Maysir means gambling; pre-Islamic maysir players would gamble for the parts of a sacrificed animal. Here the enemies of the caliph are likened to maysir players, but the flesh they gamble for and cut apart is their own.

[3] Jinn are half-spirit creatures.

[4] Al-Taff is where an enemy leader was slain, while al-Thawiyyah was the burial site of another enemy leader.

[5] Zufar was initially an enemy of Caliph al-Malik, but by the time of this poem, he rivaled al-Akhtar and his clan, the Banu Taghlib, for the caliph's favors.

49. But take him as an enemy:
  for what you see of him
And what lies hid within
  is all corruption.

50. For in the end you'll meet
  with ancient rancor
That, like mange,[1] lies latent for a while
  only to spread the more.

51. Through us you were victorious,
  O Commander of the Faithful,
When the news reached you
  within al-Ghutah [of Damascus],

52. They identified for you the head
  of Ibn al-Hubab,

Its nose bridge now marked
  by the sword.

53. Ears deaf, never will he
  hear a voice;
Nor will he talk till stones
  begin to speak.[2]…

78. And remember the Banu Ghudanah
  like herds of young slit-eared goats,
Runty ones, for whom
  corrals are built,

79. That pee on their forelegs
  when they're hot,
And shiver with cold
  when wet with rain.[3]…

THE IMPOVERISHED BUT INVENTIVE WEST

2.10 A world explained by words: Isidore of Seville, *Etymologies* (*c*.615-*c*.630)

Isidore, bishop of Seville (*c*.560–636), gathered together much of the lore of the ancient world in his *Etymologies*, which attempted not only to explain the derivation of words but also, through their linguistic roots (which were often mistaken), to get at the nature and essence of things. A huge manuscript, divided by one of Isidore's younger colleagues into twenty books, the *Etymologies* began with the subjects of the liberal arts (grammar, rhetoric, dialectic, mathematics, music, astronomy); moved on to human institutions like law and medicine; continued with God and angels; and then considered human beings, animals, the cosmos, clothing, and tools (among other things). The section printed here, on the ages of human beings, followed a consideration of the parts of the human body and preceded a section on portents. The *Etymologies* was a major reference work for subsequent generations of medieval scholars and poets.

[Source: Stephen A. Barney, W.J. Lewis, J.A. Beach, and Oliver Berghof, with the collaboration of Muriel Hall, *The Etymologies of Isidore of Seville* (Cambridge: Cambridge University Press, 2006), pp. 241–43 (slightly modified).]

---

[1] Mange is a skin disease.

[2] Al-Akhtar here boasts that his clan defeated and beheaded al-Hubab, the leader of an enemy clan, while the caliph himself relaxed in the park of al-Ghutah.

[3] For a society that values camels above all other animals, it is a great slur to liken the Ghudanah to runty goats.

On the Ages of Human Beings

There are six stages in a lifetime: infancy, childhood, adolescence, youth, maturity, and old age. The first age, the infancy (*infantia*) of a newborn child, lasts seven years. The second age is childhood (*pueritia*), that is, a pure (*purus*) age, during which a child is not yet suited for procreating; it lasts until the fourteenth year. The third age, adolescence (*adolescentia*), is mature (*adultus* is the past participle of *adolescere*) enough for procreating and lasts until the twenty-eighth year. The fourth age, youth (*iuventus*), is the strongest of all ages, ending in the fiftieth year. The fifth is the age of an elder person (*senior*), that is, maturity (*gravitas*), which is the decline from youth into old age; it is not yet old age, but no longer youth…. This age begins in the fiftieth and ends in the seventieth year. The sixth age is old age (*senectus*), which has no time limit in years; rather, however much life is left after the previous five ages is allotted to old age. *Senium*, however, is the last part of old age, so called because it is the end of the sixth (cf. *seni*, "six") age.

Into these six intervals, therefore, the philosophers have divided human life—ages in which life is changed, runs its course, and reaches the final point of death. Let us therefore proceed briefly through the aforementioned stages in a lifetime, demonstrating their etymologies with regard to the terms used for a human being.

A human being of the first age is called an infant (*infans*); it is called an infant, because it does not yet know how to speak (*in-*, "not"; *fari*, present participle of *fans*, "speaking"), that is, it cannot talk. Not yet having its full complement of teeth, it has less ability to articulate words. A boy (*puer*) is so called from purity (*puritas*), because he is pure and still retains, without the hint of a beard, the bloom of the cheeks. They are ephebes (*ephebus*), so called after Phoebus, gentle youths, not yet [grown] men. The word child (*puer*), however, is used in three ways: in reference to birth, as in Isaiah, "A child (*puer*) is born to us."[1] To indicate age, as in "an eight-year-old," "a ten-year-old"—whence the following expression.

Now he took a child's (*puerilis*) yoke on his tender neck.[2]

And finally, in reference to obedience and purity of faith, as in the words of the Lord to the prophet: "You are my child (*puer*), do not be afraid," spoken when Jeremiah had already left behind the years of childhood a long time before.[3]

Puella is "little girl" (*parvula*), as if the term were "chick" (*pulla*). Hence we use the term "wards" (*pupillus*), not because of the legal status of wards, but because of their youthful age. A ward, named like the pupil (*pupillus*) of the eye, is one bereft of parents. Those truly called *pupilli*, however, are children whose parents died before giving them a name. Other "bereft ones" (*orbus*) are called orphans (*orphanus*), the same as are those called *pupilli*; for *orphanus* is a Greek word and *pupillus* a Latin word. Thus in the psalm, where it is said, "Thou wilt be a helper to the orphan (*pupillus*)," the Greek has the word *orphanos*.[4]

Those who have reached puberty (*puberes*) are so called from *pubes*, that is, the private parts, for this is the first time that this area grows hair. There are those who calculate puberty from age, that is, they take someone who has completed his fourteenth year to have reached puberty, even though he may begin to show the signs of puberty very late; however, it is most certain that he who shows the outward signs of puberty and can already procreate has reached puberty. *Puerpera* are those who give birth at a youthful (*puerilis*) age. Whence Horace says

The young woman in labor (*puerpera*) is praised for her firstborn.[5]

And they are called *puerperae* either because they are burdened with their "first birth" (*primus partus*), or else because they first "give birth to children" (*pueros parere*). An adolescent (*adolescens*) is so called because he is "old enough" to procreate, or by derivation from "growing" (*crescere*) and "being strengthened" (*augere*). A youth (*iuvenis*) is so called because he begins to be able to help (*iuvare*), just as we name the young bullocks (*iuvencus*) among oxen, when they have separated from the calves. A youth is at the peak of his development and ready to give assistance—for a person's "helping" is his contributing

---

[1] See Isa. 9:6.

[2] From an anonymous poetic fragment in Latin.

[3] See Jer. 1: 6–8.

[4] Ps. 10: 14; Douay Ps. 9: 14. If you check these versions in Latin, you will see that many of them use *orphanus*, but Isidore's version used the word *pupillus* instead.

[5] Horace (65–8 BCE) was a Roman poet. The quotation comes from his *Odes* 4.5.23.

81

some work. As in human beings the thirtieth year is the time of full maturity, so in cattle and beasts of burden the third year is the strongest.

A man (*vir*) is so called, because in him resides greater power (*vis*) than in a woman—hence also "strength" (*virtus*) received its name—or else because he deals with a woman by force (*vis*). But the word woman (*mulier*) comes from softness (*mollities*), as if *mollier* (compare *mollior*, "softer"), after a letter has been cut and a letter changed, is now called *mulier*. These two are differentiated by the respective strength and weakness of their bodies. But strength is greater in a man, lesser in a woman, so that she will submit to the power of the man; evidently this is so lest, if women were to resist, lust should drive men to seek out something else or throw themselves upon the male sex. As I was saying, woman (*mulier*) is named for her feminine sex, not for a corruption of her innocence,[1] and this is according to the word of Sacred Scripture, for Eve was called woman as soon as she was made from the side of her man, when she had not yet had any contact with a man, as is said in the Bible: "And he formed her into a woman (*mulier*)."[2]

The term "virgin" (*virgo*) comes from "a greener (*viridior*) age," just like the words "sprout" (*virga*) and "calf" (*vitula*). Otherwise it is derived from lack of corruption, as if the word were formed from "heroic maiden" (*virago*), because she has no knowledge of female desire. A "heroic maiden" is so called because she "acts like a man" (*vir* + *agere*, "to act"), that is, she engages in the activities of men and is full of male vigor. The ancients would call strong women by that name. However, a virgin cannot be correctly called a heroic maiden unless she performs a man's task. But if a woman does manly deeds, then she is correctly called a heroic maiden, like an Amazon.

She who is nowadays called a woman (*femina*) in ancient times was called *vira*; just as "female slave" (*serva*) was derived from "male slave" (*servus*) and "female servant" (*famula*) from "male servant" (*famulus*), so also woman (*vira*) from man (*vir*). Some people believe that the word for "virgin" (*virgo*) is from *vira*. The word "woman" (*femina*) is derived from the parts of the thighs (*femur*, plural *femora* or *femina*) where the appearance of

the sex distinguishes her from a man. Others believe that through a Greek etymology *femina* is derived from "fiery force," because she desires more vehemently, for females are said to be more libidinous than males, both in human beings and in animals. Whence among the ancients excessive love was called feminine (*femineus*) love.

The "elder" (*senior*) is still fairly vigorous. In the sixth book Ovid speaks of the elder, who is

Between the youth and the old man (*senex*).[3]

And Terence

By the privilege I enjoyed when I was younger (*adulescentior*).[4]

...

The term "old man" (*senex*), however, some believe to be derived from decay of the senses (*sensus*), because from that time on they act foolishly due to old age. Physiologists maintain that human beings are stupid due to colder blood, wise due to warm blood. Hence also old people, in whom blood has turned cold, and children, in whom it has not yet warmed up, are less wise. This is the reason why infancy and old age resemble one another: old people dote because they are too old, while children have no insight into their actions due to playfulness and childishness.…

Old age brings with it much that is good and much that is bad. Much that is good, because it frees us from despotic masters, imposes moderation on desires, breaks the drive of lust, augments wisdom, and imparts riper counsel. Much that is bad, however, because of the weakness and unpopularity it brings, for

Diseases and sorrowful old age creep up.[5]

Indeed, there are two things whereby the forces of the body are diminished: old age and disease.

Death (*mors*) is so called, because it is bitter (*amarus*), or by derivation from Mars, who is the author of death; [or else, death is derived from the bite (*morsus*) of the first human, because when he bit the fruit of the forbid-

---

[1] The word *mollities*, softness, could also connote sexual licentiousness.

[2] See Gen. 2: 22.

[3] Ovid (43 BCE–17 CE) was a Roman poet. The quotation comes from his *Metamorphoses* 12.464.

[4] Terence (*c*.195–159? BCE) was a Roman comic playwright. The quotation comes from his *The Mother-in-Law* 11.

[5] Virgil (70–19 BCE) was a Roman poet. The quotation comes from his *Georgics* 3.67.

den tree, he incurred death].[1] There are three kinds of death: heartrending, premature, and natural death. That of children is heartrending, that of young people premature, that of old people merited, that is, natural. However, it is uncertain from which part of speech *mortuus* ("dead, a dead person") is inflected. Indeed, as Caesar says, because it is the perfect participle of *morior* ("die")

it ought to end in *-tus*—that is, it ought to have one *u* only, not two. Where the letter *u* is doubled, it is inflected substantively, not as a participle, as in *fatuus* ("foolish") and *arduus* ("difficult"). This makes sense in this way: just as what *mortuus* means cannot be "declined" by any behavior of ours (i.e. we cannot avoid death), so the term itself cannot be "declined" grammatically.

....

2.11 A modern martyr in Francia: *The Passion of Leudegar* (680s). Original in Latin.

The martyrs of the pre-Constantinian Church were replaced by heroic ascetics such as St. Antony (see his *Life* above, p. 27) and St. Martin (see his *Life* above, p. 34). Hagiographers of late-seventh-century Merovingian Francia (as we may now call Gaul) created a new generation of martyrs, portraying men and women embroiled in the violent political life of the period as saints. Leudegar (Saint-Léger in French) was one of these. Brother of Gaerin, the count of Paris, and appointed to the bishopric of Autun (an important see in Burgundy that Leudegar held *c.*662–*c.*677?) by Queen Balthild, regent for her son Clothar III (r.657–673), Leudegar was an important man at court. But he had a falling out with Ebroin, mayor of the palace, who eventually had him executed in *c.*678. His *Passion*, which means "suffering" or "martyrdom," was written soon thereafter by an anonymous author who dedicated the work to Hermenar, Leudegar's successor at Autun and originally his rival. The cult of Leudegar was evidently becoming so strong that Hermenar needed to try to claim it, and he appears in the *Passion* as a sympathetic figure. How have the roles and virtues of the bishop changed from the time of St. Martin to that of Leudegar? How might you explain the reasons for these changes?

[Source: *From Roman to Merovingian Gaul: A Reader*, ed. and trans. Alexander Callander Murray (Toronto: University of Toronto Press, 2000), pp. 509–18, 524–26 (slightly modified).]

[1] Glorious and renowned Leudegar, bishop of the city Autun, has been created a new martyr in Christian times. Just as he was nobly born according to earthly descent, so, accompanied by divine grace and growing in manly strength from an early age, he stood out prominently ahead of others no matter what the office or order in life to which he was promoted. His uncle Dido, bishop of Poitiers,[2] who was provided with a notable abundance of prudence and wealth beyond that of his neighbors, took great pains to raise him; and so, thoroughly polished in

all respects by the file of instruction in the various studies that the powerful of the world are accustomed to undertake, Leudegar was chosen to assume the burden of the archdiaconate of the same city.

His courage and wisdom became so conspicuous that he appeared to have no equal among his predecessors. Especially because he was not unacquainted with the penalties of the temporal law, he was a terrifying judge of secular matters. And since he was filled with the doctrines of the church canons, he emerged as a distinguished

---

[1] The words in brackets are found in some, but not all, of the manuscripts of the *Etymologies*.
[2] Bishop Dido of Poitiers died in 669.

teacher of clerics. He was also spirited in the punishment of offenders and never tried to be lenient with excesses of the flesh. He was vigilant, keenly concerned with the duties of church personnel, energetic in keeping accounts, prudent in giving advice, and glowing with eloquence.

[2] Meanwhile it became necessary to ordain him bishop of the city of Autun. For lately a dispute between two candidates for the episcopal office of that city had erupted and had reached the point of bloodshed. When one of the candidates lay dead on the spot and the other had been exiled for committing the crime, Balthild, who with her son Clothar [III] was in charge of the palace of the Franks, at that point, inspired, I believe, by divine counsel, sent this energetic man to that city to be its bishop. The church which, as if widowed, had already been left to the uncertainties of the world for almost two years, would now be protected by his direction and strength and defended against those who were attacking it.

How much more should be said? All the enemies of the church and the town, as well as those who endlessly disputed among themselves with hateful acts and killings, were so afraid on his arrival that they did not want to hear the outrage that had taken place recalled. Those whom his preaching could not persuade to accept peace, the terror of justice forced to do so.

Now that he was in office by God's will, he lavished such concern on giving alms to the poor that it would take too long to recount it in detail. But if we are silent, his works are a witness: the station for poor relief that he established stands at the doors of the church; the beauty of the precious objects which glow with the flash of gold in the service of the church; and also the decorations of the baptistery made with marvelous workmanship. The tomb of Saint Symphorian and the translation of his body reveals to those who remain silent the extent to which he was devoted to the love of the martyrs.[1] Moreover the pavement and the golden awning of the church, the construction of a new atrium, the repair of the town walls, the restoration of buildings and his reconstruction of whatever had deteriorated through great age, suggest as visible reminders to onlookers the extent of his energy.

Let these few special examples among many suffice. We turn in our account to the time the champion of Christ first took up the fight against the devil....

[4] In those days Ebroin was, as we say, mayor of the palace. He ran the palace at that time under King Clothar [III, r.657–673], for the queen whom we mentioned above was now living in the monastery which she had previously prepared for herself.[2] Moreover, envious men came to Ebroin and roused his anger against Leudegar the man of God, and whereas they found no charge to lay that was true, they made up a false one that, while everyone obeyed Ebroin's commands, only Bishop Leudegar defied his orders.

The aforesaid Ebroin was so inflamed by the torch of gain and so captive to the desire for money that only those who brought more money had their cause judged to be just by him. As some out of fear, and others to purchase justice, lavished immense sums of gold and silver on him, for this reason the hearts of certain people were roused against him, distressed at being robbed but especially because he not only trafficked in plunder but even shed the innocent blood of many nobles for a minor offense. And so Ebroin continued to be suspicious of Bishop Leudegar; for Ebroin could not conquer him by words, and Leudegar, unlike others, did not pay court to him with flattery. Ebroin recognized that Leudegar always remained firm in the face of all his threats.

At the time, Ebroin had issued a tyrant's edict that no one should presume to come to the palace from Burgundy without receiving his authorization.[3] Out of fear, all the leading men were now suspicious that he was contemplating adding to his crime by condemning certain people to lose their heads or by inflicting losses of property on them.

[5] While the matter remained unresolved, King Clothar, called by God, passed away [673]. But although Ebroin ought to have called the magnates together and, as is customary, solemnly raised to the kingship the king's brother, Theuderic [III, r.673, 675–690/691] by name, he was puffed up with pride and decided not to call them from this time onwards. They became more afraid because as long as he kept control of the king, whom

---

[1] Symphorian was martyred at Autun c.180. A monastery was dedicated to him there while, as we see here, his tomb was in the cathedral church. The "translation of his body" refers to the ritual in which his body was moved from one place to another.

[2] Queen Balthild was "eased" out of court and went to live at Chelles, a monastery for women that she had founded and endowed.

[3] Autun was in Burgundy, so this edict was directed at Leudegar and his flock.

he should have raised up in public for the glory of the homeland, he would be able fearlessly to inflict evil on anyone he desired in the king's name. A host of nobles were hastening to meet the new king when Ebroin sent a command for them to give up their journey. They took counsel among themselves, abandoned the king, and all sought out Childeric [II, d.675], the king's younger brother who had been allotted the kingship in Austrasia. Whoever did not want to accept this decision either escaped by flight or agreed against his will under threat of death by burning.

[6] When, out of fear of the tyrant Ebroin, they had all brought Childeric into the kingdom of Neustria as well as that of Burgundy, the tyrant recognized that it was his own villainy that brought this about and took refuge at the altar of the church; his treasure was at once broken into many pieces and what the wicked man had gathered together wrongly for so long was immediately well dispersed. They did not kill him because certain bishops stepped in between them, and especially because the bishop Leudegar intervened; but they sent him to the monastery of Luxeuil in exile so that, through penance, he might escape the consequences of the crimes he had committed. But since the eyes of his heart were blinded by the dust of earthly desire, spiritual wisdom did not prevail in his spiteful soul.

Childeric ordered his brother, against whom he had been asked to come, brought into his presence so he could speak with him. That is when certain leaders in the kingdom who wanted to dissuade Childeric from bloodshed through flattery had the audacity to order the hair of their lord cut and took pains to deliver him before his brother in this condition.[1] But when Theuderic was asked by his brother what he wished done to him, he declared only that he was awaiting the swift judgment of God because he had been unjustly degraded from his position as king. Then orders were given that Theuderic live in the monastery of the holy martyr Dionysius;[2] and he was kept safe there until such time as he grew back the hair they cut off. And the God of heaven, whom he had declared as his judge, happily allowed him to reign afterwards.

[7] Meanwhile everyone asked King Childeric to issue throughout the three kingdoms he had acquired[3] edicts to the following effect. Judges must, as in antiquity, preserve the law and custom of each of the homelands. Officials (rectores) must not pass from one province into another. And one person must not be allowed to usurp power in the fashion of Ebroin and then, like him, hold his peers in disdain; as long as it was recognized that advancement to the top offices would take place by turns, no one would dare set himself before another. Although the king granted the requests freely, he was corrupted by foolish, almost heathen, counselors—for the superficiality of youth got the better of him—and immediately opposed what he had authorized with the advice of wise men.

[8] The king kept holy Leudegar constantly by his side in the palace because he had seen that the bishop outshone everyone in wisdom. For this reason the envy of evil men revived and grew. Again they looked for grounds for making accusations against him, so that whatever the king did, whatever just or unjust decision he made, they accused Leudegar of doing it. Had the king complied with Leudegar's advice, he would have acted with divine authority. But by now the sentence laid down by heaven had overtaken him, so that his heart could not comprehend the teachings of justice; instead he deserved that a swift sentence carry out the judgment that Theuderic declared he was awaiting from God.

When the man of God saw the envy of the devil heat up once more against him, following the apostle, he took up the armor of faith, the helmet of salvation, and the sword of the Spirit, which is the word of God, and went into single combat with the ancient enemy. And since priestly integrity knows not how to fear the threats of a king, Leudegar censured him for suddenly altering the customs of the kingdoms after he had ordered them to be preserved; and likewise, it is said, he told him that the queen [Bilichild], his wife, was the daughter of his uncle [Sigibert III]; and, if he did not emend these deeds as well as other transgressions, he should know truly that divine vengeance would immediately be at hand.

Indeed, at first the king began to listen willingly, but the advice of his followers got the better of him. At the

---

1   "The audacity to order the hair of their lord cut" means that they tonsured him—the sign of the monk. He could not reign until his hair grew back.

2   This was Saint Denis, near Paris.

3   I.e., Austrasia, Neustria, and Burgundy—the whole of the Frankish Kingdom. Childeric had become king of Austrasia in 662; now, 673–675, he ruled over all of them.

same time as he should have been using Leudegar's words to reform himself, the king began to look for pretexts for bringing about the bishop's death. This was on the advice of those who wanted to overturn justice and, disorderly themselves, were in favor of the king acting in an immature fashion, as well as of those who enticed the king into breaking his own decree. All of them, and others like them living amidst the desires of the world, feared their works would be destroyed by the man of God, for by now they knew that he marched a straight course along the path of justice. The old world, weighed down by vices, could not withstand the manly power of the heavenly citizen.

[9] There was in those days a certain nobleman called Hector, who had taken up the fasces of office over the patriciate of Marseille.[1] He was endowed beyond others with nobility of birth and worldly wisdom, being descended from a famous lineage. He had come to see King Childeric about a certain legal case and hoped to gain what he was seeking through the intercession of the man of God. The holy man of God had welcomed Hector to his city and provided him with lodging, waiting for the time when he could recommend Hector to the king and speak on his behalf, as Hector had requested. For Leudegar had asked Childeric to come to the church of his city[2] during the celebration of Easter. The envious ones found this the pretext by which they might fill the king's heart to the full with the vileness they had lately been pouring into it. They brought the then mayor of the palace, who was called Wulfoald, into their subterfuge and made up a lying story that Leudegar and Hector had joined together to overthrow royal authority and usurp for themselves the reins of power.

[10] There was also at the time in the monastery of Saint Symphorian a certain man in the garb of a religious by the name of Marcolinus, a recluse in body but not in mind and, as was publicly revealed afterwards, rather too eager to seek human praise and honors through the false appearance of religion. Of his way of life I think it better to be silent than to speak, especially since it was revealed to everyone. The king, therefore, mistook this fellow for

a prophet of God in all matters because Marcolinus flattered his desire to be favored above all else with accusations against the man of God.

And so on the night when the holy vigils of Easter were celebrated in the city, the king, by now suspicious, refused to come there, but with a few flatterers sought the advice of the aforesaid hypocrite; and since the king bore ill feelings towards the servant of God, he had no qualms about receiving the Easter sacrifice at the right time where he was.

But afterwards, shamefully drunk on wine, he entered the church while others, fasting, were awaiting the holy services. He looked for Leudegar, shouting out his name, trying to put him to flight; all the while he terrified those who now relayed messages, threatening to strike them with the sword. Frequently calling for Leudegar, the king learned that he was in the baptistery, and when he entered it, stood amazed at the brightness of the light and the aroma of the chrism that was used by those conducting baptisms there to give blessings. But although Leudegar answered the shouting by saying, "I am here,"[3] the king completely failed to see him. He crossed the baptistery and took up quarters in the bishop's mansion of the church, which had been made ready.

The other bishops who were celebrating the vigils with the man of God returned to their quarters. But when Leudegar finished the holy office, showing no sign of fear, he approached the angry king and gently asked him why he had not come before the vigils and why he stayed so angry through the celebrations of such a holy night. Disturbed, the king could only answer the ineffable wisdom of Leudegar by saying that he had suspicions about him concerning a certain matter.

[11] Leudegar the man of God saw that the king had not changed his mind. The king, at the urging of his followers, would inflict death on him and Hector, just as he had resolved; or Hector, with no place to turn, would rise up against the despised king, just as the king's men feared. Leudegar was not concerned for his own life but for those who had come to him for protection, and looking for safety, chose for the time being to find refuge in flight rather than offer a pretext for the church to be

---

1. The patriciate of Marseille was the major governmental authority in the city. "Fasces of office": rods bound together with an ax were carried before ancient Roman magistrates, and although this had for centuries ceased to be the case, it remained a literary image of authority.

2. I.e., Autun.

3. See 1 Sam. 3: 4.

bloodied by his martyrdom or to be ravaged during the celebrations of Christ's resurrection, or for those who had turned to him to lose their lives without any consideration. For surely there is no one who thinks that he was afraid even of martyrdom.

In fact, when earlier he got word of his own destruction through a monk by the name of Berthar on the day of the Lord's supper, the next day, that of the passion of the Lord, he went to the king's palace, and, bursting in uninvited, tried to offer his blood to Christ on the very day that Christ poured forth his own blood for the salvation of the world. On the same day the king even tried to strike him with his own hand, but, because of the respect due the day, was prevented from doing so by the wise advice of certain magnates. One must believe without doubt that he was saved at that moment by heaven so that the furnace of lengthy persecution would purify any impurity he might have acquired from living a human life, which cannot be led without fault. And placed like pure gold in the crown of his own king, he would afterward shine like gleaming jewels by the power of miracle.

Those who were waiting to exploit this opportunity thereupon mounted a swift pursuit of him. Hector was killed on the spot; and since he manfully tried to defend himself, as was God's will, it took large numbers to overcome him and some of those accompanying him. And it is believed to be not impossible that indulgence can be obtained from God through the merits of the holy martyr for those souls who along with him tried innocently to ward off the storm of persecution.

[12] As soon as Leudegar, the servant of God, had been taken into custody by certain of his pursuers, they immediately sent word to Childeric that the deed was done; he who had successfully arrested Leudegar thought that he would enjoy the utmost favor of the king. On the advice of the magnates and bishops, orders were given for Leudegar to be taken to the monastery of Luxeuil until such time as they could deliberate together as to what to do with a man of such rank.

In the meantime, Childeric inquired of all the chief officials of the palace together what judgment they would determine for this saint of God, and they answered unanimously that, if the king granted him his life, he should order Leudegar to remain in perpetual exile in Luxeuil. The king immediately authorized the judgment decreed against him. Some bishops and priests, for their part, agreed to it to free Leudegar for the moment from the anger of the king.

For, led astray by the advice of the wicked, the king had given orders for him to be taken from Luxeuil and placed at the disposal of his accusers as an object of mockery for them to have killed as they wished, as formerly Herod had intended the Jews to do to Peter.[1] Now there was present a venerable abbot of the church of Saint Symphorian by the name of Hermenar—it was to him that the king assigned the city at the request of the people after the death of the man of God—and he repeatedly threw himself at the feet of the king begging him over and over again to allow Leudegar to remain in Luxeuil and not to have him led into the waiting arms of cruel men whose anger the devil had inflamed against him. Because of entreaties of this kind, Leudegar was at that time at last saved from death. But some were of the false belief that Hermenar often visited the lodging of the king to be first among Leudegar's accusers and thereby more readily get permission to hold the bishopric. At length the truth emerged, and because the eye of the flesh does not see spiritual love, the deeds of that man afterwards bore witness, for as long as Leudegar was still alive he tended to his needs with devout charity as best he could.

[13] In those days Ebroin was still lodged as an exile in Luxeuil, tonsured and in a monk's garb, pretending to act with the peaceable intention that as long as both he and Leudegar were serving the same but separate sentences of exile they would lead their lives in harmony.

In the meantime, after these events had taken place, divine vengeance did not refrain long from imposing its judgment on Childeric. For his loose behavior among the palace magnates grew worse. Then one of them, who found this more troubling than the others, gave him his death wound as he was hunting in safety in the forest.

[14] But before that happened, while a certain two dukes to whom the orders had been given to remove Leudegar from Luxeuil were waiting to do that, one of their servants agreed to put Leudegar to the sword if he saw him outside Luxeuil. When the time came to do it, an unbearable trembling so engulfed the man's heart that he not only said in a public confession that he was contemplating such a momentous deed but also told why. Trembling, he threw himself at Leudegar's feet begging to be forgiven by him for this wickedness.

---

1 See Acts 12: 3–4.

[15] As soon as Childeric's death was suddenly announced, certain of those who had been sentenced to exile at his command returned without fear, like poisonous snakes after wintertime that come forth from their caves in the spring. Their wild rage caused a huge disturbance in the homeland, so that it was openly believed that the approach of the Antichrist was at hand.[1] As for those who should have been in charge of the regions, they rose against each other, and those who should have kept the bonds of peace together began to provoke each other with hateful deeds. And as long as the king was not established on top, each one did what seemed right according to his own desires, without fear of punishment. Indeed we recognized at that time that the anger of God became manifest, so that even a star that the astrologers call a comet was seen in the sky [August 676]: on its rising, they say, the land is thrown into confusion by famine, by the succession of kings, and by disturbance among the nations, and destruction by the sword is imminent. It is certain that all these events plainly happened after that. But as it is written that the foolish cannot be corrected by words, much less by portents, they returned from exile with evil intent. They made the claim that whatever they had suffered for their crimes was the fault of Leudegar's supporters.

[16] In these days the man of God was held in custody by the aforementioned dukes for safety's sake and had by now recently been taken by them from Luxeuil. At that very moment divine grace had granted its servant a venerable honor whereby those same dukes, their wives, all their servants and their households, and also the common people in those districts, were joined together in such love of him that, if the need had arisen, they would not have hesitated to sacrifice themselves on his behalf. When those who were holding the servant of God in their custody informed the other authorities round about that they could see that divine grace was upon the servant of God, they now came together in pious Christian love to support him. Reaching an agreement among themselves, they affirmed that, as long as the disorderly confusion that had arisen prevailed in those districts, holy Leudegar would be protected with their help should anyone try to do harm to him before they had also raised Theuderic to the kingship.

In those days Ebroin also came forth from Luxeuil, like Julian [the Apostate] who pretended to live the life of a monk.[2] And since he was immediately mobbed by a swarm of friends as well as servants, the aforesaid exiles, who were seeking to serve him—and an evil service it was, tacked together from their own claim of injustice—made him leader. This way they could use Ebroin's help and advice to take vengeance on the man of God all together. Ebroin himself raised his venomous head, and like a viper restoring its poison, he pretended to be a follower of Theuderic, hurrying to his side for that reason as quickly as possible.

[17] As the man of God was traveling quickly along the same road with his above-mentioned allies, it happened that, when they were less than a day's journey from the city of Autun, Ebroin, forgetting the pledge of friendship he had once made and at the urging of his associates, would have seized him at that point, had he not been prevented by the advice of Genesius, metropolitan of Lyon, or been frightened by the strong band accompanying Leudegar. Again Ebroin feigned friendship, and joining forces they reached the city together.

The church rejoiced at the restored presence of its shepherd, the streets were strewn with fresh boughs, the deacons prepared candles, the clergy celebrated with singing, the whole city rejoiced at the advent of its bishop after the storm of persecution. And not undeservedly was the display of praise offered to him, for in the presence of God he rushed toward the crown of martyrdom, and there, as part of the advent of their pastor, they made ready pleasures for his enemies.

The next day Leudegar and Ebroin moved on together so that they might arrive at a meeting with Theuderic united.

[18] The journey begun, they went to meet the king, but in the meantime, almost in the middle of the trip, the tyrant Ebroin abandoned their company and pressed straight on to his own people, tossing aside his clerical status and returning to his wife behind the holy veil [i.e., she was now a nun] "as a dog returns to its vomit."[3] He who could not serve in the camp of Christ took up the weapons of the world with his enemies. And whereas he had now abandoned faith and God, he showed himself an open enemy of his earthly lord.

---

[1]   The false Christ who was expected to rule as an antagonist to Christ before the Second Coming—and triumph—of Christ himself.

[2]   Emperor Julian (r.361–363), called "the Apostate," was vilified by Christians. He was never a monk.

[3]   Prov. 26: 11.

Now Theuderic had already recovered the kingdom and was staying safely at the time at the villa of Nogent-les-Vierges when Ebroin attacked swiftly with Austrasians. Who can recount fully the plundering that then took place of the royal treasury and of the vessels of the church that previous Catholic princes had devoutly conferred on the Lord's sanctuary out of Christian love, and who can recount the killing of Theuderic's mayor of the palace?

[19] The reason Ebroin committed this evil was that he was furnished with advice by diabolical and envious men. Their complaint was that they had been brought down by the punishment they deserved. Since they saw that the whole realm had faithfully taken Theuderic's side, that he was now established in the kingship, and that Leudegar the servant of God was living in his own city with the king's favor, envious, they began to be tormented by spite again. For as long as the just were standing tall, the wicked would be unable to make a comeback. Under the influence of the devil, who stripped them of faith, and now blinded, they could devise no truthful strategy for bringing about the ruin of the man of God; and so they resorted to greater destruction by inventing a lie: with this they introduced into the kingdom great evil and devastating slaughter in persecuting many people....

[Ebroin and his faction controlled the kingdom in the name of a "certain young lad," Clovis, who was said to be the son of Clothar III and rightful king. They now carried through the plan to get rid of Leudegar by bringing him to trial at the palace.]

[33] ... When Leudegar had been brought forward into the midst of the assembly [of bishops], they tried to get from him a confession that he had been privy to the killing of Childeric. Then realizing that again conflict threatened him because of a diabolical fiction, Leudegar said that, just as he did not absolve himself from human wrongdoing, so too he had never advised this deed, but declared that God knew this rather than man. They interrogated him for some time but could not get anything else out of him. So they tore apart his tunic from top to bottom, and the impious tyrant gave orders for him to be handed over to a certain Chrodobert, who was count of the palace at the time, and for his life in this world to be taken from him by a stroke of the sword.

The martyr of God found joy in all his suffering, for he could sense the approach of the martyr's crown that was due to him as a reward from God. Now Chrodobert took him to his own residence. And he obtained such a

heavenly blessing on his arrival that, when all those living there saw this plainly, they abandoned their own sins by confessing and eagerly took refuge in the healing medicine of penance. God had adorned his servant with this gift so that whenever he was handed over as an exile to be treated badly, those who received him, on the contrary, all paid him the reverence due from servants.

[34] At last arrived the day of death on which his persecution came to an end. At that time the results of a judicial decision were issued by the palace that Leudegar must live no longer. The impious Ebroin, fearing that faithful Christians would pay Leudegar the respect of a martyr, gave orders for a well to be found deep in the woods and his mutilated corpse to be sunk in it so that, once the mouth of the well was filled in with earth and stones, people would not know where he was buried.

Meanwhile Leudegar, by his preaching to Chrodobert, had already begun to some extent to bring about the latter's conversion. Because Chrodobert could not bear to look at the death of the man of God, he charged two of his servants to carry out the orders he had been given. When this news reached his house, his wife began to weep in bitter distress because such a cruel and shameful act had become the duty of her husband.

[35] When the man of God saw that his end was now at hand, he began to comfort the weeping woman, saying, "Please do not weep over my passing. No demand for vengeance will ever be made against you for my death, but rather a blessing will be given by God from heaven if you devoutly bury my body in its grave."

And when he had spoken these words, he said goodbye at the urging of the servants and was taken to the woods for them to carry out the sentence of the order.

Now they had previously found a well where they could hide his body as they had been told; but they never found it again. While looking for the well, they wandered hopelessly about and on this account put off killing him. In the meantime the martyr of God was allowed to prostrate himself in prayer and to entrust his passing to God. To both of his killers, who were looming over him, he began to predict the future through the spirit of prophecy. One of them, sparked by the ancient enemy, was quite anxious to carry out the deed. But the other, who was a gentle man, tremblingly begged him not to take vengeance on Leudegar.

Leudegar addressed the two of them

"You, who follow orders against your will," he said, "confess your previous sins immediately to a priest and by doing penance you shall also escape the consequences of this deed."

To the other he said, "And as for you, if you do not do the same, you shall have to be delivered up immediately to God for swift vengeance."

Again, prostrating himself in prayer, he confidently entrusted his soul to Christ the lord. And getting up, he extended his neck and bade the executioner do what he had been ordered to do. And when the man we mentioned above suddenly cut off his head, a chorus of angels, rejoicing, conducted the spirit of the blessed martyr to heaven to be presented to the Lord so he might reign in heaven with all the saints. There in joyful company of the saints is our lord Jesus Christ, who with the Father and holy Spirit lives and reigns through the course of the ages.

2.12 The settlement of disputes: *Judgment of Childebert III* (709 or 710). Original in Latin.

In the Merovingian period, as today, most disputes were probably settled out of court. Nevertheless, some did lead to formal action in assemblies or meetings. Normally a document was drawn up, called a *placitum*, reporting on the proceedings and the outcome. These were kept by the institution that won the case. In the judgment below, King Childebert (r.694–711) presided over an assembly at which Abbot Dalfinus of the monastery of Saint-Denis (near Paris) litigated against Grimoald, mayor of the palace. Dalfinus claimed for his monastery all the tolls collected from merchants at the annual fair held at Saint-Denis. While most such disputes were real, this one seems to have been "fictive"—a way for the abbot of Saint-Denis to get public reaffirmation of rights that had long been granted to his monastery. As in real cases, the proceedings included the testimony of witnesses and the production of written documents, in this case "the directives" of former kings who had issued such grants to Saint-Denis against the interest of the "fisc"—the king's own treasury. What factors might lead you to argue that the fair at Saint-Denis generated a lot of income? What might lead you to conclude the opposite—that these revenues were negligible? What might be the uses of a fictive dispute for the abbot—or even for the mayor of the palace?

[Source: *From Roman to Merovingian Gaul: A Reader*, ed. and trans. Alexander Callander Murray (Toronto: University of Toronto Press, 2000), pp. 585–87.]

Childebert [III], king of the Franks, to those of illustrious rank.

Representatives of the venerable Dalfinus, abbot of the basilica of our own special patron Saint Dionysius [i.e., Saint-Denis], wherein lies the precious body of this lord, came before us and our leading men in our palace at Montmacq. They claimed in opposition to the representatives of the illustrious Grimoald, mayor of our palace, that over a long period of time our grandfather the late Clovis [II], and after him our uncle Childeric [II] and our father Theuderic [III], as well as our brother Clothar [III, IV, Clovis III?] had issued directives granting to that basilica of Saint Dionysius the entire toll collected from all merchants, whether of Saxon or other nationality, who attend the fair held on the holy feast of Lord Dionysius [9 October]; as a consequence of the grant, they said, the fisc was precluded at that time [of Clovis II] and later from exacting or collecting on its own behalf tolls from those merchants either there, at the fair, or within the district of Paris or within the city of Paris; the basilica of Saint Dionysius, they said, had been granted and awarded this right in its entirety for all time.

They then produced the directives of the aforesaid

princes to that effect for the court to read. Those directives were deposited and examined, and it was determined that such a grant in its entirety had been made to that house of God by those princes.

Then the representatives of Dalfinus said that the representatives of Grimoald, mayor of our palace as well as count of the district of Paris, collected half the toll from them, removing its benefits from the basilica.

The representatives of the mayor of our palace Grimoald replied on the contrary that for a long time it had been customary for the house of Saint Dionysius to receive one half the toll and the count the other on behalf of the fisc.

The representatives of Saint Dionysius contended in reply that Gaerin,[1] the late count of Paris, introduced this custom by force and at times collected half the toll from them; but those representatives informed the palace of this and, they said, always renewed their royal directives without diminution of the grant.

Again an examination was undertaken of numerous people and of the directives that the aforesaid princes had granted originally and had subsequently confirmed without diminution of the grant.

And so, with Grimoald's agreement and that of many other loyal followers of the king, a determination was made and judgment given that the representatives of Grimoald were on behalf of our fisc to invest that toll in its entirety once again upon the agents of the abbot by means of a pledge. And so they did.

Whereas it is known that the suit has been brought forward and settled, investigated and adjudicated, in just such a fashion as the illustrious count of our palace Rigofred has reported, it is our command, now that the previous directives granted to the monastery have been examined, that for all time the aforesaid monastery of Saint Dionysius, wherein that most precious lord's body rests, and abbot Dalfinus and his successors have successfully sued for and laid claim to that entire toll collected at the feast of Saint Dionysius, both that which arises on the lands of the basilica and later in Paris.

In earlier times, the market was moved on account of a catastrophe from the site of Saint Dionysius and was established in the city of Paris between the basilicas of Saints Martin and Laurence. The abbey received directives from the aforesaid princes to the effect that the aforesaid basilica of Saint Dionysius should get the toll in its entirety either there or wherever it set up to conduct business and commerce on the occasion of that feast. In view of these circumstances, if it happens that on account of some catastrophe or interruption the fair should be moved somewhere else, let that aforesaid toll, because of our devotion to that holy place, in present and future times, remain granted to and bestowed upon that house of God to offset the cost of lighting. And between our fisc and the representatives of Saint Dionysius, may all dispute and contention be laid to rest.

Actulius has been ordered to certify this.

Given, under auspicious signs, in December, on the thirteenth day, in the sixteenth year of our reign at Montmacq.

2.13 Reforming the Continental church: *Letters to Boniface* (723–726). Original in Latin.

Born in Wessex, England, Boniface (672/675–754) entered a monastery at the age of seven, where he received an excellent education. In 716 he undertook the first of his missionary efforts, going to Frisia, where he followed in the footsteps of earlier English evangelists. In 717 he traveled to Rome—where he changed his name from the Anglo-Saxon "Wynfrith" to the Latinate "Boniface"—and received a commission from Pope Gregory II (715–731) to evangelize the people living east of the Rhine—in Bavaria and Thuringia. In fact, these regions had already been Christianized, and Boniface spent most of his time reforming churches already established rather than preaching the Word to pagans. In all of his work he was avidly supported by Charles Martel (d.741), the powerful mayor of the palace in Francia (as we may now call Gaul). After Charles's death, Boniface focused on reforming the Frankish church itself, which he did through a series of church councils

---

[1] Leudegar's brother; see above, p. 83.

that he called between 742 and 744. A year later he became archbishop of Mainz, but not long thereafter he returned to Frisia, which had not yet been Christianized, and there suffered a martyr's death in 754. The letters below come from Boniface's earliest period in Germany. In the first, Charles Martel offers him protection. In the second, Gregory II commends him to the Thuringians, whose Christianization he does not recognize. In the third, the pope instructs Boniface on particular matters of Christian practice. Why did Gregory II support Boniface's work? In what ways did the model of Pope Gregory the Great's missionary work in England (see the letters in Bede, p. 94) inspire Gregory II? What might explain Charles Martel's support of Boniface?

[Source: *The Letters of Saint Boniface*, trans. Ephraim Emerton (New York: W.W. Norton, 1940), pp. 47, 52–56.]

[CHARLES MARTEL COMMENDS BONIFACE TO ALL FRANKISH OFFICIALS, 723]

To the holy and apostolic bishops, our fathers in Christ, and to the dukes, counts, vicars, palace officials, all our lower agents, our circuit judges [missi] and all who are our friends, the noble Charles, mayor of the palace, your well-wisher, sends greeting.

Be it known to you that the apostolic man in Christ, Father Boniface, a man of apostolic character and a bishop, came to us with the request that we should take him under our guardianship and protection. Know that we have acquiesced with pleasure and, hence, have granted his petition before witnesses and commanded that this written order signed by our own hand be given him, that wheresoever he may choose to go, he is to be left in peace and protected as a man under our guardianship and protection to the end that he may render and receive justice. If he shall be in any need or distress which cannot be remedied according to law, let him and those dependent upon him come in peace and safety before our presence, so that no person may hinder or do him injury, but that he may rest at all times in peace and safety under our guardianship and protection.

And that this may the more surely be given credit, I have signed it with my own hand and sealed it with our ring.

[POPE GREGORY II COMMENDS BONIFACE TO THE THURINGIANS, DECEMBER 724]

Gregory, servant of the servants of God, to all the people of the Thuringians.

The Lord Jesus Christ, Son of God and very God, descended from Heaven, was made man, deigned to suffer and be crucified for us, was buried, rose from the dead on the third day, and ascended into Heaven. To His holy Apostles and disciples He said: "Go forth and teach all peoples, baptizing them in the name of the Father, the Son, and the Holy Spirit (Matt. 28:19)"; and He promised those who believed in Him eternal life.

We, therefore, desiring that you may rejoice with us forever where there is no ending, neither sorrow nor any bitterness, but eternal glory, have sent to you our most holy brother, Bishop Boniface, that he may baptize you and teach you the doctrine of Christ and lead you out of error into the way of safety, that you may win salvation and life eternal. But do you be obedient unto him in all things, honor him as your father, and incline your hearts to his instruction, for we have sent him to you, not for any temporal gain, but for the profit of your souls. Therefore love God and receive baptism in his name, for the Lord our God has prepared for those who love him things which the eye of man hath not seen, and which have never entered into the heart of man. Depart from evil doing, and do what is right. Worship not idols, neither sacrifice offerings of flesh to them, for God does not accept such things, but observe and do as our brother Boniface shall direct, and you and your children shall be in safety forever.

Build also a house where this your father and bishop may live and churches where you may offer up your prayers, that God may forgive your sins and grant you eternal life.

[REPLIES OF POPE GREGORY II TO QUESTIONS OF BONIFACE, NOVEMBER 22, 726]

Gregory, servant of the servants of God, to his most reverend and holy brother and fellow bishop Boniface.

Your messenger, the pious priest Denuald, has brought us the welcome news that you are well and prospering, with the help of God, in the service for which you were sent. He also brought a letter from you showing that the field of the Lord which had been lying fallow, bristling with the thorns of unbelief, has received the plowshare of your instruction, plowing in the seed of the word, and is bringing forth an abundant harvest of true belief.

In this same letter you inserted several paragraphs of inquiries as to the faith and teaching of this Holy and Apostolic Roman Church. And this was well done; for the blessed apostle Peter stands as the fountainhead of the apostolate and the episcopate. And to you who consult us about ecclesiastical matters we show what decision you have to take according to the teaching of apostolic tradition, and we do this not as if by our own personal authority, but by the grace of Him who opens the mouth of the dumb and makes eloquent the tongues of infants.

You ask first within what degrees of relationship marriage may take place. We reply: strictly speaking, in so far as the parties know themselves to be related they ought not to be joined together. But since moderation is better than strictness of discipline, especially toward so uncivilized a people, they may contract marriage after the fourth degree.

As to your question, what a man is to do if his wife is unable, on account of disease, to fulfill her wifely duty: it would be well if he could remain in a state of continence. But, since this is a matter of great difficulty, it is better for him who cannot refrain to take a wife. He may not, however, withdraw his support from the one who was prevented by disease, provided she be not involved in any grievous fault.

In regard to a priest or any cleric accused by the people: unless the evidence of the witnesses to the charge against him is positive, let him take oath before the assembly, calling as witness of his innocence Him to whom all things are plain and open; and so let him keep his proper standing.

In the case of one confirmed by a bishop, a repetition of this rite is prohibited.

In the celebration of the Mass, the form is to be observed which our Lord Jesus Christ used with his disciples. He took the cup and gave it to them, saying: "This cup is the new testament in my blood; this do ye as oft as ye take it." Wherefore it is not fitting that two or three cups should be placed on the altar when the ceremony of the Mass is performed.

As to sacrificial foods: You ask whether, if a believer makes the life-giving sign of the cross above them, it is permitted to eat them or not. A sufficient answer is given in the words of the blessed apostle Paul: "If any man say unto you, This is offered in sacrifice unto idols, eat not for his sake who showed it, and for conscience' sake."[1]

You ask further, if a father or mother shall have placed a young son or daughter in a cloister under the discipline of a rule, whether it is lawful for the child after reaching the years of discretion to leave the cloister and enter into marriage. This we absolutely forbid, since it is an impious thing that the restraints of desire should be relaxed for children offered to God by their parents.

You mention also that some have been baptized by adulterous and unworthy priests without being questioned whether they believe, as it is in the ritual. In such cases you are to follow the ancient custom of the Church. He who has been baptized in the name of the Father, Son, and Holy Spirit may on no account be baptized again; for he has received the gift of His grace not in the name of the one who baptizes, but in the name of the Trinity. Let the word of the Apostle be observed: "One God, one faith, one baptism."[2] We require you to convey spiritual instruction to such persons with especial zeal.

As to young children taken from their parents and not knowing whether they have been baptized or not, reason requires you to baptize them, unless there be someone who can give evidence in the case.

Lepers, if they are believing Christians, may receive the body and blood of the Lord, but they may not take food together with persons in health.

You ask whether, in the case of a contagious disease or plague in a church or monastery, those who are not yet attacked may escape danger by flight. We declare this to be the height of folly; for no one can escape from the hand of God.

Finally, your letter states that certain priests and bishops are so involved in vices of many sorts that their lives are a blot upon the priesthood and you ask whether it is lawful for you to eat with or to speak with them, supposing them not to be heretics. We answer, that you by apostolic authority are to admonish and persuade them and so bring them back to the purity of church discipline. If they obey, you will save their souls and win reward for yourself. You are not to avoid conversation or eating at the same table with them. It often happens that those who are slow in coming to a perception of the truth under strict discipline may be led into the paths of righteousness by the influence of their table companions and by gentle admonition. You ought also to follow this same rule in dealing with those chieftains who are helpful to you.

This, my dear brother, is all that need be said with the authority of the Apostolic See. For the rest we implore the mercy of God, that He who has sent you into that region in our stead and with apostolic authority and has caused the light of truth to shine into that dark forest by means of your words may mercifully grant the increase, so that

---

[1] 1 Cor. 10: 28.

[2] Eph. 4: 5.

you may reap the reward of your labors and we may find remission for our sins.

God keep you in safety, most reverend brother.

Given on the tenth day before the Kalends of Decem- ber, in the tenth year of our most pious and august Lord Leo, by God crowned emperor, in the tenth year of his consulship and the seventh of the Emperor Constantine his son, in the tenth indiction.[1]

2.14 Creating a Roman Christian identity for England: Bede, *The Ecclesiastical History of the English People* (731). Original in Latin.

A child of the cloister—he entered the monastery of Wearmouth-Jarrow in the north of England at the age of seven—Bede (673–735) was among the best-educated men of his day in the Roman, papal tradition and the expertise in Latin that went with it. Because his monastery was extraordinarily well stocked with books—brought back from the Continent (mainly Rome) by Wearmouth and Jarrow's founder, Benedict Biscop—Bede was able to consult a wide range of sources for his numerous writings. These included biblical commentaries, the lives of saints, liturgical works, sermons, scientific texts (his *Computation of Time* was particularly important for calculating the date of Easter and other movable feasts), and histories, including a *History of the Abbots of Wearmouth and Jarrow* and *The Ecclesiastical History*. Although Christianity came to England in a variety of ways, Bede emphasized the Roman contribution. How did Bede's writings enhance the reputation of Gregory the Great?

[Source: Bede, *The Ecclesiastical History of the English People*, ed. Judith McClure and Roger Collins (Oxford: Oxford University Press, 1994), pp. 37–41, 55–59, 65–71, 152–59, 370–75, 397 (slightly modified).]

Book 1

CHAPTER 23

In the year of our Lord 582 Maurice,[2] the fifty-fourth from Augustus, became emperor; he ruled for twenty-one years. In the tenth year of his reign, Gregory,[3] a man eminent in learning and in affairs, was elected pontiff of the apostolic see of Rome; he ruled for thirteen years, six months, and ten days. In the fourteenth year[4] of this emperor and about 150 years after the coming of the Angles to Britain, Gregory, prompted by divine inspiration, sent a servant of God named Augustine[5] and several more God-fearing monks with him to preach the word of God to the English race. In obedience to the pope's commands, they undertook this task and had already gone a little way on their journey when they were paralyzed with terror. They began to contemplate returning home rather than going to a barbarous, fierce, and unbelieving nation whose language they did not even understand. They all agreed that this was the safer course; so forthwith they

---

[1] The letter is thus dated by the reign of Byzantine Emperor Leo III (r.717–741) and his son Constantine, for whom see *The Synod of 754* (above, p. 65) and the *Chronicle of Theophanes* (above, p. 69).

[2] Emperor Maurice Tiberius (r.582–602).

[3] Pope Gregory the Great (590–604).

[4] August 595 to August 596.

[5] Augustine—who should not be confused with St. Augustine (d.430), the bishop of Hippo—had been prior (just below the abbot in administrative status) of the monastery that Gregory founded on his own family property on the Caelian Hill in Rome.

sent home Augustine whom Gregory had intended to have consecrated as their bishop if they were received by the English. Augustine was to beg St. Gregory humbly for permission to give up so dangerous, wearisome, and uncertain a journey. Gregory, however, sent them an encouraging letter in which he persuaded them to persevere with the task of preaching the Word and trust in the help of God. The letter was in these terms:

Gregory, servant of the servants of God, to the servants of our Lord.

My dearly beloved sons, it would have been better not to have undertaken a noble task than to turn back deliberately from what you have begun: so it is right that you should carry out with all diligence this good work which you have begun with the help of the Lord. Therefore do not let the toilsome journey nor the tongues of evil speakers deter you. But carry out the task you have begun under the guidance of God with all constancy and fervor. Be sure that, however great your task may be, the glory of your eternal reward will be still greater. When Augustine your prior returns, now, by our appointment, your abbot, humbly obey him in all things, knowing that whatever you do under his direction will be in all respects profitable to your souls. May Almighty God protect you by His grace and grant that I may see the fruit of your labors in our heavenly home. Though I cannot labor with you, yet because I should have been glad indeed to do so, I hope to share in the joy of your reward. May God keep you safe, my dearly loved sons.

Given on July 23, in the fourteenth year of the reign of our most religious emperor Maurice Tiberius, and the thirteenth year after his consulship, and the fourteenth indiction.[1] [July 23, 596]

CHAPTER 24

The venerable pontiff at the same time also sent a letter to Etherius of Arles,[2] asking him to receive Augustine kindly on his return to Britain. This is the text:

To his most reverend and holy brother and fellow bishop Etherius, Gregory, servant of the servants of God.

Although religious men stand in need of no recommendation with those bishops who have that love which is pleasing to God, yet because a suitable occasion for writing presents itself, we think fit to send this letter to you our brother, informing you that we have directed thither the bearer of this document, Augustine, the servant of God, of whose zeal we are assured, together with other servants of God devoted to winning souls with the Lord's help. It is essential that your holiness should assist him with episcopal zeal and hasten to provide him with what he needs. And in order that you may be the more prompt with your help, we have specially enjoined him to tell you of his mission. We are sure that when you know this you will be prepared with all zeal to afford him your help for the Lord's sake as the occasion requires. We also commend to your charity the priest Candidus,[3] a son of both of us, whom we have sent to take charge of a small patrimony of our church. God keep you safe, most reverend brother.

Given on July 23, in the fourteenth year of the reign of our most religious emperor, Maurice Tiberius, and the thirteenth year after his consulship and the fourteenth indiction. [July 23, 596]

CHAPTER 25

So Augustine, strengthened by the encouragement of St. Gregory, in company with the servants of Christ, returned to the work of preaching the word, and came to Britain. At that time Ethelbert, king of Kent [d.616], was a very powerful monarch. The lands over which he ruled stretched as far as the great river Humber, which divides the northern from the southern Angles. Over against the eastern districts of Kent there is a large island called Thanet which, in English reckoning, is 600 hides[1] in extent. It is divided from the mainland by the river Wantsum, which is about three furlongs wide,[5] can be

---

[1] "Indiction" was a regular cycle of fifteen years, used initially for tax-assessment purposes, but which remained a conventional way of dating documents in the late Roman Empire.

[2] Etherius was actually bishop of Lyon (r.586–602), not of Arles. Bede adopts the term "archbishop" used in the Anglo-Saxon Church, but the Frankish equivalents were called metropolitan bishops. Similar letters were sent to the bishops of Marseille, Arles, and Tours to secure assistance and safe passage for the mission.

[3] Candidus was being sent as Rector of the papal Patrimony, to take charge of the running of the estates owned by the Roman Church in southern Gaul.

[4] The "hide" was theoretically the amount of land that supported one family, its extent varying from place to place.

[5] A furlong is one-eighth of a mile.

crossed in two places only, and joins the sea at either end. Here Augustine, the servant of the Lord, landed with his companions, who are said to have been nearly forty in number. They had acquired interpreters from the Frankish race according to the command of Pope St. Gregory. Augustine sent to Ethelbert to say that he had come from Rome bearing the best of news, namely the sure and certain promise of eternal joys in heaven and an endless kingdom with the living and true God to those who received it. On hearing this the king ordered them to remain on the island where they had landed and be provided with all things necessary until he had decided what to do about them. Some knowledge about the Christian religion had already reached him because he had a Christian wife of the Frankish royal family whose name was Bertha.[1] He had received her from her parents on condition that she should be allowed to practice her faith and religion unhindered, with a bishop named Liudhard whom they had provided for her to support her faith.

Some days afterwards the king came to the island and, sitting in the open air, commanded Augustine and his comrades to come there to talk with him. He took care that they should not meet in any building, for he held the traditional superstition that, if they practiced any magic art, they might deceive him and get the better of him as soon as he entered. But they came endowed with divine not devilish power and bearing as their standard a silver cross and the image of our Lord and Savior painted on a panel.[2] They chanted litanies and uttered prayers to the Lord for their own eternal salvation and the salvation of those for whom and to whom they had come. At the king's command they sat down and preached the word of life to himself and all his officials and companions there present. Then he said to them: "The words and the promises you bring are fair enough, but because they are new to us and doubtful, I cannot consent to accept them and forsake those beliefs which I and the whole people of the Angles have held so long. But as you have come on a long pilgrimage and are anxious, I perceive, to share with us things which you believe to be true and good, we do not wish to do you harm; on the contrary, we will

receive you hospitably and provide what is necessary for your support; nor do we forbid you to win all you can to your faith and religion by your preaching." So he gave them a dwelling in the city of Canterbury, which was the chief city of all his dominions; and, in accordance with his promise, he granted them provisions and did not refuse them freedom to preach. It is related that as they approached the city in accordance with their custom carrying the holy cross and the image of our great King and Lord, Jesus Christ, they sang this litany in unison: "We beseech Thee, O Lord, in Thy great mercy, that Thy wrath and anger may be turned away from this city and from Thy holy house, for we have sinned. Alleluia."

CHAPTER 26

As soon as they had entered the dwelling-place allotted to them, they began to imitate the way of life of the apostles and of the primitive church. They were constantly engaged in prayers, in vigils and fasts; they preached the word of life to as many as they could; they despised all worldly things as foreign to them; they accepted only the necessaries of life from those whom they taught; in all things they practiced what they preached and kept themselves prepared to endure adversities, even to the point of dying for the truths they proclaimed. To put it briefly, some, marveling at their simple and innocent way of life and the sweetness of their heavenly doctrine, believed and were baptized. There was nearby, on the east of the city, a church built in ancient times in honor of St. Martin,[3] while the Romans were still in Britain, in which the queen who, as has been said, was a Christian, used to pray. In this church they first began to meet to chant the psalms, to pray, to say mass, to preach, and to baptize, until, when the king had been converted to the faith, they received greater liberty to preach everywhere and to build or restore churches.

At last the king, as well as others, believed and was baptized, being attracted by the pure life of the saints and by their most precious promises, whose truth they confirmed by performing many miracles. Every day more and more began to flock to hear the Word, to forsake

---

[1] Bertha was the daughter of the Merovingian king Charibert I (r.561–567), whose short-lived realm had been centered on Paris. As Bede points out, she was a Catholic Christian who brought her own bishop, Liudhard, with her.

[2] How might Bede's emphasis on this image be an indirect critique of Byzantine iconoclasm? Bede was writing at the very beginning of that movement.

[3] The western section of the chancel (the space around the altar) of the extant church of St. Martin in Canterbury is thought to have formed part of the church of Queen Bertha. This reference, like that to Liudhard, hints at the survival of Christian worship in post-Roman lowland Britain prior to the arrival of Augustine.

their heathen worship, and, through faith, to join the unity of Christ's holy Church. It is related that the king, although he rejoiced at their conversion and their faith, compelled no one to accept Christianity; though nonetheless he showed greater affection for believers since they were his fellow citizens in the kingdom of heaven. But he had learned from his teachers and guides in the way of salvation that the service of Christ was voluntary and ought not to be compulsory. It was not long before he granted his teachers a place to settle in, suitable to their rank, in Canterbury, his chief city, and gave them possessions of various kinds for their needs....

CHAPTER 29

Since Bishop Augustine had advised him that the harvest was great and the workers were few, Pope Gregory sent more colleagues and ministers of the word together with his messengers. First and foremost among these were Mellitus, Justus, Paulinus, and Rufinianus; and he sent with them all such things as were generally necessary for the worship and ministry of the Church, such as sacred vessels, altar cloths and church ornaments, vestments for priests and clerks, relics of the holy apostles and martyrs, and very many manuscripts. He also sent a letter in which he announced that he had dispatched the pallium[1] to him and at the same time directed how he should organize the bishops in Britain. Here is the text of this letter:

To the most reverend and holy brother Augustine, our fellow-bishop, Gregory, servant of the servants of God.

While it is certain that untold rewards in the eternal kingdom are laid up for those who labor for Almighty God, nevertheless it is necessary that we should bestow rewards and honors upon them so that they may be encouraged by this recognition to toil more abundantly in their spiritual work. And because the new church of the English has been brought into the grace of Almighty God through the bounty of the Lord and by your labors, we grant to you the use of the pallium in the church but only for the performance of the solemn rites of the mass, so that you may ordain twelve bishops in various places who are to be subject to your jurisdiction. However, the bishop of London[2] shall, for the future, always be consecrated by his own synod and receive the honor of the pallium from that holy and apostolic see which, by the guidance of God, I serve. We wish to send as bishop to the city of York one whom you yourself shall decide to consecrate. But if this city together with the neighboring localities should receive the Word of the Lord, he [the bishop of York] is also to consecrate twelve bishops and enjoy the honorable rank of a metropolitan. For it is our intention, God willing, if we live, to give him the pallium too. Nevertheless, brother, we wish him to be subject to your authority. But after your death, he should preside over the bishops he has consecrated, being in no way subject to the authority of the bishop of London. There is, however, to be this distinction in honor, in future, between the bishops of London and York, that he who was first consecrated is to be reckoned senior. But let them agree to do whatever has to be done, taking counsel together and acting out of zeal for Christ. Let them judge rightly and with one mind and so carry out their decisions without disagreement.

You, brother, are to have under your subjection those bishops whom you have consecrated as well as those who shall be consecrated by the bishop of York, and not those only but also all the bishops of Britain, under the guidance of our Lord God, Jesus Christ, so that they may see from the words and actions of your Holiness what true faith and good living are like and so, fulfilling their office in faith and righteousness, may attain to the heavenly kingdom when it shall please the Lord. May God keep you safe, most reverend brother.

Given June 22 in the nineteenth year of the reign of our most religious emperor Maurice Tiberius, the eighteenth year after his consulship and in the fourth indiction. [June 22, 601]

CHAPTER 30

When these messengers had departed, St. Gregory sent after them a letter which is worth recording, in which he plainly showed his eager interest in the salvation of our race. This is what he wrote:

To my most beloved son, Abbot Mellitus, Gregory, servant of the servants of God.

---

[1] The "pallium" was a thin band of white wool worn by the popes in the performance of the liturgy, the use of which could be conferred on approved metropolitan bishops. It was regularly given to the archbishops of Canterbury.

[2] Gregory, relying on the former Roman administrative structures, assumed that London (actually in the kingdom of the East Saxons) would be the seat of the new archbishopric; contemporary political realities had already led to Canterbury's taking this role instead.

Since the departure of our companions and yourself I have felt much anxiety because we have not happened to hear how your journey has prospered. However, when Almighty God has brought you to our most reverend brother Bishop Augustine, tell him what I have decided after long deliberation about the English people, namely that the idol temples of that race should by no means be destroyed, but only the idols in them. Take holy water and sprinkle it in these shrines, build altars and place relics in them. For if the shrines are well built, it is essential that they should be changed from the worship of devils to the service of the true God. When the people see that their shrines are not destroyed they will be able to banish error from their hearts and be more ready to come to the places they are familiar with, but now recognizing and worshiping the true God. And because they are in the habit of slaughtering many cattle as sacrifices to devils, some solemnity ought to be given them in exchange for this. So on the day of the dedication or the festivals of the holy martyrs, whose relics are deposited there, let them make themselves huts from the branches of trees around the churches which have been converted out of shrines, and let them celebrate the solemnity with religious feasts. Do not let them sacrifice animals to the devil, but let them slaughter animals for their own food to the praise of God, and let them give thanks to the Giver of all things for His bountiful provision. Thus while some outward rejoicings are preserved, they will be able more easily to share in inward rejoicings. It is doubtless impossible to cut out everything at once from their stubborn minds, just as the man who is attempting to climb to the highest place, rises by steps and degrees and not by leaps. Thus the Lord made Himself known to the Israelites in Egypt, yet he preserved in his own worship the forms of sacrifice which they were accustomed to offer to the devil and commanded them to kill animals when sacrificing to him. So with changed hearts they were to put away one part of the sacrifice and retain the other; even though they were the same animals as they were in the habit of offering, yet since the people were offering them to the true God and not to idols, they were not the same sacrifices. These things then, dearly beloved, you must say to our brother so that in his present position he may carefully consider how he should order all things. May God keep you in safety, most beloved son.

Given July 18 in the nineteenth year of the reign of our most religious emperor Maurice Tiberius, and in the eighteenth year after his consulship and in the fourth indiction. [July 18, 601]

CHAPTER 31

At the same time Pope Gregory heard that Augustine had been performing miracles and sent him a letter on the subject, in which he exhorts Augustine not to incur the danger of being elated by their great number:

I know, most beloved brother, that Almighty God out of love for you has worked great miracles through you for the race which it was his will to have among the chosen. It is therefore necessary that you should rejoice with trembling over this heavenly gift and fear as you rejoice. You will rejoice because the souls of the English are drawn by outward miracles to inward grace: but you will fear lest among these signs which are performed, the weak mind may be raised up by self-esteem and so the very cause by which it is raised to outward honor may lead through vainglory to its inward fall. We ought to remember that when the disciples were returning from their preaching full of joy, they said to their heavenly Master, "Lord, even the devils are subject to us through thy name (Luke 10: 17)." And forthwith they received the reply, "In this rejoice not, but rather rejoice that your names are written in heaven (Luke 10: 20)." They had set their minds on personal and temporal joys when they rejoiced over their own miracles, but they are recalled from private to common joys and from temporal to eternal joys by his words, "Rejoice in this that your names are written in heaven." For not all the elect work miracles, but nevertheless all their names are written in heaven. Therefore those who are true disciples ought not to rejoice except in that good thing which they have in common with all the elect and which they will enjoy for ever. So it remains, most dear brother, that amidst those outward deeds which you perform through the Lord's power you should always judge your inner self carefully and carefully note within yourself what you are and how great is the grace shown to that people for whose conversion you have received the gift of working miracles. And if you remember that you have at any time sinned against your Creator either in word or deed, always call this to mind in order that the memory of your guilt may suppress the vainglory which arises in your heart. And whatever power of working miracles you have received or shall receive, consider that these gifts have been conferred not on you, but on those for whose salvation they have been granted you.

CHAPTER 32

Pope Gregory at the same time also sent a letter to King Ethelbert as well as numerous gifts of every kind. He was anxious to glorify the king with temporal honors, while at the same time he rejoiced to think that Ethelbert had attained to the knowledge of heavenly glory by Gregory's own labor and industry....

Book 2

CHAPTER 1

About this time, in the year of our Lord 605,[1] Pope St. Gregory, who had reigned in great glory over the apostolic Roman see for thirteen years, six months, and ten days, died and was taken up to reign for ever in the kingdom of heaven. Well indeed may we, the English nation converted by his efforts from the power of Satan to the faith of Christ, give a somewhat full account of him in this *History*. We can and should by rights call him our apostle, for though he held the most important see in the whole world and was head of Churches which had long been converted to the true faith, yet he made our nation, till then enslaved to idols, into a Church of Christ, so that we may use the apostle's words about him, "If he is not an apostle to others yet at least he is to us, for we are the seal of his apostleship in the Lord (see 1 Cor. 9: 2)."

He was of Roman race, his father's name being Gordianus. He traced his descent from ancestors who were not only noble but also devout. Felix,[2] for example, who was once bishop of the apostolic see and a man of great reputation both in Christ and in the Church, was his forefather. That ancestral tradition of religion he followed with the same religious devotion as his parents and kinsmen, while the noble position which was accounted his, according to the standards of the world, was by God's grace entirely sacrificed to winning glory and honor of a higher kind. He promptly renounced his secular habit and entered a monastery,[3] in which he proceeded to live with such grace and perfection—as he used afterwards to declare with tears—that his soul was then above all transitory things, and he soared beyond all things subject to change. He used to think nothing but thoughts of heaven so that, even though still imprisoned in the body, he was able to pass in contemplation beyond the barriers of the flesh. He loved death, which in the eyes of almost everybody is a punishment, because he held it to be the entrance to life and the reward of his labors.

He used to relate all this, not boasting over his progress towards moral perfection, but rather bewailing the loss which he seemed to have incurred as the result of his pastoral cares. Once, for instance, when he was talking privately with his deacon Peter and enumerating the former virtues of his soul, he added mournfully that now on account of his pastoral cares he had to trouble himself with the business of men of this world, and after the enjoyment of peace so lovely, he was soiled by the dust of earthly activities. After dissipating his strength on outward things by descending to the affairs of all and sundry, even when he sought the things of the spirit, he inevitably returned to them impaired. "I realize," he said, "what I endure and what I have lost; and when my mind turns to what I have lost, then what I endure becomes so much the more burdensome."

The holy man said all this in a spirit of great humility. We need not believe, however, that he had lost any of his monastic perfection by reason of his pastoral cares. It would appear that he profited more by his efforts over the conversion of many than he had done from the quiet retirement of his earlier way of life. This was largely because, while fulfilling his pontifical duties, he turned his own house into a monastery; and when he was first taken from the monastery and was ordained to the ministry of the altar, having been sent to Constantinople as delegate of the apostolic see, he never ceased from his heavenly manner of life, though he had to live in an earthly palace. He even used some of the brothers from his monastery who had followed him out of brotherly love to the royal city [Constantinople] to protect him in his observance of the Rule. Thus, as he himself writes, through their unremitting example he could bind himself, as it were by an anchor cable, to the calm shores of prayer, while he was being tossed about on the ceaseless tide of secular affairs. So his mind, shaken by worldly business, could be strengthened by the encouragement derived from daily reading and contemplation in their company. By their fellowship he was thus not only defended against worldly assaults, but was also encouraged more and more to the activities of the heavenly life.

They urged him to unfold by spiritual interpretation the Book of Job, a work which is shrouded in great obscurity. Nor could he refuse the task imposed on him

---

[1] Gregory died on 12 March 604; otherwise Bede is right about the length of his pontificate. But Bede's facts and dates are not always accurate.

[2] Felix IV was pope 526–530.

[3] Gregory turned his own family home on the Caelian Hill in Rome into the monastery of St. Andrew.

by his loving brethren, seeing that it was likely to be of great use to many. So in thirty-five books[1] of exposition he taught in a marvelous manner the literal meaning of the book, its bearing on the mysteries of Christ and the Church, and the sense in which it applies to each of the faithful. He began this work while he was delegate in the royal city and finished it after he was made pope at Rome. While he was still in the royal city, helped by the grace of the catholic truth, he crushed at its birth a new heresy which arose there concerning our state at the resurrection. Eutychius, the bishop of the city, taught that our body in its resurrection glory, would be impalpable and more subtle than wind or air.[2] When Gregory heard this he proved both by sound reasoning and by the example of our Lord's resurrection that this dogma was contrary in every particular to the orthodox belief. For the catholic faith maintains that our body, while it is indeed exalted by the glory of immortality and made subtle by the effectual working of the spirit, is palpable by the reality of its nature as was our Lord's body, concerning which he said to his disciples, when it had been raised from the dead, "Touch me and see, for a spirit has not flesh and bones as you see me have (Luke 24: 39–40)." The venerable father Gregory strove so earnestly in his declaration of the faith against this newborn heresy and, with the help of the most religious emperor Tiberius Constantine,[3] suppressed it with such resolution, that no one has since been found to resuscitate it.

He composed another remarkable book called the *Pastoral Care*, in which he set forth in the clearest manner what sort of persons should be chosen to rule the Church and how these rulers ought to live; with how much discrimination they should instruct different types of listeners; and how earnestly they ought each day to reflect on their own frailty. He composed forty *Homilies on the Gospel*, which he divided into two volumes of equal size, and made four books of *Dialogues* in which, at the request of Peter his deacon, he collected the virtues of the most famous saints he knew or could learn of in Italy as an example of life to posterity; as in his expository works he taught what virtues men ought to strive after, so, by describing the miracles of the saints, he showed how glorious those virtues are. He also showed in twenty-two homilies how much inner light is to be found within the most obscure sections of the prophet Ezekiel, namely the first part and the last. There is also a useful Synodal book which he composed in collaboration with the bishops of Italy, dealing with some of the Church's vital problems, together with familiar letters to certain individuals, not to mention the book of answers to the questions of St. Augustine, the first bishop of the English race, which I have described above and of which the whole is included in this *History*. It is all the more wonderful that he was able to produce so many books and of such length, since almost continually throughout his early manhood he had been, to use his own words, tortured with frequent pains in the bowels, and every moment of the day he was exhausted by a weakness of the internal organs, and his breathing was affected by a low but unremitting fever. Yet always amid these troubles, when he carefully reflected on the testimony of the scriptures that, "He scourges every son whom he receives,"[4] the more severely he was oppressed by present evils, the more surely he was refreshed by eternal hope.

This much may be said of his immortal spirit, which could not be quenched by so much bodily pain. Other popes applied themselves to the task of building churches and adorning them with gold and silver, but he devoted himself entirely to winning souls. Whatever money he had he took diligent care to distribute and give to the poor, so that "his righteousness might endure for ever and his horn be exalted with honor,"[5] so that the words of the blessed Job might truly be said of him: "When the ear heard me, then it blessed me and when the eye saw me it gave witness to me because I delivered the poor that cried and the fatherless also that had none to help him. The blessing of him that was ready to perish came upon me and I consoled the widow's heart. I put on righteousness and I clothed myself with my judgment as with a robe and a diadem. I was eyes to the blind and feet was I to the lame. I was a father to the poor and the cause which I knew not,

---

[1] This was the *Moralia in Job*.

[2] Eutychius was the Patriarch of Constantinople 552–565.

[3] Tiberius Constantine became Caesar and regent in 574, when Justin II (r.565–578) became insane; he was sole emperor from 578 to 582.

[4] Heb. 12: 6.

[5] Ps. 112: 9; Douay Ps. 111: 9.

I diligently searched out. I broke the jaws of the wicked and plucked the spoil out of his teeth."[1] And again a little further on he says, "If I have withheld their desire from the poor or have caused the eyes of the widow to fail; if I have eaten my morsel myself alone and the fatherless has not eaten thereof; for from my youth my compassion grew up with me and from my mother's womb it came forth with me."[2]

To his works of piety and justice this also belongs: that he snatched our race from the teeth of the ancient foe and made them partakers of everlasting freedom by sending us preachers. Rejoicing in their faith and commending them with worthy praise he says in his commentary on the blessed Job: "Lo, the mouth of Britain, which once only knew how to gnash its barbarous teeth, has long since learned to sing the praises of God with the alleluia of the Hebrews. See how the proud Ocean has become a servant, lying low now before the feet of the saints, and those barbarous motions, which earthly princes could not subdue with the sword, are now, through the fear of God, repressed with a simple word from the lips of priests; and he who, as an unbeliever, did not flinch before troops of warriors, now, as a believer, fears the words of the humble. For having received the heavenly Word and being enlightened by miracles as well, he is filled with the grace and the knowledge of God. He is restrained by the fear of God so that he dreads to do evil and with all his heart he longs to attain to everlasting grace." In these words St. Gregory also declares that St. Augustine and his companions led the English race to the knowledge of the truth, not only by preaching the Word but also by showing heavenly signs.

Among other things, Pope St. Gregory arranged that masses should be celebrated in the churches of the apostles St. Peter and St. Paul over their bodies. And in the celebration of the mass, he added three quite perfect petitions, "Dispose our days in peace, and command that we be saved from eternal damnation, and that we be numbered among the flock of thine elect."

He ruled the Church during the days of the Emperors Maurice and Phocas.[3] He departed this life in the second year of Phocas and passed to the true life in heaven. His body was buried in the church of St. Peter the Apostle, before the sanctuary, on 12 March; and in that body he will one day rise again in glory together with the other pastors of the Church. His epitaph written on his tomb runs as follows:

Earth, take this corpse—'tis dust of thine own dust:
When God shall give new life, restore thy trust.
Star-bound his soul: for Death's writ does not run
Where grave's but gateway to life new-begun.
A great high-priest this sepulcher inherits,
Who lives for ever by uncounted merits;
Hunger with meat, winter with clothes he ended,
Souls with sound learning from the foe defended;
Whate'er he taught, himself fulfilled in act—
Mystic his words, but his example fact.
Anglia to Christ at piety's dictation
He turned, won thousands from an unknown nation.
Thus that great shepherd labored, thus he wrought;
To increase his Master's flock was all his thought.
Take thy reward in triumph and in joy,
Who in God's council sits eternally!

We must not fail to relate the story about St. Gregory which has come down to us as a tradition of our forefathers. It explains the reason why he showed such earnest solicitude for the salvation of our race. It is said that one day, soon after some merchants had arrived in Rome, a quantity of merchandise was exposed for sale in the market place. Crowds came to buy and Gregory too among them. As well as other merchandise he saw some boys put up for sale, with fair complexions, handsome faces, and lovely hair. On seeing them he asked, so it is said, from what region or land they had been brought. He was told that they came from the island of Britain, whose inhabitants were like that in appearance. He asked again whether those islanders were Christians or still entangled in the errors of heathenism. He was told that they were heathen. Then with a deep-drawn sigh he said, "Alas that the author of darkness should have men so bright of face in his grip, and that minds devoid of inward grace should bear so graceful an outward form." Again he asked for the name of the race. He was told that they were called *Angli*. "Good," he said, "they have the

---

[1] Job 29: 11–17.

[2] Job 31: 16–18.

[3] Emperor Maurice (r.582–602) was overthrown in a military revolt led by Phocas (r.602–610).

face of angels [*angeli* in Latin], and such men should be fellow heirs of the angels in heaven." "What is the name," he asked, "of the kingdom from which they have been brought?" He was told that the men of the kingdom were called *Deiri*. "*Deiri*," he replied. "*De ira!* [=From anger!] good! snatched from the wrath of Christ and called to his mercy. And what is the name of the king of the land?" He was told that it was Ælle;[1] and playing on the name, he said, "Alleluia! the praise of God the Creator must be sung in those parts." So he went to the bishop of Rome and of the apostolic see, for he himself had not yet been made pope, and asked him to send some ministers of the word to the race of the Angles in Britain to convert them to Christ. He added that he himself was prepared to carry out the task with the help of the Lord provided that the pope was willing. But he was unable to perform this mission, because although the pope was willing to grant his request, the citizens of Rome could not permit him to go so far away from the city. Soon after he had become pope, he fulfilled the task which he had long desired. It is true that he sent other preachers, but he himself helped their preaching to bear fruit by his encouragement and prayers. I have thought it proper to insert this story into this Church *History*, based as it is on the tradition that we have received from our ancestors....

Book 3

CHAPTER 25

Meanwhile, after Bishop Aidan's death,[2] Finan succeeded him as bishop,[3] having been consecrated and sent over by the Irish. He constructed a church on the island of Lindisfarne suitable for an episcopal see, building it after the Irish method, not of stone but of hewn oak, thatching it with reeds; later on the most reverend Archbishop Theodore[4] consecrated it in honor of the blessed apostle Peter. It was Eadberht,[5] who was bishop of Lindisfarne, who removed the reed thatch and had the whole of it, both roof and walls, covered with sheets of lead.

In those days there arose a great and active controversy about the keeping of Easter. Those who had come from Kent or Gaul declared that the Irish observance of Easter Sunday was contrary to the custom of the universal church. One most violent defender of the true Easter was Ronan[6] who, though Irish by race, had learned the true rules of the church in Gaul or Italy. In disputing with Finan he put many right or at least encouraged them to make a more strict inquiry into the truth; but he could by no means put Finan right. On the contrary, as he was a man of fierce temper, Ronan made him the more bitter by his reproofs and turned him into an open adversary of the truth. James, once the deacon of the venerable Archbishop Paulinus, as we have already said,[7] kept the true and catholic Easter with all those whom he could instruct in the better way. Queen Eanfleda[8] and her people also observed it as she had seen it done in Kent, having with her a Kentish priest named Romanus who followed the Catholic observance. Hence it is said that in these days it sometimes happened that Easter was celebrated twice in the same year, so that the king had finished the fast and was keeping Easter Sunday, while the queen and her people were still in Lent and observing Palm Sunday. This difference in the observance of Easter was patiently tolerated by all while Aidan was alive, because they had clearly understood that although he could not keep Easter otherwise than according to the manner of those who had sent him, he nevertheless labored diligently to practice the works of faith, piety, and love, which is the mark of all the saints. He was therefore deservedly loved by all, including those who had other views about Easter. Not only was he respected by the ordinary people but also by bishops, such as Honorius of Kent and Felix of East Anglia.

---

[1] Ælle was king of the Deirans (in England) 559–588.

[2] Aidan (d.651) was the bishop of Lindisfarne (in northern England). He had come from Ireland to teach the Christian faith at the request of Oswald, king of Northumbria (d.642).

[3] Finan (d.661).

[4] Theodore was archbishop of Canterbury 668–690.

[5] Eadberht was bishop of Lindisfarne 688–698.

[6] Nothing else is known of Ronan. The church in the south of Ireland had by this time largely adopted Continental practices with respect to the dating of Easter.

[7] Paulinus (d.644) was bishop of York and Rochester.

[8] Eanfleda (d.c.704) was the daughter of Edwin, king of Deira, and Ethelburg Tata, daughter of Ethelbert and Bertha of Kent. She married Oswiu, king of Bernicia (r.642–670).

When Finan, Aidan's successor, was dead and Colman,[1] who had also been sent from Ireland, had become bishop, a still more serious controversy arose concerning the observance of Easter as well as about other matters of ecclesiastical discipline. This dispute naturally troubled the minds and hearts of many people who feared that, though they had received the name of Christian, they might have done so in vain. All this came to the ears of the rulers [of Northumbria] themselves, Oswiu [d.670] and his son Alhfrith. Oswiu, who had been educated and baptized by the Irish and was well versed in their language, considered that nothing was better than what they had taught. But Alhfrith had as his instructor in the Christian faith one Wilfrid, a most learned man who had once been to Rome to study church doctrine and had spent much time at Lyon with Dalfinus,[2] archbishop of Gaul, having received there his ecclesiastical tonsure in the form of a crown. So Alhfrith rightly preferred his teaching to all the traditions of the Irish and had therefore given him a monastery of forty hides in the place called Ripon. He had presented the site, a short time before, to those who followed Irish ways, but because, when given the choice, they preferred to renounce the site rather than change their customs, he gave it to one who was worthy of the place both by his doctrine and his way of life. At that time there had come to the kingdom of Northumbria Agilbert, bishop of the West Saxons, whom we have mentioned before, a friend of Alhfrith and of Abbot Wilfrid; he stayed some time with them and, at the request of Alhfrith, he ordained Wilfrid priest in his own monastery. Agilbert had with him a priest called Agatho.

When this question of Easter and of the tonsure and other ecclesiastical matters was raised, it was decided to hold a council [in 664] to settle the dispute at a monastery called *Streanæshealh* (Whitby), a name which means the bay of the lighthouse, at this time Hild, a woman devoted to God, was abbess.[3] There came to the council the two kings, both father and son, Bishop Colman with his Irish clergy, and Agilbert with the priests Agatho and Wilfrid. James and Romanus were on their side while the Abbess Hild and her followers were on the side of the Irish; among these also was the venerable Bishop Cedd, who, as has been mentioned, had been consecrated long before by the Irish and who acted as a most careful interpreter for both parties at the council.

First King Oswiu began by declaring that it was fitting that those who served one God should observe one rule of life and not differ in the celebration of the heavenly sacraments, seeing that they all hoped for one kingdom in heaven; they ought therefore to inquire as to which was the truer tradition and then all follow it together. He then ordered his bishop Colman to say first what were the customs which he followed and whence they originated. Colman thereupon said, "The method of keeping Easter which I observe, I received from my superiors who sent me here as bishop; it was in this way that all our fathers, men beloved of God, are known to have celebrated it. Nor should this method seem contemptible and blameworthy seeing that the blessed evangelist John, the disciple whom the Lord specially loved, is said to have celebrated it thus, together with all the churches over which he presided." When he had said all this and more to the same effect, the king ordered Agilbert to expound the method he observed, its origin, and the authority he had for following it. Agilbert answered, "I request that my disciple, the priest Wilfrid, may speak on my behalf, for we are both in agreement with the other followers of our church tradition who are here present; and he can explain our views in the English tongue better and more clearly than I can through an interpreter." Then Wilfrid, receiving instructions from the king to speak, began thus: "The Easter we keep is the same as we have seen universally celebrated in Rome, where the apostles St. Peter and St. Paul lived, taught, suffered, and were buried. We also found it in use everywhere in Italy and Gaul when we traveled through those countries for the purpose of study and prayer. We learned that it was observed at one and the same time in Africa, Asia, Egypt, Greece, and throughout the whole world, wherever the Church of Christ is scattered, amid various nations and languages. The only exceptions are these men and their accomplices in obstinacy, I mean the Picts and the Britons, who in these, the two remotest islands of the Ocean, and only in some parts of them, foolishly attempt to fight against the whole world."

Colman answered, "I wonder that you are willing to call our efforts foolish, seeing that we follow the example of that apostle who was reckoned worthy to recline on

---

[1] Colman was bishop of Lindisfarne 661–664.

[2] Bede confused Dalfinus, who was the prefect (secular ruler) of Lyon, with his brother Annemundus, the bishop of Lyon (c.650–660). Wilfrid (d.709), bishop of York and Hexham, was the chief proponent of the Roman date for Easter.

[3] Under Hild, Whitby was a double monastery with both men and women (in separate quarters). Hild presided over both.

the breast of the Lord; for all the world acknowledges his great wisdom." Wilfrid replied, "Far be it from me to charge John with foolishness: he literally observed the decrees of the Mosaic law when the Church was still Jewish in many respects, at a time when the apostles were unable to bring to a sudden end the entire observance of that law which God ordained in the same way as, for instance, they made it compulsory on all new converts to abandon their idols which are of devilish origin. They feared, of course, that they might make a stumbling-block for the Jewish proselytes dispersed among the Gentiles. This was the reason why Paul circumcised Timothy, why he offered sacrifices in the temple, and why he shaved his head at Corinth in company with Aquila and Priscilla; all this was of no use except to avoid scandalizing the Jews. Hence James said to Paul, 'Thou seest, brother, how many thousands there are among the Jews of them which have believed; and they are all zealous for the law (Acts 21: 20).' But in these days when the light of the Gospel is spreading throughout the world, it is not necessary, it is not even lawful for believers to be circumcised or to offer God sacrifices of flesh and blood. So John, in accordance with the custom of the law, began the celebration of Easter Day in the evening of the fourteenth day of the first month, regardless of whether it fell on the sabbath or any other day. But when Peter preached at Rome, remembering that the Lord rose from the dead and brought to the world the hope of the resurrection on the first day of the week, he realized that Easter ought to be kept as follows: he always waited for the rising of the moon on the evening of the fourteenth day of the first month in accordance with the custom and precepts of the law, just as John did, but when it had risen, if the Lord's Day, which was then called the first day of the week, followed in the morning, he proceeded to celebrate Easter as we are accustomed to do at the present time. But if the Lord's Day was due, not on the morning following the fourteenth day of the moon but on the sixteenth or seventeenth or any other day until the twenty-first, he waited for it, and began the holy Easter ceremonies the night before, that is, on the Saturday evening; so it came about that Easter Sunday was kept only between the fifteenth day of the moon and the twenty-first. So this evangelical and apostolic tradition does not abolish the law but rather fulfils it, by ordering the observance of Easter from the evening of the fourteenth day of the moon in the first month up to the twenty-first of the moon in the same month. All the successors of St. John in Asia since his death and also the whole church throughout the world have followed this observance. That this is the true Easter and that this alone must be celebrated by the faithful was not newly decreed but confirmed afresh by the Council of Nicaea as the history of the Church informs us.[1] So it is plain, Colman, that you neither follow the example of John, as you think, nor of Peter, whose tradition you knowingly contradict; and so, in your observance of Easter, you neither follow the law nor the gospel. For John who kept Easter according to the decrees of the Mosaic law, took no heed of the Sunday; you do not do this, for you celebrate Easter only on a Sunday. Peter celebrated Easter Sunday between the fifteenth and the twenty-first day of the moon; you, on the other hand, celebrate Easter Sunday between the fourteenth and the twentieth day of the moon. Thus you very often begin Easter on the evening of the thirteenth day of the moon, which is never mentioned in the law. This was not the day—it was the fourteenth, in which the Lord, the author and giver of the Gospel, ate the old passover in the evening and instituted the sacraments of the new testament to be celebrated by the church in remembrance of his passion. Besides, in your celebration of Easter you utterly exclude the twenty-first day, which the law of Moses specially ordered to be observed. So, as I have said, in your celebration of the greatest of the festivals you agree neither with John nor Peter, neither with the law nor the Gospel."

Colman replied, "Did Anatolius, a man who was holy and highly spoken of in the history of the Church to which you appeal, judge contrary to the law and the Gospel when he wrote that Easter should be celebrated between the fourteenth and the twentieth day of the moon? Or must we believe that our most reverend father Columba and his successors,[2] men beloved of God, who celebrated Easter in the same way, judged and acted contrary to the holy scriptures, seeing that there were many of them to whose holiness the heavenly signs and the miracles they performed bore witness? And as I have no

---

[1] This is a reference to the account of the First Council of Nicaea of 325 in Rufinus' translation and in the continuation in Eusebius' *History of the Church*.

[2] Columba (d.597) was an Irish monk who left his homeland to found the monastery of Iona (in Scotland), which he used as a base for missionary work. Though he was highly praised in the Irish world, Wilfrid seems to have known very little about him—or, at least, he is presented as knowing little by Bede.

doubt that they were saints, I shall never cease to follow their way of life, their customs, and their teaching."

Wilfrid replied, "It is true that Anatolius was a most holy and learned man, worthy of all praise; but what have you to do with him since you do not observe his precepts? He followed a correct rule in celebrating Easter, basing it on a cycle of nineteen years, of which you are either unaware or, if you do know of it, you despise it, even though it is observed by the whole Church of Christ. He assigned the fourteenth day of the moon to Easter Sunday, reckoning after the Egyptian manner that the fifteenth day of the moon began on the evening of the fourteenth. So also he assigned the twentieth day to Easter Sunday, reckoning that after evening it was the twenty-first day. But it appears that you are ignorant of this distinction, in that you sometimes clearly keep Easter Day before full moon, that is on the thirteenth day of the moon. So far as your father Columba and his followers are concerned, whose holiness you claim to imitate and whose rule and precepts (confirmed by heavenly signs) you claim to follow, I might perhaps point out that at the judgment, many will say to the Lord that they prophesied in His name and cast out devils and did many wonderful works, but the Lord will answer that He never knew them. Far be it from me to say this about your fathers, for it is much fairer to believe good rather than evil about unknown people. So I will not deny that those who in their rude simplicity loved God with pious intent, were indeed servants of God and beloved by Him. Nor do I think that this observance of Easter did much harm to them while no one had come to show them a more perfect rule to follow. In fact I am sure that if anyone knowing the Catholic rule had come to them they would have followed it, as they are known to have followed all the laws of God as soon as they had learned of them.

But, once having heard the decrees of the apostolic see or rather of the universal Church, if you refuse to follow them, confirmed as they are by the holy Scriptures, then without doubt you are committing sin. For though your fathers were holy men, do you think that a handful of people in one corner of the remotest of islands is to be preferred to the universal Church of Christ which is spread throughout the world? And even if that Columba of yours—yes, and ours too, if he belonged to Christ—was a holy man of mighty works, is he to be preferred to the most blessed chief of the apostles, to whom the Lord said, 'Thou art Peter and upon this rock I will build my Church and the gates of hell shall not prevail against it, and I will give unto thee the keys of the kingdom of heaven.'"?[1]

When Wilfrid had ended, the king said, "Is it true, Colman, that the Lord said these words to Peter?" Colman answered, "It is true, O King." Then the king went on, "Have you anything to show that an equal authority was given to your Columba?" Colman answered, "Nothing." Again the king said, "Do you both agree, without any dispute, that these words were addressed primarily to Peter and that the Lord gave him the keys of the kingdom of heaven?" They both answered, "Yes." Thereupon the king concluded, "Then, I tell you, since he is the doorkeeper I will not contradict him, but I intend to obey his commands in everything to the best of my knowledge and ability. Otherwise, when I come to the gates of the kingdom of heaven, there may be no one to open them, because the one who on your own showing holds the keys has turned his back on me." When the king had spoken, all who were seated there or standing by, both high and low, signified their assent, gave up their imperfect rules, and readily accepted in their place those which they recognized to be better.

---

[1] Matt. 16: 18.

TIMELINE FOR CHAPTER TWO

600

c.610–22 *QUR'AN SURAS* ———

——— c.615– c.630 *ISIDORE, ETYMOLOGIES*

BEF. 625 AL-A'SHA, *BID HURAYRA FAREWELL* ———

650

——— 7TH C. *LIFE OF ST. THEODORE OF SYKEON*

680S *PASSION OF LEUDEGAR* ———

——— c.692 AL-AKHTAL, *THE TRIBE HAS DEPARTED*

709/710 *JUDGMENT OF CHILDEBERT III* ———
700

——— 710 *TAX DEMAND IN EGYPT*

713 *TREATY OF TUDMIR* ———

——— 723–26 *LETTERS TO BONIFACE*

——— 730S/EARLY 750S *JOHN OF DAMASCUS,*

731 BEDE, *ECCLESIASTICAL HISTORY* ———
ON HOLY IMAGES

750

754 *ICONOCLASTIC SYNOD* ———

800

BEF. 818 *CHRONICLE OF THEOPHANES* ———
CONFESSOR

To test your knowledge and gain deeper understanding of this chapter,
please go to www.utphistorymatters.com for Questions for Reflection.

III

Creating New Identities (c.750–c.900)

THE MATERIAL BASIS OF SOCIETY

3.1 Manors in the West: *Polyptyque of the Church of Saint Mary of Marseille* (814–815). Original in Latin.

In the very year that Charlemagne died (814), an enterprising official began to make an inventory of 13 of the estates (*villae*; sing. *villa*) held by the cathedral of Marseille—Saint Mary, the seat of the bishop—and the monastery of Saint-Vincent of Marseille. Since the properties of Saint-Vincent were administered by the bishop of Marseille, there tended to be some overlap. The resulting register, called a *polyptyque*, provides a partial snapshot of some peasant households and the products and taxes that they owed. Each villa consisted of tenements, or small landholdings. In this polyptyque they are called *colonicae* (sing. *colonica*); in other regions they were called *mansi* (sing. *mansus*).

The entries (which are labeled A, B, and so on) follow a predictable pattern. First the villa is named, and then there are entries for each holding (*colonica*). First comes the holding's location, followed by the name and status of the male tenant (*colonus, mancipium*), the name of his wife and children, the age of the children (if under 14 or 15) or indication that the child is grown (here translated as "adult"). Sometimes the entry indicates which of the children are in school (precious evidence of village schooling in the period) and which are in holy orders, that is, ordained as priests, deacons, and so on. The adult children's husbands and wives are sometimes named, and sometimes we learn whether they were "foreigners"—that is, from outside the village. Dues are mentioned occasionally, but sometimes not. How does this document compare with a modern census? What evidence does it provide for the size and composition of peasant households in early-ninth-century Provence? In the welter of names, can you discover any family naming patterns?

[Source: *Carolingian Civilization: A Reader*, ed. Paul Edward Dutton, 2nd ed. (Toronto: University of Toronto Press, 2004), pp. 214–18 (slightly modified).]

B: *Description of the Dependents of Saint Mary of Marseille from the Villa Domado of that Third Part, Made in the Time of the lord bishop Waldus [r.814–818], from the seventh indiction [814]*

1. Holding [colonica] at Nemphas. Martinus, colonus. Wife Dominica. Bertemarus, an adult son. Desideria, an adult daughter. It pays the tax: 1 pig, 1 suckling [pig]; 2 fattened hens; 10 chickens; 40 eggs. Savarildis, an adult woman. Olisirga, a daughter 10 years old. Rica, a daughter 9 years old.
2. Holding of a colonus in vineyards. Ingoaldus, a dependent [mancipium]. Wife Unuldis. Martinus, a son; wife Magna. Onoria, a daughter, with a foreign husband. Deda, a daughter. Danobertus, an adult son. Ingolbertus, an adult son. Arubertus, an adult son.
3. Holding at Code: 1 lot without tenant.
4. Holding at Ruinolas: 1 lot without tenant.
5. In total these make 4 holdings.
6. Holding at Ursiniangas: 1 lot without tenant.

F. *Description of the Dependents of Saint Mary of Marseille from the Villa of Betorrida,[1] Made in the Time of the lord bishop Waldus, from the seventh indiction*

1. Holding in Cenazello. Dructaldus, tenant (*accola*); with his foreign wife. Druefomus, a son. Dutberta, an adult daughter. Drueterigus, a son at school. Sinderaldus, a son at school. Joannis. For pasturage: 1 denarius.[2]
2. Holding in Albiosco. Teodorus, colonus. Wife Eugenia. Marius, a deacon. Teobaldus, an adult son. Teodericus, a cleric. Ing…dus, a son 7 years old. Teodesia, a daughter 7 years old. For pasturage: 1 denarius.
3. Therein a holding: 1 lot without tenant. 2 denarii.[3]
4. Holding in Asaler. Candidus, colonus. Wife Dominica. Celsus, a son: information required. Mariberta, an adult daughter. Regitrudis, an adult daughter. Gennarius, a son, shepherd. Saviniana, a daughter: information required. It pays in tax: 1 pig, 1 sucking [pig]; 2 fattened hens; 10 chickens; 40 eggs; for pasturage: 1 castrated ram; in tribute: 1 denarius.
5. Holding without tenant in Nonticlo, which Bertarius,

priest, holds in benefice. It pays tax and tribute similarly: [plus] a castrated ram.
6. Holding in the same place: 1 lot without tenant. Paulus and Valeriana, with their infants: information required. It pays tax and tribute similarly; for pasturage: 1 castrated ram.
7. Holding in Albiosco: information required.
8. Holding in Curia. Calumniosus, colonus, with a foreign wife. It pays tax: 1 denarius and similarly in tribute. Saumo, with his infants: information required.
9. Holding in the same place. Colonus Martinus. Wife Primovera. Felicis, an adult son. Deidonus, an adult son. Leobertga, an adult daughter. Martina, a daughter 6 years old. An infant at the breast. It pays tax and tribute similarly; for pasturage: 1 denarius.
10. Holding [in] Cusanulas, which Nectardus holds in benefice. It pays tax and tribute similarly.
11. Holding in Carmillo Sancto Promacio, held by the priest of the local church. It pays for pasturage: 1 denarius.
12. Holding in Cumbis: 1 lot without tenant, which Dructebertus has. For pasturage: 2 denarii.
13. Holding in Massimana. Donaldus, dependent. Wife Dominica. Domnildis, daughter. Bertarius, an adult son. Bertulfus, an adult son. Bertelaicus, an adult son. Saisa, an adult daughter. It pays for pasturage: 2 denarii.
14. Holding in Asinarius: 1 lot without tenant. For pasturage: 1 castrated ram.
15. Holding in Terciago, which Martinus holds in benefice. For pasturage: 2 denarii.
16. Holdings in Cenazellis: 2 lots without tenants. For pasturage: 1 castrated ram.
17. Holding in Tullo: 1 lot without tenant. For pasturage: 1 castrated ram. Vuarmetrudis, with her infants: information required.
18. Holding in Galiana. Cannidus, colonus. Wife Inguildis. An infant at the breast. Domecianus, a cleric. Laurada, a daughter 8 years old. It pays tax and tribute similarly. For pasturage: 2 denarii.
19. Holding in Cleo. Aquilo, an equitarius [a serf performing messenger duty on horseback]. Wife Vumiberga. Candidus, a son 6 years old. An infant at the breast. For pasturage: 1 denarius.
20. Holding in Gencianicus. Ursius, cleric. The dependent Lubus, son, with foreign wife, who ought to

---

1   Today Bezaudun, near Grasse.
2   A denarius (pl. denarii) was a silver penny.
3   Presumably this means that it pays 2 denarii when occupied by a tenant.

manage that holding…. Gencuonca, an adult daughter. Teodo, an adult son.

21. Holding in Nidis: 1 lot without tenant. Bernarius, cotidianus [owing daily service to the lord]. Wife Dominica. Magnildis, daughter: information required. Dominico, son. Bernardus, son. Teodranus, son: information required. In tribute: 1 denarius. Montigla, a female [serf], with foreign husband. Cenazello, son: information required.

22. Holding in Vencione. Ildebertus, a dependent. Wife Luborfolia. It pays tax: 2 denarii.

23. Holding in Cumbis: 1 lot without tenant. It pays for pasturage: 2 denarii.

24. Holding in Tasseriolas: 1 lot without tenant. For pasturage: 1 denarius.

25. Holding in Massimiana Sancto Promacio: belonging to the office of the local priest. Donobertus, Babilda: information required.

26. Holding in Camarjas, which Bertaldus, priest, holds.

27. We have a holding in Sugnone, a third part of that small village, and there are 10 holdings [there].

28. Holding in Camarja: 1 lot without tenant. 29. We have in Salo a third part of that small village, and there are three holdings without tenants.

30. Holding in Puncianicus: 1 lot without tenant.

31. Holding in Campellis: 1 lot without tenant.

32. Holding in Rosolanis: 1 lot without tenant.

33. Holding in Speluca: 1 lot without tenant.

34. Vualdebertus, Guirbertus, Ragnebertus: information required.

35. In total that makes 49 holdings.

3.2 Byzantine guilds: *The Book of the Prefect* (886–912). Original in Greek.

Constantinople teemed with merchants, craftsmen, and notaries (the ancient version of lawyers). Organized into collective professional organizations—guilds—the people who plied these trades were regulated by the chief official of the city, the Prefect. *The Book of the Prefect*, an imperial edict issued by Emperor Leo VI (r.886–912), shows how tightly the economy of the capital was controlled—or supposed to be controlled—by the state. What evidence does this document provide for arguing that the early-tenth-century economy of Constantinople was well organized and vibrant? What evidence does it offer for the contrary argument: that the economy of the capital was stifled by rules and regulations?

[Source: Arthur E.R. Boak, "Notes and Documents: The Book of the Prefect," *Journal of Economic and Business History* 1 (1929): 600–602, 604–6 (slightly modified).]

Preface

God, after having created all things that are and given order and harmony to the universe, with his own finger engraved the Law on the tables and published it openly so that men, being well directed thereby, should not shamelessly trample upon one another and the stronger should not do violence to the weaker but that all things should be apportioned with just measure. Therefore it has seemed good for Our Serenity also to lay down the following ordinances based on the statutes in order that the human race may be governed fittingly and no person may injure his fellow.

I. The Notaries

1. Whoever wishes to be appointed a notary must be elected by a vote and decision both of the *primicerius*[1] and the notaries acting with him to ensure that he has a

---

[1]   The chief of the guild of the notaries.

knowledge and understanding of the laws, that he excels in handwriting, that he is not garrulous or insolent, and that he does not lead a corrupt life, but on the contrary is serious in his habits, guileless in his thoughts, eloquent, intelligent, a polished reader, and accurate in his diction, to guard against his being easily led to give a false meaning in places to what he writes or to insert deceptive clauses. And if at any time a notary is found to be doing something contrary to the law and the authorized written regulations, those who have acted as his witnesses shall be responsible.

2. The candidate must know by heart the forty titles of the *Manual of Law*[1] and must also know the sixty books of the Basilika.[2] He shall also have received a general education so that he may not make mistakes in formulating his documents and be guilty of errors in his reading. He shall also have abundant time to give proof of his ability both mental and physical. Let him prepare a handwritten document in a meeting of the guild, so that he may not later commit unforeseen errors; but if he should then be detected in any, let him be expelled from the order.

3. The election of the candidate shall be carried out as follows. After the hearing of the witnesses and the examination he shall present himself wearing a cloak before the most glorious Prefect of the City accompanied by the guild of the notaries and the *primicerius*. These shall swear before God and by the safety of the emperors that he is being enrolled in the order not through any favor, influence, family connection, or friendship, but by reason of his good conduct, knowledge, ability, and general fitness. After the oaths have been taken, by means of a sign the Prefect in office shall elect him in the prefectural bureau, and he shall be enrolled in the guild and numbered among the notaries. Then he shall go to the church nearest his residence, while all the notaries wear their cloaks, and doffing his cloak and donning a white surplice shall be consecrated by a prayer of the priest. He shall be escorted on his way by all the notaries clad in their cloaks, while the *primicerius* himself holds a censer[3] and directs the fumes towards the newly elect, who carries the Bible openly before him. This signifies that his ways shall be made straight as the incense ascending before the face of God. In this glorious fashion he shall proceed to the seat to which he has been allotted and then return home

with the same pomp, there to feast and rejoice with his associates.

4. Any notary who intends to absent himself from a royal procession or ceremony in the hippodrome or a meeting or assembly summoned by the most glorious Prefect or from any other gathering of this sort shall pay four *keratia*[4] to the officers of the Prefect and an equal sum to the members of the guild. But if he shows a clear and reasonable ground for his absence, which is not for his own profit, he shall be excused from the penalty if the *primicerius* approves.

5. If a notary has been summoned by the *primicerius* for a necessary purpose and has failed to come once, twice, or thrice, he shall pay on the first occasion two *keratia*, on the second, four, and on the third, six. But if he does this out of bravado and a spirit of contempt, he shall be punished by whipping at the Prefect's order.

6. If a notary should be summoned to draw up a contract, and afterwards another should be called in, let them both do the work and share the fee equally. But if one should come uninvited, let him not only be chased out without pay but also be punished by whipping. And if one of the two should leave voluntarily while the work is being completed, he shall not receive any part of the fee.

7. If a notary who is called in to draw up a contract wishes to leave for some adequate reason and calls in another, the one thus summoned shall receive two thirds of the fee, while the one first called in shall get a third.

8. If a notary has been called in and has completed the agreement, and then another has been summoned and has both completed the agreement and finished the work, the latter shall receive the whole fee if he is ignorant that it had previously been completed by the other. But if he came with knowledge of this, he shall receive one third, while the former received two thirds. And if two have been called in together, the junior shall yield to his senior in rank, but they shall share the fee equally.

9. If a notary approaches the seat of another and the latter does not greet him respectfully, or if one seats himself at table without regard to precedence, or if one is convicted of having verbally abused another, the guilty one shall in each case pay six *keratia*. But if one also lays violent hands upon another, he shall be punished by the Prefect....

---

[1] A brief compilation of laws in forty titles published by Basil I between 870 and 878.

[2] The great codification of Byzantine Law begun under Basil I and completed and published by Leo VI (r.886–912).

[3] A vessel for burning incense.

[4] The Byzantine coins mentioned in the Edict are the following: the *nomisma* (pl. *nomismata*), a gold coin; the *miliarision* (pl. *miliarisia*), a silver coin equal to 1/12 of a *nomisma*; the *keration* (pl. *keratia*) also of silver, equal to 1/12 of a *miliarision* or 1/24 of a *nomisma*; the copper *follis* or *obol* worth about 1/12 of a *keration*.

II. The Jewelers

1. We ordain that the jewelers may, if any one invites them, buy the things that pertain to them, such as gold, silver, pearls, or precious stones; but not bronze and woven linens or any other materials which others should purchase rather than they. However, they are not hereby prevented from buying anything they wish for private use.

2. They must not depreciate or increase the price of things for sale to the detriment of the vendors, but shall appraise them at their just value. If anyone acts deceitfully in this, he shall forfeit the appraised value of the things to the vendor.

3. Following the old custom, on the regular market days the jewelers shall take their seats in their shops along with their statores or attendants in charge of their sales tables. Their money is to be counted out in *miliarisia* so that if anyone tries to sell some jewelers' ware they may purchase it.

4. If a jeweler discovers a woman offering for sale objects of gold or silver, or pearls, or precious stones, he shall inform the Prefect of these things to prevent their being exported to foreign peoples.

5. If anyone adulterates uncoined metal and manufactures things for sale from it, he shall have his hand cut off.

6. If any foreigner sells gold or silver in a worked or unworked state, he is to be questioned as to its origin and to be reported to the chief of the guild, in order that stolen goods may be detected.

7. If any jeweler is found to have bought a sacred object, whether damaged or intact, without having shown it to the Prefect, both he and the seller shall suffer confiscation.

8. We command that no goldsmith, whether slave or free, shall purchase for his work more than a single pound of unminted gold, be it unwrought or wrought.

9. And if one does take from somebody more than a pound of uncoined gold for his work, and does not declare it at once to the chief of the goldsmiths, if he is a slave he shall be confiscated by the state, but if a freeman he shall be whipped and subjected to a fine of a pound of gold.

10. A slave who is going to be set up in a jeweler's shop shall be sponsored by his own master if the latter is a man of means. But a freeman shall be vouched for by five persons, who shall assume the same risk as he whom they have nominated.

11. We order that no goldsmith shall have the right to work gold or silver in his home, but only in the shops on the Mese.[1] Also that no one shall be nominated as a goldsmith without the knowledge of the Prefect.

12. The jewelers shall not undertake any work of evaluation without the knowledge of the Prefect, nor shall they when making appraisals stir up strife with one another. If they are caught doing any of these things, they shall be whipped; shorn;[2] and removed from the roll of their guild.

IV. The Silk-Garment Merchants[3]

1. The silk-garment merchants shall buy silk garments but not any other merchandise except something for their personal needs which they may not sell to others. They shall not give foreigners any of the prohibited articles, such as red or purple silk goods of large size, so that these may not be transported to strange peoples. Whoever violates these regulations shall be flogged and suffer confiscation of goods.

2. Silk-garment merchants, whether slaves or free persons, when purchasing garments valued at ten *nomismata* from persons of any sort whatsoever, even from princes or silk weavers, shall declare this to the Prefect so that he may know where they are to be sold. Those who fail to do so are liable to the aforesaid punishment.

3. Whoever fails to declare to the Prefect cloaks or robes of a blue color or purple two-thirds red, shall be liable to punishment.

4. Whoever fails to show to the Prefect goods that are to be exported to foreign peoples so that they may receive his seal, shall suffer punishment.

5. Whoever is to be enrolled in the craft of the silkgarment merchants shall first be declared by five persons of the same guild in the presence of the Prefect to be worthy to be in this trade. He shall then be entered on the roll, shall open a shop, and engage in trade. He shall also pay to the corporation six *nomismata*.

6. Whoever wishes to become the owner of a silk garment shop, shall pay ten *nomismata*. He must also have the approval of the Prefect.

7. One who is both a silk-garment merchant and a silk weaver shall be allowed to choose one of these trades but must give up the other. If he dares to practice both, he

---

[1] The Middle Street, the main industrial and commercial thoroughfare of Constantinople.

[2] That is, their hair and beard cut off.

[3] *Vestiopratai*: dealers in manufactured articles of clothing and the like, as opposed to raw or spun silk.

111

shall come under the punishment mentioned above [i.e., flogging and confiscation of goods].

8. Strangers who reside in the inns of the city must be carefully prevented from purchasing either prohibited articles of clothing or those woven in a single piece, except something for personal use and that prepared in the imperial city. Upon their departure they shall declare such articles to the Prefect so that he may know the goods that they have bought. Whoever helps them to conceal such things shall be flogged and suffer confiscation of goods.

9. Any silk-garment merchant who secretly or openly seeks to raise the rental of another, shall be flogged, shorn, and suffer confiscation of goods....

[Further sections include regulations for dealers in raw silk, silk weavers, linen merchants, perfume dealers, candle makers, grocers, leather cutters, butchers (except pork), pork dealers, fishmongers, bakers, tavern keepers, and contractors (such as joiners, plasterers, locksmiths, and painters).]

Map 3.1: Major European Slave Exports (700–900).

Coin hoard evidence suggests that Islamic—and, to a lesser extent, Byzantine—money came into Europe in considerable abundance during the period 700–900. What did the Europeans provide in return? Swords is one answer; slaves is another, as this map demonstrates. It shows where European slaves were captured and the places to which they were transported. Some remained in Europe (as *A Contract of Sale*, below, p. 113 attests); many others were traded to the Islamic world. Note the convergence of many routes at Córdoba. As you read through the other documents in this book, take note of how often slaves are mentioned. How differently were they treated from free men and women?

[Based on Michael McCormick, *Origins of the European Economy: Communications and Commerce* a.d. 300–900 (Cambridge: Cambridge University Press, 2001), p. 562, Map 25.1, modified by, and with many thanks to, Michael McCormick.]

3.3 The sale of a slave in Italy: *A Contract of Sale* (725). Original in Latin.

This is an absolutely ordinary record of a sale, much like many others drawn up at the same time in the Lombard kingdom of Italy for land and animals. In this case, however, the item sold was a boy. What does this transaction add to the information presented in the map of Major European Slave Exports on p. 112?

[Source: *Medieval Trade in the Mediterranean World*, trans. and ed. Robert S. Lopez and Irving W. Raymond (New York: Columbia University Press, 2001), pp. 45–46 (notes modified).]

Milan, June 6, 725

In the thirteenth year of the reign of our lord, most excellent man, King Liutprand,[1] on the eighth day before the Ides of June, eighth indiction; good fortune. I, Faustino, notary by royal authority, wrote this document of sale, invited by Ermedruda, honorable woman, daughter of Lorenzo, acting jointly with consent and will of that parent of hers, and being the seller. And she acknowledges that she has received, as indeed she at the present time is receiving from Totone, most distinguished man, 12 new gold solidi [coins] as the full price for a boy of the Gallic people named Satrelano, or by whatever other name the boy may be called. And she declared that it[2] had come to her from her father's patrimony. And she, acting jointly with her aforesaid father, promises from this day to protect that boy against all men on behalf of the buyer. And if the boy is injured or taken away and they [Ermedruda and Lorenzo] are in any way unable to protect it against all men, they shall return the solidi in the double to the buyer, [including all] improvements in the object.[3] Done in Milan, in the day, reign, and in the eighth indiction mentioned above.

The sign[4] of the hand of Ermedruda, honorable woman, seller, who declared that she sold the aforesaid Frankish boy of her own good will with the consent of her parent; and she asked this sale to be made.

The sign of the hand of Lorenzo, honorable man, her father, consenting to this sale.

The sign of the hand of Theoperto, honorable man, maker of cuirasses, son of the late Giovannace, relative of the same seller, in whose presence she proclaimed that she was under no constraint, giving consent.

The sign of the hand of Ratchis, honorable man, Frank, witness.

Antonino, devout man, invited by Ermedruda, honorable woman, and by her father giving his consent, undersigned as a witness to this record of sale.

I, the above Faustino, writer of this [record] of sale, after delivery gave [this record].

---

[1]   Liutprand, King of the Lombards 712–744, ruled over much of northern Italy.

[2]   A slave in Lombard as well as in Roman law was not considered as a person but as a thing (*res*); hence the document uses the neuter pronoun when referring to the boy.

[3]   Again, the boy is considered as a thing. He may learn some skill and hence become more valuable.

[4]   Ermedruda could not write her name, but she indicated her assent to the terms of the contract with a cross or other sign, recorded by the notary as her "sign." He himself supplied her name.

THE ABBASID RECONFIGURATION

3.4 An early view of the Prophet: Muhammad ibn Ishaq, *Life of Muhammad* (754–767). Original in Arabic.

Writing under the patronage of the Abbasid Caliph al-Mansur, Ibn Ishaq (*c*.704–767), who was born in Medina, wrote the first extant life of Muhammad. It was soon attacked for including spurious poetry and for lacking sufficient *isnad*—the chains of named sources that were, by the end of the eighth century, considered essential to prove the authenticity of any narrative about the Prophet (hadith). (For hadith considered authoritative, see al-Bukhari, *On Fasting*, below, p. 117). Ibn Ishaq was also accused of Shi'ite sympathies. It is thus not surprising that his original work is lost. The version that we have today is an edition by Ibn Hisham (d.833), a scholar who, though somewhat critical of the original, also considered it of great value. Throughout, Ibn Ishaq calls Muhammad "the apostle of God" and emphasizes how fully he fulfilled the Christian and Jewish prophecies. In what ways were the mission, virtues, and lifestyle of Muhammad in Ibn Ishaq's account similar to—and different from—those of saints in Christian hagiography, such as the *Life of St. Antony*, above, p. 27?

[Source: *The Life of Muhammad: A Translation of Ishaq's* Sirat Rasul Allah, trans. and ed. Alfred Guillaume (London: Oxford University Press, 1955), pp. 81–83, 104–7 (slightly modified).]

The apostle of God grew up, God protecting him and keeping him from the vileness of heathenism because he wished to honor him with apostleship, until he grew up to be the finest of his people in manliness, the best in character, most noble in lineage, the best neighbor, the most kind, truthful, reliable, the furthest removed from filthiness and corrupt morals through loftiness and nobility, so that he was known among his people as "The trustworthy" because of the good qualities which God had implanted in him. The apostle, so I was told, used to tell how God protected him in his childhood during the period of heathenism, saying, "I found myself among the boys of Quraysh[1] carrying stones such as boys play with; we had all uncovered ourselves, each taking his shirt and putting it round his neck as he carried the stones. I was going to and fro in the same way, when an unseen figure slapped me most painfully saying, 'Put your shirt on'; so I took it and fastened it on me and then began to carry the stones upon my neck wearing my shirt alone among my fellows."…

The Apostle of God Marries Khadija

Khadija was a merchant woman of dignity and wealth. She used to hire men to carry merchandise outside the country on a profit-sharing basis, for Quraysh were a people given to commerce. Now when she heard about the prophet's truthfulness, trustworthiness, and honorable character, she sent for him and proposed that he should take her goods to Syria and trade with them, while she would pay him more than she paid others. He was to take a lad of hers called Maysara.

The apostle of God accepted the proposal, and the two set forth until they came to Syria. The apostle stopped in the shade of a tree near a monk's cell, when the monk came up to Maysara and asked who the man was who was resting beneath the tree. He told him that he was of Quraysh, the people who held the sanctuary; and the monk exclaimed: "None but a prophet ever sat beneath this tree."

Then the prophet sold the goods he had brought and bought what he wanted to buy and began the return jour-

---

1   The tribe at Mecca to which Muhammad also belonged.

ney to Mecca. The story goes that at the height of noon, when the heat was intense as he rode his beast, Maysara saw two angels shading the apostle from the sun's rays. When he brought Khadija her property she sold it and it amounted to double or thereabouts. Maysara for his part told her about the two angels who shaded him and of the monk's words. Now Khadija was a determined, noble, and intelligent woman possessing the properties with which God willed to honor her. So when Maysara told her these things, she sent to the apostle of God and—so the story goes—said: "O son of my uncle I like you because of our relationship and your high reputation among your people, your trustworthiness and good character and truthfulness." Then she proposed marriage. Now Khadija at that time was the best born woman in Quraysh, of the greatest dignity and, too, the richest. All her people were eager to get possession of her wealth if it were possible.

Khadija was the daughter of Khuwaylid b. Asad b. 'Abdu'l-'Uzza b. Qusayy b. Kilab b. Murra b. Ka'b b. Lu'ayy b. Ghalib b. Fihr.[1] Her mother was Fatima bt. Za'ida b. al-Asamm b. Rawaha b. Hajar b. 'Abd b. Malis b. 'Amir b. Lu'ayy b. Ghalib b. Fihr. Her mother was Hala bt. 'Abd Manaf b. al-Harith b. 'Amr b. Munqidh b. 'Amr b. Ma'is b. 'Amir b. Lu'ayy b. Ghalib b. Fihr. Hala's mother was Qilaba bt. Su'ayd b. Sa'd b. Sahm b. 'Amr b. Husays b. Ka'b b. Lu'ayy b. Ghalib b. Fihr.

The apostle of God told his uncles of Khadija's proposal, and his uncle Hamza b. 'Abdu'l-Muttalib went with him to Khuwaylid b. Asad and asked for her hand and he married her.

She was the mother of all the apostle's children except Ibrahim, namely al-Qasim (whereby he was known as Abu'l-Qasim); al-Tahir, al-Tayyib, Zaynab, Ruqayya, Umm Kulthum, and Fatima.

Al-Qasim, al-Tayyib, and al-Tahir died in paganism. All his daughters lived into Islam, embraced it, and migrated with him to Medina.

Khadija had told Waraqa b. Naufal b. Asad b. 'Abdu'l-'Uzza, who was her cousin and a Christian who had studied the scriptures and was a scholar, what her slave Maysara had told her that the monk had said and how he had seen the two angels shading him. He said, "If this is true, Khadija, then truly Muhammad is the prophet of this people. I knew that a prophet of this people was to be expected. His

time has come," or words to that effect. Waraqa was finding the time of waiting wearisome and used to say "How long?" Some lines of his on the theme are:

I persevered and was persistent in remembering
An anxiety which often evoked tears. And
Confirmatory evidence kept coming from Khadija.
Long have I had to wait, O Khadija,
In the vale of Mecca in spite of my hope
That I might see the outcome of thy words.
I could not bear that the words of the monk
You told me of should prove false
That Muhammad should rule over us
Overcoming those who would oppose him.
And that a glorious light should appear in the land
To preserve men from disorders.
His enemies shall meet disaster
And his friends shall be victorious.
Would that I might be there then to see,
For I should be the first of his supporters,
Joining in that which Quraysh hate
However loud they shout in that Mecca of theirs.
I hope to ascend through him whom they all dislike
To the Lord of the Throne though they are cast down.
Is it folly not to disbelieve in Him
Who chose him Who raised the starry heights?
If they and I live, things will be done
Which will throw the unbelievers into confusion.
And if I die, 'tis but the fate of mortals
To suffer death and dissolution....

The Prophet's Mission

When Muhammad the apostle of God reached the age of forty, God sent him in compassion to mankind, "as an evangelist to all men."[2] Now God had made a covenant with every prophet whom he had sent before him that he should believe in him, testify to his truth, and help him against his adversaries. He required His prophets to transmit that to everyone who believed in them, and they carried out their obligations in that respect. God said to Muhammad, "When God made a covenant with the prophets, [He said], 'This is the scripture and wisdom which I have given you; afterwards an apostle will come

---

[1] The abbreviation b. means "Ibn," son of, while bt. means "bint," daughter of. Through this string of names, the author is authenticating Khadija's lineage. Compare Matt. 1: 1–11.

[2] Sura 34: 27.

confirming what you know that you may believe in him and help him.' He said, 'Do you accept this and take up my burden?' i.e., the burden of my agreement which I have laid upon you. They said, 'We accept it.' He answered, 'Then bear witness and I am a witness with you.'"[1] Thus God made a covenant with all the prophets that they should testify to his truth and help him against his adversaries, and they transmitted that obligation to those who believed in them among the two monotheistic religions.

Al-Zuhri related from 'Urwa b. Zybayr that 'A'isha[2] told him that when Allah [God] desired to honor Muhammad and have mercy on His servants by means of him, the first sign of prophethood granted to the apostle was true visions, resembling the brightness of daybreak, which were shown to him in his sleep. And Allah, she said, made him love solitude so that he liked nothing better than to be alone.

'Abdu'l-Malik b. 'Ubaydullah b. Abu Sufyan b. al-'Ala' b. Jariya the Thaqafite, who had a retentive memory, related to me from a certain scholar that the apostle at the time when Allah willed to bestow His grace upon him and endow him with prophethood would go forth for his affair and journey far afield until he reached the glens of Mecca and the beds of its valleys where no house was in sight; and there was no stone or tree that he passed that didn't say, "Peace unto thee, O apostle of Allah." And the apostle would turn to his right and left and look behind him and he would see nothing but trees and stones. Thus he stayed seeing and hearing so long as it pleased Allah that he should stay. Then Gabriel came to him with the gift of God's grace while he was on Hira'[3] in the month of Ramadan.

Wahb b. Kaisan, a client of the family of al-Zubayr, told me: I heard 'Abdullah b. al-Zubayr say to 'Ubayd b. 'Umayr b. Qatada the Laythite, "O 'Ubayd tell us how began the prophethood which was first bestowed on the apostle when Gabriel came to him." And 'Ubayd in my presence related to 'Abdullah and those with him as follows: The apostle would pray in seclusion on Hira' every year for a month to practice *tahannuth* as was the custom of Quraysh in heathen days. *Tahannuth* is religious devotion. Abu Talib said:

By Thaur and him who made Thabir firm in its place
And by those going up to ascend Hira' and coming down.[4]

Wahb b. Kaisan told me that 'Ubayd said to him: Every year during that month the apostle would pray in seclusion and give food to the poor that came to him. And when he completed the month and returned from his seclusion, first of all before entering his house he would go to the Ka'ba[5] and walk round it seven times or as often as it pleased God; then he would go back to his house until, in the year when God sent him, in the month of Ramadan in which God willed concerning him what He willed of His grace, the apostle set forth to Hira' as was his custom, and his family with him. When it was the night on which God honored him with his mission and showed mercy on His servants thereby, Gabriel brought him the command of God. "He came to me," said the apostle of God, "while I was asleep, with a coverlet of brocade whereon was some writing, and said, 'Read!' I said, 'What shall I read?' He pressed me with it so tightly that I thought it was death; then he let me go and said, 'Read!' I said, 'What shall I read?' He pressed me with it again so that I thought it was death; then he let me go and said 'Read!' I said, 'What shall I read?' He pressed me with it the third time so that I thought it was death and said 'Read!' I said, 'What then shall I read?'—and this I said only to deliver myself from him, lest he should do the same to me again. He said:

Read in the name of thy Lord who created,
Who created man of blood coagulated.
Read! Thy Lord is the most beneficent,
Who taught by the pen,
Taught that which they knew not unto men.[6]

So I read it, and he departed from me. And I awoke from my sleep, and it was as though these words were written on my heart. When I was midway on the mountain, I heard a voice from heaven saying, 'O Muhammad! thou art the apostle of God and I am Gabriel.' I raised my head towards heaven to see (who was speaking), and lo, [there was] Gabriel in the form of a man with feet astride the

---

[1]   Sura 3: 75.

[2]   One of Muhammad's wives.

[3]   A nearby mountain.

[4]   Thaur and Thabir are mountains near Mecca.

[5]   This was Mecca's holy site. At this time, before Mecca became Muslim, it was filled with images of many gods.

[6]   Sura 96: 1–5. For a different translation, see "The Embryo" above, p. 75.

horizon, saying, 'O Muhammad! thou art the apostle of God and I am Gabriel.' I stood gazing at him, moving neither forward nor backward; then I began to turn my face away from him, but towards whatever region of the sky I looked, I saw him as before. And I continued standing there, neither advancing nor turning back, until Khadija sent her messengers in search of me and they gained the high ground above Mecca and returned to her while I was standing in the same place; then he parted from me and I from him, returning to my family. And I came to Khadija and sat by her thigh and drew close to her. She said, 'O Abu'l-Qasim,[1] where have you been? By God, I sent my messengers in search of you, and they reached the high ground above Mecca and returned to me.' Then I told her of what I had seen; and she said, 'Rejoice, O son of my uncle, and be of good heart. Truly, by Him in whose hand is Khadija's soul, I have hope that you will be the prophet of this people.'" Then she rose and gathered her garments about her and set forth to her cousin Waraqa b. Naufal b. Asad b. 'Abdu'l-'Uzza b. Qusayy, who had become a Christian and read the scriptures and learned from those that follow the Torah and the Gospel. And when she related to him what the apostle of God told her he had seen and heard, Waraqa cried, "Holy! Holy! Truly, by Him in whose hand is Waraqa's soul, if you have spoken the truth to me, O Khadija, then the greatest Namus [i.e., Gabriel], who came to Moses in the past, has come to him [Muhammed], and lo, he is the prophet of this people. Bid him be of good heart." So Khadija returned to the apostle of God and told him what Waraqa had said. And when the apostle of God had finished his period of seclusion and returned [to Mecca], in the first place he performed the circumambulation of the Ka'ba, as was his custom. While he was doing it, Waraqa met him and said, "O son of my brother, tell me what you have seen and heard." The apostle told him, and Waraqa said, "Surely, by Him in whose hand is Waraqa's soul, you are the prophet of this people. Unto you has come the greatest Namus, who came unto Moses. You will be called a liar, and they will use you spitefully and cast you out and fight against you. Truly, if I live to see that day, I will help God in such ways as He knows." Then he brought his head near to him and kissed his forehead; and the apostle went to his own house.

Isma'il b. Abu Hakim, a freedman[2] of the family of al-Zubayr, told me on Khadija's authority that she said to the apostle of God, "O son of my uncle, are you able to tell me about your visitor, when he comes to you?" He replied that he could, and she asked him to tell her when he came. So when Gabriel came to him, as he was wont, the apostle said to Khadija, "This is Gabriel who has just come to me." "Get up, O son of my uncle," she said, "and sit by my left thigh." The apostle did so, and she said, "Can you see him?" "Yes," he said. She said, "Then turn round and sit on my right thigh." He did so, and she said, "Can you see him?" When he said that he could she asked him to move and sit in her lap. When he had done this she again asked if he could see him, and when he said yes, she disclosed her form and cast aside her veil while the apostle was sitting in her lap. Then she said, "Can you see him?" And he replied, "No." She said, "O son of my uncle, rejoice and be of good heart, by God he is an angel and not a satan."

I told 'Abdullah b. Hasan this story and he said, "I heard my mother Fatima, daughter of Husayn, talking about this tradition from Khadija, but as I heard it she made the apostle of God come inside her shift, and thereupon Gabriel departed, and she said to the apostle of God, 'This truly is an angel and not a satan.'"

3.5 Hadith: Al-Bukhari, *On Fasting* (9th c.). Original in Arabic.

The hadith are the traditions about the prophet handed down by authoritative transmission. There are two parts to every hadith: the first consists of the chain of oral transmitters (*isnad*), with the most recent one listed first; the second part consists of the text of the tradition, which is always about the Prophet, his family, and his close associates.

---

[1] Abu'l-Qasim means "Father of Qasim," and Muhammad was so called because Qasim was the name of his first-born son. It was Muhammad's "name of honor."

[2] I.e., a former slave who has been freed.

(Shiʿite hadith also include traditions about the imams—those few leaders who possessed the "Muhammadan light.") Numerous questions occurred to Muslims after the time of Muhammad; they attempted to answer them by recourse to "what the Prophet would do in such-and-such situation," for that was the guide to "right behavior" (*sunna*). By the early Abbasid period, numerous, sometimes conflicting, answers to these questions were circulating. Al-Bukhari (810–870) and other scholars who followed him attempted in their collections (though not entirely successfully) to include only the "authentic" hadith. The *isnad*—which should be unbroken and come from reliable sources close to Muhammad—were an important element in their winnowing process. The section below, on fasting, illustrates their attempt to account for every possible situation.

[Source: *A Reader on Islam: Passages from Standard Arabic Writings Illustrative of the Beliefs and Practices of Muslims*, ed. Arthur Jeffery (ʿS-Gravenhage: Mouton & Co., 1962), pp. 88–90, 92–94, 98–101.]

1. ON THE NECESSITY OF THE FAST OF RAMADAN, AND ON THE VERSE (II, 183/179): "O YOU WHO HAVE BELIEVED, FASTING IS PRESCRIBED FOR YOU, JUST AS IT WAS PRESCRIBED FOR THOSE WHO WERE BEFORE YOU. MAYBE YOU WILL SHOW PIETY."

Qutaiba related to us, saying: Ismaʿil b. Jaʿfar related to us from[1] Abu Suhail, from his father, from Talha b. ʿUbaidallah, that a nomad Arab came to the Apostle of Allah—on whom be Allah's blessing and peace—with dishevelled head, saying: "O Apostle of Allah, inform me of what Allah has laid on me as incumbent duty in the matter of saying prayers." He answered: "The five prayer-services, unless you would voluntarily add thereto." Then [the Arab] said: "O Apostle of Allah, inform me of what Allah has laid on me as incumbent duty in the matter of fasting." He answered: "The month of Ramadan, unless you would voluntarily add thereto." Said [the Arab]: "Inform me of what Allah has laid on me as incumbent duty in that matter of alms [i.e. charity]." So the Apostle of Allah informed him of the legal prescriptions of Islam [with regard to alms]. Said he: "By Him who has honored you with the truth, I will not voluntarily add anything, but neither will I come short of what Allah has prescribed as incumbent duties for

me." Then the Apostle of Allah—upon whom be Allah's blessing and peace—said: "He will be one of the fortunate ones, if he means that." Or [according to another version, he said]: "He will be brought into Paradise, if he means that."

Musaddad related to us, saying: Ismaʿil related to us from Ayyub, from Nafiʿ, from Ibn ʿUmar, who said: "The Prophet—upon whom be Allah's blessing and peace—fasted ʿAshura'[2] and bade it be kept as a fast, but when Ramadan was made an incumbent duty [on the Muslims], it was abandoned. ʿAbdallah[3] used not to fast therein save when it happened to coincide with his [voluntary] fasts."

Qutaiba b. Saʿid said: al-Laith has related to us from Yazid b. Abi Habib, that ʿIrak b. Malik related to him that ʿUrwa informed him from ʿA'isha[4] that the Quraysh[5] used to fast the Day of "Ashura" in the pre-Islamic days, and then the Apostle of Allah—upon whom be Allah's blessing and peace—bade it be kept as a fast, [which it was] till Ramadan was made an incumbent duty. Said the Apostle of Allah—upon whom be Allah's blessing and peace—: "If anyone so wishes, let him still keep it as a fast, but if anyone so wishes, let him eat thereon."

---

[1] The particle ʿan used in these *isnad*s really means "on the authority of," but as the transmission of the Tradition was "from" one authority to another, it is translated throughout by "from" for brevity's sake. The b. in names means "son of."

[2] A fast said to have been observed by the Jews and some of the Arabs in the pre-Islamic days as commemoration of their deliverance from their enemies.

[3] Probably the companion of the Prophet ʿAbdallah ibn ʿAbbas.

[4] The Prophet's youngest wife, who is quoted as the source for a vast number of Traditions.

[5] The ruling Arab tribe in Mecca in the days of the Prophet.

2. ON THE MERITS OF THE FAST.

'Abdallah b. Maslama related to us from Malik, from Abu'z-Zinad, from al-A'raj, from Abu Huraira,[1] that the Apostle of Allah—upon whom be Allah's blessing and peace—said: "Fasting is a protective covering [from the fires of Hell], so let there be no unseemly speech, no foolish acting [during it]. If a man is attacked or vilified [during it], let him say twice: 'I am fasting;' for by Him in whose hand is my soul, the odor from the mouth of him who fasts is sweeter to Allah than the perfume of musk. [Allah says to Himself]: 'He is giving up his food and his drink and his body lusts for My sake when he is fasting unto Me, so I shall reward him, and for each good deed [that he does] grant him the merit of ten.'"

3. ON FASTING AS AN EXPIATION.

'Ali b. 'Abdallah related to us, saying: Sufyan related to us, saying: several have related to us from Abu Wa'il, from Hudhaifa, who said: "Umar once asked: 'Who is there who has memorized a Tradition from the Prophet—upon whom be Allah's blessing and peace—about discord?' Hudhaifa answered: 'I heard him say that discord arises for a man from [three sources: from] his family, from his property, and from his neighbor; but prayer, fasting and gifts of charity may be its expiation.' Said ['Umar]: 'I am not asking about this [general matter of discord arising among men], but about that [which will come at the Last Days] billowing like the billows of the sea.' 'Facing that,' said [Hudhaifa], 'there is a gate shut.' 'Will it be opened,' asked ['Umar], 'or broken down?' 'It will be broken down,' answered [Hudhaifa]. 'Then,' said he, 'it is not likely to be shut again until the Day of Resurrection.'" We said to Masruq: "Ask him if 'Umar knew who the 'Gate' would be?"[2] So he asked him, and he answered: "Yes, [he knew that] just as he knew that night is before morning."...

8. ON HIM WHO DOES NOT GIVE UP SAYING FALSE WORDS AND DOING FALSE DEEDS DURING RAMADAN.

Adam b. Abi Iyas related to us, saying: Ibn Abi Dhi'b related to us, saying: Sa'id al-Maqburi related to us from his father, from Abu Huraira, who said: Said the Prophet—upon whom be Allah's blessing and peace—: "If one does not give up saying false words and doing false deeds in Ramadan, his giving up eating and drinking means nothing to Allah."

9. ON WHETHER, IF ONE IS REVILED, HE SHOULD SAY: "I AM FASTING."

Ibrahim b. Musa related to us, saying: Hisham b. Yusuf informed us from Ibn Juraij, who said: 'Ata' informed me from Abu Salih az-Zayyat, that he heard Abu Huraira say: The Apostle of Allah—upon whom be Allah's blessing and peace—said: "Allah, mighty and majestic is He, has said: 'Every deed of a child of Adam is his [and will be recorded and rewarded in due measure] save fasting, which is Mine, and which I will reward [in My own measure].' Fasting is a protective covering, so when the day comes for anyone of you to fast, let there be no unseemly speech, no clamoring. If anyone reviles such a person, or attacks him, let him say: 'I am fasting.' By Him in whose hand is my soul, the odor from the mouth of him who fasts is sweeter to Allah than the perfume of musk. He who fasts has two occasions of rejoicing. He will have joy when he breaks his fast, and when he meets his Lord he will have joy because of his fasting."

10. ON FASTING [AS A HELP] FOR ONE WHO FEARS [THE TEMPTATIONS OF ONE WHO REMAINS] CELIBATE.

'Ubdan related to us from Abu Hamza, from al-A'mash, from Ibrahim, from 'Alqama, [who said]: While I was walking with 'Abdallah he said: "I was once with the Prophet—upon whom be Allah's blessing and peace—when he said: 'Let him who is able to marry take a wife, for it is the best way of averting lascivious glances and of providing chaste enjoyment, but let him who is not able [to marry] fast, for it will be a remover [of unseemly passions] for him.'"

11. ON THE SAYING OF THE PROPHET—UPON WHOM BE ALLAH'S BLESSING AND PEACE—: "WHEN YOU SEE THE NEW MOON, FAST, AND WHEN YOU SEE IT, BREAK YOUR FAST."

Sila quoted from 'Ammar: "Whosoever fasts on a doubtful

---

[1] Abu Huraira was a highly celebrated "Companion" of the Prophet. Thousands of hadith named him as the final transmitter in the isnad.

[2] The technical word in this Tradition is *fitna*, "dissension," "discord," and in Muslim accounts of the events of the Last Days preceding the great Day of Judgment there are innumerable stories about the dissensions that will arise among the people. The "gate" (*bab*) is the individual who will usher in any particular dissension.

day is disobeying Abu'l-Qasim,[1]—upon whom be Allah's blessing and peace.

'Abdallah b. Maslama related to us from Malik, from Nafi', from 'Abdallah b. 'Umar, that the Apostle of Allah—upon whom be Allah's blessing and peace—mentioned Ramadan, and said: "Do not fast until you see the new moon, and do not break the fast until you see it, and if it is cloudy make a computation for it."

'Abdallah b. Maslama related to us, saying: Malik related to us from 'Abdallah b. Dinar, from 'Abdallah b. 'Umar, that the Apostle of Allah—upon whom be Allah's blessing and peace—said: "The month is twenty-nine nights, so do not fast till you see it (i.e., the new moon), and if it is cloudy then compute the number to thirty."

Abu'l-Walid related to us, saying: Shu'ba related to us from Jabala b. Suhaim, who said: "I heard Ibn 'Umar say that the Prophet—upon whom be Allah's blessing and peace—said: 'The month is so-and-so,' and he tucked in [his] thumb the third time."

Adam related to us, saying: Shu'ba related to us, saying: Muhammad b. Ziyad related to us, saying: I heard Abu Huraira say that the Prophet—upon whom be Allah's blessing and peace—said:—or maybe he said: Abu'l-Qasim, upon whom be, etc. said:—"Fast when it (i.e., the moon) becomes seeable, and break your fast when it becomes seeable, and if it is cloudy then complete the number of Sha'ban,[2] [i.e.,] thirty."

Abu 'Asim related to us from Ibn Juraij, from Yahya b. 'Abdallah b. Saifi, from 'Ikrima b. 'Abd al-Rahman from Umm Salama, that the Prophet—upon whom be Allah's blessing and peace—took an oath to abstain from his women for a month. When twentynine days had elapsed be came in the morning—or maybe it was in the evening—to 'A'isha. Someone objected, "But you swore that you would not enter for a month," and he replied: "A month has twentynine days."

'Abd al-'Aziz b. 'Abdallah related to us, saying: Sulaiman b. Bilal related to us from Humaid, from Anas, who said: "The Apostle of Allah—upon whom be Allah's blessing and peace—took an oath to abstain from his women. As his foot was injured he stayed in an upper chamber for twenty-nine nights. Then he came down, but they said: 'O

Apostle of Allah, you took an oath for a month', whereat he said: 'The month is twenty-nine [days].'"

12. ON HOW THE TWO MONTHS OF FESTIVAL MAY NOT BE CURTAILED.

Musaddad has related to us, saying: Mu'tamir related to us, saying: I heard Ishaq b. Suwaid [quoting] from 'Abd al-Rahman b. Abi Bakra, from his father, from the Prophet—upon whom be Allah's blessing and peace—[or according to another *isnad*], Musaddad related to me, saying: Mu'tamir related to us from Khalid al-Hadhdha', who said: 'Abd al-Rahman b. Abi Bakra related to me from his father, from the Prophet—upon whom be Allah's blessing and peace—who said: "There are two months which may not be curtailed, the two months of festival, Ramadan and Dhu'l-Hijja."[3] Said Abu 'Abdallah: "Ishaq said: 'Twenty-nine complete days.' Ahmed b. Jundub said: 'If Ramadan is curtailed, complete Dhu'l-Hijja, and if Dhu'l-Hijja is curtailed, complete Ramadan.' Abu'l-Hasan said: 'Ishaq b. Rahuwaih used to say, 'Let neither be curtailed in [their] meritoriousness, whether it is twenty-nine or thirty [days].'"…

22. ON THE FASTER WHO AWAKES IN THE MORNING IN A STATE OF SEXUAL POLLUTION.

'Abdallah b. Maslama related to us from Malik, from Sumayy, a client of Abu Bakr b. 'Abd al-Rahman b. al-Harith b. Hisham b. al-Mughira, that he heard Abu Bakr b. 'Abd al-Rahman say: "I was with my father when we entered to 'A'isha and Umm Salama," [or as another *isnad* has it], Abu'l-Yaman related to us, saying: Shu'aib informed us from al-Zuhri, who said: Abu Bakr b. 'Abd al-Rahman b. al-Harith b. Hisham informed me that his father 'Abd al-Rahman informed Marwan that 'A'isha and Umm Salama had both informed him, that the Apostle of Allah—upon whom be Allah's blessing and peace—would be overtaken by the dawn while he was still in a state of pollution from [sexual contact with] his wives, but he would bathe and then fast. Marwan said to 'Abd al-Rahman b. al-Harith: "I swear by Allah you shall surely [go and] disturb Abu Huraira by that [information]." Marwan was at that time [Governor] over Medina. Said Abu Bakr: "'Abd al-

---

[1] Abu'l-Qasim means "Father of Qasim," and Muhammad was so called because Qasim was the name of his first-born son. It was Muhammad's "name of honor."

[2] Sha'ban is the month that precedes the fasting month of Ramadan.

[3] Ramadan, the month of fasting, is the ninth month in the Islamic calendar, and Dhu'l-Hijja is the twelfth month, the month during which the annual pilgrimage to Mecca—the *hajj*—takes place.

Rahman, however, disliked [the idea of doing] that, so it was decided among us that we would gather together at Dhu'l-Hulaifa, where Abu Huraira had some land. Then 'Abd al-Rahman said to Abu Huraira: 'I am about to mention to you a matter that I should never have mentioned to you had not Marwan sworn that I should.' Then he mentioned what 'A'isha and Umm Salama had said. Said [Abu Huraira]: 'That is so. Al-Fadl b. 'Abbas related [it] to me, and no one would know better than him.'" Said Hammam and Ibn 'Abdallah b. 'Umar [quoting] from Abu Huraira: "The Prophet—upon whom be Allah's blessing and peace—used to order [in such a case that] the fast be broken," but the first [version] has the better *isnad*.

23. ON THE [RESTRICTIONS OF] SEX RELATIONS FOR ONE WHO IS FASTING.
'A'isha said: "It is her vulva which is forbidden to him."

Sulaiman b. Harb related to us from Shu'ba, from al-Hakam, from Ibrahim, from al-Aswad, from 'A'isha, who said: "The Prophet—upon whom be Allah's blessing and peace—used to kiss and handle [his wives] while he was fasting, but he had more control over his *irb* than any of you." [As to this word *irb*], Ibn 'Abbas said that [the derivative from it] *ma'arib* means "need," and Tawus used to use the phrase "one who possesses no *irba*" for a defective who has no need of women. Jabir b. Zaid said: "If one looks [at a woman] and has an emission let him go on with his fast."

24. ON THE [LEGITIMACY OF] KISSING FOR ONE WHO IS FASTING.
Muhammad b. al-Muthanna related to us, saying: Yahya related to us from Hisham, who said: My father informed me from 'A'isha—with whom may Allah be pleased—from the Prophet—upon whom be Allah's blessing and peace—[or by another *isnad*], 'Abdallah b. Maslama related to us from Malik, from Hisham, from his father, from 'A'isha—with whom may Allah be pleased—who said: "There were times when the Apostle of Allah—upon whom be Allah's blessing and peace—would kiss certain of his wives while he was fasting." Then she laughed.

Musaddad related to us, saying: Yahya related to us from Hisham b. Abi 'Abdallah, who said: Yahya b. Abi Kathir related to us from Abu Salama, from Zainab daughter of Umm Salama, from her mother,[1] who said: "While I was with the Prophet—upon whom be Allah's blessing and peace—in bed, my menses started, so I slipped out and put on my menstrual clothes. He asked: 'What is the matter with you? has your period come on?' 'Yes,' I replied, and I entered the bed with him again." Now she and the Apostle of Allah—upon whom be Allah's blessing and peace—used both to bathe at the same [water] vessel, and he used to kiss her when he was fasting.

25. ON THE BATHING OF ONE WHO IS FASTING.
Ibn 'Umar soiled his garment with urine but put it on him while he was fasting. Ash-Sha'bi entered the [public] baths while he was fasting. Ibn Abbas said: "There is no harm in tasting [what is in] the cooking pot [while fasting] or [any other] thing." Al-Hasan said: "There is no harm in the faster gargling or cooling himself off" (i.e., provided he does not drink the water). Ibn Mas'ud said: "When the day comes around for any one of you to fast he may, as he rises in the morning, use oil and comb." Anas said: "I had a copper wash-basin in which I used to plunge even while I was fasting, and Ibn 'Umar used to brush his teeth at the beginning and at the end of the day [while he was fasting]." Ibn Sirin said: "There is no harm in the use of the tooth-brush if it is fresh." The objection was raised: "But it has taste," and [he replied]: "and so does the water have taste when you gargle with it, [yet that is not considered to be breaking the fast]. Anas, al-Hasan and Ibrahim also saw no harm in the faster making use of kohl [for the eyes].

Ahmad b. Salih related to us, saying: Ibn Wahb related to us, saying: Yunus related to us, from Ibn Shihab, from 'Urwa and Abu Bakr, who said: 'A'isha—with whom may Allah be pleased—said: "The dawn used to overtake the Prophet in Ramadan when he was polluted—and not from an [erotic] dream—but he would bathe and [then commence the] fast."

Isma'il related to us, saying: Malik related to me from Sumayy, a client of Abu Bakr b. 'Abd al-Rahman b. al-Harith b. Hisham b. al-Mughira, that he heard Abu Bakr b. 'Abd al-Rahman say: "I was with my father and went along with him till we entered to 'A'isha—with whom may Allah be pleased—who said: 'I bear witness of the Apostle of Allah—upon whom be Allah's blessing and peace—that he used to wake up in the morning polluted [by sperm] from intercourse, not from dreaming, and then he would fast [that day].' Then we entered to Umm Salama, who said the same thing."

---

[1] Her mother was one of the Prophet's wives.

26. ON THE FASTER WHO EATS AND DRINKS FROM FORGETFULNESS.

'Ata' said: "If one snuffs up water and some of it enters the throat so that one is not able to reject it, no harm is done [thereby to one's fast]." Also al-Hasan said: "If a fly should get into one's throat, that is nothing," and al-Hasan and Mujahid both said: "If one should have sexual intercourse forgetfully, that is nothing."

'Abdan related to us [saying], Yazid b. Zurai' informed us, saying, Hisham related to us, saying: Ibn Sirin related to us from Abu Huraira, from the Prophet—upon whom be blessing and peace—that he said: "If anyone forgets and eats or drinks, let him complete his fast, for it was Allah who caused him thus to eat or drink."

27. ON THE FRESH AND THE DRY TOOTHBRUSH FOR HIM WHO IS FASTING.

It is reported from 'Amir b. Rabi'a, who said: "I have seen the Prophet—upon whom be Allah's blessing and peace—using the toothbrush while he was fasting more times than I can reckon or count." 'A'isha said, quoting the Prophet—upon whom be Allah's blessing and peace—: "The toothbrush is a purifier for the mouth and a thing well-pleasing to the Lord." 'Ata' and Qatada said: "One may swallow one's saliva [without thereby breaking one's fast]." Abu Huraira said, quoting the Prophet—upon whom be Allah's blessing and peace—: "Were it not that I might be causing distress to my community I should bid them use the toothbrush at every ablution." The like of this Tradition is transmitted from Jabir and Zaid b. Khalid from the Prophet—upon whom be Allah's blessing and peace—who [in this matter] did not particularize the one fasting from anyone else.

'Abdan related to us, saying: 'Abdallah informed us, saying: Ma'mar informed us, saying: al-Zuhri related to us from 'Ata' b. Yazid, from Humran, who said: "I saw 'Uthman [i.e., the third Caliph] performing ablutions. He poured [the water out] over his hands three times. Then he gargled and snuffed up [the water]. Then he washed his face three times. Then he washed his right arm up to the elbow three times. Then he washed his left arm up to the elbow three times. Then he rubbed his head [with his moist hands]. Then he washed his right foot three times. Then he washed his left foot three times. Then he said: 'I have seen the Apostle of Allah—upon whom be Allah's blessing and peace—performing ablution just like this ablution of mine, after which he [i.e., the Prophet] said: Whosoever performs [his] ablutions as I have done here, and prays a two-bow prayer, not allowing anything to distract him during them, will have all his past sins forgiven him.'"

3.6 The "New Poetry": Abu Nuwas, *Turning the Tables* (*c.*800). Original in Arabic.

Umayyad poetry (see above p. 78) added eulogies of the caliphs and the rhythms of the Qur'an to the forms of pre-Islamic poetry. Abbasid poetry was even more experimental, playing with traditional structures and vocabularies and adding poems of the hunt, satire, and obscenity to the traditional genres of wine songs, laments, elegies, and love poems. Abu Nuwas (d.813/815) was an exceptionally versatile poet who lived a relatively short and irreverent life. He was a lover of beardless boys yet also taken with a slave girl; a boon companion of al-Amin, heir to the caliphate, yet imprisoned by al-Amin and his father at least twice; an impious pilgrim to Mecca, yet well-versed in the Qur'an and hadith (see above, p. 117). In *Turning the Tables,* he portrays a servant who turns his masters into sex slaves during the night. But the tables are turned once again as the poem ends, with a longing lament that suggests real love.

[Source: Philip F. Kennedy, *Abu Nuwas: A Genius of Poetry* (Oxford: One World, 2005), pp. 40–42 (note added).]

Turning the Tables

Young men assembled,
  Sterling coins at the count
    To whom chance time delivered me
"Sunday is close," they said; so I ambled to the promised location
  And was the first to arrive   5
Dressed like a preacher, in full-covering robes
  Kept fast by a plaited cord.
When they had purchased what they wanted,
  Eager to slake their desire,
I approached and offered: "I'll carry this stuff;   10
  I have the necessary saddle bags:
My ropes are sturdy, and I am brisk and dependable."
"Take it," they said, "You seem to be what you claim
  And we'll reward you according to your efforts."
So I advanced in their company   15
  And was told to climb with them [to the spot we were making for];
There vessels were unveiled for them (like wives exposed for the first time)
  While a bird warbled in a melancholy strain.
I skipped up to the glasses, and polished them,
  Leaving them like dazzling snow;   20
My dexterity impressed the beardless young men
  (Though with my skill I intended no good for them);
I served them without respite wine mixed with water
  —It was as warming and bright as kindled fire—
Until I noticed their heads incline,
  Bent and crooked with drunkenness   25

And their tongues tied and heavy,
  They now either slept or reclined;
I got up trembling to have sex with them
  (All those who creep stealthily tremble [at the thought]!);
Their trouser-bands stymied my pleasure [at first]   30
  But then, with subtle art, I untied them
To reveal each man's quivering backside
  Oscillating supply like a green bough.
O for this night which I spent enraptured
  In continual enjoyment and excess,   35
Making from this to that man,
  Screwing whomever I could find in the house
Until the first one awoke and got up
  Feeling bruised at the thighs;
Then I rose with fear to wake up the others,   40
  Saying: "Do you feel the same thing as me?
Is this sweat we've all been stained with?"
  They said: "It looks more like butter."
And when I saw them now alert
  I went off to relieve myself;   45
And when the *majlis*[1] came to life anew
  I joined them, as the cups passed briskly around,
Draped in the finest colored robes,
  All spanking new;
I was asked: "Who are you?" And replied: "Your servant;   50
  From whom you need fear no rude behavior."
Then I sang a love song, captured by the mood:
  "O would that Salma discharged her vows."

AL-ANDALUS

3.7 The minority—that is, Christian—view: *Chronicle of Albelda* (*c.*883). Original in Latin.

The *Chronicle of Albelda* is generally considered to be the earliest of the surviving histories from Asturias, one of the small Christian kingdoms in the very north of the Spanish Peninsula. Most of it apparently dates from 881, with an additional section that we know was completed in November 883. Its author(s) and place of composition are unknown, but given that the work promoted the legitimacy of the Asturian monarchy we can safely assume its author was connected in some way to the Asturian court.

---

[1] The assembly, the group.

The *Chronicle of Albelda* has come down to us as part of a broader historical mélange containing geographical information, genealogies, lists of bishops, and curious prophetic materials. The chronicle proper begins with a summary of the reigns of Roman rulers from Romulus to Tiberius II (r.698–705), followed by a similar outline of the reigns of the Visigothic kings. It ends with entries describing Pelayo and his descendants, the rulers of Asturias. We begin here with the entry for Ordoño I.

[Source: *Medieval Iberia: Readings from Christian, Muslim, and Jewish Sources*, ed. Olivia Remie Constable (Philadelphia: University of Pennsylvania Press, 1997), pp. 67, 70–74. Translated and introduced by Kenneth B. Wolf.]

[Ordoño I: 850–866]

Ordoño, the son of Ramiro, ruled for seventeen years. He increased the kingdom of the Christians with the help of God. He populated León and Astorga as well as Tuy and Amaya and he garrisoned many other fortresses. Many times he emerged victorious over the Saracens.[1] He took the city of Talamanca in battle and he permitted its king, Mozeror, whom he captured there, to go freely to Peña Santa with his wife, Balkaiz. He likewise stormed the strong city of Albelda. He ambushed its exceedingly powerful king Musa[2] at Mt. Laturce and weakened [Musa's] army with the sword. Musa himself was wounded with a lance, but was saved by a certain friend—who was known to have been one of our [men]—and was carried to a safe place by this friend on horseback. In Ordoño's time, the Northmen came again to the shores of Galicia, where they were killed by a count named Peter. The Moors,[3] coming in their ships, were also defeated on the coasts of Galicia. Such gentleness of soul and mercy [was attributed] to this prince, being so pious to everyone, that he was worthy of being called a father to his people. He died a peaceful death in Oviedo on the sixth day before the Kalends of June [May 27], in the era 904 [866].

[Alfonso III: 866–910]

Alfonso, the son of Ordoño, assumed the kingship in his eighteenth year. In the first flower of his adolescence—in the first year of his kingship and the eighteenth since his birth—he was deprived of his rule as the result of a rebellion by the apostate count of Galicia, Fruela. The king left for Castile. After a short time, this same rebel and unfortunate king, Fruela, was killed by those faithful to our prince [Alfonso] in Oviedo, and the glorious young man was brought back from Castile. He rejoiced, ruling happily from the throne of his father. From the outset of his reign he always enjoyed victory over his enemies. Twice he humiliated and overcame the fierceness of the Basques with his army. During his reign, in a year long past, the Ishmaelite host advanced toward León under the command of Almundar, son of King Abd al-Rahman [II][4] and brother of King Muhammad [I][5] of Córdoba. No sooner had Almundar arrived than he was impeded [from achieving his goal], for after losing many of his soldiers there, the rest of the army left in flight. Another army approached Bierzo at that time and was completely annihilated. This happened in many regions controlled by the enemy. [Alfonso] took the fortress Deza and then acquired Atienza peacefully. He depopulated Coimbra, which was held by the enemy, and afterward peopled it with Galicians. He subjected many more fortresses to his rule. In his time the church grew and his

---

[1] *Saraceni* is the most common Latin designation for "Arabs." It is somewhat misleading in the context of Spanish history since the bulk of the original invading force was made up not of Arabs but of Berbers from Morocco.

[2] Musa ibn Musa, one of the leaders of the Banu Qasi, a clan of *muwallads* (converts to Islam) that controlled much of the Ebro region in the ninth century.

[3] Berbers.

[4] Emir of Córdoba (r.822–852). The "Ishmaelite host" refers to the Islamic army.

[5] Emir of Córdoba (r.852–886).

kingdom increased in size. The cities of Braga, Oporto, Orense, Eminio, Viseo, and Lamego were populated with Christians. By means of yet another victory, he depopulated and destroyed Coria, Idanha, and the rest of the territory of Lusitania[1] all the way to Mérida and the sea, consuming it with the sword as well as hunger. Shortly before that, in the era 915 [877], Abuhalit, the consul of Spain and counselor to King Muhammad, was captured in battle in the territory of Galicia and was taken to our king in Oviedo. Afterward he redeemed himself, handing over his two brothers, his son, and his nephew [to be held as hostages], until he paid the king 100,000 gold *solidi*. During that same time in the era 916 [878], Almundar, son of King Muhammad,[2] came from Córdoba to Astorga and León with the general Ibn Ganim and an army of Saracens. One contingent of the enemy forces, following opposite the army—a force of 13,000 from Toledo, Talamanca, Guadalajara and other fortresses—was destroyed by our prince in Polvorosa at the river Orbigo. The [king] knew that Almundar wanted to press on to the fortress of Sublancio because of what happened in Polvorosa. Once Almundar learned that our king was waiting with his entire army to do battle with him in the fortress of Sublancio, he fearfully fled before the light of dawn. At the instigation of Abuhalit, there was a three-year truce between the two kings. Afterward our king, waging war against the Saracens, mobilized his army and entered [Muslim] Spain, in the era 919 [881]. After plundering the castle of Nefza, Alfonso pressed on through the province of Lusitania and, after crossing the Tagus River, advanced to the territory of Mérida. Ten miles outside of Mérida, he crossed the Guadiana River and came to Mt. Oxiferio, which no one before him had ever tried to approach.[3] There he triumphed over enemies with a glorious victory: for more than 15,000 others are known to have been killed at the same mountain. Thus our prince returned to his royal throne in victory. All of the churches of the Lord were restored by this prince and a city was built in Oviedo with a royal palace. He was brilliant in his knowledge and placid in his appearance, dress, and stature. The Lord always inclined [Alfonso's] soul to rule his people piously. After his long rule, he passed from his earthly kingdom to his heavenly one. Amen.

[Continuation]

While this king [Alfonso] was ruling, in the era 920 [882], the above-mentioned Almundar, son of King Muhammad, set out from Córdoba to Zaragoza, accompanied by the general Abuhalit and an army from [Muslim] Spain numbering 80,000. [This was because] Ismail ibn Musa[4] of Zaragoza had become an enemy of the Cordobans. When the army arrived at Zaragoza, it fought there for twenty-two days but won no victory. From there it advanced to Tudela and attacked a fortress held by Fortun ibn Musa,[5] but accomplished nothing. Then Ababdella—also known as Muhammad ibn Lope,[6] who had always been, like his father, a friend to us—made peace with the Cordobans and sent the strongest of his [men] to their army out of envy for his uncles to whom the king [Alfonso] had entrusted his son Ordoño to be reared. Thus the army of the Chaldeans,[7] entering the confines of our kingdom, first attacked the fortress at Cellorigo but accomplished nothing except to lose many of their own men. Vigila Jimenez was the count in Alava at that time. This same army, coming to the frontier of Castile, attacked the fortress called Poncorbo for three days, but won no victory and lost many of its own [men] to the avenging sword. Diego, son of Roderic, was the count in Castile [at that time]. Munio, son of Nuño, left the fortress of Castrojeriz deserted on account of the

---

[1] The old Roman province that corresponds more or less with modern-day Portugal but that also included the cities of Mérida and Salamanca.

[2] It is not clear whether this is a different Almundar from the brother (of the same name) of Muhammad mentioned above, or simply an error on the part of the chronicler.

[3] The success of this long-distance raid in particular seems to have been regarded by the chronicler (and presumably his royal patrons) as a sign that the days of Muslim rule in Spain were numbered. Hence the flurry of self-promoting historical literature produced in Asturias in the 880s.

[4] Son of Musa ibn Musa (a member of the Banu Qasi).

[5] Another son of Musa ibn Musa.

[6] A grandson of Musa ibn Musa.

[7] Yet another synonym for Saracens, this one emphasizing the biblical role of the "scourge" that Christians often invoked when trying to make sense out of their defeat at the hands of Muslims.

advance of the Saracens, because it was not yet heavily fortified. Our king, formidably garrisoned in the city of León with his army, waited for the enemy forces so that he might fight them in the suburbs of the city. But when the [Saracen] forces learned that our king was eagerly and daily anticipating their approach to the city, they, on the advice of Abuhalit, who had spied the king's men [in the city], crossed the river Esla fifteen miles from the city and burned a number of garrisoned fortresses. From the plains of Alcoba, [Abuhalit] sent envoys to the Orbigo River to meet our king, asking for the release of his son Abulkazim, whom the king had been holding [as a hostage] up to that time. So Abuhalit sent [as a hostage], for the sake of peace, the son of Ismail ibn Musa, who had been sent to his father from Córdoba, along with Fortun ibn Alazela, whom they had captured by trickery in Tudela. And so, entreating [King Alfonso] and giving him many gifts, [Abuhalit] received his son and made his way across the river Orbigo to Cea. Then he returned to Córdoba. They arrived in Córdoba, whence they had set out the previous March, in September. Later our king handed over the [hostages] from the Banu Qasi—whom he had received from Abuhalit in exchange for his son—to their friends without ransom. The above-mentioned Ababdella, the son of Lope, turned in hate against his uncles and cousins on account of his friendship with the Cordobans, and the question of war arose between them. That winter, on account of the insolence of Ababdella, his uncle Ismail ibn Musa and his cousin Ismail ibn Fortun moved their armies about seven miles wanting to do battle against Ababdella. Ababdella waited for them in rough terrain. Both Ismails, with light escorts, came to the same rugged mountain where they knew him to be, and ascended it with a few men and servants. Ababdella rushed toward them at full speed and, as they broke into flight, Ismail ibn Fortun fell from his horse and was immediately captured. Likewise Ismail ibn Musa was captured as he tried to seize his nephew. Many of the nobles of the Banu Qasi were also captured. The rest of the army, which had been waiting in the plain, escaped in flight. Having won a victory, Ababdella transported those whom he had captured, bound in chains, to his fortress called Viguera. From there he proceeded to Zaragoza, and took it in the name of peace without resorting to the sword, thus subjecting it to his authority. He sent messengers to Córdoba at once, acting as if he had done all of this for the sake of the king, so as to appear faithful in all things. But when the Cordoban king requested the city of Zaragoza itself along with the others that Ababdella had captured, and Ababdella would by no means consent to do this, the Cordobans were moved to anger. As a result, [Ababdella and his kinsmen] were reconciled. He released his uncle and received the fortress of Valtierra from him. Likewise Ababdella released his cousin and on account of this received Tudela and the fortress of St. Stephan from him. Ababdella retained (and still holds) Zaragoza, which he had taken before. During this same period, Ababdella sustained many raids and attacks from the counts of Castile and Alava, Diego and Vigila. When he saw that he was hard pressed by them, he immediately sent legates to our king [Alfonso] for the sake of peace and indeed he still sends them, but as yet he has not received any firm peace from the prince. Still he remains friendly toward us and wants to remain that way even if our king does not consent [to a formal peace].

3.8 An Islamic Andalusian voice: Ibn 'Abd Rabbihi, *I Have Never Seen* (before 940). Original in Arabic.

Arabic poetry in al-Andalus, as in the rest of the Arabic world, became newly experimental and free when the Umayyad caliphate fell. Having lost regular contact with the eastern half of the Islamic world, Andalusian poets abandoned the imagery of the desert, concentrating on urban life and metaphors of leisure and opulence. Ibn 'Abd Rabbihi (860–940) was a Córdoban poet of great renown, and his poetry is exemplary for its simplicity. Compare it with Abu Nuwas, *Turning the Tables*, above p. 122.

[Source: *Poems of Arab Andalusia*, trans. Cola Franzen from the Spanish versions of Emilio Garcia Gómez (San Francisco: City Lights Books, 1989), pp. 3–4.]

White Skin

I have never seen
nor heard of such a thing

her modesty turns
pearl into carnelian.

Her face is so clear
that when you gaze
on its perfections

you see your own face
reflected.

....

3.9 A Jewish poet in al-Andalus: Dunash ben Labrat, *There Came a Voice* (mid-10th c.). Original in Hebrew.

Born in Fez (today Morocco), Dunash ben Labrat (*fl.* mid-10th c.) became a rabbi in Spain (perhaps at Córdoba). He was one of many scholars and writers to flourish under the patronage of Hasdai ibn Shaprut, the first Jew to be an important figure at the Islamic Spanish court. Under these favorable conditions, ben Labrat and others debated Hebrew grammar, compiled Hebrew dictionaries, and created a new, secular form of Hebrew poetry. Mastering the traditions of Arabic poetic meter and rhyme, ben Labrat took up many of the same themes as the Arabic poets while invoking a very specific Jewish identity.

[Source: *Wine, Women, & Death: Medieval Hebrew Poems on the Good Life*, trans. and ed. Raymond P. Scheindlin (Oxford: Oxford University Press, 1986), pp. 41–42.]

There came a voice: "Awake!
Drink wine at morning's break.
'Mid rose and camphor make
A feast of all your hours,

'Mid pomegranate trees   5
And low anemones,
Where vines extend their leaves
And the palm tree skyward towers,

Where lilting singers hum
To the throbbing of the drum,   10
Where gentle viols thrum
To the plash of fountains' showers.

On every lofty tree
The fruit hangs gracefully.
And all the birds in glee   15
Sing among the bowers.

The cooing of the dove
Sounds like a song of love.

Her mate calls from above—
Those trilling, fluting fowls.   20

We'll drink on garden beds
With roses round our heads.
To banish woes and dreads
We'll frolic and carouse.

Dainty food we'll eat.   25
We'll drink our liquor neat,
Like giants at their meat,
With appetite aroused.

When morning's first rays shine
I'll slaughter of the kine   30
Some fatlings; we shall dine
On rams and calves and cows.

Scented with rich perfumes,
Amid thick incense plumes,
Let us await our dooms,   35
Spending in joy our hours."

I chided him: "Be still!	The Torah, God's delight 45
How can you drink your fill	Is little in your sight,
When lost is Zion hill[1]	While wrecked is Zion's height,
To the uncircumcised. 40	By foxes vandalized.
You've spoken like a fool!	How can we be carefree
Sloth you've made your rule.	Or raise our cups in glee, 50
In God's last judgment you'll	When by all men are we
For folly be chastised.	Rejected and despised?"

THE WESTERN CHURCH AND EMPIRE

3.10 The pope and the Carolingians: Pope Stephen II, *Letters to King Pippin III* (755–756). Original in Latin.

The letters from Pope Stephen II (752–757) to King Pippin III (r.752–768) are crucial sources for the commencement and early years of the Franco-papal alliance, the emergence of the Papal States, the development of papal administration in and around Rome, and the political history of central Italy in the eighth century. Contained in the so-called *Codex Carolinus* (or "Charlemagne's Book"), these letters form part of a collection of 99 letters sent by a series of popes to the Carolingian mayors of the palace and kings from 739 to about 791. The *Codex* survives in a single late-ninth-century manuscript prepared on the order of Archbishop Willibert of Cologne, but not all of the papal letters survive in the *Codex*. The excerpt here represents only some of the letters that Pope Stephen sent to Pippin. Why did he put great emphasis on the role of Saint Peter? What, exactly, did he want from the Carolingians? Why did he represent himself as "shedding tears and beating our breast"? Do you think such rhetoric was effective? Why?

[Source: *Codex Carolinus*, *Epistolae* 6–10, ed. Wilhelm Gundlach, Monumenta Germaniae Historica, Epistolae 3, Epistolae Merovingici et Karolini Aevi 1 (Berlin: Weidmann, 1892), pp. 488–503. Translated and introduced by Thomas F. X. Noble.]

1 (6): *Stephen II to Pippin III (755)*

Pope Stephen to the most excellent lords and sons, Pippin, king and our spiritual co-father,[2] and Charles and Carloman, likewise kings and all of them Patricians of the Romans.[3]

So long as your realm's reputation for sincere faith in blessed Peter will shine brilliantly among other peoples because of your sincere faith in the blessed Peter, prince of the apostles, it is crucial to pay particular attention that, even as all Christians declare that you are more glorious than

---

[1] A reference to the land of Israel, "lost" to the Jews of the Diaspora.

[2] Stephen anointed Pippin's sons Charles and Carloman as kings of the Franks and thus entered a spiritual relationship that made Stephen and Pippin "co-fathers" of the two boys. Compaternity was normally associated with baptismal sponsorship.

[3] "Patrician" was a Roman honorific title that conferred no specific rights. In principle, only the Roman (i.e Byzantine) emperor could confer this title, but the popes began conferring it on the Carolingians.

other peoples in the service of blessed Peter, you should in the same way please the almighty Lord, "who gives salvation to kings,"[1] more perfectly in the defense of his holy church, so that you might have as a helper in all things the faith which you cherish for that same prince of the apostles.

Indeed, we had hoped, most exceptional sons, to delay a while longer amplifying our discourse, but because our heart is terribly worn down by sadness and our spirit grieves because of the many trials borne upon us by the wicked King Aistulf of the Lombards, so we have turned away from the wordiness of many speeches and we have been keen to bring one thing, because it is necessary, to the attention of your most excellent Christianity.

Our spiritual co-father, protected by God, and you, our sweetest sons, for the benefit of your souls, just as our merciful God has deigned to bestow victories upon you from heaven, you have been diligent to demand, as far as you could, the rights of blessed Peter, and through a charter of donation your goodness has confirmed that restitution should be made.[2] Now, however, just as we previously instructed your Christianity about the malice of this same wicked king, behold how his deceit and wicked perversity and perjury have been proclaimed recently. Indeed, the devil, the ancient enemy of the human race, has invaded his wicked heart and what was affirmed by the bond of an oath he has been seen to render worthless, and he has not suffered to return one hand's-breadth of land to blessed Peter and to his holy church, the Republic of the Romans.[3] Indeed, since that day when we [the pope and Pippin] parted from one another, he has attempted to afflict us and to hold the holy church of God in great disgrace to such an extent that the tongues of men cannot describe it, since the very stones themselves, if it may be said, cry out with great lamentation at our tribulation.[4] And he has been seen to afflict us to such a degree that our weakness has been renewed in us once again. For I deeply lament, most excellent sons, that not hearing the words of our unhappiness, you, deceiving yourselves and mocking, have chosen to believe falsehood [spread by Aistulf] rather than truth. Whence even without having achieved the justice of blessed Peter we have returned to our own flock and to the people committed to us.

Finally, all Christians used to believe so firmly that blessed Peter, the prince of the apostles, would now have received his justice through your most potent right arm, since through the intercession of his prince of the apostles the Lord God and Savior Jesus Christ has displayed such a great and resplendent miracle in your most blessed times and has deigned to bestow such an immense victory upon you for the defense of his holy church. But nevertheless, good sons, trusting that same wicked king in what he promised through the bond of an oath, by your own will you have confirmed by a charter of donation that the cities and localities of blessed Peter and of the republic of the holy church of God ought to be restored. But he, having forgotten the Christian faith and the God who ordered him to be born, has been seen to have rendered empty what was confirmed by an oath. Wherefore "his iniquity falls upon his own head";[5] indeed, the trap that he has dug has been revealed, and he is caught in it for his mendacity and perjury.

I implore you most excellent and God-protected sons, through the Lord our God and his holy, glorious and ever virgin mother Mary, our lady, and all the powers of heaven, and through blessed Peter the prince of the apostles, who anointed you as kings, that you grieve for the holy church of God, and that according to that donation which you ordered to be offered to your very protector, our lord, the blessed Peter, you eagerly restore and hand over everything to the holy church of God, and that by no means would you now trust the seductive words or lying illusion of that most wicked king, or his representatives. Behold, his mendacity is indeed manifest such that it ought not by any means to have any further capacity to attract belief but rather, his wicked spirit and wicked will being known, his treachery is uncovered. Indeed, what you once promised blessed Peter, and what was confirmed through a donation in your own hand, for the good of your soul, hasten to restore and hand over to blessed Peter. Finally, the blessed apostle Paul says "It is better not to make a vow than, having made a vow, not to fulfill it."[6]

---

[1] Ps. 144: 10; Douay Ps. 143: 10

[2] Stephen refers to the so-called "Quierzy Document" (754), which spelled out the lands that Pippin would make Aistulf restore to the pope.

[3] Historically only the Roman Empire could be designated this way; the pope is calling the lands assigned to him by Pippin the "Republic" of the Romans.

[4] See Luke 19. 40.

[5] Ps. 7: 17; Douay Ps. 6: 17.

[6] Actually, not Paul but Eccles. 5: 4.

For truly we commend to your heart all the causes of the holy church of God, and you will render account to God and to blessed Peter on the day of the fearful judgment for exactly how you struggled in the cause of that same prince of the apostles and for the restoration his cities and localities. For ultimately this good work has been reserved for you already for a long period of time now, so that through you the holy church might be exalted, and the prince of the apostles might obtain his justice. None of your ancestors merited such a magnificent gift, but God chose and foreknew you before all time, just as is written "Those whom he foreknew and predestined, those he also called; and those whom he called, he also justified."[1] You have been called. Attend with all haste to effect the justice of this very prince of the apostles because it is written "Faith is justified by works."[2]

Concerning all our tribulations, which we have suffered or are yet suffering, with God's help, let our son Fulrad,[3] your counselor, and his associates inform you. And so act then in the cause of blessed Peter so that in this life you may be victorious with the Lord's favor and, in the future life, through the intercession of that very same prince of the apostles, blessed Peter, you may possess eternal joys.

Farewell, most excellent sons.

3 (8) *Stephen II to Pippin (c.Feb. 24, 756)*

Pope Stephen to his most excellent lord son and spiritual co-father Pippin, king of the Franks and patrician of the Romans.

We believe that the very creation of the whole universe would declare by what great, mournful, and extremely bitter sadness we are on every side surrounded, and by what great anxiety and difficulty we are hemmed in, and what great tears our streaming eyes pour forth as unceasing evils increase. Who, seeing these tribulations, would not mourn? Who, hearing of the calamities weighing upon us, would not wail? Wherefore we speak in the words of a certain good and modest woman, Susannah: "Difficulties lie upon our every side and we do not know what to do."[4] O, most excellent and Christian sons, just as

the almighty creator of all things, the Lord, in former times had sent the prophet Habakkuk, carried thence suddenly by an angel to revive and console the distinguished prophet Daniel who was concealed in the lion's den, so also now, if I may say so, if only his most merciful patience had made your God-preserved excellence present here even for the space of a single hour so that you might behold the miserable and mournful hardships and tribulations which we are suffering helplessly at the hands of the Lombard people and their wicked king! Behold, the days of hardship have come upon us. Days of weeping and bitterness, the day of anxiety and groans of grief are at hand, for what we feared is happening, and what we dreaded is coming to pass. And so, attacked, afflicted, and overwhelmed and surrounded on every side by their most wicked king and their Lombard people, shedding tears and beating our breast we say, calling upon the Lord with the prophet "Help us, Lord of our salvation, and for the honor of your name, deliver us."[5] And again "Take up arms and a shield and rise up in our assistance; Lord, condemn those who are harming us and defeat those who are attacking us."[6] Indeed, though we seem often to bring our tribulations to the attention of your goodness, now however we have taken care to relate the perils of the evils that we have suffered from that same shameless king and his Lombard people, since the magnitude of the danger compels us.

We believe, most Christian and excellent son, and spiritual co-father, that everything is already known to your nobility: How the peace treaty has been overthrown by the wicked King Aistulf and his people; and how we have been able to obtain nothing in the way that he agreed to and which was confirmed through the bond of an oath; and even that no gain has come to us but instead after the desolation of our whole region even more murders have been perpetrated by that same people. And now may you recognize what we are saying with great tears and sorrow in our heart, most excellent son and spiritual co-father. On the very first of January the entire army of that same King Aistulf of the Lombards mustered from the area of Tuscany against this Roman city and camped right at the gate of Saint Peter, and the gate of Saint Pancras, and the gate of Portuensis. Indeed Aistulf himself joined with other troops from a different area and pitched his tents at

---

[1] A paraphrase of Rom. 8: 29–30.

[2] James 2: 24.

[3] Abbot of Saint-Denis and key adviser to Pippin and later to his son Charlemagne.

[4] Dan. 13: 22.

[5] Ps. 78: 9; Douay Ps. 77: 9 (slightly paraphrased).

[6] See Ps. 34: 2; Douay Ps. 33: 2.

the Salarian gate and at other gates too and he sent to us, saying "Open the Salarian Gate to me that I might enter the city, and hand over to me your pontifical office, and I might have mercy on you.[1] Otherwise, overturning the walls, I shall kill you with a single sword and we shall see who can rescue you from my hands." And indeed all the Beneventans as a whole mustering against this Roman city have taken up a position at the gate of blessed John the Baptist, at the gate of blessed Paul the apostle, and at the rest of the gates of this Roman city.

To be sure, they have laid waste with fire and sword all the estates far and wide outside the city and, burning up all the houses, they have razed them almost to their foundations. They have set fire to the churches of God, and, casting the most holy images of the saints into the fire, they have destroyed them with their swords. And as for the holy gifts, that is the body of our Lord Jesus Christ, they have put them in their foul vessels that they call bags, and stuffed with abundant food of flesh, they eat those same gifts.[2] Carrying off the veils or all the ornaments of the churches of God, which it is too cruel to have to relate, they have used them for their own purposes. Beating the monks, the servants of God who live in monasteries for the sake of the divine office,[3] with immense blows, they have mutilated quite a few. They have dragged away and polluted with great cruelty the nuns and recluses who, for the love of God, handed themselves over to be cloistered from infancy or the age of puberty, and they seem in that same contamination even to have killed some of them. They have put to the torch all the *Domuscultae*[4] of blessed Peter or, as is reported, they have utterly destroyed by fire the houses of all the Romans outside the city, stolen all the flocks, cut the vines almost to the roots, and completely destroyed the crops by grinding them down. Neither to the house of our holy church nor to anyone living in this Roman city has there remained any hope of surviving because, as it is reported, they have destroyed everything with fire and sword and have killed many. And they have also slain the abundant family[5] of blessed Peter and of all the Romans, both men and women, and they have led away many others as captives. These same

wicked Lombards have killed the innocent little children whom they have snatched from their mothers' breasts as well as the mothers themselves, whom they have polluted by force. Indeed they have committed such evils in this Roman province as certainly not even the pagan peoples ever before perpetrated so that, as one could say, even the very stones, seeing our losses, cry out with us.[6]

Besieging this suffering Roman city and surrounding it on every side for five and fifty days, they have waged the fiercest battles against us at the walls of this Roman city incessantly, day and night, and they do not stop attacking us with the aim of subjecting all the people to his power—may God prevent it!—so that wicked king Aistulf may kill them with a single sword. For in such a way, mocking us with great fury, they were proclaiming: "Behold, you are surrounded by us and you will not escape our hands. Let the Franks come now and save you from our hands."

Now they have seized the city of Narni, which your Christianity conceded to us, and they have taken certain cities of ours. Afflicted in such a way, we have barely been able, through great cleverness and by using a sea route, to send our envoys and our present letter, which we have written with great tears, to your excellent Christianity. We even—we speak with the truth bearing us out—would express through each and every letter tears mixed with blood; and if only the Lord would grant it to us, at the moment when you read our mournful exhortation a tear filled with blood might flow in your presence through every letter of this message.

Whence, most excellent son and spiritual co-father, I ask you, and as though appearing in your very presence bowed down upon the ground and prostrating myself at your feet, with the divine mysteries, I adjure you before the living and true God and blessed Peter his prince of the apostles, that you come to our assistance with all possible haste and the greatest speed, lest we perish, for after God, it is in your hands that we have placed all our souls, those of all the Romans. Do not abandon us; so also may the Lord not abandon you in all your works and deeds. Do not spurn us; so also may the Lords not spurn you when you call upon his power. Do not withdraw your aid

---

[1] The Latin is tortured here but it seems that Aistulf was asking Stephen to resign.

[2] This is a reference to the consecrated bread of the altar, the Eucharist.

[3] Monks gathered several times each day to pray the *Opus Divinum,* the Divine Office.

[4] Beginning with Pope Zachary (741–752) the papacy began reorganizing some of its scattered rural estates into large-scale farms called *Domuscultae.*

[5] *Familia* means household more than a small group of related people. The word here relates to the peasants who worked the lands of the Roman Church.

[6] See Luke 19: 40.

from us, most Christian son and spiritual co-father; so also may the Lord not withdraw his aid and protection from us and your people when you have marched out to fight against your enemies. Come to our assistance and help us with great speed, most Christian one: Thus may you receive support from almighty God who anointed you into kingship above all the masses of the peoples through the disposition of blessed Peter. Hasten, hasten, son, hasten to help us before the enemy's sword reaches our heart; I plead with you, lest we perish, lest the peoples who are in all the earth have occasion to say "What has become of the trust of the Romans which they used to place, after God, in the kings and people of the Franks?" Do not suffer us to perish and do not hold back or delay to relieve us or cut us off from your support; thus may you not be a stranger from the kingdom of God and be cut off by force from your dearest wife, the most excellent queen and our spiritual co-mother. Do not permit us to be worried and endangered any further and to continue in mourning and weeping, fine excellent son and spiritual co-father; in the same way, may sorrow not come upon you over your and my sweetest sons, the lords Charles and Carloman, most outstanding kings and patricians. Do not shut your ear from hearing us and do not turn your face from us lest we be disappointed in our petitions and we be imperiled to the very extremity. In the same way, may the Lord not shut his ear from hearing your prayers and may he not turn his face from you on that day of judgment to come when, with the blessed Peter and with the rest of his apostles, he shall sit to judge through fire every order, both sexes, and every human and worldly power and—God forbid it!—may he not say to you "I do not know you because you have not helped to defend the church of God and you scarcely took any care to rescue his special people in their time of danger."

Hear me, son, hear me and come to our assistance. Behold, the time for saving us has arrived. Save us, before we perish, most Christian king. For what could be better, or finer, or more outstanding than to save those who are in grave danger and caught in dire straits? For it is written: "He who saves is like he who builds up."[1] On this point indeed the eminent prophet Isaiah said: "Relieve the oppressed."[2] For all peoples who are located all around you and have sought protection from your people of the Franks, most mighty through the power of God, have been made safe, and if you do not hesitate

to bestow assistance upon all peoples and they are made safe by you, you ought much more to have freed the holy church of God and his people from the attack of their enemies. O how much confidence there was in our heart when we were worthy to behold your honeyed countenance and we were bound and connected in a bond of love that we would remain in great peace and comfort! But while we were expecting to see the light from you, darkness burst forth[3] and our new situation became worse than the former one. Consider, son, consider and reflect deeply, I adjure you through the living God, how our soul and the souls of all the Roman people, committed to you by God, depend, after God and his prince of the apostles, upon your God-protected excellence and the people of the Franks, for as has already been related, we have committed our souls into your keeping. And if it should happen that we perish—let it not be so and may divine mercy prevent it—weigh carefully, I beseech you, and in every way consider upon whose soul the sin shall lie. Believe with all certainty, most Christian one, that if some perilous disaster shall befall us—may it not happen—you, of all people, protected by God, and most beloved to us, will be destined to give account before the tribunal of God with all your officials because, as has been related, we have, through the precept of God and of blessed Peter, committed the holy church of God and our people of the republic of the Romans for protection to no one else but only to your most beloved excellence and to your sweetest sons and to the whole people of the Franks.

Behold, we have made known all our sorrows and anxieties and difficulties to your God-protected goodness. As for you, most excellent son and spiritual co-father, act, and after God, free those who are fleeing to you so that, bearing good fruit, on the day of future judgment you shall be worthy to say "My lord, blessed Peter, prince of the apostles, behold I, your unworthy servant, having run the race, having kept faith with you, having defended the church of God commended to you by heavenly mercy, I freed it from the hands of its persecutors and, standing unblemished before you, I offer you the sons whom you committed to me for the purpose of rescuing them from the hands of enemies, standing here now unharmed and safe." Then, both holding the helm of the kingdom in this present life and also reigning with Christ in the world to come, you would deserve to obtain the joys of heavenly rewards, hearing without doubt that longed-for fatherly

---

[1] Although reminiscent of passages in Psalms and Proverbs, this quotation cannot be identified.

[2] Isa. 1: 17.

[3] See Job 30: 26.

voice of the one who says "Come, blessed of my father, and receive the kingdom that has been prepared for you from the beginning of the world."[1]

May heavenly grace keep your Excellency safe and sound.

4 (9) Pope Stephen II to Pippin, Charles, and Carloman (c.Feb. 24, 756)

To the most excellent lords Pippin, Charles, and Carloman, three kings and our patricians of the Romans, and also to all the bishops, abbots, priests and monks, and to the glorious dukes, counts, and to the entire army of the kingdom and provinces of the Franks, Pope Stephen and all the bishops, priests, deacons, and dukes, soldiers, counts, tribunes, and the whole people and army[2] of the Romans, all placed in affliction.

[The rest of this letter repeats the previous one almost verbatim. What is different is the address to all the officials of the Frankish world and the letter's dispatch from all the religious and secular officials of Rome.]

5 (10) Pope Stephen II writes in the name of Saint Peter to Pippin, Charles, and Carloman (c.Feb. 24, 756)

Peter, called to be an apostle by Jesus Christ the son of the living God who, reigning before all time with the Father in the unity of the Holy Spirit, in the last days became incarnate and was made a man for the salvation of us all and redeemed us by his precious blood through the will of the Father's glory, just as he ordained through his holy prophets in the holy scriptures; and through me the entire catholic and apostolic Roman church of God, the head of all the churches of God, founded by the blood of our very redeemer upon a solid rock, and Stephen, prelate of that same nourishing church: May Grace, peace, and strength for rescuing from the hands of its persecutors that same holy church of God and its Roman people committed to me, be bestowed fully upon you by our Lord God, most excellent men, Pippin, Charles, and

Carloman, all three kings, and also upon the most holy bishops, abbots, priests and all the religious monks, as well as upon the dukes, counts, and all the rest of the armies and people living in Francia.

I, Peter the Apostle, when I was called by Christ, the son of the living God, by the will of divine clemency, was foreordained as the teacher of the whole world by his power, as that very same Lord our God confirmed: "Go, teach all nations, baptizing them in the name of the Father and of the Son and of the Holy Spirit";[3] and again "Receive the Holy Spirit; whose sins you shall remit, they are remitted for them."[4] And commending his sheep in particular to me, his meager servant yet called as an apostle, he said: "Feed my sheep, feed my lambs." And again "You are Peter and upon this rock I shall build my church, and the gates of Hell will not prevail against it, and I shall give you the keys of the kingdom of heaven; whatever you will have bound on earth will also be bound in heaven and whatever you will have loosed on earth will also be loosed in heaven."[5] Wherefore, let all those who, hearing my teaching, fulfill it, believe with certainty that in this world their sins are forgiven by the precept of God and they shall proceed clean and without blemish into that life. Thus, because the inspiration of the Holy Spirit has shone forth in your gleaming hearts and you have been made lovers of his unique and holy Trinity by receiving the word through the preaching of the gospel, your hope of future reward is held bound up in this holy Roman church of God that has been committed to us.

Therefore, I, Peter, the apostle of God, who regard you as adopted sons, appealing to the love of all, I implore you to defend from the hands of its enemies this Roman city and the people committed to me by God, and also to rescue the house where I lie at rest according to the flesh from the defilement of the nations, and bearing witness I warn you to liberate the church of God commended to me by the divine power of God because they are suffering immense afflictions and oppressions from the awful nation of the Lombards. May you by no means believe otherwise, most beloved, but instead trust in it as a certainty: Through my very own self, just as if I were standing alive in the flesh before you, we constrain and bind with mighty adjurations through this exhortation

---

[1] Matt. 25: 34.

[2] The presence of these military figures may be surprising, but the popes seem to have retained something of the military establishment of the formerly Byzantine Duchy of Rome. They were neither numerous nor effective, as these letters make clear.

[3] Matt. 28: 19.

[4] John 20: 22–23.

[5] Matt. 16: 18–19.

because, according to the promise which we received from that same Lord God, our redeemer, we consider all you peoples of the Franks to be a special people among all the nations. So I bear witness and I warn you as if through a mysterious vision and with firm obligation I adjure you, most Christian kings Pippin, Charles, and Carloman, and also all the archbishops, bishops, abbots, priests, and all the religious monks, and all the officials, and the dukes, counts, and the whole people of the kingdom of the Franks, and believe, all of you, just as firmly that the words of the exhortation are addressing you as you would if I, Peter, the apostle of God, were standing before you alive in the flesh in person, because, even if I am not there in the flesh, I am not absent from you spiritually, for it is written: "He who receives a prophet in the name of a prophet, receives the prophet's reward."[1]

And also our mistress, the mother of God, the ever-virgin Mary, bears witness, warns, and commands you, along with us, adjuring by great obligations, likewise also thrones and dominions, and all the troops of the heavenly host, not to mention the martyrs and confessors of Christ, and everyone wholly pleasing to God. And these, urging and imploring along with us, testify to how much you grieve for this Roman city committed to us by the Lord God, and for the Lord's flocks dwelling within it, and also for the holy church of God commended to me by the Lord. So, defend and free it, with great haste, from the hands of the persecuting Lombards, lest—may it never be!—my body which suffered torments for the sake of the Lord Jesus Christ, and my house, where by God's command it lies at rest, be contaminated by them and lest my special people be further maimed or they be butchered by that very people of the Lombards who stand guilty of such a great crime of treachery and are proven to be transgressors of the divine scriptures. Offer therefore to my Roman people, committed to me by God in this life, your own brothers, protection with all your strength, with the Lord assisting you, so that I, Peter, called to be an apostle of God, may extend in turn patronage to you in this life and on the day of future judgment, so that in the kingdom of God the most shining and distinguished tents may be prepared for you and that I, giving my word, may bestow upon you in turn the rewards of eternal recompense and the endless joys of paradise, provided that you will have defended my Roman city and my special people, your brothers, the Romans, with great swiftness, from the hands of the wicked Lombards.

Hasten, hasten, I urge and protest by the living and true God, hasten and assist, before the living font whence you were nourished and reborn dries up; before that little spark that remains from the most blazing flame, from which you have known your light, is extinguished; before your spiritual mother, the holy church of God, in which you hope to receive eternal life, is humiliated, overwhelmed, and is violated and contaminated by the impious. I witness before you, my most beloved adoptive sons, through the grace of the Holy Spirit, I bear witness and I greatly urge and admonish before God the terrible creator of all, I, the apostle of God, Peter, and together with me the holy, catholic, and apostolic church of God, which the Lord committed to me: Do not suffer this Roman city to perish in which the Lord laid my body and which he commended to me and established as the foundation of the faith.

Free it and its Roman people, your brothers, and in no way permit it to be invaded by the people of the Lombards; thus may your provinces and possessions not be invaded by peoples of whom you know nothing. Let me not be cut off from my Roman people; thus may you not be foreign and cut off from the kingdom of God and eternal life. In whatever you have demanded of me, I shall come to your aid, that is to say, I shall also bestow my patronage. Come to the aid of my Roman people, your brothers, and struggle more perfectly and achieve final success in freeing them. For no one receives the crown except he who has genuinely struggled. And you, struggle bravely for the liberation of the holy church of God lest you perish for eternity. I adjure you, I adjure you, most beloved, as I have already said, by the living God, and I stand true witness: Do not in the slightest permit this my Roman city and the people living in it to be mutilated any further by the people of the Lombards; thus may your bodies and souls not be slashed and tormented in the eternal and inextinguishable fire of Tartarus with the devil and his stinking angels. And let not the sheep of the Lord's flock, committed to me by God, that is the Roman people, be further scattered; may the Lord not scatter and drive you out just as the Israelite people has been scattered.

For it has been declared that your people of the Franks is devoted to me, to the apostle of God, Peter, beyond all peoples who are under heaven; thus I have commended to you through the hand of my vicar the church, which the Lord handed to me, so that you might free it from the hands of its enemies. Believe most confidently that I, the servant of God, called to be an apostle, have lent my aid in all your needs when you have called on me, and I have bestowed victory upon you, through the power of

---

[1] Matt. 10: 41.

God, over your enemies, and in the future I shall bestow no less, believe me, if you make haste with great dispatch to free this my Roman city. Remember this as well: How I also caused the enemies of the holy church of God to be struck down by you when they threatened battle against you who were few in number against them. Therefore, struggle; fulfill this warning of mine quickly, that you may more perfectly deserve to obtain my help through the grace that has been given to me by Christ, our Lord God.

Behold, dearest sons, for in preaching I have warned you. If you shall have obeyed quickly it will lead to great reward for you and assisted by my intercession you will overcome your enemies in the present life and you will endure to a great age, and you will have the goods of the earth at your disposal and beyond doubt you will enjoy eternal life. If not, however, which we do not believe, you will have made some delay or excuse for making no haste to fulfill this our exhortation to defend this Roman city of mine and the people living in it and the holy apostolic church of God committed to me by the Lord, and likewise his prelate, then know this: That by the authority of the holy and unique Trinity, through the grace of the apostolic office, a grace that has been given to me by the Lord Christ, we disinherit you from the kingdom of God and from eternal life for your transgression of our exhortation.

But may our God and Lord Jesus Christ who, redeeming us by his precious blood, has led us to the light of truth and established us as preachers and teachers for the whole world, grant it to you to judge these things wisely, and to understand and to make arrangements concerning them exceedingly quickly so that you may more swiftly hasten to rescue this Roman city and its people and the holy church of God committed to me by the Lord and, with my intercession intervening on your behalf, may he keep you safe and victorious with the mercy he shows to those who are faithful to his power, and in the world to come may he make you worthy many times over of the gifts of his reward with his saints and chosen ones.

Farewell.[1]

3.11 Charlemagne as Roman emperor: Einhard, *Life of Charlemagne* (825–826?). Original in Latin.

Born to an elite Frankish family, Einhard (*c.*770–840) received a good education in biblical studies and Latin classics at the monastery of Fulda, which was founded in 744 by Saint Sturm, a disciple of Boniface, a religious reformer closely tied to the early Carolingians (see above, p. 91). Einhard was probably in his early twenties when he started to serve at the court of Charlemagne (r.768–814). There he was known by the other courtiers as "little Nard" – probably to rhyme with the "hard" of his name and to stress his tiny stature – and also as "Bezaleel," Moses' wonderful craftsman (see Exod. 31: 1–5). But Einhard's expertise extended beyond the arts to elegant writing. This allowed him to serve as an ambassador and administrator under Charlemagne and also, for a time, under Charlemagne's heir, Louis the Pious (r.814–840). He did not produce any major writings while living at court, but later, after retiring with his wife, Emma, to the estates that he received for his service to the king, he began to write books. He was so taken with classical Latin models that his *Life of Charlemagne* was, to some degree, patterned on *The Lives of the Caesars*, portraits of the first Roman emperors written by the Roman writer and imperial official Suetonius (69–after 122).

[Source: *Charlemagne's Courtier: The Complete Einhard*, ed. and trans. Paul Edward Dutton (Toronto: University of Toronto Press, 1998), pp. 15–39 (notes added).]

---

[1] Soon after this letter Pippin mustered his army, marched into Italy, defeated Aistulf, and drew up the Second Peace of Pavia, better known as the "Donation of Pippin."

[Preface]

After I decided to describe the life and character, and many of the accomplishments, of my lord and foster father, Charles, that most outstanding and deservedly famous king, and seeing how immense this work was, I have expressed it in as concise a form as I could manage. But I have attempted not to omit any of the facts that have come to my attention, and [yet I also seek] not to irritate those who are excessively critical by supplying a long-winded account of everything new [I have learned]. Perhaps, in this way, it will be possible to avoid angering with a new book [even] those who criticize the old masterpieces composed by the most learned and eloquent of men.

And yet I am quite sure that there are many people devoted to contemplation and learning who do not believe that the circumstances of the present age should be neglected or that virtually everything that happens these days is not worth remembering and should be condemned to utter silence and oblivion. Some people are so seduced by their love of the distant past, that they would rather insert the famous deeds of other peoples in their various compositions, than deny posterity any mention of their own names by writing nothing. Still, I did not see why I should refuse to take up a composition of this sort, since I was aware that no one could write about these things more truthfully than me, since I myself was present and personally witnessed them, as they say, with my own eyes. I was, moreover, not sure that these things would be recorded by anyone else.

I thought it would be better to write these things down [that is, his personal observations], along with other widely known details, for the sake of posterity, than to allow the splendid life of this most excellent king, the greatest of all the men in his time, and his remarkable deeds, which people now alive can scarcely equal, to be swallowed up by the shadows of forgetfulness.

There is still another reason, an understandable one, I believe, which even by itself might explain why I felt compelled to write this account; namely, the foster care [Charlemagne] bestowed on me and the constant friendship [I had] with him and his children after I began living at his court. Through his friendship he so won me over to him and I owed him so much both in life and death, that I might both seem and be fairly criticized as ungrateful if I

forgot the many kindnesses he conferred upon me. Could I keep silent about the splendid and exceedingly brilliant deeds of a man who had been so kind to me and could I allow his life to remain without record and proper praise, as if he had never lived? But to write and account [for such a life] what was required was [an almost] Ciceronian eloquence,[1] not my feeble talent, which is poor and small, indeed almost non-existent.

Thus [I present] to you this book containing an account of the most splendid and greatest of all men. There is nothing in it that you should admire but his accomplishments, except perhaps that I, a German with little training in the language of Rome, should have imagined that I could write something correct and even elegant in Latin. Indeed, it might seem [to you] that my headlong impudence is very great and that I have willfully spurned the advice of Cicero [himself], since in the first book of his *Tusculan* [*Disputations*], when speaking of Latin authors, he had said: "for people to set their thoughts down in writing when they cannot organize them, make them clear, or charm their readers with any style is a complete waste of time and energy."[2] Indeed, this opinion of the famous orator might have stopped me from writing [this book, at all], if I had not decided in advance that it was better to risk the criticisms of people and to endanger my own small reputation by writing [this book], than to neglect the memory of so great a man and [instead] say myself.

[The Life of Charlemagne]

1. The family of the Merovingians, from which the Franks used to make their kings, is thought to have lasted down to King Childeric [III], whom Pope Stephen [II] ordered deposed. His [long] hair was shorn and he was forced into a monastery. Although it might seem that the [Merovingian] family ended with him, it had in fact been without any vitality for a long time and [had] demonstrated that there was nothing of any worth in it except the empty name of 'king'. For both the [real] riches and power of the kingdom were in the possession of the prefects of the palace, who were called the mayors of the palace [*maiores domus*], and to them fell the highest command. Nothing was left for the king [to do] except sit on his throne

---

1   In fact Cicero (106–43 BCE), a Roman orator and writer whose Latin style was (and continues to be) greatly admired, was a major influence on Einhard. Note his reference to Cicero's *Tusculan Disputations* in the next paragraph.

2   Cicero, *Tusculan Disputations*, 1.3.6.

with his hair long and his beard uncut, satisfied [to hold] the name of king only and pretending to rule. [Thus] he listened to representatives who came from various lands and, as they departed, he seemed to give them decisions of his own, which he had [in fact] been taught or rather ordered [to pronounce]. Except for the empty name of 'king' and a meager living allowance, which the prefect of the court extended to him as it suited him, he possessed nothing else of his own but one estate with a very small income. On that estate, he had a house and servants who ministered to his needs and obeyed him, but there were few of them. He traveled about on a cart that was pulled by yoked oxen and led, as happens in the countryside, by a herdsman to wherever he needed to go.[1] In this way he used to go to the palace and so also to the public assembly of his people, which was held annually for the good of the kingdom, and in this manner he also returned home. But it was the prefect of the court [the mayor of the palace] who took care of everything, either at home or abroad, that needed to be done and arranged for the administration of the kingdom.

2. When Childeric was deposed, Pepin [III, the Short], the father of King Charles, held the office [of mayor of the palace], as if by hereditary right. For his father Charles [Martel] had brilliantly discharged the same civil office, which had been laid down for him by his father Pepin [II, of Herstal]. This Charles overthrew those oppressors who claimed personal control over all of Francia and he so completely defeated the Saracens,[2] who were attempting to occupy Gaul, in two great battles—the first in Aquitaine near the city of Poitiers [in 732] and the second near Narbonne on the River Berre [in 737]—that he forced them to fall back into Spain. For the most part, the people [that is, the Frankish nobles] only granted the office [of mayor of the palace] to those men who stood out above others because of the nobility of their birth and the magnitude of their wealth.

For a few years Pepin, the father of King Charles, had held, as if under that [Merovingian] king, the office [of mayor of the palace], which was left to him and his brother Carloman by his grandfather and father. He shared that office with his brother in splendid harmony. [Then in 747] Carloman walked away from the oppressive

chore of governing an earthly kingdom. It is not clear why he did this, but it seems that he was driven by a desire to lead a contemplative life. [Hence] he went to Rome in search of a quiet life and there changed his way [of dress and life] completely and was made a monk. With the brothers who joined him there, he enjoyed for a few years the quiet life he so desired in the monastery [he] built on Mount Soracte near the church of St-Sylvester. But since many nobles from Francia frequently visited Rome in order to fulfill their solemn vows and did not wish to miss [seeing] the man who had once been their lord, they interrupted the peaceful life he so loved by constantly paying their respects and so forced him to move. For when he realized that this parade [of visitors] was interfering with his commitment [to the monastic life], he left Mount [Soracte] and retreated to the monastery of St. Benedict located on Monte Cassino in the province of Samnium. There he spent what was left of his earthly life [until 755] in religious contemplation.[3]

3. Moreover, Pepin, who had been mayor of the palace, was established as king [in 751] by the decision of the Roman pope [Zacharias] and he ruled the Franks by himself for fifteen years or more. When the Aquitainian war, which Pepin waged against Waifar, the duke of Aquitaine, for nine straight years, was over, he died of edema in Paris [in 768]. He was survived by two sons, Charles and Carloman, and upon them, by divine will, fell the succession of the kingdom. Indeed, the Franks at a general assembly solemnly established both of them as their kings, but on the condition, agreed to in advance, that they should divide up the entire territory of the kingdom equally. Charles was to take up and govern that part [of the kingdom] which their father Pepin had held and Carloman that part which their uncle Carloman had [once] governed. Both of them agreed to these conditions and each of them received the portion of the kingdom allotted to him by the plan. That peaceful agreement of theirs held fast, but with the greatest strain, since many on Carloman's side sought to drive the brothers apart. Some went so far as to plot to turn them [against each other] in war. But the outcome of things proved that the threat [of war] was more suspected than real in this case, and when Carloman died [in 771] his wife and sons, along with some of

---

[1] Although Einhard presents the Merovingians as ridiculous, in fact the cart as well as their right to wear long hair and beard had been signs of their royal and religious status.

[2] Muslims.

[3] For the Rule that St. Benedict wrote for this monastery, see above, p. 17.

his chief nobles, took refuge in Italy. For no reason at all, she spurned her husband's brother and placed herself and her children under the protection of Desiderius, the king of the Lombards. In fact, Carloman had died [naturally] from disease after ruling the kingdom for two years with his brother. After his death, Charles was established as king by the agreement of all the Franks.

4. I believe it would be improper [for me] to write about Charles's birth and infancy, or even his childhood, since nothing [about those periods of his life] was ever written down and there is no one still alive who claims to have knowledge of these things. Thus, leaving aside the unknown periods [of his life], I have decided to pass straight to the deeds, habits, and other aspects of his life that should be set forth and explained. Nevertheless, so that I might not skip anything either necessary or worth knowing, I shall first describe his deeds inside and outside [the kingdom], then his habits and interests, and finally his administration of the kingdom and his death.

5. Of all the wars he waged, [Charles] began first [in 769] with the one against Aquitaine, which his father had started, but left unfinished, because he thought that it could be quickly brought to a successful conclusion. His brother [Carloman] was [still] alive at the time and [Charles] even asked for his help. And despite the fact that his brother misled him [by not delivering] the promised help, he pursued the campaign with great energy. He refused to back away from a war already in progress or to leave a job undone, until he had by sheer determination and persistence completely achieved the goal he had set for himself. For he forced Hunold, who had tried to take possession of Aquitaine after Waifar's death and to revive a war that was almost over, to give up Aquitaine and seek [refuge in] Gascony. But [Charles], unwilling to allow him to settle there, crossed the River Garonne and through messengers commanded Lupus, the duke of the Gascons, to hand over the fugitive. If he did not do this quickly, [Charles] would demand his surrender by waging war. Lupus not only gave way to wiser counsel and returned Hunold, but he even entrusted himself and the territory he governed to [Charles's] power.

6. With things settled in Aquitaine and the war over, and since the co-ruler [of Francia, his brother Carloman] was now also dead, [Charles] took up war against the Lombards [in 773]. Hadrian [I], the bishop of the city of Rome, [had] asked and appealed to him to do this. Indeed, his father had previously taken up this war at the request of Pope Stephen [II], [but] with great trouble, since some of the chief Franks, whom he regularly consulted, were so opposed to his plan that they openly stated that they would abandon the king and return home. Despite that [threat], [Pepin] took up the war against King Haistulf and quickly finished it at that time. But, although [Charles] and his father seem to have had a similar or, rather, identical reason for taking up this war, all agree that the [actual] fighting and conclusion [of the two conflicts] were different. For in fact, after laying siege to King Haistulf for a short time [in 756] in Pavia, Pepin forced him to surrender hostages, to restore the cities and fortified places seized from the Romans, and to swear that he would not try to regain the things he had returned. But Charles after he had begun the war did not stop until he had, by means of a long siege [in 774], worn King Desiderius down and had accepted his complete surrender. He forced [Desiderius's] son Adalgis, on whom the hopes of all [the Lombards] seemed to rest, to depart not only from the kingdom, but also from Italy. [Charles] restored everything that had been seized from the Romans. He also overcame Rotgaud, the duke of Friuli, who was plotting new [uprisings in 776], and brought all Italy under his control. He set up his own son Pepin as the king of this conquered land.

I would relate here how difficult it was for one to enter Italy across the Alps and what a struggle it was for the Franks to overcome unmarked mountain ridges, upthrust rocks, and rugged terrain, were it not my intention in this book to record the manner of his life, rather than the details of the wars which he waged. Nevertheless, the end result of this war [against the Lombards] was that Italy was conquered, King Desiderius was sent into permanent exile, his son Adalgis was driven out of Italy, and the properties stolen by the Lombard kings were returned to Hadrian, the head of the Roman church.

7. At the conclusion of this campaign, the Saxon war, which had seemed merely postponed, was begun again. No war taken up by the Frankish people was ever longer, harder, or more dreadful [than this one], because the Saxons, like virtually all the peoples inhabiting Germany, were naturally fierce, worshiped demons, and were opposed to our religion. Indeed, they did not deem it shameful to violate and contravene either human or divine laws. There were underlying causes that threatened daily to disturb the peace, particularly since our borders and theirs ran together almost everywhere in open land except for a few places where huge forests or mountain ridges came between our respective lands and

established a clear boundary. Murder, theft, and arson constantly occurred along this border. The Franks were so infuriated by these [incidents], that they believed they could no longer respond [incident for incident], but that it was worth declaring open war on the Saxons.

Thus, a war was taken up against them, which was waged with great vehemence by both sides for thirty-three straight years [772–804]. But the damage done to the Saxons was greater than that suffered by the Franks. In fact, the war could have been brought to a close sooner, if the faithlessness of the Saxons had [but] allowed it. It is almost impossible to say how many times they were beaten and pledged their obedience to the king. They promised [on those occasions] to follow his orders, to hand over the hostages demanded without delay, and to welcome the representatives sent to them by the king. At different times, they were so broken and subdued that they even promised to give up their worship of demons and freely submit themselves to Christianity. But though they were on occasion inclined to do this, they were always so quick to break their promises, that it is not possible to judge which of the two ways [of acting] can be said to have come more naturally to them. In fact, since the start of the war with the Saxons there was hardly a single year in which they did not reverse themselves in this way. But the king's greatness [of spirit] and steadfast determination—both in bad times and good—could not be conquered by their fickleness or worn down by the task he had set himself. Those perpetrating anything of this sort were never allowed to go unpunished. He took vengeance on them for their treachery and exacted suitable compensation either by leading the army [against them] himself or by sending it under [the charge of] his counts. Finally, when all those who were in the habit of resisting had been crushed and brought back under his control, he removed ten thousand men who had been living with their wives and children along both sides of the Elbe river and he dispersed them here and there throughout Gaul and Germany in various [small] groups. Thus, that war which had lasted for so many years ended on the terms laid down by the king and accepted by the Saxons, namely that they would reject the worship of demons, abandon their ancestral [pagan] rites, take up the Christian faith and the sacraments of religion, and unite with the Franks in order to form a single people....

9. While he was vigorously pursuing the Saxon war, almost without a break, and after he had placed garrisons at selected points along the border, [Charles] marched into Spain [in 778] with as large a force as he could [mount]. His army passed through the Pyrenees and [Charles] received the surrender of all the towns and fortified places he encountered. He was returning [to Francia] with his army safe and intact, but high in the Pyrenees on that return trip he briefly experienced the treachery of the Basques. That place is so thoroughly covered with thick forest that it is the perfect spot for an ambush. [Charles's] army was forced by the narrow terrain to proceed in a long line and [it was at that spot], high on the mountain, that the Basques set their ambush. They fell upon the last part of the baggage train and drove the men of the rear guard, who were protecting the troops in front, down into the valley below. In the skirmish that followed, they slaughtered every last one of those men. Once they had looted the baggage train, the Basques, under the cover of darkness, since night was then coming on, quickly dispersed in every direction. The Basques had the advantage in this skirmish because of the lightness of their weapons and the nature of the terrain, whereas the Franks were disadvantaged by the heaviness of their arms and the unevenness of the land. Eggihard, the overseer of the king's table, Anselm, the count of the palace, and Roland, the lord of the Breton March, along with many others died in that skirmish.[1] But this deed could not be avenged at that time, because the enemy had so dispersed after the attack that there was no indication as to where they could be found.

10. [Charles] also conquered the Bretons, who live along the sea in the westernmost part of Gaul. Since they were not subject to him, he sent a force against them [in 786]. The Bretons were forced to surrender hostages and to promise that they would follow his orders....

11. Then the Bavarian war suddenly broke out, but it was brought to a quick end. That war was a product of the pride and foolishness of Duke Tassilo. His wife, who urged him to it, was the daughter of King Desiderius and she thought that she could take revenge for [Charles's] expulsion of her father [from the kingdom of Lombardy] through her husband. Thus, after Tassilo had struck a deal with the Huns,[2] who lived to the east of the Bavarians, he

---

[1] This battle of Roncevaux formed the core of the later epic poem, *The Song of Roland*.

[2] There were no longer any Huns; it was the name Einhard sometimes used for the Avars, a group from Central Asia who had taken the place of the Huns in East Central Europe.

attempted not only to disobey the king, but to provoke him to war. The king in his fury could not abide [the duke's] defiance, which seemed outrageous [to him], and so he gathered troops from all over [Francia] and prepared to invade Bavaria. He himself led that great force [in 787] to the River Lech, which separates the Bavarians from the Alemannians. Before entering the province [of Bavaria], he set up camp on the bank of the river [Lech] and sent representatives to learn the duke's intentions. But Tassilo [now] realized that holding out would benefit neither himself nor his people and so he humbly surrendered to the king. He submitted the hostages demanded, among whom was his own son Theodo, and he also swore with an oath that he would not [in the future] listen to anyone who advised him to rebel against the king's authority. And so this war, which [had] seemed likely to be the greatest conflict of all, was brought to the quickest end. But a little later [that was in 788] Tassilo was summoned before the king and not allowed to leave. The province, which he had [once] held, was not given to another duke to rule, but to [a series of] counts.

12. After [Tassilo's] insurrection had been settled in this way, [the king] declared war against the Slavs, whom we normally refer to as the Wilzi, but who are properly called the Welatabi in their own language. In that war the Saxons fought as auxiliaries alongside the other peoples who were ordered to march in the king's army, but the obedience [of the Saxons] was insincere and lacking in complete commitment. That war came about because [the Slavs] were constantly harassing and attacking the Abodrites, who had once allied themselves with the Franks. [The Slavs] were not inclined [in this matter] to listen to the [king's] commands.

A certain gulf [the Baltic Sea] with an unknown length and a width no more than a hundred miles wide and in many places [much] narrower runs from the western ocean towards the east. Many peoples live around this sea. In fact, the Danes and Swedes, whom we call Northmen, live along the northern shore [of the Baltic] and on all the islands located there. The Slavs, Estonians, and other peoples live along the southern shore [of the Baltic]. The Welatabi were the most prominent of these peoples and it was against them that the king now took up war. He beat them so [badly] and brought them under his control in the one and only campaign he personally waged [against them], that from that point on they never thought of refusing to obey his commands.

13. Aside from the war against the Saxons, the greatest of all the wars waged by [Charles] was the one against the Avars or Huns, which came next [in 791]. He managed that war with greater attention and preparation than his other wars. Even then, he still led one campaign himself into Pannonia, a province then occupied by the Avars. He turned the other campaigns over to his son Pepin, to the governors of the provinces, and to the counts and even their representatives. These men very vigorously conducted this war and finally brought it to a close in its eighth year [it actually ended in 803]. How many battles occurred in that war and how much blood was spilled is indicated by the utter depopulation of Pannonia and the desertion of the khan's palace; in fact, there is hardly a trace [now] that people once lived there. All the nobility of the Huns died out in this war and all their glory vanished. All the wealth and treasure they had collected over many years was seized. No one can recall any war against the Franks that left them richer or better stocked with resources. Until then they had seemed almost impoverished. So much gold and silver was found in the [khan's] palace and so many precious objects were taken in this war, that it might be fairly said that the Franks had justly seized from the Huns what the Huns had unjustly seized from other peoples. Only two Frankish leaders died in that war: Eric, the duke of Friuli, who was ambushed by the people of Tersatto, a seaside city in Liburnia and Gerold, the governor of Bavaria....

14. Charles's final war was the one taken up against the Northmen who are called Danes. First they had operated as pirates, but then they raided the coasts of Gaul and Germany with larger fleets. Their king, Godefrid, was so filled with vain ambition, that he vowed to take control of all Germany. Indeed, he already thought of Frisia and Saxony as his own provinces and had [first] brought the Abodrites, who were his neighbors, under his power and [then] made them pay tribute to him. He even bragged that he would soon come to Aachen, where king [Charles] held court, with a vast army. Some stock was put in his boast, although it was idle, for it was believed that he was about to start something like this, but was suddenly stopped by death. For he was murdered by one of his own attendants and, thus, both his life and the war he had begun came to a sudden end [at the same time].

15. These [then] were the wars that that mighty king waged with great skill and success in many lands over the forty-seven years he reigned. In those wars he so splendidly added to the Frankish kingdom, which he had received

in great and strong condition from his father Pepin, that he nearly doubled its size....

16. He also increased the glory of his kingdom by winning over kings and peoples through friendly means. In this way he so completely won over Alfonso [II], the king of Galicia and Asturias, that when he sent letters or emissaries to Charles, he ordered that in Charles's presence he was only to be referred to as his subject. By his generosity he had so impressed the Irish kings with his goodwill, that they publicly declared that he was certainly their lord and they were his subjects and servants. Some letters they sent to [Charles] still survive and testify to this sort of feeling toward him.

He had such friendly relations with Harun-al-Raschid, the king of the Persians,[1] who held almost all the east except India, that [Harun] counted the favor of his friendship as more valuable than that of all the kings and rulers in the world and thought that only [Charles] was worthy of receiving his honor and generosity. Indeed, when [Charles's] representatives, whom he had sent loaded with gifts for the most Holy Sepulcher of our Lord and Savior [in Jerusalem] and for the place of his resurrection, came before [Harun] and informed him of their lord's wishes, he not only allowed them to complete their mission, but even handed over that sacred and salvific place, so that it might be considered as under Charles's control.[2] [Harun] sent his own representatives back with [Charles's] and he sent magnificent gifts for him, among which were robes, spices, and other riches of the east. A few years before this he had sent an elephant, the only one he then possessed, to Charles who had asked him [for such an animal].

The emperors of Constantinople, Nicephorus [I], Michael [I], and Leo [V], who were also voluntarily seeking friendship and an alliance with Charles, sent many representatives to him. But when he took up the title of emperor, [it seemed] to them that he might want to seize their empire. Thus, [Charles] struck a very strong treaty [with them], so that no [potential] source of trouble of any sort might remain between them. For the Romans and Greeks were always suspicious of Frankish power; hence that Greek proverb which still circulates: "Have a Frank as a friend, never as a neighbor."

17. Despite being so committed to increasing the size of the kingdom and to subduing foreign peoples and being so constantly preoccupied with business of this kind, [Charles] still took up many projects in different places to improve and beautify the kingdom. He achieved some of them, but not all. Probably the most outstanding of these [projects] are the church of the Holy Mother of God in Aachen, which is a remarkable edifice, and the bridge spanning the Rhine River at Mainz, which was half a mile long, the width of the river at that point. But that bridge burned down the year before Charles died. Although he thought of rebuilding it, this time in stone rather than wood, his sudden death prevented that. He also began [to build two] splendid palaces, one not far from the city of Mainz, on the [royal] estate of Ingelheim, and the other at Nijmegen on the River Waal, which passes along the south side of the island of the Batavians. Even then, if he learned that sacred churches had fallen into ruin because of their age anywhere in his kingdom, he ordered the bishops and priests responsible for them to repair them and charged his representatives with insuring that his orders had been followed.

He [also] constructed a fleet for use against the Northmen. Ships were built for this purpose near the rivers that flow from Gaul and Germany into the North Sea. Since the Northmen were constantly raiding and ravaging the coasts of Gaul and Germany, fortifications and guards were set up at all the ports and at the mouth of every river that seemed large enough to accommodate ships. With such fortifications he stopped the enemy from being able to come and go [freely]. He took the same [precautions] in the south, along the coasts of the province of Narbonne and Septimania and along the whole coast of Italy up to Rome, where the Moors[3] had recently taken to plundering. Through these measures, Italy suffered no great harm from the Moors while [Charles] lived, nor did Gaul and Germany suffer from the Northmen. The Moors did, however, through betrayal capture and pillage Civitavécchia, a city of Etruria, and the Northmen raided some islands in Frisia not far from the German coastline.

18. It is widely recognized that, in these ways, [Charles] protected, increased the size of, and beautified his kingdom. Now I should begin at this point to speak of the

---

[1] Harun (r.786–809) was the caliph at Baghdad.

[2] One of Charlemagne's ambassadors had obtained the keys of the Holy Sepulcher from the Patriarch of Jerusalem in 799. Harun had nothing to do with this, and Jerusalem was never under Charlemagne's control.

[3] Muslims.

character of his mind, his supreme steadfastness in good times and bad, and those other things that belong to his spiritual and domestic life.

After the death of his father [in 768], when he was sharing the kingdom with his brother [Carloman], he endured the pettiness and jealousy of his brother with such great patience, that it seemed remarkable to all that he could not be provoked to anger by him. Then [in 770], at the urging of his mother [Bertrada], he married a daughter of Desiderius, the king of the Lombards, but for some unknown reason he sent her away after a year and took Hildegard [758–783], a Swabian woman of distinct nobility. She bore him three sons, namely Charles, Pepin, and Louis, and the same number of daughters, Rotrude, Bertha, and Gisela. He had three other daughters, Theoderada, Hiltrude, and Rothaide, two by his wife Fastrada, who was an eastern Frank (that is to say, German), and a third by some concubine, whose name now escapes me. When Fastrada died [in 794], [Charles] married Liutgard, an Alemannian woman, who bore no children. After her death [in 800], he took four concubines: Madelgard, who gave birth to a daughter by the name of Ruothilde; Gersvinda, a Saxon, by whom a daughter by the name of Adaltrude was born; Regina, who bore Drogo and Hugh; and Adallinda who gave him Theoderic.

[Charles's] mother, Bertrada, also spent her old age in great honor with him. He treated her with the greatest respect, to the point that there was never any trouble between them, except over the divorce of King Desiderius's daughter, whom he had married at her urging. She died [in 783], not long after Hildegard's death, but [had lived long enough] to have seen three grandsons and the same number of granddaughters in her son's house. [Charles] saw to it that she was buried with great honor in St-Denis, the same church where his father lay.

He had only one sister, whose name was Gisela. She had devoted herself to the religious life from the time she was a girl. As he had with his mother, he treated her with the greatest affection. She died a few years before him [in 810] in the monastery [that is, the convent of Chelles where she was abbess] in which she had spent her life.

19. [Charles] believed that his children, both his daughters and his sons, should be educated, first in the liberal arts, which he himself had studied. Then, he saw to it that when the boys had reached the right age they were trained to ride in the Frankish fashion, to fight, and to hunt. But he ordered his daughters to learn how to work

with wool, how to spin and weave it, so that they might not grow dull from inactivity and [instead might] learn to value work and virtuous activity.

Out of all these children he lost only two sons and one daughter before he himself died: Charles, his eldest son [who died in 811], Pepin, whom he had set up as king of Italy [died in 810], and Rotrude, his eldest daughter, who [in 781] was engaged to Constantine, emperor of the Greeks [she died in 810]. Pepin left behind only one surviving son, Bernard [who died in 818], but five daughters: Adelhaid, Atula, Gundrada, Berthaid, and Theoderada. The king displayed a special token of affection toward his [grandchildren], since when his son [Pepin] died he saw to it that his grandson [Bernard] succeeded his father [as king of Italy] and he arranged for his granddaughters to be raised alongside his own daughters. Despite the surpassing greatness [of his spirit], he was deeply disturbed by the deaths of his sons and daughter, and his affection [toward his children], which was just as strong [a part of his character], drove him to tears.

When he was informed of the death of Hadrian, the Roman pontiff [d.795], he cried so much that it was as if he had lost a brother or a deeply loved son, for he had thought of him as a special friend. [Charles] was, by nature, a good friend, for he easily made friends and firmly held on to them. Indeed, he treated with the greatest respect those he had bound closely to himself in a relationship of this sort.

He was so attentive to raising his sons and daughters, that when he was home he always ate his meals with them and when he traveled he always took them with him, his sons riding beside him, while his daughters followed behind. A special rearguard of his men was appointed to watch over them. Although his daughters were extremely beautiful women and were deeply loved by him, it is strange to have to report that he never wanted to give any of them away in marriage to anyone, whether it be to a Frankish noble or to a foreigner. Instead he kept them close beside him at home until his death, saying that he could not stand to be parted from their company. Although he was otherwise happy, this situation [that is, the affairs of his daughters] caused him no end of trouble. But he always acted as if there was no suspicion of any sexual scandal on their part or that any such rumor had already spread far and wide.

20. Earlier I chose not to mention with the others [Charles's] son Pepin [the Hunchback] who was born to him by a concubine [named Himiltrude]. He was hand-

some in appearance, but hunchbacked. When his father had taken up the war against the Huns [in 792] and was wintering in Bavaria, [Pepin] pretended to be sick and entered into a conspiracy against his father with certain leading Franks who had enticed him with the false promise of a kingdom [of his own]. After the plot was uncovered and the conspirators were condemned, [Pepin] was tonsured and allowed to pursue the religious life he had always wanted in the monastery of Prüm [where he died in 811].

Another powerful conspiracy against Charles had arisen even earlier [in 785–786] in Germany, but all its perpetrators [led by Hardrad] were sent into exile; some blinded, others unharmed. Only three conspirators lost their lives, since to avoid arrest they had drawn their swords to defend themselves and had even killed some men [in the process]. They were cut down themselves, because there was [simply] no other way to subdue them. But it is [widely] believed that the cruelty of Queen Fastrada was the cause and source of these conspiracies, since in both cases these men conspired against the king because it looked as if [Charles] had savagely departed from his usual kind and gentle ways by consenting to the cruel ways of his wife. Otherwise, [Charles] passed his whole life with the highest love and esteem of everyone, both at home and abroad, and not the least charge of cruelty or unfairness was ever brought against him by anyone....

22. [Charles] had a large and powerful body. He was tall [at slightly over six feet or 1.83 meters], but not disproportionately so, since it is known that his height was seven times the length of his own foot. The crown of his head was round, his eyes were noticeably large and full of life, his nose was a little longer than average, his hair was grey and handsome, and his face was attractive and cheerful. Hence, his physical presence was [always] commanding and dignified, whether he was sitting or standing. Although his neck seemed short and thick and his stomach seemed to stick out, the symmetry of the other parts [of his body] hid these [flaws]. [When he walked] his pace was strong and the entire bearing of his body powerful. Indeed, his voice was distinct, but not as [strong as might have been] expected given his size. His health was good until four years before he died, when he suffered from constant fevers. Toward the very end [of his life] he also became lame in one foot. Even then he trusted his own judgment more than the advice of his physicians, whom he almost loathed, since they urged

him to stop eating roast meat, which he liked, and to start eating boiled meat [which he did not].

He kept busy by riding and hunting frequently, which came naturally to him. Indeed, there is hardly a people on earth who can rival the Franks in this skill. [Charles] also liked the steam produced by natural hot springs and the exercise that came from swimming frequently. He was so good at swimming that no one was considered better than him. For this reason [that is, the existence of the hot springs], he built his palace in Aachen and lived there permanently during the final years of his life until he died. He invited not only his sons to the baths, but also his nobles and friends. Sometimes he invited such a crowd of courtiers and bodyguards, that there might be more than a hundred people bathing together.

23. He normally wore the customary attire of the Franks. [Closest] to his body he put on a linen shirt and underwear, then a silk-fringed tunic and stockings. He wrapped his lower legs with cloth coverings and put shoes on his feet. In winter he covered his shoulders and chest with a vest made of otter or ermine skin, above which he wore a blue cloak. He was always armed with a sword, whose handle and belt were made of gold or silver. On occasion he bore a jeweled sword, but only on special feast days or if the representatives of foreign peoples had come [to see him]. He rejected foreign clothes, however gorgeous they might be, and never agreed to be dressed in them, except once in Rome when Pope Hadrian had requested it and, on another occasion, when his successor Leo had begged him to wear a long tunic, chlamys [a Greek mantle], and shoes designed in the Roman [that is to say, Greek] fashion. On high feast days he normally walked in the procession dressed in clothes weaved with gold, bejeweled shoes, in a cloak fastened by a golden clasp, and also wearing a golden, gem-encrusted crown. But on other days his attire differed little from people's usual attire.

24. [Charles] was moderate when it came to both food and drink, but he was even more moderate in the case of drink, since he deeply detested [seeing] anyone inebriated, especially himself or his men. But he was not able to abstain from food, and often complained that fasting was bad for his health. He seldom put on [large] banquets, but when he did it was for a great number of people on special feast days. His dinner each day was served in four courses only, not including the roast, which his hunters used to carry in on a spit. He preferred [roast meat] over all other food. While eating, he was entertained or

listened to someone read out the histories and deeds of the ancients. He was fond of the books of Saint Augustine, particularly the one called the *City of God*.[1]

He was so restrained in his consumption of wine and other drinks, that he seldom drank more than three times during a meal. After his midday meal in the summertime, he would eat some fruit and take a single drink. Then, after he had removed his clothes and shoes, just as he did at night, he would lie down for two or three hours. While sleeping at night, he would not only wake four or five times, but would even get up. [In the morning] while putting on his shoes and dressing, he not only saw friends, but if the count of the palace informed him that there was some unresolved dispute that could not be sorted our without his judgment, he would order him to bring the disputing parties before him at once. Then, as if he were sitting in court, he heard the nature of the dispute and rendered his opinion. He not only looked after cases such as this at that time, but also matters of any sort that needed to be handled that day or to be assigned to one of his officials.

25. [Charles] was a gifted and ready speaker, able to express clearly whatever he wished to say. Not being content with knowing only his own native tongue [German], he also made an effort to learn foreign languages. Among those, he learned Latin so well, that he spoke it as well as he did his own native language, but he was able to understand Greek better than he could speak it. Indeed, he was such a fluent speaker, that [at times] he actually seemed verbose.

He avidly pursued the liberal arts and greatly honored those teachers whom he deeply respected. To learn grammar, he followed [the teaching of] Peter of Pisa, an aged deacon. For the other disciplines, he took as his teacher Alcuin of Britain, also known as Albinus, who was a deacon as well, but from the [Anglo-]Saxon people. He was the most learned man in the entire world. [Charles] invested a great deal of time and effort studying rhetoric, dialectic, and particularly astronomy with him. He learned the art of calculation [arithmetic] and with deep purpose and great curiosity investigated the movement of the stars. He also attempted to [learn how to] write and, for this reason, used to place wax-tablets and notebooks under the pillows on his bed, so that, if he had any free time, he might accustom his hand to forming letters. But his effort came too late in life and achieved little success.

26. With great piety and devotion [Charles] followed the Christian religion, in which he had been reared from infancy. For this reason he constructed a church of stunning beauty at Aachen and adorned it with gold and silver, with lamps, grillwork, and doors made of solid bronze. When he could not obtain the columns and marble for this building from any place else, he took the trouble to have them brought from Rome and Ravenna. As long as his health allowed him to, [Charles] regularly went to church both morning and evening, and also to the night reading and to the morning Mass. He was particularly concerned that everything done in the church should be done with the greatest dignity and he frequently warned the sacristans that nothing foul or unclean should be brought into the church or left there. He made sure that his church was supplied with such an abundance of sacred vessels made of gold and silver and with such a great number of clerical vestments, that, indeed, in the celebration of the Mass not even those looking after the doors, who hold the lowest of all ecclesiastical orders, found it necessary to serve in their normal clothes. He very carefully corrected the way in which the lessons were read and the psalms sung, for he was quite skilled at both. But he himself never read publicly and would only sing quietly with the rest of the congregation.

27. [Charles] was so deeply committed to assisting the poor spontaneously with charity, which the Greeks call alms, that he not only made the effort to give alms in his own land and kingdom, but even overseas in Syria, Egypt, and Africa. When he learned that the Christians in Jerusalem, Alexandria, and Carthage were living in poverty, he was moved by their impoverished condition and used to send money. It was chiefly for this reason that he struck up friendships with kings overseas, so that the poor Christians living under their rule might receive some relief and assistance.

He loved the church of St. Peter the Apostle in Rome more than all other sacred and venerable places and showered its altars with a great wealth of gold, silver, and even gems. He [also] sent a vast number of gifts to the popes. During his whole reign he regarded nothing as more important than to restore through his material help and labor the ancient glory of the city of Rome. Not only did he protect and defend the church of St. Peter, but with his own money he even embellished and enriched it above all other churches. Despite holding it in

---

[1] See the excerpt from this book above, p. 14.

such high regard, he only traveled there four times during the twenty-seven years he reigned [in 774, 785, 787, and 800–801] to fulfill his vows and pray.

28. The reasons for his last visit [to Rome] were not just those [that is, his religious vows and for prayer], but rather because residents of Rome had attacked Pope Leo [III]. They had inflicted many injuries on him, including ripping out his eyes and cutting off his tongue.[1] This [attack] forced him to appeal to the loyalty of the king [in 799 at Paderborn]. Thus, [Charles] traveled to Rome to restore the state of the church, which was extremely disrupted, and he spent the whole winter there [until April 801]. It was at that time that he received the title of emperor and augustus, which at first he disliked so much that he stated that, if he had known in advance of the pope's plan, he would not have entered the church that day, even though it was a great feast day [Christmas 800]. But he bore the animosity that the assumption of this title caused with great patience, for the Roman [that is, Greek] emperors were angry over it. He overcame their opposition through the greatness of his spirit, which was without doubt far greater than theirs, and by often sending representatives to them and by calling them his brothers in his letters.

29. After assuming the imperial title, [Charles] realized that there were many deficiencies in the laws of his own people, for the Franks have two sets of laws that differ tremendously at a number of points. He decided, therefore, to fill in what was lacking, to reconcile the disagreements, and also to set right what was bad and wrongly expressed. He did nothing more about this than to add a few items to these laws, but even those were left in an imperfect state. But he did direct that the unwritten laws of all the peoples under his control should be gathered up and written down.

[Charles] also [ordered] that the very old Germanic poems, in which the deeds and wars of ancient kings were sung, should be written down and preserved for posterity. He began [as well] a grammar of his native language. He even gave [German] names to the months, since before then the Franks were used to referring to them by a mix of Latin and Germanic names. He also assigned individual names to the twelve winds, since until then scarcely more than four of them had been named....

30. At the very end of his life, when he was already weighed down by poor health and old age, [Charles] summoned his son Louis [the Pious], the king of Aquitaine and the only one of Hildegard's sons still alive, to come to him. When all the leading Franks from the entire kingdom had solemnly assembled and had given their opinion, he established Louis as the co-ruler of the entire kingdom and the heir to the imperial title. Then [on 11 September 813] he placed a crown upon his [son's] head and ordered that he should [henceforth] be addressed as emperor and augustus. This decision of his was widely approved by all who were present, for it seemed to have been divinely inspired in him for the general good of the kingdom. This act [the elevation of Louis] enhanced his powerful reputation and filled foreign peoples with great fear.

[Charles] then sent his son back to Aquitaine and, despite being slowed down by old age, went hunting, as was his usual habit. But he did not travel far from the palace at Aachen and passed what was left of the autumn hunting. He returned to Aachen around the beginning of November [813]. While spending the winter there, he was overcome by a strong fever and took to his bed in January. He immediately decided to abstain from food, as he usually did when he had a fever, because he thought that he could overcome the sickness by fasting or, at least, relieve [its symptoms]. But on top of the fever he developed a pain in his side, which the Greeks call pleurisy. Still he continued his fast and sustained his body with nothing more than an occasional drink. On the seventh day after taking to his bed, he died after receiving Holy Communion. It was nine o'clock in the morning on 28 January [814]. He died in the seventy-second year of his life and in the forty-seventh year of his reign.

31. His body was washed and looked after in a solemn manner and was [then] carried into the church and interred while everyone there wept. At first there had been some uncertainty about where he should be laid to rest, since when he was alive he had specified nothing about it. Finally everyone agreed that the most honorable place for him to be entombed was, in fact, in the very cathedral that he himself had built out of his own resources in Aachen, for the love of God and our Lord Jesus Christ and to honor his mother, the holy and eternal Virgin. He was buried in that church on the same day on which he died and a gilded arch with an image and

---

[1]   The attack attempted to mutilate the pope, but it did not succeed.

inscription was erected above his tomb. That inscription ran as follows:

> UNDER THIS TOMB LIES THE BODY OF
> CHARLES, THE GREAT AND CATHOLIC
> EMPEROR, WHO GLORIOUSLY INCREASED
> THE KINGDOM OF THE FRANKS AND
> REIGNED WITH GREAT SUCCESS FOR
> FORTY-SEVEN YEARS. HE DIED IN HIS
> SEVENTIES, IN THE SEVENTH INDICTION,
> ON THE TWENTY-EIGHTH DAY OF
> JANUARY, IN THE YEAR OF THE LORD 814.

32. There were so many signs of his approaching death, that not only other people, but even he himself knew that the end was near. For three straight years near the end of his life there were frequent eclipses of the sun and moon and a dark mark was seen on [the face of] the sun for a space of seven days. The arcade that he had erected with great effort between the church and palace fell to the ground in unexpected ruin on the day of the Ascension of our Lord. Similarly, the bridge over the Rhine River at Mainz, which he built, had taken ten years to complete. Though it was built out of wood with such great labor and remarkable skill that it seemed that it might last forever, it accidentally caught on fire and burned down in three hours [in May 813]. In fact, not a single piece of the bridge's wood survived, except some that was below water.

He himself, when he was waging his last campaign [in 810] in Saxony against Godefrid, the king of the Danes, was leaving camp before dawn one morning, when he saw a brilliant meteor suddenly fall from the sky. It cut across the open sky from right to left. As everyone pondered what this sign meant, the horse on which [Charles] was sitting suddenly fell down headfirst and threw him to the ground with such a bang that the clasp holding his cloak snapped and his sword belt was ripped off. The attendants who were present rushed to his side and lifted him up without his weapons or mantle. Even the javelin that he had been grasping tightly in his hand had fallen and now lay twenty feet or more distant from him.

Added to these events, the palace at Aachen frequently shook [from earthquakes] and the [wooden] ceilings of the buildings in which he lived constantly creaked. The church in which he was later entombed was hit by lightning and the golden apple that stood at the peak of the roof was struck by lightning and landed on top of the bishop's house next door. In that same church an inscrip-

tion written in red letters that ran between the upper and lower arches along the inside of the building [the inner octagon] gave the name of the builder of the church. In the last line of that inscription [the words] KAROLVS PRINCEPS[1] were to be read. But it was observed by some people that in the very year he died, a few months before his death, the letter that formed PRINCEPS became so faint that they were almost invisible. Yet Charles either rejected all these things or acted as if none of them had anything to do with him.

33. [Charles had] decided to draw up a will, so that he might make his daughters and illegitimate children heirs to some part of his estate. But the will was left too late and could not be completed. Nevertheless, three years before he died, he divided up his precious possessions, money, clothes, and other moveable goods in the presence of his friends and officials. He called on them to insure that, with their support, the division he had made would remain fixed and in force after his death. He described in a charter what he wanted done with the goods he had [so] divided. The terms and text of this [division of properties] are such:

In the name of the Lord God Almighty—the Father, Son, and Holy Spirit—[this] inventory and division [of goods] was made by the most glorious and pious Lord Charles, emperor and augustus, in the eight hundred and eleventh year from the Incarnation of our Lord Jesus Christ [that is, 810], in the forty-third year of his reign in Francia and thirty-sixth in Italy, [and] in the eleventh year of his empire, and in the fourth Indiction.

With pious and prudent reflection he decided to make this inventory and division of his precious possessions and the wealth that was located in his treasury on that day and with God's support he accomplished it. In this division he particularly wanted to insure that not only the gift of alms, which Christians solemnly provide for from their own resources, would be looked after on his behalf out of his own wealth and in an orderly and reasonable manner, but also that his heirs should be in no doubt as to what would come to them and so that they might plainly know and divide without legal strife or dispute those things among themselves in an appropriate partition [of goods].

Therefore, with this intention and purpose in mind, he first divided all the wealth and moveable goods (that is, all the gold, silver, precious stones, and royal vestments), that were found in the treasury on that day, into three lots. Then he subdivided two of those [three] lots into twenty-one parts, but kept the other lot whole. He divided those two lots into twenty-one parts because

---

[1] I.e., Prince Charles.

there are twenty-one metropolitan cities in his kingdom. In the name of charity his heirs and friends should pass one of those [twenty-one] parts to each metropolitan city. The archbishop then presiding over that church should receive the part given to his church and divide it among his suffragans [i.e. his bishops] in this way: one third should remain with his own church, two thirds should be divided among the suffragans [of his diocese]. Each of these divisions, which was made from the first two lots according to the recognized existence of the twenty-one metropolitan cites, has been separated off from the others and lies individually stored in its own repository under the name of the city to which it should be carried. The names of the metropolitan cities to which these alms or gifts should be given are: Rome, Ravenna, Milan, Cividale del Friuli [Aquiliea], Grado, Cologne, Mainz, Salzburg, Trier, Sens, Besançon, Lyons, Rouen, Rheims, Arles, Vienne, Moutiers-en-Tarantaise, Embrun, Bordeaux, Tours, and Bourges.

He wished the third lot to be kept intact so that, while the [other] two lots had been stored under seal in the [twenty-one] parts described, this third lot might serve his own daily needs as if it were property which he was under no obligation to part with or see alienated from his direct possession. This [arrangement] should hold for as long as he lived or he deemed the use [of the property] necessary for his well-being. But after his death or voluntary withdrawal from the world [into a monastery], this [third] lot should be divided into four parts and one of them should be added to the already [allotted] twenty-one parts. Another [the second] part should be taken up and divided by his sons and daughters, and by the sons and daughters of his sons in a fair and reasonable partition [of goods]. The third part, in keeping with Christian practice, should be set aside for the poor. The fourth part should, in like charitable fashion, be set aside to support the male and female servants of the palace itself. It was his wish to add to the third lot of his complete wealth, which also consists of gold and silver, everything else that was found in his treasury and wardrobe on the day [of his death]: namely, all the vessels and utensils of bronze, iron, and other metals, along with the arms, garments, and other moveable goods, both precious and ordinary, used for various things, such as curtains, bedspreads, tapestries, woolen goods, leather articles, and saddles. [He hoped] in this way that the size of the parts of the third lot would increase and that the distribution of charity would reach more people.

He arranged that his chapel, that is to say its church property, both that which he himself had provided and gathered together, and that which had come by way of family inheritance, should remain whole and not be divided up in any way. If, however, any vessels, books, or other objects should be found in the chapel which he had not indisputably given to the chapel, these could be purchased and retained by anyone who wished to have them after a fair price was determined. He similarly stipulated that the books that he had collected in great number in his personal library could be sold for a fair price to people who wished to own them and that the money [so raised] should be distributed among the poor.

Among his other possessions and riches, it is known that there are three silver tables and a gold one of great size and weight. He arranged and ordered that one of the silver tables, a square-shaped one containing an outline of the city of Constantinople, was to be sent to Rome to the church of St. Peter the Apostle along with the other gifts assigned to the saint. Another [silver table], this one having a round shape and bearing a likeness of the city of Rome, was to be transported to the episcopal seat of Ravenna. The third [silver table], which far surpasses the others in the beauty of its workmanship and its weight, contains a delicate and fine line drawing of the whole universe set within three linked circles. He stipulated that it and the gold table, which is referred to as the fourth, should be used to increase the third lot among his heirs and to increase the share of charity to be distributed from it.

[Charles] made and established this disposition and arrangement [of his goods] in the presence of the bishops, abbots, and counts who were able to be present at that time. Their names are inscribed here. The bishops [were] Hildebald [archbishop of Cologne], Richolf [archbishop of Mainz], Arn [archbishop of Salzburg], Wolfar [archbishop of Rheims], Bernoin [archbishop of Clermont], Leidrad [archbishop of Lyons], John [archbishop of Arles], Theodulf [bishop of Orléans], Jesse [bishop of Amiens], Heito [bishop of Basel], [and] Waltgaud [bishop of Liège]. The abbots [were] Fridugis [of St-Martin of Tours], Adalung [of Lorsch], Angilbert [of St-Riquier], Irmino [of St-Germain-des-Prés]. The counts were Wala, Meginher, Otulf, Stephen, Unruoc, Burchard, Meginhard, Hatto, Rihwin, Edo, Ercangar, Gerold, Bero, Hildigern, Hroccolf.

After examining this same charter his son Louis, who succeeded by divine right, saw to it that [this division of properties] was fulfilled as quickly and faithfully as possible after his [father's] death.

3.12 Modeling the state on Old Testament Israel: *The Admonitio Generalis* (789). Original in Latin.

Eleven years before he was crowned emperor, King Charlemagne drew up a set of general instructions, *The Admonitio Generalis*, for the great men of his realm, both lay and ecclesiastical, "to lead the people of God to the pastures of eternal life." He took as his model the biblical King Josiah, who discovered a copy of "the book of the law," realized how badly his people deviated from what was written therein, and immediately took steps to reform his kingdom (see 2 Kings 22–23). In effect, the many laws set forth by *The Admonitio Generalis*, only some of which are excerpted here, were Charlemagne's attempts to govern his kingdom according to the laws of God.

[Source: *Christianity through the Thirteenth Century*, ed. Marshall W. Baldwin (New York: Harper and Row, 1970), pp. 115–19.]

Our Lord Jesus Christ ruling forever.

I, Charles by the grace of God and the gift of His mercy, king and ruler of the kingdom of the Franks, devout defender and humble supporter of holy church, give greetings of lasting peace and beatitude to all grades of the ecclesiastical order and to all ranks of the secular power, in Christ our Lord, eternal God. Reflecting with dutiful and calm consideration, along with our priests and councilors, on the abundant mercy of Christ the King toward us and our people, we have considered how necessary it is not only with our whole heart and voice to offer thanks for His goodness unceasingly, but also to persist in the continuous exercise of good works in His praise so that He who has given our kingdom such honors may deign to preserve and protect us and our kingdom forever. Accordingly it has pleased us to solicit your efforts, O pastors of the churches of Christ and leaders of His flock and distinguished luminaries of the world, to strive to lead the people of God to the pastures of eternal life by watchful care and urgent advice and stir yourselves to bring back the wandering sheep within the walls of ecclesiastical constancy on the shoulders of good example or exhortation, lest the wolf, plotting against anyone who transgresses the canonical laws or evades the fatherly traditions of the ecumenical councils—which God forbid!—find him and devour him. Thus they must be admonished, urged, and even forced by the great zeal of piety, to restrain themselves within the bonds of paternal sanctions with staunch faith and unrelenting constancy. Therefore, we have sent our missi who by the authority of our name are to correct along with you what should be corrected. And we append herewith certain

chapters from canonical ordinances which seem to us to be particularly necessary.

Let no one judge this admonition to piety, by which we endeavor to correct errors, remove superfluous matter, and condense those things which are right, to be presumptuous. I entreat him rather to accept it with a benevolent spirit of charity. For we read in the book of Kings how the holy Josiah, traveling around the kingdom bestowed on him by God, correcting and admonishing, labored to recall it to the worship of the true God: not that I hold myself equal to his holiness, but because the examples of the saints are always to be followed by us, and we must bring together whomsoever we can to a devotion to the good life in the praise and glory of our Lord Jesus Christ....

Chapter 70, to the Clergy

Bishops should carefully see to it that throughout their dioceses (*parochiae*) the priests observe their Catholic faith and baptism and understand well the prayers of the mass; and that the psalms are chanted properly according to the divisions of the verses and that they understand the Lord's Prayer and preach that it is to be understood by all, so that each person may know what he is asking of God; and that the "Glory be to the Father" be sung with all dignity by everyone and that the priest himself with the holy angels and all the people of God with one voice intone the "Holy, Holy, Holy." And it should in every way be made clear to priests and deacons that they should not bear arms but trust in the protection of God rather than in arms.

Chapter 71, *Something to the Priest, Something to People*

It is likewise our will to urge your reverences that each throughout his diocese see that the church of God is held in His honor and the altars venerated with suitable dignity, and that the house of God is not used as a pathway for dogs and that the vessels consecrated to God are kept with great care or used with honor; and that secular or mundane affairs are not transacted in churches because the house of God must be a house of prayer and not a den of thieves;[1] and that the people when they come to the solemnities of the mass are attentive and do not leave before the completion of the priest's blessing.

Chapter 72, *to the Clergy*

And we also demand of your holiness that the ministers of the altar of God shall adorn their ministry by good manners, and likewise the other orders who observe a rule and the congregations of monks. We implore them to lead a just and fitting life, just as God himself commanded in the Gospel. "Let your light so shine before men that they may see your good works and glorify your Father which is in heaven,"[2] so that by their example many may be led to serve God; and let them join and associate to themselves not only children of servile condition, but also sons of free men. And let schools be established in which boys may learn to read. Correct carefully the Psalms, the signs in writing (*notas*), the songs, the calendar, the grammar in each monastery or bishopric, and the catholic books; because often some desire to pray to God properly, but they pray badly because of the incorrect books. And do not permit your boys to corrupt them in reading or writing. If there is need of writing the Gospel, Psalter, and Missal, let men of mature age do the writing with all diligence.

Chapter 73, *to the Clergy*

We have likewise taken pains to ask that all, wherever they are, who have bound themselves by the vow of a monastic life live in every way regularly in a monastic manner according to that vow. For it is written, "Render your vows to the Lord God";[3] and again, "it is better not to vow than not to fulfill."[4] And let those coming to monasteries according to the regular manner be first tested in the examination room and so accepted. And let those who come to the monastery from the secular life not be sent immediately on monastic tasks outside before they are well educated within. And monks are not to seek worldly pleasures. Likewise, those who are admitted to that clerical state which we call the canonical life, we desire that they live such a life canonically and in every way according to its rule; and the bishop should govern their life as the abbot does the monks.

Chapter 74, *to All*

Let all have equal and correct weights and just and equal measures, whether in the towns or in the monasteries, whether in giving in them or in receiving, as we have the command in the law of the Lord,[5] and likewise in Solomon, when the Lord says, "[Different] weight and [different] measure, my soul abhors."[6] …

Chapter 80, *to All the Clergy*

Let them teach fully the Roman chant and let the office be followed according to the direction of the nocturnal or gradual as our father Pepin, of blessed memory, ordered done when he suppressed the Gallican use for the sake of unity with the apostolic see and the peaceful harmony of the holy church of God.[7]

---

[1] See Matt. 21: 13.

[2] Matt. 5: 16.

[3] Deut. 23: 21.

[4] Eccles. 5: 4.

[5] See Lev. 19: 35–36.

[6] Prov. 20: 10.

[7] The "Gallican use" refers to the words and melodies used in Church liturgy in Francia under the Merovingians. Although Charlemagne here attributes the suppression of this liturgy to his father, Pippin III (d.768), in fact it was Charlemagne himself who was most instrumental in reforming the chants used in his kingdom along Roman models.

Chapter 81, *to All*

And we also decree, according to what the Lord ordained in the law,[1] that there be no servile work on Sundays, as my father, of good memory, ordered in the edicts of his synods, that is: that men do no farm work, either in plowing fields or in tending vineyards, in sowing grain or planting hedges, in clearing in the woods or in cutting trees, in working with stone or in building houses, or in working in the garden; nor are they to gather for games or go hunting. Three tasks with wagons may be performed on Sunday, the arms' cart or the food wagon, or if it is necessary to bear someone's body to the grave.

Likewise, women are not to work with cloth nor cut out clothes, nor sew or embroider; nor is it permissible to comb wool or crush flax or wash clothes in public, or shear sheep, to the end that the honor and quiet of the Lord's day be kept. But let people come together from all places to the church for the solemnities of the mass and praise God on that day for all the good things He has done for us.

Chapter 82, *to All*

And you are to see to it, O chosen and venerable pastors and rulers of the church of God, that the priests whom you send through your dioceses (*parochiae*) for ruling and preaching in the churches to the people serving God, that they rightly and justly preach; and you are not to allow any of them to invent and preach to the people new and unlawful things according to their own judgment and not according to Holy Scripture. And you too are to preach those things which are just and right and lead to eternal life, and instruct others that they are to preach these same things.

3.13 Ideals of family and fidelity: Dhuoda, *Handbook for Her Son* (841–843). Original in Latin.

A precious document for the values of the Carolingian laity—or, more precisely, for aristocratic lay women of the time—Dhuoda's *Handbook for Her Son* was written in the time of crisis just before the Treaty of Verdun (843). Her husband, Bernard, count of the Spanish March (Septimania), had once been an important courtier under Louis the Pious, but, accused of adultery with the queen, he was expelled from the court by Louis's sons. Her son William, to whom she wrote, was being held hostage at the court of Charles the Bald, partly to guarantee his father's "good behavior" and partly to ensure William's own advancement at court. Dhuoda herself was in the south of the Frankish kingdom, attempting, as she put it, "to defend the interests of my lord and master, Bernard." She had just given birth to another son, whom Bernard had "brought to him in Aquitaine." In her *Handbook*, motherhood, politics, and religion mingle as she tries to define a righteous and honorable rule of conduct for this life and the next. Just as Carolingian court scholars wrote "Mirrors of Princes" for kings to model themselves upon (see Einhard, p. 135 above), so Dhuoda wrote a "mirror" for her son in which he could "contemplate the health" of his soul, measuring it against the mirror's standard. We have no idea how William responded to Dhuoda's advice. Bernard was executed by the king shortly after she wrote, and William was executed in 850. Dhuoda may have died before she knew about these sad events; she was certainly contemplating death as she wrote her *Handbook*'s near-final section (Book 10). Compare the sources of conduct and the ideals of behavior that Dhuoda presents to William with those in *The Benedictine Rule* (p. 17 above). What evidence can you find

---

[1] See Exod. 20: 8–10.

in Dhuoda's writings to suggest that the Carolingian laity was influenced by the norms of monasticism? What evidence is there for other—and divergent—ideals, and where might they have come from? What does Dhuoda's writing suggest about the nature of lay aristocratic education in the Carolingian empire?

[Source: *Handbook for William: A Carolingian Woman's Counsel for Her Son*, trans. Carol Neel (Washington, DC: Catholic University of America Press, 1991), pp. 1, 5–6, 21–23, 95–100, and corresponding notes (notes slightly modified).]

The little book before you branches out in three directions. Read it through and, by the end, you will understand what I mean. I would like it to be called three things at once, as befits its contents—rule, model, and handbook.[1] These terms all mirror each other. The rule comes from me, the model is for you, and the handbook is as much from me as for you—composed by me, received by you....

Here Begins the Prologue.

Things that are obvious to many people often escape me. Those who are like me lack understanding and have dim insight, but I am even less capable than they.[2] Yet always there is he at my side who "opened the mouths of the dumb, and made the tongues of infants eloquent."[3] I, Dhuoda, despite my weakness of mind, unworthy as I am among worthy women—I am still your mother, my son William, and it is to you that I now address the words of my handbook. From time to time children are fascinated by dice more than all the other games that they enjoy. And sometimes women are absorbed in examining their faces in mirrors, in order then to cover their blemishes and be more beautiful for the worldly intention of pleasing their husbands. I hope that you may bring the same care, burdened though you may be by the world's pressures, to reading this little book addressed to you by me. For my sake, attend to it—according to my jest—as children do to their dice or women to their mirrors.

Even if you eventually have many more books, read this little work of mine often. May you, with God's help, be able to understand it to your own profit. You will find in it all you may wish to know in compact form. You will find in it a mirror in which you can without hesitation contemplate the health of your soul, so that you may be pleasing not only in this world, but to him who formed you out of dust.[4] What is essential, my son William, is that you show yourself to be such a man on both levels that you are both effective in this world and pleasing to God in every way.

My great concern, my son William, is to offer you helpful words. My burning, watchful heart especially desires that you may have in this little volume what I have longed to be written down for you, about how you were born through God's grace. I shall best begin there.

Preface.

In the eleventh year of the imperial rule of our lord Louis, who then reigned by Christ's favor—on the twenty-ninth of June 824—I was given in marriage at the palace of Aachen to my lord Bernard, your father, to be his legitimate wife.[5] It was still in that reign, in its thirteenth year on the twenty-ninth of November,[6] that with God's help,

---

[1] Dhuoda begins by describing her own work as threefold, reflecting the trinity of the one Christian God—Father, Son, and Holy Spirit. In doing so, she affirms her adherence to this central element in Catholic doctrine.

[2] See 2 Cor. 11: 23.

[3] Wisd. of Sol. 10: 21.

[4] See Gen. 1: 7.

[5] The marriage of Bernard and Dhuoda at the Carolingian capital, Aachen, suggests that they were children of families of great importance.

[6] The year was 826.

as I believe, you were born into this world, my firstborn and much-desired son.

Afterward, as the wretchedness of this world grew and worsened, in the midst of the many struggles and disruptions in the kingdom, that emperor followed the path common to all men. For in the twenty-eighth year of his reign, he paid the debt of his earthly existence before his time.[1] In the year after his death, your brother was born on the twenty-second of March in the city of Uzès.[2] This child, born after you, was the second to come forth from my body by God's mercy. He was still tiny and had not yet received the grace of baptism when Bernard, my lord and the father of you both, had the baby brought to him in Aquitaine in the company of Elefantus, bishop of Uzès, and others of his retainers.

Now I have been away from you for a long time, for my lord [Bernard] constrains me to remain in this city. Nonetheless I applaud his success. But, moved by longing for both of you, I have undertaken to have this little book—a work on the scale of my small understanding—copied down and sent to you. Although I am besieged by many troubles, may this one thing be God's will, if it please him—that I might see you again with my own eyes. I would think it certain that I would, if God were to grant me some virtue. But since salvation is far from me, sinful woman that I am,[3] I only wish it, and my heart grows weak in this desire.[4]

As for you, I have heard that your father, Bernard, has given you as a hostage to the lord king Charles.[5] I hope that you acquit yourself of this worthy duty with perfect good will. Meanwhile, as Scripture says, "Seek ye therefore the kingdom of God … and all these things shall

be added unto you,"[6] that is all that is necessary for the enjoyment of your soul and your body.

So the preface comes to an end.

[In Book One, Dhuoda expounds on William's primary task: to love God. In Book Two, she discusses the Trinity, the trinity of virtues (faith, hope, and charity), and the importance of prayer.]

Book Three

1. ON THE REVERENCE YOU SHOULD SHOW YOUR FATHER THROUGHOUT YOUR LIFE.

Now I must do my best to guide you in how you should fear, love, and be faithful to your lord and father, Bernard, in all things, both when you are with him and when you are apart from him. In this, Solomon is your teacher and your wisest authority. He chastises you, my son, and says to you in warning, "For God hath made the father" who flourishes in his children "honorable."[7] And likewise: "He that honoreth his father shall have joy in his own children"[8] and "shall enjoy a long life. He that obeyeth the father shall be a comfort to his mother."[9] "As one that layeth up good things,"[10] so is he who honors his father. "He that feareth the Lord, honoreth his parents."[11] "So honor thy father," my son, and pray for him devoutly, "that thou mayest be longlived upon the land,"[12] with a full term of earthly existence. "Remember that thou hadst not been born" but through him.[13] In every matter be obedient to your father's interest and heed his judgment.[14] If by God's help you come to this, "support the old age of thy father and grieve him

---

[1]   Louis the Pious died in 840, in his late sixties, so Dhuoda's comment is polite.

[2]   The year was 841. It is possible, given the long period between the births of Dhuoda's two sons, that she saw little of her husband in the interim. Bernard was heavily involved in politics and warfare across the Frankish dominions throughout their marriage.

[3]   See Ps. 119: 155; Douay Ps.118: 155.

[4]   See Job 30: 16.

[5]   William had been entrusted to Charles the Bald after the battle of Fontenoy in 841.

[6]   Matt. 6: 33.

[7]   Ecclus. 3: 3. Dhuoda here assumes a traditional attribution of this Old Testament book to David's son Solomon.

[8]   Ecclus. 3: 6.

[9]   Ecclus. 3: 7.

[10]   Ecclus. 3: 5.

[11]   Ecclus. 3: 8.

[12]   Exod. 20: 12.

[13]   Ecclus. 7: 30.

[14]   See Ecclus. 3: 2.

not in his life."[1] "Despise him not when thou art in thy strength."[2]

May you never do this last, and may the earth cover my body before such a thing might happen. But I do not believe that it will. I mention it not because I fear it but rather so that you may avoid it so completely that such a crime never comes to your mind, as I have heard that it indeed has done among many who are not like you.[3] Do not forget the dangers that befell Elias's sons, who disobediently scorned the commands of their father and for this met with a bitter death.[4] Nor should I fail to mention the tree of Absalom, who rebelled against his father and whom a base death brought to a sudden fall. Hung from an oak and pierced by lances, he ended his earthly life in the flower of his youth, with a groan of anguish. Lacking as he did an earthly kingdom, he never reached that highest of kingdoms promised to him.[5]

What of the many more who behave as he did? Their path is perilous. May those who perpetrate such evil suffer accordingly. It is not I who condemn them, but Scripture that promises their condemnation, threatening them terribly and saying, "Cursed is he that honoreth not his father."[6] And again, "He who curseth his father, dying let him die"[7] basely and uselessly. If such is the punishment for harsh, evil words alone, what do you think will happen to those who inflict real injury upon their parents and insult the dignity of their fathers? We hear of many in our times who, thinking their present circumstances unjust, consider such crimes without taking into account the past. On them and on those like them fall hatred, jealousy, disaster, and calamity, and "nourishment to their envy."[8] They lose rather than keep those goods of others that they seek, and they are scarcely able even to keep their own property. I say these things not because I have seen them happen, but because I have read about such matters in books. I have heard of them in the past, you hear about them yourself, and I am hearing them even now. Consider what will happen in the future to those who treat others in this fashion. But God has the power to bring even these people—if there are such—to lament their evil ways and, in their conversion, to do penance and be worthy of salvation. May anyone who behaves so ill stay away from you, and may God give him understanding.

Everyone, whoever he may be, should consider this, my son: if the time comes that God finds him worthy to give him children of his own, he will not wish them to be rebellious or proud or full of greed, but humble and quiet and full of obedience, so that he rejoices to see them. He who was a son before, small and obedient to his father, may then be fortunate in his own fatherhood. May he who thinks on these things in the hope that they will happen consider too what I have said above. Then "all his limbs" will work "in concert, peacefully."[9]

Hear me as I direct you, my son William, and "listen carefully," follow the "instructions … of a father."[10] Heed the words of the holy Fathers, and "bind them in thy heart"[11] by frequent reading so that "years of life may be multiplied to thee"[12] as you grow continually in goodness. For "they that wait upon"[13] God, blessing him, obeying the Fathers and complying freely with their precepts—such men "shall inherit the land."[14] If you listen to what I say above and if you put it into worthy practice, not only will you have success here on this earth, but also you will be found worthy to possess with the saints what the Psalmist describes: "I believe to see the good things

---

[1] Ecclus. 3: 14.

[2] Ecclus. 3: 15.

[3] Dhuoda here clearly refers to the conflict among Louis the Pious and his sons

[4] 1 Sam. 4: 11.

[5] See 2 Sam 18: 15.

[6] Deut. 27: 16.

[7] Lev. 20: 9.

[8] Gen. 37: 8.

[9] See *The Benedictine Rule*, chap. 34 above, p. 22: "all the members will be at peace." See as well 1 Cor. 12: 12–30.

[10] Here Dhuoda recalls the opening words of *The Benedictine Rule*. See above, p. 18.

[11] Prov. 16: 21.

[12] Prov. 4: 10.

[13] Ps. 37: 9; Douay Ps. 36: 9.

[14] Ibid.

of the Lord in the land of the living."[1] So that this other land may be your inheritance, my son, I pray that he who lives eternally may deign to prepare you to dwell there.

2. ON THE SAME TOPIC, ON REVERENCE FOR YOUR FATHER.

In the human understanding of things, royal and imperial appearance and power seem preeminent in the world, and the custom of men is to account those men's actions and their names ahead of all others, as though these things were worthy of veneration and as though worldly power were the highest honor. This attitude is testified in the words of him who said, "whether it be to the king as excelling, or to the governors."[2] But despite all this, my wish is as follows, my son. In the smallness of my understanding—but also according to God's will—I caution you to render first to him whose son you are special, faithful, steadfast loyalty as long as you shall live. For it is a fixed and unchangeable truth that no one, unless his rank comes to him from his father, can have access to another person at the height of power.

So I urge you again, most beloved son William, that first of all you love God as I have written above. Then love, fear, and cherish your father. Keep in mind that your worldly estate proceeds from his. Recognize that from the most ancient times, men who have loved their fathers and have been truthfully obedient to them have been found worthy to receive God's benediction from those fathers' hands....

[Dhuoda continues Book Three by citing examples of good sons in the bible and then turning to how William should act toward Charles the Bald and the magnates at court. In Books Four through Nine, Dhuoda takes up in turn the moral life; sin, punishment, and God's justice; the beatitudes; the two deaths of man (of body and spirit); prayer; and biblical and numerical metaphors.]

Book Ten

1. ON THE AGE YOU HAVE ATTAINED.

1 You have now reached four times four years.
    If my second son too were of this age,
    I would have another copy of this little book made
        for him.

2 And if in twice as many years and half again
    I were to see your image,
    I would write to you of more difficult things, and in
        more words.

3 But because the time of my parting hastens,
    And the suffering of pains everywhere wears my
        body down,
    I have in haste gathered this book for your benefit
        and your brother's.

4 Knowing that I cannot reach that time I have
        mentioned,
    I urge you to taste this as if it were the food of your
        mouth,
    Like a sweetened drink mixed with grain.

5 For the time at which I came to your father,
    Or when you were born of us into this earthly
        world—
    All this is known to us according to the dates of the
        months.

6 From the first line of this little book
    To its last syllable, know that
    All this is written for your salvation.

7 To find what is included here,
    Read the chapter headings
    So that you may easily take up what follows.

8 All the verses here—above and below, with all the
        rest—
    I have dictated for the good of your spirit and your
        body.
    I never cease directing you to read them aloud and
        keep them in your heart.

2. ON THE VERSES I HAVE BEGUN WITH THE LETTERS OF YOUR NAME.[3]

1 So that you may flourish and be strong, best of
        children,
    Do not hesitate to read the things I have spoken,
    Written down, and addressed to you.
        There you will easily find what is pleasing for you.

---

[1] Ps. 27: 13; Douay Ps. 26: 13.

[2] 1 Pet. 2: 13–14.

[3] The first letters of the following stanzas spell VERSI AD VVILHELMUM F[ILIUM], or "verses to William, my son." These verses form a synopsis of the preceding text.

2 God's word is living.[1] Seek it out.
　Diligently study its sacred learning.
　For your mind will be filled with great joy
　　　Throughout all time.

3 May that great and strong king, the good, bright
　　　Lord,
　Deign to nurture your mind through all that befalls
　　　you,
　My young son. May he protect you and defend you
　　　In every hour.

4 May you be humble of mind and chaste
　Of body, ready to do good service,
　So that you can readily accommodate yourself to all,
　　　Both great and small.

5 Foremost, fear and love the Lord God
　With all your mind and heart, and all your strength,
　And then honor your father
　　　In every way.[2]

6 As for that bountiful descendant of a line,
　Scion of his race and lineage,
　Him who shines in his great deeds—
　　　Never hesitate to serve him constantly.[3]

7 Love the great magnates; esteem
　Those who are first in the court, and act as the equal
　　　of those of low degree.
　Join yourself to those of good will, and take care
　　　Not to yield to the proud and the evil.

8 Always hold in honor the rightly constituted ministers
　　　of the divine rites,
　Those who are worthy of the prelate's status.
　With simple sincerity, commend yourself always with
　　　outstretched hands
　　　To those who keep the altars.

9 Help widows and orphans often,
　And be generous to pilgrims with food and drink,
　Prepare lodgings for them, and extend your hand
　　　with
　　　Clothing for the naked.

10 Be a strong and fair judge in legal matters,
　Never take a bribe from anyone,
　Nor oppress anyone. For he who has been your
　　　benefactor
　　　Will repay you.

11 Generous in gift giving, always watchful and
　　　prudent,
　Agreeable to all, with a winning manner,
　Profoundly joyful—such a countenance
　　　Will always be yours.

12 There is one who weighs out, who gives out in one
　　　direction or another.
　He returns for the merits of all what their deeds
　　　deserve,
　Granting the greatest reward, the stars of heaven,[4]
　　　For words and works.

13 And so, my noble son, seek diligently.
　Take care to hasten to receive
　Such great rewards, and turn away your eyes
　　　From the fires of blackened wood.

14 Although you count to your flourishing youth
　Only four times four years' growth,
　Your tender limbs grow older
　　　As you travel your course.

15 It seems very far from me,
　Wishing as I do to see the shape of your face—
　If strength were given me, still my merits
　　　Are not enough to win it.

16 May you live for him who made you
　With a clear mind, and join the worthy company of
　　　his servants,
　So that you may rise again in joy
　　　After your course is ended.

17 Although my mind is wrapped in shadows,
　Nevertheless I urge this, that you constantly read
　The pages of this little book written out above,
　　　And that you fix them in your mind.

---

[1] See Heb. 4: 12.

[2] See Mark 12: 33.

[3] Dhuoda here refers to Charles the Bald.

[4] Compare Rev. 2: 28.

18 With God's help these verses end,
  Now that eight years have twice gone by,
  At the beginning of December, feast of St. Andrew,
    The season of the coming of the Word.

  The verses end.

3. A POSTSCRIPT ON PUBLIC LIFE.

Here the words of this little book conclude. I have dictated them with an eager mind and have had them copied down for your benefit, as a model for you.

For I wish and urge that, when with God's help you have grown to manhood, you may arrange your household well, in appropriate order. As is written of another man who lived in this fashion, a man "like the most tender little worm of the wood,"[1] perform all the duties of your public life with loyalty, in a well-ordered fashion.

As for whether I survive to that time when I may see this with my own eyes, I am uncertain—uncertain in my own merits, uncertain in my strength, battered as I am among the waves in my frail toil. Although such is what I am, all things are possible for the Almighty. It is not in man's power to do his own will; rather whatever men accomplish is according to God's will. In the words of Scripture, "it is not of him that willeth, nor of him that runneth, but of God that showeth mercy."[2] Now, trusting in him, I say nothing else but "as it shall be the will of God in heaven so it be done."[3] Amen.

4. RETURNING TO MYSELF, I GRIEVE.

The sweetness of my great love for you and my desire for your beauty have made me all but forget my own situation. I wish now, "the doors being shut,"[4] to return to my own self. But because I am not worthy to be numbered among those who are mentioned above,[5] I still ask that you—among the innumerable people who may do so—pray without ceasing for the remedy of my soul on account of your special feeling for me, which can be measured.

You know how much, because of my continual illnesses and other circumstances, I have suffered all these things and others like them in my fragile body—according to the saying of a certain man, "in perils from my own nation, in perils from the Gentiles"[6]—because of my pitiful merits. With God's help and because of your father, Bernard, I have at last confidently escaped these dangers, but my mind still turns back to that rescue. In the past I have often been lax in the praise of God, and instead of doing what I should in the seven hours of the divine office, I have been slothful seven times seven ways.[7] That is why, with a humble heart and with all my strength, I pray that I may take my pleasure in continually beseeching God for my sins and my transgressions. May he deign to raise even me into heaven, shattered and heavy though I am.

And since you see me as I live in the world, strive with watchful heart—not only in vigils and prayer but also in alms to the poor—that I may be found worthy, once I am liberated from the flesh and from the bonds of my sins, to be freely received by the good Lord who judges us.

Your frequent prayer and that of others is necessary to me now. It will be more and more so in time to come if, as I believe, my moment is upon me. In my great fear and grief about what the future may bring me, my mind casts about in every direction. And I am unsure how, on the basis of my merits, I may be able to be set free in the end. Why? Because I have sinned in thought and in speech. Ill words themselves lead to evil deeds. Nevertheless I will not despair of the mercy of God. I do not despair now and I will never despair. I leave no other such as you to survive me, noble boy, to struggle on my behalf as you do and as many may do for me because of you, so that I may finally come to salvation.

I acknowledge that, to defend the interests of my lord and master Bernard, and so that my service to him might not weaken in the March and elsewhere[8]—so that he not abandon you and me, as some men do—I know that I have gone greatly into debt. To respond to great necessities, I have frequently borrowed great sums, not only from Christians but also from Jews. To the extent that I have been able, I have repaid them. To the extent that I

---

[1] 2 Sam 23: 8.

[2] Rom. 9: 16.

[3] 1 Macc. 3: 60.

[4] John 20: 26.

[5] Dhuoda may mean William's deceased ancestors, for whom he should pray; or she may mean the great men of the past.

[6] 2 Cor. 11: 26.

[7] See Gen. 7: 2.

[8] Dhuoda refers to her support for Bernard's position as count of the Spanish March.

can in the future, I will always do so. But if there is still something to pay after I die, I ask and I beg you to take care in seeking out my creditors. When you find them, make sure that everything is paid off either from my own resources, if any remain, or from your assets—what you have now or what you eventually acquire through just means, with God's help.

What more shall I say? As for your little brother, I have above directed you time and again concerning what you should do for him. What I ask now is that he too, if he reaches the age of manhood, deign to pray for me. I direct both of you, as if you were together here before me, to have the offering of the sacrifice and the presentation of the host made often on my behalf.

Then, when my redeemer commands that I depart this world, he will see fit to prepare refreshment for me. And if this transpires through your prayers and the worthy prayers of others, he who is called God will bring me into heaven in the company of his saints.

This handbook ends here. Amen. Thanks be to God....

[The book does not end, however. Dhuoda continues with the names of the dead in William's family; an epitaph that Dhuoda writes for her tombstone; and the psalms that William should recite on important occasions and how they should be said "with the heart's concentration."]

5. NAMES OF THE DEAD.

Here, briefly, are the names of those persons whom I failed to mention above. They are William, Cunigund, Gerberge, Witburgis, Theoderic, Gotzhelm, Guarnarius, Rothlindis.[1]

Other members of your lineage still flourish in this world with God's help. It is entirely at the will of him who made them to summon them too. Son, what should you do in regard to them but say with the Psalmist, "we that live bless the Lord: from this time now and for ever"?[2]

When a member of your family passes on, this does not befall except through God's power. When the Lord so commands, as in the case of your uncle the lord Aribert, you who survive must effect that his name be written down among the others, and you must pray for him.

6. I ASK THAT YOU WRITE THIS EPITAPH ON MY GRAVE.[3]

When I too have reached the end of my days, see to it that my name as well be written down among the names of those dead persons. What I wish and what I yearn for with all my might, as though it were happening now, is that you order the following verses to be cut in the stone of the place where I am buried, on the slab that hides my body. Then those who see this epitaph on my burial place may pour out worthy prayers to God for my unworthy self.

And as for any other who may someday read the handbook you now peruse, may he too ponder the words that follow here so that he may commend me to God's salvation as if I were buried beneath these words.

Find here, reader, the verses of my epitaph:[4]

† D † M †[5]

Formed of earth, in this tomb
Lies the earthly body of Dhuoda.
  Great king, receive her.

The surrounding earth has received in its depths
The flimsy filth of which she was made.
  Kind king, grant her favor.

The darkness of the tomb, bathed with her sorrow,
Is all that remains to her.
  You, king, absolve her failings.

You, man or woman, old or young, who walk back
  and forth
In this place, I ask you, say this:
  Holy one, great one, release her chains.

Bound in the dark tomb by bitter death,
Closed in, she has finished life in earth's filth
  You, king, spare her sins.

---

[1] The names here seem to refer to members of Bernard's family, not Dhuoda's, and thus contribute to the mother's emphasis on William's obligation to his patrilineage. Dhuoda surely does not wish her son to ignore his spiritual duty toward the other side of his family, however, for she argues that prayer on her behalf is among his primary responsibilities.

[2] Ps. 115: 18; Douay Ps. 113: 18.

[3] Other Carolingian authors, such as Alcuin, likewise composed their own epitaphs.

[4] Dhuoda here offers another acrostic. The initial letters of the following verses spell dhuodane, perhaps an alternate Latin spelling of her name or an adjectival form.

[5] Dhuoda abbreviates *dis manibus*, "to the Manes," the spirits of the dead.

So that the dark serpent
Not carry away her soul, say in prayer:
    Merciful God, come to her aid.

Let no one walk away without reading this.
I beseech all that they pray, saying:
    Give her peace, gentle father,

And, merciful one, command that she at least be enriched
With your saints by your perpetual light.
    Let her receive your amen after her death.

α † ω[1]

[In the final book, Eleven, Dhuoda copies a work by Alcuin on how to read and use the psalms.]

EXPANDING CHRISTIANITY

3.14 The Slavic conversion: Constantine/Cyril, *Prologue to the Gospel* (863–867). Original in Old Church Slavonic.

In 863 the brothers Constantine and Methodius were sent to Moravia at the behest of the Byzantine Patriarch Photius and at the invitation of the Moravian ruler Ratislav. They stayed about four years, translating the Scriptures into the Slavic dialect they had learned in Macedonia, which was not the language of Moravia but was nevertheless comprehensible to the people living there. Today this language is called Old Church Slavonic. In the prologue to his translation of the Gospels, Constantine speaks of the importance of literacy: "The soul lacking letters / Grows dead in human beings."

[Source: Roman Jakobson, "St. Constantine's Prologue to the Gospel," *St. Vladimir's Seminary Quarterly* 7 (1963): 16–19.]

I am the Prologue to the Holy Gospels:
As the prophets prophesied of old—
"Christ comes to gather the nations and tongues,
Since He is the light of the world"[2]—
So it has come to pass in this seventh millennium.   5
Since they have said, "The blind shall see,
The deaf shall hear the Word of the Book,
For it is proper that God be known."[3]
Therefore hearken, all ye Slavs!
For this gift is given by God,   10
The gift on God's right hand,
The incorruptible gift to souls,
To those souls that will accept it.
Matthew, Mark, Luke, and John
Teach all the people, saying: 15
"If you see and love the beauty of your souls,
And hence are striving
To dispel the darkness of sin,
And to repel the corruptness of this world,
Thus to win paradise life   20
And to escape the flaming fire,
Then hear now with your own mind,
Since you have learned to hear, Slavic people,
Hear the Word, for it came from God,

---

[1]   Dhuoda uses the Greek letters alpha and omega to invoke Christ. See Rev. 1: 8.

[2]   See Isa. 66: 8 and John 8: 12.

[3]   See Isa. 29: 18.

The Word nourishing human souls, 25
The Word strengthening heart and mind,
The Word preparing all to know God."
As without light there can be no joy—
For while the eye sees all of God's creation,
Still what is seen without light lacks beauty— 30
So it is with every soul lacking letters,
Ignorant of God's law,
The sacred law of the Scriptures,
The law that reveals God's paradise.
For what ear not hearing 35
The sound of thunder, can fear God?
Or how can nostrils which smell no flower
Sense the Divine miracle?
And the mouth which tastes no sweetness
Makes man like stone; 40
Even more, the soul lacking letters
Grows dead in human beings.
Thus, considering all this, brethren,
We speak fitting counsel
Which will divide men 45
From brutish existence and desire,
So that you will not have intellect without intelligence,
Hearing the Word in a foreign tongue,
As if you heard only the voice of a copper bell.
Therefore St. Paul has taught: 50
"In offering my prayer to God,
I had rather speak five words
That all the brethren will understand
Than ten thousand words which are incomprehensible."[1]
What man will not understand this? 55
Who will not apply the wise parable,
Interpreting to us the true message?
As corruption threatens the flesh,
Decaying and rotting everything worse than pus
If there is no fit nourishment, 60
So each soul no longer lives
Deprived of Divine Life,
Hearing not the Divine Word.
Let another very wise parable
Be told, ye men that love each other 65
And wish to grow toward God!
Who does not know this true doctrine?

As the seed falls on the field,
So it is upon human hearts
Craving the divine shower of letters 70
That the fruit of God may increase.
What man can tell all the parables
Denouncing nations without their own books
And who do not preach in an intelligible tongue?
Even one potent in all tongues 75
Lacks power to tell their impotence.
Let me add my own parable
Condensing much sense into few words:
Naked indeed are all nations without their own books
Who being without arms cannot fight 80
The Adversary of our souls
And are ripe for the dungeon of eternal torments.
Therefore, ye nations whose love is not for the Enemy
And who truly mean to fight him:
Open eagerly the doors of your intelligence— 85
You who have now taken up the sturdy arms
That are forged through the Lord's Books,
And who mightily crush the head of the Enemy.
Whoever accepts these letters,
To him Christ speaks wisdom, 90
Feeds and strengthens your souls,
And so do the Apostles with all the Prophets.
Whoever speak their words
Will be fit to slay the Foe,
Bringing God good victory, 95
Escaping the suppurant corruption of flesh—
Flesh that lives as in a sleep;
These will not fall but hold fast,
And come forth before God as men of valor,
Standing on the right hand of God's throne, 100
When He judges the nations with fire,
And rejoicing throughout the ages with the angels,
Eternally praising God the merciful,
Always with songs from the holy books,
Singing to God who loves man: 105
To Him befits all glory,
To the Son of God, honor and praise forever,
With the Father and the Holy Ghost,
Unto the ages of ages, from all creatures!

---

[1] See 1 Cor. 14: 19.

3.15 The Bulgarian Khan in Byzantine guise: *Seal of Boris-Michael* (864–889).

The Bulgars established themselves in Bulgaria in the 670s, as Byzantine control over the region south of the Danube weakened. The Bulgar khans (khan means "supreme ruler") and nobles subjected both Slavs and Greek-speaking Byzantines to their rule; they employed the Greek speakers in administering their new state. Influenced by Byzantine practices, these administrators affixed seals to official documents sent out in the name of the seal's owner. The seals were made of lead, a common metal. They were locally stamped and decorated with monograms or inscriptions or even human heads. Lead was used not only because it was malleable, but also to indicate the low-level, routine, and administrative, nature of the correspondence involved. Use of the inferior metal also acknowledged the lower status of the Bulgarian ruler within the Byzantine political hierarchy. Only the Byzantine emperor had the right to use gold seals, while notables with the highest titles were allowed, in exceptional circumstances, to use silver. Lower-ranking rulers who recognized the superior position of the emperors used lead.

When Khan Boris converted to the Christian religion and adopted the name Michael and the title of "prince" (see below, p. 161) he had seals made to advertise his new faith. On the seal shown here, the "obverse"—or "heads," as in "heads or tails"—side of the seal has a circle with the inscription, "Christ help your servant Michael ruler of Bulgaria." Inside the circle is the head of a long-haired and bearded Christ with a cross nimbus (halo) behind him. His right hand gives a sign of blessing, while his left hand holds the gospels. On the "reverse"—or tails—side is, again, a circle with an inscription, this time reading: "Mother of God help your servant Michael ruler of Bulgaria." Inside the circle is the head of Mary, mother of God, wearing a *maphorion* (a mantel with a hood), her hands upraised in prayer. Note that, influenced by Byzantine notions of rulership, the seal presents Boris-Michael as a territorial ruler (over "Bulgaria") rather than ruler of the Bulgar people (the "Bulgarians").

See Plate 11, p. 247, for a color reproduction of the seal.

(Kiril Petkov, ed. and trans., *The Voices of Medieval Bulgaria, Seventh–Fifteenth Century: The Records of a Bygone Culture* [Leiden: Brill, 2008], p. 33. Images courtesy of Dr. Ivan Jordanov.)

3.16 The Bulgarians adopt Christianity: Pope Nicholas I, *Letter to Answer the Bulgarians' Questions* (866). Original in Latin.

Christians mingled with Bulgars in the Bulgar state, and more arrived gradually in the course of the ninth century via Greek captives and deserters. In *c.*864 Boris converted to the Byzantine form of Christianity, taking the baptismal name of Michael, after Emperor Michael III (r.842–867). (See one of his seals in Plate 11, pictured on p. 247 in Reading through Looking.) But Boris-Michael did not intend to be subservient to the emperor. Thus in 866, seeking to reconcile Bulgar practices with Christian, he turned to Pope Nicholas I to clarify various points of the faith and how they should apply to the Bulgarians. His original questions have been lost, but the pope's advice suggests what they were.

[Source: Nicholas I, *Epistola* 99, in *Epistolae* 6, ed Ernest Perels, Monumenta Germaniae Historica (Berlin, 1925), pp. 568–600. Translated by William L. North.]

Not much needs to be said in response to your inquiries nor have we considered it necessary to pause long over each question, since we, with God's aid, are going to send to your country and to your glorious king,[1] our beloved son, not only the books of divine law but also suitable messengers of ours[2] who will instruct you concerning the details insofar as time and reason dictate; to them, as well, we have committed books that we thought they would need.

Chapter I.

Now then, at the very beginning of your questions, you state in excellent and praiseworthy fashion that your kind seeks the Christian law. If we tried to explain this law fully, countless books would have to be written. But in order to show briefly in what things it chiefly consists, you should know that the law of Christians consists in faith and good works….

Chapter IV.

We do not think we need to explain to you, who are rough and in some ways children in the faith, how many times or days in the course of a year one should abstain from meat. For the time being, on the days of fasting when one should especially supplicate the Lord through abstinence and the lamentation of penance, one should completely abstain from meat. For, although it is fitting to pray and abstain at all times, one should nevertheless be even more of a slave to abstinence during times of fasting. This is to say that he who recalls that he has committed illicit deeds, should abstain on these days even from licit things in accordance with the sacred decretals, namely during Lent, which is before Easter, on the fast before Pentecost, at the fast before the assumption of the holy mother of God and the ever virgin Mary, our Lady, as well as on the fast before the feast of the birth of our Lord Jesus Christ: these are the fasts which the holy Roman church received in antiquity and maintains. But on the sixth day of every week, and on all the vigils of famous feasts one should cease from eating meat and should apply oneself to fasting….

Chapter VII.

You further inquire, whether a clean or unclean person is allowed to kiss or carry the cross of the Lord when he holds it. [We answer] that for the person who is clean, it is completely permissible; for what is indicated in a kiss if

---

[1] Boris-Michael. Note that the pope bestows the title of king on him.

[2] Paul, bishop of Populonia, and Formosus, bishop of Porto.

not the love with which someone burns for these things? And in carrying it, what else is expressed if not the mortification or fellow-suffering of the flesh? Indeed, the Lord also ordered him to carry this cross, but in his mind; but when it is performed with the body, one is more easily reminded that it should also be performed in the mind....

Chapter IX.

You ask whether you should partake of the body and blood of the Lord every day during greater Lent.[1] We humbly pray to omnipotent God and exhort you all most vehemently that you do so, but not if your mind is disposed towards sin, or if your conscience—because it is unrepentant or unreconciled perhaps—accuses your mind of criminal sins; or if one of you is not reconciled to a brother through his own fault....

Chapter X.

You wish to know if anyone is permitted to perform any labor on Saturday or Sunday. Concerning this matter the oft-remembered holy Pope Gregory said, while addressing the Romans: "It has come to my attention that certain men of a perverse spirit have sowed some depraved things among you which are contrary to the holy faith, so that they forbid anything to be done on Saturday. What else should I call such people except preachers of the Antichrist, who shall, when he comes, make Saturday and Sunday be kept free from any work?... But on Sundays one should cease from earthly labor and devote oneself to prayers in every way, in order that whatever act of negligence has been committed during the other six days, may be expiated with prayers throughout the day of the Lord's resurrection.[2]

Chapter XI.

You ask whether you should cease from earthly work on the feast days of these apostles, martyrs, confessors, and virgins. Yes, [you should cease from work] on the feasts of the blessed virgin Mary, of the twelve apostles, of the evangelists and of their precursor, the lord John, of St. Stephen the Protomartyr as well as on the birthdays of those saints whose celebrated memory and feast day shall be held among you by God's favor. You should know clearly, that worldly work should cease on feast days in order for Christians to attend church more easily; to engage in psalms, hymns, and spiritual songs; to spend time in prayer; to offer oblations; to share in the remembrance of the saints; to rise to imitate them; to concentrate on divine scriptures, and to distribute alms to the needy....

Chapter XII.

Because you ask whether it is permitted to carry out judgment on the feasts of the saints, and whether the person, if he deserves it, should be sentenced to death on this same day, you should know that on those feasts when, as we have shown, one should cease from all worldly labor, we think that one should abstain all the more from secular affairs and especially from executions...

Chapter XIII.

Among your questions and inquiries, you said that you are requesting secular laws.[3] Regarding this matter, we would willingly have sent the volumes that we thought you might need at present, if we had learned that one among you could interpret them for the rest; if we have given some books concerning secular law to our messengers, we do not want them to be left [with you] when they return, lest by chance someone interpret them for you in a perverse way or violate them with some falsehood....

Chapter XVII.

Now then, you have told us about how you received the Christian religion by divine clemency and made your

---

[1]   The forty days preceding Easter.

[2]   Here Nicholas is thinking of Gregory the Great, Letter 13.1 to the citizens of Rome.

[3]   Note the close association that newly converted kings made between becoming Christian and gaining secular laws: see, for example, King Stephen's *Laws* for Hungary (below, p. 205). But the Bulgarians, who (as Nicholas implies) were more familiar with Greek than with Latin, did not write a written law code until the ninth century. It was based on an eighth-century Byzantine code that in turn depended on the law codes sponsored by Justinian.

entire people be baptized, and how these people, after they had been baptized, fiercely rose up against you with one spirit, claiming that you had not given them a good law and wishing to kill you and establish another king. [You then recounted] how you, prepared to oppose them with the help of divine power, conquered them from the greatest to the least and held them captives in your hands, and how all the leaders and magnates along with every one of their children were slaughtered by the sword, though the mediocre and lesser persons suffered no evil. Now you desire to know whether you have contracted any sin on account of those who were deprived of their lives. Clearly what did not escape sin nor could have happened without your fault was that a child who was not privy to their parents' plot nor is shown to have born arms against you, was slaughtered along with the guilty, even though he was innocent.... You also should have acted with greater mildness concerning the parents who were captured, that is, [you should have] spared their lives out of love for the God Who delivered them into your hands. For thus you might be able to say to God without hesitation in the Lord's Prayer: "Forgive us our debts, as we forgive our debtors."[1] But you also could have saved those who died while fighting, but you did not permit them to live nor did you wish to save them, and in this you clearly did not act on good advice; for it is written: "There shall be judgment without mercy for the person who does not exercise mercy."[2]... But because you erred more because of your zeal for the Christian religion and your ignorance than because of any other vice, with subsequent penance seek mercy and indulgence for these sins through the grace of Christ....

Chapter XXVI.

With regard to those who have slaughtered their kinsman, that is, someone related by blood such as a brother, cousin, or nephew, the venerable laws [of the Bulgarians] should be properly enforced. But if they have fled to a church, they should be saved from the laws of death but they should also submit without hesitation to the penance which the bishop or priest of the place has decided. "I do not want the death of the sinner," says the Lord, "but rather wish that he be converted and live."[3]...

Chapter XXXIII.

When you used to go into battle, you indicated that you carried the tail of a horse as your military emblem, and you ask what you should carry now in its place. What else, of course, but the sign of the cross?...

Chapter XXXIV.

You also asked, if, when a messenger arrives, you should set off immediately in order to get to the fighting or whether there are any days when it is not fitting to go forth into battle. On this matter we answer: there is no day which should be kept completely free from beginning or carrying out any kind of business, except (if too great a necessity does not compel you) the most celebrated days mentioned above, which are venerated by all Christians. But this is not because it is forbidden to do such things on these days. For our hope should be placed not in days nor determined by days, but all salvation should be expected absolutely from the true and living God alone. Rather it is because on these days, if the necessity is not unavoidable, one should spend time in prayer and the mysteries of so great a festival should be attended more zealously than usual....

Chapter XXXV.

You say that when you went forth into battle, you used to watch the days and hours and perform incantations, games, songs and some auguries, and you wish to be instructed on what you should do now. Regarding this matter, we would of course instruct you, if we did not think that you have been divinely instructed on this matter; for atop the divine foundation, we cannot build anything. Therefore, when you decide to go forth into battle, do not fail to do what you yourselves have recalled, i.e. go to the churches, carry out prayers, forgive sinners, be present at the solemnities of the Mass, offer oblations, make a confession of your sins to the priests, receive the reconciliation and communion, open the jails, loose the fetters and grant liberty to servants and especially to those who are broken and weak and captives, and distribute alms to the needy,

---

[1] Matt. 6. 12.

[2] James 2: 3.

[3] Ezek. 33: 11.

so that you may fulfill what the Apostle admonishes when he says: "Do everything, whether it be in word or deed, do it all in the name of the Lord Jesus."[1] For the things that you mentioned, that is, the observations of days and hours, the incantations, the games, iniquitous songs, and auguries are the pomp and workings of the devil, which you already renounced, thank God, in baptism and you cast off all these things completely along with the old man and his actions, when you put on the new….

Chapter XLI.

With regard to those who refuse to receive the good of Christianity but instead sacrifice to and bow down before idols, we can write nothing more to you than that you win them over to the correct faith with warnings, exhortations, and reason rather than with force. For they have knowledge but it is in vain: although they are people with capable intellects, they adore the products of their own hands and senseless elements, or to speak more truly, they bend their necks and sacrifice to demons….

Chapter XLVII.

You ask whether it is permitted to play games during Lent. Christians are not permitted to do this not only during Lent but also at any other time. But you are weak and are not yet strong enough to climb to the mountain to receive the highest commandments of God but instead have been placed in the flatlands like the former children of Israel, so that you may at least receive some of the simpler, lesser commandments. Therefore, because we cannot yet to convince you to refrain from games at all times, you should at least abstain from games, from the vain conversation and scurrility that do not befit the occasion, and idle chatter during the time of Lent and fasting when you should be spending more time and be more intent on prayer, abstinence, and every kind of penance….

Chapter XLIX.

Furthermore, you ask whether you are permitted to show your wives gold, silver, cattle, horses, etc. as dowry just

as [you did] before. Because it is no sin and the laws do not forbid it, we, too, do not forbid this from occurring; and not only this, but also whatever else you did before baptism, you are now clearly permitted to do….

Chapter LI.

You ask if you are permitted to have two wives at the same time; if this is not permitted, you know what the person in this situation should do at this point. Neither the origin of the human condition nor any Christian law allows a man to have two wives at once. For God, Who made the human being, made one male and one female at the very beginning. Of course, he could have given him two wives, if he wished but he did not want to do so….

Chapter LVII.

You claim that the Greeks forbid eunuchs to kill your animals, so that they assert that anyone who has eaten [meat] from animals killed by them has committed a grave sin. This sounds truly strange and silly to us. But because we have not heard the reasoning of the people who say these things, we cannot decide anything definitive concerning their assertion, since it is not yet fully known….

Chapter LXIV.

The number of days after a woman gives birth to a child that a man should abstain from [having intercourse] with her is proclaimed not by the products of our own wit but by the words of the Roman Pope and apostle of the English nation, Gregory [the Great] of blessed memory. Among other things, he says when he writes to Bishop Augustine, whom he had sent to [the Anglo-Saxons]: "A woman's husband should not come to lie with her until the infants to whom she has given birth, have been weaned….[2]

Chapter XCV.

You ask what we think should be done about those who flee to a church because of certain crimes. Now then,

---

[1] Col. 3: 17.

[2] Gregory the Great, in a set of letters transmitted by Bede (see above, p. 94).

although the sacred canons require that the decrees of the worldly laws be upheld and these laws appear to be without mercy towards certain persons, we who do not accept the spirit of this world nevertheless say that if someone flees to a church, he should not be removed unless he wishes [to come out] voluntarily.[1] For if long ago robbers and those guilty of various crimes fled to the Temple of Romulus for asylum and received protection from harm, so much more should those who flee to the Temple of Christ receive remission for their sins and be restored to their original state of complete safety, once the suspect has offered an oath on his own behalf.

[Closing]

… We have given these responses to your questions and proposals, insofar as the Lord has given them to us. It is not as much as we could say but rather as much as we thought could satisfy you for the time being. But when, by God's concession, you shall possess a bishop through the ministry of our prelacy, he shall teach you everything that pertains to his office. And if there are things that he does not understand, he shall receive them again from the authority of the apostolic see. May God, who has worked the greatest salvation among you, bring this to completion, make it solid, and give it stability and strength to the end [of time]. Amen.

---

[1]   Compare with the provisions on asylum in *The Theodosian Code* (above, p. 4).

TIMELINE FOR CHAPTER THREE

700

725 SALE OF A SLAVE IN ITALY ——————

750

754–67 ISHAQ, *LIFE OF MUHAMMAD* ——————

—————— 755–56 STEPHEN II, *LETTERS TO KING PIPPIN III*

—————— 789 *ADMONITIO GENERALIS*

*c.*800 ABU NUWAS, *TURNING THE TABLES* ——————   **800**

—————— 9TH C. AL-BUKHARI, *ON FASTING*

814–15 *POLYPTYQUE OF THE CHURCH* ——————
OF SAINT MARY OF MARSEILLE

—————— 825–26? EINHARD, *LIFE OF CHARLEMAGNE*

841–43 DHUODA, *HANDBOOK* ——————   **850**

863–67 CONSTANTINE/CYRIL, ——————
PROLOGUE TO THE GOSPEL

—————— 864–89 *SEAL OF BORIS-MICHAEL*

866 NICHOLAS I, *LETTER TO* ——————
ANSWER THE BULGARIANS' QUESTIONS

—————— *c.*883 *CHRONICLE OF ALBELDA*

700–900 MAJOR EUROPEAN ——————   **900**
SLAVE EXPORTS (MAP)

—————— 886–912 *BOOK OF THE PREFECT*

BEF. 940 IBN ʿABD RABBIHI, *I HAVE NEVER SEEN* ——————

950

MID-10TH C. DUNASH BEN LABRAT, ——————
THERE CAME A VOICE

To test your knowledge and gain deeper understanding of this chapter,
please go to www.utphistorymatters.com for Questions for Reflection.

IV

Political Communities Reordered (c.900–c.1050)

REGIONALISM: ITS ADVANTAGES AND ITS DISCONTENTS

4.1 Fragmentation in the Islamic world: Al-Tabari, *The Defeat of the Zanj Revolt* (*c*.915). Original in Arabic.

Al-Tabari (839–923) was born in Amul, on the southern shore of the Caspian Sea. His education took him to Baghdad, Basra, and Egypt before he returned to Baghdad (*c*.870) to write and teach. He was a prolific author, producing works on jurisprudence, the Qur'an, and history. His universal history, from which the excerpt below comes, began with Creation and continued to 915. He modestly called this extremely long work *The Short Work on the History of Messengers, Kings, and Caliphs*. The section printed here covers the last part of the reign of Caliph al-Mu'tamid (r.870–892), a period through which al-Tabari himself lived. Key to the events of this period was the revolt of the Zanj, black slaves who were put to work removing the salt from the marshes formed by the Tigris and Euphrates rivers. Led by 'Ali b. Muhammad, whom al-Tabari calls "the abominable" and "the traitor," the Zanj pillaged the cities around Basra and incited some local groups to challenge the caliph's authority. In response, al-Mu'tamid called on his brother al-Muwaffaq Abu Ahmad and Abu Ahmad's son Abu al-Abbas (later Caliph al-Mu'tadid) to wage war against the Zanj. The passage here begins in 880 with a victory by Abu al-Abbas. Although ruthlessly killing all the captives in this instance, father and son also offered amnesty and "robes of honor" to those who deserted the Zanj cause, severely dividing and weakening the opposition. They ultimately won the war against the Zanj in 883, but al-Tabari hints of other local defections from the caliphate, presaging its eventual decline.

Let us use this document to discuss once again how to read a primary source. Al-Tabari's account of the Zanj revolt is very different from the *Edict of Milan* on p. 1. Nevertheless, it should be subjected to the same series of questions. The answers lead to new questions that work just for al-Tabari (and perhaps for a small cluster of similar documents as well), in the same way as the answers to the questions about the *Edict of Milan* led to questions largely pertinent to it alone.

Who wrote it, and for what audience was it written? In this case, the answer is quite simple: the author was al-Tabari, and you know a bit about his career from the introductory note above. You can easily guess that his audience was meant to be his students and other educated readers in the Islamic world.

When was it written? Your editor has given you the date *c*.915. At this point in your studies, you need not worry much about how this date was arrived at. It is more important to consider the circumstances and historical events in the context of which a date such as 915 takes on meaning. Here you should be considering how, even as the caliphate was weakening, the Islamic world was open to wandering students and supported scholarly work.

Where was it written? The answer is, no doubt, Baghdad. But you should not be content with that. You should consider its significance at the time. Was it still the capital of the Islamic world? If not, why do you suppose al-Tabari settled there?

Why was it written? Al-Tabari begins this voluminous history with an extended passage in praise of God. He then says that he intends to begin with the Creation of the world and to continue by chronicling all the kings, messengers, and caliphs that he has heard about. But the first topic that he addresses in some detail is philosophical: "What is Time?" Thus, although al-Tabari does not say precisely why he wrote, he clearly wished to produce both a comprehensive chronicle about the powerful men in the world and a reflective work on the nature of history itself. But you should go beyond this answer to ask what other motives might have been at work. For example, might al-Tabari have thought that there were moral, practical, and religious—even doctrinal—lessons to be learned from history? Might he have been interested in legitimizing the Abbasids or other caliphs?

What is it? Clearly it is a history; the word is in the title. But what sort of history? Al-Tabari was careful to document many of his facts by citing the chain of sources (*isnad*) that attested to them. This technique was important in Islamic religious studies (see above, p. 114) and legal studies as well. Al-Tabari's work thus assimilates history with the scholarly traditions of other disciplines. Moreover his history might be called "universal," given its huge time frame. On the other hand, it is not a history of everything but rather of certain key figures.

What does it say? This is the most important question of all. To answer it, you need to analyze the text (or, here, the excerpt) carefully, taking care to understand what the author is describing and seeking further information (if necessary) about the institutions that he takes for granted.

What are the implications of what it says? This requires you to ask many questions about matters that lie behind the text. Important questions to ask are: *What does the document reveal about such institutions as family, power, social classes and groups, religion,* *and education and literacy in the world that produced it? What are its underlying assumptions about gender; about human nature, agency, and goals; about the nature of the divine?*

How reliable is it? Certainly al-Tabari's citations of his sources suggest that he was interested in reliability. On the other hand, you may ask if al-Tabari included everything that he knew, or if he had a certain "slant" on the events.

Are there complicating factors? In the Middle Ages authors often dictated their thoughts and then reworked them over time. Al-Tabari apparently finished lecturing on his *History* in about 915, but he continued to rework it. After his death, the work was copied numerous times—by hand. Paper was prevalent in the Islamic world, and it was cheaper and more abundant than parchment, which the West and the Byzantine Empire relied on. Nevertheless today we have no complete manuscript of al-Tabari's history, and scholars have had to reconstruct the full text from the various parts that are extant.

If you compare the questions and answers here with those introducing the *Edict of Milan*, you should be convinced that reading primary sources is both complex and fascinating.

[Source: *The History of al-Tabari*, vol. 37: *The 'Abbasid Recovery*, trans. Philip M. Fields, annotated by Jacob Lassner (Albany: State University of New York Press, 1987), pp. 24–27, 65–66, 132–36.]

Abu Ahmad remained in al-Firk for several days to permit his troops, and any others who wanted to proceed with him, to join on. He had prepared the barges, galleys, ferries and boats. Then, on Tuesday, the second of Rabi' I [October 11, 880], he and his clients, pages, cavalry and infantry reportedly left al-Firk, bound for Rumiyat al-Mada'in. From there they journeyed on, stopping at al-Sib, Dayr al-'Aqul, Jarjaraya, Qunna, Jabbul, al-Silh and a place one *farsakh* [about four miles] from Wasit.[1] He remained at the latter for one day and one night and was met by his son Abu al-'Abbas and a squadron of cavalry including his leading officers and men. Abu Ahmad inquired about the state of his men, and getting from his son a picture of their gallantry and devotion in fighting, he ordered that robes of honor be bestowed upon them and Abu al-'Abbas. Thereupon, the son returned to his camp at al-'Umr where he remained throughout the day. In the early morning of the next day, Abu Ahmad took to the water where he was met by his son, Abu al-'Abbas, and all his troops in military formation, as fully equipped as they would be when confronting the traitor's forces. Abu Ahmad sailed on until he reached his camp on the waterway called Shirzad, where he stopped. On Thursday, the twenty-eighth of Rabi' I [November 6, 880], he departed

from there and stopped at the canal called Nahr Sindad, opposite the village called 'Ab-dallah. He instructed his son Abu al-'Abbas to halt on the eastern side of the Tigris, opposite the mouth of the Barduda, and put him in charge of the vanguard. Then he allotted the soldiers' allowances and paid them. Following that, he instructed his son to advance in front of him with the equipment that he had in his possession, toward the mouth of the Bar Musawir Canal.

Abu al-'Abbas set out with the best of his officers and troops, including Zirak al-Turki, the commander of his vanguard, and Nusayr Abu Hamzah, the commander of the barges and galleys. After this it was Abu Ahmad who set out with his selected cavalry and infantry, leaving the bulk of his army and many of his horsemen and foot soldiers behind in his place of encampment.

His son Abu al-'Abbas met him with a show of captives, heads and bodies of slain enemies from among the troops of al-Sha'rani. For, on that same day, before the arrival of his father Abu Ahmad, Abu al-'Abbas had been attacked by al-Sha'rani who came upon the former's camp. Abu al-'Abbas dealt him a severe blow, killing a great many of his men and taking captives. Abu Ahmad ordered that the captives be beheaded, which was

---

1. The places mentioned in this document are in or near Iraq.

done. Then Abu Ahmad descended to the mouth of the Bar Musawir, where he stayed for two days. From there, on Tuesday, the eighth of Rabi' II [November 17, 880], he departed from Suq al-Khamis with all his men and equipment bound for the city which the leader of the Zanj had named al-Mani'ah bi-Suq al-Khamis. He proceeded with his ships along the Bar Musawir while the cavalry marched before him along the eastern side of the waterway until they reached the waterway called Baratiq, which led to Madinat al-Sha'rani. Abu Ahmad preferred to begin fighting against Musa al-Sha'rani before he fought Sulayman b. Jami' because he feared that al-Sha'rani, who was to his rear, might attack and thus divert him from the adversary in front of him. That is why he set out against al Sha'rani. He ordered the cavalry to cross the canal and proceed along both banks of the Baratiq. Abu Ahmad also instructed his son Abu al-'Abbas to advance with a flotilla of barges and galleys, and he himself followed with barges along with the bulk of his army.

When Sulayman, his Zanj troops and others noticed the cavalry and infantry proceeding on both banks of the canal and the ships advancing along the waterway—this was after Abu al-'Abbas had met them and engaged them in a skirmish—they fled and scattered. The troops of Abu al-'Abbas climbed the walls killing those who opposed them. When the Zanj and their supporters scattered, Abu al-'Abbas and his forces entered the city, killed a great many of its people, took many prisoners and laid hold of whatever was there. Al-Sha'rani and the others who escaped with him fled; they were pursued by Abu Ahmad's men up to the marshes where many drowned. The rest saved themselves by fleeing into the thickets.

Thereupon, Abu Ahmad instructed his troops to return to their camp before sunset of that Tuesday, and he withdrew. About five thousand Muslim women and some Zanj women, who were taken in Suq al-Khamis, were saved. Abu Ahmad gave instructions to take care of all the women, to transfer them to Wasit and return them to their families.

Abu Ahmad spent that night opposite the Baratiq Canal and in the early morning of the next day, he entered the city and gave the people permission to take all the Zanj possessions there. Everything in the city was seized. Abu Ahmad ordered the walls razed, the trenches filled, and the remaining ships burned. He left for his camp at Bar Musawir with booty taken in the districts and villages previously possessed by al-Sha'rani and his

men; this included crops of wheat, barley and rice. He ordered that the crops be sold and the money realized from the sale be spent to pay his mawla's pages,[1] the troops of his regular army, and other people of his camp.

Sulayman al-Sha'rani escaped with his two brothers and others, but he lost his children and possessions. Upon reaching al-Madhar he reported to the traitor [that is, the leader of the Zanj] what had befallen him and that he had taken refuge in al-Madhar.

According to Muhammad b. al-Hasan—Muhammad b. Hisham, known as Abu Wathilah al-Kirmani: I was in the presence of the traitor—he was having a discussion—when the letter from Sulayman al-Sha'rani arrived with the news of the battle and his flight to al-Madhar. As soon as he had the letter unsealed and his eye fell on the passage describing the defeat, his bowel muscles loosened and he got up to relieve himself, then he returned. As his Assembly came to order, he took the letter and began reading it again, and when he reached the passage which had disturbed him the first time, he left once more. This repeated itself several times. There remained no doubt that the calamity was great, and I refrained from asking him questions. After some time had elapsed, I ventured to say, "Isn't this the letter from Sulayman b. Musa?" He replied, "Yes, and a piece of heartbreaking news, too. Indeed, those who fell upon him dealt him a crushing blow 'that will not spare nor leave unburned.' He has written this letter from al-Madhar, and he has barely saved his own skin."

I deemed this news momentous and only God knows what a joy filled my heart, but I concealed it and refrained from rejoicing at the prospect of the approaching relief. However, the traitor regained self-control in face of vicissitude, and showed firmness. He wrote to Sulayman b. Jami', cautioning him against al-Sha'rani's fate and instructing him to be vigilant and watchful concerning what might lie before him....

On Tuesday, the first day of al-Muharram [August 12, 881], Ja'far b. al-Ibrahim, who was known as al-Sajjan, sought safe-conduct from Abu Ahmad al-Muwaffaq. It is mentioned that the reason for this was Abu Ahmad's battle at the end of Dhu al-Hijjah 267 [July 3–31, 881], to which we have referred above, as well as the flight of Rayhan b. Salih al-Maghribi and his men from the camp of the deviate, and their linking up with Abu Ahmad. The abominable one became completely discouraged at this; al-Sajjan was, reportedly, one of his trustworthy associates.

---

[1] A mawla could mean either master or servant. Here it undoubtedly refers to a servant or dependent.

Abu Ahmad conferred on this al-Sajjan robes of honor, various gifts, as well as a military allotment, and a place of lodging. Al-Sajjan was assigned to Abu al-'Abbas, who was ordered to transport him in a barge to a position in front of the abominable one's fortress so his [former] compatriots could see him. Al-Sajjan addressed them and told them that they were misled by the abominable one; he informed them what he had experienced because of the latter's lies and immoral behavior. The same day that al-Sajjan was placed in front of the abominable one's camp, a great many Zanj officers and others sought guarantees of safety; all of them were treated kindly. One after another the enemy sought safety and abandoned the abominable one.

After that battle which I have mentioned as having taken place on the last day of Dhu al-Hijjah of the year 267 [July 31, 881], Abu Ahmad did not cross over to fight the abominable one, thus giving his troops a respite until the month of Rabi' II [November 9–December 7, 881].

In this year, 'Amr b. al-Layth went to Fars to fight Muhammad b. al-Layth, his own governor in this province. 'Amr routed Muhammad b. al-Layth and auctioned off the spoils of his camp; the latter escaped with a small group of his men. 'Amr entered Istakhr, which was looted by his troops, and then sent a force to chase after Muhammad b. al-Layth. They seized him, and then delivered him to 'Amr as a prisoner. Thereupon, 'Amr went to Shiraz where he remained....

Now [August, 883] Abu Ahmad was sure of victory, for he saw its signs, and all the people rejoiced at what God had granted—namely, the rout of the profligate and his men. They rejoiced as well at God's having made it possible to expel the enemy from their city, and seize everything in it, and distribute what had been taken as booty—that is the money, treasures and weapons. Finally there was the rescue of all the captives held by the rebels. But Abu Ahmad was angry at his men because they disobeyed orders and abandoned the positions in which he had placed them. He ordered that the commanders of his mawlas and pages and the leading men among them be gathered together. When they were assembled for him, he scolded them for what they had done, judging them weak and castigating them in harsh language. Then they made excuses; they supposed that he had returned, and they had not known about his advance against the profligate, nor about his having pressed so far into the rebel's camp. Had they known this, they would have rushed toward him. They did not leave their places until they had taken a solemn oath and covenant that, when sent against the abominable one, none of them would

withdraw before God had delivered him into their hands; and should they fail, they would not budge from their positions until God had passed judgment between them and him. They requested of al-Muwaffaq that, after they had left al-Muwaffaqiyyah to fight, he order the ships transporting them to return and, thus, eliminate any temptation to those who might seek to leave the battle against the profligate.

Abu Ahmad accepted their apologies for their wrong-doing and again took them into his favor. Then he ordered them to prepare for crossing and to forewarn their troops just as they themselves had been forewarned. Abu Ahmad spent Tuesday, Wednesday, Thursday and Friday preparing whatever he would need. When this was completed, he sent word to his entourage and the officers of his pages and mawlas, instructing them as to their tasks when crossing [into combat]. Friday evening he sent word to Abu al-'Abbas and the officers of his pages and mawlas to set out for places which he, that is, Abu Ahmad, had specified.

Al-Muwaffaq instructed Abu al-'Abbas and his troops to set a course for a place known as 'Askar Rayhan, which lay between the canal known as Nahr al-Sufyani and the spot where the rebel sought refuge. He and his army were to follow the route along the canal known as Nahr al-Mughirah, so that they would exit where the canal intersects the Abu al-Khasib and reach 'Askar Rayhan from this direction. He forwarded instructions to an officer of his black pages to reach the Nahr al-Amir and cross at its center. At the same time, he ordered the rest of his officers and pages to pass the night on the eastern side of the Tigris, opposite the profligate's camp, and be prepared to attack him in the early morning.

During Friday night, al-Muwaffaq made the rounds among the officers and men in his barge. He divided amongst them key positions and locations which he had arranged for them in the profligate's camp. According to the assigned plan, they were to march towards these places in the morning. Early Saturday morning, on the second of Safar, 270 [August 11, 883], al-Muwaffaq reached the Abu al-Khasib Canal in his barge. He remained there until all his men had crossed [the waterway] and disembarked from their vessels, and the cavalry and infantry had assumed their positions. Then, after giving instructions for the vessels and ferries to return to the eastern side, he gave the troops the go-ahead to march against the profligate. He himself preceded them until he reached the spot where he estimated the profligate's would make a stand in an attempt to repel the government army. Meanwhile, on Monday, after the army had withdrawn, the traitor and his men returned to the city and stayed there, hoping to prolong their defense and repel the attack.

Al-Muwaffaq found that the fastest of his cavalry and infantry among the pages had preceded the main force of the army and had attacked the rebel and his companions, dislodging them from their positions. The enemy force fled and dispersed without paying attention to one another, and the government army pursued them, killing and capturing whomever they managed to catch. The profligate, with a group of his fighting men, was cut off from [the rest] of his officers and troops— among them was al-Muhallabi. Ankalay, the rebel's son, had abandoned him, as had Sulayman b. Jami'. Moving against each of the contingents which we have named was a large force of al-Muwaffaq's mawlas, and cavalry and infantry drawn from his pages. Abu al-'Abbas's troops, assigned by al-Muwaffaq to the place known as 'Askar Rayhan, met the rebel's fleeing men and put them to the sword. The officer assigned to the Amir Canal also arrived there, and having blocked the rebels' path he attacked them. Encountering Sulayman b. Jami', he took the fight to him, killing many of his men and seizing Sulayman. He made Sulayman a captive and delivered him to al-Muwaffaq without conditions. The people were glad to learn of Sulayman's capture, and there were many cries of "God is Great!" and great clamor. They felt certain of victory, since Sulayman was known to be the most able of the rebel's companions. After him, Ibrahim b. Ja'far al-Hamdani, one of the field commanders of the rebel's army, was taken captive; then Nadir al-Aswad, the one known as al-Haffar, one of the earliest companions of the rebel, was captured.

Upon al-Muwaffaq's order, precautionary measures were taken, and the captives were transferred in barges to Abu al-'Abbas.

Following this, those Zanj who had separated from the main body, together with the profligate, assaulted the government force, dislodging them from their positions and causing them to lose the initiative. Al-Muwaffaq noticed the loss of initiative, but he pressed on with the search for the abominable one, advancing quickly in the Abu al-Khasib Canal. This bolstered his mawlas and pages, who hastened to pursue (the enemy) with him. As al-Muwaffaq reached the Abu al-Khasib Canal, a herald arrived with the good news of the rebel's death; before long another herald arrived carrying a hand, and claimed that this was the hand of the rebel. This seemed to lend

credence to the report of the rebel's demise. Finally a page from Lu'lu''s troops arrived, galloping on a horse and carrying the head of the abominable one. Al-Muwaffaq had the head brought closer, and then showed it to a group of former enemy officers who were in his presence. They identified it, and al-Muwaffaq prostrated himself in adoration to God for both the hardships and bounties He had conferred upon him. Abu al-'Abbas, the mawlas and the officers of al-Muwaffaq's pages then prostrated themselves, offering much thanks to God, and praising and exalting Him. Al-Muwaffaq ordered the head of the rebel raised on a spear and displayed in front of him. The people saw it and thus knew that the news of the rebel's death was true. At this, they raised their voices in praise to God.

It is reported that al-Muwaffaq's troops surrounded the abominable one after all his field commanders had abandoned him save al-Muhallabi; the latter now turned away from him and fled, thus betraying the rebel. The rebel then set off for the canal known as Nahr al-Amir and plunged into the water, seeking safety. Even before that, Ankalay, the son of the abominable one, had split off from his father and fled in the direction of the canal known as Nahr al-Dinari, where he entrenched himself in the swampy terrain.

Al-Muwaffaq retired, with the head of the abominable one displayed on a spear mounted in front of him on a barge. The vessel moved along the Abu al-Khasib Canal, with the people on both sides of the waterway observing it. When he reached the Tigris, he took his course along the river and gave the order to return the vessels, with which he had crossed to the western side of the Tigris at daylight, to the eastern side of the river. They were returned to ferry the troops [back] across the river.

Then al-Muwaffaq continued his trip, with the abominable one's head on the spear before him, while Sulayman b. Jami' and al-Hamdani were mounted for display. When he arrived at his fortress in al-Muwaffaqiyyah, he ordered Abu al-'Abbas to sail the barge, keeping the rebel's head and Sulayman b. Jami' and al-Hamdani in place, and to take his course to the Jatta Canal where the camp of al-Muwaffaq began. He was to do this so that all the people of the camp could have a look at them. Abu al-'Abbas did this, and then returned to his father, Abu Ahmad, whereupon the latter imprisoned Sulayman b. Jami' and al-Hamdani and ordered that the rebel's head be properly prepared and cleaned.

4.2 The powerful in the Byzantine countryside: Romanus I Lecapenus, *Novel* (934). Original in Greek.

In Byzantine legal terms, a "novel" is a "new law." Emperor Romanus I Lecapenus (r.920–944) issued one such law on behalf of the poor in the countryside in 934. Newly powerful provincial landowners, collectively known as *dynatoi*, were taking advantage of a recent famine to buy up whole villages, enhancing both their economic and social positions. Romanus tried to set back the clock—he wanted the land to stay in the hands of the original peasant families or at least in the hands of their village neighbors. He insisted that the powerful "return [the land] without refund to the owners." What reasons can you give for Romanus's opposition to the powerful?

[Source: *The Land Legislation of the Macedonian Emperors*, trans. and ed. Eric McGeer (Toronto: Pontifical Institute of Mediaeval Studies, 2000), pp. 53–56, 59–60 (notes modified).]

Novel of the Lord Emperor Romanus the Elder

PROLOGUE

To dispose the soul in imitation of the Creator is the desire and ardent endeavor of those for whom it is a great and blessed thing to regard and to call themselves the work of the all-creating hand. As for those by whom this has not been accounted great and holy, they have the task of denying the Creation and the reckoning of Judgment, and, as with persons wholly content with life on earth and who choose to live their lives upon the earth alone, the display of their choice has been left in their wake.[1] Hence the great confusion of affairs, hence the great tide of injustices, hence the great and widespread oppression of the poor, and the great sighing of the needy, for whose sake the Lord rose from the dead. For He says, "For the oppression of the poor, for the sighing of the needy, now will I arise, saith the Lord."[2] If God, our Creator and Savior, Who made us emperor, rises in retribution, how will the poor man, who awaits only the eyes of the emperor for intercession, be neglected and altogether forgotten by us? Therefore, not only upon examination of the actions taken against them in the recent past or attempts to make amends, but also administering a common and lasting remedy to the matter, we have issued the present law to avenge them, having prepared this as a purgative and a cleansing of the predilection of greed. We have considered it advantageous

that now no longer will anyone be deprived of his own properties, nor will a poor man suffer oppression, and that this advantage is beneficial to the common good, acceptable to God, profitable to the treasury, and useful to the state. Careful attention to this subject, for the sake of which decrees and judgments restraining the wickedness of the will and curtailing the reach of the grasping hand have streamed down to all the officials under our authority, has not been long neglected, nor has [our concern] arisen inappropriately. But since evil is versatile and multifarious, and all evils—not least greed, if indeed not even more so—contrive to evade the grip of laws and edicts and to regard the inescapable eye of divine justice as of no account, these measures, ejecting and excising the crafty workings of the will of the evildoers, have as a result now warranted more secure and rigorous codification.

1.1. We ordain therefore that those living in every land and district, where after God our rule extends, are to keep the domicile which has come down to them free and undisturbed. If time continues to preserve this arrangement, let the subsequent acquisition by the offspring or relatives through testamentary disposition, or the intention of the owner's preference, be fulfilled. If, though, given the course of human life and the ebb and flow of time, the pressure of necessity or even the prompting of the will alone, be it as it may, the owner embarks on the alienation

---

[1] The general sense seems to be this: people who see themselves as part of God's Creation try to act in accordance with God's ways, while people who do not venerate the Creation will have to reckon with the Last Judgment; such people have left ample evidence behind them of their choice to ignore divine justice and to lead their lives in pursuit of earthly, not eternal, rewards.

[2] Ps. 12: 5; Douay Ps. 11: 6.

of his own lands either in part or in whole, the purchase must first be set before the inhabitants of the same or adjacent fields or villages. We do not introduce this legislation out of animosity or malice towards the powerful; but we issue these rulings out of benevolence and protection for the poor and for public welfare. Whereas those persons who have received authority from God, those risen above the many in honor and wealth, should consider the care of the poor an important task, these powerful persons who regard the poor as prey are vexed because they do not acquire these things more quickly. Even if such impious conduct is not true of all, let adherence to the law be common to all, lest the tare [weeds] brought in with the wheat escape notice.[1]

1.2. As a result, no longer shall any one of the illustrious *magistroi*[2] or *patrikioi*,[3] nor any of the persons honored with offices, governorships, or civil or military dignities, nor anyone at all enumerated in the Senate,[4] nor officials or ex-officials of the themes nor metropolitans most devoted to God, archbishops, bishops, *higoumenoi* [abbots], ecclesiastical officials, or supervisors and heads of pious or imperial houses,[5] whether as a private individual or in the name of an imperial or ecclesiastical property, dare either on their own or through an intermediary to intrude into a village or hamlet for the sake of a sale, gift, or inheritance—either whole or partial—or on any other pretext whatsoever. As this sort of acquisition has been ruled invalid, the acquired properties, along with the improvements since added, are to return without refund to the owners or, if they or their relatives are no longer alive, to the inhabitants of the villages or hamlets. For the domination of these persons has increased the great hardship of the poor, bringing upheavals, persecutions, coercion, and other concomitant afflictions and difficulties through the multitude of their servants, hirelings or other attendants and followers, and, to those able to see it, will cause no little harm to the commonwealth unless the present legislation puts an end to it first. For the settlement[6] of the population demonstrates the great benefit of its function—the contribution of taxes and the fulfillment of military obligations—which will be completely lost should the common

people disappear. Those concerned with the stability of the state must eliminate the cause of disturbance, expel what is harmful, and support the common good.

2.1. Let time hereafter maintain these measures for the common benefit and settled order of our subjects; but it is necessary to apply the approved remedy not only to the future, but also to the past. For many people seized upon the indigence of the poor—which time bringer of all things brought, or rather, which the multitude of our sins, driving out divine charity, caused—as the opportunity for business instead of charity, compassion, or kindness; and when they saw the poor oppressed by famine, they bought up the possessions of the unfortunate poor at a very low price, some with silver, some with gold, and others with grain or other forms of payment. Harsher than the duress at hand, in those times which followed they were like a pestilential attack of disease to the miserable inhabitants of the villages, having entered like gangrene into the body of the villages and causing total destruction....

EPILOGUE It is our desire that these regulations remain in force for the safety of our subjects for whose sake great and constant care is our concern. For if we have expended so much care for those under our authority, so as to spare nothing that contributes to freedom, on account of which lands, towns, and cities have, with the help of God, come into our hands from the enemy, some as the result of war, while others have passed over to us by the example [of the conquered towns] or through fear of capture and were taken before the trumpet's call to battle; and if we have striven, with the help of God, to provide our subjects with such great freedom from enemy attack, setting this as the goal of our prayers and exertions, how will we, after accomplishing so much against the onslaught of external enemies, not rid ourselves of our own enemies within, enemies of the natural order, of the Creation, and of justice, by reviling and repressing insatiety [endless desire], by excising the greedy disposition, and by liberating our subjects from the yoke of the tyrannical, oppressive hand and mind with the righteous intention to free them with the cutting sword of the present legislation? Let each of

---

[1] Echoing the parable of the wheat and the tares related in Matt. 13: 24–30; 36–43.

[2] Those holding the highest possible dignity conferred on non-imperial family members.

[3] Those who hold a high dignity conferred on governors of themes (military districts) or military leaders.

[4] The Byzantine Senate was an advisory body whose members were high civil officials and dignitaries.

[5] Philanthropic foundations administered by crown officials.

[6] The Greek word for "settlement" also embraces the notions of stability and prosperity among the rural populace.

those to whom judicial authority has fallen see to it that these provisions remain in force in perpetuity [forever], for the service of God and for the common benefit and advantage of our empire received from Him.

In the Month of September of the eighth indiction in the year 6443 from the creation of the world, Romanus, Constantine, Stephanus, and Constantine, emperors of the Byzantines and faithful to God.

4.3 Donating to Cluny: Cluny's *Foundation Charter* (910) and various charters of donation (10th–11th c.). Originals in Latin.

William, Duke of Aquitaine (875–918), and his wife Ingelberga, anxious to ensure their eternal salvation, founded the monastery of Cluny on family property in the region of Mâcon (Burgundy, France). Soon the monastery gained an astonishing reputation for piety, and the prayers of its monks were praised for sending souls to heaven. Local donors, ranging from small peasants to rich aristocrats, gave land to Cluny in order to associate themselves with the monks' redemptive work. The donations were recorded in charters. The charters below consist, first, of the original donation, made by William and Ingelberga, and then of a group of charters drawn up for one family, later known as the Grossi. The family relationships were as follows:

What reasons did people give for donating to the monastery of Cluny? What roles did women have in supporting the monastery? How do these charters show the conflicting tugs of family ties and charitable desires?

[Source: Patrick J. Geary, ed., *Readings in Medieval History*, 4th ed. (Toronto: University of Toronto Press, 2010), pp. 315–22 (slightly modified).]

[The Foundation Charter of Cluny: Charter # 112 (September 11, 910)]

To all right thinkers it is clear that the providence of God has so provided for certain rich men that, by means of their transitory possessions, if they use them well, they may be able to merit everlasting rewards. As to which thing, indeed, the divine word, showing it to be possible and altogether advising it, says: "The riches of a man are the redemption of his soul."[2] I, William, count and

---

[1]   The Majolus of this family was *not* the same person as the Majolus who was abbot of Cluny 954–994.

[2]   See Prov. 13: 8.

duke by the grace of God, diligently pondering this, and desiring to provide for my own salvation while I am still able, have considered it advisable—nay, most necessary, that from the temporal goods which have been conferred upon me I should give some little portion for the gain of my soul. I do this, indeed, in order that I who have thus increased in wealth may not, perchance, at the last be accused of having spent all in caring for my body, but rather may rejoice, when fate at last shall snatch all things away, in having reserved something for myself. Which end, indeed, seems attainable by no more suitable means than that, following the precept of Christ: "I will make his poor my friends"[1] and making the act not a temporary but a lasting one, I should support at my own expense a congregation of monks. And this is my trust, this my hope, indeed, that although I myself am unable to despise all things, nevertheless, by receiving despisers of the world, whom I believe to be righteous, I may receive the reward of the righteous. Therefore be it known to all who live in the unity of the faith and who await the mercy of Christ, and to those who shall succeed them and who shall continue to exist until the end of the world, that, for the love of God and of our Savior Jesus Christ, I hand over from my own rule to the holy apostles, Peter, namely, and Paul, the possessions over which I hold sway, the villa[2] of Cluny, namely, with the court and demesne *mansus*,[3] and the chapel in honor of St. Mary the mother of God and of St. Peter the prince of the apostles, together with all the things pertaining to it, the villas, indeed, the chapels, the serfs of both sexes, the vines, the fields, the meadows, the woods, the waters and their outlets, the mills, the incomes and revenues, what is cultivated and what is not, all in their entirety. Which things are situated in or about the county of Mâcon, each one surrounded by its own bounds. I give, moreover, all these things to the aforesaid apostles—I, William, and my wife Ingelberga—first for the love of God; then for the soul of my lord king Odo;[4] of my father and my mother; for myself and my wife—for the salvation,

namely, of our souls and bodies;—and not least for that of Ava who left me these things in her will;[5] for the souls also of our brothers and sisters and nephews, and of all our relatives of both sexes; for our faithful ones who adhere to our service; for the advancement, also, and integrity of the catholic religion. Finally, since all of us Christians are held together by one bond of love and faith, let this donation be for all,—for the orthodox, namely, of past, present or future times.

I give these things, moreover, with this understanding, that at Cluny a regular monastery shall be constructed in honor of the holy apostles Peter and Paul, and that there the monks shall congregate and live according to the rule of St. Benedict,[6] and that they shall possess, hold, have and order these same things unto all time, provided that the venerable house of prayer which is there shall be faithfully filled with vows and supplications, and that celestial converse shall be sought and striven after with all desire and with the deepest ardor; and also that there shall be diligently directed to God prayers, beseechings and exhortations both for me and for all, according to the order in which mention has been made of them above. And let the monks themselves, together with all the aforesaid possessions, be under the power and dominion of the abbot Berno, who, as long as he shall live, shall preside over them according to the Rule and consistent with his knowledge and ability. But after his death, those same monks shall have power and permission to elect any one of their order whom they please as abbot and rector, following the will of God and the rule promulgated by St. Benedict,—in such a way that neither by the intervention of our own or of any other power may they be impeded from making a purely canonical election. Every five years, moreover, the aforesaid monks shall pay to the church of the apostles at Rome ten *solidi*[7] to supply them with lights; and they shall have the protection of those same apostles and the defense of the Roman pontiff; and those monks may,

---

[1] Luke 16: 9.

[2] In this instance, the word *villa* means an estate, which included an enclosed area (the "court"), land, waste, meadow and various other appurtenances. In many of the other charters of Cluny, however, the word *villa* refers to a small district in which many landowners held land.

[3] A *mansus* (pl. *mansi*) was a farming unit. A "demesne *mansus*" was an outsize farming unit belonging to the lord (in this case William, and soon the monastery of Cluny), which included the *mansi* of dependent peasants.

[4] Odo, related to the later Capetians, was king of the west Franks 888–898.

[5] Ava was a sister of the donor.

[6] For *The Benedictine Rule* see above, p. 17.

[7] A *solidus* was a coin, in this case silver.

with their whole heart and soul, according to their ability and knowledge, build up the aforesaid place. We will, further, that in our times and in those of our successors, according as the opportunities and possibilities of that place shall allow, daily, works of mercy towards the poor, the needy, strangers, and pilgrims will be performed with the greatest zeal. It has pleased us also to insert in this document that, from this day, those same monks there congregated shall be subject neither to our yoke, nor to that of our relatives, nor to the sway of any earthly power. And, through God and all his saints, and by the awful day of judgment, I warn and abjure that no one of the secular princes, no count, no bishop whatever, not the pontiff of the aforesaid Roman see, shall invade the property of these servants of God, or alienate it, or diminish it, or exchange it, or give it as a benefice to any one, or constitute any prelate over them against their will. And that such unhallowed act may be more strictly prohibited to all rash and wicked men, I subjoin the following, giving force to the warning. I adjure you, oh holy apostles and glorious princes of the world, Peter and Paul, and you, oh supreme pontiff of the apostolic see, that, through the canonical and apostolic authority which you have received from God, you remove from participation in the holy church and in eternal life, the robbers and invaders and alienators of these possessions which I do give to you with joyful heart and ready will; and be protectors and defenders of the aforementioned place of Cluny and of the servants of God abiding there, and of all these possessions—on account of the clemency and mercy of the most holy Redeemer. If any one—which Heaven forbid, and which, through the mercy of the God and the protection of the apostles I do not think will happen—whether he be a neighbor or a stranger, no matter what his condition or power, should, through any kind of wild attempt to do any act of violence contrary to this deed of gift which we have ordered to be drawn up for the love of almighty God and for reverence of the chief apostles Peter and Paul; first, indeed, let him incur the wrath of almighty God, and let God remove him from the land of the living and wipe out his name from the book of life, and let his portion be with those who said to the Lord God: Depart from us; and, with Dathan and Abiron whom the earth, opening its jaws, swallowed up, and hell absorbed while still alive, let him incur everlasting damnation.[1] And being made a companion of Judas let him be kept thrust down there with eternal tortures, and, lest it seem to human eyes that he pass through the present world with impunity, let him experience in his own body, indeed, the torments of future damnation, sharing the double disaster with Heliodorus and Antiochus, of whom one being coerced with sharp blows and scarcely escaped alive; and the other, struck down by the divine will, his members putrefying and swarming with worms, perished most miserably.[2] And let him be a partaker with other sacrilegious persons who presume to plunder the treasure of the house of God; and let him, unless he come to his senses, have as enemy and as the one who will refuse him entrance into the blessed paradise, the key-bearer of the whole hierarchy of the church,[3] and, joined with the latter, St. Paul; both of whom, if he had wished, he might have had as most holy mediators for him. But as far as the worldly law is concerned, he shall be required, the judicial power compelling him, to pay a hundred pounds of gold to those whom he has harmed; and his attempted attack, being frustrated, shall have no effect at all. But the validity of this deed of gift, endowed with all authority, shall always remain inviolate and unshaken, together with the stipulation subjoined. Done publicly in the city of Bourges. I, William, commanded this act to be made and drawn up, and confirmed it with my own hand.

[Here follow the names of Ingelberga and 42 other people, mainly bishops, nobles, and members of William's family.]

[Charters of the Grossi Family: Charter # 802 (March, 951)]

To all who consider the matter reasonably, it is clear that the dispensation of God is so designed that if riches are used well, these transitory things can be transformed into eternal rewards. The Divine word showed that this was possible, saying "Wealth for a man is the redemption of

---

[1] For Dathan and Abiron, Hebrews who challenged Moses in the desert and were swiftly swallowed up by the earth, see Num. 16: 12–15, 25–34.

[2] Judas is the betrayer of Christ. In 2 Macc. 3: 7–27, Heliodorus, minister of King Seleusis of Syria, is sent to plunder the Temple at Jerusalem but is beaten up by mysterious persons sent by divine will. In 2 Macc. 9: 7–9, King Antiochus of Syria falls from a chariot and suffers horribly thereafter.

[3] The "key-bearer of the whole hierarchy of the church" is Saint Peter.

his soul," and again, "Give alms and all things will be clean unto you."[1]

We, that is, I, Doda, a woman, and my son Letbald [II], carefully considering this fact, think it necessary that we share some of the things that were conferred on us, Christ granting, for the benefit of our souls. We do this to make Christ's poor our friends, in accordance with Christ's precept and so that He may receive us, in the end, in the eternal tabernacle.

Therefore, let it be known to all the faithful that we—Doda and my son Letbald—give some of our possessions, with the consent of lord Aquin [I], my husband, for love of God and his holy Apostles, Peter and Paul,[2] to the monastery of Cluny, to support the brothers [i.e., monks] there who ceaselessly serve God and His apostles. [We give] an allod[3] that is located in the *pagus*[4] of Mâcon, called Nouville.[5] The serfs [*servi*] that live there are: Sicbradus and his wife, Robert, Eldefred and his wife and children, Roman and his wife and children, Raynard and his wife and children, Teutbert and his wife and children, Dominic and his wife and children, Nadalis with her children, John with his wife and children, Benedict with his wife and children, Maynard with his wife and children, another Benedict with his wife and children, and a woman too…[6] with her children.

And we give [land in] another *villa*[7] called Colonge and the serfs living there: Teotgrim and his wife and children, Benedict and his wife and children, Martin and his children, Adalgerius and his wife and children, [and] Sicbradus.

And [we give] a *mansus*[8] in Culey and the serfs there: Andrald and his wife and children, Eurald and his wife and children. And [we give] whatever we have at Chazeux along with the serf Landrad who lives there. We also give a little harbor on the Aar river and the serfs living there: Agrimbald and Gerald with their wives and children.

In addition, we give an allod in the *pagus* of Autun, in the *villa* called Beaumont and the serfs living there, John,

Symphorian, Adalard and their wives and children, in order that [the monks] may, for the love of Christ, receive our nephew, Adalgysus, into their society.[9]

[We give] all the things named above with everything that borders on them: vineyards, fields, buildings, serfs of every sex and age, ingress and egress, with all mobile and immobile property already acquired or to be acquired, wholly and completely. We give all this to God omnipotent and His apostles for the salvation of our souls and for the soul of Letbald [I], the father of my son, and for the salvation of Aquin [I], my husband, and of all our relatives and finally for all the faithful in Christ, living and dead.

Moreover, I, the aforesaid Letbald, uncinch the belt of war, cut off the hair of my head and beard for divine love, and with the help of God prepare to receive the monastic habit in the monastery [of Cluny]. Therefore, the property that ought to come to me by paternal inheritance I now give [to Cluny] because of the generosity of my mother and brothers. [I do so] in such a way that while [my mother and brothers] live, they hold and possess it. I give a *mansus* in Fragnes, along with the serf Ermenfred and his wife and children, to [my brother] Theoderic, *clericus*,[10] and after his death let it revert to [Cluny]. And I give another *mansus* at Verzé with the serf Girbald and his wife and children to my brother Hugo. In the *pagus* of Autun I give to [my brother] Aquin [II] the allod that is called Dompierre-les-Ormes, and the serf Benedict and his wife and their son and daughter. [I give Aquin also] another allod in Vaux, and the serfs Teutbald and his wife and children and Adalgarius. [I give all this] on condition that, if these brothers of mine [Hugh and Aquin], who are laymen, die without legitimate offspring, all these properties will go to the monastery as general alms.

If anyone (which we do not believe will happen) either we ourselves (let it not happen!) or any other person, should be tempted to bring a claim in bad faith against

---

[1] Prov. 13: 8 and Luke 11: 41.

[2] As William's foundation charter stipulated, Cluny had been handed over to the apostles Saints Peter and Paul.

[3] An allod in this region was land that was owned outright, in contrast to land held in fief, for example.

[4] A *pagus* was a Roman administrative subdivision.

[5] Almost all the places mentioned in these charters are within about ten miles of the monastery of Cluny.

[6] Effaced in the manuscript.

[7] Here the word *villa* refers to a district.

[8] The reference here is no doubt to a demesne *mansus*.

[9] Possibly Adalgysus is to become a monk; but it is more likely that he is to become a special "friend" of the monastery for whom prayers will be said.

[10] I.e., a priest.

this charter of donation, let him first incur the wrath of God, and let him suffer the fate of Dathan and Abiron and of Judas, the traitor of the Lord. And unless he repents, let him have the apostles [Peter and Paul] bar him from the celestial kingdom. Moreover, in accordance with earthly law, let him be forced to pay ten pounds. But let this donation be made firm by us, with the stipulation added. S[ignum][1] of Doda and her son Letbald, who asked that it be done and confirmed. S. of Aquin, who consents. S. of Hugo. S. of Evrard. S. of Walo. S. of Warembert. S. of Maingaud. S. of Giboin. S. of Leotald. S. of Widald. S. of Hemard. S. of Raimbald. Dated in the month of March in the 15th year of the reign of King Louis.[2] I, brother Andreas, *levite*,[3] undersign at the place for the secretary.

[Charter # 1460 (November 12, 978–November 11, 979)][4]

I, Majolus, humble abbot [of Cluny] by the will of God, and the whole congregation of brothers of the monastery of Cluny. We have decided to grant something from the property of our church to a certain cleric, named Letbald [III] for use during his lifetime, and we have done so, fulfilling his request.

The properties that we grant him are located in the *pagus* of Mâcon, in the *ager*[5] of Grevilly, in a *villa* called Collonge: *mansi*, vineyards, land, meadows, woods, water, and serfs of both sexes and whatever else we have in that place, which came to us from Raculf.[6] And we grant two *mansi* at Boye and whatever we have there. And in Massy, one *mansus*. And in "Ayrodia" [not identified], in a place called Rocca, we give *mansi* with vineyards, land, woods, water, and serfs of every sex and age; and we grant all the property of Chassigny [a place near Lugny that has disappeared]: vineyards, land, meadows, woods, water,

mills and serfs and slaves. And at "Bussiacus" [near Saint-Huruge], similarly [we grant] *mansi*, vineyards, lands, meadows, and woods. And at "Ponciacus" [not id.] [we give] *mansi*, vineyards, and land. Just as Raculf gave these things to us in his testament, so we grant them to [Letbald] on the condition that he hold them while he lives and after his death these things pass to Cluny. And let him pay 12 dinars every year to mark his taking possession.

We also grant to him other property that came from lord Letbald [I], his uncle: a *mansus* at La Verzé and another at Bassy and another at Les Légères, and again another in Fragnes and another in Chazeux. And again a *mansus* in the *pagus* of Autun, at Dompierre-les-Ormes and another in Vaux and the serfs and slaves of both sexes that belong to those *mansi*. Let him hold and possess these properties as listed in this *precaria*[7] for as long as he lives. And when his mortality prevails—something no man can avoid—let this property fall to [Cluny] completely and without delay. [Meanwhile] let him pay 12 dinars every year, on the feast day of Apostles Peter and Paul.

I have confirmed this decree with my own hand and have ordered the brethren to corroborate it, so that it will have force throughout his lifetime. S. of lord Majolus, abbot. S. of Balduin, monk. S. of Vivian. S. of John. S. of Arnulf. S. of Costantinus. S. of Tedbald. S. of Joslen. S. of Grimald. S. of Hugo. S. of Rothard. S. of Ingelbald. S. of Achedeus. S. of Vuitbert. S. of Ingelman. Dated by the hand of Rothard, in the 25th year of the reign of King Lothar.

[Charter # 1577 (Nov. 12, 981–Nov. 11, 982)]

To this holy place, accessible to our prayers [et cetera].[8] I, Rotrudis, and [my husband] Josseran, and my sons, all of us give to God and his holy Apostles, Peter and Paul

---

1   Usually laypeople did not sign charters; rather they made a mark or sign (their *signum*) that was indicated by the scribe in front of their name. The S refers to this sign.

2   This was King Louis D'Outremer (r.936–954), one of the last of the Carolingians.

3   A *levite* was a deacon.

4   This charter has this range of dates because the scribe dated it in the 25th year of the reign of King Lothar, the son of King Louis, whose rule began on November 12, 954.

5   The *pagus* of Mâcon was divided into subdivisions called *agri* (sing. *ager*). There were perhaps ten or more *villae* in each *ager*.

6   Raculf was probably a member of the Grossi family.

7   This document is a "precarial" donation. A *precaria* was a conditional grant of land by a monastery to someone outside of the monastery for his or her lifetime.

8   This charter began with a formula considered so commonplace that it did not need to be fully written out.

and at the place Cluny, half of a church[1] that is located in the *pagus* of Mâcon, named in honor of St. Peter, with everything that belongs to it, wholly and completely, and [property in] the *villa* that is called Curtil-sous-Buffières. There [we give] a field and a meadow that go together and have the name *ad Salas*. This land borders at the east on a *via publica*[2] and a manmade wall; at the south on a meadow; at the west on a *via publica*, and similarly at the north. [I make this gift] for the salvation of the soul of my husband Josseran, and [for the soul of my son] Bernard. Done at Cluny. Witnesses: Rotrudis, Josseran, Bernard, Israel, Erleus, Hugo, Odo, Raimbert, Umbert. Ingelbald wrote this in the 28th year of the reign of King Lothar.

I will pay a tax of 12 dinars on the feast day of the Prince of the Apostles [i.e., St. Peter]. After my death, let [the property] go to Cluny without delay.

But if anyone wants to bring any bad-faith claim against this donation, let him first incur the wrath of the Omnipotent and all His saints; and unless he returns to his senses, let him be thrust into Hell with the devil. As in the past, let this donation remain firm and stable, with the stipulation added. Done publicly at Cluny. S. of Majolus, who asks that it be done and confirmed. S. of Bernard, S. of Israel, S. of Arleius, S. of Bernard, S. of Hubert. Aldebard, *levita*, wrote this in the 4th year of the reign of Hugh [Capet].

[Charter # 1845 (990–991)]

By the clemency of the Savior a remedy was conceded to the faithful: that they could realize eternal returns on His gifts if they distributed them justly. Wherefore, I, Majolus,[3] in the name of God, give to God and his holy apostles Peter and Paul and at the place Cluny some of my property which is located in the county of Lyon, in the *villa* "Mons" [not id.]. It consists of a demesne *mansus* with a serf named Durannus and his wife, named Aldegard, and their children, and whatever belongs or appears to belong to this *mansus*, namely fields, vineyards, meadows, woods, pasturelands, water and water courses, that is already acquired or will be acquired, whole and complete. I make this donation first for my soul and for my burial [in Cluny's cemetery] and for the soul of my father Josseran and of my mother Rotrudis and of my brothers, and for the souls of my *parentes*[4] and for the salvation of all the departed faithful, so that all may profit in common. [I give it] on the condition that I may hold and possess it while I live, and that every year

[Charter # 2508 (994–1030?)][5]

Notice of a quitclaim[6] that took place at Cluny in the presence of lord Rainald, venerable prior at that place; and of other monks who were there, namely Walter, Aymo, Amizon, Warner, Lanfred, Locerius, Giso; and of noblemen: Witbert, Robert, Ildinus, Gislebert, Bernard, and Hugo. In the first place, let all, present and future, know that a long and very protracted quarrel between the monks of Cluny and Majolus[7] finally, by God's mercy, came to this end result: first that he [Majolus] quit his claim to the land which Oddo and Teza [Oddo's] daughter[8] destined for us and handed over by charter: the woods in *Grandi Monte* with its borders [as follows]: on the east [it borders on] its own inheritance [namely] passing between mountains and through wasteland and across the castle of Teodoric; on the south [it borders on] *terra francorum*;[9] on the west and north [it borders on] land of St. Peter. [Majolus] draws up this notice at this time so that he may reunite himself with the favor of St. Peter and the brothers, and so that he may persevere in future

---

[1] Churches could be given in whole or in part—since the revenues could be divided—and with or without their tithes (which often belonged not to the holder of the church but to the local bishop).

[2] In this region, a *via publica* was a dirt road. There was a very extensive network of roads in the area around Cluny left over from the Roman period.

[3] Not the Cluniac abbot but rather a member of the Grossi family.

[4] The *parentes* were much broader than the nuclear family but perhaps not quite as large as a clan.

[5] The scribe did not give a date. But we know that Rainald was prior at Cluny beginning in 994 and that Majolus died *c.*1030. These give us, respectively, the *terminus post quem* [time after which] and the *terminus ante quem* [the time before which] the document must have been drawn up.

[6] That is, this gives notice that a claim has been dropped ("quit").

[7] The donor from the Grossi family.

[8] Oddo and Teza were probably relatives of Majolus.

[9] This probably refers to land of free peasants.

as a faithful servant in the service of St. Peter. S. Hugo, S. Witbert, S. Robert, S. Ildinus, S. Gislebert, S. Bernard.

[Charter # 2946 (1018–1030?)][1]

In the name of the incarnate Word. I, Raimodis, formerly the wife of the lord Wichard, now dead, and now joined in matrimony to lord Ansedeus, my husband; with the consent and good will [of Ansedeus], I give or rather give again some land which is called Chazeux to St. Peter and Cluny. [I give it] for the soul of my husband Wichard. This land once belonged to St. Peter and Cluny. But the abbot and monks gave it as a precarial gift to lord Letbald [III], a certain cleric who afterwards became bishop of Mâcon. Letbald, acting wrongly, alienated [the land] from St. Peter and gave it to Gauzeran to make amends for killing Gauzeran's relative, Berengar.

Therefore I give it again to St. Peter for the soul of my husband Wichard, and for Gauzeran, Wichard's father. I also give a slave named Adalgarda and her children, and [I give] the whole inheritance for the soul of my husband Wichard, and of my daughter Wiceline, and for my own soul.

If anyone wants to bring false claim against this donation, let him not prevail, but let him pay a pound of gold into the public treasury. S. of Raimodis, who asked that this charter be done and confirmed. S. of Ansedeus. S. of another Ansedeus. S. of Achard. S. of Walter. S. of Costabulus. S. of Ugo.

4.4 Love and complaints in Angoulême: *Agreement between Count William of the Aquitanians and Hugh IV of Lusignan* (1028). Original in Latin.

This document of a series of disputes and their eventual settlement is written from the point of view of Hugh, who was the castellan (the lord of a castle and its garrison) of Lusignan, although he here calls himself Chiliarch—"leader of one thousand." The events described may be dated between about 1022 and 1028. The chief protagonists of Hugh's drama are Hugh himself and William, whom he calls "count of the Aquitainians" but who was, more importantly, count of Poitou (he ruled from *c*.995–1030). The center of his county was Poitiers, which included Lusignan (about 15 miles southwest of Poitiers) and many of the other locations mentioned in this document. Other characters who appear are mainly laymen, laywomen, and a few bishops. The *Agreement* presents an admittedly one-sided picture of the activities of the French aristocracy in the early eleventh century. As you read this document, consider what it meant to be the "man" of a lord. In what ways were legal and quasi-legal proceedings essential institutions in the Poitou? What were the meanings of "love," "anger," and "sorrow" in early eleventh-century Poitou? Try writing an account of the agreements between Hugh and the count from the *count's* point of view.

[Source: Jane Martindale, "Conventum inter Guillelmum Aquitanorum comitem et Hugonem Chiliarchum," in *Status, Authority and Regional Power: Aquitaine and France, 9th to 12th Centuries* (Aldershot: Variorum, 1997), Paper VIIb, pp. 541–52. Translated by Thomas Greene and Barbara H. Rosenwein from the Latin text, in consultation with translations by George Beech, "Hugh of Lusignan: Agreement between Lord and Vassal," in *Readings in Medieval History*, ed. Patrick J. Geary, 4th ed. (Toronto: University of Toronto Press, 2010), pp. 377–81; Martindale, "Conventum," pp. 542a–552; and Paul Hyams and others, "Agreement between Duke William V of Aquitaine and Hugh IV of Lusignan" at http://www.fordham.edu/halsall/source/agreement.asp]

---

[1] This date, which is quite uncertain, is suggested on the basis of other charters that tell us at what date Raimodis, the donor in this charter, became a widow.

William, called count of the Aquitainians, had an agreement with Hugh the Chiliarch that when Viscount Boso died, William would give Boso's honor in commendation to Hugh.[1] Bishop Roho saw and heard this and kissed the arm of the count.[2] But Viscount Savary seized from Hugh land which Hugh held from Count William.[3] When the viscount died the count promised Hugh that he would make no agreement or accord with Ralph, the brother of the dead viscount, until the land had been restored. He said this in the presence of all, but afterwards he secretly gave the land to Ralph. For that land itself, or for a larger one, or for other things, Hugh had an agreement with Viscount Ralph that he would accept Ralph's daughter as his wife. When the count heard this he was greatly angered and he went humbly to Hugh and said to him, "Don't marry Ralph's daughter. I will give to you whatever you ask of me, and you will be my friend before all others except my son." Hugh did what the count ordered, and out of love and fidelity for the count he secretly rejected the woman.

At that time it happened that Joscelin of Parthenay castle died.[4] The count said that he would give Joscelin's honor and wife to Hugh, and if Hugh refused to accept them, he would no longer have confidence in him. Hugh did not entreat or request this from the count, either for himself or for anyone else. Thinking it over, he said to the count, "I will do all that you have ordered." The count, however, after holding a public meeting with Count Fulk,[5] promised to give Fulk something from his own benefices, and Fulk promised that he would give Hugh what belonged to him. At the meeting, the count called for Viscount Ralph and said to him: "Hugh will not keep the agreement he has with you because I forbid him to. But Fulk and I have an agreement that we will give to Hugh the honor and wife of Joscelin. We do this to mess up your life, because you are not faithful to me." When he heard this Ralph was very hurt and he said to the count, "For God's sake do not do that." So the count said, "Pledge

to me that you will not give Hugh your daughter, nor keep your agreement with him, and in turn I will arrange that he not possess the honor and wife of Joscelin." And they so acted that Hugh got neither the one nor the other. Ralph went to Count William, who was at Montreuil castle, sending a message to Hugh that they should talk together. That was done. And Ralph said to Hugh, "I tell you this in confidence so that you will not give me away. Pledge to me that you will help me against Count William, and I will keep your agreement for you and will aid you against all men." But Hugh refused all of this out of his love for Count William. Hugh and Ralph parted unhappily. Then Ralph began to prosecute a public dispute with Count William, while Hugh, out of love for the count, started one with Ralph. And Hugh suffered great harm.

When Ralph died, Hugh asked the count to restore to him the land which Ralph had seized from him. Moreover the count said to Hugh, "I will not make an agreement with Viscount Josfred, the nephew of Ralph, nor with the men of Thouars castle, until I return your land." Yet none of this was done, and the count went and made an agreement with Viscount Josfred and with the men of Thouars castle. He never made an agreement with Hugh, and Hugh did not get his land. And because of the misdeeds which Hugh committed on the count's behalf, Josfred got into a dispute with Hugh, and he burned Mouzeuil castle and captured Hugh's horsemen and cut off their hands and did many other things. The count did not help Hugh at all nor did he broker a good agreement between Josfred and Hugh, but Hugh even now has lost his land, and for the sake of the count he has lost still other land that he was holding peacefully. And when Hugh saw that he was not going to get his land he took forty-three of the best horsemen of Thouars. He could have had peace and his land and justice for the wrongdoing; and if he had been willing to accept a ransom he could have had 40,000 *solidi*.[6]

When the count heard this he should have been glad, but he was sad and sent for Hugh, saying to him, "Give

---

[1] Boso (d. by 1033) was viscount of Chatellerault, 20 miles northeast of Poitiers. An "honor" referred to property.

[2] Roho was bishop of Angoulême (r.1020–1036). Formal agreements were often concluded by a kiss of peace; sometimes witnesses participated in this gesture of concord and, as here, the kiss might function as well as a sign of deference.

[3] Savary was viscount of Thouars.

[4] The "castles" that this document refers to were not luxurious chateaux but rather strongholds or fortresses. Some of them were thrown up haphazardly and minimally fortified; others were built more solidly and sometimes included a stone tower. Armed garrisons of horsemen guarded the castles and were important players—as victims, hostages, and guarantors—in the disputes and negotiations between regional lords. Included in the notion of the castle was the surrounding district that it dominated.

[5] Fulk was count of Anjou (r.987–1040).

[6] A *solidus* (pl. *solidi*) is here a silver coin.

me back the men." Hugh answered him, "Why do you ask these things of me, Lord? I am a loser only because of my loyalty to you." Then the count said, "I do not ask this of you to hurt you, but in fact because you are mine to do my will. And as all will know by our agreement, I will take over those men on condition that I make a settlement with you that your lands will be secured and the wrongdoing compensated, or I will return the men to you. Do this without doubting my credibility and good faith, and if anything should turn out badly for you, you can be sure that I will hand them over to you." Hugh put his trust in God and the count and handed the men over to the count according to this agreement. Later on Hugh got neither the men nor justice, and he lost his land.

The count of the Poitevins[1] and Bishop Gilbert[2] had an agreement among themselves with Joscelin, Hugh's uncle.[3] It was about the castle at Vivonne, and it said that after the death of Bishop Gilbert it was to be Joscelin's castle. During his lifetime, the bishop made the men of that castle commend themselves to Joscelin, and he gave Joscelin the tower. And after the death of both men, the count made an agreement between Hugh and Bishop Isembert[4] that Hugh would get half of the castle and half of the demesne and two shares of the vassals' fiefs.[5] Then the count made Hugh commend himself to Bishop Isembert—but now he has taken the better estate from them.

A certain official named Aimery seized the castle called Civray from Bernard, his lord, but this castle was rightly Hugh's, as it had been his father's. Because of his anger at Aimery, Count William urged Hugh to become the man[6] of Bernard for the part of the castle that had belonged to his father, so that together they might wage a dispute with Aimery. But it seemed wrong to Hugh that he become Bernard's man, and he did not want to do it. The count persisted in this admonition for a year, and the more he got angry, the more he urged Hugh to become the man of Bernard. After a year passed, the count came to Hugh as if in anger and said to him, "Why don't you make an agreement with Bernard? You owe so much to me that if I should tell you to make a peasant into a lord

you should do it. Do what I say, and if it should turn out badly for you, come and see me about it." Hugh believed him and became the man of Bernard for the fourth part of Civray castle. But Bernard made the count a guarantor to Hugh, as well as four hostages. The count said to Hugh, "Commend those hostages to me under such conditions that if Bernard does not faithfully keep your agreements, I will turn them over to your custody and I will faithfully aid you." How strongly the count promised this to Hugh he himself knows very well. Hugh trusted in his lord and began a fierce dispute on account of Civray castle and suffered great losses in men and many other things. The count started to build a castle, which he called Couhé, but he did not finish it for Hugh. Instead, he talked it over with Aimery, abandoned the castle, and in no way aided Hugh.

Afterwards the count grew even more unhappy with Aimery on account of the castle called Chizé, which Aimery had seized, and Hugh and the count joined together in a dispute against Aimery. The count besieged the castle called Mallevault because of the injuries that Aimery had done to him and captured it, and Hugh aided him as best he could. Before Hugh left the count, the count promised him—just as a lord ought rightly to promise to his man—that he would make no agreement or alliance with Aimery without Hugh, and that Mallevault would not be rebuilt without his advice. But the count did make an agreement with Aimery and allowed him to rebuild Mallevault without the advice of Hugh. As long as Aimery lived, none of the property mentioned above came to Hugh.

After the death of Aimery a great dispute began between his son Aimery and Hugh. At the same time Hugh went to the count and said to him, "Things are going badly for me now, my Lord, because I have none of the property that you acquired for me." The count answered him, "I am going to hold a public hearing with them so that if they act well, good; if not, I will turn over to you the castle which I started." And the castle was constructed on the advice of Bernard, who thus far had helped Hugh in the dispute. When they saw the heavy

---

1   That is, Count William.
2   Gilbert was bishop of Poitiers (r.975–1023/1024).
3   This is presumably a different Joscelin from the one of Parthenay.
4   Isembert was Gilbert's successor as bishop of Poitiers.
5   It was possible to have "half a castle" because what was at stake were the revenues due the castle, not the stronghold itself. The demesne was land belonging to the fortress directly; other land pertaining to it was granted out in fief.
6   The word used here is *homo*, which may be translated as "man" or "vassal," depending on your view of the relations among these aristocrats and the implications of these words.

demands Hugh was making on them, the men of Civray were not able to hold out, and they made an agreement with Bernard and returned the castle to him. He received it without the advice of Hugh. Now both Bernard and Aimery were in dispute with Hugh, and he was alone against them. Coming to the count, Hugh said to him, "Lord, I am doing very badly because the lord whom I got upon your advice has just taken away my property. I beg and urge you by the faith which a lord owes to aid his man: either let me have a proper public hearing or my property, just as you pledged to me; or return to me the hostages which I commended to you; and above all help me as you pledged to me." The count, however, neither aided him, nor made an agreement with him, nor returned the hostages but released them and gave them back to Bernard. And after that the dispute between Bernard and Aimery and Hugh increased.

And since Hugh saw that the count aided him in no way, he went to seek the advice of Gerald, the bishop of Limoges. Gerald and Hugh went together into La Marche against Bernard and built a castle. But the count, who ought to have aided Hugh, seized the castle from him and burned it. And the count and his son ordered all their men not to help Hugh unless they wished to die. Then Bernard accepted the council of his men that they should do harm to Hugh on the advice of the count, and they appointed a deadline fifteen days away. During those fifteen days the count arranged a truce between Bernard and Hugh. Three days into the truce the count took Hugh along with his army to Apremont castle, and a meeting was held in his castle. From there the count went to Blaye, where he was to have a meeting with Count Sancho, and he told Hugh that he should come along. And Hugh responded, "Lord, why do you ask me to go with you? You yourself know how short the truce is which I have with Bernard, and he himself is threatening to do me harm." The count said to him: "Do not fear that they will do anything to you as long as you are with me." And the count took Hugh with him by force and against Hugh's will.

While they were staying at the meeting place, Hugh's men heard that Bernard was coming against him; they sent a message to Hugh to come. Then Hugh said to the count, "Bernard is attacking me." And the count said, "Don't be afraid that they will dare attack you; and, besides, you need them to attack so that I can destroy them and aid you." In that same hour the count sent orders through his men, and he told Hugh to go on ahead, and he followed him. When Hugh reached Lusignan, Bernard was at Confolens castle. He had captured the suburb and the outskirts and burned everything; he

had taken spoils, captured men, and done plenty of other evil deeds. A messenger ran up to Hugh and said to him, "Bernard has your wife besieged in the old castle which survived the fire." Hugh came to the count and said to him: "My lord, help me now, because my wife is now being besieged." But the count gave him no aid or advice at all. And Bernard turned back, and he and his men did so much harm to Hugh and his men that 50,000 *solidi* would not have paid for it. And Hugh suffered this damage during the truce that the count offered to him at Blaye.

Not long after this Hugh went to Gençay castle and burned it and seized the men and women and took everything with him. Hastening to the count, he said to him, "Lord, give me permission to build the castle which I burned." And the count said to him, "You are the man of Fulk, how can you build the castle? Fulk will demand it of you, and you will not be strong enough to keep it from him." Hugh said, "Lord, when I became Fulk's man I told him that his men were seizing what was my right and that if I was able to regain possession of them, I would do it, but I would only hold it in his fealty, which is what I want to do. And Fulk said to me, 'If you take anything from them, don't take from me.'" When the count heard that Fulk and Hugh had such an agreement, he was pleased. And the count said to Hugh: "Build the castle under such an agreement that if I am able to negotiate with Count Fulk about my price and yours, one part will be mine and the other yours."

And Hugh built the castle. Then Fulk asked the count for it. The count responded to him, "Ask Hugh for it." And Fulk did that. Hugh answered him, "When I became your man, I said to you that if I would be strong enough to take castles from my enemies, I should take them and hold them in your fealty, and I wanted to do that because the castle which you are demanding belonged to my relatives, and I have a better right to it than those who were holding it." But Fulk said, "You who are mine, how can you hold against my will something I didn't give to you?" And Hugh sought advice from the count. The count told him, "If he is willing to give you guarantees that your enemies will not have the castle, then you cannot keep it. If not, keep it, because he will not be able to accuse you of anything." Hugh asked that Fulk give hostages to him, and Fulk gave him nothing, but said, "I will make my demands known to the count and give hostages to him and he will give you some of his own." Then the meeting turned angry. Fulk demanded Hugh's castle from the count. Hugh said, "I will not give it up without assurances." The count said to him, "I will give an assurance, and he has told me what sort to give." Hugh said, "Take what you want from Count Fulk and give me what I'm asking for. Give me the man who has custody of the tower at Melle, so that if Aimery should get the castle without my advice, and harm should befall me, that man will turn the tower over to me." The count said to him, "I will not do this, because I cannot." Hugh said, "If you don't want to do this with Melle, make the same agreement with regard to Chizé." But the count didn't want to do either.

It seemed to Hugh and his men that the count was treating him badly. And they parted in anger. Then Hugh sent all kinds of necessities into the castle and intended to hold it against all comers if they would not give him assurances. The count came out of the city,[1] asked Hugh to come to him, and commanded through Count William of Angoulême that he submit himself to the mercy of the count, because the count could not change the fact that he had to aid Fulk; and he was afraid to lose either Fulk or Hugh. Then Hugh committed himself to the trust and friendship of the count his lord, and he did this out of love for him because he was assured that he would not suffer harm at Fulk's hands. And the count said: "Let Hugh do this for me and I will keep the faith with him that a lord ought to keep with his man. If he suffers harm, he will know that I have betrayed him, and he will never trust me again." And Hugh said, "My lord has spoken similarly to me about many things by which he has deceived me." And not a single one of Hugh's men would advise him to trust the count. But the count reminded Hugh of all the good things which he had done for him, and Hugh, holding back the count by his love and entreaties—that is by their common oath—said to the count, "I will put all my trust in you, but watch out that you do not do me wrong, for if you do, I will not be faithful to you nor will I serve you, nor will I render fidelity to you. But, on account of the fact that I will be separated from you and you are not able to give me guarantees, I want you to give me my fief as a pledge that then I will no longer serve you, and release me from the oath which I have made to you." The count answered, "Gladly."

Hugh returned the castle to the count, against the wishes of his men, on condition that Aimery would not have it without Hugh's advice and that Hugh would suffer no harm. On account of hearing those lies, Hugh accepted his fief as a pledge, and the count gave it to him on condi-

tion that if he should suffer harm because of the agreement about Gençay, Hugh would never again serve him. And the count released him from his oaths, so that he would no longer do anything for the count on account of them, but not out of ill will. [But] the count handed over Gençay without the advice of Hugh and got money and some demesne land. It went very badly for Hugh, with men killed, houses burned, booty taken, land seized and many other things which in truth cannot be enumerated. When this had ended the count gave Hugh a respite and promised that he would give him a benefice either of something that was his by right or something that would be pleasing to him. But when this period passed the count did nothing for Hugh. He sent an order to him: "Don't wait, because I am not going to do anything for you. Even if the whole world were mine I would not give you as much as a finger could lift with regard to this matter."

When Hugh heard this he went to the court of the count and made the case for his rights, but it did him no good. This saddened Hugh, and in the hearing of all he renounced his fealty[2] to the count, except what he owed for the city [of Poitiers] and his own person. Before either Hugh or his men did any harm, the men of the count seized a benefice from Hugh's men in the name of war. When Hugh saw this he went to Chizé castle, which had been his uncle's but which Peter[3] was holding unjustly, and from which much harm was being done to Hugh. He seized the tower and threw out Peter's men. Hugh did this because he thought he had the right—because it had belonged to his father or others of his relatives—which he was losing. When the count heard of this he was greatly saddened and sent an order to Hugh that he turn over the tower that he had taken away from Peter. Hugh demanded that the count return the honor of his father and the other things which belonged to his relatives and to which he had right, and he would surrender the tower and all the things that he had taken within it, and in addition the entire honor which had belonged to Joscelin[4] and which the count had given him. The count thought this over and they arranged for a hearing. And the count said to Hugh, "I will not give you those honors which you ask of me, but I will give you that honor which was your uncle's—the castle, the tower and the entire honor—on

---

1   Presumably Poitiers.

2   The Latin word here is *defidavit*, which means defied. The root of the word is "faith"; a man declares his faith (*fides*=fidelity) to his lord, but if he formally renounces that fealty, as here, he "defies"—"de-fealties"—him.

3   Peter has not been identified.

4   This Joscelin was Hugh's uncle.

condition that you no longer demand of me that honor which was your father's, or others of your relatives, nor anything which you claim as your right."

When he heard this Hugh greatly mistrusted the count, because through evil trickery in the past the count had deceived Hugh in many things. He said to the count, "I don't dare do this, because I fear that you will threaten me with harm, as you have done with regard to many other things." The count said to Hugh, "I will give such assurances to you that you will no longer distrust me." Hugh said to him, "What kind of assurances?" The count said, "I will produce a serf who will undergo an ordeal for you so that you will not doubt that the agreement which we make among ourselves will be good and firm. And with regard to all the affairs of the past, no harm will ever again be done to you, but the agreement will be kept firmly without any evil trickery." When Hugh heard what the count was saying in this way, he said, "You are my lord. I will not take a guarantee from you, but I will simply rely on the mercy of the Lord and yourself." The count said to Hugh, "Give up all those claims that you have demanded from me in the past and swear fidelity to me and my son, and I will give you your uncle's honor

or something else of equal value in exchange for it." And Hugh said, "Lord, I beg you by God and this blessed crucifix which is made in the figure of Christ that you do not make me do this if in future you and your son intend to threaten me with evil trickery." The count said, "My son and I will do this in faith and without evil trickery." Hugh said, "And when I have sworn fidelity to you, you will ask me for Chizé castle, and if I should not turn it over to you, you will say that it is not right that I deny you the castle which I hold from you; but if I should turn it over to you, you and your son will take it away from me because you will have given me no guarantee except the mercy of God and yourself." The count said, "We will not do that, but if we should demand it of you, don't turn it over to us."

They received Hugh as their man in faith and trust under the terms of the agreement as it was finally pronounced: that the count and his son should bear faith to Hugh without evil trickery. And they made Hugh give up everything that he claimed from the past. And he swore fidelity to them, and they gave him the honor of his uncle Joscelin, just as Joscelin held it one year before he died.

Here end the agreements between the count and Hugh.

4.5 The Peace of God at Bourges: Andrew of Fleury, *The Miracles of St. Benedict* (1040–1043). Original in Latin.

The Peace of God was a movement initiated by bishops, and eventually declared by kings as well, to protect unarmed people (including clerics) and property (including church property) from armed predators. At church synods, laypeople and churchmen alike met to proclaim the Peace. Those who fought (the *bellatores* or *milites*: the knights) swore oaths not to violate the Peace. In the late 1030s, at one such synod, Aimon, the archbishop of Bourges from 1030 to 1070, organized a militia consisting of clergy, peasants, and a few nobles that succeeded in forcing most of the nobility of the region to take the oath. The militia even enforced the Peace by going to war against breakers of the oath. But it ran into opposition from one holdout, Odo, lord of Déols, who defeated it soundly. Andrew, a monk at the monastery of Fleury, recounted the incident in the course of his work on the *Miracles of St. Benedict*, written 1040–1043. He praised the militia's initial promise but berated it for its "ambition" and confidence in its own power rather than God's. From this document, consider what might have been the interest of common people in the Peace of God. How might the sorts of disputes described in the *Agreement between Count William and Hugh* (above, p. 181) have contributed to the Peace of God movement?

[Source: *The Peace of God: Social Violence and Religious Response in France around the Year* 1000, ed. Thomas Head and Richard Landes (Ithaca, NY: Cornell University Press, 1992), pp. 339–42.]

5.1 In the 1038th year after the incarnation of the Lord, on the eighth day of August, in the middle of the day, the sun was darkened and hid the rays of its splendors for a space of almost two hours. Again the following morning it remained under the same appearance for the entire day and unremittingly gave off bloody flames.

5.2. At this very same time, Archbishop Aimon of Bourges wished to impose peace in his diocese through the swearing of an oath. After he had summoned the fellow bishops of his province and had sought advice from these suffragans, he bound all men of fifteen years of age and over by the following law: that they would come forth with one heart as opponents of any violation of the oath they had sworn, that they would in no way withdraw secretly from the pact even if they should lose their property, and that, what is more, if necessity should demand it, they would go after those who had repudiated the oath with arms. Nor were ministers of the sacraments excepted, but they often took banners from the sanctuary of the Lord and attacked the violators of the sworn peace with the rest of the crowd of laypeople. In this way they many times routed the faithless and brought their castles down to the ground. With the help of God they so terrified the rebels that, as the coming of the faithful was proclaimed far and wide by rumor among the populace, the rebels scattered. Leaving the gates of their towns open, they sought safety in flight, harried by divinely inspired terror. You would have seen [the faithful] raging against the multitude of those who ignore God, as if they were some other people of Israel. Presently they trampled [the rebels] underfoot so that they forced them to return to the laws of the pact which they had ignored.

We thought it fitting to insert in writing that which was agreed to in the pact which the archbishop himself, along with various fellow bishops, promised under oath in the following way: "I Aimon, by the gift of God archbishop of Bourges, promise with my whole heart and mouth to God and to his saints that I shall discharge with my whole spirit and without any guile or dissimulation everything that follows. That is, I will wholeheartedly attack those who steal ecclesiastical property, those who provoke pillage, those who oppress monks, nuns, and clerics, and those who fight against holy mother church, until they repent. I will not be beguiled by the enticement of gifts, or moved by any reason of bonds of kinship or neighborliness, or in any way deviate from the path

of righteousness. I promise to move with all my troops against those who dare in any manner to transgress the decrees and not to cease in any way until the purpose of the traitor has been overcome."

He swore this over the relics of Stephen, the first martyr for Christ, and urged the other [bishops] to do likewise. Obeying with one heart, his fellow bishops made among everyone age fifteen or older (as we already said) in their separate dioceses subscribe [the pact] with the same promise. Fear and trembling then struck the hearts of the unfaithful so that they feared the multitude of the unarmed peasantry as if it were a battle line of armored men. Their hearts fell so that, forgetting their status as knights and abandoning their fortified places, they fled from the humble peasants as from the cohorts of very powerful kings. The prayer of David fitted the situation most aptly: "For thou dost deliver a humble people, but the haughty eyes thou dost bring down, for who is God but the Lord?"[1] ... Odo of Déols remained alone among the whole multitude [of rebels], reserved by the judgment of God for the punishment of evil doers.

5.3. When by the will of God they had, trusting in the help of divine strength, established peace in every direction, ambition (the root and aid of all evil) began to seep along the stalks of such good works. They forgot that God is the strength and rampart of his people and ascribed the power of God to their apostate power.... Thus the aforementioned bishop was touched by the sting of mammon[2] and raged around and around in blind ambition. Unmindful of his episcopal dignity, he attacked Beneciacum, the castle of one Stephen, along with a multitude of the people of Bourges. He reproached Stephen for the fault of having ignored the peace, he tried to burn the castle with flames and ordered it to be leveled to the ground, as if he were exacting the vengeance of God upon it. They burned the castle, which was hemmed in on all sides by the siege, with more than one thousand four hundred people of both sexes inside. Stephen alone of that great number escaped, although his brothers, wife, and sons were all consumed by the fire, and he placed the laurel wreath of his great victory on their wretched heads. The inhabitants of that region for a radius of fourteen miles had fled to this castle and, since they feared the theft of their possessions, they had brought them along. The cruel victors were hardly moved by the laments of

---

[1]   Ps. 18: 27, 31; Douay, Ps. 17: 28, 32.

[2]   The false god personifying riches and avarice.

the dying, they did not take pity on women beating their breasts; the crowd of infants clinging to their mothers' breasts did not touch any vein of mercy.... And so the just bore responsibility for the crime of the iniquitous and the just perished in place of the impious. Having been granted this great triumph, the people returned to their homes dancing with a pitiable joy. Stephen was placed under guard in a prison in Bourges.

5.4. Almighty God wished to avenge the blood of his servants and, not long after this, set the aforesaid bishop against Odo, the sole rebel. The bishop sought to force Odo to join in the pact common to all, but he would not delay in making an armed attack. Discovering that Odo's spirit remained inflexible, as was God's will, Aimon began—while the blood of the innocents was not yet dry—to collect allies together from all sides, including a large contingent of God's ministers. Confiding in lesser things, he directed his battleline against the enemy. When both armies stood almost at grips, a sound was made heavenward [indicating that Aimon's forces should] retreat, since they no longer had the Lord with them as a leader. When they made no sign of following this advice, an enormous globe of flashing light fell in their midst. Thus it came to pass, as it is said, "Flash forth the lightning and scatter them, send out the arrows and rout them!"[1] Then the people perceived that they were much inferior to their adversaries, since those exceeded in number the sands of the sea. They decided that some foot soldiers should be mounted on various animals and mixed into the cohorts of mounted warriors [*milites*] so that they would be judged mounted warriors by their opponents, more because of the appearance of their being mounted than because of the setting of their weapons. Without delay up to two thousand of the plebeian rabble were mounted on asses and arrayed as knights among the order of knights. But these men were terrified and they took flight along the banks of the Cher. They were killed in such numbers that they blocked the river in such a way that they made a bridge out of the bodies of the dying over which their enemies proceeded. More fell by their own swords than by those of their pursuers.... The number of the dying could not be comprehended: in one valley seven hundred clerics fell. Thus the most tempered judgment of God made those people—who had refused obedience to any requests for mercy, and had not been moved by the smell of their brothers' being burned, and had rejoiced more than was just to have their hands in an unfortunate victory—lost their lives along with that victory.

4.6 A castellan's revenues and properties in Catalonia: *Charter of Guillem Guifred* (1041–1075). Original in Latin.

Some time between 1041 and 1075 Bishop Guillem Guifred had a memorandum drawn up of the dues, properties, and services that were owed him as one of the lords of Sanahuja, a castle in Catalonia (today Spain). Although other castellans, such as Hugh of Lusignan (see p. 181), could not claim precisely the same mix that Guillem commanded, this list provides a good example of the sort of resources that holders of fortifications might count on. Compare it with the revenues that the bishop of Marseille could command in the Carolingian period, as evidenced by the *Polyptyque of the Church of Saint Mary of Marseille*, above, p. 107.

[Source: Pierre Bonnassie, "The Banal Seigneury and the 'Reconditioning' of the Free Peasantry," in *Debating the Middle Ages: Issues and Readings*, ed. Lester K. Little and Barbara H. Rosenwein (Oxford: Basil Blackwell, 1988), pp. 114–15.]

---

[1] Ps.144: 6; Douay Ps. 143: 6.

This is a brief reminder of what the bishop ought to have in his castellany of Sanahuja, by use and by right.

In the first place, half of the revenue of the courts without deceit. From the market, half of what comes to the lords, by justice and by right, that is to say of the fines, with the exception of rights on the udders of the cows, which belong to the castle. Of the oven, half. Of rights on minting, half.

And the bishop agrees with the lords of Sanahuja that they should bring before him the men [of the castellany], and that he should levy on them, every year, the *queste* [a tax] of bread and meat. The bailiff of the lord should go with the bailiff of the bishop to the cellars of Sanahuja, and they should judge the barrels together for levying the *compra* [a tax] of the bishop. And that the bailiffs of the lords should assess the service of those who owe army service with donkeys and other equipment, that it should be estimated under oath, and when it has been estimated, the revenue should be shared by the lord and the *castlà* [the head of the garrison that guards the castle], and the *castlà* should give the bishop his part....

In the houses of Sanahuja, the bishop has the use of the wood, cabbages, chard, cheese, ewes, except in the houses of the priests, the *cabalers* [horsemen] and the bailiffs of the lords; and all this he may use in all the other houses of Sanahuja.... And the peasants of Sanahuja who work with a team should give the bishop a *sextarius* [a unit of measure] of oats and a sheaf, those who share a team with several others should give a *hemina* [another unit of measure] of oats, and a sheaf.

And if an animal enters into the bishop's *dominicatura* [demesne—the land belonging to the lord] in Sanahuja, and is retaken there, his master should buy him back for as many pennies as the animal has feet. And the bishop's woods enjoy a franchise [a privilege] such that no man may hunt within a stone's throw of it... and a man of Sanahuja who catches a rabbit in the woods must give an ox, a pig, and nine pairs of live rabbits to the bishop in reparation.

And all the men of Sanahuja must work for the bishop on the construction of his houses and owe him transport services on the back of their beasts, with the exception of priests, *cabalers*, the lords' bailiffs, and merchants.

And no lord may award any franchise at Sanahuja without the consent of the bishop.

And the men of Sanahuja must carry the bishop's bulls and messages at his command, to any place he may desire....

And in all the mills in the territory of Sanahuja already constructed, or those to be constructed, the bishop should have the quarter [of the revenues?], and in all the use of *destre mugar* [free use of the mill for his grain], under compulsion....

This was enacted by Guillem Guifred, bishop.

BYZANTINE EXPANSION

4.7 Military life: Constantine VII Porphyrogenitus, *Military Advice to His Son* (950–958). Original in Greek.

Emperor Constantine VII Porphyrogenitus (r.913–959) was a major force behind the revival of art and learning at Byzantium known as the Macedonian Renaissance. Likely the author of a famous book on the ceremonies of the court, he also wrote other treatises including the shorter work on military expeditions excerpted here, intended for his son but never finished. Here, as in his book on ceremonies, he concentrated on the formal aspects of the job: the requisitioning of materiel, the opportunities for gift-giving, the triumphal return, and the officials involved in all of these events. What would Dhuoda (p. 150 above) say about Constantine's advice to his son? What would Constantine say about Dhuoda's?

[Source: *Constantine Porphyrogenitus: Three Treatises on Imperial Military Expeditions*, ed. and trans. John F. Haldon (Vienna: Österreichischen Akademie der Wissenschaften, 1997), pp. 95, 97, 99, 101, 107, 109, 123, 141, 143, 145 (slightly modified).]

Constantine, Emperor of the Romans in Christ the Eternal King, Son of Leo the Most Wise Emperor of Blessed Memory, Descendant of Basil the Most Courageous and Most Brave Emperor, to Romanus, God-Crowned Emperor, His Son

What Should Be Observed When the Great and High Emperor of the Romans Goes on Campaign

Listen, son, to the words of your father, Solomon exhorts you. For you will hear about duties from many, but you will not reap the lessons of virtue by nature alone unless you hear the best things from your father. For when you have accepted his words as genuinely truthful, you will have what amounts to a paternal legacy, always promoting your salvation. For the words of others, spoken for favors, often lack truth; whereas those from a father's heart, being honest, bestow upon their sons perpetual advantage. Listen, therefore, son, to your father, whose advice it is not good to ignore; for if ignorance is bad, it is clear that a knowledge of practical matters is good, and most especially of those things touching upon the affairs of the state, to which much care has been devoted. For what could be more important than courage in warfare and the ancient discipline of our forefathers, the order of things to which they held formerly in imperial wartime expeditions?…

When the great and high emperor is about to go on an expedition and to mobilize arms and troops against the enemy, he orders first of all that a *lorikion*[1] and a sword and shield should be hung up on the Chalke, outside the gates.[2] From this, the preparation of an imperial expedition is made clear to all, and from this moment each officer and soldier begins to prepare his weapons and such things as are necessary and required of a soldier. Then, after this has taken place, he orders the *logothetes* of the herds that a fair distribution and rationing (of baggage animals) from the *mitata*[3] of Asia and Phrygia, and according to the strength and capacity of each *mitaton*, should be carried out in the fear of God and in all truth and piety. For each of the above-mentioned *mitata* has a specific number of animals

due from it according to its status, which is set down clearly for all: from Asia and Phrygia 200 mules at 15 *nomismata*, 200 pack-horses at 12 *nomismata*, in total 5,424 *nomismata*, which is 76 lbs. gold.[4]

ON THE CUSTOMARY DUES OF THE OFFICERS OF THE IMPERIAL STABLES, BOTH IN THE CITY AND IN THE PROVINCIAL STABLES:

From the *komes* of the stable, 4 mules and 4 pack-horses; from the *chartoularios* and the *epeiktes* 4 mules and 4 pack-horses; from the provincial *chartoularios* 2 mules and 2 pack-horses; from the commissariat 1 mule and 1 pack-horse; from the 4 *komites* 1 mule.[5] Altogether from the officers, 322 *nomismata*, which is 4 lbs. 26 *nomismata*. In sum, 80 lbs. 26 *nomismata*.

The *logothetes* of the herds brings the 200 mules and likewise the 200 pack-horses down to Malagina, and the *komes* of the stable and the inner *chartoularios* of the stable select five-, six- and seven-year old animals, with no blemishes on their flanks. These 400 are then branded with the imperial seal on both sides of the forequarters. The same requisition and branding takes place furthermore in the following year. All the packhorses are castrated and thus become geldings, and serve as a supplement for the expedition's needs. The *logothetes* brings the 200 pack-animals fully harnessed, with felt coverings over their saddle-cloths, carrying ropes for the loads, equipped with leggings, horseshoes and with their halters.…

FROM THE METROPOLITANS AND ARCHBISHOPS:

Fifty-two fully-harnessed mules from the metropolitans; 52 mules from the fifty-two archbishops. These 104 fully harnessed mules, with their loads, are also to be shoed. The *komes* of the stable, together with the *chartoularios* of the inner stable takes them, and brands them with the rest of the baggage train, in all 104 mules. And the grand total from both sources, the *mitata* of the *logothetes* of the herds, and the (animals provided as) gifts, 585 mules.

---

[1] A *lorikion* was a suit of mail. Special clothing was often displayed to signal a special event.

[2] The Chalke was the bronze gate of the imperial palace in Constantinople.

[3] *Logothetes* was a bureaucrat of high position. The *logothetes* of the herds was the man in charge of the farms (*mitata* [sing: *mitaton*]) that supplied horses and pack animals for military expeditions.

[4] *Nomismata* were Byzantine gold coins.

[5] The *komes* (pl. *komites*), or "count," of the stable was the chief officer of the imperial stable, who purchased the animals from the *mitata* at a set price. The *chartoularios* and *epeiktes* were the titles of other officials of the stable. The "inner chartoularios," referred to in the next paragraph, is, by contrast with the "provincial chartoularios," in charge of the office in the capital.

FROM THE PIOUS MONASTERIES:

One hundred complementary horses, led before the emperor to left and right. They should be castrated and gelded; but they are not branded, since when the emperor orders a gift to be made, it is from among these that animals are presented wherever he commands. Likewise from the animals brought as gifts to the emperor during the course of the expedition. The *komes* of the stable, along with the *chartoularios* of the stable takes 3 lbs. of gold from the *eidikon* for expenses.[1]...

FOR THE PERSONAL IMPERIAL VESTIARION AND FOR THOSE SECONDED BY THE BEDCHAMBER FOR THE BAGGAGE OF THE SAME IMPERIAL VESTIARION, 30 PACK-ANIMALS:[2]

All the imperial clothing and the remaining regalia in vessels encased in purple leather and burnished iron chains and straps likewise burnished, so that they can be carried by the pack-animals; eight silver coolers with covers, for scented wine, rose-water, and water: of these, one small cooler for white wine, two large ones for rosewater, and four large ones for water. Two silver pails for water; various water-skins, large and small; four other coolers, large, of burnished copper, like earthenware pots, for water; two burnished copper pails; and sacred vessels for the chapel, which the *minsourator* transports.[3]

Books: the liturgy of the Church, military manuals, books on mechanics, including siege machinery and the production of missiles and other information relevant to the enterprise, that is to say, to wars and sieges; historical books, especially those of Polyainos and Syrianos;[4] an oneirocritical book;[5] a book of chances and occurrences; a book dealing with good and bad weather and storms, rain and lightning and thunder and the vehemence of the winds; and in addition to these a treatise on thunder and a treatise on earthquakes, and other books, such as those to which sailors are wont to refer. Note that such a book was researched and compiled from many books by myself, Constantine emperor of the Romans in Christ the eternal King.

Tufted rugs for reclining, so that guests may rest;... theriac, serapium juice, other antidotes, both mixed and unmixed, for those who have been poisoned; receptacles with all kinds of oils and remedies; and diverse salves and unguents and ointments and other medical substances, herbs and whatever else is necessary for the curing of men and beasts. Small silver pails and sprinklers with covers for the emperor, and others of polished bronze for officers and distinguished refugees; thick and thin double-bordered cushions for the emperor to recline upon; two chairs for the cortège [procession], chairs for the chamberpot, of metal gilded with beaten gold, with covers, and with other covers above concealing the space for the latrine; and for the distinguished refugees two other, similar, seats, bound in silver; imperial chalices for the guests invited to dine with the emperor; two imperial swords, one ceremonial, one for the campaign; one sabre; ointments, various perfumes: incense, mastic, frankincense, sachar, saffron, musk, amber, bitter aloes, moist and dry, pure ground cinnamon of first and second quality, cinnamon wood, and other perfumes. Silken sheets, rough linen blankets, linen towels, sheets, "western" patchwork covers, "western" towels.

FROM THE UNTAILORED CLOTHS DISPATCHED TO FOREIGNERS AS GIFTS:

Skaramaggia of different colors and patterns:[6] all-white, all-yellow and all-blue *skaramaggia;* tunics of high value, produced in the imperial workshops; undergarments of middling value produced in the imperial workshops; undergarments of lower value produced in the imperial workshops; undergarments of lower value of varying colors and patterns produced in the imperial workshops; off-white coats, two-tone silk garments of white and violet; triple-warped striped garments of violet, of purple and a selection of different hues. Note that all these are carried in containers encased in purple leather and burnished chains, with straps similarly burnished....

Once the emperor has passed into the *themata*, he is welcomed by each *thema*, when the *thema* is drawn up in

---

[1] The *eidikon* was an imperial office for fiscal matters.

[2] The *vestiarion*, also part of fiscal administration, was in charge of cloth production as well as metals and bullion.

[3] The *minsourator* was responsible for the imperial tent.

[4] Polyainos (*fl.* 2nd c. CE) wrote a book on military strategy for the Roman emperors that was highly prized later at Constantinople. Syrianos was a later (perhaps 9th c.) writer on the same topic.

[5] I.e., a book that interprets dreams.

[6] *Skaramaggia* were silk tunics decorated with embroidery. They might be worn or used as altar cloths or banners.

parade order, of course.[1] When the emperor approaches, the *strategos* and the *protonotarios* of the *thema* and the *tourmarchai* and the *drouggarokomites* and the *merarches* and the *komes* of the tent and the *chartoularios* and the *domestikos* of the *thema* dismount from their horses while the emperor is still some distance from reaching them, and form a reception party.[2] And when the emperor passes through, all the aforementioned fall to the ground, paying homage to the emperor; but the soldiers all remain mounted. After the *strategoi* and the officers referred to have paid homage to the emperor, the latter makes a short detour from the road, saying to them: "Well met!" Then he asks them: "How are you, my children? How are your wives, my daughters-in-law, and the children?" And they reply that "In the life of your Majesty, so we, your servants, are well." And again, the emperor responds: "Thanks be to Holy God who keeps us in health." When all have acclaimed the emperor, he commands the *strategos* and all the above-mentioned officers to mount up, and to leave with their army for their own ordained position....

THE VICTORIOUS RETURN OF THE CHRIST-LOVING EMPEROR BASIL [I] FROM CAMPAIGN IN THE REGIONS OF TEPHRIKE AND GERMANIKEIA[3]

When the emperor returned victorious from the war against Tephrike and Germanikeia, he passed via Hiereia to the Hebdomon, where citizens of every age met him, with crowns prepared from flowers and roses.[4] Likewise the whole senate then in the City received him there also, and the emperor greeted them verbally. And when he had entered and prayed in the Church of the Baptist in the Hebdomon, and lit candles, he went out; and donning a triple-bordered *skaramaggion*, and riding together with his son Constantine, they came to the Church of the All-Holy Virgin of the Abramites, with the whole senate going ahead with the people of the City, and with processional banners. Dismounting from their horses, they entered the Church of the Virgin; and having prayed and lit candles, they sat for a short time.

In the meantime, the Eparch of the City had prepared the City in advance, garlanding the route from the Golden Gate as far as the Chalke with laurel and rosemary and myrtle and roses and other flowers, also with a variety of *skaramaggia* and silk hangings and candelabra; he similarly strewed the ground, which was completely covered in flowers.[5]...

On the meadow outside the Golden Gate, tents were set up, and they brought over the noble and important Hagarene prisoners[6] together with the best of the booty of war, banners, and weapons. When it had been deposited in the tents, this was divided up and paraded triumphally along the Mese from the Golden Gate to the Chalke of the palace, for the central, great Golden Gate was then opened.

After the booty had been paraded, the emperors rose and, changing out of their *skaramaggia*, the autocrat and great emperor donned a gold-embroidered breastplate-tunic covered in pearls set in a criss-cross pattern, and with perfect pearls along the hems; girding himself also with a belted sword, bearing upon his head a Caesar's diadem.... His son Constantine wore a gold *klibanion*[7] and a belted sword, golden greaves, and in his hand a gilded spear decorated with pearls. On his head he wore a low turban with a circlet of white embroidered with gold, having on the forehead a likeness of a gold-embroidered crown. Both rode mounted on white horses equipped with gem-encrusted caparisons. While mounted, they received the demarchs and the two factions, wearing deme tunics and segmented diadems on their heads, with other garlands made from roses and flowers around their necks,

---

[1] The *themata* (sing. *thema*) are the themes.

[2] The *strategos* (pl. *strategoi*) and the *protonotarios* were the chief military officers of the theme, while the other officials named here were their subordinates.

[3] The emperor that Constantine is referring to here is Basil I the Macedonian (r.867–886). The "regions of Tephrike and Germanikeia" were in southeastern Anatolia.

[4] The Hebdomon palace complex was outside the walls of Constantinople on the Sea of Marmara, by the route to the Golden Gate.

[5] The Mese, the main boulevard from the Golden Gate, led to the Chalke. The Eparch of Constantinople was in effect the "mayor" of the city.

[6] The "Hagarene prisoners" were the Muslims who were captured in the wars.

[7] A *klibanion* was sleeveless body armor, in this case of gold, covering the chest to the waist. At this point in the procession, the emperor and his son were still outside the Golden Gate.

carrying kerchiefs in their hands.[1] The demarchs wore their triumphal mantles, and their officials tunics and ordinary mantles. The acclamations were to begin with as follows: "Glory to God, who returns our own Lords to us victorious! Glory to God, who exalts you, autocrats of the Romans! Glory to you, All-Holy Trinity, that we see our own Lords victorious! Welcome as conquerors, most courageous Lords!" Then other acclamations in praise of victory were made, and processional military hymns were sung, as the two factions processed before (the emperor).

When they had come from the Church of the Abramites to the Golden Gate, as we said, which was open to them, they stood before the entry to it, and were similarly acclaimed. They received then the Eparch of the City and the emperor's representative who, falling to the ground, paid homage, and presented to the emperor a golden crown, after the old custom, along with other crowns of laurel, as symbols of victory. And they then received from the emperor coin to the value and above of the golden crown. When the demes had completed their acclamations, the emperors went in procession through the great Golden Gate.

4.8 Imperial rule: Michael Psellus, *Portrait of Basil II* (*c*.1063). Original in Greek.

Michael Psellus (1018–1078), probably born and certainly educated in Constantinople, served at the courts of many of the emperors and empresses of the second half of the eleventh century. Among his many writings was the *Chronographia*, a book containing the biographies of the very Byzantine emperors and empresses whom he had known personally. Its first subject, however, was Basil II the Bulgar-Slayer, whose rule (976–1025) just barely overlapped Psellus's birth and early childhood. In his account, Psellus suggested that Basil's military successes and autocratic attitude went hand in hand. How might you put this document together with Constantine [VII]'s description of the military activities of the emperor, in the treatise above, p. 189 to help explain Byzantium's extraordinary expansion in the early eleventh century?

[Source: *Fourteen Byzantine Rulers: The* Chronographia *of Michael Psellus*, trans. Edgar R.A. Sewter (New York: Penguin Books, 1966), pp. 28–30, 43–48.]

Once invested with supreme power over the Romans, Basil was unwilling to share his designs with anyone else; he refused advice on the conduct of public affairs. On the other hand, having had no previous experience of military matters or of good civil administration, he discovered that to rely on his own unaided judgment was impossible. He was compelled to turn for help to the *parakoimomenus* (Lord Chamberlain).[2] This man, called Basil, happened at that time to be the most remarkable person in the Roman Empire, outstanding in intellect, bodily stature, and regal appearance. Although he was born of the same father as the father of Basil and Constantine [VIII], on his mother's side he came of different stock. In early infancy he had suffered castration—a natural precaution against a concubine's offspring, for as a eunuch he could never hope to usurp the throne from a legitimate heir. Actually he was resigned to his fate and was genuinely attached to the Imperial house—after all, it was his own family. He was particularly devoted to his nephew Basil, embracing the young man in the most affectionate manner and watching over his progress like some kindly foster-parent. One should not be surprised,

---

[1]   The demarchs were the leaders of the Blues and the Greens, the two traditional hippodrome factions—the chariot-racing teams and their supporters (the demes)—at Constantinople.

[2]   Son of Emperor Romanus I Lecapenus (r.920–944), he was promoted by Emperor Nicephorus II Phocas (r.963–969).

then, that Basil placed on this man's shoulders the burden of Empire. The older man's serious nature, too, had its influence on the emperor's character. The *parakoimomenus*, in fact, was like an athlete competing at the games while Basil watched him as a spectator—not a spectator present merely to cheer on the victor, but rather one who trained himself in the running and took part in the contests himself, following in the other's footsteps and imitating his style. So the *parakoimomenus* had the whole world at his feet. It was to him that the civilian population looked, to him that the army turned, and he was responsible, indeed solely responsible, for the administration of public finance and the direction of government. In this task he was constantly assisted by the emperor both in word and in deed, for Basil not only backed up his minister's measures, but confirmed them in writing.

To most men of our generation who saw the Emperor Basil he seemed austere and abrupt in manner, an irascible person who did not quickly change his mind, sober in his daily habits and averse to all effeminacy, but if I am to believe the historians of that period who wrote about him, he was not at all like that when his reign began. A change took place in his character after he acceded to the throne, and instead of leading his former dissolute, voluptuous sort of life, he became a man of great energy. The complete metamorphosis was brought about by the pressure of events. His character stiffened, so to speak. Feebleness gave way to strength and the old slackness disappeared before a new fixity of purpose. In his early days he used to feast quite openly and frequently indulged in the pleasures of love; his main concern was with his banqueting and a life spent in the gay, indolent atmosphere of the court. The combination of youth and unlimited power gave him opportunities for self-indulgence, and he enjoyed them to the full. The change in his mode of living dates from the attempted revolutions of the notorious Sclerus[1] and of Phocas.[2] Sclerus twice raised the standard of revolt, and there were other aspirants to the throne, with two parties in opposition to the emperor. From that time onward, Basil's carefree existence was forgotten and he wholeheartedly applied himself to serious objects. Once the first blow had been struck against those members of his family who had seized power, he set himself resolutely to compass their utter destruction.

[Psellus discusses the rebellion of Phocas, the two rebellions of Sclerus, and downfall of the eunuch Basil, the Lord Chamberlain. He then turns to Basil II's reconciliation with Sclerus.]

As soon as he saw Sclerus enter, Basil rose and they embraced one another. Then they held converse, the one excusing his revolt and explaining the reason why he had plotted and carried it out, the other quietly accepting the apology and attributing to bad luck what had occurred. When they shared a common drinking-bowl, the emperor first put to his own lips the cup offered to Sclerus and took a moderate sip of its contents before handing it back to his guest. Thus he relieved him of any suspicion of poison, and at the same time proved the sanctity of their agreement. After this Basil questioned him, as a man accustomed to command, about his Empire. How could it be preserved free from dissension? Sclerus had an answer to this, although it was not the sort of advice one would expect from a general; in fact, it sounded more like a diabolical plot. "Cut down the governors who become over-proud," he said. "Let no generals on campaign have too many resources. Exhaust them with unjust exactions, to keep them busied with their own affairs. Admit no woman to the imperial councils. Be accessible to no one. Share with few your most intimate plans."

On this note their conversation came to an end. Sclerus went off to the country estate which had been apportioned him, and soon afterwards he died. We will leave him and return to the emperor. In his dealings with his subjects, Basil behaved with extraordinary circumspection. It is perfectly true that the great reputation he built up as a ruler was founded rather on terror than on loyalty, for as he grew older and became more experienced, he relied less on the judgment of men wiser than himself. He alone introduced new measures, he alone disposed his military forces. As for the civil administration, he governed, not in accordance with the written laws, but following the unwritten dictates of his own intuition, which was most excellently equipped by nature for the purpose. Consequently he paid no attention to men of learning; on the contrary, he affected utter scorn—towards the learned folk, I mean. It seems to me a wonderful thing, therefore, that while the emperor so

---

[1] Bardas Sclerus had been brother-in-law of Emperor John I Tzimisces (r.969–976), who had married his sister Maria. He had expected to succeed John, for he had been promised the throne by the emperor on his deathbed.

[2] The Phocas family came from Cappadocia and for several generations had enjoyed high repute as soldiers. Bardas Phocas's uncle was Emperor Nicephorus.

despised literary culture, no small crop of orators and philosophers sprang up in those times. One solution of the paradox, I fancy, is this: the men of those days did not devote themselves to the study of letters for any ulterior purpose—they cultivated literature for its own sake and as an end in itself, whereas the majority nowadays do not approach the subject of education in this spirit, but consider personal profit to be the first reason for study. Perhaps I should add that though gain is the object of their zeal for literature, if they do not immediately achieve this goal, then they desist from their studies at once. Shame on them!

However, we must return to the emperor. Having purged the Empire of the barbarians, he dealt with his own subjects and completely subjugated them too—I think "subjugate" is the right word to describe it. He decided to abandon his former policy, and after the great families had been humiliated and put on an equal footing with the rest, Basil found himself playing the game of power-politics with considerable success. He surrounded himself with favorites who were neither remarkable for brilliance of intellect, nor of noble lineage, nor too learned. To them were entrusted the imperial rescripts,[1] and with them he was accustomed to share the secrets of State. However, since at that time the emperor's comments on memoranda or requests for favors were never varied, but only plain, straightforward statements (for Basil, whether writing or speaking, avoided all elegance of composition), he used to dictate to his secretaries just as the words came to his tongue, stringing them all together, one after the other. There was no subtlety, nothing superfluous in his speech.

By humbling the pride or jealousy of his people, Basil made his own road to power an easy one. He was careful, moreover, to close the exit-doors on the monies contributed to the treasury. So a huge sum was built up, partly by the exercise of strict economy, partly by fresh additions from abroad. Actually the sum accumulated in the imperial treasury reached the grand total of 200,000 talents. As for the rest of his gains, it would indeed be hard to find words adequately to describe them. All the treasures amassed in Iberia and Arabia, all the riches found among the Celts or contained in the land of the Scyths[2]—in brief, all the wealth of the barbarians who surround our borders—all were gathered together in one place and depos-

ited in the emperor's coffers. In addition to this, he carried off to his treasure-chambers, and sequestrated there, all the money of those who rebelled against him and were afterwards subdued. And since the vaults of the buildings made for this purpose were not big enough, he had spiral galleries dug underground, after the Egyptian style, and there he kept safe a considerable proportion of his treasures. He himself took no pleasure in any of it; quite the reverse, indeed, for the majority of the precious stones, both the white ones (which we call pearls) and the colored brilliants, far from being inlaid in diadems or collars, were hidden away in his underground vaults. Meanwhile Basil took part in his processions and gave audience to his governors clad merely in a robe of purple, not the very bright purple, but simply purple of a dark hue, with a handful of gems as a mark of distinction. As he spent the greater part of his reign serving as a soldier on guard at our frontiers and keeping the barbarian marauders at bay, not only did he draw nothing from his reserves of wealth, but even multiplied his riches many times over.

On his expedition against the barbarians, Basil did not follow the customary procedure of other emperors, setting out at the middle of spring and returning home at the end of summer. For him the time to return was when the task in hand was accomplished. He endured the rigors of winter and the heat of summer with equal indifference. He disciplined himself against thirst. In fact, all his natural desires were kept under stern control, and the man was as hard as steel. He had an accurate knowledge of the details of army life, and by that I do not mean the general acquaintance with the composition of his army, the relative functions of individual units in the whole body, or the various groupings and deployments suited to the different formations. His experience of army matters went further than that: the duties of the *protostates*, the duties of the *hemilochites*,[3] the tasks proper to the rank immediately junior to them—all these were no mysteries to Basil, and the knowledge stood him in good stead in his wars. Accordingly, jobs appropriate to these ranks were not devolved on others, and the emperor, being personally conversant with the character and combat duties of each individual, knowing to what each man was fitted either by temperament or by training, used him in this capacity and made him serve there.

---

[1] Laws written in response to particular cases.

[2] Iberia was an eastern theme of the Byzantine empire. The "riches of the Celts" refers to the riches of western states. The Slavs were called "Scyths" by classicizing authors such as Psellus.

[3] Military ranks, junior officers.

Moreover, he knew the various formations suited to his men. Some he had read of in books, others he devised himself during the operations of war, the result of his own intuition. He professed to conduct his wars and draw up the troops in line of battle, himself planning each campaign, but he preferred not to engage in combat personally. A sudden retreat might otherwise prove embarrassing. Consequently, for the most part he kept his troops immobile. He would construct machines of war and skirmish at a distance, while the maneuvering was left to the light-armed soldiers. Once he had made contact with the enemy, a regular military liaison was established between the different formations of the Roman army. The whole force was drawn up like a solid tower, headquarters being in touch with the cavalry squadrons, who were themselves kept in communication with the light infantry, and these again with the various units of heavy-armed foot [soldiers]. When all was ready, strict orders were given that no soldier should advance in front of the line or break rank under any circumstances. If these orders were disobeyed, and if some of the most valiant or daring soldiers did ride out well in front of the rest, even in cases where they engaged the enemy successfully, they could expect no medals or rewards of valor when they returned. On the contrary, Basil promptly discharged them from the army, and they were punished on the same level as common criminals. The decisive factor in the achievement of victory was, in his opinion, the massing of troops in one coherent body, and for this reason alone he believed the Roman armies to be invin-cible. The careful inspections he made before battle used to aggravate the soldiers and they abused him openly, but the emperor met their scorn with common sense. He would listen quietly, and then with a gay smile point out that if he neglected these precautions, their battles would go on for ever.

Basil's character was twofold, for he readily adapted himself no less to the crises of war than to the calm of peace. Really, if the truth be told, he was more of a villain in wartime, more of an emperor in time of peace. Outbursts of wrath he controlled, and like the proverbial "fire under the ashes" kept anger hidden in his heart, but, if his orders were disobeyed in war, on returning to his palace he would kindle his wrath and reveal it. Terrible then was the vengeance he took on the miscreant. Generally he persisted in his opinions, but there were occasions when he did change his mind. In many cases, too, he traced crimes back to their original causes, and the final links in the chain were exonerated. So most defaulters obtained forgiveness, either through his sympathetic understanding, or because he showed some other interest in their affairs. He was slow to adopt any course of action, but never would he willingly alter the decision once it was taken. Consequently his attitude to friends was unvaried, unless perchance he was compelled by necessity to revise his estimate of them. Similarly, where he had burst out in anger against someone, he did not quickly moderate his indignation. Whatever estimate he formed, indeed, was to him an irrevocable and divinely-inspired judgment.

SCHOLARSHIP ACROSS THE ISLAMIC WORLD

4.9 Education: Al-Qabisi, *A Treatise Detailing the Circumstances of Students and the Rules Governing Teachers and Students* (before 1012). Original in Arabic.

Abu al-Hasan Ali ibn Khalaf al-Qabisi (935–1012) was an important leader of one school of Islamic legal thought, the Maliki, named after its founder, Malik ibn Anas (d.796). After studying with scholars at Mecca and Cairo, al-Qabisi settled in Tunisia. Among his many writings were collections of hadith (traditions about the Prophet: see above, p. 117) and commentaries on the Qur'an. Above all, al-Qabisi was interested in law, and his treatise on students, parents, and teachers, some of which is presented here, formed part of his legal corpus. Teachers were under contract to parents and students, so al-Qabisi was concerned to clarify their obligations and to justify payments for instruction. (In the thirteenth century, western scholastics would take up similar issues.) The treatise was written in the form of a response to "an urgent questioner"; the views of al-Qabisi and other authorities were given in the third person in chains of transmission in the same way that the hadith were transmitted by *isnad*. In al-Qabisi's view, it was the obligation of parents and guardians to teach their children (usually by sending them to a teacher), and if they could not be responsible, it was up to the state to educate the young. However, al-Qabisi limited the kinds of education girls should have.

[Source: *Classical Foundations of Islamic Education Thought*, ed. Bradley J. Cook with Fathi H. Malkawi (Provo, UT: Brigham Young University Press, 2010), pp. 45–51, 54. Translated by Michael Fishbein. (Notes modified.)]

In the name of God, the Merciful, the Compassionate; God Bless Muhammad.

25. Abu al-Hasan [al-Qabisi] said: What I have told you about the merit a father can be expected to acquire from teaching his child the Qur'an should serve to encourage the father to teach his young child who, being unable to help or harm himself and unable to distinguish for himself what to take up and what to turn away, has only his father as a refuge, whose duty it is to provide his means of support....

27. Muslims throughout their history have diligently taught their children the Qur'an and provided them with teachers. This is something that no father refrains from doing for his child if he has the means to do so, unless he is following his soul's avarice. The latter is no excuse for him, for God, who is praised, has said: "Souls are very prone to avarice."[1] And, "whosoever is guarded against the avarice of his own soul—they are the prosperers."[2] Not one father would leave off doing this, deeming its omission trivial and insignificant, except a coarse father with no desire for good....

28. A child's religious status, as long as he is a minor, is the status of his father. Will the father then leave his minor child, not teaching him religion, when his teaching him the Qur'an will make his knowledge of religion firm? Has he not heard the words of the Messenger of God, on whom be peace? "Every infant is born in a state

of nature; then his parents make him a Jew or a Christian. It is just as camels are brought forth as beasts intact. Do you discern any that are mutilated?"[3] ...

29. If the children of unbelievers experience harm from their parents, it behooves the children of believers to benefit religiously from their parents. The first generations of believers had no need to trouble themselves arguing about this; they made do with the desire that had been placed in their hearts; they acted according to it, and they left it as customary practice that each generation passed on from the previous one. No father was ever reproved regarding this, nor did any father ever turn out to have omitted to do so from desire or from negligence. That is no attribute of a believing Muslim! Had it ever become evident that someone had omitted to teach his child the Qur'an out of negligence, his condition would have been deemed one of ignorance, ugliness, and deficiency, beneath that of people of contentment and satisfaction. Sometimes, however, lack of means causes parents to lag behind in this matter; then their behavior is excusable—depending on how sound their excuse turns out to be.

30. If the child has property, his father or his guardian (if his father has died) should not leave him. Let him enter the primary school and engage the teacher to teach him the Qur'an from his wealth, as is due. If the orphan has no guardian, the ruler[4] of the Muslims should oversee his affairs and proceed with his instruction as the father or guardian would have proceeded. If the child

---

[1] Qur'an 4: 128.

[2] Qur'an 64: 16.

[3] After they were born, the ears of camels were notched (and thus mutilated) to brand them.

[4] The word used here was *hakim*, which could refer to a leader of any sort, from the ruler of a country to a judge to a community official.

is in a town where there is no ruler, oversight would be exercised for him in a matter such as this if the town's righteous people came together to oversee the interests of the town's people, for overseeing this orphan is one of those interests.

31. If the orphan has no property, his mother or next of kin should be encouraged to take charge of teaching him the Qur'an. If someone else volunteers to bear the burden for them, that person shall have his reward. If the orphan has no kin to care for him, any Muslim who cares for him shall have his reward. If the teacher, reckoning on a heavenly reward, teaches him solely for God's sake, bearing it patiently, his reward for it, God willing, shall be doubled, especially since it is his craft from which he supports himself....

32. As for teaching a female the Qur'an and learning, it is good and of benefit to her. However, her being taught letter-writing or poetry is a cause for fear. She should be taught only things that can be expected to be good for her and protect her from temptation. It would be safer for her to be spared learning to write. When the Prophet (may God bless him and grant him peace) permitted women to attend the festival, he commanded them to bring out adolescent girls and those who normally are secluded behind a curtain.[1] At the same time he commanded menstruating women to avoid the place where people pray. He said, "Let women be present where there is blessing and at the prayers of Muslims." On this basis it is acceptable to teach them good things that are safe for them; as for things from which harm to them can be feared, it is preferable that such things be kept away from them, and this is the duty of their guardian. Understand what I have explained to you. Seek guidance from God, and He will guide: He is a sufficient guide and helper for you.

33. Know that God, who is mighty and exalted, has imposed certain duties on believing women, just as He has imposed certain duties on believing men. This may be inferred from God's words: "It is not for any believer, man or woman, when God and His Messenger have decreed a matter, to have the choice in the affair."[2] And, "The believers, the men and the women."[3] In more than one verse of His Book He has joined men and women together in being well rewarded. For example, "God has promised the believers, men and women, gardens underneath which rivers flow, forever therein to dwell, and goodly dwelling-places in the Gardens of Eden; and greater God's good pleasure, that is the mighty triumph."[4] And He commanded the wives of His Prophet (on whom be peace) to remember what they had heard from the Prophet: "And remember that which is recited in your houses of the signs of God and the Wisdom."[5] How should they not be taught the good and what helps to its attainment? But whoever is in charge of them should turn from them anything of which one should beware on their behalf, since he is their protector and responsible for them....

37. Know that there was not one of the religious leaders[6] of the Muslims in the first days of this community but who gave thought to what would be of benefit to Muslims in all their affairs, private and public. We have never heard that any of them appointed teachers to teach people's children in elementary schools[7] during their childhood or gave such teachers a share from the public treasury, as they did for anyone they charged to serve the Muslims either by judging between them in lawsuits, calling them to prayer in the mosque, or anything else that they established to protect Muslims and guard their affairs. They could not have neglected the business of teachers for young children. However—and God only knows—they thought it was a matter that concerned each individual personally, inasmuch as what a person taught his child was part of his own welfare that was of special concern to him. They therefore left it as one of the tasks of fathers, something that it was not fitting for someone else to do for them if they were able to do it themselves. Since the religious leaders of the Muslims had made no provision for the matter and it was one that Muslims had to carry out for their children and without which they would not feel at ease, they got themselves a teacher for their children, someone to devote himself to them on a regular basis and to care for them as he would care for his own young children. Since

---

[1] An "adolescent girl" (*awatiq*) had begun puberty and was kept behind the curtain in the tent of her family, but she was not yet married.

[2] Qur'an 33: 36.

[3] Qur'an 9: 71.

[4] Qur'an 9: 72.

[5] Qur'an 33: 34.

[6] The word used here was *a'immah*, the plural of *imam*, a religious scholar and especially the founder of a legal school.

[7] The word used here was *katatib*, the plural of *kuttab*, a school in which students learned to read the Qur'an.

it was unlikely that anyone could be found to volunteer for the Muslims, teach their children for them, devote himself entirely to them, and give up seeking his own livelihood and his profitable activities and other needs, it was appropriate for Muslims to hire someone to take care of teaching their children on a constant basis, to the exclusion of any other business. Such a teacher would relieve the children's parents of the burden of educating them; he would make them understand how to live upright lives, and he would increase their understanding of the good and turn them away from evil.

38. This is an occupation that few people volunteer to perform free of charge. If one had waited for people to volunteer to teach young children the Qur'an, many children would have been neglected and many people would not have learned the Qur'an. This would necessarily have led to loss of the Qur'an from people's hearts. It would have caused Muslim children to be confirmed in ignorance.

39. Yet there is no good reason to cause a shortage where there is no scarcity, and no injunction to abstain [from being paid to teach the Qur'an] has been confirmed as coming from the Messenger of God (may God bless him and grant him peace).

40. Al-Harith ibn Miskin,[1] in a report dated to the year [789–90], said: "Ibn Wahb gave us the following report: 'I heard Malik say, "None of the scholars I have known saw anything wrong with paying teachers—teachers of the Qur'an school."'"[2]

41. The following is also attributed to Ibn Wahb in his *Muwatta* from 'Abd al-Jabbar ibn 'Umar: "No one I asked in Medina sees anything wrong in teachers teaching for pay."…

53. The aforementioned people disagreed only about paying the teacher to teach something other than the Qur'an and writing. They did not disagree about subjects meant to reinforce the Qur'an, such as writing and penmanship.

54. Ibn Sahnun[3] mentioned: "It is fitting for the teacher to teach his students [the correct reading of] the case-endings of [the words of] the Qur'an—it is his duty to

do so—and vocalization, spelling, good handwriting, good reading, when to pause [in recitation], and how to articulate clearly; it is his duty to do so. It is his duty to teach them the good reading that has become well-known, namely the reading of Nafi',[4] but there is no harm in his having them read according to another [authority] if [the reading] is not considered disagreeable. There is no harm in his teaching them homilies, if they desire.

55. "He should teach them good manners, for it his duty toward God to give good advice, protect them, and care for them. The teacher should command them to perform the ritual prayer when they are seven years old and beat them for [omitting to pray] when they are ten. That is what Malik said…."

56. [Malik also said:] "Let him take care to teach them supplications,[5] that they may make their humble petitions to God; and let him teach them God's greatness and majesty, that they may magnify Him for it. If the people suffer from drought and the imam leads them in prayers for rain, I would have the teacher bring the children out [those of them who know how to pray], and let them beseech God with supplications and make their humble petitions to Him, for I have been told that when the people to whom Jonah was sent (may God's blessing be upon our Prophet and upon him) saw the chastisement with their own eyes, they brought out their children and entreated God by means of them, and the chastisement was lifted. He should teach them arithmetic, but it is not his duty unless it has been stipulated for him; and likewise poetry, obscure words, Arabic language, and the whole of grammar—in these matters he acts voluntarily. There is no harm in his teaching them poetry—words and reports of the [ancient] Arabs that contain nothing indecent—but it is not incumbent upon him." According to Sahnun there is nothing wrong if the person who teaches Qur'an and writing teaches all this, whether voluntarily or by stipulation. However, as for paying the teacher to teach these things with no intent to teach the Qur'an and writing, Sahnun, as mentioned previously, rejects it based on Malik's saying that he did not like payment for the teaching of poetry.

---

[1]   Al-Harith ibn Miskin was an earlier scholar of the Maliki school.

[2]   Because ibn Wahb (743–812) here transmitted the words of Malik ibn Anas, founder of the Maliki school, this passage and others like it linked al-Qabisi himself to the founder.

[3]   Ibn Sahnun (817–870) was an earlier scholar of the Maliki school and a student of ibn Wahb. Al-Qabisi was much influenced by ibn Sahnun's writings on education and quoted him extensively.

[4]   The Maliki school considered the reading of Nafi', i.e., the Qur'anic text cited as correct by Nafi' of Medina, to be best.

[5]   That is, prayers on various occasions that were not part of the five obligatory times of ritual prayers.

57. Ibn Habib, on the other hand, said: "There is nothing wrong with paying a teacher to teach poetry, grammar, letter-writing, the Days of the Arabs, and similar things, such as the knowledge of famous men and of chivalrous knights: there is nothing wrong with paying for the teaching of all this. I, however, am opposed to the teaching, learning, or recitation by an adult or child of any poetry containing accounts of unbridled violence, obscenity, or foul satire."

4.10 Political theory: Al-Farabi, *The Perfect State* (*c.*940–942). Original in Arabic.

Abu Nasr al-Farabi (872–950) was born in Turkestan, spent most of his adulthood in Baghdad, where he made a very modest living as a philosopher and writer, and joined the court of the emir of Aleppo in Syria toward the end of his life. His *Perfect State* engaged a long tradition of Greek thought on a great variety of spiritual, biological, and social topics; al-Farabi wanted to show their importance for a Muslim audience. His work thus began with God, angels, the heavens, the "bodies below the heavens," and so on, leading to the chapters below, which deal with human societies and their different degrees of excellence. How does al-Farabi's view of the "excellent and ignorant cities" compare with Augustine's notion of the "cities of God and Man" in *The City of God*, above, p. 14?

[Source: *Al-Farabi on the Perfect State*, ed. and trans. Richard Walzer (Oxford: Clarendon Press, 1985), pp. 231, 235, 239, 241, 253, 255, 257, 259.]

Chapter 15
Perfect Associations and Perfect Ruler; Faulty Associations

…§3. The most excellent good and the utmost perfection is, in the first instance, attained in a city, not in a society which is less complete than it. But since good in its real sense is such as to be attainable through choice and will and evils are also due to will and choice only, a city may be established to enable its people to cooperate in attaining some aims that are evil. Hence felicity is not attainable in every city. The city, then, in which people aim through association at cooperating for the things by which felicity in its real and true sense can be attained, is the excellent city, and the society in which there is a cooperation to acquire felicity is the excellent society; and the nation in which all of its cities cooperate for those things through which felicity is attained is the excellent nation. In the same way, the excellent universal state will arise only when all the nations in it cooperate for the purpose of reaching felicity.

§4. The excellent city resembles the perfect and healthy body, all of whose limbs cooperate to make the life of the animal perfect and to preserve it in this state. Now the limbs and organs of the body are different and their natural endowments and faculties are unequal in excellence, there being among them one ruling organ, namely the heart, and organs which are close in rank to that ruling organ, each having been given by nature a faculty by which it performs its proper function in conformity with the natural aim. So, too, the parts of the city are by nature provided with endowments unequal in excellence which enable them to do one thing and not another. But they are not parts of the city by their inborn nature alone but rather by the voluntary habits which they acquire such as the arts and their likes; to the natural faculties which exist in the organs and limbs of the body correspond the voluntary habits and dispositions in the parts of the city.

§5. The ruling organ in the body is by nature the most perfect and most complete of the organs in itself and in its specific qualification, and it also has the best of everything of which another organ has a share as well; beneath it, in turn, are other organs which rule over organs inferior to them, their rule being lower in rank than the rule of the first and indeed subordinate to the rule of the first; they rule and are ruled. In the same way, the ruler of the city is the most perfect part of the city in his specific qualification and has the best of everything which anybody else shares with him; beneath him are people who are ruled by him and rule others.

The heart comes to be first and becomes then the cause of the existence of the other organs and limbs of the body, and the cause of the existence of their faculties in them and of their arrangement in the ranks proper to them, and when one of its organs is out of order, it is the heart which provides the means to remove that disorder. In the same way the ruler of this city must come to be in the first instance, and will subsequently be the cause of the rise of the city and its parts and the cause of the presence of the voluntary habits of its parts and of their arrangement in the ranks proper to them; and when one part is out of order he provides it with the means to remove its disorder.

The parts of the body close to the ruling organ perform of the natural functions, in agreement—by nature—with the aim of the ruler, the most noble ones; the organs beneath them perform those functions which are less noble, and eventually the organs are reached which perform the meanest functions. In the same way the parts of the city which are close in authority to the ruler of the city perform the most noble voluntary actions, and those below them less noble actions, until eventually the parts are reached which perform the most ignoble actions. The inferiority of such actions is sometimes due to the inferiority of their matter, although they may be extremely useful—like the action of the bladder and the action of the lower intestine in the body; sometimes it is due to their being of little use; at other times it is due to their being very easy to perform. This applies equally to the city and equally to every whole which is composed by nature of well ordered coherent parts: they have a ruler whose relation to the other parts is like the one just described.

§6. This applies also to all existents,[1] For the relation of the First Cause to the other existents is like the relation of the king of the excellent city to its other parts.[2] For the ranks of the immaterial existents are close to the First [Cause]. Beneath them are the heavenly bodies, and beneath the heavenly bodies the material bodies. All these existents act in conformity with the First Cause, follow it, take it as their guide and imitate it; but each existent

does that according to its capacity, choosing its aim precisely on the strength of its established rank in the universe: that is to say the last follows the aim of that which is slightly above it in rank, equally the second existent, in turn, follows what is above itself in rank, and in the same way the third existent has an aim which is above it. Eventually existents are reached which are linked with the First Cause without any intermediary whatsoever. In accordance with this order of rank all the existents permanently follow the aim of the First Cause. Those which are from the very outset provided with all the essentials of their existence are made to imitate the First [Cause] and its aim from their very outset, and hence enjoy eternal bliss and hold the highest ranks; but those which are not provided from the outset with all the essentials of their existence, are provided with a faculty by which they move towards the expected attainment of those essentials and will then be able to follow the aim of the First [Cause]. The excellent city ought to be arranged in the same way: all its parts ought to imitate in their actions the aim of their first ruler according to their rank.

§7. The ruler of the excellent city cannot just be any man, because rulership requires two conditions: (a) he should be predisposed for it by his inborn nature, (b) he should have acquired the attitude and habit of will for rulership which will develop in a man whose inborn nature is predisposed for it. Nor is every art suitable for rulership, most of the arts, indeed, are rather suited for service within the city, just as most men are by their very nature born to serve. Some of the arts rule certain [other] arts while serving others at the same time, whereas there are other arts which, not ruling anything at all, only serve. Therefore the art of ruling the excellent city cannot just be any chance art, nor due to any chance habit whatever. For just as the first ruler in a genus cannot be ruled by anything in that genus—for instance the ruler of the limbs cannot be ruled by any other limb, and this holds good for any ruler of any composite whole—so the art of the ruler in the excellent city of necessity cannot be a serving art at all and cannot be ruled by any other art, but his art must be an art towards the aim of which all the other arts tend, and for which they strive in all the actions of the excellent city....

[Al-Farabi now explores the qualities of the ruler of the excellent city: his Passive Intellect (the only sort of

---

[1] I.e., that which exists, whether thing, action, or quality.

[2] The First Cause is God. The term "First Cause" is found in Aristotle's *Physics*, book 8, and his *Metaphysics*, book 12. However, the hierarchy of Being that al-Farabi describes here is neo-Platonic.

intellect that human beings have) learns all the intelligibles—all that can be understood by the intellect alone—from the Active Intellect, which is God.]

§15. In opposition to the excellent city are the "ignorant" city, the wicked city, the city which has deliberately changed its character and the city which has missed the right path through faulty judgment. In opposition to it are also the individuals who make up the common people in the various cities.

§16. The "ignorant" city is the city whose inhabitants do not know true felicity, the thought of it never having occurred to them. Even if they were rightly guided to it they would either not understand it or not believe in it. The only good things they recognize are some of those which are superficially thought of as good among the things which are considered to be the aims in life such as bodily health, wealth, enjoyment of pleasures, freedom to follow one's desires, and being held in honor and esteem. According to the citizens of the ignorant city each of these is a kind of felicity, and the greatest and perfect felicity is the sum total of all of them. Things contrary to these goods are misery such as deficiency of the body, poverty, no enjoyment of pleasures, no freedom to follow one's desires, and not being held in honor.

§17. The ignorant city is divided into a number of cities. One of them is the city of necessity, that is the city whose people strive for no more food, drink, clothes, housing and sexual intercourse than is necessary for sustaining their bodies, and they cooperate to attain this. Another is the city of meanness; the aim of its people is to cooperate in the acquisition of wealth and riches, not in order to enjoy something else which can be got through wealth, but because they regard wealth as the sole aim in life. Another is the city of depravity and baseness; the aim of its people is the enjoyment of the pleasure connected with food and drink and sexual intercourse, and in general of the pleasures of the senses and of the imagination, and to give preference to entertainment and idle play in every form and in every way. Another is the city of honor; the aim of its people is to cooperate to attain honor and distinction and fame among the nations, to be extolled

and treated with respect by word and deed, and to attain glory and splendor either in the eyes of other people or among themselves, each according to the extent of his love of such distinction or according to the amount of it which he is able to reach. Another is the city of power; the aim of its people is to prevail over others and to prevent others from prevailing over them, their only purpose in life being the enjoyment which they get from power. Another is the "democratic" city: the aim of its people is to be free, each of them doing what he wishes without restraining his passions in the least.

§18. There are as many kings of ignorant cities as there are cities of this kind, each of them governing the city over which he has authority so that he can indulge in his passion and design.

We have herewith enumerated the designs which may be set up as aims for ignorant cities.

§19. The wicked city is a city whose views are those of the excellent city; it knows felicity, God Almighty, the existents of the second order, the Active Intellect and everything which as such is to be known and believed in by the people of the excellent city; but the actions of its people are the actions of the people of the ignorant cities.

The city which has deliberately changed is a city whose views and actions were previously the views and actions of the people of the excellent city, but they have been changed and different views have taken their place, and its actions have turned into different actions.

The city which misses the right path [the "erring" city] is the city which aims at felicity after this life, and holds about God Almighty, the existents of the second order, and the Active Intellect pernicious and useless beliefs, even if they are taken as symbols and representations of true felicity. Its first ruler was a man who falsely pretended to be receiving "revelation"; he produced this wrong impression through falsifications, cheating and deceptions.

§20. The kings of these cities are contrary to the kings of the excellent cities: their ways of governing are contrary to the excellent ways of governing. The same applies to all the other people who live in these cities.

4.11 Logic: Ibn Sina (Avicenna), *Treatise on Logic* (1020s or 1030s). Original in Persian.

The study of logic as a discipline was the original achievement of the ancient Greek philosopher Aristotle (384–322 BCE). His treatises on the topic, later grouped together under the title *Organon*, dealt with what would remain the classic issues of the topic: the relationship of words to reality, the valid forms by which we may derive new truths from what is already known, and the criteria by which we may make and judge inferences. Aristotelian logic was a topic of keen interest in the pre-Christian world and remained important even into the Christian era, with the commentaries of Boethius (d. 524/526). After that, its study continued in the Islamic world, beginning in the ninth century and gaining real momentum in the tenth. The Muslim Persian scholar Ibn Sina (980–1037), known as Avicenna in the West, was one of the most important scholars in this tradition. He was able to draw on translations of Aristotle, made from the original Greek mainly by Christians living in Muslim societies. In the excerpt below he talks about the importance of logic for attaining a particularly high-grade form of knowledge that he calls "science," and he argues that such knowledge is concerned with universals such as "human being" rather than with singulars such as "Mohammed" or "Zid." For Ibn Sina, logic—and philosophy more generally—was essential for understanding Islam itself. Compare the conception and role of logic in the text of al-Farabi above, p. 200, with Ibn Sina's view.

[Source: *Avicenna's Treatise on Logic*, ed. and trans. Farhang Zabeeh (The Hague: Martinus Nijhoff, 1971), pp. 13–17 (slightly modified).]

The Purpose and Use of Logic

There are two kinds of cognition: One is called intuitive or perceptive or apprehensive. For example, if someone says, "Man," or "Fairy," or "Angel," or the like, you will understand, conceive, and grasp what he means by the expression. The other kind of cognition is judgment. As for example, when you acknowledge that angels exist or human beings are under surveillance and the like.

Cognition can again be analyzed into two kinds. One is the kind that may be known through Intellect; it is known necessarily by reasoning through itself. For example, there are the intuitive cognitions of the whatness of the soul, and judgments about what is grasped by intuitive cognition, such as, the soul is eternal.

The other kind of cognition is one that is known by intuition. Judgments about these intuitions, however, are made, not by Intellect, or by reason but by the First Principle.[1] For example, it is known that if two things are equal to the same thing then those things are equal to each other. Then there is the kind of cognition known by the senses, such as, the knowledge that the sun is bright. Also, there is the knowledge that is received from authority such as those received from sages and prophets. And the kind that is obtained from the general opinion and those we are brought by it, for example, that it is wrong to lie and injustice ought not to be done. And still other kinds—which may be named later.

Whatever is known by Intellect, whether it is simple intuitive cognition, or judgment about intuitive cognition, or cognitive judgment, should be based on something which is known prior to the thing.

An example of an intuitive or perceptual cognition is this: If we don't know what "man" means, and someone tells us that man is an animal who talks, we first have to know the meaning of "animal" and "talking," and we must have intuitive cognition of these things before we can learn something we didn't know before about man.

---

[1] The First Principle, as defined by Aristotle, was that which was self-evident.

An example of a judgment acquired by Intellect is this: If we don't know the meaning of "the world was created," and someone tells us that the world possesses color, and whatever possesses color is created; then, and only then, can we know what we didn't know before about the world.

Thus, whatever is not known but desired to be known, can be known through what is known before. But it is not the case that whatever is known can be a ground for knowing what is unknown. Because for everything that is unknown there is a proper class of known things that can be used for knowing the unknown.

There is a method by which one can discover the unknown from what is known. It is the science of logic. Through it one may know how to obtain the unknown from the known. This science is also concerned with the different kinds of valid, invalid, and near valid inferences.

The science of logic is the science of scales. Other sciences are practical, they can give direction in life. The salvation of men lies in their purity of soul. This purity of soul is attainable by contemplating the pure form and avoiding this-worldly inclinations. And the way to these two is through science. And no science which cannot be examined by the balance of logic is certain and exact. Thus, without the acquisition of logic, nothing can be truly called science. Therefore, there is no way except learning the science of logic. It is characteristic of the ancient sciences that the student, at the beginning of his study, is unable to see the use or application of the sciences. This is so, because only after a thorough study of the whole body of science will the real value of his endeavor become apparent. Thus I pray that the reader of this book will not grow impatient in reading things which do not appear of use upon first sight.

The Beginning of the Science of Logic, and a Discussion of What is Called Simple Expressions and Simple Meanings

It should be known that there are two kinds of expressions: One is simple, the other compound.[1] A simple expression is one which has no part signifying a part of the meaning of the expression, e.g., "Zid," "Mohammed," "Man," and "Wise." A compound expression is one which has some part of it denoting some part of the meaning of the expression, such as when you say, "Human beings are wise," or "The wise people." An inquiry into the nature of compound expressions first requires a discussion of the nature of simple expressions.

A Discussion of Simple and Compound Expressions

Every simple expression is either universal or individual. A universal expression is one whose meaning applies to many entities. For example, "man" signifies the same meaning when applied to Zid, Omar and Mohammed. However, even if a universal expression applies to only one entity it can be used in such a way as to indicate many entities, since it is possible to imagine, by understanding the meaning of that term, many other entities. For example, by knowing the meaning of "sun" and "moon," you can imagine many suns and moons.

An individual expression is one which signifies a single entity. It is such that it cannot be imagined that the same expression could be applied to many entities. When you say "Zid," "Zid" signifies only Zid. If you call some other entities "Zid" you are giving the term another meaning. The business of the scientist is not to deal with individual expressions and their meanings, but to investigate the nature of universals. No doubt, each universal has many particular instances.

A Discussion of Essential and Accidental Universals

The universal contains its particulars either (a) essentially or (b) accidentally. The Essential Universal and its Particulars are apprehended if, at least, three conditions are fulfilled:

(1) The particular has meaning. Thus, if you know the meaning of "animal," "man," "number," and "number four," you cannot help knowing the meaning of the expressions, "man is an animal" and "four is a number." But if you add "exists" or "is white" to the word "animal" and "number," you will not understand the meaning of the resulting expressions "man exists," "number four exists," or "man is not white" or "man is white."

(2) The existence of the Essential Universal is prerequisite for the existence of its Particular. For example, there should first be animal in order that animal be man,

---

[1] The topic of simple and complex expression and universal or individual or common name and proper name corresponds to Aristotle's statements in the *Categories*.

and first there should be number in order that number be four, and first there should be human being in order that human being be Zid.

(3) Nothing gives meaning to a particular; rather its meaning is derived from its essence. For example, nothing makes human being animal, and nothing makes four number, except its essence. For if it were otherwise, if the essence of a thing did not exist, there could be a man which is not animal, and there could be four, but no number; but this is impossible.

To further elaborate what has been said, take the saying "something may make some other thing." Its meaning is this: a thing can not be in its essence another thing, but only could be that other thing by means of something else which is accidental to it. If it is impossible for a thing to be what another thing is, nothing could make it that thing. That thing which makes man, man, makes animal, animal. But it does not make man, animal, since man in itself is animal, and four in itself is number. But this relation does not exist between whiteness and man. Hence, there should be something which makes man, white.

Thus, when every meaning has the above three characteristics it is essential. Whatever does not have all these characteristics is accidental. Accidental qualities are those which can never arise from the essence of a thing, not even by imagination. Therefore, they are unlike kinds of deduction that are made in the case of number thousand which is an even number or in the case of a triangle, the sum total of whose angles is equal to two right angles. An example of an accidental quality is laughter, an attribute of men. This problem will be discussed later on.

And I should have mentioned also that a human being has two characteristics: essential and accidental. His essential characteristic may be exemplified by his ability to speak, because this property is the essence of his soul. An accidental quality of his is laughter, because it is the character of man, on seeing or hearing a strange and unfamiliar thing, (unless hindered by instinct or habit), to perchance laugh. But before there be wonder and laughter there must be a soul for a man, in order that this soul be united with a body and man becomes a man. First, there should be a soul in order that there be a man; not first, there should be laughter in order that there be a soul. Thus, the characteristic which comes first is essential, and whatever does not come from a man is not essential, but accidental. When you say, "Zid is seated," "Zid slept," "Zid is old," and "Zid is young," these characteristics, without doubt, are accidental, no matter what their temporal sequence be.

KINGDOMS IN EAST CENTRAL EUROPE

4.12 Hungary as heir of Rome: King Stephen, *Laws* (1000–1038). Original in Latin.

The Bulgarians entered a largely Byzantine orbit when they settled in the region just south of the Danube. By contrast, the Magyars (called Hungarians in the rest of Europe), entered a region contested by both the Byzantines and the Germans. When they arrived in the Pannonian plains (north of the Danube), they contributed to the dismantling of the formerly powerful Moravian empire, which had kept its independence from Germany, in part by converting to Christianity under the aegis of the Byzantines (it was for the Moravians that Cyril and Methodius—see above, p. 158—first made their translations). The Hungarians, by contrast, eventually allied themselves with Germany and with the Catholicism that its emperor represented. Thus Hungarian prince Géza (r.972–997) converted under the auspices of German churchmen and invited German priests to spread the religion, using Christianity to enforce his rule. His son Stephen (r.997–1038), married to the sister of Duke Henry IV of Bavaria (who later became Emperor Henry II), defeated his chief rival for rule with the help of German warriors, and around the year 1000, with the approval of Emperor Otto III, received a royal crown and a blessing from Pope Sylvester II. As king, Stephen adopted many of the institutions of the post-Roman successor states, including written laws. Those excerpted below are from the oldest of the laws that he promulgated. The code was clearly concerned above all with moral and religious issues and should be compared with Charlemagne's *Admonitio generalis* (above, p. 148) and the near-contemporary Anglo-Saxon legislation of King Æthelred (below, p. 222).

[Source: *The Laws of the Medieval Kingdom of Hungary*, vol 1: 1000–1301, trans. and ed. János M. Bak, György Bónis, and James Ross Sweeney (Bakersfield, CA: Charles Schlacks, Jr. Publisher, 1989), pp. 1, 3–8, 80–83 (slightly modified).]

Preface to the Royal Law

The work of the royal office subject to the rule of divine mercy is by custom greater and more complete when nourished in the Catholic faith than any other office. Since every people use their own law, we, governing our monarchy by the will of God and emulating both ancient and modern caesars, and after reflecting upon the law, decree for our people too the way they should lead an upright and blameless life. Just as they are enriched by divine laws, so may they similarly be strengthened by secular ones, in order that as the good shall be made many by these divine laws so shall the criminals incur punishment. Thus we set out below in the following sentences what we have decreed....

6. ROYAL CONCESSIONS OF FREE DISPOSITION OF GOODS.

We, by our royal authority have decreed that anyone shall be free to divide his property, to assign it to his wife, his sons and daughters, his relatives, or to the church;[1] and no one should dare to change this after his death.

7. THE PRESERVATION OF ROYAL GOODS.

It is our will that just as we have given others the opportunity to master their own possessions, so equally the goods, warriors,[2] bondmen,[3] and whatever else belongs to our royal dignity should remain permanent, and no one should plunder or remove them, nor should anyone dare to obtain any advantage from them.

8. THE OBSERVANCE OF THE LORD'S DAY.

If a priest or *ispán* [local lord], or any faithful person find anyone working on Sunday with oxen, the ox shall be confiscated and given to the men of the castle to be eaten;[4] if a horse is used, however, it shall be confiscated, but the owner, if he wishes, may redeem it with an ox which should be eaten as has been said. If anyone uses other equipment, this tool and his clothing shall be taken, and he may redeem them, if he wishes, with a flogging.

9. MORE ON THE SAME.

Priests and *ispánok* shall enjoin village reeves[5] to command everyone both great and small, men and women, with the exception of those who guard the fire, to gather on Sundays in the church. If someone remains at home through their negligence let them be beaten and shorn.

---

[1] The king seems to have wanted to transform the undivided property of clans into the personal property of freemen and nobles, as was the case in western European societies of the time. But he was not successful.

[2] The Latin word used here was *milites* (sing. *miles*), the same word for "fighters" or "warriors" that was used in the Peace Movement. In the *Laws of Hungary* the *milites* seem to have been armed servants of the king and magnates.

[3] The Latin word used here was *servi*, (sing. *servus*), which could mean either "slave" or "serf." Since the meaning here is not clear, the neutral term "bondmen" is used.

[4] The "men of the castle" (*cives* in Latin) were dependent men attached to the castles of the royal *ispánok* (the plural of *ispán*) for their defense and maintenance, much like the garrisons that guarded the castles in the document about Hugh of Lusignan and his lord (above, p. 181).

[5] In this period the reeves (*villici* in Latin) were free peasants in charge of enforcing some laws.

10. THE OBSERVANCE OF EMBER DAYS.[1]

If someone breaks the fast known to all on the Ember day, he shall fast in prison for a week.

11. THE OBSERVANCE OF FRIDAY.

If someone eats meat on Friday, a day observed by all Christianity, he shall fast incarcerated during the day for a week.

12. THOSE WHO DIE WITHOUT CONFESSION.

If someone has such a hardened heart—God forbid it to any Christian—that he does not want to confess his faults according to the counsel of a priest, he shall lie without any divine service and alms like an infidel. If his relatives and neighbors fail to summon the priest, and therefore he should die unconfessed, prayers and alms should be offered, but his relatives shall wash away their negligence by fasting in accordance with the judgment of the priests. Those who die a sudden death shall be buried with all ecclesiastical honor, for divine judgment is hidden from us and unknown.

13. THE OBSERVANCES OF CHRISTIANITY.

If someone neglects a Christian observance and takes pleasure in the stupidity of his negligence, he shall be judged by the bishops according to the nature of the offense and the discipline of the canons.[2] If he rebelliously objects to suffer the punishment with equanimity, he shall be subject to the same judgment seven times over. If, after all this, he continues to resist and remains obdurate, he shall be handed over for royal judgment, namely to the defender of Christianity.[3]

14. ON HOMICIDE.

If someone driven by anger and arrogance, willfully commits a homicide, he should know that according to the decrees of our [royal] council he is obliged to pay one hundred ten gold pensae,[4] from which fifty will go to the royal treasury, another fifty will be given to relatives, and ten will be paid to arbiters and mediators. The killer himself shall fast according to the rules of the canons.

MORE ON THE SAME.

If someone kills a person by chance, he shall pay twelve pensae and fast as the canons command.

THE KILLING OF SLAVES.

If someone's slave kills another's slave, the payment shall be a slave for a slave, or he may be redeemed and do penance as has been said.

MORE ON THE SAME.

If a freeman kills the slave of another, he shall replace him with another slave or pay his price, and fast according to the canons.

15. THOSE WHO KILL THEIR WIVES.

If an ispán with a hardened heart and a disregard for his soul—may such remain far from the hearts of the faithful—defiles himself by killing his wife, he shall make his peace with fifty steers[5] to the kindred of the woman, according to the decree of the royal council, and fast according to the commands of the canons. And if a warrior or a man of wealth commits the same crime he shall pay according to that same council ten steers and fast, as has been said. And if a commoner has committed the same crime, he shall make his peace with five steers to the kindred and fast.

16. DRAWING THE SWORD.

In order that peace should remain firm and unsullied among the greater and the lesser of whatever station, we forbid anyone to draw the sword with the aim of injury. If anyone in his audacity should put this prohibition to the test, let him be killed by the same sword.

17. ON PERJURY.

If a powerful man of stained faith and defiled heart be found guilty of breaking his oath by perjury, he shall atone for the perjury with the loss of his hand; or he may redeem it with fifty steers. If a commoner commits perjury, he shall be punished with the loss of his hand or may redeem it by twelve steers and fast, as the canons command.

---

[1] The observance of three days' fast during the weeks following Ash Wednesday, Pentecost, the Exaltation of the Holy Cross, and the feast of St. Lucy was widespread in the Carolingian realm and, as we see here, adopted in Hungary.

[2] This chapter in fact authorizes the introduction of canon (church) law into Hungary.

[3] The "defender of Christianity" was Stephen himself.

[4] The pensa aurí was a coin equivalent to the contemporary Byzantine gold solidus.

[5] Steers were valued at one gold pensa each; hence fifty oxen, that is fifty pensa, here reflect the cost of legal compensation for the death of a woman by a man of the ispán class.

18. ON MANUMISSION.

If anyone, prompted by mercy, should set his male and female slaves free in front of witnesses, we decree that no one out of ill will shall reduce them to servitude after his death. If, however, he promised them freedom but died intestate, his widow and sons shall have the power to bear witness to this same manumission and to render *agape*[1] for the redemption of the husband's soul, if they wish.

19. GATHERING AT CHURCH AND THOSE WHO MUTTER OR CHATTER DURING MASS.

If some persons, upon coming to church to hear the divine service mutter among themselves and disturb others by relating idle tales during the celebration of mass and by being inattentive to Holy Scripture with its ecclesiastical nourishment, they shall be expelled from the church in disgrace if they are older, and if they are younger and common folk they shall be bound in the narthex of the church[2] in view of everyone and punished by whipping and by the shearing off of their hair.

20. INADMISSIBILITY OF ACCUSATIONS AND TESTIMONY OF BONDMEN OR BONDWOMEN AGAINST THEIR MASTERS OR MISTRESSES.

In order that the people of this kingdom may be far removed and remain free from the affronts and accusations of bondmen and bondwomen, it is wholly forbidden by decree of the royal council that any servile person be accepted in accusation or testimony against their masters or mistresses in any criminal case.

21. THOSE WHO PROCURE LIBERTY FOR BONDMEN OF OTHERS.

If anyone thoughtlessly brings the bondman of another, without the knowledge of his master, before the king or before persons of higher birth and dignity in order to procure for him the benefits of liberty after he has been released from the yoke of servitude, he should know that if he is rich, he shall pay fifty steers of which forty are owed to the king and ten to the master of the bondman, but if he is poor and of low rank, he shall pay twelve steers of which ten are due to the king and two to the master of the bondman.

22. THOSE WHO ENSLAVE FREEMEN.

Because it is worthy of God and best for men that everyone should conduct his life in the vigor of liberty, it is established by royal decree that henceforth no *ispán* or warrior should dare to reduce a freeman to servitude. If, however, compelled by his own rashness he should presume to do this, he should know that he shall pay from his own possessions the same composition, which shall be properly divided between the king and the *ispánok*, as in the other decree above.

SIMILARLY ON THE SAME.

But if someone who was once held in servitude lives freely after having submitted to a judicial procedure[3] held to consider his liberty, he shall be content with enjoying his freedom, and the man who held him in servitude shall pay nothing.

23. THOSE WHO TAKE THE WARRIORS OF ANOTHER FOR THEMSELVES.

We wish that each lord have his own warriors and no one shall try to persuade a warrior to leave his longtime lord and come to him, since this is the origin of quarrels.

24. THOSE WHO TAKE GUESTS OF ANOTHER FOR THEMSELVES.[4]

If someone receives a guest with benevolence and decently provides him with support, the guest shall not leave his protector as long as he receives support according to their agreement, nor should he transfer his service to any other.

25. THOSE WHO ARE BEATEN WHILE LOOKING FOR THEIR OWN.

If a warrior or a bondman flees to another and he whose warrior or man has run away sends his agent to bring him back, and that agent is beaten and whipped by anyone,

---

[1] The *agape* was a memorial meal shared by the manumitted (those released from slavery) or an offering made in memory of the dead.

[2] The entrance hall or porch.

[3] The "judicial procedure" refers to the ordeal by hot iron: the subject (in this case a person claiming to be free) must carry a hot iron for a few paces, and then put it down. His hand is bandaged. After three days the wound is inspected. If "clean," he is judged to have told the truth (or, in criminal cases, he is judged not guilty); if discolored or infected, he is judged to have lied.

[4] The "guests" were foreigners, most of whom were Western clerics and knights.

we decree in agreement with our magnates that he who gave the beating shall pay ten steers.

26. WIDOWS AND ORPHANS.

We also wish widows and orphans to be partakers of our law in the sense that if a widow, left with her sons and daughters, promises to support them and to remain with them as long as she lives, she shall have the right from us to do so, and no one should force her to marry. If she has a change of heart and wants to marry and leave the orphans, she shall have nothing from the goods of the orphans except her own clothing.[1]

MORE ABOUT WIDOWS.

If a widow without a child promises to remain unmarried in her widowhood, she shall have the right to all her goods and may do with them what she wishes. But after her death her goods shall go to the kin of her husband, if she has any, and if not, the king is the heir.

27. THE ABDUCTION OF GIRLS.

If any warrior debased by lewdness abducts a girl to be his wife without the consent of her parents, we decree that the girl should be returned to her parents, even if he raped her, and the abductor shall pay ten steers for the abduction, although he may afterwards have made peace with the girl's parents. If a poor man who is a commoner should attempt this, he shall compensate for the abduction with five steers.

28. THOSE WHO FORNICATE WITH BONDWOMEN OF ANOTHER.

In order that freemen preserve their liberty undefiled, we wish to warn them. Any transgressor who fornicates with a bondwoman of another, should know that he has committed a crime, and he is to be whipped for the first offense. If he fornicates with her a second time, he should be whipped and shorn; but if he does it a third time, he shall become a slave together with the woman, or he may redeem himself. If, however, the bondwoman should conceive by him and not be able to bear but dies in childbirth, he shall make compensation for her with another bondwoman.

THE FORNICATION OF BONDMEN.

If a bondman of one master fornicates with the bond-woman of another, he should be whipped and shorn, and if the woman should conceive by him and dies in childbirth, the man shall be sold and half of his price shall be given to the master of the bondwoman, the other half shall be kept by the master of the bondman.

29. THOSE WHO DESIRE BONDWOMEN AS WIVES.

In order that no one who is recognized to be a freeman should dare commit this offense, we set forth what has been decreed in this royal council as a source of terror and caution so that if any freeman should choose to marry a bondwoman of another with her master's consent, he shall lose the enjoyment of his liberty and become a slave forever.

30. THOSE WHO FLEE THEIR WIVES BY LEAVING THE COUNTRY.

In order that people of both sexes may remain and flourish under fixed law and free from injury, we establish in this royal decree that if anyone in his impudence should flee the country out of loathing for his wife, she shall possess everything which her husband rightfully possessed, so long as she is willing to wait for her husband, and no one shall force her into another marriage. If she voluntarily wishes to marry, she may take her own clothing leaving behind other goods, and marry again. If her husband, hearing this, should return, he is not allowed to replace her with anyone else, except with the permission of the bishop.

31. THEFT COMMITTED BY WOMEN.

Because it is terrible and loathsome to all to find men committing theft, and even more so for women, it is ordained by the royal council, that if a married woman commits theft, she shall be redeemed by her husband, and if she commits the same offense a second time, she shall be redeemed again; but if she does it a third time, she shall be sold.

32. ARSON OF HOUSES.

If anyone sets a building belonging to another on fire out of enmity, we order that he replace the building and whatever household furnishings were destroyed by the fire, and also pay sixteen steers which are worth forty *solidi*.[2]

---

[1] Here women apparently did not have a right to their dower — the gift that a husband gave his new wife — after the death of their husbands, though in later laws that right was recognized.

[2] In this particular case, Bavarian silver *solidi* are meant, of which 25 were equal to a Byzantine gold *solidus*.

33. ON WITCHES.

If a witch is found, she shall be led, in accordance with the law of judgment into the church and handed over to the priest for fasting and instruction in the faith. After the fast she may return home. If she is discovered in the same crime a second time, she shall fast and after the fast she shall be branded with the keys of the church in the form of a cross on her bosom, forehead, and between the shoulders. If she is discovered on a third occasion, she shall be handed over to the judge [of the secular court].

34. ON SORCERERS.

So that the creatures of God may remain far from all injury caused by evil ones and may not be exposed to any harm from them—unless it be by the will of God who may even increase it—we establish by decree of the council a most terrible warning to magicians and sorcerers that no person should dare to subvert the mind of any man or to kill him by means of sorcery and magic. Yet in the future if a man or a woman dare to do this he or she shall be handed over to the person hurt by sorcery or to his kindred, to be judged according to their will.

If, however, they are found practicing divination as they do in ashes or similar things, they shall be corrected with whips by the bishop.

35. THE INVASION OF HOUSES.

We wish that peace and unanimity prevail between great and small according to the Apostle: Be ye all of one accord, etc.,[1] and let no one dare attack another. For if there be any *ispán* so contumacious that after the decree of this common council he should seek out another at home in order to destroy him and his goods, and if the lord of the house is there and fights with him and is killed, the *ispán* shall be punished according to the law about drawing the sword.[2] If, however, the *ispán* shall fall, he shall lie without compensation. If he did not go in person but sent his warriors, he shall pay compensation for the invasion with one hundred steers. If, moreover, a warrior invades the courtyard and house of another warrior, he shall pay compensation for the invasion with ten steers. If a commoner invades the huts of those of similar station, he shall pay for the invasion with five steers.

4.13 Coming to terms with Catholic Poland: Thietmar of Merseburg, *Chronicle* (1013–1018). Original in Latin.

Poland, like Hungary, became a state in the wake of Moravia's collapse. Mieszko I (r.c.960–992) was the first leader to unite a region that was (roughly speaking) between the Oder and Vistula rivers. Baptized in 966, he expanded his realm by taking advantage of Bohemian and German rivalries. In 990 or 991 he placed his duchy under the direct protection of the pope. Mieszko's son and successor, Boleslaw the Brave (r.992–1025), maintained good relations with Emperor Otto III (r.996–1002) and helped him destabilize Bohemia. Thus he welcomed the exiled bishop of Prague, Saint Adalbert. Two years later he retrieved the relics of Adalbert, who had been martyred on a mission to convert the Prussians. When Otto III came on pilgrimage to see those relics at Gniezno, Poland's capital city, Boleslaw orchestrated a synod that raised Gniezno to an archbishopric. The major sources for this early history come not from Poland, however, but from Germany. An example is the *Chronicle* of Thietmar of Merseburg (975–1018). Thietmar came from a prominent Saxon family. Educated in the classics and Christian texts at Magdeburg, Thietmar was (like Ruotger and Bruno, see below, p. 216) a product of the Ottonian Renaissance, groomed to serve the king as well as to preside in a high

---

[1] See Phil. 2: 2–4.

[2] See chapter 16 of this same law code, above.

church office. In 1009, he became bishop of Merseburg, a key bishopric created by the Ottonians to strengthen the empire's control over its eastern border. Thietmar was well aware of events in Poland; he rather admired Mieszko, but he vilified Boleslaw even while recording Boleslaw's acts of piety. Why might a bishop near the eastern edge of Germany be wary of a contemporary Polish ruler?

[Source: *Ottonian Germany: The Chronicon of Thietmar of Merseburg*, trans. David A. Warner (Manchester: Manchester University Press, 2001), pp. 171–72, 191–93, 361–63 (notes modified).]

4.28 In the beginning of the summer, Adalbert, bishop of the Bohemians, arrived.[1] He had received the name Woyciech at his baptism, the other name, at his confirmation, from the archbishop of Magdeburg. He was educated in letters, in that same city.... As he was unable to separate his flock from the ancient error of wickedness through godly teaching, he excommunicated them all and came to Rome to justify himself before the pope. For a long time, with the pope's permission, he lived an exemplary life according to the strict rule of Abbot Boniface.[2] With the same pope's permission, he later tried to subdue the Prussians, their thoughts still estranged from Christ, with the bridle of holy preaching. On 23 April, pierced by a spear and beheaded, he alone received the best martyrdom, without a groan. This occurred just as he himself had seen it in a dream and had predicted to all the brothers, saying: "I thought I saw myself celebrating mass and communicating alone." Seeing that he had now died, the authors of this wicked crime increased both their wickedness and the vengeance of God by throwing the blessed body in the water. His head, however, they scornfully transfixed with a stake. They returned home in great joy. After learning of this, Boleslaw, Mieszko's son, immediately purchased both the martyr's celebrated body and his head. In Rome, after the emperor [Otto III] had been informed, he humbly offered praises to God because, during his lifetime, he had taken such a servant for himself through the palm of martyrdom....

4.55 I cannot place in its correct order everything that ought to be treated within the context of this book. In

what follows, therefore, I will not be embarrassed to add a few recollections. Indeed, I rejoice in the change of pace much as the traveller who, because of its difficulty or perhaps from ignorance, leaves the course of the more direct road and sets out on some winding secondary path. Hence, I will relate the remaining deeds of Mieszko [I], the celebrated duke of the Poles, who has already been treated in some detail in the previous books. He took a noble wife from the region of Bohemia, the sister of Boleslaw the Elder. Her life corresponded to her name—she was called Dobrawa in Slavic, which, in German, means 'the good'. For this one, faithful to Christ, and realizing that her husband was mired in various heathen errors, turned her humble spirit to the task of binding him to the faith as well. She tried in every way to conciliate him, not because of the threefold appetite of this evil world but rather for the sake of the admirable and, to all the faithful, desirable fruit of future salvation.[3]

4.56 She sinned willingly for a while, that she might later be good for a long time. For during Lent, which closely followed her marriage, though she intended to offer an acceptable tithe to God by abstaining from meat and through the affliction of her body, her husband asked and tried to coax her into giving up her plan. She consented, thinking that he might therefore be more willing to listen to her on some other occasion. Some say that she only ate meat during a single Lenten period, others say three. Now, O reader, you have heard her sin, now also consider the attractive fruit of her pious will. She labored for the sake of her husband's conversion and was heard by the Creator in

---

[1] Adalbert (956–997), of Bohemian noble birth, was (like Thietmar) educated at Magdeburg (Germany) and became bishop of Prague in 983. He was martyred in 997.

[2] That is, Adalbert spent time at the monastery of Santi Bonifacio e Alessio in Rome. That Boniface was a martyr saint of the early church.

[3] For the "three-fold" appetites, see 1 John 2: 16.

his kindness; and through his infinite goodness that most zealous persecutor came to his senses. After being admonished frequently by his beloved wife, he vomited out the poison of his unbelief and, in holy baptism, wiped away the stain of his birth. Immediately, members of his hitherto reluctant people followed their beloved head and lord and, after accepting the marriage garments, were numbered among the wards of Christ. Jordan, their first bishop, labored much with them, while he diligently invited them by word and deed to the cultivation of the heavenly vineyard. Then the couple rightly rejoiced, namely the man and the noble woman, and all who were subject to them rejoiced at their marriage in Christ. After this, the good mother gave birth to a son who was very different from her and the misfortune of many mothers. She named him Boleslaw [the Brave], after her brother. He first revealed his innate evil to her and then raged against his own flesh and blood, as I will reveal in the following.

4.57 But when his mother died [977], his father married Margrave Dietrich's daughter, a nun at the convent called Calbe, without the approval of the church. Oda was her name and great was her presumption. She rejected her celestial spouse in favor of a man of war, which displeased all the pastors of the church but most of all her own bishop, the venerable Hildeward.[1] But the welfare of the land, and the need to strengthen the peace, kept this from leading to a break; rather it provided a healthy and continuous incentive for reconciliation. For she increased the service of Christ in every way: many captives were returned to their homeland, prisoners were released from their chains, and the prisons of those who had been accused were opened. I hope that God will forgive her the magnitude of her sin, since such love of pious deeds was revealed in her. We read, however, that he who does not entirely abandon the evil he has begun, will try in vain to placate the Lord. She bore her husband three sons: Mieszko, Swentepulk and [...]. She passed her life there, highly honored, until her husband's death. She was beloved among those with whom she lived and useful to those from whom she had come.

4.58 But on 25 May, in the year of the Incarnation 992, in the tenth year of Otto III's kingship,[2] the aforementioned duke [Mieszko], now old and feverish, went from this place of exile to his homeland,[3] leaving his kingdom to be divided among many claimants. Yet, with fox-like cunning, his son Boleslaw unified it once more in the hands of one ruler, after he had expelled his stepmother and brothers, and had their familiars Odilien and Przibiwoj blinded. That he might be able to rule alone, he ignored both human and divine law. He married the daughter of Margrave Rikdag, but later sent her away and took a Hungarian woman as his wife. She bore him a son, named Bezprym, but he also sent her away. His third wife was Emnilde, a daughter of the venerable lord, Dobromir. Faithful to Christ, she formed her husband's unstable character completely for the better and strove unceasingly to wash away both of her sins through the generous dispersal of alms and abstinence. She bore two sons, Mieszko and another one whom the father named after his beloved lord.[4] She also produced three daughters of whom one was an abbess, the second married Count Herman, and the third the son of King Vladimir. I will say more about them later....

8.1 In the year 1018 of the Incarnation, in the second indiction, in the sixteenth year of Lord Henry's reign, and his fourth as emperor, the same Henry celebrated the Circumcision and Epiphany of the Lord in Frankfurt, with great solemnity.[5] On 25 January, Ezzelin the Lombard was granted his liberty. He had been held in custody for four years. Afterwards, on 30 January, Bishops Gero and Arnulf, the counts Herman and Dietrich, and the emperor's chancellor Frederick agreed to a sworn peace at the burg Bautzen. The agreement was made at the emperor's order and in response to Boleslaw's constant supplications. This was not as it should have been, however. Rather, it was the best that could be accomplished under the circumstances. In the company of a select group of hostages, the aforesaid lords returned. After four days, Oda, Margrave Ekkehard's daughter, whom Boleslaw had long desired, was escorted to Zützen by Otto, the duke's son.[6] When they arrived, they were greeted by a large

---

[1] A nun was supposed to be married to Christ and thus could not take another husband.

[2] In fact, the ninth year.

[3] I.e., he died.

[4] Referring to Otto III.

[5] Thietmar here refers to Emperor Henry II (r.1014–1024), the successor of Otto III.

[6] This Oda was Boleslaw's fourth wife.

crowd of men and women, and by many burning lamps, since it was night-time. Contrary to the authority of the canons, Oda married the duke after Septuagesima.[1] Until now, she has lived outside the law of matrimony and thus in a manner worthy only of a marriage such as this one.

8.2 In her husband's kingdom, the customs are many and varied. They are also harsh, but occasionally quite praise-worthy. The populace must be fed like cattle and punished as one would a stubborn ass. Without severe punishment, the prince cannot put them to any useful purpose. If anyone in this land should presume to abuse a foreign matron and thereby commit fornication, the act is immediately avenged through the following punishment. The guilty party is led on to the market bridge, and his scrotum is affixed to it with a nail. Then, after a sharp knife has been placed next to him, he is given the harsh choice between death or castration. Furthermore, anyone found to have eaten meat after Sep-tuagesima is severely punished, by having his teeth knocked out. The law of God, newly introduced in these regions, gains more strength from such acts of force than from any fast imposed by the bishops. There are also other customs, by far inferior to these, which please neither God nor the inhabitants, and are useful only as a means to inspire terror. To some extent, I have alluded to these above. I think that it is unnecessary for me to say any more about this man whose name and manner of life, if it please Almighty God, might better have remained concealed from us. That his father and he were joined to us, through marriage and great familiarity, has produced results so damaging that any good preceding them is far outweighed, and so it will remain in the future. During false periods of peace, Boleslaw may temporarily regard us with affection. Nevertheless, through all kinds of secret plots, he constantly attempts to sow dis-sension, diminish our inborn freedom, and, if time and place permit, rise up and destroy us.

8.3 In the days of his father,[2] when he still embraced hea-thenism, every woman followed her husband on to the funeral pyre, after first being decapitated. If a woman was found to be a prostitute, moreover, she suffered a particularly wretched and shameful penalty. The skin around her genitals was cut off and this 'foreskin', if we may call it that, was hung on the door so that anyone who entered would see it and be more concerned and prudent in the future. The law of the Lord declares that such a woman should be stoned, and the rules of our ancestors would require her beheading.[3] Nowadays, the freedom to sin dominates everywhere and to a degree that is not right or normal. And so it is not just a large number of frustrated girls who engage in adultery, hav-ing been driven by the desire of the flesh to harmful lust, but even some married women and, indeed, with their husbands still living. As if this were not enough, such women then have their husbands murdered by the adul-terer, inspiring the deed through furtive hints. After this, having given a wicked example to others, they receive their lovers quite openly and sin at will. They repudiate their legal lord in a most horrible fashion and prefer his retainer, as if the latter were sweet Abro or mild Jason.[4] Nowadays, because a harsh penalty is not imposed, I fear that many will find this new custom more and more acceptable. O you priests of the Lord, forcefully rise up and let nothing stop you! Take a sharp ploughshare and extirpate this newly sprouted weed, down to the roots! You also, lay people, do not give aid to such as these! May those joined in Christ live innocently and, after these supplanters have been rooted out, forever groan in shame. Unless these sinners return to their senses, may our helper, Christ, destroy them with a powerful breath from his holy mouth and scatter them with the great splendor of his second coming.[5]

---

[1] Septuagesima was supposed to inaugurate a period of fasting before Easter and was therefore not an appropriate time to celebrate a marriage.

[2] I.e., in the days of Mieszko I.

[3] For the "law of the Lord," see John 8: 5.

[4] Abro was a rich ancient Greek proverbially known for high living; Jason was the mythological leader of the Argonauts.

[5] For the image of the Lord slaying sinners with his breath, see 2 Thess. 2: 8.

4.14 Poland's self-image: *Boleslaw's Coin* (992–1000).

Although we have few written sources from tenth-century Poland, we do have material sources, including this coin, which was issued by Boleslaw the Brave (r.992–1025) either right after 992, when he ousted his half brothers and ascended to rulership, or around the year 1000, when Emperor Otto III met Boleslaw at Gniezno and the city was established as a archbishopric. In the emperor's eyes, Boleslaw was subservient to Germany. But Boleslaw clearly had other ideas about himself. His coin shows him in profile, like a Roman emperor (obverse). He wears a helmet with earflaps, cultivating a martial image. On the other side of the coin (reverse) is a cross, proclaiming his Christian religion, and the Latin inscription reads "Gnezdun civitas" (City of Gniezno), elevating the status of his chief city to a Christian center (whether or not the coin was struck after Gniezno was declared an archbishopric by Otto).

See Plate 12, p. 248, for a color reproduction of the coin.

(From the collection of the National Museum in Kraków)

4.15 Kievan Rus': *The Russian Primary Chronicle* (*c.*1113, incorporating earlier materials). Original in Russian.

The Russian Primary Chronicle is one of the earliest sources that we have for Russian history. Composed *c.*1113 by an anonymous monk of the Crypt Monastery near Kiev, it was clearly tied to the history of the princes of Kiev. In the excerpt below, Kievan Prince Yaroslav the Wise (r.1019–1054) is portrayed as following the model of the Christian ruler, especially the Byzantine emperor, even to the point of naming the church that he founded "St. Sophia," after the church built by Justinian at Constantinople. The passage says that Yaroslav not only patronized monks but had the learned among them copy books to be distributed in turn to new monasteries. Russian dates, which counted the years from the time of the Creation, followed the Byzantine dating system. In parentheses are the corresponding dates CE. Consider other ways in which Rus' was the child of Byzantium. In what ways was it rather more like Poland and Hungary, even though its Christianity did not come from Rome?

[Source: *The Russian Primary Chronicle: Laurentian Text*, trans. and ed. Samuel Hazzard Cross and Olgerd P. Sherbowitz-Wetzor (Cambridge, MA: Medieval Academy of America, 1953), pp. 136–38 (slightly modified).]

6544 (1036) Thereafter Yaroslav assumed the entire sovereignty, and was the sole ruler in the land of Rus'. Yaroslav went to Novgorod, where he set up his son Vladimir as prince, and appointed Zhidyata bishop.[1] At this time, a son was born to Yaroslav, and he named him Vyacheslav. While Yaroslav was still at Novgorod, news came to him that the Pechenegs were besieging Kiev.[2] He then collected a large army of Varangians[3] and Slavs, returned to Kiev, and entered his city. The Pechenegs were innumerable. Yaroslav made a sally from the city and marshaled his forces, placing the Varangians in the center, the men of Kiev on the right flank, and the men of Novgorod on the left. When they had taken position before the city, the Pechenegs advanced, and they met on the spot where the metropolitan church of St. Sophia now stands. At that time, as a matter of fact, there were fields outside the city. The combat was fierce, but toward evening Yaroslav with difficulty won the upper hand. The Pechenegs fled in various directions, but as they did not know in what quarter to flee, they were drowned, some in the Setoml',[4] some in other streams, while the remnant of them disappeared from that day to this. In the same year, Yaroslav imprisoned his brother Sudislav in Pskov because he had been slanderously accused.

6545 (1037). Yaroslav built the great citadel at Kiev, near which stands the Golden Gate. He founded also the metropolitan Church of St. Sophia, the Church of the Annunciation over the Golden Gate, and also the Monastery of St. George and the convent of St. Irene. During his reign, the Christian faith was fruitful and multiplied, while the number of monks increased, and new monasteries came into being. Yaroslav loved religious establishments and was devoted to priests, especially to monks. He applied himself to books, and read them continually day and night. He assembled many scribes, and translated from Greek into Slavic. He wrote and collected many books through which true believers are instructed and enjoy religious education. For as one man plows the land, and another sows, and still others reap and eat food in abundance, so did this prince. His father Vladimir[5] plowed and harrowed the soil when he enlightened Rus' through baptism, while this prince sowed the hearts of the faithful with the written word, and we in turn reap the harvest by receiving the teaching of books. For great is the profit from book-learning.

Through the medium of books, we are shown and taught the way of repentance, for we gain wisdom and continence from the written word. Books are like rivers that water the whole earth; they are the springs of wisdom. For books have an immeasurable depth; by them we are consoled in sorrow. They are the bridle of self-restraint. For great is wisdom. As Solomon said in its praise, "I (wisdom) have inculcated counsel; I have summoned reason and prudence. The fear of the Lord is the beginning of wisdom. Mine are counsel, wisdom, constancy, and strength. Through me kings rule, and the mighty decree justice. Through me are princes magnified and the oppressors possess the earth. I love them that love me, and they who seek me shall find grace."[6] If you seek wisdom attentively in books, you obtain great profit for your spirit. He who reads books often converses with God or with holy men. If one possesses the words of the prophets, the teachings of the evangelists and the apostles, and the lives of the holy fathers, his soul will derive great profit therefrom. Thus Yaroslav, as we have said, was a lover of books, and as he wrote many, he deposited them in the Church of Saint Sophia which he himself had founded. He adorned it with gold and silver and churchly vessels, and in it the usual hymns are raised to God at the customary seasons. He founded other churches in the cities and districts, appointing priests and paying them out of his personal fortune. He bade them teach the people, since that is the duty which God has prescribed them, and to go often into the churches. Priests and Christian laymen thus increased in number. Yaroslav rejoiced to see the multitude of his churches and of his Christian subjects, but the devil was afflicted, since he was now conquered by this new Christian nation.

---

[1] The first bishop of Novgorod died in 1030 after designating his successor. Yaroslav, however, insisted on Luka Zhidyata, who presided over the see from 1036 to 1055.

[2] The Pechenegs were a Turkic nomadic people who in the tenth century occupied the region between the Don and the Danube but, squeezed by other nomadic groups and the expanding Byzantines and Rus, raided into Rus' only to be repulsed by Yaroslav.

[3] The Varangians were the Scandinavian settlers of Rus'.

[4] The Setoml' was a small stream in Kiev.

[5] Saint Vladimir I (r.c.980–1015) converted to Christianity under the influence of Byzantine Emperor Basil II, took the baptismal name of Basil, and married Basil's sister.

[6] Prov. 8: 12, 13, 14–17.

6546 (1038). Yaroslav attacked the Yatvingians.[1]

6547 (1039). The Church of the Blessed Virgin, which had been founded by Vladimir, Yaroslav's father, was consecrated by the Metropolitan Theopemptos.

6548 (1040). Yaroslav attacked Lithuania.

6549 (1041). Yaroslav attacked the Mazovians by boat.

NORTHERN EUROPE

4.16 An Ottonian courtier-bishop: Ruotger, *Life of Bruno, Archbishop of Cologne* (late 960s). Original in Latin.

Bruno (925–965) was the youngest of the three sons of King Henry I of Saxony (r.919–936). Destined from an early age for the church, Bruno first studied in Utrecht, a city in the present-day Netherlands. In the tenth century Utrecht was part of Lotharingia, a turbulent territory that Henry occupied the year Bruno was born. In his teens, Bruno was summoned by his brother, Henry's successor Otto I (r.936–973), to be a member of the royal court. The court had no fixed capital; rather, the king and his entourage were constantly on the move. In effect, the king ruled on horseback! Bruno continued and extended his studies as he met learned people across his brother's realm. At age 28, he became archbishop of Cologne, in Lotharingia, and a few months later Otto made him duke of Lotharingia, the highest civilian authority there, amidst a rebellion against Otto. Bruno served his brother as general and chief administrator of Lotharingia while he served the church as archbishop of Cologne, pastor, and reformer, until his death at the age of 40.

By contrast, little is known about Bruno's biographer Ruotger. He was a monk in Cologne; from comments in the *Life of Bruno*, it is clear that he knew Bruno personally. Certainly Ruotger was staggeringly learned, likely a member of Bruno's intellectual circle, and perhaps his student. Besides more than twenty biblical citations or echoes, the excerpts of the *Life of Bruno* below include allusions to eight pagan Roman authors, nine Latin Christian authors, mentions of the pagan Roman orator and statesman Cicero (106–43 BCE) and Christian Latin poet Prudentius (348–after 405), and a paraphrase of the Roman historian Sallust (86–35/34 BCE). Highly conscientious, Ruotger produced a reliable account of a prince who was unique: at one and the same time a courtier, a warrior, and an archbishop.

[Source: *Ruotgers Lebensbeschreibung des Erzbischofs Bruno von Köln* (*Ruotgeri Vita Brunonis Archiepiscopi Coloniensis*), ed. Irene Ott, Monumenta Germaniae Historica, Scriptores rerum Germanicarum, Nova series, 10 (Cologne: Böhlau-Verlag, 1958), pp. 3–4, 5–7, 11, 20–21, 23–24, 31–32, 33–34, 38–39, 55. Translated and introduced by Bruce L. Venarde.]

---

[1] The Yatvingians were a Lithuanian people. Attacks on them and on Lithuania and the Mazovians (below) were evidently designed both to protect Rus's northwest flank and to keep open access to eastern Poland, on which Yaroslav made claim.

2. ... He was born in the time when his father, the glorious king Henry, was very zealously rebuilding what had been destroyed after he had quelled the ferocity of the barbarians and subdued the menace of civil strife.[1] Now at last Henry ruled a willing people with the reins of justice and, now at last, amidst a most secure and long-awaited peace. Thus the time of Bruno's birth already heralded, as it were, the future signs of his good will. For since he always approached every good thing very vigorously, he very carefully sought out the gift of peace as the nourishment and adornment of other virtues, because he knew it would benefit all good things. In tranquil times, virtues can be nourished and strengthened. Then in any disturbance, they will not allow a man to be weakened in the force of his power....

4. When he was about four years old, the noble progeny of kings was sent to Utrecht and to the venerable Bishop Baldric (who still survives) to be steeped in study of the liberal arts.[2] There, while he progressed as befits a boy of good character, with excellent discipline and according to a wise nature, at long last, as if by a considerable siege on the hateful tyranny of the Normans,[3] churches and other buildings of which scarcely ruins had survived were restored on this occasion.

Thus he passed through no stage of his life without benefit to the holy Church of God. Through him, although he did not know it yet, the Christian populace, freed from its enemies, rejoiced in the praise of God. When he had learned the first rudiments of grammar—as we often heard from him as he meditated on the glory of the almighty God—next he began to read the poet Prudentius as taught by his master.[4] Because Prudentius is catholic in faith and purpose, outstanding in eloquence and truth, and most elegant in the variety of his meters and his books, such sweetness was so immediately pleasing to the taste of Bruno's heart that he drank in with greater eagerness than can be described not only knowledge of the external words but also the marrow of inner meaning and its purest nectar, if I may put it that way.

After that there was nearly no type of liberal study in Greek or Latin that escaped the vitality of his genius. Never, which is unusual, did great riches or the abundance of clamoring crowds or the approach of any other bother turn his spirit from this noble leisure. Perpetual meditation and tireless eagerness for mental exercise testified to the purity of his heart, since already nearly all disposition of this sort became habit, as it is written: "A boy is known from his inclinations, if his behavior is pure and righteous" [Prov. 20: 11]. It reached the point that just as he did not allow the fire of his soul to be put out by the idleness and frivolity of others nor be corrupted by empty and unnecessary conversation, he bore it very sorrowfully if the books he was studying or any that were in his sight were carelessly handled or creased or treated in any way with too little attention. Indeed, he considered that nothing that pertained to him should be neglected since indeed, as Solomon says, "He who neglects the small things dies little by little" [Eccles. 19: 1].

5. After his father, Henry, who had founded and pacified his realm to the last detail, went the way of all flesh, his first-born son Otto, blessed by the Lord and anointed with the oil of happiness, with the full will and consent of his chief men began to reign in the 188th lustrum and the 63rd cycle of the indiction since the birth of our lord Jesus Christ.[5] Otto was a man on whom the spirit of God had conferred a gift of singular truthfulness and faithfulness. If I promised that I would catalogue his virtues, I would take too much on myself and be tolerated little, for praise and glory owed him exceed whatever eloquence Cicero himself might offer. Otto honorably called his brother Bruno, dedicated to God, still a youth but as if an equal, from the schools to his court, a place fitting for such a bright mirror where whatever was unseemly in almost the whole world showed itself more

---

1   The "barbarians" are the Vikings, who had frequently raided Utrecht and its vicinity. A less partisan description of civil strife would emphasize the struggles King Henry had in establishing full authority in Lotharingia.

2   Bishop Baldric of Utrecht, a relative of Bruno's mother, lived for several years after the composition of Ruotger's account; he was bishop from 918 to 975! Utrecht was a center of learning.

3   I.e., the Vikings (Norsemen).

4   The Spanish poet Prudentius was a highly placed imperial official who withdrew to the ascetic life in his 40s. It was during this period that he wrote the Christian epics for which he was best known, including the *Psychomachia*, an allegory of the duels between personified virtues and vices.

5   Ruotger's dating method, which derived from ancient Rome, refers only to a range of years. The precise date is July 2, 936.

clearly through studies.[1] From all of Otto's borders came everything that seemed important. Likewise, all harassed by any accusation sought this sole refuge [Otto's court]. For there presided a model of wisdom, piety, and justice beyond human memory. Returning from the court, those who just before had seemed to themselves very learned, blushingly approached the rudiments of the liberal arts as if saying, "Now I begin." When nothing stirred on the left side of the breast, he thereafter modestly abstained from that high tribunal, so to speak.[2] The Lord filled this his vessel with the spirit of wisdom and thoughtfulness. It did not suffice to him to gather what he had ready at hand in the treasury of his own heart; he additionally considered foreign puzzles, and whatever philosophic matter he thought remote from earthly understanding he drew forth from wherever it came. He unveiled the seven liberal arts long forgotten. Whatever historians, orators, poets, and philosophers trumpeted was the great new thing he examined with great diligence along with teachers of whatever language it was in, and there where a master exceled in genius, he humbly offered himself as a student....

11. Then Wicfrid,[3] shepherd of the holy church of Cologne, for a long time quite feeble, yet faithful to the majesty of the kingdom and fatherland, at last returning his exhausted body to earth, was joined with heavenly spirits. The people, deprived of a shepherd, in grief chose for consolation, neither ambivalently nor wavering among candidates, the one solely hoped for: Lord Bruno, a splendid and most experienced man, following the counsel of great men and the whole clergy.[4] Youthful in body, he was mature in habits, humble and gentle despite the greatest nobility, at the height of his wisdom, which had taught him not to think himself wiser than is fitting to think, but wise in measure. Sparing of himself in his royal affluence, he was a rich man to his friends....

20. The emperor, disturbed about this event,[5] so sudden and unforeseen, and grieving more for the misery of its citizens than his own loss, lifted the siege of Mainz, having finally gotten the treaty he wanted. Turning from his camp toward the east along with those he knew to be loyal, Otto decided quickly to make a plan for the region he was leaving [i.e., Lotharingia] and made his brother [Bruno] the guardian and supervisor in the west, an archduke, so to speak, in such dangerous times. He gave him these orders. [The king said to Bruno,] "How much I rejoice, my dearest brother, that we have always understood matters as one and the same, and that it cannot be said we ever had different desires in any matter. It is the thing that greatly comforts me most of all in bitter times: I see royal priesthood, by the grace of almighty God, come into our kingdom. Both priestly religion and royal power are mighty in you, in that you know how to give everyone his due, which is justice, and you are able to withstand the dread and deceit of enemies, which is power and justice. For a long time now you have investigated the very mother of the liberal arts and truly its virtue, philosophy, which has trained you in modesty and greatness of spirit...."

23. Some people ignorant of divine will may object: why did a bishop assume public office and the dangers of war when he had undertaken only the care of souls? If they understand any sane matter, the result itself will easily satisfy them, when they see a great and very unaccustomed (especially in their homelands) gift of peace spread far and wide through this guardian and teacher of a faithful people, lest in this matter those objecting further stumble around in darkness where there is no light. Nor was governing this world new or unusual for rectors of the holy Church, previous examples of which, if someone needs them, are at hand. But we, moving on to other things, leave it to the judgment of each what he wants to say concerning this pious man, in the knowledge that nobody of sound mind would strive to blacken the

---

[1] The summons was in 939 or 940, when Bruno was a teenager. Otto's itinerant court allowed Bruno to travel widely during the next dozen or so years. The unseemliness here apparently refers to poor Latin, since the rest of the paragraph focuses on Bruno's intellectual pursuits, as teacher and learner, while a member of his brother's entourage.

[2] The right side of the breast is the seat of wisdom; here Ruotger is paraphrasing the Latin poet Juvenal. The meaning appears to be that if a line of study did not seem fruitful for him, he left it to others.

[3] Archbishop of Cologne (924–953).

[4] Bruno became archbishop of Cologne in 953.

[5] Bruno was elected amidst a rebellion against Otto I led by his son Liudolf and Duke Conrad (duke since 944 and also Otto's son-in-law), as described in chapters 18 and 19, omitted here. Chapter 20 picks up with Otto besieging rebels in Mainz. Although Otto did not take the title of emperor until 962, Ruotger calls him such retrospectively.

most evident blessing with the curse of reproach. Everything that Bruno did was honorable and useful for our republic.[1] In his deeds he by no means had as object that by gaining favor, news of his actions should fly through the mouths of men, but rather he lived this way: he regulated all his works before men so that they would be a horror to the worst and a reward for the best. He made it clear to all that in the episcopate he sought a good work, in which he could not easily be censured by the hostile and jealous, but that it worked even more to his credit that he displeased such people. Therefore, engaged in this wonderful occupation, the ever watchful manager of the highest head of the household and chief priest, bearing in his hands a burning lamp, namely an example of good work, he led some willing and dragged others unwilling to the ways of God....

31. Bruno gathered from everywhere the bodies of the saints and relics and other kinds of monuments in order to increase protection for his people and by means of this glory spread the glory of the Lord among peoples near and far. He arranged places and service for them very copiously, at great expense and in great sumptuousness, concerning each of which many things could be said if my promised brevity would allow it. These are signs of invincible faith, through which he sought not what was his but what was Jesus Christ's. Everyone knows with what care, fervor, and joy he brought the staff and chain of St. Peter to Cologne, the former from Metz and the latter from Rome. In honor of St. Peter, he wondrously expanded his most honorable house, which he changed from beautiful to very beautiful.[2]...

33. Meanwhile, in many places in the parishes of his diocese, this faithful and wise servant of the Lord built churches, monasteries and other buildings suited for the service of his one lord God and in honor of God's saints. Certain other structures already founded he enlarged and others long ruined he restored. With the foreseeing skill of his nature, he placed in each one those who would serve almighty God by the rule of canonical life, and in so doing generously provided for them, lest anything be lacking to carry out this way of life.[3] The memorials of his work and most salutary zeal, lasting as the air, remain fixed in place where he put them, so that for the praise and glory of Jesus Christ the memory of such a great man never suffer a time of obscurity. He poured out the same effort for foreign people; in the kingdom entrusted to his wisdom he provided sometimes by example, sometimes through his works, sometimes through qualities in other people and in repeated exhortation.[4] He did not allow any of his people to be occupied in vain or be inactive in lazy leisure, specifying, as he often said, that a lazy beast ought to be blocked from the trough and that according to the apostle [Paul], he who does not work does not eat [see 2 Thess. 3: 10]. All the good things he did, taught, and loved cannot be written out one by one. So much material would remain for those attending to it that they would quickly leave off in exhaustion before finishing what they had undertaken. In preaching the word of God and in the subtlety of his debates concerning the truth of the scriptures, we can marvel at such and so great a man, but we cannot sum him up....

37. The merciful shepherd Bruno, champion of truth, sower of the gospel, with the greatest care sought out zealous and diligent men who would keep watch over the republic, in loyalty and strength, each in his own place. He took great care that neither advice nor resources would be lacking to them. At Bruno's most beneficial urgings, all the princes and regional chiefs and others who had to do with the interests of the kingdom agreed to treaties in full faith for the common good of the property of all people. He considered them among the highest men and his intimates, and especially won over his brother the emperor to them, thinking—not foolishly—about a maxim of a wise man: "A good man gets slower when you ignore him, but a bad one is made more wicked." He cherished above all with great honor Archbishop Henry of Trier, a man of great merit and the highest integrity, who succeeded the great prelate Ruotbert, who died during a serious epidemic at Cologne when the emperor, too, was there; and also William of Mainz, an archbishop of most brilliant and agreeable excellence,

---

[1] Ruotger does not distinguish between kingdom and republic, which in the Roman tradition he knew so well meant simply "public sphere."

[2] That is, the cathedral of Cologne, which was dedicated to St. Peter. The chain was from Peter's imprisonment in Rome before his execution.

[3] The canonical rule was that of Saint Benedict, from which this sentence quotes to underline the connection.

[4] Bruno's rebuilding, reforming, and evangelizing efforts, then, went beyond his diocese and into other parts of Lotharingia.

Bruno's nephew and successor to Frederick: both of them outstanding men, both wholly trained in the Lord's law, both closely connected in friendship, the one through blood relation to the emperor, the other for his integrity.[1] Bruno often turned for advice to these two very illustrious men, so wise and religious and learned in all the good arts, lest he alone chance to stray anywhere off the path of truth, as is the way in human affairs. We saw them together with him not only in reading, counsel, and debate, but even in the line of battle, caring for good not only before God but before men. For there was in the western parts of Lotharingia a nearly untamable barbarism, which seemed a race of the church, begrudging the salvation of others no less than their own, scornful of gentle paternal admonition, nearly without fear of power.[2] Had they been allowed their own judgment, they would have seemed evil to their own and the worst thing for themselves. Bruno before all things practiced a forethoughtful way of governing, so that according to the nature of times and places, he pondered the rule of our very wise emperor in the elevation of shepherds for the peace and harmony of the Lord's flock.[3] He preferred those who understood several matters fully: a shepherd's duty, the vice of hirelings, the taking up of ministry, and what should be done or hoped for in this service. Some, like richly dyed curtains, would adorn the interiors of the Lord's house and others, like hair shirts, would guard against the violence of external storms....

49. [A lament for the now deceased Bruno]

Hearts, pour out prayers, send forth tearful words
Behold the father of his fatherland shut up in stone.
Royal stock to be remembered in all lands,
Bruno the peacemaker, a good and pious man.
Archbishop whose seat was famed Cologne,
He seemed dear to all good people everywhere.
His long-lasting light struck out against foul darkness.
The envious tongue falls silent; only true praise
   satisfies.
This world was not worthy of so rare a gift:
Taken from this world's shortcomings, he now rejoices
   in the company of the Lord.
On the ides of October in his twelfth year as bishop[4]
He gave up this life, hope his loving companion.

4.17 Literacy: King Alfred, *Prefaces* to Gregory the Great's *Pastoral Care* (*c.*890). Original in Old English.

Alfred the Great (r.871–899), the king of Wessex, energetically beat back Viking invaders, promulgated a code of law that drew from all the others in England—thus establishing a "common" law—and undertook a program to translate major works of Latin into the vernacular, Anglo-Saxon (also known as Old English), so that everyone could understand them. The text below presents Alfred's twin prefaces to his translation of Gregory the Great's *Pastoral Care* (590), a handbook for bishops.

[Source: *Alfred the Great: Asser's* Life of King Alfred *and Other Contemporary Sources*, trans. Simon Keynes and Michael Lapidge (New York: Penguin Books, 1983), pp. 124–27, 294–96 (slightly modified).]

---

[1]   Cologne, Trier, and Mainz were the seats of the three archbishops of Lorraine. Ruotbert was Bruno and Otto's uncle, and William was the natural son of Otto and thus Bruno's nephew. Frederick was archbishop of Mainz from 937 to 954, not unstintingly loyal to Otto, which explains why Otto's son succeeded him.

[2]   That is, they were nominally Christians but so savage and destructive to themselves and others as to be Christians in name only.

[3]   This sentence refers to Bruno's consultation with Otto about the appointment of bishops in the cities of western Lorraine.

[4]   I.e., October 15, 965.

Prose Preface

King Alfred sends words of greeting lovingly and amicably to [...].[1]

And I would have it known that very often it has come to my mind what men of learning there were formerly throughout England, both in religious and secular orders; and how there were happy times then throughout England; and how the kings, who had authority over this people, obeyed God and his messengers; and how they not only maintained their peace, morality and authority at home but also extended their territory outside; and how they succeeded both in warfare and in wisdom; and also how eager were the religious orders both in teaching and in learning as well as in all the holy services which it was their duty to perform for God; and how people from abroad sought wisdom and instruction in this country; and how nowadays, if we wished to acquire these things, we would have to seek them outside.[2] Learning had declined so thoroughly in England that there were very few men on this side of the Humber who could understand their divine services in English, or even translate a single letter from Latin into English: and I suppose that there were not many beyond the Humber either. There were so few of them that I cannot recollect even a single one south of the Thames when I succeeded to the kingdom. Thanks be to God Almighty that we now have any supply of teachers at all! Therefore I beseech you to do as I believe you are willing to do: as often as you can, free yourself from worldly affairs so that you may apply that wisdom which God gave you wherever you can. Remember what punishments befell us in this world when we ourselves did not cherish learning nor transmit it to other men.[3] We were Christians in name alone, and very few of us possessed Christian virtues.

When I reflected on all this, I recollected how—before everything was ransacked and burned—the churches throughout England stood filled with treasures and books. Similarly, there was a great multitude of those serving God. And they derived very little benefit from those books, because they could understand nothing of them, since they were not written in their own language.[4] It is as if they had said: "Our ancestors, who formerly maintained these places, loved wisdom, and through it they obtained wealth and passed it on to us. Here one can still see their track, but we cannot follow it." Therefore we have now lost the wealth as well as the wisdom, because we did not wish to set our minds to the track.

When I reflected on all this, I wondered exceedingly why the good, wise men who were formerly found throughout England and had thoroughly studied all those books, did not wish to translate any part of them into their own language. But I immediately answered myself, and said: "They did not think that men would ever become so careless and that learning would decay like this; they refrained from doing it through this resolve, namely they wished that the more languages we knew, the greater would be the wisdom in this land." Then I recalled how the Law was first composed in the Hebrew language, and thereafter, when the Greeks learned it, they translated it all into their own language, and all other books as well. And so too the Romans, after they had mastered them, translated them all through learned interpreters into their own language. Similarly all the other Christian peoples turned some part of them into their own language.[5] Therefore it seems better to me—if it seems so to you—that we too should turn into the language that we can all understand certain books which are the most necessary for all men to know, and accomplish this, as with God's help we may very easily do provided we have

---

[1] It is probable that in Alfred's original, no name was given at this point, but that the name of the bishop to whom a particular copy was to be sent would be added as the copy was being made. If each bishop in Alfred's kingdom of Wessex were to receive a copy, at least ten would have been needed; and we may assume that other important monastic centers would have been sent copies as well.

[2] Alfred is here alluding to his own activities in the 880s, when it was necessary to seek learned men from outside the kingdom of Wessex—from Mercia (to the north), Francia (across the English Channel), and Wales (to the west).

[3] This is presumably a reference to the Viking invasions of the central decades of the ninth century; in common with many Christian authors before and after him, Alfred regarded the invasion of hostile peoples as a form of divine punishment for decadence and decay.

[4] The books were written in Latin.

[5] There is no certainty about what translations Alfred is referring to here. The Bible was translated into Gothic by Ulfila in the fourth century, but Alfred is unlikely to have known of this work. It is more likely that he knew of one of the translations made in Germany during the ninth century: a prose translation of the gospel story in East Franconian made at the monastery of Fulda c.830; a metrical version of the same gospel story in Old Saxon made during the decade 830–840, known as the *Heliand*; and a metrical version of the gospels in Rhenish Franconian made by the monk Otfrid of Weissenburg sometime between 863 and 871.

peace enough, so that all the free-born young men now in England who have the means to apply themselves to it, may be set to learning (as long as they are not useful for some other employment) until the time that they can read English writings properly. Thereafter one may instruct in Latin those whom one wishes to teach further and wishes to advance to holy orders.

When I recalled how knowledge of Latin had previously decayed throughout England, and yet many could still read things written in English, I then began, amidst the various and multifarious afflictions of this kingdom, to translate into English the book which in Latin is called *Pastoralis*, in English "Shepherd-book,"[1] sometimes word for word, sometimes sense for sense, as I learnt it from Plegmund my archbishop, and from Asser my bishop, and from Grimbald my mass-priest and from John my mass-priest. After I had mastered it, I translated it into English as best I understood it and as I could most meaningfully render it; I intend to send a copy to each bishopric in my kingdom; and in each copy there will be an *Æstel* worth fifty mancuses.[2] And in God's name I command that no one shall take that *Æstel* from the book, nor the book from the church. It is not known how long

there shall be such learned bishops as, thanks be to God, there are now nearly everywhere. Therefore I would wish that they [the book and the *Æstel*] always remain in place, unless the bishop wishes to have the book with him, or it is on loan somewhere, or someone is copying it.

Verse Preface

Augustine brought this work from the south over the salt sea to the island-dwellers, exactly as the Lord's champion, the pope of Rome, had previously set it out. The wise Gregory was well versed in many doctrines through his mind's intelligence, his hoard of ingenuity. Accordingly, he won over most of mankind to the guardian of the heavens, this greatest of Romans, most gifted of men, most celebrated for his glorious deeds.

King Alfred subsequently translated every word of me into English and sent me south and north to his scribes;[3] he commanded them to produce more such copies from the exemplar, so that he could send them to his bishops, because some of them who least knew Latin had need thereof.

4.18 Law: King Æthelred, *Law Code* (1008). Original in Old English.

Written law codes were, among other things, a way for early medieval kings to signal that their realms were part of the "Roman" tradition. That is why *The Theodosian Code* (see above, p. 4) was of enduring importance. Although these codes were drawn up to seem timeless, they were very much products of local conditions and circumstances. Æthelred the Unready's reign was beset by Viking invasions and internal feuds. The nickname "Unready" came from the Anglo-Saxon word *unræd*, meaning "no-counsel." But Æthelred's code says that it was issued with the approval of his "ecclesiastical and lay councilors." In fact, one of those councilors was the most distinguished churchman of his age, Archbishop Wulfstan of York (r.1002–1023), whose handwriting may be detected in several of the entries in the manuscripts of this code. What evidence can you find in this code of military crisis? How does it compare with the roughly contemporary law code of King Stephen of Hungary (above, p. 205)?

[Source: *English Historical Documents*, Vol. 1: *c.* 300–1042, ed. Dorothy Whitelock, 2nd ed. (London: Routledge, 1979), pp. 442–46 (slightly modified).]

---

[1] Today in English it is ordinarily known as *Pastoral Care*.

[2] An *æstel* was a "book-mark." A mancus (pl. mancuses) was a coin or a unit of value equal to 30 pennies.

[3] In Old English poetry, it is a common convention to have the book speak in the first person.

PROLOGUE. This is the ordinance which the king of the English and both ecclesiastical and lay councilors have approved and decreed.

1. First, namely, that we all shall love and honor one God and zealously hold one Christian faith and entirely cast off every heathen practice; and we all have confirmed both with word and with pledge that we will hold one Christian faith under the rule of one king.

1.1. And it is the decree of our lord and his councilors that just practices be established and all illegal practices abolished, and that every man is to be permitted the benefit of law;

1.2. and that peace and friendship are to be rightly maintained in both religious and secular concerns within this country.

2. And it is the decree of our lord and his councilors that no Christian and innocent men are to be sold out of the country, and especially not among the heathen people, but care is earnestly to be taken that those souls be not destroyed which God bought with his own life.

3. And it is the decree of our lord and his councilors that Christian men are not to be condemned to death for all too small offences.

3.1. But otherwise life-sparing punishments are to be devised for the benefit of the people, and God's handiwork and his own purchase which he paid for so dearly is not to be destroyed for small offences.

4. And it is the decree of our lord and his councilors that men of every order are each to submit willingly to that duty which befits them both in religious and secular concerns.

4.1 And especially God's servants—bishops and abbots, monks and nuns, priests and women dedicated to God—are to submit to their duty and to live according to their rule and to intercede zealously for all Christian people.

5. And it is the decree of our lord and his councilors that every monk who is out of his monastery and not heeding his rule, is to do what behooves him: return readily into the monastery with all humility, and cease from evil-doing and atone very zealously for what he has done amiss; let him consider the word and pledge which he gave to God.

6. And that monk who has no monastery is to come to the bishop of the diocese, and pledge himself to God and men that from that time on he will at least observe three things, namely his chastity, and monastic garb, and serve his Lord as well as ever he can.

6.1. And if he keeps that, he is then entitled to the greater respect, no matter where he dwell.

7. And canons,[1] where there is property such that they can have a refectory and dormitory, are to hold their minster [church] with right observance and with chastity, as their rule directs; otherwise it is right that he who will not do that shall forfeit the property.

8. And we pray and instruct all mass-priests to protect themselves from God's anger.

9. They know full well that they may not rightly have sexual intercourse with a woman.

9.1. And whoever will abstain from this and preserve chastity, may he have God's mercy and in addition as a secular dignity, that he shall be entitled to a thegn's wergild and a thegn's rights, in life as well as in the grave.[2]

9.2. And he who will not do what belongs to his order, may his dignity be diminished both in religious and secular concerns.

10. And also every Christian man is zealously to avoid illegal intercourse, and duly keep the laws of the Church.[3]

10.1. And every church is to be under the protection of God and of the king and of all Christian people.

10.2. And no man henceforth is to bring a church under subjection, nor illegally to traffic with a church,[4] nor to expel a minister of the church without the bishop's consent.

11. And God's dues are to be readily paid every year.

11.1. Namely, plough-alms 15 days after Easter, and the tithe of young animals by Pentecost, and of the fruits

---

[1] Canons here refer to priests who live together in common.

[2] The wergild was the price of compensation, which varied with the status of the victim. Thegns were noblemen, and they had the high wergild of 1200 shillings.

[3] This provision involves not marrying within six degrees of relationship, or with the widow of so near a kinsman, or a close relative of a previous wife, or a nun, or anyone related by spiritual affinity, or a deserted woman.

[4] This refers to buying a church office or bartering a church.

of the earth by All Saints' day, and "Rome money" by St. Peter's day and light-dues three times a year.[1]

12. And it is best that payment for the soul be always paid at the open grave.

12.1. And if any body is buried elsewhere, outside the proper parish, the payment for the soul is nevertheless to be paid to the minster to which it belonged.

12.2. And all God's dues are to be furthered zealously, as is needful.

12.3. And festivals and fasts are to be properly observed.

13. The Sunday festival is to be diligently observed, as befits it.

13.1. And one is readily to abstain from markets and public meetings on the holy day.

14. And all the festivals of St. Mary are to be diligently observed, first with a fast and afterwards with a festival.

14.1. And at the festival of every Apostle there is to be fasting and festivity, except that we enjoin no fast for the festival of St. Philip and St. James, because of the Easter festival.

15. Otherwise other festivals and fasts are to be kept diligently just as those kept them who kept them best.

16. And the councilors have decreed that St. Edward's festival is to be celebrated over all England on March 18th.[2]

17. And there is to be a fast every Friday, except when it is a feast day.

18. And ordeals and oaths are forbidden on feast days and the legal Ember days, and from the Advent of the Lord until the octave of Epiphany, and from Septuagesima [Lent] until 15 days after Easter.

19. And at these holy seasons, as it is right, there is to be peace and unity among all Christian men, and every suit is to be laid aside.

20. And if anyone owes another a debt or compensation concerning secular matters, he is to pay it readily before or after [these seasons].

21. And every widow who conducts herself rightly is to be under the protection of God and the king.

21.1. And each [widow] is to remain unmarried for twelve months; she is afterwards to choose what she herself will.

22. And every Christian man is to do what is needful for him, heed zealously his Christian duties, form the habit of frequent confession, and freely confess his sins and willingly atone for them as he is directed.

22.1. And everyone is to prepare himself often and frequently for going to communion;

22.2. and to order words and deeds rightly and keep carefully oath and pledge.

23. And every injustice is to be zealously cast out from this country, as far as it can be done.

24. And deceitful deeds and hateful abuses are to be strictly shunned, namely, false weights and wrong measures, and lying witnesses and shameful frauds,

25. and horrible perjuries and devilish deeds of murder and manslaughter, of stealing and spoliation, of avarice and greed, of over-eating and over-drinking, of deceits and various breaches of law, of injuries to the clergy and of breaches of the marriage law, and of evil deeds of many kinds.

26. But God's law henceforth is to be eagerly loved by word and deed; then God will at once become gracious to this nation.

26.1. And people are to be zealous about the improvement of the peace, and about the improvement of the coinage everywhere in the country, and about the repair of boroughs in every province and also about military service,[3] according to what is decreed, whenever it is necessary,

27. and about the supplying of ships, as zealously as possible, so that each may be equipped immediately after Easter every year.

28. And if anyone deserts without leave from an army that the king himself is with, it is to be at the peril of his life and all his property.

28.1. And he who otherwise deserts from the army is to forfeit 120 shillings.

29. And if any excommunicated man—unless it be a suppliant for protection—remain anywhere in the king's

---

[1] "Rome money" refers to Peter's Pence, dues sent to Rome to support the papacy. "Light-dues" were revenues to pay for church candles.

[2] St. Edward was the martyred King Edward (r.975–978), the brother of Æthelred.

[3] Boroughs, or burhs, were fortifications.

neighborhood before he has submitted readily to eccle-siastical penance, it is to be at the peril of his life and all his possessions.

30. And if anyone plots against the king's life, he is to forfeit his life; and if he wishes to clear himself, he is to do it by [an oath of the value of] the king's wergild or by the three-fold ordeal in [the area under] English law.[1]

31. And if anyone commit obstruction or open resistance anywhere against the law of Christ or the king, he is to pay either wergild or fine or *lahslit*,[2] ever in proportion to the deed.

31.1. And if he illegally offers resistance with assault, and so brings it about that he is killed, no wergild is to be paid to any of his friends.

32. And ever henceforth the abuses are to cease which hitherto have been too common far and wide.

33. And every abuse is to be zealously suppressed.

33.1. For [only] as a result of suppressing wrong and loving righteousness will there be improvement at all in the country in religious and secular concerns.

34. We must all love and honor one God and entirely cast out every heathen practice.

35. And let us loyally support one royal lord, and all together defend our lives and our land, as well as ever we can, and pray Almighty God from our inmost heart for his help.

4.19 Christianity comes to Denmark: *The Jelling Monument* (960s).

The Jelling Monument is a large boulder with writing and carvings on it. It is important for understanding how Christianity became incorporated into the networks of power and prestige in Scandinavia.

Powerful people with great resources had long lived in Jelling, close to what is today Vejle, on the Jutland peninsula. During the Bronze age, before 500 BCE, they built an earthen mound, and, just south of the mound, they lined up several large standing stones to suggest the outline of a ship.

In 958 the Viking King Gorm died at Jelling. His son Harald Bluetooth buried his father in the old mound, adding more soil to make it taller. He also constructed another mound a short distance to the south, in the process destroying the "ship." The con-struction of mounds was a newly resuscitated custom in the tenth century. It was a self-conscious appeal to old traditions in the face of Christian customs spreading from Denmark's southern neighbors, the Germans. Accompanying Gorm in his tomb were a horse, riding gear, an elegant silver cup, a chest, a small wooden cross, and other artifacts A powerful man or woman was not to arrive in the afterlife without suitable equipment. This was entirely the opposite of Christian customs, which by the tenth century prohib-ited burying goods with bodies: the Christian afterlife was supposed to be immaterial.

Harald took over his father Gorm's kingdom. Then, in the 960s, he became a Christian. The reminders in Jelling of his pagan past, including his father, became an embarrassment, so Harald built a large wooden church close to the northern mound. He dug up the

---

[1] In the "three-fold" ordeal, the hot iron weighed three times more than its usual weight. For the ordeal, see above, p. 208, n. 3.

[2] *Lahslit* meant "breach of the law". It was the term given in the Danelaw (the law in the eastern region of England heavily settled by the Danes) to a fine varying with the rank of the offender, 10 half-marks for the king's thegn, 6 half-marks for other landowners, 12 ores (there were 8 ores to the mark) for the ordinary freeman.

body of his father and moved him to an honored place in the middle of the church, thus posthumously Christianizing Gorm. The centerpiece of the new Christian compound was a piece of art, a large granite boulder situated exactly at the midpoint between the two mounds—the "Jelling Monument." Harald had the boulder inscribed on three sides with large pictures and a text in runic characters, a special alphabet. When they were new, the pictures and the text would have been painted in bright colors. The stone proudly proclaimed that this was a Christian site. One side depicts a great rampant animal (a dragon? a lion?) entwined by a snake. Another side (see photo) portrays Christ cruci-fied. Remarkably, the cross itself is lacking. Instead, interlacing bands surround Christ.

The inscription reads: "King Harald had this monument made in memory of his father Gorm and in memory of his mother Thyre; that Harald who won for himself all of Denmark and Norway and made the Danes Christian." The last words are visible on the photo under the figure of Christ.

Thousands of runestones still dot the landscape of Scandinavia, most put up in the eleventh century, when most of the population had converted to Christianity. The text of these runestones was usually along the lines of the formula of Jelling: "X had this stone made/raised in memory of Y, his/her mother/father/brother/companion-at-arms." Many stones added "God save his (or her) soul," and others had crosses.

These inscriptions may appear to be selfless acts of remembrance of loved ones, but they served at least as much to remind all who passed of the power and wealth of the sponsor of the inscription, the person who was able to afford such a great monument. Certainly Harald did not hide behind any false humility; he forthrightly included his name twice to drive the point home. Harald, no one else, was the powerful conqueror and the religious benefactor of those he conquered. In this he appeared both as a traditional warlord and as a good Christian ruler.

The Jelling compound was part of Harald's efforts to consolidate his power, which also included the construction of forts all over his kingdom. It did not help. His son Svein Fork-beard rebelled against him in 986 or 987. Harald had to go into exile, where he soon died. The tomb that he had reserved for himself in the church next to his father Gorm is still empty. Taking this monument together with Bede's account of the Christianization of England, above, p. 94, consider how the new religion was—and was not—compatible with pre-Christian forms of kingship. Why, do you suppose, interlace was used in place of the cross?

See Plate 13, p. 249, for a color reproduction of *The Jelling Monument*.

(Caption by Anders Winroth. Image courtesy of the Nationalmuseet, Denmark)

TIMELINE FOR CHAPTER FOUR

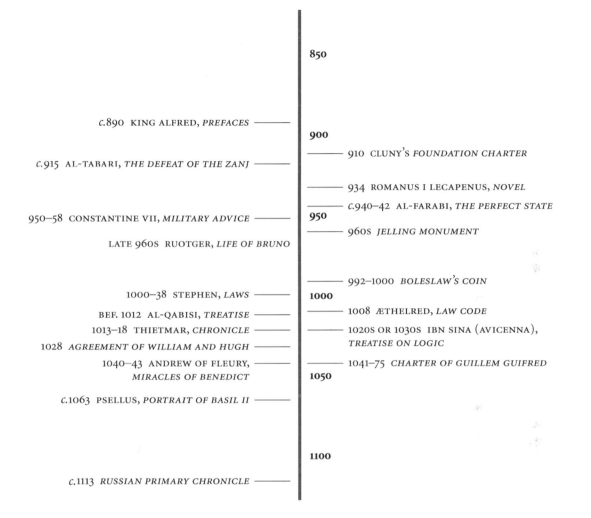

850

*c.*890 KING ALFRED, *PREFACES* ————

900

———— 910 CLUNY'S *FOUNDATION CHARTER*

*c.*915 AL-TABARI, *THE DEFEAT OF THE ZANJ* ————

———— 934 ROMANUS I LECAPENUS, *NOVEL*

———— *c.*940–42 AL-FARABI, *THE PERFECT STATE*

950–58 CONSTANTINE VII, *MILITARY ADVICE* ———— 950

———— 960S *JELLING MONUMENT*

LATE 960S RUOTGER, *LIFE OF BRUNO*

———— 992–1000 *BOLESLAW'S COIN*

1000–38 STEPHEN, *LAWS* ———— 1000

BEF. 1012 AL-QABISI, *TREATISE* ————

———— 1008 ÆTHELRED, *LAW CODE*

1013–18 THIETMAR, *CHRONICLE* ————

———— 1020S OR 1030S IBN SINA (AVICENNA),
TREATISE ON LOGIC

1028 *AGREEMENT OF WILLIAM AND HUGH* ————

1040–43 ANDREW OF FLEURY, ————
MIRACLES OF BENEDICT

———— 1041–75 *CHARTER OF GUILLEM GUIFRED*

1050

*c.*1063 PSELLUS, *PORTRAIT OF BASIL II* ————

1100

*c.*1113 *RUSSIAN PRIMARY CHRONICLE* ————

To test your knowledge and gain deeper understanding of this chapter,
please go to www.utphistorymatters.com for Questions for Reflection.

Containing the Holy

The theme "containing the holy" applies to all three of the major religions of the Western Middle Ages: Islam, Judaism, and Christianity in both its Greek Orthodox and Catholic traditions. Each object included in this insert should be treated in much the same way as a written primary source. A procedure for using them fruitfully might include:

1. Reading the caption for each plate.
2. Looking carefully at each object and considering what ideas (and even feelings) it evokes in you.
3. Asking (and trying to answer) the following general questions:
   a. When and where was the object made? See if you can find written sources in *Reading the Middle Ages* from the same region and/or time period. Read up on the object's larger context in *Short History of the Middle Ages* and/or other texts.
   b. Who made the object? In many cases you will not know the exact identity of the creator, but you will know (or at least you will be able to speculate about) the status (monk, craftsman, mosaicist) of both the person who made the object and the person or corporation (very often a nobleman or noblewoman, a ruler, or a person affiliated with the church) who paid for it or asked that it be made.
   c. For what purpose(s) was the object made? Consider the possible audiences that saw the object and how they might have understood and used it.
   d. What does the object say about the nature of holiness? Can holiness indeed be "contained," according to that object? Does the object imply a "theory" of the holy that can be teased out and analyzed?
   e. Does the container itself just "contain" the holy? To what extent is the container itself holy?
4. Asking specific questions (and seeking answers) that apply just to the particular object you are analyzing.

PLATE 1

Dome of the Rock (692)

While Caliph 'Abd al-Malik's forces were defeating a rival caliph, *c*.692, he ordered and paid for the building of a shrine in Jerusalem known as the Dome of the Rock. Its site had once held the Jewish Temple, destroyed by the Romans in 70 CE. Some Christian and Jewish traditions held that the rock within the edifice had been the place where the Messiah would appear at the end of time. Islamic *hadith* reported that after the creation, God had left earth and ascended to heaven from that very place.

Still other traditions, today largely accepted in the Islamic world, held that Muhammad ascended to heaven from the rock. The building itself is in the style of a centrally planned Christian *martyrium*—a church built over the tomb of a saint. Octagonal, its exterior walls (see the exterior view in Plate 1A) were originally covered with mosaics (replaced by tiles in the Ottoman period), while its dome was made of wood and gilded. The interior (see the interior view in Plate 1B) is still covered with mosaics reflecting the original program of the founder. These appear for the most part above two arcades of piers and columns. The imagery on the interior arcade spandrels (the triangular space between the arch curves) reuses and reinterprets traditional forms: vegetation and other decorative elements are combined with representations of Persian and Byzantine crowns, jewels, and breastplates. Across the entire circumference of the shrine are quotations from the Qur'an. Typical is this one: "O People of the Book, do not exaggerate in your religion, and say only the truth about God. The messiah, Jesus, son of Mary, was only a messenger of God, and His word, which He committed to Mary, and a spirit from Him. So believe in God and His messengers, and do not say 'three.'" What sorts of claims were being made by the caliph via the Dome and its decoration?

Icon with Saint Demetrios (2nd half 10th c.)

Icons are images believed to be holy. In the second half of the tenth century, when this one was probably carved, some icons were painted on panels, while others were composed of mosaics. Still others were represented in stained glass or, as here, made of ivory. (Personal icons, which were small, might be made of gold or silver, embellished with gems, and decorated with cloisonné enamel.) Demetrios, the patron saint of Thessalonica and popular elsewhere as well, was a late-third-century martyr. A church was built in his honor at the end of the fifth century, the earliest collection of miracle stories about him was composed at the beginning of the seventh century, and stories about his life and death began to be written in the ninth century. Above all, he was known as the protector of his city. In this relatively large (7 ¼ x 4 ¾ x ⅜ in.) plaque, he is dressed in the splendid armor of a high imperial military officer. He holds a spear (broken today) and a shield. Slung diagonally over his shoulder is the scabbard for his sword. The inscription on either side of his head says "Saint Demetrios." Although carved in relief (i.e., not in the round), the relief is so deep that Demetrios appears almost three-dimensional. The icon was probably originally nailed (you can see the four holes at the corners) alongside images of other saints. Later the area between the saint's feet was carved out to allow the plaque to be clamped to a pole during processions on the saint's feast day. Why did the artist show Demetrios so large that his halo required carving out the frame of the icon? What sort of power do you suppose this icon had on and for its devotees? How does the icon present a warrior as a holy man? What was happening to Byzantium in the tenth century that might help explain this imagery?

PLATE 3
Reliquary Locket (10th–11th c.)

This pendant, made of silver, gold, and niello (the black areas), was produced at Constantinople in the 10th or 11th century. On one side is a scene of the nativity, with the Christ Child (watched over by an ox and ass) in the space above the reclining Virgin. Saint Joseph sits by the foot of her bed. Below is a scene showing the Magi bearing gifts to the Child. The other side of the pendant shows a cross; the symbols on the two ends of the arms are ambiguous. The inscription on the rim says: "Secure deliverance and aversion from all evil," while the edge of the lid shows that the saints invoked were the twin doctors Cosmas and Damian, third-century martyrs renowned by this time throughout the Christian world for their ability to cure and heal and their refusal to take money for their work. The cavity in the locket held a relic, probably to ward off illnesses. What does this locket suggest about the importance of relics even in post-iconoclastic Byzantium? What other forms did reliquaries take—in both the East and the West—apart from lockets? (For some ideas, see below, Plates 7, 8, and 10.) What sorts of powers did relics have? What made them holy?

PLATE 4
Page from a Qur'an (993)

Each Qur'an not only contains the word of God but is itself a holy object. The script used to write it, therefore, had to be special: this is why the art of calligraphy was so highly valued in the Islamic world. Precious materials, too, were used in the making of the Qur'an: parchment at first and later paper, the formula for which was learned from Chinese prisoners of war captured during the Umayyad conquest of Transoxiana. The design of the page was also important. The large (about 9 ½ × 13 ¼ in.) page shown here is from a Qur'an manuscript copied in 993 in Isfahan (Iran). It was written on paper in the so-called "New Style" of script, making it quite untraditional. But it also drew on highly traditional elements. The very fact that the page is wider than it is long from top to bottom is a throwback to an early Qur'an format. The band of gold across the page is also traditional. The

writing on that band announces the number of the sura (chapter) to come, its familiar name, and the number of verses that it contains. The band's decorative "handle" at one end (on your left) is a motif ultimately derived from one kind of Roman tablet. The small gold rosettes (in the lines above the band) mark the end of each verse. Diacritical marks (in colors) hark back to an older way to indicate vowels and consonants. Given all this, and considering the sacred nature of the text of the Qur'an and of the container of the text itself, what variants were nevertheless possible? Compare the "holiness" of a Qur'an with that of a Christian reliquary. Usually the Qur'an was learned by heart and chanted, so why would Muslims want to have one as costly and beautiful as this is?

PLATE 5
A Holy Vestment (late 10th–early 11th c.)

The outermost vestment worn by a Christian priest during the Mass was the chasuble. Although the poncho-like garment developed from a humble late-Roman cape (called a *paenula*), by the Carolingian era the priestly chasuble was often highly ornamented and made of precious fabrics. This splendid example (Plate 5A) is made of a patterned golden silk produced in Byzantine Anatolia (perhaps Syria) in the late tenth or early eleventh century. The heavy weave, called samite, is in a complex repeat pattern with ovals enclosing palm-fronds linked by floral motifs (for these details, see Plate 5B). This vestment is one of

two surviving "holy Willigis chasubles" associated with Willigis, Archbishop of Mainz (r.975–1011): this one was preserved in the castle chapel at Aschaffenburg, where the archbishop had supported a school to train clerics. The other is from the church Willigis founded in honor of Saint Stephen in 990 in the city of Mainz (where Willigis was buried). Willigis served as chancellor to Emperor Otto I, whose son and heir Otto II raised him to the see of Mainz and made him arch-chancellor. Otto II's Byzantine bride, Theophanu, supported Willigis in the building of several churches, including Saint Stephen's, and she is the most likely source for the beautiful Byzantine silk of this chasuble. The empress's generosity was repaid during the crisis provoked by the death of Otto II in 983: Archbishop Willigis orchestrated the election of her son Otto III, consecrated him as king at Aachen on Christmas day, and then negotiated the three-year-old monarch's release and return to his regent mother after he was seized by the usurper Henry the Quarrelsome. Although never officially canonized, Willigis's date of death, February 23, was commemorated as a feast at Mainz, and the woven golden bands decorating the chasuble, which date from the thirteenth to the fifteenth centuries, attest to the continued use of this "holy Willigis chasuble" by the clergy of Mainz. Why might this garment be called "holy"? What does it tell us about how objects become holy? In what ways is it similar to or different from the holiness of the Reliquary Locket (Plate 3)? Try to imagine the feelings of priests who donned the Holy Willigis Chasuble long after Willigis had died. In light of your readings of the clergy in action (see below, p. 262), what various possible motives—and qualms— might these priests have had?

(Caption by Maureen C. Miller. Images by permission of the Bayerisches Nationalmuseum)

PLATE 6A

PLATE 6B

PLATE 6
Tlemcen, Great Mosque (1236)

The congregational mosque in Tlemcen, Algeria, rebuilt in 1136 by the Almoravids, provides a nice example of the general layout of a mosque. Most mosques are rectangular in plan, but an adjacent fortress forced the builders at Tlemcen to make a diagonal adjustment when they extended the mosque in 1236. This mosque, like most others, has several entrances (see the plan in Plate 6A) labeled (1), a minaret (2) added in 1236, adjacent to an internal courtyard with a fountain for ablutions (3). The prayer hall (4) is characterized by evenly placed piers that hold up the arcades and the roof. The focus of the mosque, and of all who pray within it, is the *qibla* wall (5), which points in the direction of Mecca. The *mihrab* (6) is a niche set off by a lobed horseshoe arch. A dome marks the space before the *mihrab* and the place of the *minbar* (7), a stepped pulpit that is brought out for the Friday noon sermon.

Plate 6B shows the dome, which was made of stucco and decorated with pierced arabesque patterns.

Plate 6C shows the *mihrab*, normally in the center of the *qibla* and the holiest spot of all. It is symbolic, perhaps, of the place where the Prophet Muhammad once stood when leading prayers in his house/mosque at Medina. In some ways, the *mihrab* is analogous to the ark in a Jewish synagogue (see Plate 9) or the altar in a medieval church.

What does the organization of space in the mosque communicate about the holy? How does this organization compare to the plan of a Christian church (see, for example, Plate 7)? How does it compare with the layout of a synagogue (see Plate 9)?

(Images courtesy of Jonathan Bloom and Sheila Blair)

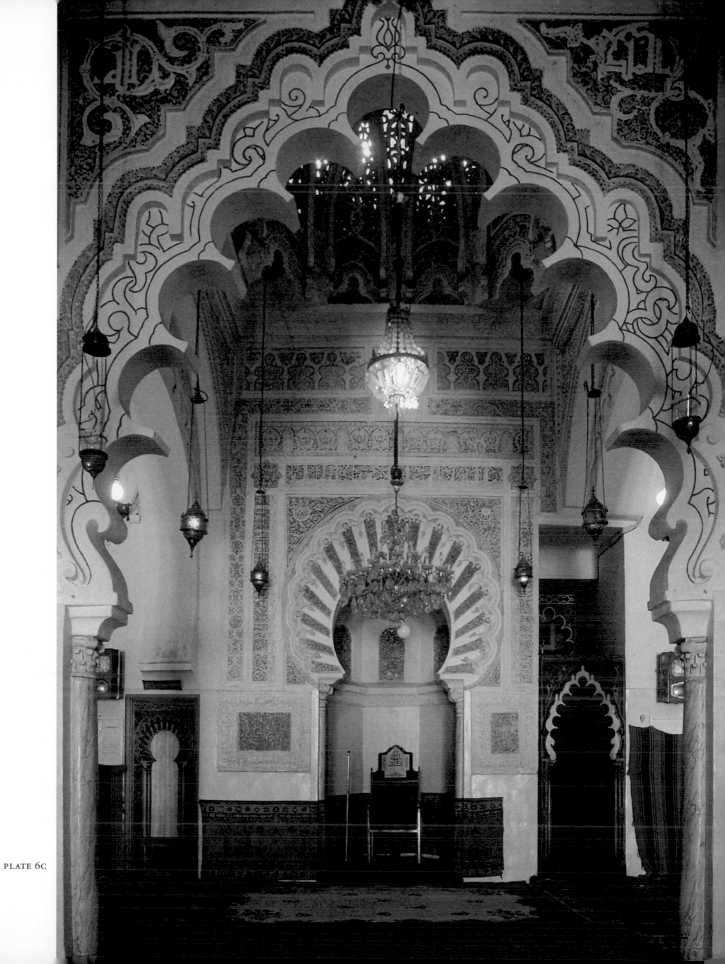

PLATE 6C

PLATE 7

The Church as Reliquary: Sainte-Chapelle (1248)

Completed in 1248, the Sainte-Chapelle (Holy Chapel) in Paris was built to house many of the sacred objects of Christ's Passion—the Crown of Thorns, pieces of the True Cross, and so on—that had once been part of the Byzantine emperor's relic collection. These had once been kept in the Pharos (lighthouse) Chapel—an architectural reliquary that held both relics and reliquaries—within the imperial palace. After the conquest of Constantinople by the crusaders of the Fourth Crusade (1202–1204), the weak rulers of the Latin Empire, needing money, sold the relics to Western rulers, including French King Louis IX (r.1226–1270). Between 1239 and 1241 Louis amassed 22 of these relics. He brought them to Paris with great fanfare. To house them fittingly, he commissioned Sainte-Chapelle right within the royal palace (mimicking in this way the Pharos Chapel). The architect was probably Thomas de Cormont, who had worked on the cathedral at Amiens. Sainte-Chapelle had two stories: a relatively somber first floor for the members of the court, and an upper story, glowing with the bright colors of its stained glass wall-to-ceiling windows, for the royal family. Every consecrated church is in a sense a reliquary (and all altars contain a relic), but the Sainte-Chapelle was built to *look* like a reliquary. Within it was another, smaller reliquary, the Grande Châsse (destroyed during the French Revolution). Kept behind the altar of the upper story, it held the precious objects of the Passion. (Some, like the Crown of Thorns, were also broken up into smaller pieces, put into smaller reliquaries, and sent off as gifts to other notables.) The instruments of the Passion were now in Paris, and pilgrims flocked to see them. How might the acquisition of these relics and the building of the Sainte-Chapelle have influenced the urban space around it and the status of the city of Paris? What messages did the Sainte-Chapelle communicate about the kings of France and their power?

(Copyright © Bernard Acloque / Centre des monuments nationaux)

240

PLATE 8

Monstrance (*c.*1430)

The word "monstrance" comes from a Latin word meaning "to show." In the later Middle Ages, priests wanted to "show"—and their flocks wanted to "see"—the central mystery of the Christian religion: the host. Bread turned into the body of the crucified Christ took on new importance in a society that was intensely focused on Christ's life and death and that found salvation in the act of Holy Communion. The monstrance was designed to hold and show the host. This particular example, made in Cologne (Germany) *c.*1430 of silver gilt, is, at about 20 inches in height, relatively small. In the precise center, measuring top to bottom, is a crystal cylinder for the host itself; the rest exists to honor and frame Christ's body. Around the cylinder, a golden circle decorated with flowers is itself framed—as if it were a Gothic church—by delicate buttresses that rise up to a central tower topped by a crucifix. (The tiny figure of the Virgin within the tower is a much later addition.) The whole is meant to echo the Heavenly Jerusalem, which Rev. 21: 11, 18–19 describes as lighted "like to a precious stone … even as crystal," while "the city itself [was] of pure gold.… And the foundations of the wall of the city were adorned with all manner of precious stones." In the Cologne monstrance the six-part base is engraved with images of saints and the Virgin and Child alongside a petition for prayers on behalf of the monstrance's donor and his family. Why would a donor want his monstrance to look like a church? How was the host like (and unlike) a relic?

(Copyright © Rheinisches Bildarchiv Köln, rba_c012396)

242

PLATE 9

Synagogue and Ark (1435)

This full-page illumination is in a manuscript made at Mantua, Italy, in 1435. Not a holy object itself, the illumination represents what is very hard to find today: the interior of a medieval synagogue. Unlike churches, which persisted (though often much changed) into the modern period, most medieval synagogues were destroyed over time. Yet the synagogue was a container of holiness. Symbolically, it replaced the Temple at Jerusalem (whose most recent incarnation was destroyed by the Romans in 70 CE). Within the synagogue was the Torah ark (here on the right), which replaced the Temple's Inner Holy of Holies. The Torah scroll—consisting of the first five books of the Hebrew Bible and itself a holy object—is about to be replaced in the ark after the reading for the day. (The reader and his lectern are in the middle of the room.) The faithful, even the women, are clothed in special prayer shawls. On the four corners of the page are the animals invoked by Judah ben Tema (a 2nd-c. CE Talmudic scholar) ("Be strong as a leopard, swift as the eagle, fleet as the gazelle, and brave as the lion.") Compare the architecture of this synagogue and its ark with the architecture of Sainte-Chapelle and its Grande Châsse (see Plate 7) and with the mosque and its *mihrab* at Tlemcen (see Plate 6C). What commonalities and what differences do you see?

PLATE 10
The Wienhausen Sepulcher (15th c.)

In the later Middle Ages, numerous churches in Europe wanted to have replicas of the Holy Sepulcher, Christ's tomb in Jerusalem. As "props" for liturgical dramas, these sepulchers played an especially important role in Easter celebrations. In 1448, the abbess Katherina von Hoya consecrated an elaborately decorated sepulcher (Plate 10A) for her convent at Wienhausen, in northern Germany. For the body, the nuns used a thirteenth-century wooden effigy of

Christ, his side wound gaping open and blood dripping down his hands and spurting out holes in the soles of his feet. The tomb was generally opened only for the Easter rituals, so that the nuns could see scenes of the infancy of Christ (here sheltering Christ's left side) and Christ's passion (the lid that hangs down on Christ's right.) Small doors at Christ's head and feet (Plate 10B) were opened during the course of the celebrations to allow the whole of

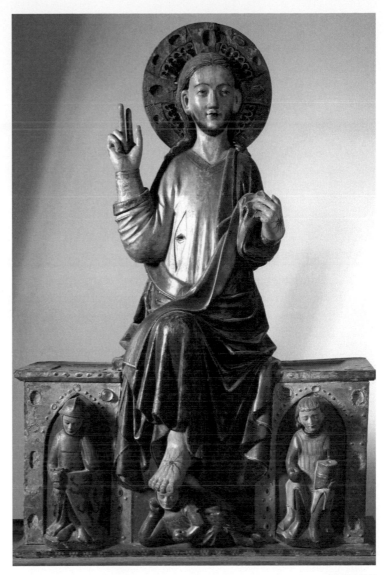

PLATE 10B   PLATE 10C

Christ's bleeding body to be eventually revealed. A hole in his head and the wounds on the soles of his feet once held relics, while the Good Friday host was tucked into his side wound. On Easter Sunday, the nuns removed the effigy of the dead Christ and substituted an image of the resurrected Christ (Plate 10C). Thus the sepulcher served as a site not only for holy objects but also for the re-enactment of the holiest of Christian rites: Christ's resurrection and with it the promise of the salvation of all Christians. What

transformations in Christian "containers of the holy" do you see taking place over time? Compare the meanings of the Wienhausen tomb with those of the Grande Châsse of Sainte-Chapelle (Plate 7), the *mihrab* of the mosque at Tlemcen (Plate 6C), and the ark of the Torah (Plate 9). How do their various decorative programs compare? What might explain the differences?

(Images courtesy of the Kloster Wienhausen/Lüneburger Klosterarchive and Elina Gertsman)

245

Reading through Looking

The plates in this section are meant to complement some of the readings; they represent another way to understand the topic at hand. For example, Plate 14, a portion of *The Bayeux Tapestry,* should be considered alongside the texts from William of Jumièges, "Florence of Worcester," and the *Domesday Book* in order to explore the many ways in which the Norman Conquest of England was understood and portrayed.

OBVERSE

REVERSE

PLATE 11
Seal of Boris-Michael (864–889)

When the Bulgarian Khan Boris converted to the Christian religion in *c*.864, he had seals such as this made to advertise his link to that faith. On its obverse (or "heads") side, an image of Christ is encircled by the inscription: "Christ help your servant Michael ruler of Bulgaria."

(Images courtesy of Dr. Ivan Jordanov)

OBVERSE

REVERSE

PLATE 12
Boleslaw's Coin (992–1000)

Boleslaw the Brave of Poland (r.992–1225) issued coins that celebrated his rulership. On the obverse ("heads") side he is shown in profile, like a Roman emperor; on the reverse ("tails"), a cross is surrounded by an inscription referring to his chief city, Gniezno.

(From the collection of the National Museum in Kraków)

PLATE 13
The Jelling Monument (960s)

In the 960s, when Danish King Harald Bluetooth converted to Christianity, he "Christianized" his father's burial place by building a church on the site and marking the spot with this granite monument depicting the crucified Christ.

(Courtesy of the Nationalmuseet, Denmark)

The text visible within the tapestry reads: BAGIAS · VBI · hAROLD : SACRAMENTVM : FECIT : · hIC hA— · VVILLELMO · DVCI :·

PLATE 14
The Bayeux Tapestry (end of the 11th c.)

This detail from a long embroidery commissioned by a supporter of Duke William of Normandy depicts a crucial moment in the Duke's conquest of England. It shows his chief competitor to English kingship swearing fealty to him.

(Detail of the Bayeux Tapestry—11th Century. With special permission from the City of Bayeux)

250

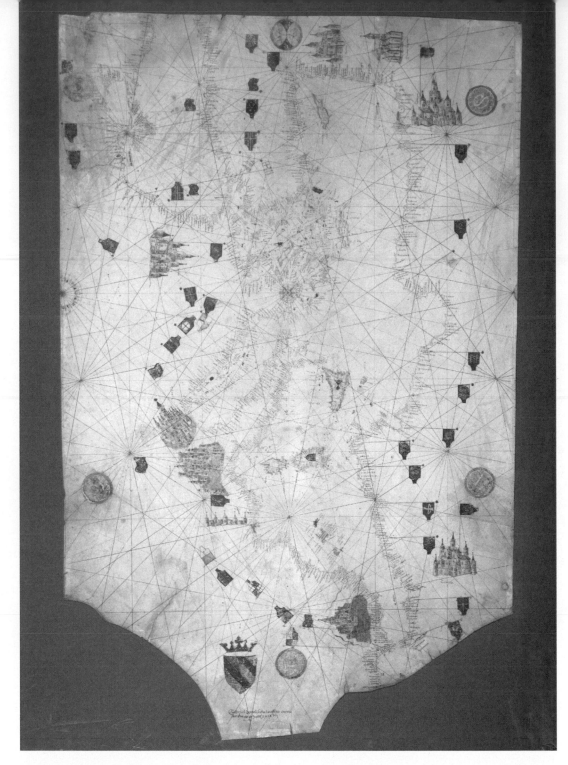

Gabriel de Valseca, *Portolan Map* (1447)

Unlike many earlier maps, which were meant to symbolize the world rather than to be practical guides for travelers, portolan maps such as this one showed coastlines with considerable precision, allowing sailors to skirt headlands where they might run aground and find estuaries that supplied fresh water.

(By permission of the Bibliothèque nationale de France)

V

The Expansion of Europe (c.1050–c.1150)

COMMERCIAL TAKE OFF

5.1 Cultivating new lands: *Frederick of Hamburg's Agreement with Colonists from Holland* (1106). Original in Latin.

The commercial revolution took place in both town and countryside. In the countryside it depended on the enterprise of peasants and the support of people in power. In this charter the archbishop of Hamburg-Bremen, Frederick (r.1105–1123), granted swamp land in his diocese to colonists from Holland willing to undertake the backbreaking, collective work of drainage. (They were used to this sort of work; much of Holland itself was swampland.) The bishop required payments in return, not only for the produce of the land but also for the right of the colonists to hear their own court cases. His call to settlers was part of a wider movement. Hamburg-Bremen was on the Slavic frontier. Bringing Christians to settle it was one way that German leaders meant to subdue the polytheistic natives. For a contemporary account of a later phase of this development, see Helmold, *Chronicle of the Slavs*, p. 303 in *Reading the Middle Ages*, Vol. II.

[Source: *Ausgewählte Urkunden zur Erläuterung der Verfassungsgeschichte Deutschlands im Mittelalter*, ed. Wilhelm Altmann and Ernst Bernheim, 5th ed. (Berlin: Weidmannsche Buchhandlung, 1920), pp. 161–62, no. 80. Translated by Barbara H. Rosenwein.]

[1] In the name of the holy and individual Trinity, Frederick, bishop of the church of Hamburg by grace of God, [gives] to all the faithful in Christ, present and future, perpetual benediction. We wish to notify all of a certain agreement that certain people living on this side of the Rhine, who are called Hollanders, made with us.

[2] The aforementioned men came to Our Majesty resolutely asking us to concede to them territory for them

to cultivate. This land is situated in our bishopric and has hitherto been uncultivated, marshy, and useless to our locals. And so, having taken counsel with our vassals (*fideles*) and thinking it would be beneficial for us and our successors not to refuse their petition, we gave [our] assent.

[3] Moreover, the agreement of their petition was that they give to us a single denar [a silver coin] each year for every manse of this land.[1] We have thought it necessary to write down here the dimensions of a manse, lest there be a dispute later on among the people: a manse is 720 royal rods long and 30 wide, including the streams which flow through the land, which we grant in similar manner.

[4] Finally, they promised to give us a tithe according to our decree, that is, the eleventh part of the fruit of the earth, the tenth of the lambs, similarly of pigs, similarly of goats, the same of geese, and also they will give in the same way a tenth of the amount of honey and flax. They will render a dinar for each foal on the feast of St. Martin [November 11], and an obol [a coin worth less than a dinar] for each calf.

[5] They promised that they would obey us always in all matters pertaining to ecclesiastical law according to the decrees of the holy fathers, canon law, and the customs of the church of Utrecht [the home diocese of the colonists].

[6] With regard to judgments and court hearings involving secular law, they affirm that they will pay 2 marks [a gold or silver coin worth a substantial amount] each year for every 100 manses so that they may try all disputes themselves, lest they suffer from the prejudice of foreign [judges]. If they are unable to settle the more serious hearings or judgments, they shall refer them to the tribunal of the bishop. If they bring him with them to decide the case, for however long he remains [with them] they shall provide for him at their own expense in this manner: they shall keep two thirds of the court fees and give the last third to the bishop.

[7] We have allowed them to construct churches on said territory wherever it seems appropriate to them. We have offered to each church, for the express use of the priests serving God there, a tithe from our tithes of those parish churches. They confirm that the parishioners of each church will give no less than one manse to each church as an endowment for the use of the priest.

[8] The names of the men who came together to make and confirm this agreement are: Heinricus, the priest, to whom we have granted the aforesaid churches for life, and other laymen: Helikinus, Arnoldus, Hiko, Fordoltus, and Referic. To them and their heirs after them we concede the said land according to the secular laws and abovementioned agreement.

[9] The affirmation of this agreement was made in the year of our Lord's incarnation 1106, in the sixth indiction, in the reign of Lord Henry IV, Emperor Augustus of the Romans. To confirm this document with our affirmation, it pleases us that the charter be affixed with the impression of our seal. If anyone says anything against it, let him be anathema.

[10] In confirmation of this document, I, Bishop Wernherus was present and signed. I, Bishop Marquardus. I, Bishop Hasoko. I, Bishop Hujo. I, Adelbero. I, Thieto was present and signed. I, Gerungus, *advocatus* [a lay protector of a church] was present and witnessed. I, Hericus, was present. I, Thidericus. I, Willo, was present. I, Erpo, was present and witnessed. I, Adelbertus. I, Gerwardus. I, Ermbertus. I, Reinwardus. I, Ecelinus.

5.2 Ibn 'Abdun, *Regulations for the Market at Seville* (early 12th c.). Original in Arabic.

Muslim Spain was urbanized before most other Western regions and, as the document here demonstrates, its economic life was integrated into its notions of religion and morality. Ibn 'Abdun may well have been a market inspector—a *muhtasib*—responsible not only for making sure that products sold were up to a certain standard and that prices were legitimate but also for regulating relations between Christians, Muslims, and Jews

---

[1] A manse (*mansus*) was a farming unit: it often included a house, waste, meadow, a garden, and, of course, land for crops. Here its dimensions are standardized and declared because the land is considered "virgin" and ready to be parceled out at will.

and enforcing Muslim rules regarding sexuality and purity. Compare these regulations to those in the Byzantine *Book of the Prefect*, above, p. 109, from an earlier period, and to the later ordinances at Pistoia in response to the plague, p. 448 in *Reading the Middle Ages*, Vol. II. What are the similarities, what are the differences, and what do these comparisons reveal about economic life in the different periods and cultures?

[Source: Bernard Lewis, ed. and trans., *Islam: From the Prophet Muhammad to the Capture of Constantinople*, vol. 2: *Religion and Society* (New York: Oxford University Press, 1987), pp. 157–65.]

Shopkeepers must be forbidden to reserve regular places for themselves in the forecourt of the great mosque or elsewhere, for this amounts to a usurpation of property rights and always gives rise to quarrels and trouble among them. Instead, whoever comes first should take his place.

The *muhtasib* [market inspector] must arrange the crafts in order, putting like with like in fixed places. This is the best and most orderly way.

There must be no sellers of olive oil around the mosque, nor of dirty products, nor of anything from which an irremovable stain can be feared.

Rabbits and poultry should not be allowed around the mosque, but should have a fixed place. Partridges and slaughtered barnyard birds should only be sold with the crop plucked, so that the bad and rotten can be distinguished from the good ones. Rabbits should only be sold skinned, so that the bad ones may be seen. If they are left lying in their skins, they go bad.

Egg sellers must have bowls of water in front of them, so that bad eggs may be recognized.

Truffles should not be sold around the mosque, for this is a delicacy of the dissolute.[1]

Bread should only be sold by weight. Both the baking and the crumbs must be supervised, as it is often "dressed up." By this I mean that they take a small quantity of good dough and use it to "dress up" the front of the bread which is made with bad flour....

The cheese which comes from al-Madāin[2] should not be sold, for it is the foul residue of the curds, of no value. If people saw how it is made, no one would ever eat it. Cheese should only be sold in small leather bottles, which can be washed and cleaned every day. That which is in bowls cannot be secured from worms and mold.

Mixed meats should not be sold on one stall, nor should fat and lean meat be sold on one stall. Tripe should only be sold dry on boards, for water both spoils it and increases its weight. The entrails of sheep must be taken out, so that they should not be sold with the meat and at the same price, which would be a fraud. The heads of sheep should not be skinned, except for the young. The guts must always be removed from the bodies of animals, except lambs, and should not be left there, for this too would be an occasion for fraud.

No slaughtering should take place in the market, except in the closed slaughterhouses, and the blood and refuse should be taken outside the market. Animals should be slaughtered only with a long knife. All slaughtering knives should be of this kind. No animal which is good for field work may be slaughtered, and a trustworthy and incorruptible commissioner should go to the slaughterhouse every day to make sure of this; the only exception is an animal with a defect. Nor should a female still capable of producing young be slaughtered. No animal should be sold in the market which has been brought already slaughtered, until its owner establishes that it is not stolen....

Women should be forbidden to do their washing in the gardens, for these are dens for fornication.

Grapes in large quantities should not be sold to anyone of whom it is known that he would press them to make wine. This is a matter for supervision.

Fruit must not be sold before it is ripe for this is bad, except only for grapes, which are good for pregnant women and for the sick....

The seller of grapes should have baskets and nets in which to arrange them, as this is the best protection for them.

Cakes should be properly baked and should only be made wide, as thin ones are good only for the sick.

If someone assays gold or silver coins for a person,

---

[1] Apparently a common view. A Spanish Arabic proverb includes the large consumption of truffles among the signs by which the dissolute may be recognized.

[2] A term applied to the fertile islands in the lower Guadalquivir, below Seville.

and later it emerges that there is base metal in them, the assayer must make good, for he deceived and betrayed the owner of the coins, who placed his trust in him. Swindlers when detected must be denounced in all crafts, but above all in assaying coin, for in this case the swindler can only be a person who is expert in matters of coin.

Women should not sit by the river bank in the summer if men appear there.

No barber may remain alone with a woman in his booth. He should work in the open market in a place where he can be seen and observed.

The cupper.[1] He should only let blood into a special jar with graduation marks, so that he can see how much blood he has let. He should not let blood at his discretion, for this can lead to sickness and death.

The water wheel. Most of the holes for the spindles should be wedged, as this is best for its working.

No one may be allowed to claim knowledge of a matter in which he is not competent, especially in the craft of medicine, for this can lead to loss of life....

Only a skilled physician should sell potions and electuaries and mix drugs. These things should not be bought from the grocer or the apothecary whose only concern is to take money without knowledge; they spoil the prescriptions and kill the sick, for they mix medicines which are unknown and of contrary effect....

Only good and trustworthy men, known as such among people, may be allowed to have dealings with women in buying and in selling. The tradespeople must watch over this carefully. The women who weave brocades must be banned from the market, for they are nothing but harlots.

On festival days men and women shall not walk on the same path when they go to cross the river....

The basins in the public baths should be covered. If they are left uncovered, they cannot be protected from pollution, yet this is a place of purity. The bath attendant, the masseur, and the barber should not walk about in the baths without a loincloth or drawers.

A Muslim must not massage a Jew or a Christian nor throw away his refuse nor clean his latrines. The Jew and the Christian are better fitted for such trades, since they are the trades of those who are vile. A Muslim should not attend to the animal of a Jew or of a Christian, nor serve him as a muleteer, nor hold his stirrup. If any Muslim is known to do this, he should be denounced.

Muslim women shall be prevented from entering their abominable churches for the priests are evil-doers, fornicators, and sodomites. Frankish[2] women must be forbidden to enter the church except on days of religious services or festivals, for it is their habit to eat and drink and fornicate with the priests, among whom there is not one who has not two or more women with whom he sleeps. This has become a custom among them, for they have permitted what is forbidden and forbidden what is permitted. The priests should be ordered to marry, as they do in the eastern lands. If they wanted to, they would....

A Jew must not slaughter meat for a Muslim. The Jews should be ordered to arrange their own butcher's stalls.

A garment belonging to a sick man,[3] a Jew, or a Christian must not be sold without indicating its origin; likewise, the garment of a debauchee. Dough must not be taken from a sick man for baking his bread. Neither eggs nor chickens nor milk not any other foodstuff should be bought from him. They should only buy and sell among themselves.

The sewer men must be forbidden to dig holes in the streets, as this harms them and causes injury to people, except when they are cleaning the entire street.

Itinerant fortune-tellers must be forbidden to go from house to house, as they are thieves and fornicators.

A drunkard must not be flogged until he is sober again.

Prostitutes must be forbidden to stand bareheaded outside the houses. Decent women must not bedeck themselves to resemble them. They must be stopped from coquetry and party making among themselves, even if they have been permitted to do this [by their husbands]. Dancing girls must be forbidden to bare their heads.

No contractor,[4] policeman, Jew, or Christian may be allowed to dress in the costume of people of position, of a jurist, or of a worthy man. They must on the contrary be abhorred and shunned and should not be greeted with the formula, "Peace be with you," for the devil has gained mastery over them and has made them forget the name

---

[1] Muslims practiced "wet" bloodletting. A cup was applied to the skin to create a mild suction, and then the swollen area was cut with the proper tools. A second application of the cup drew out the blood.

[2] That is, Christians from outside Spain and from those parts of Spain not under Muslim rule.

[3] Probably lepers are meant.

[4] I.e., tax farmer.

of God. They are the devil's party, "and indeed the devil's party are the losers."[1] They must have a distinguishing sign by which they are recognized to their shame.

Catamites[2] must be driven out of the city and punished wherever any one of them is found. They should not be allowed to move around among the Muslims nor to participate in festivities, for they are debauchees accursed by God and man alike.

When fruit or other foodstuffs are found in the possession of thieves, they should be distributed in prisons and given to the poor. If the owner comes to claim his goods and is recognized, they should be returned to him.

5.3 The role of royal patronage: Henry I, *Privileges for the Citizens of London* (1130–1133). Original in Latin.

Towns were permanent commercial centers, and their citizens often demanded and received special privileges that gave them considerable autonomy. In this charter, Henry I, king of England (r.1100–1135), grants privileges to the citizens of London *c.*1130, basing them on grants handed out by previous kings. The Londoners have the right to the "farm" or revenues of their own borough, Middlesex, holding it, as a vassal might hold a fief, of the king and his heirs. The citizens are also allowed to have their own courts and freedom from various duties and tolls (called "customs" here). The reference to "sokes" in this text means "jurisdictions," which, among other things, were sources of revenues. Compare the freedoms granted by King Henry to those granted by Bishop Frederick in his *Agreement with Colonists*, p. 253 above.

[Source: *English Historical Documents*, vol. 2: 1042–1189, ed. David C. Douglas and George W. Greenaway, 2nd ed. (London: Routledge, 1981), pp. 1012–13 (slightly modified).]

Henry, by the grace of God, king of the English, to the archbishop of Canterbury, and to the bishops and abbots, and earls and barons and justices and sheriffs, and to all his liegemen, both French and English, of the whole of England, greeting. Know that I have granted to my citizens of London that they shall hold Middlesex at "farm" for 300 pounds "by tale" for themselves and their heirs from me and my heirs, so that the citizens shall appoint as sheriff from themselves whomsoever they may choose, and shall appoint from among themselves as justice whomsoever they choose to look after the pleas of my crown and the pleadings which arise in connection with them. No other shall be justice over the men of London.

And the citizens shall not plead outside the walls of the city in respect of any plea; and they shall be quit of scot and of Danegeld and the murder-fine.[3] Nor shall any of them be compelled to offer trial by battle.[4] And if any one of the citizens shall be impleaded [sued] in respect of the pleas of the crown, let him prove himself to be a man of London by an oath which shall be judged in the city. Let no one be billeted within the walls of the city, either of my household, or by the force of anyone else. And let all the men of London and their property be quit and free from toll and passage and lestage and from all other customs throughout all England and at the seaports. And let the churches and barons and citizens

---

[1] Qur'an 57: 22.

[2] A young man who has sexual relationships with men.

[3] The "murder-fine" (*murdrum*) penalized an entire community for the death of any Norman. It dated from the period after the Norman Conquest, when feelings ran high against the invaders. The Londoners are here exempt from paying this.

[4] This was a duel to determine which party was in the right; the tradesmen of London preferred other forms of trial.

hold and have well and in peace their sokes, with all their customs, so that those who dwell in these sokes shall pay no customs except to him who possesses the soke, or to the steward whom he has placed there. And a man of London shall not be fined at mercy[1] except according to his "were,"[2] that is to say, up to 100 shillings: this applies to an offence which can be punished by a fine. And there shall no longer be "miskenning"[3] in the hustings court, nor in the folk-moot,[4] nor in other pleas within the city. And the hustings court shall sit once a week, to wit, on Monday. I will cause my citizens to have their lands and pledges and debts within the city and outside it. And in respect of the lands about which they make claim to me, I will do them right according to the law of the city. And if anyone has taken toll or custom from the citizens of London, then the citizens of London may take from the borough or village where toll or custom has been levied as much as the man of London gave for toll, and more also may be taken for a penalty. And let all debtors to the citizens of London discharge their debts, or prove in London that they do not owe them; and if they refuse either to pay or to come and make such proof, then the citizens to whom the debts are due may take pledges within the city either from the borough or from the village or from the county in which the debtor lives. And the citizens shall have their hunting chases, as well and fully as had their predecessors, namely, in Chiltern and Middlesex and Surrey. Witness: the bishop of Winchester; Robert, son of Richer; Hugh Bigot; Alfred of Totnes; William of Aubigny; Hubert the king's chamberlain; William of Montfiquet; Hagulf "de Tani"; John Belet; Robert, son of Siward. Given at Westminster.

CHURCH REFORM

5.4 The royal view: Henry IV, *Letter to Gregory VII* (1075). Original in Latin.

The movement for church reform was initially supported by both popes and emperors. But as the issue of church leadership came to the fore, the two powers inevitably clashed. When, in 1075, King Henry IV (r.1056–1106) "invested"—put into office—his episcopal candidate at Milan, Pope Gregory VII (1073–1085) complained. Henry reacted vigorously. He met with his bishops at Worms, and the assembly denounced Gregory (called by his old name, Hildebrand) as a usurper of the papal throne. The letter below, which was circulated within Germany, charges Gregory with throwing the church into chaos and calls upon him to resign. A milder version was sent to the pope himself.

[Source: *Imperial Lives and Letters*, ed. Robert L. Benson; trans. Theodor E. Mommsen and Karl F. Morrison (New York: Columbia University Press, 2000), pp. 150–51.]

Henry, King not by usurpation, but by the pious ordination of God,[5] to Hildebrand, now not Pope, but false monk:

You have deserved such a salutation as this because of the confusion you have wrought; for you left untouched no order of the Church which you could make a sharer

---

[1] I.e., fined at discretion, and to an unlimited amount.

[2] The "were" was the wergild, the price a murderer had to pay as compensation to the kin of his victim. In this case, the price of 100 shillings is slightly higher than the "were" of a commoner but lower than that of a thegn.

[3] A "miskenning" was a verbal error in reciting the formal oaths protesting innocence; this entailed the loss of the case.

[4] The "hustings court" and the "folk-moot" were both judicial assemblies, but the folk-moot was slightly larger.

[5] Rom. 13: 2.

of confusion instead of honor, of malediction instead of benediction.

For to discuss a few outstanding points among many: Not only have you dared to touch the rectors of the holy Church—the archbishops, the bishops, and the priests, anointed of the Lord as they are[1]—but you have trodden them under foot like slaves who know not what their lord may do.[2] In crushing them you have gained for yourself acclaim from the mouth of the rabble. You have judged that all these know nothing, while you alone know everything. In any case, you have sedulously used this knowledge not for edification, but for destruction,[3] so greatly that we may believe Saint Gregory, whose name you have arrogated to yourself, rightly made this prophesy of you when he said: "From the abundance of his subjects, the mind of the prelate is often exalted, and he thinks that he has more knowledge than anyone else, since he sees that he has more power than anyone else."[4]

And we, indeed, bore with all these abuses, since we were eager to preserve the honor of the Apostolic See. But you construed our humility as fear, and so you were emboldened to rise up even against the royal power itself, granted to us by God. You dared to threaten to take the kingship away from us—as though we had received the kingship from you, as though kingship and empire were in your hand and not in the hand of God.

Our Lord, Jesus Christ, has called us to kingship, but has not called you to the priesthood. For you have risen by these steps: namely, by cunning, which the monastic profession abhors, to money; by money to favor; by favor to the sword. By the sword you have come to the throne of peace, and from the throne of peace you have destroyed the peace. You have armed subjects against their prelates; you who have not been called by God have taught that our bishops who have been called by God are to be spurned; you have usurped for laymen the bishops' ministry over priests, with the result that these laymen depose and condemn the very men whom the laymen themselves received as teachers from the hand of God, through the imposition of the hands of bishops.

You have also touched me, one who, though unworthy, has been anointed to kingship among the anointed. This wrong you have done to me, although as the tradition of the holy Fathers has taught, I am to be judged by God alone and am not to be deposed for any crime unless—may it never happen—I should deviate from the Faith. For the prudence of the holy bishops entrusted the judgment and the deposition even of Julian the Apostate not to themselves, but to God alone. The true pope Saint Peter also exclaims, "Fear God, honor the king."[5] You, however, since you do not fear God, dishonor me, ordained of Him.

Wherefore, when Saint Paul gave no quarter to an angel from heaven if the angel should preach heterodoxy,[6] he did not except you who are now teaching heterodoxy throughout the earth. For he says, "If anyone, either I or an angel from heaven, preach any other gospel unto you than that which we have preached unto you, let him be accursed."[7] Descend, therefore, condemned by this anathema and by the common judgment of all our bishops and of ourself. Relinquish the Apostolic See which you have arrogated. Let another mount the throne of Saint Peter, another who will not cloak violence with religion but who will teach the pure doctrine of Saint Peter.

I, Henry, King by the grace of God, together with all our bishops, say to you: Descend! Descend!

---

[1] Ps. 105: 15; Douay Ps. 104: 15; 2 Sam. 1: 14.

[2] See John 15: 15.

[3] See 2 Cor. 10: 8, 13: 10.

[4] Gregory I, *Pastoral Care* 2. 6.

[5] 1 Pet. 2. 17.

[6] That is, doctrine that diverges from correct belief.

[7] Gal. 1: 18.

5.5 The papal view: Gregory VII, *Letter to Hermann of Metz* (1076). Original in Latin.

Soon after receiving Henry's letter, the pope met with *his* bishops and excommunicated Henry. Many of Henry's supporters abandoned the king, and Bishop Hermann of Metz, one of a handful of bishops at Worms who had opposed the condemnation of Gregory, was important in fomenting the resulting war. Yet Hermann needed arguments to back up the actions of the pope and convince others to separate themselves from the excommunicated king. Gregory supplied some reasons in this letter, downgrading the dignity of kingship and maintaining that the act of excommunicating kings had a long and illustrious history.

[Source: Herbert E.J. Cowdrey, *The Register of Pope Gregory VII*, 1073–1085: *An English Translation* (Oxford: Oxford University Press, 2002), pp. 208–11 (notes modified).]

Gregory, bishop, servant of the servants of God, to Hermann, bishop of Metz, greeting and apostolic blessing.

By your questioning you are seeking many things of me who am exceedingly busy, and you send a messenger who presses me too much at his own pleasure. Accordingly, if I do not reply sufficiently, I ask you to bear it with patience.

Therefore how I am in my bodily health, or how the Romans and the Normans[1] who are proving themselves to be with regard to me, the bearer of this letter may tell you. But as regards the other matters about which you have questioned me, would that blessed Peter[2] might answer through me, for he is often honored or suffers injury in me, his servant such as I am.

Now, who the excommunicated bishops, priests, or laymen are there is no need that you should inquire of me, for undoubtedly they are those who are known to have held communion with the excommunicated King Henry, if it is right that he should be called king. For they do not scruple to set human favor or fear before the precept of the eternal King, nor do they fear by their support to drive their king towards the wrath of Almighty God.

He, however, by communicating with his own courtiers who were excommunicated for the simoniac heresy[3] has not feared to incur excommunication, and has not been ashamed to draw others to be excommunicated by communicating with him. Concerning such men, what else is there that we might think except what we have learnt in the Psalms: "The fool has said in his heart, 'There is no God,'" and again, "All have together been made unprofitable" in their intentions?[4]

Now, as for those who say, "it is not right that the king should be excommunicated," although in view of their great folly we have no need so much as to answer them, yet lest we seem to pass impatiently over their foolishness we direct them to the words or deeds of the holy fathers, in order that we may call them back to sound teaching. Let them, therefore, read what blessed Peter commanded to the Christian people at the ordination of St. Clement about him whom they knew not to have the favor of the pontiff.[5] Let them learn why the Apostle says, "Ready to avenge every act of disobedience,"[6] and of whom he says, "With such a man not even to take food."[7] Let them ponder why Pope Zacharias deposed the king of the Franks

---

[1] When Gregory spoke of the Romans, he meant the people—and above all the nobles—of Rome. By the Normans he meant the rulers of Southern Italy, with whom the papacy had been allied since 1059.

[2] This refers to St. Peter, whose "servant" but also spokesman Gregory considered himself.

[3] Gregory called the purchasing of church offices "simony" or the "simoniac heresy" after Simon Magus, who in Acts 8: 18–24 offered money to Peter and John if they would give him the power to confer the Holy Spirit.

[4] Ps. 14: 1–3; Douay Ps. 13: 1–3.

[5] *Epistola Clementis prior*, chap. 18.

[6] 2 Cor. 10: 6.

[7] 1 Cor. 5: 11.

and absolved all the Frankish people from the bond of the oath that they had taken to him.[1] Let them also learn in the Register of blessed Gregory that in privileges that he drew up for certain churches he not only excommunicated kings and dukes who contravened his words but also adjudged that they should forfeit their office.[2] Nor let them overlook that blessed Ambrose not only excommunicated Theodosius—not only a king but indeed an emperor in habitual conduct and power, but even debarred him from remaining in church in the place of the priests.[3]

But perhaps these men wish to have it thought that, when God three times committed his church to blessed Peter saying, "Feed my sheep,"[4] he made an exception of kings. Why do they not take notice, or rather shame-facedly confess, that, when God gave principally to blessed Peter the power of binding and loosing in heaven and upon earth,[5] he excepted nobody and withheld nothing from his power. For when a man denies that he can be bound by the chain of the church, it remains that he must deny that he can be loosed by its power; and whoever brazenly denies this altogether separates himself from Christ. And if the holy apostolic see, deciding through the pre-eminent power that is divinely conferred upon it, settles spiritual matters, why not also secular matters? In truth, as for the kings and princes of this world who place their own honor and temporal gains before the righteousness of God, and who by neglecting his honor seek their own, whose members they are or to whom they cleave your charity is not in ignorance. For just as those who set God before their own entire will and obey his command rather than men[6] are members of Christ,[7] so also those of whom we have been speaking above are members of Antichrist. If, then, spiritual men are judged when it is necessary, why are not secular ones the more under constraint concerning their wicked deeds?

But perhaps they think that the royal dignity excels the episcopal. From their origins they can gather how greatly they each differ from the other. For human pride has instituted the former; divine mercy has instituted the latter. The former ceaselessly snatches at vain glory; the latter always aspires to the heavenly life. And let them learn what the blessed Pope Anastasius wrote to the Emperor Anastasius about these dignities,[8] and how blessed Ambrose distinguished between these dignities in his pastoral letter: "The episcopal honor and excellence," he said, "if you compare them with the splendor of kings and the diadem of emperors, leave them much more inferior than if you compare the metal of lead with the splendor of gold."[9] Being not unaware of these things, the Emperor Constantine the Great chose not the principal but the least place to sit amongst the bishops; for he knew that "God resists the proud, but he gives favor to the humble."[10]

Meanwhile, brother, we are letting you know that, having received letters from certain of our brother bishops and dukes, by the authority of the apostolic see we have given licence to these bishops to absolve those excommunicated by us who are not afraid to keep themselves from communion with the king. As regards the king himself, [Henry IV] we have absolutely forbidden that anyone should venture to absolve him until his assured penitence and sincere satisfaction shall have been reported to us by trustworthy witnesses, so that we may at the same time ascertain how, if divine mercy shall look upon him, we may absolve him to the honor of God and to his own salvation. For it is not hidden from us that there are some of you who, seizing any pretext that might seem to come from us, would be led astray by fear or human favor and presume to absolve him if we were not to forbid, and to add wound to wound in place of medicine. If any who are bishops in truth should forbid them, they would conclude that they were not defending righteousness but pursuing enmities.

---

[1] In 751, Pope Zacharias (741–752) sanctioned the deposition of Childeric III (r.743–c.751), the last of the Merovingian kings.

[2] This refers to the letters of Pope Gregory the Great (590–604).

[3] The reference is to St. Ambrose's measures against the Emperor Theodosius I (r.379–395) after the emperor responded to a revolt at Thessalonica by massacring its inhabitants.

[4] John 21: 15–17.

[5] See Matt. 16: 19. The power of binding and loosing, as interpreted by the papacy, was the priestly power to impose penance and to administer absolution.

[6] See Acts 5: 29.

[7] See 1 Cor. 6: 15.

[8] This refers to a letter from Pope Anastasius II (496–498) to the Emperor Anastasius I (r.491–518).

[9] We now know that the work in question was not written by St. Ambrose.

[10] James 4: 6. The reference is to Emperor Constantine I (r.306–337) at the Council of Nicaea (325).

Now, as for the ordination and consecration of bishops who venture to communicate with the excommunicated king, as blessed Gregory testifies, before God they become an execration.[1] For when they proudly resist to obey the apostolic see, as Samuel is witness, they fall into the crime of idolatry.[2] For if he is said to be of God who is stirred up by the zeal of divine love to destroy vices, he assuredly denies that he is of God who refuses, so far as he is able, to reprove the life of carnal men. And if he is accursed who withholds his sword from blood,[3] that is, the word of preaching from the slaying of carnal life, how much more is he accursed who from fear or favor drives the soul of his brother to eternal perdition [damnation]? In sum, that the accursed and excommunicated can bless and bestow upon anyone the divine grace that they do not fear to deny by their own works, can be discovered in no ruling of the holy fathers.

Meantime, we order you to have a word with the venerable archbishop of Trier,[4] our brother that is, who is to forbid the bishop of Toul[5] from intruding into the affairs of the abbess of the monastery of Remiremont,[6]

and who, in concert with you, is to annul whatever he has decided against her. Now, as regards Matilda,[7] the daughter of us both and the faithful handmaid of blessed Peter, what you wish, I wish. But in what state of life she should continue under God's direction, I do not yet grasp for certain. But of Godfrey her late husband,[8] you may know for a certainty that I, although a sinner, frequently make memorial before God; for neither his enmity nor any vain consideration holds me back and, moved by your own brotherly love and Matilda's pleading, I long for his salvation.

May Almighty God, by the intercession of the queen of heaven, Mary ever-virgin, and by the authority of the blessed apostles Peter and Paul which is granted by him to them, absolve from all sins both you and all our brothers in whatever order who are defending the Christian religion and the dignity of the apostolic see; and, giving to you the increase of faith, hope, and charity, may he make you strong in the defense of his law, so that you may deserve to attain to eternal salvation. Given at Tivoli on August 25th, in the fourteenth indiction.

....

THE CLERGY IN ACTION

5.6 *Vesting Prayers* (*c.*1000?). Original in Latin.

Even before the Gregorian reform, clerics themselves developed devotions to prepare spiritually for their sacramental duties. One practice used the special garments that the priest wore to celebrate the Mass to help him cultivate purity and virtue, prescribing prayers to be said as each liturgical vestment was put on. These vesting prayers developed into a pre-Mass ritual performed in the sacristy: the clerics participating in the liturgy chanted a few psalms to put them in the proper frame of mind and then recited prayers as they donned their vestments. This clerical devotion emerged in response to ninth-century Carolingian reforms (as the manuscript excerpted below, dated to the late tenth century or the beginning of the eleventh, demonstrates), but was more widely disseminated through the eleventh-century Gregorian movement. Vesting prayers proved

---

[1] This is a reference to a letter of Gregory the Great.

[2] See 1 Sam. 15: 23.

[3] See Jer. 48: 10.

[4] Bishop Udo.

[5] Bishop Pibo.

[6] Gisela.

[7] Matilda was countess of Tuscany and a staunch supporter of Gregory.

[8] Godfrey, duke of Lorraine, was killed on February 26, 1076.

incredibly popular with clerics and were required until the Second Vatican Council in 1965 made them optional. Brief prayers such as these were sometimes recorded before the text or *ordo* of the Mass, but they were also copied into margins and on blank spaces at the beginning and ends of liturgical manuscripts. Often, as in the example below, variant prayers are given so that clerics could choose versions that spoke to them.

[Source: Biblioteca Apostolica Vaticana, Ottoboniensis Latinus 6, fol. 9v. Translated and introduced by Maureen C. Miller.]

Here begins the rite (*ordo*) for a bishop or priest to prepare himself to say Mass.

First, chant the psalms "Quam dilecta," "Benedixisti," "Inclina," and "Credidi."[1] Then recite the "Kyrie eleison" and the Lord's Prayer.[2] Then pray,

Let your mercy, O God, be upon us
You will turn, O God, and bring us to life
Show us, O Lord, your mercy
And enter not into judgment with your servant
Hear, O Lord, my prayer.[3]

To the amice:[4] Rend, O Lord, my garment and wrap me in joy. To the same: Protect my shoulders, O Lord, with the grace of the Holy Spirit and gird my spirit, all sins having been removed, [so that I might] sacrifice to you, O God, [who] lives and reigns forever.

To the alb:[5] Clothe me, O Lord, in the vestment of salvation and gird me with the breastplate of fortitude. To the same: Gird me, O Lord, with the armor of faith, so that having been shielded from the arrows of iniq-

uity, I might have the strength to preserve righteousness and justice. To the same: Omnipresent and eternal God, I humbly beseech you in order that having cast off the deception of all evasions and put on this white garment, I might be worthy to follow you into the realm of true joy.

To the cincture:[6] Equip me, O Lord, with a watchfulness for my soul, lest my mind be warped by a prideful spirit. To the same: Gird me, O Lord, with virtue and make my soul immaculate. To the same: Fasten most powerfully upon my thigh, O Lord, your sword, so that I may be able manfully to vanquish your enemies with the steadfast hope of eternal truth.

To the stole:[7] Place the stole of justice around my neck, O Lord, and purify my soul of all sinful corruption; break the chain of my sins, so that having taken up the yoke of your service, I might be worthy to attend you with fear and reverence.

To the chasuble:[8] Robe me, O Lord, with the ornament of humility, love, and peace so that having been completely fortified with virtues I might be able to withstand sins and enemies of mind and body, through you, Jesus Christ.

---

[1] Psalms 84, 85, 86, and 116; Douay 83, 84, 85, and 115, here identified by their opening word or words in the Latin in which they would have been chanted.

[2] The "Kyrie eleison" is a brief Greek prayer incorporated into the Latin Mass during the early Middle Ages. Meaning "Lord have mercy," the phrase appears in the Greek translation of the Old Testament (the Septuagint) and in the New Testament. The Lord's Prayer is thus called because the gospels of Matthew (6: 9–15) and Luke (11: 2–4) describe Jesus teaching it to his disciples. It is also known by its opening phrase as the Our Father (in Latin, *Pater noster*).

[3] All of these are lines from the Psalms: 33: 22, 85: 7-8, 143: 2, 143: 1; Douay 32: 22, 84: 7–8; 142: 2; 142: 1.

[4] The amice, the first vestment to be put on, was a rectangular piece of linen or cotton with ties extending from the long ends of one side. It was draped over the shoulders with the ties crossing the chest, crossing again in back, and then tied in front. It likely served to protect the neckline of other vestments from grime (the amice being more easily washable).

[5] A white line or cotton long-sleeved tunic that was the base garment worn for the Mass and other ceremonies.

[6] A belt worn over the alb and used to adjust its length by pulling fabric up over the belt.

[7] A sort of liturgical scarf worn by deacons and priests, but especially associated with priestly status. Usually eight to ten feet long and two to three inches wide, the stole was put on over the alb, resting on the neck with both ends falling down straight over the front of the body.

[8] See Plate 5, p. 236, in Containing the Holy.

5.7 *The Star of Clerics* (*c.*1200?). Original in Latin.

Church reformers in the eleventh century demanded that priests be celibate, obtain their offices without payment, and generally be more devout and better prepared than before to minister to their flocks. In response to these demands, many new educational aids were produced to help bishops to train priests and clerics to study. The *Stella clericorum* was one of the most popular, surviving in over 450 manuscript copies. Although the earliest-known manuscript dates from the late thirteenth or early fourteenth century, internal evidence indicates that this anonymously authored miscellany of admonitions was a product of innovations *c.*1200 in theology and clerical spirituality. The entire text is brief—26 small manuscript pages, and about the same today in its published form—and its content unoriginal, but it offered pithy summaries and memorable adages to help priests meet the pastoral expectations of the post-Gregorian church.

[Source: *Stella clericorum*, ed. Eric H. Reiter (Toronto: Pontifical Institute of Medieval Studies, 1997), pp. 22–24. Translated and introduced by Maureen C. Miller.]

[5.] Every pastor or priest should cultivate three things, namely: knowledge, eloquence, and a good [manner of] life. He ought to have knowledge and understanding of divine books, through which he may first learn about himself and then others. He who does not know himself, knows nothing. This excellent maxim is found among worldly philosophers: as they say, "know yourself." Moreover, Augustine in his book on the Holy Trinity preferred knowledge of his own infirmity to knowledge of the heavens or of earthly or infernal places.[1] Whence also Bernard [said]: "O Lord, let me know you, understand myself, [and] love you."[2]

He ought also to have discreet eloquence so that he may preach to others those things that he knows and understands, lest he "hide his lord's money,"[3] and lest he be a mute dog[4] in God's house (that is, in church).

Whence Isaiah: "Cry, cease not, lift up your voice like a trumpet and show my people their wicked doings,"[5] and Cicero: "It is better that I speak at length and prudently than someone without eloquence keenly hold forth."[6]

Therefore, let a priest have knowledge with eloquence. Whence Gregory: "The ignorance of a priest is neither forgiven nor excused."[7] Daniel [too wrote]: "But they who are learned shall shine as the brightness of the firmament" (that is, the sun) "and those that instruct many to justice are like stars for all eternity."[8] Whence another: "Doubly honored are priests, first by the dignity of their office [and] second by doctrine, especially those who faithfully labor in the Gospel because the order of faithful preachers is distinguished."[9]

Let a priest have a good [manner of] life so that what he preaches with his mouth he may fulfill in his works.

---

[1] This expression is actually not from the esteemed fourth-century Bishop of Hippo and Father of the Church, but from a work (*De spiritu et anima liber unus*, 50) that circulated under his name during the Middle Ages.

[2] The author probably is intending to quote the twelfth-century Cistercian abbot Bernard of Clairvaux, but this sentence is not found in his works.

[3] Matt. 25: 18.

[4] Isa. 56: 10.

[5] Isa. 58: 1.

[6] Citation not found.

[7] Pope Gregory the Great (590–604), as quoted in the important collection and textbook of ecclesiastical law, Gratian's *Decretum* D.38 c.3.

[8] Dan. 12: 3.

[9] 1 Tim. 5: 17.

Luke: "Jesus began to do and to teach."[1] Jerome: "Does not the one who speaks or preaches well but lives perversely not condemn himself with his own mouth?"[2] Origen: He who does not instruct others [through his manner of life] cannot himself teach it.[3] Gregory: "Let the preacher glory not in the splendor of words but in works of virtue."[4] Jerome: "The helping hand of the learned reaches out to the fallen and shows the way of truth to the erring."[5] Gregory: "The good teacher is the one who humbly serves learning and through discipline does not fall into pride."[6] Chrysostom: "Is holy strength evident? You shall be strict regarding your own life, and merciful regarding the sins of others. Let men hear you commanding small things, and doing burdensome things."[7] Gregory: "He whose life is despised finds his preaching condemned."[8] …

[13] Accordingly, O you prelates and priests, the souls of your subordinates, having been committed to you[r care], weigh upon you. He is called priest (*presbiter*), as it were, "one showing the way" (*prebens iter*) for the flock committed to him, through his word and the example of his life, and even by offering temporal help—although he seeks not so much the gain of temporal things as the profit of souls from whom the Son of God endured death.

5.8 *A Visitation Record* (1268). Original in Latin.

Reformers not only disseminated "best practices" for the clergy, but they also made more rigorous and systematic efforts to enforce these standards. An important tool was the visitation of parishes. Church councils from the fifth century set out the requirement that bishops, or their delegates, visit the churches of their dioceses to inspect their physical condition, their equipment (the books and ceremonial objects essential to delivering pastoral care), their ministers, and more generally the spiritual and moral condition of both clergy and laity. Sporadic prescriptive and documentary sources reveal episcopal attempts to carry out visitations from the ninth through the twelfth centuries, but it is only in the thirteenth century that we begin to get detailed records produced by visitations. Usually the checklist or questionnaire that the prelate carried into the field does not survive, but the notes taken down by the scribe or notary accompanying the visitor reveal ecclesiastical concerns and the standards being enforced. Translated below are the records of a visitation of the churches in the deanery (an ecclesiastical district within a large diocese) of Demouville in the Norman see of Bayeux. It was conducted in 1268 by Henri de Vézelay, then archdeacon of Bayeux, on behalf of his bishop. Henri went on to have a brilliant career in royal administration, serving as chancellor and advisor to French kings Louis IX (Saint Louis, r.1226–1270) and his son Philip III the Bold (r.1270–1285).

[Source: L. Delisle, "Visites pastorales de maître Henri de Vezelai, archidiacre d'Hiémois en 1267 et 1268," *Bibliothèque de l'École des Chartres* 54 (1893): 465–67. Translated and introduced by Maureen C. Miller.]

---

1. Acts 1: 1.
2. In fact not Jerome but Pseudo-Isidore of Seville, *Commandments of Divine Scripture and of the Fathers* (*Testimonia divinae scripturae <et patrum>*), 6.3.
3. Citation not found.
4. Gregory the Great, in his commentary on the first book of Kings (*In librum I Regum*), 6.16.
5. Jerome (*c*.347–419/420) in his commentary on the book of Jonah at Jon. 4: 10–11.
6. Isidore, bishop of Seville (d.636), *Three Books of Sentences*, 3.41.1.
7. Pseudo-Chrysostom, *Opus imperfectum* 43, quoted in Gratian's *Decretum* C.26 q.7 c.12.
8. Gregory the Great, *Forty Gospel Homilies* 12.1, quoted in Gratian's *Decretum* C.3 q.7 c.2.

1268, ON THE MONDAY BEFORE THE FEAST OF BLESSED MICHAEL [24 SEPTEMBER 1268], DEANERY OF DEMOUVILLE.

At Robehomme the *chrismatorium*[1] should be restored and a Gradual and Psalter[2] ought to be bought. The spider cloth[3] above the altar ought to be removed, the blessed altar renewed and repaired, and thus we ordered the people of the place and their treasurers to do this. Garinus Hayche, a married man, is defamed[4] of Johanna, the unmarried daughter of William Viel.

TUESDAY [25 SEPTEMBER 1268]

At Bavent a few things are lacking in the church and its ornaments. A lantern ought to be bought for doing the viaticum.[5] Henry Hemet, a cleric, is defamed of Maltide, daughter of the deceased Noel and he has a child by her. Henry Prestrel is defamed of the wife of Hormont, she whom he had abjured, and he threw out his own wife. Master Gelscuel of Bigarz, a cleric, keeps his own concubine at home.

At Petiville the church gate is falling down and very dangerous. Neither the tabernacle where the body of the Lord [is kept] nor the font are secured due to the negligence of the priest.

At Varaville the Missal[6] is old and unreadable.

At Sallenelles we did not enter the church because the priest was absent and the key to the church could not be found.

At Amfreville the priest was absent, however we visited the church and came upon the chalice in a bag without any other cloth [protecting it]. The church was uncovered[7] through the negligence of the priest. Neither the receptacle where the body of the Lord is kept nor the [baptismal] font was secured. The vestments are very dirty and horrible. Finally, the priest arrived and everything was shown [to us] by him. He was ordered on pain of suspension to get a key for the receptacle for the body of Christ by the following Monday and to correct other things.

At Colombelles the church is being re-roofed; books are lacking.

At Giberville nothing is lacking in the church's ornaments, [but] the church is uncovered. The two chaplains frequent taverns. Thomas Diaconus, a cleric, is denounced for usury and for keeping a kitchen maid. William Synemande, an excommunicate, has been excommunicated several times for a long time. The cleric Aliotus keeps a kitchen maid. Regnaudus Basile, a cleric, is defamed of Petronilla, the widow of the deceased Martin son of Philip.

At Demouville nothing is lacking in the church or its ornaments. The cleric Henry, brother of the dean, is defamed of the widow Florencia. Herbert Boet has a child by Matilda. The cleric Richard Boti still has Marieta. Richard Carsanoz is defamed of Juliana, wife of Selle Guerart and took her to his native land.[8] The cleric Robert Biquet has Matilda and has a child with her. Men don't keep feast days.

THURSDAY [27 SEPTEMBER 1268]

At Banneville-la-Campagne the ornaments, corporals,[9] and

---

1 A *chrismatorium* is a vessel for storing chrism, a mixture of olive oil and balsam consecrated by the bishop that is used in the administration of several sacraments.

2 The Gradual was a book containing the chants to be sung by the choir at Mass. It takes its name from the step (*gradus*) on which the cantor stood to lead the responsorial psalms intoned after the reading of the Epistle and before the Gospel. The Psalter was a book of the psalms used to recite the cycle of daily prayer known as the Divine Office, a devotion increasingly enjoined on priests from the twelfth century. It was also used to teach reading.

3 A cloth protecting the altar from spiders and other potential sources of contamination.

4 The visitor's inquiries allowed parishioners to comment on the conduct and morals of their pastor, but they also brought their own behavior under scrutiny. The passive verb *diffamatur* (here translated "defamed"), from *diffamo*, to accuse or slander, indicates that someone made an accusation of immoral, usually sexual, conduct.

5 The viaticum was the Eucharist administered to those on the verge of death. The term originally denoted traveling provisions and in Christian usage conveyed the idea that the Eucharist would aid believers on the journey into eternal life. The concern registered here seems to be that if the clergy were summoned in the middle of the night to administer the viaticum, they would have a lamp to light their way in carrying the sacrament.

6 The Missal is the liturgical book containing all the texts (prayers, readings) need for saying Mass.

7 *Ecclesia discooperta* likely comments on the state of the building's roofing.

8 The text uses *patria*—fatherland, country—suggesting that Richard was not from Normandy.

9 A corporal is a piece of linen upon which the chalice and paten are placed on the altar.

vestments are dirty. The Breviary[1] is old and unreadable.

At Guillerville the church is poor. The ornaments are good enough.

At Émiéville [the church] lacks a key for the font and chrismatorium; the cemetery is not enclosed. These things ought to be corrected within three years. A Psalter and Manual[2] are also lacking. The person assigned to the church does not want to live here so the bishop holds the church. Robert Hardiz still has Luceta au Tabour, whom he is unable to have as his wife because of their consanguinity.

At Manneville the chrismatorium lacks a key through the priest's negligence. He also owes the church treasury three *sextaria* [of grain].

At Cagni all that was lacking in the church has been corrected.

At Vimont the person assigned to the church is still defamed of Petronilla, his blood relative whom he had abjured, and she goes about with him. We ordered a person to remove his straw from the church.

THE CRUSADES AND RECONQUISTA

5.9 Martyrs in the Rhineland: Rabbi Eliezer b. Nathan ("Raban"), *O God, Insolent Men* (early to mid-12th c.). Original in Hebrew.

In the spring of 1096, irregular crusader armies passed through the Rhine valley. They were responding to Pope Urban II's call to regain the Holy Land from the Muslim "infidels" who ruled it, but they also decided to attack the "infidels in their midst"—the Jews. Confronting their persecutors with a new and unprecedented religious fervor, the Jews actively sought martyrdom rather than submit to the enemy's demand that they convert. Indeed, not only did hundreds of Jews meet their death at the hands of the crusaders, but many preferred to kill themselves and their children rather than be defiled by the crusaders' swords. These suicide-martyrdoms became a rallying image for northern European Jews over the next century. Three short chronicles dramatized the resistance and martyrdom of the Rhineland Jews in 1096. In addition, dozens of liturgical poems—including *O God, Insolent Men* by Rabbi Eliezer b. Nathan (*c*.1090–1170), known as the "Raban"—described the martyrdoms of 1096 and those of subsequent persecutions.

Poems such as Rabbi Eliezer's, excerpted here, were written as hymns and often performed in commemorative liturgies that were rich in symbolic display. The texts were written for a highly literate audience, men deeply immersed in the study of Jewish texts and trained to recognize the shorthand allusions to them in the verses. *O God, Insolent Men* taps all the motifs of the new genre of Hebrew martyrological verse: it is polemical, including a number of insulting comments about Christianity; it is eschatological, interpreting historical catastrophe as a prelude to messianic redemption and overlaying

---

[1] The Breviary is a liturgical book containing all the texts (psalms, antiphons, hymns, lessons) needed to recite the Divine Office. It appears to date from the eleventh century, and Pope Gregory VII is often credited with this abridged and simplified form of the hours suited to the active lives of secular clerics. Since it could replace several books—the Psalter, Antiphonary, Lectionary—the Breviary was well suited to rural churches.

[2] A Manual is a book containing ceremonial directions for performing various liturgies or services.

images of violence with biblical images of revelation and covenant; and it offers consolation, particularly in its call for vengeance. Formally, the poem is an alphabetic acrostic; it is extremely controlled, as if to reassure its listeners that order prevails over seeming chaos.

[Source: Abraham Habermann, *Sefer gezerot ashkenaz vetzarfat* (Jerusalem: 1945, repr. 1971), pp. 84–87. Introduced and translated by Susan L. Einbinder.]

O God, insolent men have risen against me[1]
They have sorely afflicted us from our youth[2]
They have devoured and destroyed us in their wrath against us[3]
Saying, let us take [their] inheritance for ourselves.[4]
...

Their hearts were turned to plotting evil and trouble.[5]
They went to seek pollution far away:[6]
The crucified one, buried and placed in a deep pit in the depths of hell.[7]   20

And the insolent ones, alien idolators, plotted.
They stubbornly sought deceit and treachery[8]

And put their hand to leaving the House of Jacob in ruins,[9]
Saying, God will not see.

"O abandoned ones, why do you hope for relief and healing?[10]   25
Your King has abandoned you to the nations to be devoured
Do this and live: worship the icon!"[11]
Remember this, O Lord, how the enemy scoffs![12]

"Heaven forbid," cried the innocent ones.
"It would be shameful to abandon Him," they   30
proclaimed from the bare heights.[13]

---

[1] Ps. 86: 14. The Douay version will not be cited for R. Eliezer's text. R. stands for Rabbi in the notes here.

[2] Ps. 124: 3; Ps. 129: 1–2.

[3] The first half of the verse echoes Jer. 10: 25, which begins with the vengeful "pour out thy wrath upon the nations," echoed in Psalm 79 (evoked below). The end of Raban's verse is from Ps. 124: 3.

[4] Ps. 83: 12.

[5] Isa. 59: 7 (see also Isa. 55: 7 and Mic. 2: 1); 1 Sam. 25: 31.

[6] The tone is contemptuous. The speaker inverts the crusaders' mission, in its sense of a pilgrimage to the site of Jesus' life and death, to a journey toward impurity. By Jewish law, contact with a corpse, or with anything that has come into contact with a corpse or other unclean thing, is a source of pollution (See Lev. 11 and 21). Thus the crusaders, by returning to the site of Jesus' crucifixion, seek their own contamination.

[7] This verse cannot be translated literally. It is clipped from Prov. 30: 16, where it is already corrupt and caused the commentators great trouble. The great northern French commentator, R. Solomon b. Isaac ("Rashi," d.1105), referred to an exegetical tradition according to which the expression refers to Sheol, or Gehenna, i.e., hell. R. Eliezer would have known this tradition.

[8] See Num. 25: 18; Ps. 78: 57.

[9] See Isa. 24: 12.

[10] See Jer. 33: 6.

[11] The polemical literature of medieval Jews often represented Christians as worshiping "icons" or "idols." As with the case of biblical critiques of the use of idols, the writers probably understood that the image was not the actual object of worship but a representation of something immaterial. However, it served their purposes to emphasize the stupidity of those who would worship pieces of wood and stone. Here, too, R. Eliezer puts in the Christian speech the type of argument Jews must have actually heard: God's covenant with the Jews had been superseded by a new covenant with the Christians, and the flourishing of Christendom, like the abasement of the Jews, proved this.

[12] Ps. 74: 18.

[13] Perhaps an allusion to Jer. 3: 21, "a voice on the bare heights is heard, the weeping and pleading of Israel's sons...."

"We live by His favor, and his anger is but a moment to the weak,[1]
The Lord is merciful and compassionate and long-suffering."[2]

When the impure ones heard this, they were filled with poison.
They slaughtered them, they wrung their necks. No household was spared.[3]

They piled together infants and women, young and old.[4]   35
The prideful ones concealed [their] trap for me, and spread their snares.[5]

Together, with a full heart, the remnant came forth willingly.[6]
They went out to perform their worship and fulfilled it energetically.

Their lips moved as they made their peace with Heaven:[7]
"There is a God who judges the earth."[8]   40

Brides and grooms behaved identically[9]
As one they were determined to sanctify You, O Awesome and Dreadful One.
Our eyes failed [watching] them day after day[10]
For we are killed for You every day.[11]

Tender children said sweetly to their mothers,   45
"Make us whole offerings! We are desired in Heaven."
Weep for all this, weep, O daughters of Israel.
Teach your daughters mourning; let each woman teach her companion laments.[12]

Youths like saplings pleaded with their fathers:
"Hurry! Hasten to do our Maker's Will!   50
The One God is our portion and destiny
Our days are over, our end has come."[13]

---

[1] Rearranging the language of the Hebrew version of Ps. 30: 5 ("his anger is but for a moment, [but] his favor is for a lifetime"). The Hebrew word for "weak" may echo a passage in the Talmud, B.Hullin 3b, where it refers to a weakness in the hands before the slaughter of sacrificial animals.

[2] A common tribute to God: see, e.g., Exod. 34: 6.

[3] Literally, the verse says "according to the number of persons, they were counted," which is an allusion to Exod. 12: 4. The cryptic formulation makes sense when its biblical context is recalled. In Exod. 12, God orders the enslaved Israelites to slaughter a lamb per household and mark their doorposts with its blood. If "a household is too small for a lamb," two neighboring households may combine their number ("according to the number of persons") and so "make the count" for the lamb. By analogy, the medieval Jews are slaughtered "per household," meaning that no household is spared.

[4] References to the mingled blood of male and female, young and old, etc., are a common motif in 1096 poetry, including this example. The demographic variety of the martyrs is equalized in death. In the next century, this equality will disappear in the literature to emphasize the martyrdom of elite, scholarly, men.

[5] See Ps. 140: 5; Prov. 29: 5

[6] See 1 Chron. 29: 9, but evoking also Exod. 35: 21, 29. Notice how this section switches its allusions to Exodus and its tale of collective revelation and covenant. Thus the martyrological lament becomes a polemical response to the dreadful possibility voiced in Exod. 25 28. God has not abandoned the Jews but is with them and renewing his covenant precisely at this moment of suffering.

[7] Alternatively, it is possible to read this line as "they reconciled themselves in vigor" or, possibly, "they reconciled themselves in fear."

[8] Ps. 58: 11.

[9] Literally, brides and grooms "did not divide their twin-ness." The verse alludes to the allegorical readings of the Song of Songs, interpreted as the "twinned" marriage of Israel and God.

[10] Ps. 69: 3, 119: 82.

[11] Or, all day long. See Ps. 44: 22.

[12] See Jer. 9: 20. A number of Hebrew martyrological poems include a call to women to make lament, perhaps an allusion to professional laments or to the prominence of women among public mourners.

[13] See Lam. 4: 18.

"Bound on Mt. Moriah, [Isaac's] father tied him
so he would not kick and ruin his slaughter.[1]
In our love for God, we will be slaughtered without 55
being tied
Our souls will rejoice in the Lord and be glad for His
salvation."[2]

The fathers were glad when they heard these pleasing
words.
They hastened to lay hands upon the pure lambs[3]
They trilled: "God is One!" They cried out in
consolation:[4]

"My witness is in Heaven, my witness is above!"[5]   60
They took their stations and slaughtered them while
weeping
Free-will offerings as if on God's altars
Mothers swooned, naked, upon their children[6]
For this I weep.[7]

...

Their blood spatters on [God's] purple robe[8]
In exchange for silver, I bring gold.[9]

---

[1] This legend would be familiar to most medieval Jews. The ancient rabbis determined by adding and subtracting their way through the first chapters of Genesis that Isaac must have been a grown man (37!) at the time Abraham was ordered to "offer him up" in Gen. 22. How could it be that he would not have resisted? The rabbis concluded that Isaac knew very well what Abraham intended, and asked his father to tie him down tightly so as not to mar the sacrifice (comparing himself to the ritual offerings of the Temple cult). Here, R. Eliezer claims that the Jewish children slaughtered by their fathers also undertook to die willingly; moreover, their courage and piety exceeded that of the biblical Isaac because they did not flinch or require restraint. The idea of the exemplary piety of the Ashkenaz (German) communities and in particular of their martyrs is found throughout this poetry. It is a hallmark of the Ashkenazic "self-image," and undoubtedly contributed to the resistance of the communities to conversion.

[2] See Ps. 35: 9.

[3] Again, comparing the young victims to the sacrificial lambs of the Temple cult.

[4] Deut. 6: 4. This is the "battle-cry" of the Jewish martyr. According to tradition, these were the last words of the famous first-century Jewish martyr, R. Akiba, who was executed by the Romans. The stories of the so-called "Ten Martyrs" of the Roman period were well known to medieval Jews and recited annually on Yom Kippur (the Day of Atonement). Two versions of the "Ten Martyrs" were current, one in the Babylonian Talmud, Avodah Zara 18ab, and one in the long poem known as "Eleh ezkerah" ("These I shall remember").

[5] See Job 16: 19.

[6] They have been stripped by the crusaders. See Mic. 1: 11, but also the description in Ezek. 16 of God as a lover who finds Israel naked and covered in blood, pledges his love for her, and makes his covenant with her. Like the allusion to the paschal lambs in v.34, this passage would be associated with the Jewish holiday of Passover, as it is included in the Haggadah—the service book for that holiday. For medieval Jews, however, the Passover liturgy and imagery were messianic, i.e., they enacted a dramatic, sacred, narrative in which God's intervention in history and redemption of his people was an event to be anticipated as much as recalled.

[7] Lam. 1: 16.

[8] R. Eliezer alludes here to an ancient legend, which underwent a powerful revival in medieval martyrological laments. According to rabbinic legend, God would not step into history to avenge the deaths of the innocent until his coat was sufficiently saturated with their blood (hence, the "purple" coat). In the writings of the 1096 survivors and their followers, this ancient legend came to justify the suicide-martyrdoms of medieval Ashkenaz: if God's coat was not yet saturated with the blood of the martyrs, the innocent Jews who killed themselves and their families were adding to it, hoping to prod God into action. This motif is eschatological as well as a call for vengeance.

[9] Here again, as in the preceding line, R. Eliezer is "speaking in shorthand" for a complex theological argument. It was possible that Jewish communities would interpret their persecution as a deserved punishment for wrongdoing. Many did, but not in Ashkenaz (Germany). On the contrary, the rabbis would argue, the Jewish communities of Ashkenaz and their holy martyrs were exemplars of piety. Precisely because of their unimpeachable goodness, God had waited to exact from them the cost of earlier transgressions, most notably the biblical sale of Joseph by his brothers for twenty pieces of silver. In exchange for this "silver," therefore, the Rhineland Jews offer the "gold" of their own meritorious lives.

For these the Almighty's pious ones, no ransom has 95
been set.[1]
I will avenge their blood, and I will not clear the
guilty.[2]

[So] cry and call out to Your Creator always
Demand the blood of Your servants from those who
shed it[3]
Give them, O Lord, what their evil deeds deserve.[4]
Give them broken hearts, let Your curse be upon 100
them.[5]

....

5.10 A Westerner in the Holy Land: Stephen of Blois, *Letter to His Wife* (March 1098). Original in Latin.

The crusaders had moderate success in their war against the Muslims. During the long
siege of Antioch, which began in October 1097 and was not over until July 1098, one of
the crusade leaders, Count Stephen of Blois (d.1102), dictated a letter to his wife, Adela.
Full of love, bravado, false claims (e.g., that he was the leader of the "whole expedition"),
and pious sentiments, the letter betrays little sign that Stephen was about to desert the
army and return home. The letter is a good illustration of what a crusader was supposed
to think about the enterprise, whether he did or not.

[Source: *The Crusades: A Reader*, ed. S.J. Allen and Emilie Amt (Toronto: University of Toronto Press,
2003), pp. 63–66, revised from *Translations and Reprints from the Original Sources of European History*, ed.
Dana C. Munro, Ser. 1, Vol. 1 (Philadelphia: University of Pennsylvania Department of History, 1895),
no. 4, pp. 5–8.]

Count Stephen to Adela, his sweetest and most amiable
wife, to his dear children, and to all his vassals of all
ranks—his greeting and blessing.

You may be very sure, dearest, that the messenger
whom I sent to give you pleasure, left me before Antioch
safe and unharmed, and through God's grace in the greatest prosperity. And already at that time, together with all
the chosen army of Christ, endowed with great valor by
him, we had been continuously advancing for twenty-
three weeks toward the home of our Lord Jesus. You may

know for certain, my beloved, that of gold, silver and
many other kind of riches I now have twice as much
as your love had assigned to me when I left you. For
all our princes, with the common consent of the whole
army, against my own wishes, have made me up to the
present time the leader, chief and director of their whole
expedition.

You have certainly heard that after the capture of the
city of Nicaea we fought a great battle with the perfidi-
ous Turks and by God's aid conquered them. Next we

---

[1] It is critical that the survivors believe that repentance and prayer can atone for sin. In the case of the holy martyrs, however, there
was no "ransom" (this word can also be translated as "redemption," as in the redemption of slaves) because their exemplary piety
had pre-determined that their lives would pay for the sins of earlier generations.

[2] Joel 3: 21.

[3] Echoing the call for vengeance in Ps. 79: 10, "Let the avenging of the outpoured blood of thy servants be known among the
nations...." This psalm, too, is a familiar element of the Passover liturgy.

[4] Ps. 28: 4.

[5] See Lam. 3: 65, which the Revised Standard Version of the Bible translates as "dullness of heart." Rashi notes this as a secondary
meaning, and perhaps then the sense would be numbness, rather than broken-ness, of heart. His first gloss is "broken-hearted."

conquered for the Lord all Romania[1] and afterwards Cappadocia. And we learned that there was a certain Turkish prince Assam, dwelling in Cappadocia; thither we directed our course. All his castles we conquered by force and compelled him to flee to a certain very strong castle situated on a high rock. We also gave the land of that Assam to one of our chiefs and in order that he might conquer the above-mentioned Assam, we left there with him many soldiers of Christ. Thence, continually following the wicked Turks, we drove them through the midst of Armenia, as far as the great river Euphrates. Having left all their baggage and beasts of burden on the bank, they fled across the river into Arabia.

The bolder of the Turkish soldiers, indeed, entering Syria, hastened by forced marches night and day, in order to be able to enter the royal city of Antioch before our approach. The whole army of God, learning this, gave due praise and thanks to the omnipotent Lord. Hastening with great joy to the aforesaid chief city of Antioch, we besieged it and very often had many conflicts there with the Turks; and seven times with the citizens of Antioch and with the innumerable troops coming to its aid, whom we rushed to meet, we fought with the fiercest courage, under the leadership of Christ. And in all these seven battles, by the aid of the Lord God, we conquered and most assuredly killed an innumerable host of them. In those battles, indeed, and in very many attacks made upon the city, many of our brethren and followers were killed and their souls were borne to the joys of paradise.

We found the city of Antioch very extensive, fortified with incredible strength and almost impregnable. In addition, more than 5,000 bold Turkish soldiers had entered the city, not counting the Saracens, Publicans, Arabs, Turcopolitans, Syrians, Armenians and other different races of whom an infinite multitude had gathered together there. In fighting against these enemies of God and of our own we have, by God's grace, endured many sufferings and innumerable evils up to the present time.

Many also have already exhausted all their resources in this very holy passion. Very many of our Franks, indeed, would have met a temporal death from starvation, if the clemency of God and our money had not succored them. Before the above-mentioned city of Antioch indeed, throughout the whole winter we suffered for our Lord Christ from excessive cold and enormous torrents of rain. What some say about the impossibility of bearing the heat of the sun throughout Syria is untrue, for the winter there is very similar to our winter in the west.

When truly Caspian,[2] the emir of Antioch—that is, prince and lord—perceived that he was hard pressed by us, he sent his son Sensodolo[3] by name, to the prince who holds Jerusalem, and to the prince of Calep, Rodoam[4] and to Docap prince of Damascus.[5] He also sent into Arabia for Bolianuth[6] and to Carathania for Hamelnuth.[7] These five emirs with 12,000 picked Turkish horsemen suddenly came to aid the inhabitants of Antioch. We, indeed, ignorant of all this, had sent many of our soldiers away to the cities and fortresses. For there are 165 cities and fortresses throughout Syria which are in our power. But a little before they reached the city, we attacked them at three leagues' distance with 700 soldiers, on a certain plain near the "Iron Bridge."[8] God, however, fought for us, his faithful, against them. For on that day, fighting in the strength that God gives, we conquered them and killed an innumerable multitude—God continually fighting for us—and we also carried back to the army more than two hundred of their heads, in order that the people might rejoice on that account. The emperor of Babylon also sent Saracen messengers to our army with letters, and through these he established peace and concord with us.[9]

I love to tell you, dearest, what happened to us during Lent. Our princes had caused a fortress to be built before a certain gate which was between our camp and the sea. For the Turks, daily issuing from this gate, killed some of our men on their way to the sea. The city of Antioch is about five leagues' distance from the sea. For this rea-

---

[1] "Romania" here refers to the Byzantine Empire; at the time Stephen was writing, much of Anatolia had been taken by the Seljuk Turks.

[2] This was Yaghi Siyan, appointed emir in 1087.

[3] Shams ad-Daulah.

[4] This was Ridwan of Aleppo.

[5] Docap was Duqaq, Seljuk ruler of Damascus (r.1095–1104).

[6] This was Kerbogha, the Turkish governor of Mosul (d.1102).

[7] Carathania refers to Khorasan, today in Iran.

[8] The "Iron Bridge" crossed the Orontes River, about 7 miles north of Antioch.

[9] A reference to an offer of neutrality by the Fatimid caliph of Egypt, who was Shi'a, and thus hostile to the Sunni Turks.

son they sent the excellent Bohemond[1] and Raymond, count of St. Gilles,[2] to the sea with only sixty horsemen, in order that they might bring mariners to aid in this work. When, however, they were returning to us with those mariners, the Turks collected an army, fell suddenly upon our two leaders and forced them to a perilous flight. In that unexpected flight we lost more than 500 of our footsoldiers—to the glory of God. Of our horsemen, however, we lost only two, for certain.

On that same day truly, in order to receive our brethren with joy, and ignorant of their misfortunes, we went out to meet them. When, however, we approached the above-mentioned gate of the city, a mob of horsemen and footsoldiers from Antioch, elated by the victory which they had won, rushed upon us in the same manner. Seeing these, our leaders sent to the camp of the Christians to order all to be ready to follow us into battle. In the meantime our men gathered together and the scattered leaders, namely, Bohemond and Raymond, with the remainder of their army came up and narrated the great misfortune which they had suffered.

Our men, full of fury at these most evil tidings, prepared to die for Christ and, deeply grieved for their brethren, rushed upon the sacrilegious Turks. They, the enemies of God and of us, hastily fled before us and attempted to enter their city. But by God's grace the affair turned out very differently; for, when they wanted to cross a bridge built over the great river Moscholum,[3] we followed them as closely as possible, killed many before they reached the bridge, forced many into the river, all of whom were killed, and we also slew many upon the bridge and very many at the narrow entrance to the gate. I am telling you the truth, my beloved, and you may be very certain that in this battle we killed thirty emirs, that is princes, and, three hundred other Turkish nobles, not counting the remaining Turks and pagans. Indeed, the number of Turks and Saracens killed is reckoned at 1,230, but of ours we did not lose a single man.

While on the following day (Easter) my chaplain Alexander was writing this letter in great haste, a party of our men, lying in wait for the Turks, fought a successful battle with them and killed sixty horsemen, whose heads they brought to the army.

These which I write to you are only a few things, dearest, of the many which we have done, and because I am not able to tell you, dearest, what is in my mind, I charge you to do right, to carefully watch over your land, to do your duty as you ought to your children and your vassals. You will certainly see me just as soon as I can possibly return to you. Farewell.

5.11 The Muslim reaction: Ibn al-Athir, *The First Crusade* (13th c.). Original in Arabic.

From the Muslim point of view, the conquests "for the Lord" that Stephen of Blois spoke about were, to the contrary, entirely ungodly. In the writings of Ibn al-Athir (1160–1233), the key events of the First Crusade—the siege and conquest of Antioch, the capture of Jerusalem—are told with some dispassion, for al-Athir, while drawing on earlier sources, was writing over a century after the events. His inclusion of a poem by al-Abiwardi shows that, just as a new Hebrew literature of martyrdom emerged after the massacre of the Jews, so too an Arabic literature of lamentation accompanied the Muslim experience of the First Crusade. How would you compare his account of the siege of Antioch with that of Stephen of Blois in his letter home, above, p. 271? How would you compare the sentiments in the poem of al-Abiwardi here with those of Raban in his poem above, p. 267?

[Source: *Arab Historians of the Crusades*, ed. and trans. (from Arabic) Francesco Gabrieli, trans. (from Italian) E.J. Costello (Berkeley: University of California Press, 1969), pp. 3–12 (slightly modified).]

---

[1] Bohemond of Taranto (d.1111), leader of the Norman contingent.

[2] Raymond of St. Gilles (d.1105) was the count of Toulouse and an important crusade leader.

[3] The Orontes River; this was another battle at the Iron Bridge.

The Franks Seize Antioch

The power of the Franks first became apparent when in the year 478 [1085][1] they invaded the territories of Islam and took Toledo and other parts of Andalusia, as was mentioned earlier. Then in 484 [1091] they attacked and conquered the island of Sicily[2] and turned their attention to the African coast. Certain of their conquests there were won back again but they had other successes, as you will see.

In 490 [1097] the Franks attacked Syria. This is how it all began: Baldwin, their King,[3] a kinsman of Roger the Frank who had conquered Sicily,[4] assembled a great army and sent word to Roger saying: "I have assembled a great army and now I am on my way to you, to use your bases for my conquest of the African coast. Thus you and I shall become neighbors."

Roger called together his companions and consulted them about these proposals. "This will be a fine thing both for them and for us!" they declared, "for by this means these lands will be converted to the Faith!" At this Roger raised one leg and farted loudly, and swore that it was of more use than their advice. "Why?" "Because if this army comes here it will need quantities of provisions and fleets of ships to transport it to Africa, as well as reinforcements from my own troops. Then, if the Franks succeed in conquering this territory they will take it over and will need provisioning from Sicily. This will cost me my annual profit from the harvest. If they fail they will return here and be an embarrassment to me here in my own domain. As well as all this Tamim[5] will say that I have broken faith with him and violated our treaty, and friendly relations and communications between us will be disrupted. As far as we are concerned, Africa is always there. When we are strong enough we will take it."

He summoned Baldwin's messenger and said to him: "If you have decided to make war on the Muslims your best course will be to free Jerusalem from their rule and thereby win great honor. I am bound by certain promises and treaties of allegiance with the rulers of Africa." So the Franks made ready and set out to attack Syria.

Another story is that the Fatimids of Egypt were afraid when they saw the Seljuks extending their empire through Syria as far as Gaza, until they reached the Egyptian border and Atsiz[6] invaded Egypt itself. They therefore sent to invite the Franks to invade Syria and so protect Egypt from the Muslims.[7] But God knows best.

When the Franks decided to attack Syria they marched east to Constantinople, so that they could cross the straits and advance into Muslim territory by the easier, land route. When they reached Constantinople, the Emperor of the East refused them permission to pass through his domains.[8] He said: "Unless you first promise me Antioch, I shall not allow you to cross into the Muslim empire." His real intention was to incite them to attack the Muslims, for he was convinced that the Turks, whose invincible control over Asia Minor he had observed, would exterminate every one of them. They accepted his conditions and in 490 [1097] they crossed the Bosphorus at Constantinople. Iconium and the rest of the area into which they now advanced belonged to Qilij Arslan ibn Sulaiman ibn Qutlumísh, who barred their way with his troops. They broke through in rajab 490 [July 1097], crossed Cilicia, and finally reached Antioch, which they besieged.

When Yaghi Siyan, the ruler of Antioch, heard of their approach, he was not sure how the Christian people of the city would react, so he made the Muslims go outside the city on their own to dig trenches and the next day sent the Christians out alone to continue the task. When they were ready to return home at the end of the day he refused to allow them. "Antioch is yours," he said, "but you will have to leave it to me until I see what happens between us and the Franks." "Who will protect our children and our wives?" they said. "I shall look after them for you." So they resigned themselves to their fate, and

---

[1] The first date is the Islamic one, the *anno Hejirae* (AH), named after the *hijra* or emigration of Muhammad to Medina; the second date is CE. The year 1 AH is equal to 622 CE.

[2] This date clearly refers to the end of the Norman conquest of Sicily.

[3] No "King Baldwin" led the First Crusade, but several Baldwins were involved in it, and later one of them, Baldwin of Boulogne (d.1118), was crowned King of Jerusalem.

[4] Roger Guiscard (d.1101).

[5] Tamim was the Zirid emir of Tunisia.

[6] Atsiz ibn Uwaq, a Seljuk general.

[7] The Fatimid rulers of Egypt were Shi'ite Muslims.

[8] The "Emperor of the East" refers to Byzantine Emperor Alexius (d.1118).

lived in the Frankish camp for nine months, while the city was under siege.

Yaghi Siyan showed unparalleled courage and wisdom, strength and judgment. If all the Franks who died had survived they would have overrun all the lands of Islam. He protected the families of the Christians in Antioch and would not allow a hair of their heads to be touched.

After the siege had been going on for a long time the Franks made a deal with one of the men who were responsible for the towers. He was a breast-plate maker called Ruzbih whom they bribed with a fortune in money and lands. He worked in the tower that stood over the riverbed, where the river flowed out of the city into the valley. The Franks sealed their pact with the breast-plate maker, God damn him! and made their way to the water-gate. They opened it and entered the city. Another gang of them climbed the tower with ropes. At dawn, when more than 500 of them were in the city and the defenders were worn out after the night watch, they sounded their trumpets. Yaghi Siyan woke up and asked what the noise meant. He was told that trumpets had sounded from the citadel and that it must have been taken. In fact the sound came not from the citadel but from the tower. Panic seized Yaghi Siyan and he opened the city gates and fled in terror, with an escort of thirty pages. His army commander arrived, but when he discovered on enquiry that Yaghi Siyan had fled, he made his escape by another gate. This was of great help to the Franks, for if he had stood firm for an hour, they would have been wiped out. They entered the city by the gates and sacked it, slaughtering all the Muslims they found there. This happened in jumada I [491; April/May 1098].[1] As for Yaghi Siyan, when the sun rose he recovered his self control and realized that his flight had taken him several *farsakh*[2] from the city. He asked his companions where he was, and on hearing that he was four *farsakh* from Antioch he repented of having rushed to safety instead of staying to fight to the death. He began to groan and weep for his desertion of his household and children. Overcome by the violence of his grief he fell fainting from his horse. His companions tried to lift him back into the saddle, but they could not get him to sit up, and so left him for

dead while they escaped. He was at his last gasp when an Armenian shepherd came past, killed him, cut off his head and took it to the Franks at Antioch.

The Franks had written to the rulers of Aleppo and Damascus to say that they had no interest in any cities but those that had once belonged to Byzantium. This was a piece of deceit calculated to dissuade these rulers from going to the help of Antioch.

The Muslim Attack on the Franks, and Its Results

When Qawam ad-Daula Kerbuqa[3] heard that the Franks had taken Antioch he mustered his army and advanced into Syria, where he camped at Marj Dabiq. All the Turkish and Arab forces in Syria rallied to him except for the army from Aleppo. Among his supporters were Duqaq ibn Tutush,[4] the Ata-beg Tughtikin, Janah ad-Daula of Hims, Arslan Tash of Sanjar, Sulaiman ibn Artuq and other less important emirs. When the Franks heard of this they were alarmed and afraid, for their troops were weak and short of food. The Muslims advanced and came face to face with the Franks in front of Antioch. Kerbuqa, thinking that the present crisis would force the Muslims to remain loyal to him, alienated them by his pride and ill-treatment of them. They plotted in secret anger to betray him and desert him in the heat of battle.

After taking Antioch the Franks camped there for twelve days without food. The wealthy ate their horses and the poor ate carrion and leaves from the trees. Their leaders, faced with this situation, wrote to Kerbuqa to ask for safe-conduct through his territory but he refused, saying "You will have to fight your way out." Among the Frankish leaders were Baldwin, Saint-Gilles, Godfrey of Bouillon, the future Count of Edessa, and their leader Bohemond of Antioch. There was also a holy man who had great influence over them, a man of low cunning, who proclaimed that the Messiah had a lance buried in the Qusyan, a great building in Antioch:[5] "And if you find it you will be victorious and if you fail you will surely die." Before saying this he had buried a lance in a certain spot and concealed all trace of it. He exhorted them to fast and

---

[1] June 3rd, according to European sources.

[2] One *farsakh* is about four miles.

[3] This was Kerbogha, the Turkish governor of Mosul (d.1102).

[4] Duqaq was Seljuk ruler of Damascus 1095–1104.

[5] This is a reference to the church of St. Peter in Antioch.

repent for three days, and on the fourth day he led them all to the spot with their soldiers and workmen, who dug everywhere and found the lance as he had told them.[1] Whereupon he cried "Rejoice! For victory is secure." So on the fifth day they left the city in groups of five or six. The Muslims said to Kerbuqa: "You should go up to the city and kill them one by one as they come out; it is easy to pick them off now that they have split up." He replied: "No, wait until they have all come out and then we will kill them." He would not allow them to attack the enemy, and when some Muslims killed a group of Franks, he went himself to forbid such behaviour and prevent its recurrence. When all the Franks had come out and not one was left in Antioch, they began to attack strongly, and the Muslims turned and fled. This was Kerbuqa's fault, first because he had treated the Muslims with such contempt and scorn, and second because he had prevented their killing the Franks. The Muslims were completely routed without striking a single blow or firing a single arrow. The last to flee were Suqman ibn Artuq and Janah ad-Daula, who had been sent to set an ambush. Kerbuqa escaped with them. When the Franks saw this they were afraid that a trap was being set for them, for there had not even been any fighting to flee from, so they dared not follow them. The only Muslims to stand firm were a detachment of warriors from the Holy Land, who fought to acquire merit in God's eyes and to seek martyrdom. The Franks killed them by the thousand and stripped their camp of food and possessions, equipment, horses and arms, with which they re-equipped themselves.

The Franks Take Ma'arrat an-Nu'man

After dealing this blow to the Muslims the Franks marched on Ma'arrat an-Nu'man and besieged it. The inhabitants valiantly defended their city. When the Franks realized the fierce determination and devotion of the defenders they built a wooden tower as high as the city wall and fought from the top of it, but failed to do the Muslims any serious harm. One night a few Muslims were seized with panic and in their demoralized state thought that if they barricaded themselves into one of the town's largest buildings they would be in a better position

to defend themselves, so they climbed down from the wall and abandoned the position they were defending. Others saw them and followed their example, leaving another stretch of wall undefended, and gradually, as one group followed another, the whole wall was left unprotected and the Franks scaled it with ladders. Their appearance in the city terrified the Muslims, who shut themselves up in their houses. For three days the slaughter never stopped; the Franks killed more than 100,000 men and took innumerable prisoners. After taking the town the Franks spent six weeks shut up there, then sent an expedition to 'Arqa, which they besieged for four months. Although they breached the wall in many places they failed to storm it. Munqidh, the ruler of Shaizar, made a treaty with them about 'Arqa and they left it to pass on to Hims. Here too the ruler Janah ad-Daula made a treaty with them, and they advanced to Acre by way of an-Nawaqir. However they did not succeed in taking Acre.

The Franks Conquer Jerusalem

Taj ad-Daula Tutush was the Lord of Jerusalem but had given it as a fief to the emir Suqman ibn Artuq the Turcoman. When the Franks defeated the Turks at Antioch the massacre demoralized them, and the Egyptians, who saw that the Turkish armies were being weakened by desertion, besieged Jerusalem under the command of al-Afdal ibn Badr al-Jamali. Inside the city were Artuq's sons, Suqman and Ilghazi, their cousin Sunij and their nephew Yaquti. The Egyptians brought more than forty siege engines to attack Jerusalem and broke down the walls at several points. The inhabitants put up a defence, and the siege and fighting went on for more than six weeks. In the end the Egyptians forced the city to capitulate, in sha'ban 489 [August 1096].[2] Suqman, Ilghazi and their friends were well treated by al-Afdal, who gave them large gifts of money and let them go free. They made for Damascus and then crossed the Euphrates. Suqman settled in Edessa and Ilghazi went on into Iraq. The Egyptian governor of Jerusalem was a certain Iftikhar ad-Daula, who was still there at the time of which we are speaking.[3]

After their vain attempt to take Acre by siege, the Franks moved on to Jerusalem and besieged it for more

---

[1] The finding of the Sacred Lance at the instigation of Peter Bartholomew was a major turning point for the crusade armies. Western sources do not accuse Peter of burying it.

[2] In fact, the Fatimids took Jerusalem in August 1098.

[3] The crusaders' attack on Jerusalem began in June 1099.

than six weeks. They built two towers, one of which, near Sion, the Muslims burnt down, killing everyone inside it. It had scarcely ceased to burn before a messenger arrived to ask for help and to bring the news that the other side of the city had fallen. In fact Jerusalem was taken from the north on the morning of Friday 22 sha'ban 492 [15 July 1099]. The population was put to the sword by the Franks, who pillaged the area for a week. A band of Muslims barricaded themselves into the Oratory of David[1] and fought on for several days. They were granted their lives in return for surrendering. The Franks honored their word, and the group left by night for Ascalon. In the Masjid al-Aqsa the Franks slaughtered more than 70,000 people, among them a large number of Imams and Muslim scholars, devout and ascetic men who had left their homelands to live lives of pious seclusion in the Holy Place. The Franks stripped the Dome of the Rock[2] of more than forty silver candelabra, each of them weighing 3,600 drams, and a great silver lamp weighing forty-four Syrian pounds, as well as a hundred and fifty smaller silver candelabra and more than twenty gold ones, and a great deal more booty. Refugees from Syria reached Baghdad in ramadan, among them the qadi Abu Sa'd al-Harawi. They told the Caliph's ministers a story that wrung their hearts and brought tears to their eyes. On Friday they went to the Cathedral Mosque and begged for help, weeping so that their hearers wept with them as they described the sufferings of the Muslims in that Holy City: the men killed, the women and children taken prisoner, the homes pillaged. Because of the terrible hardships they had suffered, they were allowed to break the fast....

It was the discord between the Muslim princes, as we shall describe, that enabled the Franks to overrun the country. Abu l-Muzaffar al-Abiwardi[3] composed several poems on this subject, in one of which he says:

We have mingled blood with flowing tears, and there
  is no room left in us for pity.

To shed tears is a man's worst weapon when the
  swords stir up the embers of war.
Sons of Islam, behind you are battles in which heads
  rolled at your feet.
Dare you slumber in the blessed shade of safety,
  where life is as soft as an orchard flower?
How can the eye sleep between the lids at a time of
  disasters that would waken any sleeper?   5
While your Syrian brothers can only sleep on the
  backs of their chargers, or in vultures' bellies!
Must the foreigners feed on our ignominy, while you
  trail behind you the train of a pleasant life, like
  men whose world is at peace?
When blood has been spilt, when sweet girls must for
  shame hide their lovely faces in their hands!
When the white swords' points are red with blood,
  and the iron of the brown lances is stained with
  gore!
At the sound of sword hammering on lance young
  children's hair turns white.   10
This is war, and the man who shuns the whirlpool to
  save his life shall grind his teeth in penitence.
This is war, and the infidel's sword is naked in his
  hand, ready to be sheathed again in men's necks
  and skulls.
This is war, and he who lies in the tomb at Medina
  seems to raise his voice and cry: "O sons of
  Hashim!"[4]
I see my people slow to raise the lance against the
  enemy: I see the Faith resting on feeble pillars.
For fear of death the Muslims are evading the fire of
  battle, refusing to believe that death will surely
  strike them."   15
Must the Arab champions then suffer with resignation,
  while the gallant Persians shut their eyes to
  their dishonor?

---

[1] Known as the Tower of David in European sources, it was in the citadel at Jerusalem (and is not to be confused with the small sanctuary of the same name in the Temple precinct).

[2] The rock from which, Muslims believe, Muhammad ascended into heaven. Over it was built the "Dome of the Rock," the chief Islamic monument in Jerusalem. See Plate 1, p. 230.

[3] An Iraqi poet, writing after the fall of Jerusalem.

[4] The image here is of the Prophet who, from the tomb, raises his voice to rebuke his descendants (the sons of Hashim), that is, the unworthy caliphs whose opposition to the crusades is only half-hearted.

5.12 The crusade in Spain and Portugal: *The Conquest of Lisbon* (1147–1148). Original in Latin.

Many European Catholics considered the *Reconquista* of the Iberian Peninsula another theater of the crusade. In fact, one group of crusaders left for the Second Crusade by way of the North Sea and England. They arrived in Spain in 1147 and were immediately put to work conquering the Muslims at Lisbon. The anonymous author of *The Conquest of Lisbon*, evidently an Anglo-French priest with high connections in both England and Spain, personally participated in the siege. In the excerpt below he records a speech given by Peter, bishop of Oporto, who rallied the army to undertake the assault. Peter's rhetoric was precisely that of the popes and other preachers who had inspired armies for the First and now Second Crusades. The siege was, Peter said, a sacrifice, a pious pilgrimage, and a righteous use of force against robbers and murderers. Although the warriors were on their way to Jerusalem, they could do no better than pause to do God's good work in Spain first. In this text the term "Moors" refers to the first Islamic invaders of Spain, who had by 1147 been settled there for about 400 years, while the "Moabites" are the Almoravids, more recent arrivals from the Maghreb. The passage below begins as the crusaders' ships pulled into the port of Oporto on their way to the Holy Land. What justifications does Peter give for the attack on Lisbon? Compare the ways Peter and Rabbi Eliezer (in the poem above, p. 267) use passages from the Bible to make their points.

[Source: *De expugnatione Lyxbonensi: The Conquest of Lisbon*, trans. Charles Wendell David (New York: Columbia University Press, 2001), pp. 69, 71, 73, 77, 79, 81.]

Early next morning we all gathered from all the ships before the bishop on a hilltop in the cathedral churchyard, for our numbers were so great that the church would not hold us. When silence had been proclaimed of all, the bishop delivered a sermon in Latin, so that it might be made known to everyone in his own language through interpreters. Thus it begins:

"'Blessed is the nation whose God is the Lord, and the people whom he hath chosen for his own inheritance.'[1] And assuredly are they blessed on whom God has by some inestimable privilege conferred both understanding and riches: understanding, in order that they should know the ways of discipline; and riches, in order that they should be able to accomplish that which they piously desire. And truly fortunate is your country which rears such sons, and in such numbers, and unites them in such a unanimous association in the bosom of the mother church. And deservedly is the truth of that highest beatitude accomplished in you, in which it is said, 'Blessed are they that have not seen me and yet have believed.'[2]

"Christ, the mediator between God and men, when he came in person into the world, found very few who were followers of this way and of pure religion; hence, when a certain young man who said that he had fulfilled and kept the law asked him how he could be perfect, he answered, 'Go and sell all,' etc. Weigh carefully what follows: 'He was sad, for he had great possessions.'[3] Oh how great is the righteousness and mercy of our Creator! Oh how great the blindness and the hardness of the human mind! The young man spoke with Truth and about truth, and the voice of Truth was in his ears, and yet, since the hardness of his callous mind was not soft-

---

[1] Ps. 33: 12; Douay Ps. 32: 12.

[2] John 20: 29.

[3] Compare Matt. 19: 16–22; Mark 10: 17–22; Luke 18: 18–23.

ened by the word of Truth, it is not to be wondered at if, when his mind had been emptied of the joy of sincerity, sadness entered in. And what shall we say to all this? How many there are among you here who are richer in possessions than this young man! How many who are higher in the rank of honors! How many who are more fortunate in a prolific stock and a numerous offspring! Yet it is a fact that they have exchanged all their honors and dignities for a blessed pilgrimage in order to obtain from God an eternal reward. The alluring affection of wives, the tender kisses of sucking infants at the breast, the even more delightful pledges of grown-up children, the much desired consolation of relatives and friends— all these they have left behind to follow Christ, retaining only the sweet but torturing memory of their native land. Oh, marvelous are the works of the Savior! Without the urging of any preacher, with the zeal of the law of God in their hearts, led by the impulse of the [Holy] Spirit, they have left all and come hither to us, the sons of the primitive church, through so many perils of lands and seas and bearing the expenses of a long journey. They are the most recent proof of the mysterious power of the cross. Oh, how great is the joy of all those who present a more cheerful face to hardships and pain than we do, we who, alas, are vegetating here in slothful idleness. Verily, 'this is the Lord's doing, and it is marvelous in our eyes.'[1] Verily, dear brothers, you have gone forth without the camp bearing the reproach of the cross;[2] you are seeking God while he may be found,[3] in order that you may lay hold on him. For it seems not strange that men should go unto God, since for the sake of man God also came among men. Even now unto you at the ends of the earth hath the seed of the word of God been borne, for 'a sower went out to sow his seed.' 'The seed is the word of God.'[4] The word of God is God. If it ascend the throne of your mind, your mind is accordingly good, but not without it. These divine seeds have been sown in your bodies, and, if you receive them as good husbandmen, they must needs produce fruit like unto its source and the counterpart of that from which it sprang; but, if you prove bad husbandmen, the result can only be that sterile and swampy ground will destroy the seeds, and afterwards it will bring forth trash instead of fruit. And may the good God 'increase the fruits of your righteousness.'[5]

"Verily, dear sons, reborn of a new baptism of repentance, you have put on Christ once more, you have received again the garment of innocence to keep it stainless. Take care lest you wander away again after your own lusts.…

"We believe it has already become well enough known in the countries from which you come that through the presence of the Moors and Moabites divine vengeance has smitten all Spain with the edge of the sword,[6] and that but few Christians, resident in but a few cities, have been left in it, [and these] under the yoke of a grievous servitude. But these matters, of which a knowledge was brought to you by fame only, now most certainly lie open to your view more clear than day. Alas, that in all Galicia and the kingdom of Aragon and in Numantia, of the numberless cities, castles, villages, and shrines of the saints there should now remain hardly anything to be seen but the signs of ruin and marks of the destruction which has been wrought! Even this city of ours which you see, once among the populous, now reduced to the semblance of an insignificant village, has within our memory repeatedly been despoiled by the Moors. Indeed, but seven years ago it was so oppressed by them that from the church of the blessed Virgin Mary, which according to my poor talents by God's grace I serve, they carried away the insignia, the vestments, the vessels, and all the ecclesiastical ornaments, after they had slain the clergy or made them captive. And from among the citizens and from the surrounding territory as far as the church of St. James the Apostle, they bore away with them into their own country almost innumerable captives, though not without bloodshed on the part of our nobles; and everything that remained they destroyed with fire and sword. Indeed, what does the coast of Spain offer to your view but a kind of memorial of its desolation and the marks of its ruin? How many cities and churches have you discovered to be in ruins upon it, either through your own observation or through information given you by the inhabitants? To you the mother church, as it were with her arms cut off and her face disfigured, appeals for help;

---

[1] Ps. 118: 23; Douay Ps. 117: 23.

[2] See Heb. 13: 13.

[3] See Isa. 55: 6.

[4] Luke 8. 5, 11.

[5] 2 Cor. 9: 10.

[6] Compare 2 Kings 10: 25.

she seeks vengeance at your hands for the blood of her sons. She calls to you, verily, she cries aloud. 'Execute vengeance upon the heathen and punishments upon the people.'[1] Therefore, be not seduced by the desire to press on with the journey which you have begun; for the praiseworthy thing is not to have been to Jerusalem, but to have lived a good life while on the way; for you cannot arrive there except through the performance of His works. Verily, it is through good work that anyone deserves to come to a glorious end. Therefore, as worthy rivals [strive together] to raise up the fallen and prostrate church of Spain; reclothe her soiled and disfigured form with the garments of joy and gladness. As worthy sons, look not on the shame of a father nor say to a mother, 'It is a gift by whatsoever thou mightest be profited by me.'[2] Weigh not lightly your duty to your fellow men; for, as St. Ambrose says, 'He who does not ward off an injury from his comrades and brothers, if he can, is as much at fault as he who does the injury.'[3]

"Now, as worthy sons of the mother church, repel force and injury; for in law it happens that whatever anyone does in self-defense he is held to have done lawfully. Brothers, you have laid aside the arms [of violence] by which the property of others is laid waste—concerning which it is said, 'He that strikes with the sword shall perish with the sword,'[4] that is, he who, without the command or consent of any higher or legitimate power, takes up arms against the life of his brothers—but now by God's inspiration you are bearing the arms [of righteousness] by means of which murderers and robbers are condemned, thefts are prevented, acts of adultery are punished, the impious perish from the earth, and parricides are not permitted to live nor sons to act unfilially. Therefore, brothers, take courage with these arms, courage, that is to say, either to defend the fatherland in war against barbarians or to ward off enemies at home, or to defend comrades from robbers; for such courage is full of righteousness. Indeed, such works of vengeance are duties which righteous men perform with a good conscience."

THE NORMAN CONQUEST OF ENGLAND

5.13 The pro-Norman position: William of Jumièges, *The Deeds of the Dukes of the Normans* (*c.*1070). Original in Latin.

Celebrating Duke William of Normandy's victory at Hastings (1066) and justifying his anointment as king of England was William, a monk of Jumièges, a monastery near Rouen founded and supported by the Norman ducal family. William's account was enormously popular, surviving in many manuscripts and inspiring numerous other chroniclers, so that his became the predominant voice in depicting the events of 1066. In the passage below, Duke Harold is the man who was crowned king of England after the death of Edward the Confessor. William of Jumièges portrays this as a usurpation.

[Source: *The Norman Conquest*, ed. and trans. R. Allen Brown (London: Edward Arnold, 1984), pp. 13–15 (slightly modified).]

---

[1] Ps. 149: 7.
[2] Matt. 15: 5.
[3] Ambrose, *De officiis* 1.36.
[4] See Matt. 26: 52.

23 Edward, king of the English,[1] by Divine disposition lacking an heir, had formerly sent Robert [of Jumièges] archbishop of Canterbury to the duke[2] to nominate him as the heir to the kingdom which God had given him. Furthermore he afterward sent to the duke Harold,[3] the greatest of all the earls of his dominions in riches, honor and power, that he should swear fealty to him[4] concerning Edward's crown and confirm it with Christian oaths. Harold, hastening to fulfill this mission, crossed the narrow seas and landed in Ponthieu, where he fell into the hands of Guy, count of Abbeville, who at once took him and his companions prisoner. When the duke heard of this he sent envoys and angrily caused them to be released. Harold remained with the duke for some time, and swore fealty concerning the kingdom with many oaths, before being sent back to the king laden with gifts.

At length king Edward, having completed the term of his fortunate life, departed this world in the year of Our Lord 1066. Whereupon Harold immediately usurped his kingdom, perjured in the fealty which he had sworn to the duke. The duke at once sent envoys to him, exhorting him to withdraw from this madness and keep the faith which he had sworn. But he not only would not listen but caused the whole English people also to be faithless to the duke. Then there appeared in the heavens a comet[5] which, with three long rays, lit up a great part of the southern hemisphere for 15 nights together, foretelling, as many said, a change in a kingdom.

24 Duke William therefore, who himself by right should have been crowned with the royal diadem, seeing Harold daily grow in strength, quickly caused a fleet of 3,000 vessels to be built and anchored at St. Valery (sur-Somme) in Ponthieu, loaded both with splendid horses and the finest warriors, with hauberks[6] and with helmets. Thence with a following wind, sails spread aloft, he crossed the sea and landed at Pevensey, where he at once raised a strongly entrenched castle. Leaving a force of warriors in that, he hastened on to Hastings where he quickly raised another. Harold, hastening to take him by surprise,

raised an immense army of English and, riding through the night, appeared at the place of battle in the morning.

25 The duke however, in case of night attack, ordered his army to stand to arms from dusk to dawn. At daybreak he marshalled the squadrons of his warriors in three divisions and fearlessly advanced against the dread foe. He engaged the enemy at the third hour (9 a.m.) and the carnage continued until nightfall. Harold himself fell in the first shock of battle,[7] pierced with lethal wounds. The English, learning that their king had met his death, despairing of their lives, with night approaching, turned about and sought safety in flight.

26 The victorious duke returned to the battlefield from the pursuit and slaughter of his enemies in the middle of the night. Early next morning, the loot having been collected up from the fallen foe and the corpses of his own cherished men buried, he began his march towards London. It is said that in this battle many thousands of English lost their lives, Christ in them exacting retribution for the violent and unlawful death meted out to Alfred, brother of king Edward [the Confessor]. At length the fortunate war-leader, who was no less protected by good counsel, leaving the highroad, turned away from the city at Wallingford, where he crossed the river and ordered camp to be pitched. Moving on from there he came to London, where an advance-party of warriors on entering the city found a large force of rebels determined to make a vigorous resistance. At once engaging them, the warriors inflicted much sorrow upon London by the death of many of her sons and citizens. At length the Londoners, seeing that they could resist no longer, gave hostages and submitted themselves and all they had to their noble conqueror and hereditary lord. And thus his triumph duly completed in spite of so many perils, our illustrious duke, to whom our inadequate words do not begin to do justice, on Christmas Day, was chosen king by all the magnates both Norman and English, anointed with holy oil by the bishops of the kingdom and crowned with the royal diadem, in the year of Our Lord 1066.

---

1   Edward the Confessor, king 1042–1066.

2   I.e., Duke William of Normandy. Throughout this document he is the man known as the "duke."

3   Harold, son of the powerful Earl Godwine of Wessex, and thus known as Harold Godwineson.

4   I.e., Duke William.

5   This was in fact Halley's comet, which, in its orbit around the sun, passes near the earth about once every 76 years.

6   A hauberk is a long tunic made out of chain mail.

7   This is unlikely; Harold seems to have fallen at the end of the battle, not at the start.

5.14 The native position: "Florence of Worcester," *Chronicle of Chronicles* (early 12th c.). Original in Latin.

Not everyone agreed that William ruled "by right." Members of the Anglo-Saxon lay and ecclesiastical aristocracy bitterly resented their displacement by William's followers. Monks, too, were unhappy, as William imposed a new regime on English monastic life closely modeled on the elaborate round of collective prayer at Cluny. Submerged opposition may be seen in the *Chronicle of Chronicles*, produced in the early twelfth century by a monk at Worcester who was for a long time thought to be "Florence" but is now thought to have been a different monk, named John. The source is still generally known as "Florence of Worcester." In the passage below the author gives the Anglo-Saxon view of William (whom he calls "count" of Normandy) and the events of 1066. Note that Wulfstan, bishop of Worcester (d.1095), is mentioned in the text as among the few Anglo-Saxon prelates to swear fealty to William. At the same time, Wulfstan was almost certainly the person who commissioned "Florence of Worcester" to write. After analyzing the accounts of "Florence of Worcester" and William of Jumièges (p. 280, above), consider whose side you are on and explain why.

[Source: *English Historical Documents*, vol. 2: 1042–1189, ed. David C. Douglas and George W. Greenaway, 2nd ed. (London: Routledge, 1981), pp. 225–28 (slightly modified).]

1066 On Thursday the vigil of our Lord's Epiphany, in the Fourth Indiction, the pride of the English, the pacific king, Edward, son of King Æthelred, died at London, having reigned over the English twenty-three years six months and seven days. The next day he was buried in kingly style amid the bitter lamentations of all present. After his burial the under-king, Harold, son of Earl Godwine, whom the king had nominated as his successor, was chosen king by the chief magnates of all England; and on the same day Harold was crowned with great ceremony by Aldred, archbishop of York. On taking the helm of the kingdom Harold immediately began to abolish unjust laws and to make good ones; to patronize churches and monasteries; to pay particular reverence to bishops, abbots, monks and clerks; and to show himself pious, humble and affable to all good men. But he treated malefactors with great severity, and gave general orders to his earls, ealdormen, sheriffs and thegns to imprison all thieves, robbers and disturbers of the kingdom. He labored in his own person by sea and by land for the protection of his realm. On April 24th in this year a comet was seen not only in England but, it is said, all over the world, and it shone for seven days with an exceeding brightness. Shortly afterwards Earl Tosti[1] returned from Flanders and landed in the Isle of Wight. After making the islanders pay tribute he departed and went pillaging along the sea-coast until he came to Sandwich. As soon as King Harold who was then at London heard this, he assembled a large fleet and a contingent of horsemen, and prepared himself to go to Sandwich. Tosti, learning of this, took some of the shipmen of that place (whether willing or unwilling) and set his course towards Lindsey, where he burnt many villages and put many men to death. Thereupon Edwin, earl of the Mercians, and Morcar, earl of the Northumbrians, hastened up with an army and expelled them from that part of the country. Afterwards he went to Malcolm, king of Scots, and remained with him during the whole of the summer. Meanwhile, King Harold arrived at Sandwich and waited there for his fleet. When it was assembled, he crossed over with it to the Isle of Wight, and, inasmuch as William, count of the Normans, was preparing to invade England with an army, he watched all the summer and autumn for his coming. In addition he distributed a land

---

[1] Earl Tosti was King Harold's brother. He sided with the Norwegian claimant to the English throne, Harald Hardraada, and the two were killed at the battle of Stamford Bridge on September 25, 1066.

force at suitable points along the sea coast. But about the feast of the Nativity of St. Mary[1] provisions fell short so that the naval and land forces returned home. After this Harald Hardraada, king of the Norwegians and brother of St. Olaf, the king, suddenly arrived at the mouth of the river Tyne with a powerful fleet of more than five hundred large ships. Earl Tosti, according to previous arrangement, joined him with his fleet. Hastening, they entered the Humber and, sailing up the Ouse against the stream, landed at Riccall. On hearing this, King Harold marched with speed towards Northumbria. But before his arrival the two brother earls, Edwin and Morcar, at the head of a large army fought a battle with the Norwegians on the northern bank of the river Ouse near York on Wednesday[2] which was the vigil of the feast of St. Matthew the Apostle. They fought so bravely at the onset that many of the enemy were overthrown; but after a long contest the English were unable to withstand the attacks of the Norwegians and fled with great loss. More were drowned in the river than slain on the field.[3] The Norwegians remained masters of the place of carnage, and having taken one hundred and fifty hostages from York and left there the same number of their own men as hostages they went to their ships. Five days after this, namely on Monday, September 25th, as Harold, king of the English, was coming to York with many thousand well-armed fighting men, he fell in with the Norwegians at a place called Stamford Bridge. He slew King Harald and Earl Tosti with the greater part of their army and gained a complete victory. Nevertheless the battle was stoutly contested. Harold, king of the English, permitted Olaf, the son of the Norwegian king, and Paul, earl of Orkney, who had been sent off with a portion of the army to guard the ships, to return home unmolested with twenty ships and the survivors, but only after they had sworn oaths of submission and had given hostages. In the midst of these things, and when the king might have thought that all his enemies were subdued, it was told him that William, count of the Normans, had arrived with a countless host of horsemen, slingers, archers and footsoldiers, and had brought with him also

powerful help from all parts of Gaul. It was reported that he had landed at Pevensey. Thereupon the king at once, and in great haste, marched with his army to London. Although he well knew that some of the bravest Englishmen had fallen in the two former battles, and that one-half of his army had not yet arrived, he did not hesitate to advance with all speed into Sussex against his enemies. On Saturday, October 22nd,[4] before a third of his army was in order for fighting, he joined battle with them nine miles from Hastings, where his foes had erected a castle. But inasmuch as the English were drawn up in a narrow place, many retired from the ranks, and very few remained true to him. Nevertheless from the third hour of the day until dusk he bravely withstood the enemy, and fought so valiantly and stubbornly in his own defense that the enemy's forces could make hardly any impression. At last, after great slaughter on both sides, about twilight the king, alas, fell. There were slain also Earl Gyrth, and his brother, Earl Leofwine, and nearly all the magnates of England. Then Count William returned with his men to Hastings. Harold reigned nine months and as many days. On hearing of his death earls Edwin and Morcar, who had withdrawn themselves from the conflict, went to London and sent their sister, Queen Edith,[5] to Chester. But Aldred, archbishop of York, and the said earls, with the citizens of London and the shipmen planned to elevate to the throne Prince Edgar, nephew of Edmund Ironside, and promised they would renew the contest under his command.[6] But while many were preparing to go to the fight, the earls withdrew their assistance and returned home with their army. Meanwhile Count William was laying waste Sussex, Kent, Hampshire, Surrey, Middlesex and Hertfordshire, burning villages and slaying their inhabitants until he came to Berkhamsted. There Archbishop Aldred, Wulfstan, bishop of Worcester, Walter, bishop of Hereford, Prince Edgar, the earls Edwin and Morcar, the chief men of London, and many others came to him, and giving hostages they surrendered and swore fealty to him. So he entered into a pact with them, but none the less permitted his men to burn villages and keep on pillaging. But

---

[1] September 8, 1066.

[2] September 20, 1066.

[3] This was the battle of Fulford.

[4] This is an error; the battle of Hastings was fought on St. Calixtus's day, Saturday, October 14, 1066.

[5] She had married King Harold.

[6] Edmund Ironside was a son of King Æthelred II the Unready of England. For Æthelred, see the introduction to his Law Code above, p. 222.

when Christmas day drew near, he went to London with his whole army in order that he might be made king. And because Stigand, the primate of all England, was accused by the pope of having obtained the *pallium* in an uncanonical manner, William was anointed king by Aldred, archbishop of York.[1] This was done on Christmas day with great ceremony. Before this (since the archbishop made it a condition), the king had sworn at the altar of St. Peter the Apostle,[2] and in the presence of the clergy and people, that he would defend the holy churches of God and their ministers, that he would rule justly and with kingly care the whole people placed under him, that he would make and keep right law, and that he would utterly prohibit all spoliation and unrighteous judgments.

5.15 The Conquest depicted: *The Bayeux Tapestry* (end of the 11th c.).

Not a tapestry at all but rather an embroidery, this long (230 feet) and narrow (20 inches) piece of linen tells in uninterrupted pictures, comic-strip style, the story told by William of Jumièges (above, p. 280). It covers Harold's early fealty to Duke William, his usurpation of the crown, and his defeat at the Battle of Hastings. Borders at top and bottom add picturesque details to the pictures, while embroidered labels in Latin identify important people and briefly explain the action. Probably commissioned by Odo of Bayeux, Duke William's half brother and a key figure in the story, the Tapestry is a work of propaganda. The portion shown here depicts Harold taking an oath before William. On the left is Duke William, sitting in authority upon a throne. Behind him are two Norman witnesses. Each of Harold's hands touches a reliquary as he swears an oath recognizing his dependency on William. To his right, pointing a finger at him, is an English witness. Harold's going back on his oath—his perjury—justifies the invasion of England. Might William's conquest have been a dress rehearsal for the First Crusade? What does the visual evidence suggest?

See Plate 14, p. 250, for a color reproduction of *The Bayeux Tapestry*.

(Detail of the Bayeux Tapestry—11th Century. With special permission from the City of Bayeux)

---

[1] A "pallium" was a thin band of white wool worn by the popes in the performance of the liturgy, the use of which could be conferred on approved metropolitan bishops. It was regularly given to the archbishops of Canterbury.

[2] This was Westminster Abbey.

5.16 Exploiting the Conquest: *Domesday Book* (1087). Original in Latin.

In 1086 William ordered a survey of England's counties (or shires) that came to be called "Domesday." Completed in 1087, *Domesday* consists of two books. The first and longer is a well-digested and abbreviated account of the commissioners' reports for all except three counties. The second contains less reworked reports for the remaining counties. The excerpt below, from the first volume, is part of the survey of Huntingdonshire. The excerpt begins with the landholders—the king and his tenants-in-chief—in the shire. There follows an itemization of the properties of each of these landholders along with the geld, or tax, they yielded in the "time of King Edward" (= *tempore Regis Edwardi*, abbreviated TRE). For example, in the time of Edward, the lands at Cotton were assessed at 2 hides when a geld was collected. "There is land for 3 ploughs" was a way to express the acreage: "1 plough" was the theoretical amount of land that could be ploughed each year by a team of 8 oxen. The "demesne" was the lord's share of the land. The villans (sometimes spelled villains or villeins) were fairly well-off peasants, at least in comparison with bordars, who represented the poorest peasants. The whole manor at Cotton was worth 40 shillings, both in 1066 and in 1086, when the royal commissioners were asking their questions. While the tenant-in-chief holding Cotton was the bishop of Lincoln, he gave it to Tursin to "hold," probably in return for knight's service. Compare this document with the *Polyptyque of the Church of Saint Mary of Marseille*, above, p. 107, with regard to their purposes and the things they inventory. Did any women "hold" land?

[Source: *Domesday Book: A Complete Translation*, ed. Ann Williams and G.H. Martin (New York: Penguin, 2002), pp. 551–53 (slightly modified).]

Huntingdonshire

Here Are Entered the Holders of Lands in Huntingdonshire

I KING WILLIAM
II The Bishop of Lincoln
III The Bishop of Coutances
IIII The Abbey of Ely
V The Abbey of Crowland
VI The Abbey of Ramsey
VII The Abbey of Thorney
VIII The Abbey of Peterborough
IX Count Eustace
X The Count of Eu
XI Earl Hugh
XII Walter Giffard
XIII William de Warenne

XIIII Hugh de Bolbec
XV Eudo fitzHubert
XVI Swein of Essex
XVII Roger d'Ivry
XVIII Ernulf de Hesdin
XIX Eustace the sheriff
XX Countess Judith
XXI Gilbert de Ghent
XXII Aubrey de Vere
XXIII William fitzAnsculf
XXIIII Ranulph, Ilger's brother
XXV Robert Fafiton
XXVI William Engaine
XXVII Ralph fitzOsmund
XXVIII Rohais, Richard's wife
XXIX The king's thegns

I. The Land of the King

HURSTINGSTONE HUNDRED[1]

IN HARTFORD King EDWARD had 15 hides of land to the geld. [There is] land for 17 ploughs. Ranulph, Ilger's brother, has custody of it now. There are now 4 ploughs in demesne; and 30 villans and 3 bordars have 8 ploughs. There is a priest and 2 churches, and 2 mills [rendering] £4, and 40 acres of meadow, [and] woodland pasture 1 league long and half a league broad. TRE worth £24; now £15.

NORMANCROSS HUNDRED

In BOTOLPH BRIDGE [in Peterborough] King Edward had 5 hides to the geld. [There is] land for 8 ploughs. There the king now has 1 plough in demesne; and 15 villans having 5 ploughs. There is a priest and a church, and 60 acres of meadow, and 12 acres of woodland pasture in Northamptonshire. TRE worth 100s;[2] now £8 Ranulph has custody of it. In this manor of the king and in other manors the sluice of the Abbot of Thorney has flooded 300 acres of meadow.

In STILTON the king's sokemen [dependents, rather freer than villans] of Normancross [Hundred] have 3 virgates of land to the geld. [There is] land for 2 ploughs, and 5 oxen ploughing.

In ORTON WATERVILLE [in Peterborough] the king has soke [jurisdictional rights, which brought in revenue] over 3½ hides of land in the land of the Abbot of Peterborough which was Godwine's.

TOSELAND HUNDRED

In GREAT GRANSDEN Earl Ælfgar had 8 hides of land to the geld. [There is] land for 15 ploughs. There are now 7 ploughs in demesne; and 24 villans and 8 bordars having 8 ploughs. There is a priest and a church, and 50 acres of meadow and 12 acres of scrubland. From the pasture come 5s4d [5 shillings, 4 pennies]. TRE worth £40; now £30. Ranulph has custody of it.

LEIGHTONSTONE HUNDRED

In ALCONBURY and Great Gidding, a BEREWICK,[3] there were 10 hides to the geld. [There is] land for 20 ploughs. There are now 5 ploughs belonging to the hall, on 2 hides of this land; and 35 villans have 13 ploughs there, and 8

acres of meadow. TRE worth £12; now the same. Ranulph, Ilger's brother, has custody of it.

In KEYSTON King Edward had 4 hides of land to the geld. [There is] land for 12 ploughs. There are now 2 ploughs in demesne; and 24 villans and 8 bordars have 10 ploughs, and [there are] 86 acres of meadow. [There is] woodland, pasture in places, 5 furlongs long and 1½ furlongs broad. TRE, as now, worth £10. Ranulph, Ilger's brother, has custody of it.

In BRAMPTON King Edward had 15 hides to the geld. [There is] land for 15 ploughs. There are now 3 ploughs, and 36 villans and 2 bordars have 14 ploughs. There is a church and a priest and 100 acres of meadow, woodland pasture half a league long and 2 furlongs broad, and 2 mills rendering 100s. TRE, as now, worth £20. Ranulph, Ilger's brother, has custody of it.

In GRAFHAM are 5 hides to the geld. [There is] land for 8 ploughs. The soke [is] in "Leightonstone" Hundred. There 7 sokeman and 17 villans now have 6 ploughs, and 6 acres of meadow. [There is] woodland pasture 1 league long and broad. TRE worth £5: now 10s less.

In GODMANCHESTER King Edward had 14 hides to the geld. [There is] land for 57 ploughs. There are 2 ploughs now in the king's demesne, on 2 hides of this land; and 80 villans and 16 bordars have 24 ploughs. There is a priest and a church, and 3 mills [rendering] 100s, and 160 acres of meadow and 50 acres of woodland pasture. From the pasture 20s. From the meadows 70s. TRE worth £40: now the same, by tale [counting rather than weighing].

II. The Land of the Bishop of Lincoln

TOSELAND HUNDRED

In COTTON the Bishop of Lincoln had 2 hides to the geld. [There is] land for 3 ploughs. There are now 2 ploughs in demesne; and 3 villans having 2 oxen, and [there are] 20 acres of meadow. TRE, as now, worth 40s. Turstin holds it of the bishop.

In GREAT STAUGHTON the Bishop of Lincoln had 6 hides to the geld. [There is] land for 15 ploughs. There are now 2½ ploughs in demesne: and 16 villans and 4 bordars having 8 ploughs. There is a priest and a church, and 24

---

[1]   In Anglo-Saxon England the shires (i.e., counties) were divided into hundreds for administrative and other purposes.

[2]   "100s" means 100 shillings, or *solidi*.

[3]   Berewick = an outlying estate.

acres of meadow and 100 acres of woodland pasture. TRE, as now, worth £10. Eustace holds it of the bishop. The Abbot of Ramsey claims this manor against the bishop.

In DIDDINGTON the Bishop of Lincoln had 2½ hides to the geld. [There is] land for 2 ploughs. There are now 2 ploughs in demesne; and 5 villans having 2 ploughs. There is a church, and 18 acres of meadow, [and] woodland pasture half a league long and a half broad. TRE worth 60s; now 70s. William holds it of the bishop.

In BUCKDEN the Bishop of Lincoln had 20 hides to the geld. [There is] land for 20 ploughs. There are now 5 ploughs in demesne; and 37 villans and 20 bordars having 14 ploughs. There is a church and a priest and 1 mill [rendering] 30s, and 84 acres of meadow, [and] woodland pasture 1 league long and 1 league broad. TRE worth £20; now £16.10s.

NORMANCROSS HUNDRED

In DENTON Godric had 5 hides to the geld. [There is] land for 2 ploughs. There is now 1 plough in demesne; and 10 villans and 2 bordars have 5 ploughs. There is a church and a priest, and 24 acres of meadow and 24 acres of scrubland. TRE worth 100s; now £4. Turstin holds it of the bishop.

In ORTON WATERVILLE [in Peterborough] Leofric had 3 hides and 1 virgate of land to the geld. [There is] land for 2 ploughs and 1 ox. There is now 1 plough in demesne, and 2 villans, and 9 acres of meadow. TRE worth 20s; now 10s. John holds it of the bishop. The king claims the soke of this land.

In STILTON Tovi had 2 hides to the geld. [There is] land for 2 ploughs and 7 oxen. There is now 1 plough in demesne; and 6 villans with 3 ploughs, and 16 acres of meadow and 5 acres of scrubland. TRE, as now, worth 40s. John holds it of the bishop. This land was given to Bishop Wulfwine TRE.

LEIGHTONSTONE HUNDRED

In LEIGHTON BROMSWOLD Thorkil the Dane had 15 hides to the geld. [There is] land for 17 ploughs. There are now 6 ploughs in demesne; and 33 villans and 3 bordars having 10 ploughs, and 1 mill [rendering] 3s. 3 knights hold 3 hides, less 1 virgate, of this land. There they have 3 ploughs, and 3 villans with half a plough. There are 30 acres of meadow and 10 acres of scrubland. TRE, as now, the bishop's demesne was worth £20; the land of the knights, 60s. Earl Waltheof gave this manor in alms to ST. MARY of Lincoln.

In PERTENHALL Alwine had 1 virgate of land to the geld. [There is] land for half a plough. This land is situated

in Bedfordshire but renders geld and service in Hunting-donshire. The king's servants claim this [land] for his use. TRE, as now, worth 5s. William holds it of Bishop Remigius and ploughs it there with his own demesne.

III. *The Land of the Bishop of Coutances*

In HARGRAVE [Northants] Sæmær had 1 virgate of land to the geld. [There is] land for 2 oxen. The SOKE [is] in Leigh-tonstone [Hundred]. The same man himself holds it now of the Bishop of Coutances, and ploughs there with 2 oxen, and has 2 acres of meadow. TRE worth 5s; now the same.

IIII. *The Land of the Abbey of Ely*

[HURSTINGSTONE HUNDRED]

In COLNE the Abbot of Ely had 6 hides to the geld. [There is] land for 6 ploughs, and in demesne [he had] land for 2 ploughs apart from the 6 hides. There are now 2 ploughs in demesne; and 13 villans and 5 bordars having 5 ploughs; and 10 acres of meadow. [There is] woodland pasture a league long and a half broad, and as much marsh. TRE worth £6; now 100s.

In BLUNTISHAM the Abbot of Ely had 6½ hides to the geld. [There is] land for 8 ploughs and, apart from these hides, [he had] land for 2 ploughs in demesne. There are now 2 ploughs in demesne; and 10 villans and 3 bordars with 3 ploughs. There is a priest and a church, and 20 acres of meadow, [and] woodland pasture 1 league long and 4 furlongs broad. TRE, as now, worth 100s.

In SOMERSHAM the Abbot of Ely had 8 hides to the geld. [There is] land for 12 ploughs and, apart from these hides, [he had] land for 2 ploughs in demesne. There are now 2 ploughs in demesne; and 32 villans and 9 bordars having 9 ploughs. There are 3 fishponds [rendering] 8s. and 10 acres of meadow, [and] woodland pasture 1 league long and 7 furlongs broad. TRE worth £7; now £8.

In SPALDWICK the Abbot of Ely had 15 hides to the geld. [There is] land for 15 ploughs. There are now 4 ploughs in demesne, on 5 hides of this land; and 50 villans and 10 bordars having 25 ploughs. There is 1 mill [rendering] 2s, and 160 acres of meadow and 60 acres of woodland pasture. TRE worth £16; now £22.

In Little Catworth, a BEREWICK of Spaldwick, [there are] 4 hides to the geld. [There is] land for 4 ploughs. There 7 villans have 2 ploughs now.

THE TWELFTH-CENTURY RENAISSANCE

5.17 Logic: Peter Abelard, *Glosses on Porphyry* (*c.*1100). Original in Latin.

While Avicenna (see above, p. 203) could draw directly on the works of Aristotle, only a small sample of those writings was available in the West when the philosopher Peter Abelard (1079–1142) was fired up to use logic as a tool to arrive at truth. Abelard could draw on only a few of Aristotle's works on logic. He had, in addition, a treatise that the Greek neo-Platonist Porphyry (d.*c.*305) had written as an introduction to Aristotle's *Categories*; it had been commented on and translated into Latin by the late Roman philosopher Boethius (d.524/526). Like Avicenna, whose writings at the time were, however, unknown in the West, Abelard was interested in using and developing logic. He concentrated particularly on understanding the kind of reality possessed by "universals"—the "genera and species" that Aristotle spoke of in his writings on logic. Confronting William of Champeaux (d.1121), a scholar of Abelard's day who believed that universals existed outside the mind as common entities, Abelard formulated a set of arguments against this possibility. In his view, every real being outside the mind was entirely singular and in no way common. So-called universals, he concluded, were nothing more than names. They were common not because they possessed any kind of common being but simply because they could be predicated of many different subjects. We can say, for example, that Peter is human; Paul is human; Mary is human; and so on for countless others. As 'human' is thus predicable of many, it is accordingly a universal. In the selection below, we see some of Abelard's arguments against William's view, which has come to be known as realism. These arguments were apparently so successful that, much to Abelard's delight, they forced William to modify his position.

[Source: *Basic Issues in Medieval Philosophy*, ed. Richard N. Bosley and Martin Tweedale (Peterborough, ON: Broadview Press, 1997), pp. 382–83. Introduced by Blake Dutton.]

It remains now to object to those who say that each individual in that it agrees with others is universal and who allow that the same items are predicated of many, not in that many are essentially them, but because many agree with them. But if to be predicated of many is the same as agreeing with many, how is it that we say an individual is predicated of only one, since there is nothing which agrees with only one thing? Also how does being predicated of many constitute a difference between universal and singular, since Socrates agrees with many in exactly the same way as a human being agrees with many? Certainly a human being insofar as he is a human being and Socrates insofar as he is a human being agrees with others. But neither a human being insofar as he is Socrates nor Socrates insofar as he is Socrates agrees with others.

Therefore, whatever a human being has Socrates also has, and in the same way.

Besides, since human being which is in Socrates and Socrates himself are conceded to be completely the same things, there is no difference of the latter from the former. For no thing is diverse from itself at one and the same time, because whatever it has in itself it has and in entirely the same way. Thus Socrates while white and literate is not in virtue of these diverse from himself, although he has diverse things in himself, for he has both these and in entirely the same way. He is not in one way of himself literate and another way white, just as it is not one thing which of itself is white and another literate.

Also when they say that Socrates and Plato agree in human being, how is that to be understood when it is agreed that all humans differ from each other both in matter and in form? For if Socrates agrees with Plato in the thing which is human being, but no thing is human being other than Socrates himself or some other human being, he will have to agree with Plato either in himself or in someone else. But in himself he is diverse from Plato and likewise in another since he is not the other.

There are those who understand agreeing in human being negatively as if it were said: Socrates does not differ from Plato in human being. But we could also say that he does not differ from Plato in stone since neither is a stone. Then we note no greater agreement between them in human being than in stone, unless perhaps there is an earlier proposition, as though we said: They are human being because they do not differ in human being. But this cannot be since it is altogether false that they do not differ in human being. For if Socrates does not differ

from Plato in the thing which is human being, neither does he in himself. For if he differs in himself from Plato, since he is the thing which is human being, certainly he will differ from Plato in the thing which is human being.

Now that we have given the arguments why things either individually or collectively cannot be called universal, i.e. said to be predicated of many, it remains to ascribe universality to utterances alone. So just as grammarians call some nouns common and others proper, so dialecticians call some simple expressions universal, some particular, i.e. singular. A word is universal when it is apt to be predicated of many individually on account of its establishment, like the noun "human being" which is conjoinable to particular names of humans in virtue of the nature of the subject things to which it is applied. A singular word is one which is predicable of only one, like "Socrates," since it is taken to be a name of only one.

5.18 Medical science: Constantine the African's translation of Johannitius's *Isagoge* (before 1098). Original in Latin.

We know very little about Constantine the African except that he came to Salerno before 1077 and died at the monastery of Monte Cassino (near Rome) between 1085 and 1098—and that his writings initiated a wholesale revival of medical learning in the West! Among his works, excerpted here, was a translation of the *Masa'il fi-tibb* ("Questions about Medicine") by the Nestorian Christian Hunayn ibn Ishaq, who lived in Baghdad in the ninth century. That, in turn, had been a distillation of Galen's *Art of Medicine*, an important medical textbook of the ancient world. Constantine Latinized Hunayn into "Johannitius" and used the Greek word *Isagoge* ("Introduction") in place of Hunayn's Arabic title. The work soon joined other medical texts in translation—some from Hippocrates, the ancient Greek doctor, and others from more recent Byzantine writings—to form the *Articella*, the standard textbook for learning "Greek" medicine in the West. Even after the *Articella* was superseded by other medical texts, the *Isagoge* remained important in medical education, especially at Salerno.

[Source: *Medieval Medicine: A Reader*, ed. Faith Wallis (Toronto: University of Toronto Press, 2010), pp. 140–48 (notes added from glossary). Translated by Faith Wallis.]

1. Medicine is divided into two parts, namely, theory and practice. And of these, theory is further divided into three, that is to say, the consideration of things that are natural, and of things that are non-natural (whence comes knowledge of health, disease, and the neutral state), and when these natural things depart from the course of nature—that is, when the four humors increase beyond the course of nature; and from what cause and symptoms disease may arise.

[The Naturals[1]]

2. **Natural things.** There are seven natural things: the elements, the mixtures [of qualities], the humors,[2] the members [of the body], the powers,[3] the faculties, and the spirits.[4] Some people add to these four others: namely, the ages of life, the colors, the shapes, and the distinction between male and female.

3. **The four elements.** There are four elements: fire, air, water, and earth. Fire is hot and dry; air is hot and moist; water is cold and moist; earth is cold and dry.

4. **The mixtures [of qualities].** There are nine mixtures [of qualities]. Eight are unequal and one equal. Of the unequal, four are simple: namely, hot, cold, moist, and dry. And from these come four composite [mixtures], namely, hot and moist; hot and dry; cold and moist; cold and dry. [A mixture is] equal when the body is brought to a state where it is sound and intact through a balance [of all four qualities].

5. **The humors.** There are four compound [humors]: blood, phlegm, red bile, and black bile. Blood is hot and moist, phlegm is cold and moist, red bile is hot and dry, black bile is cold and dry.

6. **Phlegm.** There are five varieties of phlegm. There is the salty phlegm, hotter and drier than the other kinds, and tinged with red bile. There is the sweet phlegm, associated with warmth and moisture, and tinged with blood. There is the acrid phlegm, associated with cold and dryness, and tinged with black bile. There is the glassy phlegm, caused by great coldness and coagulation, such as occurs in old people who are destitute of natural warmth. And there is one which is cold and moist; it has no savor, but retains its characteristic coldness and moisture.

7. **Red bile.** Red bile exists in five kinds. There is red bile which is naturally and substantially clear, and it originates in the liver. There is another which is lemon-colored; it originates from the watery humor phlegm and from red bile, and therefore it is less hot. There is a bile which is like egg yolk, which originates from the mixture of coagulated phlegm and clear red bile, and which is less hot. 8. A fourth kind of bile is green, like *prasius* [*a light green semi-precious stone*] and it generally originates in the stomach; and there is another bile that is green like verdigris and it burns like a poison. It comes from too much adustion[5] and it possesses its own innate heat and innate harmful quality.

9. **Black bile.** Black bile comes in two kinds. One kind is natural—the dregs of the blood and its perturbation, so to speak. It is known from its black color when it flows out of the body from below [through the bowel] or above [from the mouth], and this kind is truly cold and dry. The other kind is unnatural and its origin is from the adustion of the choleric mixture, and so it is rightly called black (that is, black bile). It is hotter and lighter than the abovementioned kind, having in itself a vigorous action and a quality which is extremely deadly and pernicious.

10. **Kinds of members.** There are four kinds of members. Some of them are principal—the foundations and material, so to speak. These are four: the brain, the heart, the liver, and the testicles. Other members serve the aforesaid principal members, such as the nerves, which minister to the brain, and the arteries which minister to the heart, and the veins, which minister to the liver, and the sper-

---

1   In Arabic-Galenic physiology, the term "naturals" or "things natural" referred to the unalterable "givens" of the physical world and the human body: the elements, complexions, humors, organs, etc.

2   Depending on the context, the humors were either a) a moisture or fluid of some kind, or b) one of the four bodily fluids deemed to constitute the physiological basis of human life. The classic humors were blood, red bile (also called yellow bile or choler), phlegm, and black bile (or melancholy).

3   The powers were the natural principles within the body that organized and executed the three major functions of life. Natural powers were nutrition, growth, and reproduction. Spiritual or vital powers were respiration, heat, and emotion. Animal powers were sensation, voluntary motion, and cognition. The powers were manifestations of the spirits.

4   The spirits were the life forces that organized the principal functions of the body. The natural spirit, whose seat was the liver, controlled nutrition, growth, and reproduction. The vital (or spiritual) spirit, located in the heart, controlled respiration, vital heat, and, to some degree, motion and emotion. The animal spirit, which resided in the brain, governed sensation, voluntary motion, and (in humans) reason.

5   Adustion is the burning or scorching of a humor caused by excessive heat.

matic vessels, which convey sperm to the testicles. Some members have their own inherent power that governs these members and comprises their quality—for example bones, all the cartilages or the membranes that are between the skin and the flesh, the muscles, fat, and flesh. 11. There are other [members] that originate from their own innate power and derive vigor from the fundamental [members], for example, the stomach, kidneys, intestines, and all the muscles. By their own proper power, these members seek out food and transform it, and they perform their actions according to nature. They also have other inherent powers that derive from the fundamental principal [members]; sensation, life, and voluntary motion come from these.

12. **The powers.** The powers are divided into three. There is the natural power, the spiritual power, and the animal power. One natural power ministers, and another is ministered to. Sometimes it generates, at another time it nourishes, and at another time it feeds. But the power that ministers sometimes seeks out, retains, digests, and expels the things that minister to the feeding power, just as the feeding power ministers to the nourishing power. 13. The other two serve the generating power, one by altering food, the other by re-fashioning it. These differ from one another in that the first power alters, and it serves the generating power through the activity of refashioning. But the operations of the re-fashioning power are five: assimilation, hollowing out, perforating, roughening, and smoothing.

14. **Spiritual power.** From the spiritual power, two others proceed: one is operative and the other is operated upon. The operative power is that which dilates the heart and arteries and then contracts them. From the one which is operated upon come anger, indignation, triumph, domination, astuteness, and anxiety.

15. **Animal power** [*the power of* **animus** *or mind*]. Animal power encompasses three things. One animal power arranges, discriminates, and assembles; a second one moves with voluntary motions; the third is called "sensing." From the ordering, discriminating, and assembling power come these things: imagination in the front part of the head, cognition or reasoning in the brain, and memory in the occipital region. The [second animal] power moves with voluntary motion. And the sensing power consists in sight, hearing, taste, smell, and touch.

16. **Faculties.** Faculties are of two kinds. There are faculties of which each accomplishes on its own what pertains to it, such as appetite for food [which works] by means of heat and dryness; digestion [which works] by means of heat and moisture; retention [which works] by means of cold and dryness; expulsion [which works] by cold and moisture. There are also composite faculties which are composed of two [faculties]: such are desire and expulsion.

17. **Spirit.** The spirits are three. First, the natural spirit takes its origin from the liver; second, the vital spirit, [originating] from the heart; third, the animal spirit, from the brain. Of these three the first is diffused throughout the whole body in the veins which have no pulse; the second is transmitted by the arteries; and the third by the nerves. These are considered in the seventh division of the seven natural things, that is, the spirit.

18. **The ages [of life].**[1] There are four ages; namely, youth, prime of life, maturity, and old age. Adolescence is of a hot and moist complexion;[2] in adolescence the body increases and grows up to the twenty-fifth or thirtieth year. The prime of life follows, which is hot and dry, preserving the body in a perfect state, with no diminution of its powers, and it ends at age thirty-five or forty. After this comes maturity, which is cold and dry, in which the body begins to decline and decrease, although its power is not abated, and it lasts to the fiftieth or sixtieth year. After this comes old age, abounding in phlegmatic humor, cold and wet, in which it is apparent that there is a decline of power, and it ends with the end of life.

22. **The tunics of the eye.** The eye has seven coats and three humors. The first coat is called the retina, the second the secundine, the third the sclera, the fourth the web [*choroid*], the fifth the uveal, the sixth the cornea, and the seventh the conjunctiva. The first humor is the vitreous, the second the crystalline, and the third the albugineous.

---

[1] Compare these ages, derived from Galen, with those given by Isidore of Seville, above, p. 80.

[2] Complexion referred to the blending of qualities or humors natural to an individual. It is more or less equivalent to temperament. The term survives today to denote the quality of the skin because pre-modern physicians made an initial determination of the patient's complexion from examining the face.

23. **The colors of the eyes.** The colors of the eyes are four: black, whitish, varied, and grey. Black color is due to a defect of the visual spirit,[1] because it is clouded, or from a lack of crystalline humor, or because most of the crystalline humor remains on the inside [of the eye], or from abundance of the humor that is like the white of an egg [*the albugineous humor*], or because it is perturbed, or from the high quality of the uveal humor. 24. Whitish [color] comes from seven things which are the opposite of those just mentioned, namely from an abundance or clarity of the visual spirit, the magnitude and prominence of the crystalline humor, a reduction in the quantity and clarity of the albugineous humor, and a deficiency in the quality of the uveal humor. Varicolored and grey come about when the circumstances which result in black and white converge. Variable color signifies by its variety that the visual spirit is more abundant and brighter; grey color signifies by its greyness that the visual humor is less abundant, and somewhat darkened.

25. **The qualities of the body.** The qualities of the body are five in number; namely, obesity; thinness; emaciation, atrophy, and the mean state. Fatness of flesh arises from lack of heat and overabundance of moisture; thinness arises from heat and intense dryness. Emaciation arises from cold and intense dryness; atrophy from cold and intense moisture. And a mean state arises from a mean proportion of the humors. These are the shapes of the body.

26. **The difference between male and female.** The male differs from the female because he is hotter and dryer; she, on the contrary, is colder and more moist.

[The Non-naturals[2]]

27. **Changes of air.** Changes of the air come about in five different ways; from the seasons, from the rising and setting of the stars, from the winds, from the lands, and from the vapors that arise from them.

28. **The four seasons of the year.** The seasons of the year are four: spring, which is hot and moist; summer, which is hot and dry; autumn, which is cold and dry; winter, which is cold and moist. The nature of the air is changed by the stars, for when the sun approaches a star or a star the sun, the air becomes hotter. But when they separate the coldness of the air is increased.

29. **The winds.** There are four winds: the east wind, the west wind, the north wind, and the south wind. Of the latter two, the nature of the first [that is, the north wind] is cold and dry and of the second [the south wind] is hot and moist. The two others are of an equal nature, for the east wind is hot and dry and the west wind is cold and moist. The south wind is slightly hotter and moister and the north wind colder and dryer.

32. **Exercise.** Exercise produces change in the body. When it is moderate, it causes a moderate amount of heat; when it is increased, it warms it to a greater degree and afterwards cools it down.

33. **Rest.** Rest produces change in the body; if excessive, it increases cold and moisture.

34. **Baths.** Baths are either of fresh water or of water which is not fresh. A fresh-water bath softens the body, a hot bath warms it, a cold bath cools it. But a fresh-water bath dries out the body, while baths of salt or bitter or sulphurous waters heat and dry the body, and alum or alkaline baths cool and dry it.

35. **Kinds of foods.** Foods are of two kinds. Good food generates good humor and bad food generates an evil humor. That which produces a good humor is that which generates good blood; namely, that which is in a balanced state as regards mixture [of qualities] and operation, such as clean bread [with bran removed] and the flesh of yearling lamb or kid. Bad food brings about the contrary state, for example old bread, or bread with bran in it, or the flesh of old rams or goats. Foods producing good or evil humors are of two kinds, heavy or light. Pork and beef are heavy; chicken or fish are light. And of the latter, the flesh of the middle-sized and more active kinds is better than that of the fatter and scaly varieties.

---

1 The visual spirit was, according to one school of thought, a subtle ray emitted by the eye that contacted the object of sight and connected the mind to it.

2 The non-naturals referred to environmental and behavioral factors affecting health or disease. These were variable (including air, food and drink, sleep and wakefulness, rest and motion, retention and elimination, and emotional states), and they exerted an influence on the naturals.

36. Some kinds of vegetables produce an evil humor of red bile; for instance, nasturtium, mustard, and garlic. Lentils, cabbage, and the meat of old goat's flesh or beef produce black bile. Suckling pig, lamb, purslane,[1] and mountain spinach beget phlegm. Moreover, heavy foods produce phlegm and black bile, and light food produces red bile; in either case, this is bad.

37. **Kinds of drink.** Drinks are of three kinds. First, there is drink which is nothing but a drink: for example, water. Secondly, there is drink which is both drink and food, such as wine. Thirdly, there is drink which is both of these, and this is the potion [medicine] which is given to counteract the harm from a disease, such as melicrate [*honey and water*], mead, or spiced tonic. Food is useful because it restores the integrity of the body in its proper order. Drink is useful because it distributes food throughout the body. But that kind of drink which we called "potion" is useful because it changes the nature of the body into itself.[2]

[The Contra-naturals[3]]

42. **Fever.** Fever is unnatural heat, exceeding the normal course of nature, proceeding from the heart into the arteries; and it inflicts harm by its effect. There are three kinds: the first is in the spirit, and it is called "ephemeral"; the second arises from humors which putrefy, and it is called "putrid"; and the third damages the members of the body, and this one is called "hectic." Of these, the ephemeral variety arises from incidental causes, and putrid [fever] also, [which arises] from things that are putrefied. 43. Some of these are simple and not combined with others, and these are four. The first is that which arises from the putrid state of the blood, scorching both the interior and exterior of the body; for instance, a continued fever. The second is that which arises from the putrid state of red bile; for instance, tertian fever. The third arises from the putrid state of phlegm; for instance, quotidian fever. And the fourth arises from the putrid state of black bile; this attacks the sick man after an interval of two days, and this is called quartan [fever].[4]

46. **What produces health.** If each of the natural things in the human body preserves its proper nature, health is maintained. If any should lose its proper nature, this will make either for illness or the neutral state. There are three classes of illness: similar, universal, and official. 47. A [similar disease] is one affecting the similar members[5] and they have a similar name when the type of suffering is the same, for example, an *aching* head. An [official disease] befalls official members[6] such as the feet, hands, tongue, or teeth. This takes its name from the infirmity incident to them, for instance podagra [in the foot] or chiragra [in the hand]. And finally there is a universal disease, which is linked to the other two, for example dislocation of the members.

---

[1]   A succulent plant sometimes cooked as a vegetable or put into salads.

[2]   That is, the potion transforms the body to conform to the nature of the potion itself.

[3]   The contra-naturals were all the diseases and trauma that threatened the natural body.

[4]   Continuous fevers never broke; tertian fevers peaked every third day; quotidian fevers peaked every day; quartan fevers peaked every fourth day.

[5]   Similar diseases were diseases of bad mixtures of humors or qualities, while similar members referred to homogenous parts. Here Constantine gives the example of aches; they were caused by bad mixtures and could affect similar members—i.e., the head or other body parts—indifferently.

[6]   An official disease was not of bad mixture but of bad conformation, such as a deformity. Official members were parts of the body with particular, "official," functions, such as the feet, which have the function of walking. Podagra (today called gout of the foot) and chiragra (today known as gout of the hand) were seen as diseases of bad conformation.

5.19 The healing power of stones: Marbode of Rennes, *The Book of Stones* (? late 11th c.). Original in Latin.

Marbode of Rennes (*c.*1035–1123), a native of western France, studied at the cathedral school (the predecessor institution to the university that emerged in the twelfth century) in Angers and later became its director. In 1096, he was elected bishop of Rennes, a city about 80 miles to the northwest of Angers. Marbode was a distinguished author of poetry and prose, writing everything from erotic poetry to biographies of saints. His interest in stones derives from three traditions: scientific writings of the pre-medieval Mediterranean world, books on magic, and Christian commentaries explaining the symbolic meaning of the various stones that appear in the Bible. Framed as a practical guide, the *Liber lapidum* ("The Book of Stones"), excerpted below, is a self-conscious display of erudition. Written in verse and drawing in particular on medical writings, the *Liber* described the properties and powers of sixty different stones. It offered a guide to the medicinal uses of minerals that supplemented similar sorts of writings on plants. The poem was very popular in the Middle Ages, quickly translated into a number of languages, including Hebrew, from the twelfth century forward. However, its purpose is hard to figure out: a prologue claims that the mysteries the poem reveals should be shared with at most three friends but proceeds to claim it will help physicians in general. The entry on green stone begins to catalog its twelve varieties and then gives up in boredom after four or five. Some lines are very difficult to interpret. Other texts are frequently cited, but only vaguely: "it is said…" or "we read…." Some of Marbode's other poetry is openly sarcastic and satirical. Is this poem a scholarly send-up? If so, what exactly is Marbode mocking? In what ways might the *Liber* be considered among the early writings of the twelfth-century Renaissance? Does it seem to reflect some knowledge of the translation into Latin of medical texts by Constantine the African (above, p. 289)?

[Source: John M. Riddle *Marbode of Rennes'* De lapidibus: *Considered as a Medical Treatise with Text, Commentary, and C. W. King's Translation, Together with Text and Translation of Marbode's Minor Works on Stones*, Sudhoffs Archiv, Zeitschrift für Wissenschaftsgeschichte, Beihefte; Heft 20 (Wiesbaden: Franz Steiner, 1977), pp. 45, 49, 50, 51. Translated by Bruce L. Venarde.]

Green Stone (de smaragdo)[1]

Smaragdus triumphs over every green thing in its
   greenness;[2]
Its types are said to be twelve: twice five plus two.

These include Scythian, Bactrian, and Nile.[3]
There are furthermore those kinds said to appear in veins
   of copper
whose foul nature the metal makes known in its failings.[4]   5

---

[1] *Smaragdus* eventually came to mean "emerald" exclusively, but in Marbode's time and for many centuries before, it could refer to any number of green stones, including green marble and alabaster.

[2] A possible reference to texts concerning the medicinal uses of plants, which Marbode identifies as effective, but less so than gems, in the prologue to the *Liber lapidum*.

[3] That is, from what are now, roughly, Ukraine, Afghanistan, and Egypt.

[4] This seems to mean that any so-called *smaragdus* associated with the relatively common copper gathered in mines is tainted, an unsurprising association given that copper is quite liable to oxidation that turns it green.

There are also those from Chalcedon,[1] — it is annoying
    to enumerate the others.
Greatest honor and gift belongs to the Scythian stones.
Sarmatians[2] seize it with the help of guardian griffons.[3]
Those whose sight pierces the stone have greater
    reputation,
as do those whose nearby air is touched with its green
    tint of light.   10
Neither sun nor bright light nor shadows change it.
Its surface is flat or its form concave, in the way
that still water copies the face of one looking at it.
Word has it that Nero made this use of mirrors
when he watched the gladiatorial shows.[4]   15
The best structure for these stones is a flat surface.
This stone is said to be useful to those who search out its
    hidden qualities
Because they want to know things in advance, to see into
    the future.
It increases the power of anyone who carries it reverently,
granting the power of persuasion in any sort of matter
    (*causa*).[5]   20
Hung around the neck, *smaragdus* wards off frightful
    fever
and in the same way cures epilepsy.
It improves weakened vision with its gentle greenness —
and is thought able to ward off storms.
It is also said to calm lustful urges.   25
It is refined in its greenness, and its color is perfected
when it is bathed in wine and anointed with green olive
    oil.

Chrysolite (de chrysolito)[6]

Chrysolite flashes with gold and glitters like fire.
It is like the sea, suggesting a certain greenness.
Set in gold, it is said to be an amulet.
It is a strong protection against night frights.
If it is pierced and strung on donkey's hairs,   5
it scares away demons and is thought to upset them.
Thus pierced, it is fit to be worn on the left bicep.
We read that Ethiopians send us this stone.

Beryl (de berillo)[7]

A six-faceted shape makes beryls outstanding.
If not it is made weak, and seems to be pale.
People want its outstanding specimens to be like olive oil
or watery blue; knowledgeable age approves of them.[8]
This stone comes to us from India.   5
It is said to support conjugal love
and to glorify someone who carries it
and to burn the right hand of one who clutches it.
Water in which this stone lies heals weak eyes
and a drink of it relieves belching and labored
    breathing.   10
They say it cures all liver complaints.
The masters have it that there are nine kinds.

Topaz (de topazio)[9]

An island of the same name produces topaz,[10]
precious to the same degree it is rare.

---

[1] Probably a reference to a town in Asia Minor, now Turkey, but green stones with this name are most likely to have come from the south Asian subcontinent.

[2] Likely a reference to peoples of western Scythia (to the north and east of the Black Sea).

[3] The griffon is a legendary creature with the body of a lion and the head and wings of an eagle.

[4] Nero was the infamously self-absorbed and ineffective emperor of Rome, 54–68, also the first to persecute Christians in his empire. This is an especially interesting reference since Nero is said to have demanded thinly cut green stones to guard his eyes against the harsh light of the gladiatorial games; that is, Nero perhaps demanded a distant ancestor of modern sunglasses twelve centuries or so before corrective lenses as we know them appeared in Europe.

[5] The Latin word (*causa*) can refer to legal cases, and that is surely one of its meanings here; in all his writings, Marbode often chose Latin words with what had, by his time, multiple meanings.

[6] The exact identity of this stone is uncertain. It is probably what is now referred to as olivine or peridot.

[7] Here, a simple reference: this is the gem known in our times as beryl.

[8] The meaning of this phrase is somewhat obscure. "Knowledgeable age" seems to refer to the wisdom of elders.

[9] Marbode describes two types, the first of which is probably our modern topaz.

[10] This is an island in the Red Sea, known to the Greeks as Topazion and today as Zabargad or St. John's Island.

It is said to have only two varieties.
The one has a color more like pure gold,
the other is clearer and finer.
This same stone is said to help with hemorrhoids   5

and what is more wondrous, it is thought to feel the
    moon.[1]
It is further claimed to calm raging waves,
and the land of the Arabs, very rich in gems, produces it.

....

CLUNIACS AND CISTERCIANS

5.20 The Cistercian view: Saint Bernard, *Apologia* (1125). Original in Latin.

An apologia is a defense, not an apology. This one emerged from the growing tension between the competing claims of holiness of the Cistercians and the traditional Benedictines, the "black monks," particularly Cluny. Bernard's *Apologia*, written in the guise of a letter to William of Saint-Thierry, the reform-minded abbot of a Cluniac-style house, is modeled on classical rhetorical practice: first you belittle your own side and then you turn to demolish your opponent. The passage below begins at the end of Bernard's criticism of his own order, the Cistercians, which, he says, ought not to be overly proud of its own style of life. Then he turns to "certain monks of yours"—he means the black monks in general and the Cluniacs in particular—offering a bit of "friendly" advice. What follows is a scathing satire on what Bernard took to be the excess, luxury, and laxity of the Cluniacs.

[Source: *The Cistercian World: Monastic Writings of the Twelfth Century*, trans. and ed. Pauline Matarasso (New York: Penguin Press, 1993), pp. 47–51, 55–58 (notes modified).]

15 If this is to be a letter, it is time I finished it. I have taken up the pen and rebuked as vigorously as I could those monks of ours whom you, Father, complained of as having criticized your Order,[2] and have cleared myself at the same time, as it behoved me, of any unfounded suspicion on this count. However, I feel bound to add a few remarks. Because I give our own men no quarter, I might seem to condone the behavior of certain monks of yours—conduct which I know you disapprove of, and which all good monks must necessarily avoid. I refer to abuses that, if they exist in the Order, God forbid should ever be a part of it. Certainly no order can contain an element of disorder, for disorder and order are incompatible. So long, therefore, as I attack in the men I censure not the Order they belong to but their vices, I shall be seen as arguing for the Order and not against it. In doing this I have no fear of offending those who love the Order. On the contrary they will surely thank me for hunting down what they themselves detest. Any who might be displeased would prove by their refusal to condemn the vices that corrupt it that they did not have the Order's good at heart. To them I make the Gregorian rejoinder: better that scandal erupt than that the truth be abandoned.[3]

---

[1] This may mean that topaz cured or warded off lunacy, i.e., mental afflictions.

[2] Throughout the following passage Bernard plays on the meaning of "order," which can refer to the general and abstract notion of order; the monks of the Benedictine Order—that is, those who adhere to the *Benedictine Rule*—and finally, the monks of the Order of Cluny—that is, those who were juridically under the abbot of Cluny, whether at Cluny or not, or, more loosely, those who belonged to a "Cluniac-style" monastery.

[3] Gregory the Great, *Homilies on Ezechiel* 1.7.5.

Against Superfluity

VIII, 16 It is said, and quite rightly, that the Cluniac way of life was instituted by holy Fathers; anxious that more might find salvation through it, they tempered the Rule to the weak without weakening the Rule. Far be it from me to believe that they recommended or allowed such an array of vanities or superfluities as I see in many religious houses. I wonder indeed how such intemperance in food and drink, in clothing and bedding, in horses and buildings can implant itself among monks. And it is the houses that pursue this course with thoroughgoing zeal, with full-blown lavishness, that are reputed the most pious and the most observant. They go so far as to count frugality avarice, and sobriety austerity, while silence is reputed gloom. Conversely, slackness is called discretion, extravagance liberality, chattering becomes affability, guffawing cheerfulness, soft clothing and rich caparisons are the requirements of simple decency, luxurious bedding is a matter of hygiene, and lavishing these things on one another goes by the name of charity. By such charity is charity destroyed, and this discretion mocks the very word. It is a cruel mercy that kills the soul while cherishing the body. And what sort of charity is it that cares for the flesh and neglects the spirit? What kind of discretion that gives all to the body and nothing to the soul? What kind of mercy that restores the servant and destroys the mistress? Let no one who has shown that sort of mercy hope to obtain the mercy promised in the Gospel by him who is the truth: "Blessed are the merciful, for they shall receive mercy."[1] On the contrary, he can expect the sure and certain punishment which holy Job invoked with the full force of prophecy on those whom I call "cruelly kind": "Let him be no longer remembered, but let him be broken like a sterile tree." The cause—and a sufficient cause for that most proper retribution—follows at once: "He feeds the barren, childless woman and does no good to the widow."[2]

17 Such kindness is obviously disordered and irrational. It is that of the barren and unfruitful flesh, which the Lord tells us profits nothing[3] and Paul says will not inherit the kingdom of God.[4] Intent on satisfying our every whim it pays no heed to the Sage's wise and warning words: "Have mercy on your own soul and you will please God."[5] That is indeed true mercy, and must perforce win mercy, since one pleases God by exercising it. Conversely it is, as I said, not kindness but cruelty, not love but malevolence, not discretion but confusion to feed the barren woman and do no good to the widow—in other words, to pander to the desires of the profitless flesh while giving the soul no help in cultivating the virtues. For the soul is indeed bereaved in this life of her heavenly Bridegroom.[6] Yet she never ceases to conceive by the Holy Spirit and bring forth immortal offspring, which, provided they are nurtured with diligent care, will rightfully be heirs to an incorruptible and heavenly inheritance.[7]

18 Nowadays, however, these abuses are so widespread and so generally accepted that almost everyone acquiesces in them without incurring censure or even blame, though motives differ. Some use material things with such detachment as to incur little or no guilt. Others are moved by simple-mindedness, by charity or by constraint. The first, who do as they are bidden in all simplicity, would be ready to act differently if the bidding were different. The second kind, afraid of dissension in the community, are led, not by their own pleasure, but by their desire to keep the peace. Lastly there are those who are unable to stand out against a hostile majority that vociferously defends such practices as pertaining to the Order and moves swiftly and forcibly to block whatever judicious restrictions or changes the former try to bring in.

IX, 19 Who would have dreamed, in the far beginnings of the monastic order, that monks would have slid into such slackness? What a way we have come from the monks who lived in Anthony's day![8] When one of them paid on occasion a brotherly call on another, both were so avid for the spiritual nourishment they gained from the encounter that they forgot their physical hunger

---

[1] Matt. 5: 7.

[2] Job 24: 20–21.

[3] John 6: 64.

[4] 1 Cor. 15: 50.

[5] Ecclus. 30: 24; the "Sage" is the author of Ecclesiasticus, Jesus son of Sirach.

[6] The "heavenly Bridegroom" is Christ.

[7] See 1 Pet. 1: 4.

[8] A reference to St. Antony, for whose life see above, p. 27.

and would commonly pass the whole day with empty stomachs but with minds replete. And this was the right order of precedence—to give priority to what is nobler in man's make-up; this was real discretion—making greater provision for the more important part; this indeed true charity—to tend with loving care the souls for love of whom Christ died.

As for us, when we come together, to use the Apostle's words, it is not to eat the Lord's supper.[1] There is none who asks for heavenly bread and none who offers it. Never a word about Scripture or salvation. Flippancy, laughter and words on the wind are all we hear. At table our ears are as full of gossip as our mouths of festive fare, and all intent on the former we quite forget to restrain our appetite.

On Meals

20 Meanwhile course after course is brought in. To offset the lack of meat—the only abstinence—the laden fish dishes are doubled. The first selection may have been more than enough for you, but you have only to start on the second to think you have never tasted fish before. Such are the skill and art with which the cooks prepare it all that one can down four or five courses without the first spoiling one's enjoyment of the last, or fullness blunting the appetite. Tickle the palate with unaccustomed seasonings and the familiar start to pall, but exotic relishes will restore it even to its preprandial sharpness; and since variety takes away the sense of surfeit, one is not aware that one's stomach is overburdened. Foodstuffs in their pure and unadulterated state have no appeal, so we mix ingredients pell-mell, scorning the natural nutriments God gave us, and use outlandish savors to stimulate our appetite. That way we can eat far more than we need and still enjoy it.

To give but one example: who could itemize all the ways in which eggs are maltreated? Or describe the pains that are taken to toss them and turn them, soften and harden them, botch them and scotch them, and, finally serve them up fried, baked and stuffed by turns, in conjunction with other foods or on their own? What is the purpose of all this unless it be to titillate a jaded palate? Attention is also lavished on the outward appearance of a dish, which must please the eye as much as it grati-

fies the taste buds, for though a belching stomach may announce that it has had enough, curiosity is never sated. Poor stomach! the eyes feast on color, the palate on flavor, yet the wretched stomach, indifferent to both but forced to accept the lot, is more often oppressed than refreshed as a result.

On Drink

21 What can I say about the drinking of water when even watering one's wine is inadmissible? Naturally all of us, as monks, suffer from a weak stomach, which is why we pay good heed to Paul's advice to use a little wine.[2] It is just that the word *little* gets overlooked, I can't think why. And if only we were content with drinking it plain, albeit undiluted. There are things it is embarrassing to say, though it should be more embarrassing still to do them. If hearing about them brings a blush, it will cost you none to put them right. The fact is that three or four times during the same meal you might see a half-filled cup brought in, so that different wines may be not drunk or drained so much as carried to the nose and lips. The expert palate is quick to discriminate between them and pick out the most potent. And what of the monasteries—and there are said to be some—which regularly serve spiced and honeyed wine in the refectory on major feasts? We are surely not going to say that this is done to nurse weak stomachs? The only reason for it that I can see is to allow deeper drinking, or keener pleasure. But once the wine is flowing through the veins and the whole head is throbbing with it, what else can they do when they get up from table but go and sleep it off? And if you force a monk to get up for vigils before he has digested, you will set him groaning rather than intoning. Having got to bed, it's not the sin of drunkenness they regret if questioned, but not being able to face their food....

On Mounting One's High Horse

Leaving the rest aside, what evidence is there of humility when one solitary abbot travels with a parade of horse-flesh and a retinue of lay-servants that would do honor to two bishops? I swear I have seen an abbot with sixty horses and more in his train. If you saw them passing, you

---

[1] 1 Cor. 11: 20.

[2] 1 Tim. 5: 35.

would take them for lords with dominion over castles and counties, not for fathers of monks and shepherds of souls. Moreover, napery, cups, dishes and candlesticks have to be taken along, together with packs stuffed full, not with ordinary bedding, but with ornate quilts. A man cannot go a dozen miles from home without transporting all his household goods, as though he were going on campaign or crossing the desert where the basic necessities were unobtainable. Surely water for washing one's hands and wine for drinking can be poured from the same jug? Do you think that your lamp will fail to burn and shine[1] unless it stands in your very own candlestick, and a gold or silver one at that? Can you really not sleep except on a chequered blanket and under an imported coverlet? And is a single servant not capable of loading the packhorse, serving the food and making up the bed? And lastly, if we must travel with these retinues of men and beasts, can we not mitigate the evil by taking the necessary provisions instead of battening on[2] our hosts?

On the Place of Pictures, Sculpture, Gold and Silver in Monasteries

XII, 28 But these are minor points. I am coming to the major abuses, so common nowadays as to seem of lesser moment. I pass over the vertiginous height of churches, their extravagant length, their inordinate width and costly finishings. As for the elaborate images that catch the eye and check the devotion of those at prayer within, they put me more in mind of the Jewish rite of old. But let this be: it is all done for the glory of God. But as a monk I ask my fellow monks the question a pagan poet put to pagans: "Tell me, O priests, why is there gold in the holy place?"[3] "Tell me, O poor men," say I—for it is the meaning, not the measure that concerns me—"tell me, O poor men, if poor you are, what is gold doing in the holy place?" It is one thing for bishops but quite another for monks. Bishops are under an obligation both to the wise and the foolish. Where people remain impervious to a purely spiritual stimulus, they use material ornamentation to inspire devotion. But we who have separated ourselves from the mass, who have relinquished for Christ's sake all the world's beauty and all that it holds precious, we who, to win Christ, count as dung[4] every delight of sight and sound, of smell and taste and touch, whose devotion do we seek to excite with this appeal to the senses? What are we angling for, I should like to know: the admiration of fools, or the offerings of the simple? Or have we perhaps, through mixing with the Gentiles, learned their ways and taken to worshipping their idols?

To put it plainly: suppose that all this is the work of cupidity,[5] which is a form of idol-worship; suppose that the real objective is not yield but takings. You want me to explain? It's an amazing process: the art of scattering money about that it may breed. You spend to gain, and what you pour out returns as a floodtide. A costly and dazzling show of vanities disposes to giving rather than to praying. Thus riches elicit riches, and money brings money in its train, because for some unknown reason the richer a place is seen to be the more freely the offerings pour in. When eyes open wide at gold-cased relics, purses do the same. A beautiful image of a saint is on show: the brighter the colors the holier he or she will be considered. Those who hasten to kiss the image are invited to leave a gift, and wonder more at the beauty than at the holiness they should be venerating.

Instead of crowns one sees in churches nowadays great jewelled wheels bearing a circle of lamps, themselves as good as outshone by the inset gems. Massive tree-like structures, exquisitely wrought, replace the simple candlestick. Here too the precious stones glimmer as brightly as the flames above.

What is this show of splendor intended to produce? Tears of contrition or gasps of admiration? O vanity of vanities,[6] but above all insanity! The walls of the church are ablaze with light and color, while the poor of the Church go hungry. The Church revets its stones in gold and leaves its children naked. The money for feeding the destitute goes to feast the eyes of the rich. The curious find plenty to relish and the starving nothing to eat. As for reverence, what respect do we show for the images of the saints that pattern the floor we tread beneath our feet? People often spit on angels' faces, and their tramp-

---

[1] See John 5: 35.

[2] Thriving at someone else's expense.

[3] Persius, *Satires* 2.69.

[4] See Phil. 3: 8.

[5] I.e., greed.

[6] Eccles. 1: 2.

ing feet pummel the features of the saints. If we care little for the sacred, why not save at least the lovely colors? Why decorate what is soon to be defaced? Why paint what is bound to be trodden on? What good are beautiful pictures where they receive a constant coating of grime? And lastly, what possible bearing can this have on the life of monks, who are poor men and spiritual? And yet perhaps the poet's well-known line can be countered by the Prophet's words: "Lord, I have loved the beauty of your house and the place where your glory dwells."[1] Very well, we will tolerate such doings in our churches on the grounds that they harm only the foolish and the grasping and not the simple-hearted and devout.

29 But what can justify that array of grotesques in the cloister where the brothers do their reading, a fantastic conglomeration of beauty misbegotten and ugliness transmogrified? What place have obscene monkeys, savage lions, unnatural centaurs, manticores, striped tigers, battling knights or hunters sounding their horns? You can see a head with many bodies and a multi-bodied head. Here is a quadruped with a dragon's tail, there an animal's head stuck on a fish. That beast combines the forehand of a horse with the rear half of a goat, this one has the horns in front and the horse's quarters aft. With such a bewildering array of shapes and forms on show, one would sooner read the sculptures than the books, and spend the whole day gawking at this wonderland rather than meditating on the law of God. Ah, Lord! if the folly of it all does not shame us, surely the expense might stick in our throats?

30 This is a rich vein, and there is plenty more to be quarried, but I am prevented from carrying on by my own demanding duties and your imminent departure, Brother Oger.[2] Since I cannot persuade you to stay, and you do not want to leave without this latest little book, I am falling in with your wishes: I am letting you go and shortening my discourse, particularly since a few words spoken in a spirit of conciliation do more good than many that are a cause of scandal. And would to heaven that these few lines do not occasion scandal! I am well aware that in rooting out vices I shall have offended those involved. However, God willing, those I fear I may have exasperated may end up grateful for my strictures if they desist from their evil ways—that is to say, if the rigorists stop carping and the lax prune back their excesses, and if both sides act in conscience according to their own beliefs, without judging the others who hold different views. Those who are able to live austerer lives should neither despise nor copy those who cannot. As for the latter, they should not be led by admiration for their stricter brethren to imitate them injudiciously: just as there is a danger of apostasy when those who have taken a more exacting vow slip into easier ways, not everyone can safely scale the heights.

5.21 The Cluniac view: Peter the Venerable, *Miracles* (mid-1130s–mid-1150s). Original in Latin.

Peter the Venerable (1092/1094–1156) was born into a well-to-do land-owning family. When he became abbot of Cluny in 1122, he inherited a troubled institution, weakened by a revolt against a former abbot and struggling to find a way to deal with hundreds of monasteries that, in one way or another, were dependent on Cluny. After he read Bernard's *Apology*, Peter responded to it in a long letter, rebutting each point. But he also answered the Cistercian critique by regulating the Cluniac lifestyle in his *Statutes* and by praising Cluny in his *Miracles*. Written over the course of the last twenty years of his life, the *Miracles*, which contained mainly stories having to do with Cluny, had

---

1 Ps. 26: 8; Douay Ps. 25: 8.

2 Oger was Bernard's friend and a canon at Mont-Saint-Éloi, in the very north of France. The idea that Oger was a sort of messenger, on the point of taking the letter to William of Saint-Thierry, is a literary conceit. In fact, Bernard revised and polished the *Apologia* over the course of many months.

one major purpose: to praise Cluniac monks. For Peter, Cluny was the embodiment of Christian virtue on earth, the "refuge" of sinners, and the model of monastic life. In the passage below he prefaces a discussion of miraculous visions of the dead with thoughts about Cluny's particular excellence. How did his emphasis on Cluny's function as the "asylum of all Christians" implicitly belittle the Cistercians?

[Source: Peter the Venerable, *De miraculis* 1.9, ed. Denise Bouthillier (Turnhout: Brepols, 1988), pp. 35–36. Translated by Barbara H. Rosenwein.]

The monastery of Cluny is the best known in just about the entire world for its religion, the severity of its discipline, the number of its monks, and its complete observance of the monastic rule. It is the individual and collective place of refuge for sinners by means of which much harm has been inflicted on Hell and a great many profits have been gained by the Heavenly Kingdom. There [at Cluny] innumerable multitudes of men, casting off the heavy burdens of the world from their shoulders, have submitted their necks to the sweet yoke of Christ.[1] There the men of every profession, dignity, and order have changed secular arrogance and luxury into the humble and poor life of monks. There the venerable fathers of these churches [i.e., bishops], fleeing the burdens of church affairs, have chosen to live more safely and more quietly and to obey rather than to command. There the unending and turbulent struggle against spiritual evils offers daily palms of victory to the soldiers of Christ. For the inhabitants of this place, who subject their flesh to the spirit by a continuous effort, the Apostle speaks truly: "To live is Christ, and to die is gain."[2]

By the balm of spiritual virtues that is diffused from this place, the whole house of the world has been filled with the odor of ointment,[3] while the ardor of monastic religion, which at one time had grown cold, grew warm again by the example and zeal of these men. Gaul, Germany, and even Britain across the sea bear witness to this; Spain, Italy, and all of Europe acknowledge it. All of them are full of monasteries either newly founded by them or restored from their earlier decline. There [at these Cluniac houses] colleges of monks, like the celestial troops that surround God in their proper orders, with other armies of holy power, apply themselves day and night to divine praises, so that the saying of the prophet may be understood to also be about them: "Blessed are they that dwell in thy house, O Lord: they shall praise thee for ever and ever."[4] But why do I list other parts of the world, since Cluny's fame has reached from our westernmost regions all the way to the East and has not been hidden from even a corner of the Christian world? For Cluny is the vineyard, and its monks are the branches which, truly clinging to the vine, Christ, and pruned by the Father, the gardener, bear much fruit according to the words of the Evangelist.[5] We read about this vineyard in the Psalms: "It stretched forth its branches unto the sea, and its boughs unto the river."[6] Although this was said about the synagogue of the Jews brought out of Egypt, and above all about the present Church, nevertheless nothing prevents us from understanding it also about this Cluniac Church, which is not the least member of the Universal Church.

---

[1] See Matt. 11: 28–30.

[2] Phil.1: 21.

[3] See John 12: 3.

[4] Ps. 84: 4; Douay Ps. 83: 5.

[5] See John 15: 1–17.

[6] Ps. 80: 11; Douay Ps. 79: 12.

TIMELINE FOR CHAPTER FIVE

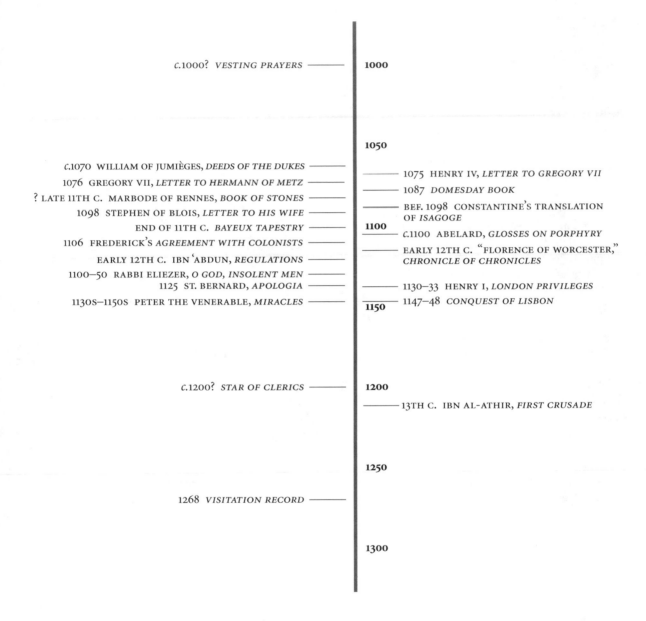

*c.*1000? *VESTING PRAYERS* ——— **1000**

1050

*c.*1070 WILLIAM OF JUMIÈGES, *DEEDS OF THE DUKES* ———
1076 GREGORY VII, *LETTER TO HERMANN OF METZ* ———
? LATE 11TH C. MARBODE OF RENNES, *BOOK OF STONES* ———
1098 STEPHEN OF BLOIS, *LETTER TO HIS WIFE* ———
END OF 11TH C. *BAYEUX TAPESTRY* ———
1106 FREDERICK'S *AGREEMENT WITH COLONISTS* ———
EARLY 12TH C. IBN ʿABDUN, *REGULATIONS* ———
1100–50 RABBI ELIEZER, *O GOD, INSOLENT MEN* ———
1125 ST. BERNARD, *APOLOGIA* ———
1130S–1150S PETER THE VENERABLE, *MIRACLES* ———

——— 1075 HENRY IV, *LETTER TO GREGORY VII*
——— 1087 *DOMESDAY BOOK*
——— BEF. 1098 CONSTANTINE'S TRANSLATION OF *ISAGOGE*
1100
——— *c.*1100 ABELARD, *GLOSSES ON PORPHYRY*
——— EARLY 12TH C. "FLORENCE OF WORCESTER," *CHRONICLE OF CHRONICLES*
——— 1130–33 HENRY I, *LONDON PRIVILEGES*
1150 1147–48 *CONQUEST OF LISBON*

*c.*1200? *STAR OF CLERICS* ——— **1200**

——— 13TH C. IBN AL-ATHIR, *FIRST CRUSADE*

1250

1268 *VISITATION RECORD* ———

1300

To test your knowledge and gain deeper understanding of this chapter, please go to *www.utphistorymatters.com* for *Questions for Reflection.*

Sources

CHAPTER I

1.1 Toleration or favoritism? *Edict of Milan* (313). Excerpts from *Church and State through the Centuries: A Collection of Historic Documents with Commentaries*, trans. and ed. Sidney Z. Ehler and John B. Morrall. Copyright © 1954, The Newman Press. Used with permission of Paulist Press, Inc., New York/Mahwah, N.J. www.paulistpress.com.

1.2 Law: *The Theodosian Code* (438). Pharr, Clyde; *The Theodosian Code and Novels and the Sermondian Constitutions.* Copyright © 1952 in the name of the author, 1980 renewed in name of Roy Pharr, executor. Reprinted by permission of Princeton University Press.

1.4 Heretics: *A Donatist Sermon* (c.318). *Donatist Martyr Stories: The Church in Conflict in Roman North Africa*, trans. Maureen A. Tilley, Translated Texts for Historians, 24. Liverpool University Press, 1996. Reprinted by permission of Liverpool University Press.

1.5 Orthodoxy's declaration: *The Nicene Creed* (325). J.N.D. Kelly, *Early Christian Doctrines*, 2nd ed. Harper and Row, 1958. Courtesy of Continuum International Publishing Group.

1.6 Relating this world to the next: Augustine, *The City of God* (413–426). *Concerning the City of God against the Pagans by St Augustine*, translated by Henry Bettenson, introduced by John O'Meara (First published in Pelican Books 1972, Reprinted in Penguin Classics, 1984). Translation copyright © Henry Bettenson, 1972. Reproduced by permission of Penguin Books Ltd.

1.7 Monasticism: *The Benedictine Rule* (c.530–c.560). Reprinted by permission of the publisher from *The Rule of Saint Benedict*, edited and translated by Bruce L. Venarde, Dumbarton Oaks Medieval Library Volume 6, pp. 3, 7, 9, 17, 19, 21, 23, 29, 31, 33, 35, 37, 45, 47, 57, 59, 61, 79, 85, 87, 89, 97, 123, 125, 139, 141, 143, 161, 163, 177, 179, 187, 189, 191, 193, 229, Cambridge, Mass.: Harvard University Press, Copyright © 2011 by the President and Fellows of Harvard College.

1.9 The eremetical life: Athanasius, *Life of St. Antony of Egypt* (357). Athanasius of Alexandria, *Life of St. Antony of Egypt*, trans. David Brakke, in *Medieval Hagiography: An Anthology*, ed. Thomas Head. Garland, 2000. Courtesy of David Brakke.

1.11 St. Radegund as ascetic: Venantius Fortunatus, *The Life of St. Radegund* (before c.600). "Radegund, Queen of the Franks and Abbess of Poitiers (ca. 525–587)," in *Sainted Women of the Dark Ages*, JoAnn McNamara, John Halborg, E. Gordon Whatley, pp. 60–106. Copyright © 1992, Duke University Press. All rights reserved. Reprinted by permission of the publisher. www.dukeupress.edu

1.12 St. Radegund as relic collector: Baudonivia, *The Life of St. Radegund* (c.600). Venantius Fortunatus, *The Life of St. Radegund* (before c.600). "Radegund, Queen of the Franks and Abbess of Poitiers (ca. 525–587)," in *Sainted Women of the Dark Ages*, JoAnn McNamara, John Halborg, E. Gordon Whatley, pp. 60–106. Copyright © 1992, Duke University Press. All rights reserved. Reprinted by permission of the publisher. www.dukeupress.edu

1.13 Gothic Italy as Rome's heir: Cassiodorus, *Variae (State Papers)* (*c.*507–536). Cassiodorus: *Variae*, trans. S.J.B. Barnish. Copyright © 1992, Liverpool University Press. Reprinted by permission of Liverpool University Press.

1.14 Gothic Spain converts: *The Third Council of Toledo* (589). *Medieval Iberia: Readings from Christian, Muslim, and Jewish Sources*, 2nd ed., Olivia Remie Constable with Damian Zurro, trans. David Nirenberg, pp. 12–20. Copyright © University of Pennsylvania Press, 2011. Reprinted with permission of the University of Pennsylvania Press.

CHAPTER II

2.1 Byzantine village life and the education of a saint: *The Life of St. Theodore of Sykeon* (7th c.). Republished with permission of St. Valdimir's Seminary Press, from *Three Byzantine Saints: Contemporary Biographies translated from the Greek*, trans. Elizabeth Dawes and Norman H. Baynes. Copyright © 1977. Permission conveyed through Copyright Clearance Center, Inc.

2.3 The iconoclastic argument: *The Synod of 754*. Republished with permission of William B. Eerdmans Publishing Company, from *A Select Library of Nicene and Post-Nicene Fathers of the Christian Church*, 2nd series, ed. Philip Schaff and Henry Wace, Vol. 14: The Seven Ecumenical Councils. Copyright © 1971. Permission conveyed through Copyright Clearance Center, Inc.

2.4 Vilifying the iconoclasts: *The Chronicle of Theophanes Confessor* (before 818). *The Chronicle of Theophanes Confessor: Byzantine and Near Eastern History*, AD 284–813, ed. and trans. Cyril Mango and Roger Scott. Copyright © 1997. By permission of Oxford University Press.

2.5 Pre-Islamic Arabic poetry: Al-A'sha, *Bid Hurayra Farewell* (before 625). Michael A. Sells, "Bid Hurayra Farewell" from *Desert Tracings: Six Classic Arabian Odes by 'Alquama, Shanfara, Labid, 'Antara, Al-A'sha, and Dhu al-Rumma* © 1989 by Michael A. Sells. Reprinted by permission of Wesleyan University Press.

2.6 The sacred text: *Qur'an Suras* 1, 53:1–18, 81, 87, 96, 98 (*c.*610–622). Republished with permission of White Cloud Press, from *Approaching the Qur'an: The Early Revelations*, trans. Michael Sells. Copyright © 1999. Permission conveyed through Copyright Clearance Center, Inc.

2.7 Umayyad diplomacy: *The Treaty of Tudmir* (713). *Medieval Iberia: Readings from Christian, Muslim, and Jewish Sources*, ed. Olivia Remie Constable, trans. David Nirenberg, pp. 37–38. Copyright © University of Pennsylvania Press, 1997. Reprinted with permission of the University of Pennsylvania Press.

2.8 Taxation: *A Tax Demand in Egypt* (710). *Islam from the Prophet Muhammad to the Capture of Constantinople, Vol. 2: Religion And Society*, ed. and trans. Bernard Lewis (1987), p. 130. Copyright © 1974 by Bernard Lewis. By permission of Oxford University Press, USA.

2.9 Praising the caliph: Al-Akhtal, *The Tribe Has Departed* (*c.*692). Republished with permission of Indiana University Press, from *The Poetics of Islamic Legitimacy: Myth, Gender, and Ceremony in the Classical Arabic Ode*, Suzanne Pinckney Stetkevych. Copyright © 2002. Permission conveyed through Copyright Clearance Center, Inc.

2.10 A world explained by words: Isidore of Seville, *Etymologies* (*c.*615–*c.*630). *The Etymologies of Isidore of Seville*, ed. Stephen A. Barney, W.J. Lewis, J.A. Beach and Oliver Berghof. Copyright © 2006 Stephen A. Barney, W.J. Lewis, J.A. Beach and Oliver Berghof. Reprinted with the permission of Cambridge University Press.

2.13 Reforming the Continental church: *Letters to Boniface* (723–726). From *The Letters of Saint Boniface*, trans. Ephraim Emerton. Copyright © 1940 Columbia University Press. Reprinted with permission of the publisher.

2.14 Creating a Roman Christian identity for England: Bede, *The Ecclesiastical History of the English People* (731). Bede, *The Ecclesiastical History of the English People*, ed. Judith McClure and Roger Collins (1994), pp. 37–41, 55–59, 65–71, 152–59, 370–75, 397. By permission of Oxford University Press.

CHAPTER III

3.2 Byzantine guilds: *The Book of the Prefect* (912). A.E.R. Boak, "Notes and Documents: The Book of the Prefect," *Journal of Economic and Business History* 1 (1929): 600–02, 604–10.

3.3 The sale of a slave in Italy: *A Contract of Sale* (725). From *Medieval Trade in the Mediterranean World*, trans. and ed. Robert S. Lopez and Irving W. Raymond. Copyright © 2001 Columbia University Press. Reprinted with permission of the publisher.

3.4 An early view of the Prophet: Muhammad ibn Ishaq, *Life of Muhammad* (754–767). *The Life of Muhammad: A Translation of Ishaq's Sirat Rasul Allah*, trans. and ed. A. Guillaume. Oxford University Press, 1955, pp. 81–83, 104–07.

3.5 Hadith: Al-Bukhari, *On Fasting* (9th c.). *A Reader on Islam: Passages from Standard Arabic Writings Illustrative of the Beliefs and Practices of Muslims*, ed. Arthur Jeffery. Mouton & Co., 1962, pp. 88–90, 92–94, 98–101.

3.6 The "New Poetry": Abu Nuwas, *Turning the Tables* (*c.*800). Republished with permission of Oneworld, from *Abu Nuwas: A Genius of Poetry*, Philip Kennedy. Copyright © 2005. Permission conveyed through Copyright Clearance Center, Inc.

3.7 The minority—that is, Christian—view: *Chronicle of Albelda* (*c.*883). *Medieval Iberia: Readings from Christian, Muslim, and Jewish Sources*, ed. Olivia Remie Constable, trans. David Nirenberg, pp. 67, 70–74. Copyright © University of Pennsylvania Press, 1997. Reprinted with permission of the University of Pennsylvania Press.

3.8 An Islamic Andalusian voice: Ibn 'Abd Rabbihi, *I Have Never Seen* (before 940). *Poems of Arab Andalusia*, trans. Cola Franzen from the Spanish versions of Emilio Garcia Gómez. City Lights Books, 1989. Copyright © by Cola Franzen. Reprinted by permission of City Lights Books.

3.9 A Jewish poet in al-Andalus: Dunash ben Labrat, *There Came a Voice* (mid-10th c.). Reprinted from *Wine, Women, and Death: Medieval Hebrew Poems on the Good Life*, translated and edited by Raymond Scheindlin, by permission of the University of Nebraska Press. Copyright © 1986 by the Jewish Publication Society.

3.12 Modeling the state on Old Testament Israel: *The Admonitio Generalis* (789). *Christianity through the Thirteenth Century*, ed. Marshall W. Baldwin. Harper and Row, 1970.

3.13 Ideals of family and fidelity: Dhuoda, *Handbook for Her Son* (841–843). Reprinted from *Handbook for William: A Carolingian Woman's Counsel for Her Son by Dhuoda*, translated by Carol Neel, by permission of the University of Nebraska Press. Copyright © 1991 by the University of Nebraska Press.

3.14 The Slavic conversion: Constantine/Cyril, *Prologue to the Gospel* (863–867). Republished with permission of St. Vladimir's Seminary Press, from Roman Jakobson, "St. Constantine's Prologue to the Gospel," *St. Vladimir's Seminary Quarterly 7*. Copyright © 1963. Permission conveyed through Copyright Clearance Center, Inc.

3.16 The Bulgarians adopt Christianity: Pope Nicholas I, *Letter to Answer the Bulgarians' Questions* (866). Nicholas I, *Epistola 99*, in *Epistolae 6*, ed. Ernest Perels, Monumenta Germaniae Historica. Berlin, 1925. Translated by William L. North. Reprinted by permission of William L. North.

CHAPTER IV

4.1 Fragmentation in the Islamic world: Al-Tabari, *The Defeat of the Zanj Revolt* (*c.*915). Reprinted by permission from *The History of al-Tabari, Vol. 37: The 'Abbasid Recovery: The War Against the Zanj Ends A.D. 879–893/A.H. 266–279*, translated by Philip M. Fields, the State University of New York Press © 1987, State University of New York. All rights reserved.

4.2 The powerful in the Byzantine countryside: Romanus I Lecapenus, *Novel* (934). *The Land Legislation of the Macedonian Emperors*, trans. and ed. Eric McGeer. Pontifical Institute of Mediaeval Studies, 2000. Reprinted by permission of the Pontifical Institute of Mediaeval Studies.

4.4 Love and complaints in Angoulême: *Agreement between Count William of the Aquitanians and Hugh IV of Lusignan* (1028). Jane Martindale, "Conventum inter Guillelmum Aquitanorum comitem et Hugonem Chiliarchum," in *Status, Authority and Regional Power: Aquitaine and France, 9th to 12th Centuries*. Variorum, 1997. Translated by Thomas Greene and Barbara H. Rosenwein. Reprinted by permission of the translators.

4.5 The Peace of God at Bourges: Andrew of Fleury, *The Miracles of St. Benedict* (1040–1043). *The Peace of God: Social Violence and Religious Response in France around the Year 1000*, ed. Thomas Head and Richard Landes. Cornell University Press, 1992.

4.6 A castellan's revenues and properties in Catalonia: *Charter of Guillem Guifred* (1041–1075). Pierre Bonnassie, "The Banal Seigneury and the 'Reconditioning' of the Free Peasantry," in *Debating the Middle Ages: Issues and Readings*, ed. Lester K.

Little and Barbara H. Rosenwein. Basil Blackwell, 1988. Reproduced by permission of Wiley.

4.7 Military life: Constantine VII Porphyrogenitus, *Military Advice to His Son* (950–958). *Constantine Porphyrogenitus: Three Treatises on Imperial Military Expeditions*, ed. and trans. John F. Haldon. Österreichischen Akademie der Wissenschaften, 1997. Reproduced by permission of the publisher.

4.8 Imperial rule: Michael Psellus, *Portrait of Basil II* (*c.*1063). *Fourteen Byzantine Rulers: The* Chronographia *of Michael Psellus*, trans. Edgar R.A. Sewter. Penguin Books, 1966.

4.9 Education: Al-Qabisi, *A Treatise Detailing the Circumstances of Students and the Rules governing Teachers and Students* (before 1012). *Classical Foundations of Islamic Education Thought*, ed. Bradley J. Cook with Fathi H. Malkawi; trans. Michael Fishbein. Brigham Young University Press, 2010.

4.10 Political theory: Al-Farabi, *The Perfect State* (*c.*940–942). *Al-Farabi: The Perfect State*, ed. and trans. Richard Walzer (1985), pp. 231, 235, 239, 241, 253, 255, 257, 259. By permission of Oxford University Press.

4.11 Logic: Ibn Sina (Avicenna), *Treatise on Logic* (1020s or 1030s). *Avicenna's Treatise on Logic*, ed. and trans. Farhang Zabeeh, pp. 13–17, Martinus Nijhoff, 1971, with kind permission from Springer Science+Business Media B.V.

4.12 Hungary as heir of Rome: King Stephen, *Laws* (1000–1038). *The Laws of the Medieval Kingdom of Hungary, vol 1: 1000–1301*, trans. and ed. János M. Bak, György Bónis, and James Ross Sweeney. Charles Schlacks, Jr. Publisher, 1989. Reprinted by permission of the publisher.

4.13 Coming to terms with Catholic Poland: Thietmar of Merseburg, *Chronicle* (1013–1018). *Ottonian Germany: The Chronicon of Thietmar of Merseburg*, trans. David A. Warner. Manchester University Press, 2001.

4.15 Kievan Rus': *The Russian Primary Chronicle* (*c.*1113, incorporating earlier materials). *The Russian Primary Chronicle: Laurentian Text*, trans. and ed. Samuel Hazzard Cross and Olgerd P. Sherbowitz-Wetzor. Medieval Academy of America, 1953.

4.17 Literacy: King Alfred, *Prefaces* to Gregory the Great's *Pastoral Care* (*c.*890). *Alfred the Great: Asser's Life of King Alfred and Other Contemporary Sources* translated with an introduction by Simon Keynes and Michael Lapidge (Penguin Classics, 1983). This translation, introduction and notes copyright © Simon Keynes and Michael Lapidge, 1983. Reproduced by permission of Penguin Books Ltd.

4.18 Law: King Æthelred, *Law Code* (1008). *English Historical Documents*, Vol. 1: c. 300–1042, ed. Dorothy Whitelock, 2nd ed. Copyright © 1979, Routledge. Reproduced by permission of Taylor & Francis Books UK.

CHAPTER V

5.2 Ibn 'Abdun, *Regulations for the Market at Seville* (early 12th c.). *Islam: From the Prophet Muhammad to the Capture of Constantinople, vol. 2: Religion and Society*, ed. and trans. Bernard Lewis. Copyright © 1974 by Bernard Lewis. By permission of Oxford University Press, USA.

5.3 The role of royal patronage: Henry I, *Privileges for the Citizens of London* (1130–1133). *English Historical Documents*, Vol. 2: 1042–1189, ed. David C. Douglas and George W. Greenaway, 2nd ed. Copyright © 1981, Routledge. Reproduced by permission of Taylor & Francis Books UK.

5.4 The royal view: Henry IV, *Letter to Gregory VII* (1075). From *Imperial Lives and Letters*, ed. Robert L. Benson, trans. Theodor E. Mommsen and Karl F. Morrison. Copyright © 2000 Columbia University Press. Reprinted with permission of the publisher.

5.5 The papal view: Gregory VII, *Letter to Hermann of Metz* (1076). *The Register of Pope Gregory VII, 1073–1085* by H.E.J. Cowdrey (2002), pp. 208–11. By permission of Oxford University Press.

5.9 Martyrs in the Rhineland: Rabbi Eliezer b. Nathan ("Raban"), *O God, Insolent Men* (early to mid-12th c.). Abraham Habermann, *Sefer gezerot ashkenaz vetzarfat*. 1945, repr. 1971. Introduced and translated by Susan L. Einbinder.

5.11 The Muslim reaction: Ibn al-Athir, *The First Crusade* (13th c.). Republished with permission of the University of California Press, from *Arab Historians of the Crusades*, ed. and trans. (from Arabic) Francesco Gabrieli, trans. (from Italian) E.J. Costello. Copyright © 1969. Permission conveyed through Copyright Clearance Center, Inc.

5.12 The crusade in Spain and Portugal: *The Conquest of Lisbon* (1147–1148). From *De expugnatione Lyxbonensi: The Conquest of Lisbon*, trans. Charles

Wendell David. Copyright © 2001 Columbia University Press. Reprinted with permission of the publisher.

5.13 The pro-Norman position: William of Jumièges, *The Deeds of the Dukes of the Normans* (*c.*1070). *The Norman Conquest*, ed. and trans. R. Allen Brown. Edward Arnold, 1984. Reprinted by permission of Boydell & Brewer.

5.14 The native position: "Florence of Worcester," *Chronicle of Chronicles* (early 12th c.). *English Historical Documents*, Vol. 2: 1042–1189, ed. David C. Douglas and George W. Greenaway, 2nd ed. Copyright © 1981, Routledge. Reproduced by permission of Taylor & Francis Books UK.

5.16 Exploiting the Conquest: *Domesday Book* (1087). *Domesday Book: A Complete Translation*, ed. Ann Williams and G.H. Martin. Penguin, 2002. Copyright © Alecto Historical Editions. Reproduced by permission.

5.17 Logic: Abelard, *Glosses on Porphyry* (*c.*1100). *Basic Issues in Medieval Philosophy*, second edition, edited by Richard N. Bosley and Martin Tweedale. Broadview Press, 2006; page 353. Reprinted with the permission of Broadview Press.

5.20 The Cistercian view: St. Bernard, *Apologia* (1125). *The Cistercian World: Monastic Writings of the Twelfth Century* translated and edited with an introduction by Pauline Matarasso (Penguin Classics, 1993). Copyright © Pauline Matarasso, 1993. Reproduced by permission of Penguin Books Ltd.

PLATES

1 Dome of the Rock (692). Dome of the Rock and Imam, Jerusalem and Dome of the Rock, View of Rock, Jerusalem. Copyright © Sonia Halliday Photographs.

2 Icon with Saint Demetrios (2nd half 10th c.). Icon with Saint Demetrios. Second half of the 10th century. Ivory, Overall: 7¾ x 4¾ x ⅜ in. (19.7 x 12.1 x 1 cm). The Cloisters Collection, 1970 (1970.324.3). The Metropolitan Museum of Art, New York, NY, USA. Image copyright © The Metropolitan Museum of Art. Image source: Art Resource, NY.

3 Reliquary Locket (10th–11th c.). Copyright © The Trustees of the British Museum.

4 Page from a Qur'an (993). KFQ 90, recto, The Nasser D. Khalili Collection of Islamic Art. Copyright © Nour Foundation. Courtesy of the Khalili Family Trust.

5 A Holy Vestment (late 10th–early 11th c.). Glockenkasel des Erzbischofs Willigis von Mainz, Inv.-Nr. 11/170.1-2, Photo No. D52112, Poto No. D31776. Reproduced by permission of the Bayerisches Nationalmuseum.

6 Tlemcen, Great Mosque (1236). Images reproduced by permission of Jonathan Bloom and Sheila Blair. Plan from Rachid Bourouiba, *L'art religieux musulman en Algerie*. S.N.E.D., 1973.

7 The Church as Reliquary: Sainte-Chapelle (1248). Sainte-Chapelle de Paris, nef de la chapelle haute, vers l'abside et la tribune des reliques. © Bernard Acloque / Centre des monuments nationaux.

8 Monstrance (*c.*1430). Monstranz, um 1430; Museum Schnutgen, G 97. Copyright © Rheinisches Bildarchiv Köln, rba_c012396.

9 Synagogue and Ark (1435). Ross.555.f.12v. Reproduced by permission of Biblioteca Apostolica Vaticana, with all rights reserved.

10 The Wienhausen Sepulcher (15th c.). The Tomb of the Holy Sepulchre and The Risen Christ, Kloster Wienhausen, reproduced by permission of Kloster Wienhausen/ Lüneburger Klosterarchive. The Tomb of the Holy Sepulchre (detail), Kloster Wienhausen, reproduced by permission of Elina Gertsman.

11 *Seal of Boris-Michael* (864–889). By kind permission of Dr. Ivan Jordanov.

12 *Boleslaw's Coin* (992–1000). Denar (typ GNEZDVN CIVITAS), MNK VII-P-798, from the collection of the National Museum in Krakow.

13 *The Jelling Monument* (960s). The Jelling Stone / Monument. Photographer unknown, Nationalmuseet, Denmark.

14 *The Bayeux Tapestry* (end of the 11th c.). Detail of the Bayeux Tapestry—11th Century. With special permission from the City of Bayeux.

15 Gabriel de Valseca, *Portolan Map* (1447). Registre C; 40333: Carte marine de la mer Méditerranée et de la mer Noire. Reproduced by permission of Bibliothèque nationale de France.

MAP

3.1 Major European Slave Exports (700–900). Michael McCormick, "Map 25.1: Main European Slave Exports: A.D. 700–900," *Origins of the European Economy: Communications and Commerce A.D. 300–900*. Cambridge University Press, 2001. Copyright © 2001 Michael McCormick. Reprinted with the permission of Cambridge University Press.

Index of Names, Places, and Readings